THE 70S & 8
NEW WAVE
& POST-PUNK
ALMANAC

PART TWO

MICHAEL KRILICH

APS BOOKS
YORKSHIRE

APS Books,
The Stables, Field Lane
Aberford, West Yorkshire,
LS25 3AE

APS Books is a subsidiary of the APS Publications imprint

www.andrewsparke.com

First published worldwide by APS Books in 2025

AUTHOR'S NOTE

There was a call from members of a Facebook group that I created that I should gather my daily blogs and consolidate them into a book. Initially, it was my intention for creating a Facebook page where I could share my passion with a few friends. However, it unexpectedly evolved into a central hub for fans of the New Wave and Post-Punk era from the '70s and '80s from all corners of the world. This group has gathered a large community of dedicated enthusiasts who visit it daily, often making it their first stop before starting their day.
https://www.facebook.com/groups/NewWaveAndPostPunkOnly .

Although it was not my original intention, the page has become a virtual meeting place for fans, enthusiasts, and even influential artists from that era. It provides a platform for sharing thoughts, memories, and opinions about the music and influential musicians of that time. Through these shared experiences, readers could immerse themselves in the memories and perspectives of others, reliving that unique period.

This almanac primarily focuses on the years between 1977 and 1987. It is a compilation of daily events, including debut performances, debut and significant record releases, and the biographies of noteworthy artists associated with the era and its various sub-genres. Because of its concept and format, I anticipate that this book will eventually be recognized as an authoritative source of information about the era, its genres, and the individuals involved.

I would like to express my gratitude to all the mentioned artists, for their willingness to participate in this project as without their contributions, this book would not exist. I am also immensely thankful to the members and administrators of my Facebook group, who have provided me with a wealth of valuable information and prompted me to discover artists I would have otherwise never known.

Over the span of more than a decade, I have gathered information from a wide array of sources. I have consulted magazines, non-fiction books, encyclopedias, and the internet for historical data. Nevertheless, the most valuable insights have come directly from the artists and personalities upon whom this book is based. I have strived to present the information as accurately as possible, and any critical evaluations are solely the opinion of the author, myself. I hope this book successfully captures the essence of this significant period in music history.

It is my hope that this book (the second part of a two volume set) will be seen as a daily companion that graces coffee tables around the world. Day by day, year by year, it will always remain 'live', informing readers about the historical events that occurred on each day.

Michael Krilich September 2025

BIBLIOGRAPHY

Baker, Glenn A & Coupe, Stuart. The New Music, 1980
Barnes, Jim. Dyer, Fred. Scanes, Stephen. The Book, 1986
Bennett, Murray. Product 45, 2015
Clifford, Mike. New Illustrated Rock Handbook, 1992
Cossar, Neil. This Day In Music, 2005
Duffy, Ged. Factory Fairy-Tales, 2021, 2023
George, B. and Defoe, Martha. International New Wave Discography, 1982
Guiness Rockopedia, The Ultimate A-Z of Rock & Pop, 1998
Heatley, Michael. The Definitive Illustrated Encyclopedia of Rock, 2007
Hennessey, Val. In The Gutter, 1978
Larkin, Colin. The Virgin Encyclopedia of 70s Music
McFarlane, Ian. Australian Rock and Pop, 1999-2017
Mackay, Andy. Electronic Music, 1981
Morrow, Bruce. Rock & Roll…and the beat goes on, 2009
Noble, Peter L. Future Pop,1983
Reynolds, Simon. Rip It Up and Start Again, 2005
Rolling Stone Encyclopedia of Rock & Roll, 1983
Robertson, Donald. The Big Beat, 2019
Spencer, Chris. Nowara, Zbig. & McHenry, Paul. Who's Who of Australian Rock! 1987-2002
The Big Australian Rock Book
The Virgin Encyclopedia of Eighties Music, 1997
Walker, Clinton. Inner City Sound, 1982-2005

INTERNET SOURCES

allmusic.com
cherryred.co.uk
jango.com
lesdisquesducrepuscule.com
liveandloudshows.com
music.metason.net
musicbrainz.org
nervejam.com
newhamvoices.co.uk
nonightsweats.com
nostalgiacentral.com
nwoutpost.com
officialcharts.com
punkjourney.com
pastemagazine.com
rateyourmusic.com
rockmusictimeline.com

rockonvinyl.blogspot.com
slicingupeyeballs.com
sheffieldvision.com
spill-label.org/fastforward
strangewaysradio.com
synthmusictimeline.com
systemsofromance.com
thegreatrockbible.com
ticketcollector.wordpress.com
trouserpress.com
tumblr.com
vinylgoldmine.blogspot.com
web.archive.org
wikipedia.org
womenofaussiemusic.blogspot.com/
1980schild.blogspot.com
45cat.com

1

○ The musical duo A.R. Kane, comprised of Alex Ayuli and Rudi Tambala, put out their first full-length album on July 1, 1988, titled *69* on the Rough Trade label. Though reminiscent of bands like My Bloody Valentine and Jesus & Mary Chain with their dreamy, melodic pop sound, *69* had a distinctive style all its own. While not as cohesive structurally as their previous EP *Lolita* from 1987, this record captured much of the same atmospheric, blissful vibe. For listeners willing to immerse themselves in it, *69* proves to be an enthralling experience.

○ Clan of Xymox's *self-titled* album hit the music scene in 1985, showcasing their unapologetic embrace of sequencers, reminiscent of New Order's iconic track 'Blue Monday', and the dark electronic soundscapes of The Sisters of Mercy. With their unique blend of gothic influences, CoX left an indelible mark on the genre. This album is widely regarded as the pinnacle of the original lineup, featuring the talents of Ronny Moorings, Pieter Nooten, Frank Weyzig, and Anke Wolbert. CoX effortlessly combines dancefloor beats with moody, introspective lyrics, creating an atmospheric experience. Tracks like 'A Day' and 'Stranger' exude a bleak and shadowy aura, while their infectious hooks keep you captivated. The funky vibes of 'No Words' demonstrate CoX's appreciation for the new romantic movement, and 'Stumble and Fall' takes you on an exotic and haunting journey. This album is an absolute must-listen for any fan of the genre.

○ The debut single 'D for Desire' by All About Eve came out in 1985 in a limited release. There are clear similarities to Cocteau Twins, most notably through Julianne Regan's vocals and Tim Brichino's guitar playing. The Cocteau Twins' influence is undeniable. The single itself is extremely hard to find these days, but don't lose hope - the tracks are included on the CD compilation *Return to Eden, Vol. One, The Early Recordings*.

○ On this day in 1982, the influential hip hop group Grandmaster Flash and the Furious Five released their groundbreaking single 'The Message' on Sugar Hill Records. The song was a revelation in hip hop, with its raw, realistic lyrics depicting the struggles of inner-city life. Unlike much of the party-orientated hip hop at the time, 'The Message' had a gritty, socially conscious message. With its aggressive rhythms and inventive vocal delivery, it showed hip hop's potential as a vehicle for social commentary. The song's refrain "*Don't push me, cause I'm close to the edge*" captured the frustration and anger of urban youth. In 2012, Rolling Stone magazine named 'The Message' the greatest hip hop song of all time, cementing its status as a landmark recording. Commercially, it became the group's biggest hit, reaching No.4 on the R&B charts. However, its success exacerbated tensions within Grandmaster Flash and the Furious Five, leading to acrimonious splintering. Grandmaster Flash had creative differences with Sugar Hill Records and sued them in 1983 for $5 million in unpaid royalties, resulting in the group's subsequent work being credited to Melle Mel and the Furious Five or Grandmaster Melle Mel. Despite the fracturing, 'The Message' remains an iconic song that showed hip hop could make a powerful statement about contemporary urban life.

○ July 1,1945, is Deborah Harry's birthdate. As the vocalist for Blondie, she had six UK No.1 singles and four US No.1 Singles. In 1978 Blondie went to No.1 worldwide with the album *Parallel Lines*. As a solo artist, she scored the 1986 UK No.8 single 'French Kissing in the USA'. Debbie was a former Playboy Bunny, with an acting career that spanned over thirty film roles and numerous television appearances. Jeffrey Lee Pierce of The Gun Club, leader of Blondie's West Coast USA fan club, cherished a handwritten note from Debbie that he always carried in his wallet.

⦿ John Francis Kennedy was born in Liverpool, England, in 1958. He was as he puts it, " *I was lucky to be born into the culture that gave the world the Beatles and the Liverpool Football Club and the misfortune in 1965 to migrate to hot suburban wastelands of Acacia Ridge, Brisbane, Australia*". As a good catholic boy, he was confirmed at the age of ten and took the middle name Francis to complete the famous JFK moniker. Inspired by British pop, Country & Western and NEW WAVE, JFK and the Cuban Crisis was formed in Brisbane in 1980. John relocated to Sydney in 1982 and enjoyed a modicum of indie success via the newly founded Waterfront Records. Then after the usual musical differences prevailed, John goes solo and forms John Kennedy's Love Gone Wrong in 1984. Despite numerous indie hits, including 'The Texan Thing', 'Miracle (in Marrickville)' and King Street on the Waterfront and Red Eye Records labels, major commercial success continued to be elusive. After the breakup of Love Gone Wrong in 1988, Kennedy chose to leave Australia to try his luck in the wider world. He lived in the USA, the UK, Berlin, and Hong Kong continuing to perform and record his Urban & Western songs on various indie labels. In 2000 he returned to Sydney's Inner West and formed John Kennedy's 68 Comeback Special performing regularly and from 2007, releasing numerous indie albums. Even though pronouncing his music career was dead, he showed signs of being alive and well since 2017, with six albums of originals, best-ofs, reissues, and two volumes of his brilliant *Raining Treasure* Australian Indie cover version collections.

THE ALBUM THAT KILLED MY CAREER
JOHN KENNEDY
(Love Gone Wrong, JFK & The Cuban Crisis)

People occasionally ask me, "*When will Always The Bridegroom (ATB) by Love Gone Wrong (LGW) be released digitally?*". My answer is usually some variation on, "*When hell freezes over*". Somehow the whole recording process and the subsequent breakup of the band not too long after the original 1987 release left a very bad taste in my mouth. I'd removed the John Kennedy's prefix from the Love Gone Wrong on the album cover in an effort to promote greater band engagement. In retrospect I thought it was a smart move, thinking that somehow this distanced me from a project that for a long time I just wanted to forget.

But over the years many people have told me that they really love this album. One slightly bizarre occasion found me backstage at a gig with Russell Crowe telling me it was one of his all-time favourites. When I pointed out that I had many reservations about it, he quickly changed the subject. You don't contradict Russ, even when it's your own album you're criticising. Moving house after 20 years forced me to consider what I wanted to do with all my old recording tapes I had stored in the attic. Through a series of online exchanges, Tony Slaughter offered to finance the re-issue of *ATB* on CD. So, it was time for me to consider whether I really did want the album buried forever.

The band that recorded this album was about the fourth lineup of John Kennedy's Love Gone Wrong (that's right! JKsLGW). I'd had some great musicians pass through the band. But many moved on when they got better offers. Most new band members arrived via some personal contact. JKsLGW Mk4 was the first lineup where members were sourced through a call out for applicants. The results were variable. In mid-1986 I restarted the band with guys who were a few years younger than me without much band experience. Barry Turnbull from the previous lineup stayed on for a while playing bass, helping steady the new band.

Cory Messenger had come down from Brisbane chasing a music career. He'd been a fan, following my band around. He joined the band on rhythm guitar after I'd earlier stolen Barry and Mark Dawson, the rhythm section from his band, The Spring Quartet. Lead guitarist Wayne Connelly was an electrical engineer living in the Palace Hotel, recording his own songs on a 4-track. He went on to do some great things. Vince Sheehan, who joined on drums, was probably the least experienced of an inexperienced bunch. He also went on to do some great things, but not necessarily in music. All in all, they were a nice bunch of guys. They were keen to commit to a band that already had a few runs on the scoreboard.

I remember one of this lineup's first big gigs was headlining at The Club in Melbourne with Weddings Parties Anything, as the support act. Despite weeks of rehearsal, the standard of our performance was underwhelming compared to WPA's punchy set. That impression stayed with me, despite the evidence of a 3LO live-to-air recording that resurfaced during the attic cleanout. The recording was made not too long after that Melbourne gig. It would have been at the end of a run of 6 or 8 shows in and around Melbourne. This live-in-the-studio performance, included as a bonus disc with this *ATB* re-issue presents a pretty tight band performing a mixture of older tunes, some substantially reworked, newer songs and a couple of covers.

So why did it take the best part of 12 months and 2 or 3 demo sessions before we went into a studio to record this album? Somewhere along the way we lost Barry. He was replaced on bass by Michael Armiger. Michael had a bit of a mixed pedigree, having been in Paul Kelly's band before accepting an offer to do a tour with ska band The Allniters. On his return he found that he'd lost his place in the soon-to-be Coloured Girls. He was a fine bass player and a decent harmony vocalist who gave the live Love Gone Wrong sound some much-needed grunt. We worked solidly playing around Sydney a few times a week and touring regularly to Melbourne and occasionally to Brisbane and Adelaide. But the initial attempts to get some decent studio recordings proved to be problematic.

One session, possibly an audition at Festival Records studio in Pyrmont, was a case in point. We spent about 12 hours in the studio recording 8 to 10 songs but never quite nailing any of them convincingly. Tempos raced. Solos never quite fired. Harmonies were strong but not too, erm, harmonious. As band leader, I couldn't quite figure out why this was (or wasn't) happening. I'd recorded with many lineups in different studios, and somehow the results were almost always satisfying. Perhaps this band just didn't believe in itself enough.

Over the course of 1987 the band, without any new releases, seemed to lose the momentum gained from the high-rotation 2JJJ hit, 'Big Country' in July 1986. Our manager, convinced that we had to move on from my indie past with Red Eye Records, pitched our lacklustre demos to all the major and some minor-major record labels in Sydney to no great response. We ended up, without any other alternative offers, accepting a deal with Mighty Boy Records (MBR), a relatively new player that was trying to break into the big league. With no advance budget on offer, we booked to record our album at a studio run by Gerard Teleman, another MBR artist. We would be paying for the sessions ourselves, so the 16-track home studio setup in his rented Surry Hills terrace was as much as we could have afforded. The studio arrangement was reasonably professional but also relatively relaxed.

One major decision made from the outset was that the drum tracks for the songs would need to be recorded to a click track. We'd had earlier recordings weakened by accelerating tempos. So, this seems to be an essential tool to achieve better quality recordings. The problem that I didn't realise at the time was that playing drums to a click track and still retaining a feel or a groove was a skill not all drummers had. As a result, our recordings were in time, but they lacked a little life. We added bass, guitars, and vocals on top of the drum tracks. I realised that once the foundation is compromised, the rest of the building won't be solid.

The sessions became a bit of a grind. There was not much fun. Not much spark. It became a chore that we needed to finish. We'd worked for a year preparing to record our first album. But now we were at that point; we just wanted it to be finished. There weren't really any arguments. We just felt that we wouldn't be capturing much magic during these sessions.

The songs? The songs were generally good. Nothing screamed Smash Hit. But there were plenty of strong songs: 'Hey Steven', 'I Want You', 'The Singing City', and 'Better Days'. Even the relatively "minor" tracks - 'The Eyes Have It', 'You Will Find', and 'When Evening Comes' - had enough detail and texture to hold interest. They were not markedly different from many of the songs in the back catalogue. The collection was more like a development on the songs that I'd released before. There were a number of co-writes with Cory and one with Wayne, adding some new accents.

The album came out in late 1987, probably a mistake, getting lost in the Christmas rush of mega releases. Mighty Boy did their job getting it out to radio and getting the band spots on ABC and commercial TV. They also got us lots of reviews from the music press and the daily newspapers. I think it sold okay, making the Indie charts. But it didn't top those charts like some of my earlier releases had. We seemed to have been caught straddling two streams. We didn't have what the commercial radio wanted - the slick, punchy stadium rock sound. And we'd lost much of our indie charm by trying to produce a more professional sound. Like an old song from Dave Warner said, we were "*Too hip for the straights. And too straight for the hips*".

The responses varied widely. To many, the album seemed to be likeable but not great. The more positive reviews said it was good but lacked a couple of "killer" songs. Others were less kind. It seems like there'd been some axe grinding going on, and now they were really going to cut us down. "*Either the finest moment of a rather mediocre band or the mediocre beginnings of a very good one*", concluded one reviewer. Battered by some of this criticism, the band staggered on for about another six months before disbanding, not waiting to see if the second of these predictions would be realised.

So, was this the album that killed my career? Because of the mixed reviews, the modest sales, and the lack of satisfaction, the band went through the motions of promoting the album. But whatever spirit we'd had was gone. There was another live concert recording done in late '87, again in Melbourne. This one was for the TV show Rockarena. The footage of that show, which is up on YouTube, sees the band at the top of its game. The songs played are mainly from *ATB*. The performances are much more confident than those on the album. But it felt as though we'd missed an opportunity. Just when things could have been taking off, they were starting to stall. The band broke up in mid-'88. I faced the choice of starting again with a new lineup or packing my bags and heading off on an adventure overseas. I chose the adventure, and it led me to Berlin and a new life. But my music career was dead. I'd never again regain the momentum I'd had with Love Gone Wrong.

And did I really want the album buried forever? Well, obviously, not. Hindsight is a wonderful thing if you can get far away enough from something you've focused too closely on. On listening to the remastered versions of these songs, I hear the care and the craft that went into them. Under the pale skin of the production, I hear the beating hearts of the songs. The songs on this album may not be as dear to me as others, but they are an important part of my back catalogue - part of my story - part of my heritage. As such, I can now listen to them without the weight of negative connotations and enjoy the melodies and lyrics again. To those who liked these songs the first-time round, listen to them and the bonus tracks and let them take you back to the joys of your well spent years in the Australian Indie landscape of the 1980s. It's unlikely any of the harsher critics will be tempted to revisit this album. But if they did, they'd find some fine moments from a band that never quite reached its potential.

P.S.: 2021 indeed did see the release of an expanded remastered CD set of *Always The Bridegroom*. I can hear the care and craft that went into making these songs, they may not be as dear to me as others in my back catalogue, but nonetheless they are part of my story, part of my legacy. *ATB* holds some fine moments of a band that never quite reached its potential. Those that liked these songs the first-time round, listen to them again; let them take you back to your well-spent years in the Australian Indie landscape of the 1980s.

● The debut LP by Mi-Sex, titled *Graffiti Crimes*, was released in July 1979. The album was quickly issued to coincide with their national tour supporting Talking Heads. The recordings had been mixed and produced just a couple of weeks prior. The single 'Computer Games' reached No.1 in Australia in October 1979 and No.5 in New Zealand, where the band originated. Mi-Sex, like many New Zealand bands, became based in Australia and tirelessly played in pubs from 1977 to 1986. They reformed in 2011, but sadly without Steve Gilpin, who was killed in a car accident in 1992. The band took their name from a track by Ultravox called 'My Sex', which appeared on that group's debut album, *Ultravox!* The original line-up of the band consisted of Gilpin as the vocalist, Murray Burns on keyboards, Kevin Stanton as the guitarist/songwriter, Richard Hodgkinson on drums, and Don Martin on bass.

● Propaganda's *A Secret Wish*, released internationally on June 1, 1985, stands as a remarkable exemplar of synthpop-NEW WAVE perfection, much like Human League's *Dare*. It exudes pure bliss, rivaling the best works of OMD, New Order, and Depeche Mode. This album excels in its song composition, experimentation, production, and design, solidifying its status as an ageless gem within the Industrial-Techno-Europop genre. Noteworthy tracks include 'Dr Mabuse', which, despite its limited chart success in the eighties, showcases courage and brilliance. 'Duel' possesses all the qualities of an earworm that lingers in the mind, while 'Sorry for Laughing', a cover version of Josef K's song, leaves an indelible mark. Undoubtedly, this album is an essential addition to any music collection. In the words of Edgar Allan Poe, "*All that we see or seem, is but a dream within a dream*".

Propaganda by permission/Propaganda by John Stoddart

● The icon Fred Schneider was born on this day in 1951. Fred is and always has been the front-man vocalist with The B-52's. Fred has said "*I didn't sing until I was in the band*"….but aren't we glad he did? The B-52's as we know have become rock music royalty. As a solo artist Fred has recorded two albums and from 2006 Fred has led a synthpop side project called The Superions recording a couple of albums and a handful of singles. Fred can also be seen and/or heard in quite a few films.

AN INTERVIEW WITH FRED SCHNEIDER III
(The B-52's)

Hi Fred, It's great to connect via face-time, gotta love technology! So, I've read and heard you say that prior to the B-52's you weren't involved in music as such, is that right?

Yes correct, I wrote, I didn't play anything. I wrote poetry and lyrics for crazy songs in high school; they had no melodies as such just threw myself into creative writing.

In those high-school years what did you listen to?

I lived in New York, and we had the Top 40, but I was easily drawn to the sounds of Motown, the likes of Martha and The Vandellas and even more-so the obscure Motown artists. I loved The Rolling Stones and The Beatles just like everyone else, of course. Soul was more my thing, when I discovered them, I was glued to the African-American stations, it took me to the Detroit radio stations… I'm there! This is me!!

Travelling back in time to the debut B-52's gig. You had Keith (Strickland) on congas, Ricky (Wilson) on guitar and the girls Kate (Pierson) and Cindy (Wilson), Ricky's sister. Were there others involved?

Oh No! There was a tape machine with added music. Keith and Ricky were whizzes, amazing with all that stuff. The tape machine actually fell off the table but luckily, we got it going again. We did four songs and then did the same four songs over again! The songs…mmmmm.. 'Killer Bees' the first song we ever wrote, maybe 'Planet Claire'…. the others seem to be gone from my memory.

Okay… you are now a band, The B-52's is now an entity. What was the feeling amongst you about the future and getting signed?

We didn't like our first manager; we felt that he was trying to take advantage of us. We just didn't know what to expect. We knew how to get a show going and just knew we could have people blown away. And whenever we did support different bands there was this thing *"oh.. the B-52's really stole the show"*. We once appeared on Saturday Night Live, we were not camera ready at all and almost paralyzed with fear! It was 1980 and it was here that my family, my mother, and grandmother first saw us, they loved us! My grandmother would say, *"That's my Freddy!"*

With so many gigs under your belt now, what is the most memorable one for you, the one that really stands out?

You can't ask that because there are just so many! Like there's Rock in Rio, that first show in Australia. OH MY GOD!! What is going on here?! Australia! We just weren't ready for our first '15 minutes', we were just a bunch of friends, like WOW! Australia was just unbelievable, patting a koala, feeding a kangaroo, this was just what we wanted! We're going here! One thing I loved and was proud of was doing 'Planet Claire' with Foo Fighters on Halloween, my favourite holiday, it was back in 2002. I love those guys; it was unrehearsed and went over really well! I thought, I can still do this stuff with these young guys!

How about touring, you are about to stop touring, has it just become too tedious?

Back in the day, we travelled on a bus, I just couldn't sleep on a bus! I needed sleeping pills! The travel... oh my! Planes…Please get me off here!

Is there anything happening recording-wise?

No not really, I have a few singles out under my name working with other groups. Nothing planned, but you never know…never say never, we never even knew from the beginning. It's just so hard and expensive to get us all together. We all want to do our own thing, yet we love each other and being together is just so good. But… You never know!

Musically what are you most proud of? You must have a favourite.

OH! Mmmmmm... tough one... my solo stuff with the Superions, yes, my solo albums. I wrote everything, except for one song. Coming up with lyrics for certain songs the B's did of course. How does one have a favourite with favourites on every album. There's 'Dreamland' that I wrote with Kate and Keith and there's 'Planet Claire', nobody writes songs like we do! 'Love Shack'! We're the only band that does it really well.

What music is playing or was the last thing played in your household? And your top five of all time?

I have so many albums and 45's I'm set for life. I turn on the radio and they say *"this is so new and different"* but no it isn't! I guess it just has to be Greatest Hits albums. Number 1 would be, Martha & The Vandellas, number 2, The Ronettes, number 3, Dusty Springfield's Greatest Hits, her first album was the first record I ever bought. Mmmmmm...so, mmmmmm number 4, The 3CD set of Petula Clark... And oh, I guess I should name one of our albums. The double Best of The B-52's, but that doesn't exist.... YET!

Away from music what are you into, what's your pastime?

I love to cook, I'm a vegetarian and I've been told I should open a restaurant! I love reading, I read a lot and at the moment I'm reading Beasts Before Us, The Untold Story of Mammals Evolution. I'm a dinosaur nut!! Ha! Surprise!!

Great to talk with you Fred, and we must thank Tom Yaz for making this happen.

Fred Schneider of The B-52s by Peter Tocher

◉ Sire Records launched the 'Don't Call It Punk' campaign in mid-1977. The goal was to replace the term "punk rock" with "NEW WAVE". Seymour Stein, Sire Records chairman, believed that using the term "punk" was hurting sales for Sire's acts. Many of these acts performed at CBGB in New York. The Dead Boys, The Ramones, and Talking Heads had early releases that didn't gain much attention. Stein wanted to promote the term "NEW WAVE" instead, which marked the beginning of the end for Punk Rock.

2

◉ In 2008, the gravestone belonging to Ian Curtis, the former lead singer of Joy Division, was taken from his burial site at Macclesfield Cemetery in Cheshire, England, where his cremated remains had been interred. The Cheshire Police reported that Curtis' memorial marker, which was inscribed with his name, birth and death dates, and the title of the Joy Division song 'Love Will Tear Us Apart', had been stolen. Both law enforcement and Curtis' family made public appeals for any information that could lead to the recovery of the original headstone, but as of now, it has still not been returned to his grave.

◉ Pete Briquette, also known as Patrick Martin Cusack, was born in 1954 in Ballyjamesduff, Ireland. He was a founding member of the Boomtown Rats in 1977, serving as the bassist.

In addition to his musical contributions, Pete is recognized as a record producer and composer. Currently, he is a member of Bob Geldof's band. The stage name Pete Briquette is inspired by his Irish roots, where peat briquettes were commonly used for heating purposes instead of coal.

⊙ On July 2nd, 1982, Topper Headon of The Clash was arrested, charged, and remanded on bail for stealing a bus stop sign on Fulham Road, London. He was a naughty boy!!

⊙ Malcom McLaren was at it again! On July 2, 1980, McLaren's cunning business mind brought us the first cassette single release with 'C·30 C·60 C·90 Go', the debut release by Bow Wow Wow. McLaren created the band himself, taking Adam and The Ants minus Adam, and adding the barely teenage Annabella Lwin, forming what would become an almost perfect pop group. McLaren produced and wrote the song, sharing writing credits with ex-Ants Matthew Ashman, Leigh Gorman, and Dave Barbarossa. It was No.1 on the cassette single chart (the only one on there), and on the official singles chart, it reached No.34 in the UK.

⊙ The San Franciscan band Romeo Void released their first album; *It's a Condition* on this day in 1981. While many attribute the success of Romeo Void to Debora Lyall's captivating voice, presentation, and lyrical content, it is important to acknowledge the contribution of the talented musicians who support her. The album showcases a combination of intricate lyrical poetry and exceptional alternative jazzy instrumentation. Despite being an overlooked gem, this debut album predates the popular song 'Never Say Never', which later became Romeo Void's most recognized work and received extensive airplay.

⊙ The Australian television series *Sweet and Sour* first screened on ABC-TV in 1984. Created by Johanna Piggott and Tim Gooding (both from the XL Capris), it tells the story of the trials and tribulations in the modern pop world of a NEW WAVE band called The Takeaways. The series starred Tracy Mann, David Reyne and Arky Michael. Deborah Conway from Do-Re-Mi, John Clifforth and Cathy McQuade of Deckchairs Overboard provided the 'singing voices' of the lead actors, and some of the music was played by the likes of Reg Mombassa, Red Symons, Todd Hunter & Rick Grossman. It's been said that during the recording of show there was 'a meeting of the minds' by Mark Callaghan, Graham Bidstrup & Chris Baily and it led to the formation of GANGgajang.

3

⊙ Brian Canham was born in 1962 in Melbourne, Australia. In 1982, he formed Pseudo Echo with his high school friend Pierre Gigliotti. Taking influence from the likes of Ultravox and Japan they created their own style of smooth rhythmic synthpop. Pseudo Echo had several top 10 hits and their album *Autumnal Park* reached No.11 on the charts. It was the cover of the Lipps Inc. disco hit Funkytown that had them being heard on dance floors across the nation, the band gave the song a new lease of life as it went No.1 nationally. The band split in 1990 but has had a few reunions. Brian has also been successful as a producer and jingle writer. Pseudo Echo still performs occasionally and released a new album, *After Party*, in 2020.

⊙ Vincent John Martin was born in 1960 in South Woodford, England and later adopted the stage name Vince Clarke. He started playing keyboards and was an original member of the bands Depeche Mode, Yazoo, The Assembly, and Erasure. He formed Depeche Mode along with schoolmates Andrew Fletcher and Martin Gore, initially performing under the names No Romance in China and Composition of Sound before settling on Depeche Mode in 1980. Their debut album *Speak & Spell* reached No.10 on the UK charts in 1981. It featured hit singles 'Just Can't Get Enough' and 'New Life'. Despite the early success, Clarke left Depeche Mode in 1981 to start the synthpop duo Yazoo with singer Alison Moyet, also known as Alf. Yazoo produced two very successful albums and multiple hit singles before splitting up in 1983. Clarke then partnered with singer Andy Bell to create Erasure, his most fruitful collaboration to date. Erasure found popularity in both the UK and US with hits like 'Sometimes', 'Chains of Love', and 'A Little Respect'. To date, they have sold over 25 million albums globally, with four reaching No.1 in the UK and are regarded as one of the most successful British pop groups ever.

Julie Mostyn of Flaming Hands photo by Stuart Spence 1981

◉ Julienne Mostyn-Gilbert was born July 3rd and as Julie Mostyn she started out as the vocalist with The Kamikaze Kids before joining up in 1980 with songwriter/guitarist Jeff Sullivan to form The Flaming Hands. The Flaming Hands had a massive following drawn in by an infectious brand of POST-PUNK styled 1960s soul, psyche R&B. Signing to Phantom records in 1980 they released the well-received single 'I Belong to Nobody' followed by 'Wake Up Screaming' early the next year. They had now formed a solid line-up consisting of Julie, Jeff Sullivan, Paul 'Sluggo' Maheno on sax, Grant Conner (bass), Peter Bull (keyboards) and Alan Brown on drums. It was this line-up that had a single night's support of The Clash during their seven-night stint at Sydney's Capitol Theatre in 1982. So impressed with the style of the band The Clash's manager, Bernie Rhodes became something of a Flaming Hands fan! Yet, even with minor success and sales the band folded by the end of '82. Julie and Jeff stayed together and got together a new band called Tunnels and Trains but soon they rebirthed the name The Flaming Hands and signed to Big Time Records and released the *self-titled* album in 1984. Two great singles were released from this LP 'Break Down and Cry' and 'Out of Our Hands', but by the end of '85 after years of hard work, blood sweat and tears Julie and Jeff retired Flaming Hands. In 2017 there was a reunion gig as support to Sunnyboys at The Enmore, the place was packed and the excitement of the early '80s was relived!! Today, Julie lives on the mid north coast of New South Wales married to former Radio Birdman bassist Warwick Gilbert.

HOW I FOUND MYSELF WHILE LOSING MYSELF IN MUSIC
JULIE MOSTYN-GILBERT
(Kamikaze Kidz, Flaming Hands)

I could tell you about the time The Flaming Hands were hired to play on The Alexander Pushkin Russian cruise ship for 10 days, the rough seas we experience, how Jeff (Sullivan) became so ill (he burst all the blood vessels around his eyes making him look like a human panda bear) he required a bucket on stage to vomit into whilst playing every night. I could perhaps bore you a little with the time we were lucky enough to play with the late great musician Billy Preston, in some down at heel Western Sydney RSL, and how he told me

"*You got soul, sister*"… a mighty nice confidence boosting compliment coming from the great man. I could even mention the time we played with The Clash at the Capitol Theatre and how Bernie Rhodes became a fan. Then there was Tom Waits at The State Theatre, these were definitely highlights, and although I've forgotten a lot, hopefully I'll keep those memories stored so as to be able to pull them out when the going gets tough. But instead, I'm going to get a little personal, dive a bit deeper and tell you how singing and making music with my buddies and compatriots makes me feel.

In some strange way, singing is a wonderful disguise. I leave myself behind and get lost in the music. Music takes you somewhere else, like a strange out of body experience and connects you with your audience.

I was a shy only child from an oddball family. How was I to learn about the world? I grew up in Kings Cross/Potts Point with my eccentric parents. Music was my saviour, it took me into another world, transported me from where I was and who I was, it was the perfect escape from everything. I could lose myself, every chance I had, in music. Thereby entering what Tim Winton has called "the infinite present". So, from a very early age I was listening. Either on my tranny with my ear pressed up against the speaker of our record player …. My father was a huge fan of music and lucky for me, would bring, fantastic vinyl LPs and singles back from his many trips to the US. There were albums likes Frank Sinatra's … *Songs for Swinging Lovers!*, Nina Simone's … *Nina at the Village Gate*, Sam Cooke's *Night Beat,* Odetta's … *Sometimes I Feel Like Crying*, and great songs like Eartha Kitt's … 'I Want to Be Evil', Ray Charles' … 'Mess Around', Henry Red Alan's … 'Wild Man Blues' and of course Aretha Franklin, etc.. All these artists spoke to me with their rhythm, melody, lyrics, and emotions.

The Beatles blew my mind, The Rolling Stones, The Animals, Them, Dusty Springfield, Sandy Shaw …… fantastic!

The Beatles tour of Australia in June 1964 was a revelation, they stayed up the road, at The Sheraton hotel in Macleay Street Potts Point, opposite The Chevron Hotel where The Rolling Stones would stay a year later in November 1965. It was an amazingly exciting time! She Loves You Yeah Yeah Yeah! I was 11 years old how could I not be swept away, they were definitely speaking to me, they understood me or so I thought … ha! The first vinyl LP I ever bought with my own money was The Beatles' *Please Please Me*. How lucky could a young girl be, I had to walk past the Sheraton on my way to school charged with hope in my heart, the myriad of screaming girls added to the excitement, it was absolutely fantastic… I might catch a glimpse of John, Paul, George or Ringo…Oh my God!!

A little over a year later in November 1965, The Rolling Stones arrived this time staying at The Chevron Hotel. By now I was 13 with all the puberty blues that age suggests. Somehow, I persuaded my mother to come with me to The Chevron for a sandwich and there they were in the dining room having a frigging food fight!... I plucked up enough courage to go over and ask for their autographs, sadly, since lost.

Fast forward to the '70s, it was a great time of change, Gough Whitlam had made so many positive changes for Australia, like indigenous recognition, free tertiary education, he made the ABC's 2JJ radio station possible etc. etc. and then 'The Dismissal' happened in 1975, I was devastated and angry, I was rebellious. Another world beckoned. Music would take me there.

Often, it's the people we meet that shape our world, in my case this was true. I met Joel Griffin, Dare Jennings and a bunch of people who had a secret, a tribe, it was Radio Birdman, now we're talking rebellion and belonging…..

Maybe I can form a band too?? First came The Jive Bombers an R&B outfit…I was listening, listening and learning, then Ron Blake asked me to form a band which became the Kamikaze Kidz early 1978. We did lots of great covers, Janis Joplin, Sex Pistols, Ike & Tina

Turner. Peter Coutanche played a mighty guitar and Ron a cool bass, we didn't do any recording besides the 2JJ recording of us, and with X one hot sweaty night at the Civic Hotel early 1979 (this recording only just surfaced...thanks Steve Lorkin). We broke up of course...too much of the usual sex, drugs, and R'n'R bought us to our knees. Not long after (sometime in 1979) Jeff Sullivan and I got together and formed The Flaming Hands.

I've always loved words. A question often asked of people is: *"what is it you like best about music, is it the melody, the rhythm, the words, the emotion, the feeling?"* Well, for me it's the whole box and dice...the rawness, the mistakes the whole catastrophe. For me it's impossible to separate one from the other. But words hold a special place in my heart. It's through words we derive meaning, metaphor and nuance. Jeff is a wonderful wordsmith and rhythm man; he and I worked together really well and with the other band members were able to create the sound of the Flaming Hands...thanks guys.

We had a soul influenced funky sound, great to dance to and packed full of rhythm, having said that, we didn't shy away from the occasional ballad either.

For me having the privilege of working on music, honing it and then presenting it to an audience was and is truly amazing. That's where I reached that state of the "infinite present" that Tim Winton talks about. This shy girl could express the same feelings and emotions we all have, I could have that intimate discussion with you through song.

Now I have the great joy of working on music with my soul mate and husband Warwick Gilbert. Warwick and I created our home and family together with our children Beau, Bridie, and Brook. Music has given me so very much; it saved me in many ways. My son Beau was born. I have met so many fantastic people who are long lasting friends. I've grown up through music and found myself.

● Lee Ranaldo's debut solo album *From Here to Infinity* arrived on record store shelves in 1987, showcasing the Sonic Youth guitarist's bold experimentation and creative ambition. The album featured Ranaldo's innovative use of the "locked groove", allowing listeners to choose the duration of the closing track. Released originally on clear and grey vinyl instead of traditional black, *From Here to Infinity* married abrasive noise with oddly listenable moments of discordant songcraft, sculpting sounds for those drawn to sonic design over structure. It was an intriguing, pioneering work.

● Tim Smith, the lead vocalist/guitarist, and keyboardist of Cardiacs, also known as Cardiac Arrest, was born in Carshalton, England in 1961. The band, which saw a constant flow of more than 20 members, could only be described as the UK's equivalent of Pere Ubu. Their live shows were hailed as incredibly surreal, blending POST-PUNK and progressive elements in a way that defied categorization. From 1980 to 1999, they released a total of eight studio albums, yet commercial success eluded them, with only one single, 'Is This the Life?', charting in 1988. Tim passed away on July 21, 2020, after battling complications resulting from a simultaneous heart attack and stroke in 2008.

4

● Any Trouble was formed in 1975 by Clive Gregson and after a handful of singles finally release their debut album *Where Are All the Nice Girls?* in 1980 on the Stiff label. This is a power-pop gem, there's no denying there are sprinklings of influences by the classic tracks of NEW WAVE luminaries Elvis Costello, Joe Jackson, and Graham Parker. Any Trouble's debut is an enjoyable and a musically varied album, a highlight of Gregson's output.

● The Clash made their live debut at The Black Swan in Sheffield, supporting the Sex Pistols on July 4, 1976.

⊙ Kirk Pengilly was born July 4, 1958, in Kew, Victoria, he is best known as the co-writer, guitarist, percussionist and saxophonist of INXS. In 1971, while in high school, Kirk met Tim Farriss and they started an amateur band called Guinness. Kirk was the main songwriter and lead singer of Guinness. After Guinness broke up, The Farriss Brothers band was formed. Initially, Kirk and Michael Hutchence shared lead vocals in the band. However, since Michael did not play an instrument, he took over as the lead singer while Kirk focused on playing the guitar and saxophone. Kirk was the band's archivist and logged daily entries in a diary. Kirk contributed greatly to the authorized INXS biography *Story to Story* and even wrote the foreword of the book.

⊙ Approximately one year after forming, The Primitives entered the studio to record their first single, 'Thru The Flowers', which was released on July 4, 1986. The upbeat, guitar-driven pop song blended the sounds of Blondie and The Jesus & Mary Chain, featuring Tracy Tracy's vocals and Paul Court's guitarwork. It was put out on their independent label Lazy Records. Court once remarked that their initial aim was to play at an extremely high volume that would nearly obscure the vocals, but this changed when they brought Tracy on board.

⊙ Talk Talk's first album *The Party's Over* came out in 1982. With its synthpop sound reminiscent of Duran Duran, it was a strong inaugural release for the new band, which would go on to make even better music over time. Though the record was of high caliber, Mark Hollis and company still saw room for growth. Tracks like 'Talk Talk', 'It's So Serious', 'Today', 'Mirror Man', 'Hate' and 'Candy' are beautiful compositions. All in all, *The Party's Over* was a very impressive first effort for Talk Talk.

5

⊙ On July 5, 1981, Belgium's Werchter Festival boasted a lineup of De Kreumers (a local band), The Undertones, Toots & The Maytals, Elvis Costello & The Attractions, The Cure and Robert Palmer, with Dire Straits topping the bill. There were a few early technical issues that meant time was running short, and while The Cure were onstage, midway through what was to be a 15-song set, Palmer's roadies insisted that they would have to cut their set short. Robert Smith later said, *"This bloke ran on stage and said, "If you don't stop playing, we're going to pull the plug".* Smith then announced, *"This is our final song as we aren't allowed to carry on anymore because everyone wants to see Robert Palmer I think".* Following jeers from the crowd, The Cure then proceeded to play a slowed version 'A Forest' stretching the 6-minute song to 15 minutes! This naturally annoyed the Palmer crew! At the end, The Cure's bassist Simon Gallup yelled, *"I hope you're not arresting me. Fuck Robert Palmer! Fuck rock 'n' roll!"* Smith later said, *"It was fucking brilliant. Unfortunately, when we finished, they threw all our stuff off the back of the stage!"*

The Cure 1985 by Petra Gall

O Terence Chimes, also known as Terry, was born on this day in 1956 in Stepney, London, England. He was the original drummer of the band The Clash. Chimes had three separate periods of time playing with the band in 1976, 1977, and 1982. He also played with other groups such as Cowboys International and Hanoi Rocks. Additionally, Chimes was a part of Billy Idol's touring band and had various other musical endeavours. In 2003, he was inducted into the Rock and Roll Hall of Fame alongside Joe Strummer, Mick Jones, Paul Simonon, and Nicky "Topper" Headon, who was the other drummer in the band. It is worth noting that Pete Howard, who only appeared on The Clash's final studio album *Cut the Crap*, did not receive the same honour.

O Chris Wardman initially gained recognition as the guitarist and songwriter for the influential Canadian NEW WAVE band Blue Peter. This band played a pivotal role in the POST-PUNK scene in Toronto and had the privilege of sharing stages with renowned acts such as The Police, Simple Minds, Blondie, The Jam, and The Boomtown Rats. Even after four decades, their song 'Don't Walk Past' continues to receive significant airplay. Wardman, born in Oshawa, Canada, in 1959, later embarked on a successful career as a producer, collaborating with numerous artists, including Art Bergmann, The Tragically Hip, Rusty, Chalk Circle, Randy Bachman, The Leslie Spit Tree-o, Emm Gryner, The Watchmen, Big Wreck, Ensign Broderick, and many others. Additionally, he has held positions as an in-house producer, A&R representative, and new media specialist at major record labels such as Capitol Records, BMG Music Canada, and Universal Music Canada.

BUMPED BY THE CLASH
CHARIS WARDMAN
(Blue Peter)

In 1977 my band Blue Peter (ironically named after a British kids show we'd never watched) was stuck between our art rock aspirations and the more realistic path of playing rock covers in the rundown bars of northern Ontario. Hearing the first albums of Elvis Costello and Talking Heads showed us a different path. By 1978 we were playing punk/NEW WAVE bars in downtown Toronto to a small but growing audience.

The following year we got the dream call to open for our heroes, the Clash, on their first North American tour. On February 29, 1979, we loaded our gear into Toronto's Rex Danforth Theatre and were sitting in the dressing room when we got the news that we'd been bumped for an all-female local punk band (which we actually thought was kinda cool). We did get to see the Clash play, though, and as we were loading out, our bass player, Geoff McOuat, had the pleasure of hailing a cab for the band.

A month later we spent two nights opening for the Boomtown Rats at the El Mocambo, getting an encore both nights. We were confined to a basement dressing room where the club stored broken chairs, but a waitress snuck us into the headliner's show, where we watched them play a brand-new song called 'I Don't Like Mondays'.

In 1980, at the record release concert for our first album, *Radio Silence*, Joni Mitchell showed up and told the press how much she liked the band, so that kind of made up for the Clash letdown.

Over the next couple of years, with constant regional touring, we did support gigs for The Jam, The Police and Simple Minds. Blue Peter went on to success in Canada, with an iconic video for the song 'Don't Walk Past' before breaking up in 1985.

O Frank Weyzig was born in 1957 in the Netherlands. Frank started his music career in the mid-'80s with the legendary Dutch electronic band Clan of Xymox (CoX) when, at the time, they were signed with the famed English label 4AD. Frank played guitar & keyboard parts on the acclaimed CoX *self-titled* debut album in 1985 and continued to join the band on stage as live guitarist and keyboard player until 1990. CoX fans will surely remember Frank's haunting guitar solo on 'Cry in the Wind'. From 1995 until 1999 he played as vocalist and guitarist with Dutch indie-wave band Born For Bliss. Frank of late has been the driving force of Vaselyne, a collaboration with Yvette Winkler.

MEETING A STARMAN
FRANK WEYZIG
(Clan of Xymox, Born For Bliss)

I have so many stories to tell about the things that I have experienced during my musical career. But one of the most precious moments was when I met the man who inspired me to become a musician... Everything became full circle for me at that moment... A small-town boy from the Netherlands ending up in Los Angeles, meeting his hero.

I grew up in a small town in the north of the Netherlands. Back in those days, when I was a teenager, there was not much of an exciting Dutch music culture happening that I wanted to be part of. So, I had to look and listen at what was going on in my neighbouring country, the UK. When I was a kid, I wasn't really thinking of becoming a musician until I heard David Bowie on the radio for the first time. It was as if a door to a new universe opened up to me. Songs like 'Starman' and 'Moonage Daydream' literally changed my life, and *The Rise and Fall of Ziggy Stardust and the Spiders from Mars* became my all-time favourite rock album. Not only did David Bowie become my number one hero, but also Mick Ronson became my hero guitar player. I no longer wanted to be a kid. I wanted to grow up to be just like them.

Years later, when I had somewhat established my own musical career by joining Clan of Xymox, I finally had the opportunity to meet with the man who had been my number one inspiration for becoming a musician.

I remember and cherish this special moment that now seems much more precious to me than ever before since he passed away... In 1989, during our Twist of Shadows tour, I played with Xymox in Los Angeles. I forgot which venue we played, but there was a rumour that someone famous was in the audience... In Los Angeles we were sharing the same hotel with The Godfathers. The day after our gig, some of our group went to The Godfather's after-party and then suddenly... there he was. I was standing face to face with my hero, the man who changed my world and inspired me to become a musician.

"*I enjoyed the show, great gig*", he said. I hardly could believe what I was hearing but obviously he was referring to our Xymox gig from the previous night. Of course, I was in shock, and I was almost paralysed, and all I could mutter was a stuttered "*Ttt...tt...thanks*"... We shook hands, and without even realising it, I must have squeezed his hand very strongly because all I wanted was to just hold his hand forever and never let go... He smiled, and very gently he pulled back his hand as if he didn't want to spoil my moment of eternal happiness... Then he just turned around and walked away, and I just stood there for the next couple of minutes as if struck by lightning, speechless! www.frankweyzig.com

6

◉ On July 6, 1979, planet Earth shook with the release of the *self-titled* B-52's debut album. Costing $35,000 to record, it's simply a classic disc, like a great comic strip; it's full of landmark moments and promises of things to come. This was pure pop NEW WAVE; it was vibrant, individualistic, and unique. No, the band members weren't great musicians technically, but the sense of mirth and irreverence in it is rich. There is an energy that radiates through when the band itself plays and writes their music, as opposed to having other musicians play as they did later. This is just a fun album and one of the most interesting sonic experiences out there. How could the fun-loving, foot-tapping types resist the magnificent hooks and grooves of this debut? The magnificent song 'Rock Lobster' remains unmatched in terms of its relentless, infectious power to move one's feet, and that goes ditto for '52 Girls', straight from sixties garage rock. From the celestial opening of 'Planet Claire' to the cheesy, corny cover of Petula Clark's 'Downtown', this debut is as close to perfect as you can get. Seriously cheeky, the album in totality is catchy and infectious with a beat that is reminiscent of the 60s surf/beach pop. Everyone has this album. EPIC!

○ In 1976 The Damned took to the stage for their debut gig using that name when they supported the Sex Pistols at the 100 Club, London. That said, they had played a few weeks earlier at a free festival in Croydon but were yet unnamed. The band became what is generally accepted as the first of the London punk bands to release a single, 'New Rose', on the new independent label Stiff.

The Damned – unknown photographer

○ John Leslie Keeble was born in 1959 in Hampstead, North London. John was a founding member and remains the drummer with Spandau Ballet. One wonders if he will ever play with Tony Hadley's solo band since his official 2017 split. John was Hadleys' drummer throughout a tour of 2006. John has his own band, I Play Rock, and they perform sporadically.

○ The *self-titled* debut album of The Lords of the New Church was released in 1982. The punk genre was considered finished, leading Stiv Bators to collaborate with guitarist Brian James, who was looking for a new project after departing from The Damned. The result was a unique blend of POST-PUNK and NEW WAVE music, entering down the road of 'Goth Glam'. Yeah, many genres but that's what happens when something is hard to pigeonhole. The music featured powerful drumming, booming basslines, and electric guitar riffs, reminiscent of a milder version of Killing Joke. Bators' distinctive vocals shone on tracks like 'New Church', 'Open Your Eyes', 'Livin' On Livin', and 'Holy War'.

7

○ Petra Gall died on 7 July 2018. Born in 1955, Petra from Berlin, Germany, was a highly regarded photo-journalist who was integral in documenting the punk, new wave, post-punk, and the alternative music scenes in Europe. She became well known for her photographic exposés of the Berlin feminist and lesbian subculture during the 1980s. Her work was eagerly sought by the mainstream and alternative press, and it was with Heidi Zimmermann that they founded the photo agency Zebra; together they published books and calendars and worked for newspapers and magazines. Petra's photographs are featured in this book, and we thank the Schwules Museum of Berlin for making her work available to us.

Petra Gall self portrait

⊙ On July 7, 1981, The Go-Go's released their debut album *Beauty and The Beat*. This album must be rated as one of the NEW WAVE pop masterpieces of the '80s. It's superbly produced, it's clear, bright, and yet not at all ostentatious. Full marks must go to the songwriting, the songs are infectious and energetic with a feel of '60s surf-rock, and a nod to bubble-gum while always remaining at a level of maturity. From 'Our Lips Are Sealed' to 'Can't Stop the World' and all stops in between we get wonderfully constructed pop. Timeless.

⊙ In 1984, David Sylvian released his first solo album, *Brilliant Trees*. It is a dazzling release where he steps away from Japan. The songs, instrumentation, and arrangements are cutting-edge. Many notable musicians contribute to this record, creating a sound that transcends genres. The music is elegant and graceful, with a relaxing calmness throughout. Each track on the album is classy, and it's difficult to choose favourites. 'Weathered Wall', featuring Jon Hassell's treated trumpet, stands out for its sophistication. 'Nostalgia' creates a mood and atmosphere that is also a peak moment. David's voice shines on 'Red Guitar', creating a sublime experience. The production, led by Steve Nye and Sylvian, is both intricate and minimalistic. The album is beautifully crafted and indeed brilliant.

⊙ The Waterboys released their *self-titled* debut album in 1983, establishing themselves as a key part of the eighties Celtic rock scene. Led by vocalist Mike Scott, whose passionate singing drew comparisons to Bono and whose anthemic tunes invited parallels with U2, The Waterboys composed hymns of energy and optimism on this record. It's easy to get swept up in rousing tracks like 'December', 'Girl in the Swing', and 'Savage Earth Heart', while 'A Girl Called Johnny' became an instant classic despite its Split Enz-esque style. Though coloured with folk hues, these advanced POST-PUNK tunes stood apart from other popular NEW WAVE bands of the era thanks to their sincerity and Scott's stirring songwriting.

8

⊙ The B-52's appeared in the UK for the first time at the Lyceum Ballroom in London on this day in 1979; the support on the bill was The Tourists, featuring Dave Stewart and Annie Lennox.

⊙ Following the transgression by Topper, the next members of The Clash to run into trouble with the authorities were Joe Strummer and Paul Simonon. On July 8, 1978, after completing a concert at the Apollo Theatre in Glasgow, Scotland, the two musicians were detained by police for public intoxication and unruly behaviour. They were eventually charged with the offences, resulting in fines of 50 British pounds each.

⊙ In 1977 DEVO took the stage for the first time in New York; the venue was Max's Kansas City. It was the first of 3 nights there; also on the bill were The Cramps and Suicide. David

Bowie was at the show and later in the night on stage proclaimed that "*this is the band of the future, I'm going to produce them this Christmas in Tokyo*". Eventually, in Conny Plank's Cologne studio, Brian Eno ended up being the dominant producer of *Q: Are We Not Men? A; We Are Devo!*, though David is credited with some production.

○ Killing Joke released their second and critically acclaimed studio album, *What's THIS For...!* in 1981. The album opens with pounding drums, chainsaw guitar, and metallic thrash that set the intense tone. More aligned with POST-PUNK than metal, the album maintains a relentlessly dark vibe throughout. With hypnotic, repetitive drumming and pulsing synths, songs like 'Unspeakable' exemplify the proto-industrial style that makes this a masterpiece. The band demonstrates the power of rhythmic repetition rather than melody. Overall, Killing Joke establishes their signature intense and hypnotic POST-PUNK/industrial sound on this seminal album.

○ Rodney Orpheus, born on July 8, 1960, in Moneymore, Northern Ireland, boasts over four decades of experience as a respected multi-instrumentalist, technology designer, and producer. He also served as the frontman of The Cassandra Complex (TCC). Formed in 1980 in Leeds, TCC has released eight albums since their impressive debut with *Grenade* in 1986. The band's music falls within the EBM, Gothic, and Industrial genres, known for their electronic sound and dance-friendly beats. Rodney's expertise at the mixing desk has led him to collaborate on remixes and productions with renowned artists such as Die Krupps and Future Sound of London.

○ The release of R.E.M.'s debut single 'Radio Free Europe' b/w 'Sitting Still' in 1981 marked the band's initial foray into the music scene. While some may now consider R.E.M. a pivotal group of the POST-PUNK era, this first single, although featuring a catchy melody and chorus, leaned more towards an AOR sound rather than aligning closely with POST-PUNK stalwarts like The Cure, XTC, or New Order. Nevertheless, the USA found in R.E.M. the birth of indie and alternative rock, a movement that they enthusiastically embraced.

○ Andrew John Fletcher, also known as Fletch, was born in Nottingham, England, in 1961. Fletch was a talented musician who played keyboards and bass, and he played a crucial role as a founding member of the iconic band Depeche Mode. From their debut album *Speak and Spell* in 1981 to their album *Spirit* in 2017, Fletch contributed his musical talents to all their albums. Not only was he a skilled musician, but he also took on various responsibilities within the band, such as handling their business, legal matters, and other non-musical interests throughout the years. Fletch was known as the 'tiebreaker' and played a vital role in bringing the band together, acting as a mediator between Dave Gahan and Martin Gore during their disagreements over songwriting duties. In addition to his contributions to Depeche Mode, Fletch was a renowned DJ. Whenever he took breaks from the band, he would perform at festivals and club gigs worldwide, delighting audiences with his DJ sets that included Depeche Mode remixes and samples. Sadly, Fletch passed away on May 26, 2022, at the age of 60.

9

○ Peter Mark Sinclair Almond, who goes by the stage name Marc Almond, was born in 1959 in Southport, England. Almond found great success starting in 1977 when he and his friend from Leeds Polytechnic, David Ball, formed the electronic duo Soft Cell. Soft Cell reached No.1 twice; first with their cover of 'Tainted Love' by the Four Preps and then again with Almond's duet with Gene Pitney on 'Something's Gotten Hold of My Heart'. Soft Cell's album *Non-Stop Erotic Cabaret* cemented their place in '80s NEW WAVE's synthpop history, with dancefloor-filling hits. Though Soft Cell amicably disbanded in 1984, they briefly reunited in 2000 for some live shows and new albums. Before the breakup, Almond had already started the project Marc and the Mambas, recording two albums with shifting members. This led to his prolific solo career spanning over twenty albums in diverse musical styles; he resists being pigeonholed. Almond is highly respected among his peers, as shown by his many collaborations with artists like John Cale, Nick Cave, Siouxsie Sioux, and Nico.

Marc Almond by Petra Gall/ Andy Fletcher by Petra Gall

THAT'S NOT WHAT I EXPECTED
MARC ALMOND
(Soft Cell, Marc and The Mambas)

If I was to look back to a point in my life when it all changed, it was when I was in my room living in Leeds in 1981, and I was called to the hallway phone, where I was told that our record 'Tainted Love' had reached number one. Everything changed after that, in ways that I could never have imagined. If someone had told me what that meant, to be a gay artist in the early eighties, I honestly might have had second thoughts. It came with so much hatefulness and misery. I remember being recognised for the first time in the off-license after the notorious Top of the Pops appearance where I was wearing thick black eyeliner (which had jammed the switchboard with complaints) and not finding fame the way I had imagined it at all. Fame isn't the answer. I soon quickly came to understand that fame is like seawater; the more we drink, the thirstier we become.

◉ Boxbury Beat from Norway first came together as Zap Zap Music in 1984. Their debut single of 1985 'Never Along with You' b/w 'Windows', out on EMI, was a missed gem of Euro synthpop; one can only think the marketing dept. at EMI let them down. The members then were Einar Øverenget (bass and synthesizer programming), Kent Maurstad (guitar), Iver Erling Arva (keyboards), and Helge Hellebustsinger (synthesizer & programming). They had a very short life, but the little product they did release is well worth trying to find.

Cocteau Twins by Petra Galll

⊙ On July 10, 1982, *Garlands*, the debut LP by Cocteau Twins, was released by the 4AD label. *Garlands* features a swirling, shimmering wall of guitar sound layered with a sharp, solid drumbeat, all the while accompanied by Liz Fraser's haunting, indecipherable vocal plane. The only thing letting the Cocteaus down here was the production quality, sometimes a little muddy. It's evident that this is where the ethereal Cocteau Twins had their birth, but as much as *Garlands* is not of the quality of *Treasure* or *Heaven or Las Vegas,* it is essential Cocteau Twins.

⊙ Tom Hingley, aka Thomas William Hingley, was born July 9, 1965, in Abingdon, England. Tom comes from a family of six siblings whose father Russian was a history scholar and university lecturer. As an early teen he learnt his licks with family members and local friends in a variety of unknown punk bands before moving to Manchester, where he studied English literature. While sharing his time studying and working at The Hacienda in 1984, Tom formed Too Much Texas, who released the debut single 'Hurry on Down' in 1988; they were good enough to earn a support of New Order. In 1989 after a victorious audition, Tom became the frontman-vocalist with the Madchester icons Inspiral Carpets, pipping the Carpets' roadie/tech Noel Gallagher for the job. After 23 years as the lead singer with the Carpets (1989-2011), he parted with them to forge a successful solo career, entering collaborations and band projects, one being The Kar-Pets, performing Inspiral Carpets songs.

THE ORANGES AND LEMONS
TOM HINGLEY
(Inspiral Carpets)

My family lived in the South Oxfordshire countryside in the 1970s in a large rambling house with the rather grand moniker of Frilford Grange. Elizabethan at the rear with a more modern Victorian colonnaded Romanesque wedding cake frontage. My father, an Oxford academic, was often away in his digs at St. Anthony's College, so the seven of us dragged one another up with the assistance of my mother, Ruth. Mother would buy year-old hens, local farm layers who would otherwise have had their necks rung. She would put them in the hen run with the much wilder bantams, who would soon teach them how to revert from battery prisoners to a free-range tree-climbing iteration. It was an idyllic, privileged childhood, I guess, but there was fuck all else to do in rural South Oxfordshire, and in 1976 we discovered Punk!

We bought electric guitars and wrote stupid two chord punk songs insulting members of the Royal Family and The Wombles, creating primitive overdub recordings by using a reel-to-reel machine which was hooked up to a cassette player. *Sgt Pepper's* it wasn't.

We watched Tony Wilson on the Granada TV show So it Goes, which debuted Siouxsie and the Banshees, Buzzcocks, Joy Division, et.al.. We followed and devoured the Pub Rock scene that featured Graham Parker and the Rumour, Doctor Feelgood, and all the Punk/NEW WAVE that followed it in the early eighties.

My sisters attended a few shows at the Oranges and Lemons. In 1978 I famously eschewed a show by The Ruts there because I was thirteen and had to stay in and finish my French homework! Alas, I missed seeing the frontman of another famous punk band of the time who was rumoured to have been found in flagrante with a man behind the venue near the bins.

We formed rubbish punk bands. Brothers Martin and Andrew in Ash Tray and the Dogends, Debbie Keeping, Will Keeping, my sister Helen and I were Albert Park and his Playmates. The Playmates performed a song about the local public school and the child abuse that was exacted on the poor boarders that attended it in the 1970s, not strictly pop music then. Many years later Radiohead and comedian David Mitchell would be students at that school.

My sister Vicki and I bought *Never Mind the Bollocks* on the day of its release, 28th October 1977, from local music shop, Haken and Bell; it was an original pressing. McLaren had put it out about that the album and record cover would get banned, but a linguistic expert paid for by Branson and Virgin Records had argued successfully that the word 'bollock' was included in the Oxford Dictionary and was therefore an accepted English word and not obscene or a swear word as the forces of censorship of the Sex Pistols would have it.

I hadn't quite turned 13 when I went to my first concert; it was Ian Dury and the Blockheads at the Oxford New Theatre on February 25th, 1978. I woke up the next day and wanted to be in The Blockheads. In 2022 I performed with The Blockheads at the London PowerHaus; my musical career had come full circle from humble 1970s rural boredom/bedroom beginnings.

Tom Hingley ©2023

◉ Jim Kerr was born in 1959 in Glasgow, Scotland. Jim was/is/will be the vocalist for Simple Minds. Jim's musical beginning was in the late '70s with Johnny and the Self-Abusers, but with guitarist Charlie Burchill, bassist Tony Donald, drummer Brian McGee and Mick McNeil on keyboards, they formed Simple Minds in 1978. With 20 albums to their credit and 8 of those top 5 releases, Simple Minds are simply rock music royalty. Jim married Chrissie Hynde in 1984, but after living together for six years and having one daughter, they got divorced in 1990.

◉ On July 9, 1977, Declan MacManus, later known as Elvis Costello, quit his day job as a computer nerd at Elizabeth Arden Cosmetics to become a full-time musician. In about three weeks time he would be arrested for illegally busking outside the London Hilton.

10

Blaine Reininger by Petra Gall

◉ Blaine L. Reininger was born in Pueblo, Colorado, USA, in 1953. Blaine was the co-founder of Tuxedomoon, a band that explored an experimental POST-PUNK path. After being signed to the Ralph label, Tuxedomoon recorded the ground-breaking albums *Half Mute* (1980) and *Desire* (1981); here, Blaine's input was dominant, contributing all manner of instruments to the band's oblique sound, notably performing on the violin, which he had studied classically. In 1984 Blaine parted ways with Tuxedomoon to concentrate on his solo career and numerous collaborations. He had already released the LP *Broken Fingers* to critical acclaim, making comparisons to David Bowie's work. The album includes a cover of Bowie's Sons of the Silent Age. Blaine returned to the fold of Tuxedomoon in the early 1990s and to date, with output mainly via the Les Disques du Crépuscule label, he has released over 20 solo albums. Today, he lives in Athens, Greece, performing solo and continuing as part of Tuxedomoon.

THE BOB STORY
BLAINE REININGER
(Tuxedomoon)

Today, in the course of doing an interview for the Athens Voice, I was asked *"What is the most bizarre story from the early days of Tuxedomoon?"*. Of course, there are many such stories, very many, but I decided it was time to tell 'The Bob Story'. I tell this story to Maria's friends and anyone else who will listen, but I think this is the first time I have written it down.

In 1980, Tuxedomoon was booked to play at a club called The Ritz in New York as part of a big bill of NEW WAVE acts, including Suicide, Indoor Life, and all sorts. The club was pretty much a Mafia front and had double booked the stage, so there were two complete sets of bands supposed to be on stage at the same time. We sat around for hours and hours; it grew late, and we still had not played. No one from our bill had. At one point, John Belushi and his crew poked their heads into our dressing room *"Got any drugs in here?"* he asked *"No"*. *"Ok. Bye"*.

I asked Alan Vega what time he was going onstage. *"Onstage? I already got paid. I'm leaving"*.

When Tuxedomoon finally took the stage at about 5 am I said into the microphone, *"This club has been treating us like animals all day long. You should all go somewhere else in the future..."* and they cut off our power. A Rolling Stone journalist offered to escort me out of the building since he didn't think the Mafia goons from the club would beat me up if he was with me. When I went to an after-hours basement club later, they asked, *"Are you the guy who told the Ritz to fuck off? You drink free tonight!* And the drinks kept coming.

After the after-hours place, my wife, JJ, and I put on our trusty Ray-Bans and went out into the morning light. We needed another drink. I saw a place just ahead. The door seemed closed, so I went and knocked. A window in the door slid up. *"Who sent you?"* asked the man.

"Uh.... Bob. Bob sent me", I replied, giving the first name that popped into my mind, not really believing anyone would ask me such a thing.

"Ok. If Bob sent you, then you must be all right! Come on in".

We went in and found ourselves in a coke dealer's party. People offered us lines out of 100-dollar bills. We drank champagne. We left about 4 in the afternoon, unable to believe our night out in New York.

The next day, we went looking for that place. Almost needless to say, it had vanished without a trace.

❂ Scars, from Edinburgh, Scotland, released their one and only album, *Author! Author!*, in 1981. The POST-PUNK flavoured music on this album is delicious, filled with beautiful melodies and clever guitar riffs. Similar to other Scottish bands like Josef K and Fire Engines, Scars managed to create some incredibly likeable songs. The combination of jangly guitars and a driving rhythm section perfectly complemented the poetic lyrics and vocals of their frontman, Robert King. *Author! Author!* has rightfully earned a spot in the Top 100 Scottish albums of all time.

❂ Neil Tennant, born on this day in 1954 in North Shields, Northumberland, England, initially pursued a career in journalism before transitioning to the music industry. During his time as an editor and critic for Smash Hits magazine, he developed a passion for dance-orientated music. In 1981, fate brought him together with Chris Lowe at an electronics store where they both worked. Discovering their shared love for this genre, they embarked on a songwriting journey. Neil assumed the role of vocalist, while Chris took charge of the electronic elements. Their unique combination of captivating melodies and cleverly crafted lyrics quickly captured the attention of NEW WAVE enthusiasts worldwide. The Pet Shop Boys, as they came to be known, achieved immense success, selling over 100 million records across the globe. Throughout his career, Neil collaborated with various artists, including David Bowie, Boy George, Electronic, and Madonna. In 1994, he publicly disclosed his homosexuality and has since become an outspoken advocate for LGBTQ+ rights. Neil also serves as a patron for the Elton John AIDS Foundation.

◉ Holly Beth Vincent was born in 1956 in Chicago, USA. Best known as a founding member of the supreme power-pop unit Holly and The Italians, her talent extends into being an acclaimed singer-songwriter, multi-instrumentalist, and record producer. The Holly and The Italians' 1979 debut release of the single 'Tell That Girl to Shut Up' on Oval Records had a huge impact critically but moderate sales, though it earned the band a recording contract with Virgin Records. This exposure saw them on tour opening for acts like The Clash and Blondie. The band went on the record a handful of singles, and only one highly regarded album, *The Right to Be Italian*. When the band split in 1981, Holly had a short tenure with The Waitresses before moving to Los Angeles, where she formed The Oblivious in 1990.

TEEN PILOTS ARE OK!
HOLLY BETH VINCENT
(Holly and The Italians)

Right, so you want a story from yesteryear.

This is so last minute, and I apologise for that. I couldn't focus, to be honest. Not that I will now. But I'll try. It's a post-COVID thing. Half a minute has passed since typing that sentence, and my mind wanders, but I'll keep going. The bulk of the story I promised actually doesn't have a lot to it, so I'll beat around the bush first. Wasting time here!

So, you know my band Holly and The Italians? Our agency in the UK was called Wasted Talent. Ha, a good name! There you see. Random. This is nothing but that. And the birthday-biography thing. I liked that idea. It gives order. Mine is July 10, and I don't know if there will be another July 10, but it would be cool. (ed: Yes, Blaine Reininger and Neil Tennant). The only other person I know of with that exact date is Jessica Simpson, the American pop singer and entertainer. Known for being occasionally ditzy or daft. I was happy to know that… it's a relief.

Anyway, July 10 and Cancer is my birth sign in astrological terms. I'm a Capricorn rising, the opposite sign, which barely saves me from drowning in the other multiple watery signs, like mostly water, I'm swimming constantly. Sometimes I reach shore. Rambling over, the story or anecdote I'll tell now. Really, it's weird how my memory works. Not much detail, mostly visuals and impressions. Like on this day, the day of the story my band and I were booked to appear playing live on a children's game show, and I don't remember what it was called. Not that that is important; I just went where they sent me. And where they sent us for this kid's show was on the other side of the English Channel. To Belgium of all places. In a plane, a small plane, no jets for us. We flew with our gear. Sitting on our gear actually, well, the bass player was. Our equipment was in flight cases and jammed into the interior of a Cessna aircraft. Makes sense it's a three-piece band. Plus, a member of the marketing department, Julie. Marketing goes in the front of the plane, next to the pilot. What airport is this? Probably Gatwick. Heathrow in the UK is meant for bigger planes and commercial flights. I'm just making that up now. It's a guess. So, we are packed into this little plane wearing our leather jackets, and who knows what is expected of us at this children's show? Playing our song 'Tell That Girl to Shut Up' it's a good song for kids anyway. OK! I'll wrap this up.

We are on this plane, and the weather is bad; there is zero visibility. The marketing person Julie looks at the pilot and says, *"How old are you anyway?"* He introduces himself *"I'm (such & such) and I'm nineteen years old and a member of the Royal Air Force"* (RAF for short). He's a kid, basically. Flying us even younger kids to an even younger show!

He hands Julie a map and says, *"Here, you're the navigator"* and grins. She says *"No! I'm not... I can't navigate a plane!"*. He assures her *"You can, it'll be fine. Anyway, I think I've flown one of these before"*. So off we go. The map took up way more than her space in the co-pilot seat. I think my band and I were amused and not scared, it was just like, *'OK, just another thing'*. *"Thanks Richard"* (Branson, our boss since we were on Virgin Records, UK).

We did a lot of fun, interesting things as recording artists, and this was pretty typical. So, then we take off; there's nothing to see in front of us as we're flying. The plane bumps around a little, but it's expertly handled by the teen RAF pilot. And we land. In Belgium. I forget where. Some airport, whatever. And on the tarmac, next to us, is a larger plane. And there is the band Spandau Ballet. Wearing New Romantics clothes and with really good haircuts with long bangs (I had that haircut on the Old Grey Whistle Test, a BBC music show) but I guess Spandau Ballet were also playing on the kids show.

Well, they are standing on the tarmac and someone or more than one, are throwing up from the flight. Their plane was bigger than ours! They likely flew with an adult pilot! Maybe there was even a crew! I don't know. Anyway, we were laughing like punks would do, and we went off to perform on the show. And that's the end of my story. Peace, everyone. Holly.

Teen Pilots rule...OK!

11

◉ Dexys Midnight Runners released their debut LP *Searching for The Young Souls Rebels*, in 1980. Tuning the radio through the crackling stations, being flipped past Deep Purple, The Pistols, Specials and the gang shouts, an exclamation... *"For God's sake, burn it down!"*. Undefinable brass, some great harmonies and Kevin Rowland's soul-orientated voice take us through a record that was close to ska and blue beat yet somewhat divorced but married to Northern Soul. Here we get some very cool R&B grooves and such tasty brassy hooks they sound like and have the class of Blood, Sweat & Tears! 'Geno' at the time sounded great, and today, still does, emotive and horn laden. 'Tell Me When My Light Turns Green' and 'Thankfully Not Living in Yorkshire It Doesn't Apply' are pure gems and album highlights. The instrumental 'The Teams That Meet in Caffs' is so good it should have been made a single and would have sold enormously well, even for an instrumental. They leave the best till last, 'There, There, My Dear'. It's like *"let's give it all we have fellas"*, Dexys does indeed! With the band in whisper behind Kevin Rowland exclaims his search for the young soul rebels and says *"I can't find them anywhere!"*, they were there with him all the time! Welcome the new soul vision.

◉ It was on this day in 2014 that producer and drummer Tommy Ramone, aka Thomas Erdelyi, from the influential New York City punk rock band the Ramones, died aged 65. His passing came following unsuccessful treatment for bile duct cancer. A little-known fact about Tommy is that in 1970, he was an assistant engineer for the production of the Jimi Hendrix album *Band of Gypsies*.

● Pete Murphy, on July 11, in Northampton, England, was the lead singer of the POST-PUNK band Bauhaus from 1978 to 1983, as well as during brief reunions in 1998, 2005-2008. He occasionally played guitar and other instruments with the band as well. The band was originally going to be called Bauhaus 1919 as a reference to the 20th century German art movement known for its minimalist aesthetic, but they shortened the name to just Bauhaus before releasing any music. After Bauhaus first split up in 1983, Murphy embarked on a solo career while guitarist Daniel Ash and drummer Kevin Haskins started a new band called Tones on Tail. Later, Ash and Haskins reunited with bassist David J to form the alternative rock band Love and Rockets. In 1984, Murphy teamed up with former Japan musician Mick Karn to create the short-lived musical project Dalis Car, which resulted in the album *The Waking Hour*. Two years later, in 1986, Murphy finally released his debut solo studio album, *Should the World Fail to Fall Apart*.

● While it's unclear if it was planned to coincide with his birthday, Peter Murphy put out his first solo record, *Should the World Fail to Fall Apart*, in the second week of July 1986. Murphy had just finished up a troubled collaboration with Mick Karn called Dalis Car, and there are noticeable similarities between the two projects. No matter what, Murphy's unique voice always shines through, and that's especially true on what might be the album's best song, 'God Sends'. It has smooth production and vocals recorded twice to give a layered effect, with the percussion really standing out. Other highlights are the opening number 'Canvas Beauty', the serenely beautiful 'Never Man', and an exceptional take on Pere Ubu's 'Final Solution'.

● Ultravox (UV) released their first album without John Foxx, *Vienna*, in 1980. Let's call them 'UV MkII'. They marked a significant shift from the earlier Ultravox! sound, with the lineup of Billy Currie, Warren Cann, Chris Cross & Midge Ure becoming the most recognised. The NEW WAVE/synthpop/new romantic direction of UV MkII was a departure from the guitar-driven POST-PUNK style. Produced by Conny Plank, *Vienna* was a commercial success, reaching the top 10 in various countries. The album demonstrated that a band could thrive even after a key member departs. While many attribute UV's "decline" to Foxx's exit, credit should also be given to Steve Shears and Robin Simon. UV MkII was a very different animal; they were among the forerunners of the electronic NEW WAVE-New Romantic movement, overshadowing bands like The Fixx, Flock of Seagulls, and Spandau Ballet. *Vienna* received critical acclaim for its fresh and genre-defying tracks. From the hypnotic instrumental 'Astradyne' to the cinematic 'Mr. X' and the energetic 'All Stood Still', the album showcased Midge Ure's versatile talents as a guitarist, keyboardist and singer. Ultravox set a standard for synthesizer use and the music style of the early 1980s NEW WAVE era.

● Suzanne Nadine Vega was born July 11, 1959, in Santa Monica, California, but has lived in New York City since the age of 2. She is hard to pigeonhole; her well-known songs 'Marlene on the Wall', 'Luka' and 'Tom's Diner' don't fit easily within any particular genre. Suzanne displays elements of electronica, pop and folk-rock. Her influences were Lou Reed and Bob Dylan. In Suzanne's early days she played to enthralled audiences at New York's Folk City venue, where Dylan coincidentally cut his teeth. Suzanne initially found it tough to secure a recording contract but eventually signed to A&M, and in time her style and songwriting has earned her sales of over seven million albums and two Grammy awards!

LOU
SUZANNE VEGA

In 2010 I was invited to perform at the Shel Silverstein memorial tribute concert in Central Park. I went alone, as usual. I ran into Lou Reed backstage, who was with Emily Haines from the band Metric and his wife, Laurie Anderson. I had known Lou for more than 20 years at that point, seeing him all over town. Which is, of course, New York City.

"What are you doing here by yourself", Why are you always alone?" he asked me. I just smiled in return, not really knowing what to say, and knowing he wouldn't wait for an answer anyway.

But seeing that I had his ear, I was lucky enough to play him a new song, 'Daddy Is White', and he really got a kick out of it. *"Did you really rhyme Latin with Manhattan?"* he said. He loved how I was raised in a radical Puerto Rican family, and yet I am so white.

"Hey!" he yelled out to anyone passing by. *"Suzanne isn't what she seems to be!"*

"But Lou, that's not true", I said to him, pointing out, *"I look as white as I really am!"*

"Hey!" he yelled again. *"Suzanne is EXACTLY what she seems to be!"* Thereby confusing more than a couple of people, who smiled at me uncertainly.

"You need to write more REAL songs", he said to me. Lou isn't really one for metaphor, and metaphor is what comes naturally to me.

"Can I try this on?" he said, grabbing my hat from my head, and attempting a cracked strained little smile. He posed in my hat for a couple of photos and allowed me to post one on Facebook.

This day became a turning point in our friendship, as we realized that we both had houses near each other in Long Island. From that day forward he was welcoming and kind. Well, for the most part.

I saw him a month before he passed. *"Just come over any time"*, he said. *"No need to be so formal. I mean it"*. Words I still treasure.

12

◉ Jim Basnight was born July 12, 1957, growing up in Seattle, Washington. Guitarist and vocalist Jim launched with The Moberlys in the late '70s; their power-pop brand sat on the fringe of garage and POST-PUNK, being pre-grunge in his native Seattle. Relocating to NYC in 1980, Jim carved a solid reputation on the strength of live performances and from the album *The Moberlys*. Reforming The Moberlys, Jim returned to Seattle in 1984, then to Los Angeles in 1985, rebirthing The Moberlys yet again along with drummer Dave Drewry, bassist Toby Keil and guitarist Glenn Oyabe. The album *Sixteen* held some raucous, catchy tunes and garnered a slew of major demo deals, but no releases, and by mid-1989 The Moberlys split. Jim then ventured into solo works and the formation of The Rockinghams. Jim's distinguished career has seen him appear and share the stage with acts such as Ramones, The Police, The Band and Billy Idol, as well as with members of Blondie, REM, and Nirvana. Jim still records, releasing *Not Changing* in 2019 and *Jokers, Idols, and Misfits* in 2020. His latest being remasters available for download and streaming only, *Seattle-NY LA* and *Makin' Bacon* in 2021, *Pop Top* and *Early Years (1977-82)* in 2022.

BLOW YOUR LIFE AWAY
JIM BASNIGHT
(The Moberlys)

I'm Jim Basnight, born July 12th, 1957, in Philadelphia, Pennsylvania, USA. After living as a small child in Philly and NYC, we moved to Seattle, where I grew up. By 1977, I had already played in an early proto-punk act called the Loverboys in 1974-75, doing a glam cover thing (Bowie's Spiders, Alice Cooper, Dolls, Stooges and T. Rex) and the Meyce, an original song band.

JULY

After one huge gig at my Roosevelt High School's talent show, which caused a fairly major stir, the Loverboys split into two bands, the Meyce and the Telepaths.

Both were heavily influenced by the burgeoning NY rock scene, as detailed in magazines like Rock Scene, and by 1976, the early issues of Punk, brought back from Manhattan by an older glam rocker who had travelled to NY and SF, with the stage name Tomata Du Plenty.

Tomata and two other older glam boys called the Tupperwares fronted a band of musicians comprised of my school-age contemporaries from the Telepaths and the Eldon Hoke Band (who by 1977 were called the Mentors). On May 1st, 1976, The Tupperwares, Telepaths and Meyce produced the first DIY "Punk" show on the west coast of the USA.

It was, of course long after the NY scene, but in fact one week before the first one in London. The Meyce (though very raw) by then were a Velvet Underground, Modern Lovers, Ramones and Television (I sent away by mail order for the 'Little Johnny Jewel' single) and further forward-leaning quirky pop-influenced original act.

The Loverboys had played all covers of our then-current glam heroes, but by fall 1975, my vocalist girlfriend Jennie Skirvin (now Brott), fellow Loverboy Paul Hood (who made his name in time with SF's Toiling Midgets) on bass, fanzine editor and drummer Lee Lumsden and I were feverishly writing songs.

The media, outside of Lee's fanzine "Chatterbox" and a couple local papers, were almost completely unaware of our groundbreaking "Punk" progeny, unlike the London kids, or for that matter the LA scene that was spawned later in the year when the three older Tupperwares moved there, became The Screamers, and started staging shows with various youngsters and freakazoids at The Masque Club.

After a year of self-staged gigs in Seattle with the Telepaths and other early Seattle original rock acts of various stripes and singer Jennie being replaced by guitarist and future Vice President of Synch Licensing at BMG Music Publishing Pam Lillig, the Meyce opened for the Ramones at the Olympic Hotel on March 6th, 1977.

Now the Fairmont Olympic, a very fancy downtown Seattle hotel for upscale tourists, because of the worldwide success of the Seattle rock scene of the early 90s, there is a stylized luxury hotel room there filled with "Grunge" and "Seattle Rock" memorabilia for affluent traveling fans looking to see where it all happened.

The Ramones, with the Meyce show, is likely the only event of historic rock and roll significance which ever happened on the property, and there are souvenirs from it included in that specialised hotel room. At that time, the show signified the first time an acknowledged "Punk Rock" national act performed in Seattle.

The Ramones loved us and, along with their road crew, urged us to come to NY, where we would be well received. The others were not prepared to move to NY, but the idea caught my fancy, so I did the next month. I survived for six months by working in record stores but found it tough to keep jobs due to my over attending nightclubs like CBGB's, Max's Kansas City and others.

After seeing incredible performances by dozens of astounding NY bands and others who travelled there to the then worldwide "Co-Mecca" of this so-called "Punk Rock," along with London, and writing many songs, I lost my last record store job and my very crummy accommodations at a horrid 79th and Broadway Manhattan hotel with a shared bathroom.

Joey Ramone and light man, graphic designer and merch guy Arturo Vega allowed me to stay in their loft around the corner from CBGB, while they were on the road doing gigs. I shared the place with Arturo's girlfriend, but the place would regularly be hijacked by rockers in the neighbourhood for before and after-show parties.

After a couple of months, I was determined to be in the way of some established groupie-types, so Joey and Arturo asked me to leave, as I was outnumbered in that opinion. I avoided leaving the neighbourhood by the good graces of a couple from France, Lizzy Mercier (later

28

Descloux) and Michele Esteban, who let me sleep in their loft a few blocks south on Broadway and Houston Street.

But eventually they needed more privacy (understandably), and I was unable to find a safe place to stay. I made a lot of good friends while there, such as Marty Thau, the former Dolls manager, and by then manager of Suicide. Marty was very kind to me, taking me to a number of great shows like the Heartbreakers at the Village Gate and Suicide and Devo at Max's.

But, unlike a number of jetsetters "Punk Rock" slumming in Lower Manhattan, I was broke, and had nowhere to stay. I moved into the YMCA uptown on the east side of Midtown Manhattan, with the last chunk of change I had left. I was trying to figure out my next move. I'd quit the Meyce, and my family told me if I came back, I'd have to quit the music business or again get out.

NYC was tough (think *Taxi Driver*), and I didn't want to sink lower into the throngs of other teenagers desperate to survive there. I had no way out. I picked up the guitar and wrote 'Blow Your Life Away', a 1-minute and 40-second-long song. I decided to go back to Seattle and throw myself at the mercy of a place I felt I had a better chance to survive on the street unscathed in.

My parents were true to their word and only let me stay there for a couple of weeks after a cross-country Greyhound bus ride. So, I got a record store job and moved into a garage which Lee had rented to rehearse in. I was able to raise the money from supporters to record and release arguably the first Seattle "Punk" 45 by the end of '77 and started looking for a band to front with my original tunes.

The band was The Moberlys, which came together by spring '78. We went through a few personnel changes, but by late '78 played Seattle's famed Paramount Theatre opening up for a touring national act. We became the most-talked about band in Seattle through 1979.
But lack of major label interest, which some local managers attempted to precipitate for us in LA, and money issues (as original music had little or no infrastructure to support NW bands then) led the band to split in late '79.

A friend from record store work named Brian Fox helped me release an album, arguably the first Seattle "NEW WAVE" album, in December '79, and the opening song was 'Blow Your Life Away'.

My hard work and dedication to move my songs forward continued through a 2nd Moberlys in NYC, after I moved back there with *The Moberlys* LP in hand in October 1980. A 3rd Moberlys happened when I moved back to Seattle in early '84 with Dave Drewry, a drummer who had come out to be part of the 2nd Moberlys in 1981.

That band stuck together after a small handful of vinyl, including one of the first European LP indie releases by a Seattle '80s rock band, *Sixteen* on the Lolita (France) Records label (1985) and a move to LA in '85. *Sixteen* also included 'Blow Your Life Away', as it was a compilation of previous work and current recordings by the new band.

The band lasted through a number of LA "Big" major label, management and producer deals without another record release until 1989, leaving a fine archive of tracks I was able to retain, many of which have since been released and enjoyed by many.

My career continued through other bands (most notably the Rockinghams, who performed 'Blow Your Life Away' from 1993-97) before settling into, for the most part, a solo career with the Jim Basnight Band (who regularly sing 'Blow Your Life Away') through to the present.

But this 'Blow Your Life Away' story goes on all the way to this month, when I released a collection of my high-energy work from 1977 to -82, as a digital album titled *Early Years*. Including 'Blow Your Life Away', its entirety has been expertly remastered by Grammy winner Garey Shelton and, better than ever captures the rock and roll spirit which refused to die in that Big Apple YMCA room.

The kids I grew up with included a lot of very talented folks, including Telepaths drummer Bill Rieflin (who appears on Early Years on drums and piano), later of Ministry, R.E.M. and King Crimson.

Other notables from our Seattle high school (Roosevelt) scene include fellow high school glam rocker and bassist Nikki Sixx, later of Motley Crue; Eldon "El Duce" Hoke; Muffs and Rockinghams drummer Criss Crass; and Meyce guitarist Lillig.

From Roosevelt High, others notably followed in our "Punk Rock" footsteps, including superstars Duff McKagan of Guns and Roses and Mike McCready of Pearl Jam.

While I have not had the kind of worldwide success and acknowledgement of all of these famous and notable folks, I've left a mark. My spirit to write, record and perform my music has not died and continues to provide rock and roll joy to new listeners at an increasing rate today.

◉ The *self-titled* debut album by The Communards was released in 1986. Jimmy Somerville and Richard Coles delivered a synthpop sound that followed a classic formula similar to Frankie Goes to Hollywood and The Eurythmics. The album highlights Jimmy Sommerville's impressive falsetto range with a diverse mix of tracks, ranging from the lively disco beats of 'Don't Leave Me This Way' to the soft, haunting ballad 'Reprise' and the soulful vibes of 'You Are My World'. While not groundbreaking, the album is far from irritating.

◉ Chris Difford and Glenn Tilbrook released their only album in 1984. The album, entitled *Difford & Tilbrook*, is witty, melodic, infectious, and full of pop sensibilities. While it may not reach the level of *Argy Bargy* or *Cool for Cats*, it is still snappy and catchy; this genius duo from Squeeze rarely disappoints. However, the production by Tony Visconti is a bit of a letdown. Nevertheless, tracks like 'Hope Fell Down', 'Man for All Seasons', and 'The Apple Tree' impress just like any other great Squeeze songs.

◉ Hunters and Collectors released the stunning single 'Talking to a Stranger' in 1982. Released with two versions, it followed their debut release, the 3-track *World of Stone* EP. It's rhythmically funk crazy, semi-industrial, and via Greg Perano's incessant ultra-tribal percussion, it's a foot-tapping treat. Mark Seymour's lyrical combination of growls, hoots and hollers is a joy to listen to. You would find it hard to find anything like this before or since. This, the first single from the *self-titled* LP, released later in the month, was accompanied by a music video directed by filmmaker Richard Lowenstein.

◉ Wilko Johnson, originally named John Wilkinson, was born in 1947 in Westcliff-on-Sea, England. He left the band Dr. Feelgood before they recorded the UK No.9 single 'Milk and Alcohol' in 1979. In 2013, while with Solid Senders, Wilko announced that he had terminal cancer and planned a farewell tour. As part of this tour, he appeared as a guest on the television show Madness Live: Goodbye Television Centre, broadcast on BBC Four. After briefly joining Ian Dury & The Blockheads in 1980, he focused on his Wilko Johnson Band and released more than a dozen albums. In a 2016 interview, he expressed his determination to continue performing as long as he felt healthy. Wilko passed away at home on November 21, 2022, leaving behind a significant legacy of influential work.

◉ Released on this day in 1985 was *Camera Obscura* by Nico + The Faction. This was an excellent swansong recording by Nico, faultlessly produced by John Cale. The album takes us down the road of what can be described as psychedelic industrial electronica. Even though essentially minimalist, it's hypnotically percussive and atmospherically dark. *Camera Obscura* is unquestionably unique; it's far removed from Nico's earlier works and a recording that will indeed broaden the listener's scope of appreciation of this incredible artist. Nico's last album may prove challenging for new listeners to fully appreciate, but in time they will see that the songs are powerful, utterly captivating, emotionally intense, and singular. This masterwork serves as a crowning artistic achievement. 5 Stars.

◉ Robin Simon was born in 1956 in Halifax, West Yorkshire, England. Robin played guitar with Ultravox! (version 1), Magazine, Humania and Visage. His CV is not incredibly excessive, but arguably everything that he played on is incredibly tasty. Robin was one of a handful of POST-PUNK guitarists that paved the way for the entire wave of music. When Simon joined Ultravox! replacing Steve Shears, in 1978, he brought a more multi-dimensional sound to the band. His co-write, Slow Motion, the first single from the subsequent album *Systems of Romance*, provided the original lineup with its only official hit. When John McGeoch split from Magazine soon after the classic album *The Correct Use of Soap*, in came Robin to the fold of another primary, seminal POST-PUNK band. It was a brief stay, but then joined up with John Foxx again for the album *The Garden,* and he continued to play on Foxx's subsequent solo albums from the first phase of his career. His next project was hooking up with Billy Currie in Currie's post-Ultravox group Humania. The band was short-lived, with Currie subsequently forming another incarnation of Ultravox, but without Simon. In January 2013, Visage announced their new line-up to consist of vocalist and founding member Steve Strange, bassist Steve Barnacle, Lauren Duvall on vocals and Robin on guitars. Robin is the brother of the highly regarded session drummer Paul Simon, who has also been part of the bands Cowboys International, Pleasure Pack, and Glen Matlock & The Philistines/Mavericks. More recently Paul and Robin teamed up to create AjantaMusic, venturing into recordings that are a blend of electronic and world sounds. 2021 and the Simon brothers current project is 'Station X present Ultrasonic', the live sound of early Ultravox with Robin Simon on guitar. Robin has also recorded with Paul on several remixes of tracks by The Fallout Club. This line-up features Thomas Dolby, Trevor Herion, Paul Simon, and the late Matthew Seligman. Matthew was also a member of Station X.

13

◉ In 1993, Björk released *Debut*. The album is technically not her first album, but as it is titled, it is generally regarded as her debut as an international modern music artist. It was her first after the dissolution of The Sugarcubes. She did release a couple of albums in Iceland, her first being when she was 12 years old! There's no denying though that *Debut* was the album that put Björk on the tip of everyone's lips. *Debut* is excellent; it's light-hearted and loaded with some out-of-this-world instrumentation. But it's the vocalisation of the Icelandic lady that makes it all worthwhile; Björk gasps, she squeals, she shrieks, and she growls as only Björk can do. With the assistance of over a dozen engineers, Björk's self-production technique is nothing short of brilliant; her desire to give us an eclectic range of tunes is so well translated through ingenious arrangements. *Debut* is arty, romantic, and seductive.

◉ Ana da Silva was born in 1948 in Madeira, Portugal. Moving to London in 1974, Ana went on to study at the Hornsey College of Art, where she met the like-minded Gina Birch and, in 1977, formed The Raincoats. It was the height of punk, but The Raincoats took a different path, being arguably one of the first units to portray POST-PUNK sensibilities. In November 1979, The Raincoats released their *self-titled* debut album, a recording stacked with irresistible grooves, intriguing instrumentation via tribal drumming, angular guitar and out-of-left-field violin. Soon after their third album, *Moving*, in 1984 The Raincoats split, but after Ana had a chance meeting with Raincoats fan Kurt Cobain, they almost reformed to be openers for a Nirvana tour, but Cobain's passing prevented that. Ten years after the last release, indeed they did a rebirth for the excellent EP, *Extended Play*, and their fourth studio album, *Looking in the Shadows*. 2004 saw Ana in her home studio for the recording of the exotic The Lighthouse album, released February 2005, it's a vast departure from The Raincoats, where Ana's voice and sparse instrumentation caresses the listener, taking you to the worlds of Laurie Anderson or Anne Clark. Tasty. Thurston Moore of Sonic Youth fame hailed Ana's collaborative album *Island* of September 2018 as the best release of the year!

Bjork by Kristan James Melik / Ana da Silva 1978 by Shirley O'Loughlin

I HEAR THE MUSIC
ANA DA SILVA
(The Raincoats)

For me, The Raincoats was about art. Art is related to life. They walk hand in hand. I resented some people reading us exclusively as a feminist band. We were definitely that, among many other things, and anyone who wants to live in a richer and more interesting world has to strive for equal opportunities for people of any gender. Prejudice creates a negativity that spreads like a virus.

We never really sat down to make big decisions, and that included what sort of music we were going to play. Things always tended to *evolve* organically. We didn't want to follow any rules of how to structure our music or how to present it. We were always exploring and risking ideas instead of learning and using that knowledge to write songs. I think this approach made our songs sound different from each other and each album very different from the one before it.

I like the idea of poetry. Lyrics have a slightly different purpose, though, but it's good if they also look good on paper. So, like with music, I tried to go as far as I could with them. Some people think that lyrics don't matter, but for me they must have a purpose, an ambition, just like the music.

The way we dressed and presented our artwork was an expression of who we were. We didn't talk a lot about clothes (at least not in a band sort of way), didn't coordinate or even dress up. Each one of us had our own personal style, and we did care about how we looked, but not as members of a band, just everyday style. And we took that to the stage. It was a charity shop second-hand style and therefore in opposition to fashion house trends. This is what we could afford anyway, but it was definitely a fun and creative way of dressing.

I would like people to remember us for our musical exploration, for having stuck to our guns and broken barriers, for having been there. We just wanted to push boundaries, look out the windows, hear the music outside, and fly the sky. We wanted to tell our fairy tales and sing our love songs.

◉ In 1979, The Flying Lizards released their first hit single, 'Money', which reached No.5 on the UK charts. There is an ironic twist to this cover version - the original singer, Barrett

Strong, claims he co-wrote the famous song with Berry Gordy and Janie Bradford back when he recorded it for Motown in the 1960s. However, three years after the song was written, Strong's name was removed from the copyright registration, thus depriving him of any royalties. His credit was briefly restored in 1987 when the copyright was renewed but then removed again the following year. Motown founder Berry Gordy has said that Strong was only originally listed as a writer due to a clerical mistake. Over the decades, 'Money' has made millions in publishing royalties through covers by bands like The Beatles and The Rolling Stones, frequent use in films and ads, and its inclusion in the Broadway musical Motown. Yet Barrett Strong, who first recorded the hit and was initially credited by the US Copyright Office as a writer, says he has never received any of those profits.

◉ Arguably the greatest music event of all time, 'LIVE AID', took place in London and Philadelphia on July 13, 1985. (What about Woodstock, you say!). The event was organised by Bob Geldof (Boomtown Rats) and Midge Ure (Ultravox) to raise funds for relief of the famine in Ethiopia. Both venues ended the concert with anti-hunger anthems, with Band Aid's 'Do They Know It's Christmas?' closing the UK concert and USA for Africa's 'We Are the World' closing the US concert. Live Aid gave us the biggest TV audience ever, with about 1.9 billion viewers in 150 countries. Promoter Harvey Goldsmith said that the concerts would raise $1 million; $70 million was closer to the mark!

◉ In 1976, the first issue of the punk zine 'Sniffin' Glue' was released in London. Created by Mark Perry in his bedroom, 'Sniffin' Glue' pioneered the DIY fanzine movement that exploded afterwards. The content was raw, passionate, and opinionated. It embodied the growing DIY ethic at the time and held nothing back. Though only 50 copies of the first issue sold, circulation quickly rose to 15,000, and it was sought after worldwide, even appearing in record stores in faraway places like Australia. Published monthly but lasting just 12 issues, it was far from a polished product. Riddled with spelling errors, basic cut-and-paste graphics, and handwritten or typed text, it nonetheless struck a chord. In August 1977, Perry ceased publication encouraging readers to start their own punk zines. Many did.

14

◉ Bob Casale, also known by his birth name, Robert Edward Pizzute, Jr, was born in Kent, USA, on July 14, 1952. He gained fame as a guitarist and keyboardist for the band DEVO. Alongside other members of Devo, Bob was part of Mutato Muzika, a musical production group involved in creating soundtracks for movies and TV. Bob's musical talents also extended to composing the music for the movie *Happy Gilmore* and working as the engineer on the first solo album *XYZ* by Andy Summers, the guitarist for the Police. Unfortunately, Bob passed away on February 17, 2014, due to heart failure.

◉ Chris Cross, aka Chris Allen, was born on this day in 1952 in London, England. Chris played bass and synths for Tiger Lily, Ultravox! & Ultravox, who had a 1981 UK No.2 single with Vienna, which he co-wrote with the rest of the band. He should not be mistaken for the Christopher Cross who is best known for the yacht-rock/smooth pop hits 'Ride Like the Wind'. In his final days Chris was working as a psychotherapist and counsellor. Chris died on March 25, 2024.

◉ In 1978, Talking Heads released their second album, titled *More Songs About Buildings and Food*. This album was recorded in March 1978 at Compass Point Studio in the Bahamas, and with Brian Eno taking on the role of producer, it marked the beginning of his production trilogy for the band. The album showcased a sharper and more polished version of Talking Heads, with outstanding songs that epitomised the New York NEW WAVE sound. It is worth noting that Eno's influence played a significant role in bringing out the best in Talking

Heads' music. Furthermore, this release showcased David Byrne's powerful vocals, as he effortlessly transitioned between different registers. Tina Weymouth, the bassist, also found her comfort zone and displayed her skills on tracks like 'Warning Sign', where she added a rhythmic sway and impactful basslines. Additionally, the album highlighted the evolving interplay between Byrne and Jerry Harrison's guitars, demonstrating their growing musical connection. This was merely the beginning, as there was much more to come from this talented five-piece band.

15

◉ With the release of their first studio album, *The Crossing*, in 1983, Big Country made a huge impact on the music scene. Their guitar-driven rock incorporated Celtic influences reminiscent of U2 and Simple Minds, with riffs that at times evoked the sound of bagpipes. This spectacular debut record introduced Big Country's one-of-a-kind, heartfelt, and soaring guitar rock style. Guitarist Stuart Adamson instantly became a hero to millions with his phenomenal playing on this powerhouse album. The songs on *The Crossing* range from rousing, anthemic tracks like 'In A Big Country', 'Fields of Fire', 'A Thousand Stars' and 'Inwards' to more grounded, surprisingly tender ballads such as 'Chance' and 'The Storm'. The combination of dual guitar lines and prominent bass and drums created an epic, oceanic sound. *The Crossing* was a brilliant first record from Big Country.

◉ Ian Curtis was born in 1956 in Stretford, England. He was the lead singer of the band Warsaw, which later became Joy Division. Sadly, Ian took his own life by hanging in his home on May 18th, 1980, at the young age of 23. At the time, he had been listening to Iggy Pop's album *The Idiot* on his record player. Ian left a suicide note that read, *"At this very moment, I wish I were dead. I just can't cope anymore"*. When Joy Division partnered with Factory Records and producer Martin Hannett, they released their debut album *Unknown Pleasures,* in 1979, having a profound impact on music for years to come. Ian Curtis' brooding intensity and baritone vocals paired with Stephen Morris' precise drumming; Peter Hook's distinctive basslines and Bernard Sumner's unique guitar style created a groundbreaking new sound. Songs like 'Disorder', 'She's Lost Control', 'Shadowplay' and 'Interzone' demonstrated the raw, haunting style that defined their POST-PUNK genre, while tracks like 'Day of the Lords', 'Candidate' and 'New Dawn Fades' showed more subdued, ominous undertones. From there they released their second and final album, *Closer*. It's impossible to know just how much further Joy Division could have taken their innovative sound.

◉ John Anthony Genzale, Jr., better known as Johnny Thunders, was born in 1952 in New York City. He made his biggest impact as a guitarist for the pioneering glam punk band the New York Dolls. After the Dolls broke up in 1975, Thunders and drummer Jerry Nolan co-founded the influential proto-punk band The Heartbreakers along with Richard Hell and Walter Lure. Hell soon left the group and was replaced by Billy Rath. Shortly after Nolan's departure, The Heartbreakers disbanded. In 1978, Thunders launched a solo career and recorded *So Alone*, collaborating with high-profile punk and rock musicians like the Sex Pistols' Steve Jones and Paul Cook, the Small Faces' Steve Marriott, the Only Ones' Peter Perrett, The Damned's Paul Gray, and Phil Lynott from Thin Lizzy. Over the next decade, Thunders put out five more solo albums before he was found dead in his New Orleans hotel room in 1991 at the age of 38. Though his albums sold poorly during his lifetime, Thunders' fusion of rock and punk influenced many musicians in the 1970s New York scene and beyond.

○ Born in 1949 in Hetton-le-Hole, England, Trevor Horn is a multi-talented English musician, songwriter, record producer, and vocalist. He has earned the title 'The Man Who Invented the Eighties' for his groundbreaking work as the architect of The Buggles and The Art of Noise and as the producer behind the hit songs of Frankie Goes to Hollywood and ABC. Horn was pivotal in the success of the maverick ZTT label, and his innovative use of technology in music production has had a lasting impact on the music industry. The prescience of his electro-pop duo with Geoff Downes, The Buggles, was evident when their 1979 worldwide No.1 hit 'Video Killed the Radio Star' became the first video broadcast by MTV upon its launch in the USA in August 1981. Horn's brief stint as the lead vocalist for rock group Yes, replacing Jon Anderson, saw him record only one album, *Drama*, on which he also played bass on one track before leaving after just seven months to focus on his production work. A wide range of artists, including Spandau Ballet, The Korgis, Malcolm McLaren, Propaganda, Pet Shop Boys, and many others, see him amassing an extensive catalogue of production work.

○ Matthew Seligman, born in London on July 15, 1955, made a name for himself as a bassist in various bands such as The Soft Boys, The Camera Club, The Fallout Club, and The Dolphin Brothers. His exceptional skills as a session musician were highly sought after, leading him to contribute to recordings for a wide range of artists, including The Thompson Twins, Sinéad O'Connor, Thomas Dolby, David Bowie, Peter Murphy, AjantaMusic, and Morrissey. Sadly, at the time of his untimely demise on April 17, 2020, he had plans underway to collaborate with John Foxx on a new project.

○ On July 15, 1978, the Rock Against Racism spectacle happened at Alexandra Park, Manchester. There was an illustrious lineup that boasted legendary artists like The Buzzcocks, Graham Parker & The Rumour, Exodus, and the resounding beats of Steel Pulse. An extraordinary gathering of 100,000 punters came together in unity and defiance against prejudice.

16

○ Stewart Copeland was born in 1952 in Alexandria, Virginia, USA. He is probably best known as the drummer for The Police but during 1974-76 he was part of the progressive rock band Curved Air. Originally Stewart was a road manager for the band and took over the drumming for a 1975 reunion tour. He was also married to the band's vocalist Sonja Kristina, having three sons. It was 1977, drawing excitement from the new "punk" fashion, that Stewart formed The Police with Henry Padovani and Sting. After seeing Andy Summers play with Strontium 90 Stewart and Sting asked him to join The Police. They played as a four-piece a couple of times before becoming that famous three-piece, we all know.

○ In 1982, Billy Idol's *self-titled* LP was released, marking a significant milestone in his career. This English popster disguised as a New York punk, embodied the essence of the NEW WAVE movement while still maintaining the edgy appearance of a few years prior. Despite his trademark snarl, Billy's music was undeniably accessible pop, evident in standout tracks like 'Dancing with Myself', 'White Wedding', and 'Hot in the City', which were flawlessly produced. The remaining songs on the album included a few other noteworthy tunes, alongside a couple of less remarkable ones. With this release and those that followed, Billy solidified his position as an iconic figure of the '80s NEW WAVE era.

○ The *self-titled* record by Marie et les Garçons (meaning 'Mary and the Boys' in English) first appeared in stores on July 16, 1980. The band started in Lyon, France, with drummer and singer Marie Girard in late 1976. Among the tracks on the album were the moderately successful singles 'Attitudes' and 'Re Bop'. The record displays the group's influences, with strong hints of The Velvet Underground and Modern Lovers. The driving force throughout is Girard's precise, powerful drumming. Side two of the album captures a live show in Paris on December 5, 1977...most remarkable is their rendition of Modern Lovers' 'Roadrunner'.

17

◉ Who was Holger Czukay? Holger was an electronic music pioneer, member of Can and collaborator with a myriad of artists, including Cluster, Brian Eno, David Sylvian, and Jah Wobble. Holger released the seminal LP *On the Way to Peak Normal* mid-year 1981, on different dates in different locations worldwide. Holger's work here has been quoted by many artists as being highly influential, and rightly so. Even though it has the element of surrealism, the recording was and remains to this day accessible electronica. 'Ode to Perfume', for instance, has an endearing feel that you wish would not stop. Essential.

◉ Wolfgang Flur was born in 1947 in Frankfurt, Germany. Wolfgang played electronic percussion for the band Kraftwerk from 1974 to 1987 and established himself as one of the most well-known musicians in electronic music. Many sources credit him as not just a pioneer but the creator of electronic drumming. However, Wolfgang has had disputes with his former Kraftwerk bandmates on a couple of occasions. First, there was a dispute over patent records that named Florian Schneider and Ralf Hütter as the creators of the electronic drum pads used by Kraftwerk. Second, a lawsuit arose after Wolfgang published a book called, *I Was a Robot*, which detailed the band's experiences with drug parties and other unsavoury events. In recent years, Wolfgang has performed as Musik Soldat, working as a music presenter, playing electronic house music at festivals, events, and clubs.

◉ In 1978, six months after dropping the moniker Johnny and The Self Abusers, Simple Minds made their first live appearance at The Satellite Club, Glasgow. The line-up consisted of Jim Kerr (vocals), Charlie Burchill (guitar, violin & keys), Duncan Barnwell (guitar), Tony Donald (bass) & Brian McGee (drums).

18

Vin and Larry Cassidy-- Section 25.

◉ Vincent Cassidy (Vin) was born on July 18 in Blackpool, England, in 1958. The third sibling of four, as an 11-year-old, he had a dream of being a drummer. He built his first drum kit piece by piece, firstly a snare drum, then a bass drum, and then, not being able to get his hands on actual drums, he made his own tom-toms from an old oil drum cut in half. Vin even made his own drumsticks in his dad's workshop; he took lessons and incessantly practiced playing along to vinyl records at home. When his brother Larry started playing bass guitar, they would jam for hours learning their chops. In 1978 they formed a band, named Section 25 with old school friend Paul Wiggin, and we gained the attention of Factory Records, Joy Division and Martin Hannett. Up to 2018, Section 25 released 9 albums, with the Hannett-produced debut release *Always Now* from 1981 often viewed as a seminal recording of POST-PUNK. Through the years the band has been through many changes, and with the passing of Larry in 2010, Vin has carried on playing in and managing the band, and to this day remains the only original member of Section 25 recording and touring. Today he manages his time between music and his family, a wife, Ita, of 40 years, his 3 children and grandchildren. Vin quotes: *"Musically I have come full circle...I started out as a kid playing for the pure joy of it and blimey...that's why I play now!"*

DON'T CROSS THAT LINE!
VINCENT CASSIDY
(Section 25)

Back in 2009, when my brother Larry was still alive... God bless him, he died in early 2010, and I miss him most days. Section 25 played a festival in Italy called 'Bats Over Milan'. The festival was over one weekend. Red Lorry Yellow Lorry were playing Friday and Section 25 and The Fall were playing on Saturday.

Of course, Section 25 and The Fall went way back together with the Manchester music scene, but strangely we had never actually played together on the same bill... until this show.

There was a good, receptive audience, and I felt it was going to be a great show! I knew, of course, that Mark E. Smith could be grumpy, as did my brother Larry... In fact, back in the day, at a televised Hacienda show where Madonna was on the bill and Angie and Jenny of S-25 were playing in 'The Factory Allstars' there had been a row in the dressing room between Larry and Mark over something... I forget what it was about, but it was probably something trivial like arguing over a seat or some bullshit... So, I was a little worried for trouble ahead.

There was only one dressing room at the Milan festival, and Mark E. Smith was really not happy; he was not prepared to share with another band, in response my brother dug his heels in and said he was not prepared to be without a dressing room; it was a total deadlock! In the end, after negotiating, the promoter had to get a piece of chalk and draw a line down the middle of the dressing room floor (it was a hard stone floor, like a disused kitchen or something), half was Section 25's and half was The Fall's. It was like a mini-Berlin wall!

The gig went off really well for us and for The Fall too, however we all kept to our territory... Still makes me laugh!... When we eventually left to go back to the hotel... our then tour manager James Nice said later that he thought he had trespassed getting a guitar during load-out.

He was so chuffed though, because he said, *"Mark E Smith has actually told me to fuck off"*.

◉ Terry Chambers was born in 1955, in Swindon, England. Terry was a founding member and drummer of XTC, part of their tours and recordings until his departure from the band during the 1982 sessions for *Mummer*. Terry had good reason for leaving XTC; he migrated to New South Wales with his new Australian wife. He became involved in session drumming while living in Australia, as well as recording and touring with the band Dragon in the mid '80s. Terry featured on the 1984 Dragon album *Body and the Beat*. He makes an appearance in the Dragon video clips 'Wilderworld', 'Cry', 'Magic' and the classic 'Rain'. After moving back to Swindon, in 2017 Terry teamed up once again with XTC bassist Colin Moulding to form TC&I, and they released the EP *Great Aspirations*.

● The debut album by Echo & the Bunnymen, *Crocodiles,* was released in 1980. Pure POST-PUNK with a touch of psychedelia. The impeccable guitars, vocals, and overall production arrangements make this album truly exceptional. Despite being a product of the dominant '80s POST-PUNK era, *Crocodiles* has managed to stand the test of time and doesn't sound outdated at all. Echo and the Bunnymen had a unique sound, yet they shared similarities with their contemporaries such as The Teardrop Explodes and The Cure. On *Crocodiles*, there are no filler tracks; it showcases a young band that had a clear sense of identity and direction. Songs like 'Rescue', 'Villiers Terrace', and 'Pride' are raw, spontaneous, and incredibly catchy. This album is where Echo made their mark, and arguably, even though their later albums achieved more commercial success, *Crocodiles* remains stronger and more consistent. It will always be regarded as one of the greatest debut albums.

● The release of Joy Division's second album, *Closer*, on this day in 1980 marked a significant moment in music history. Widely regarded as one of the most impactful and influential albums of the 1980s, *Closer* powerfully conveys the sentiments of despair, fear, depression, and anguish experienced by the vocalist Ian Curtis. Recorded and produced by Martin Hannett in the final two weeks of March, the album was made available just two months after Curtis' tragic suicide. Even though only a year apart, the distance in contrast to the guitar-centric sound of their debut album, *Unknown Pleasures*, is immense. *Closer* exhibits a richer, more textured keyboard atmosphere, foreshadowing the musical direction the surviving members would take as New Order. Hannett's production relegates guitar to the background until brought forward to give an unsettling spirit to the sound. This an album of profound density; an '80s classic, *Closer* stands as a seminal work that cemented Joy Division's legacy as one of the most compelling and innovative bands of the era.

● Julian "Keith" Levene was born in 1957 in Muswell Hill, London, England. He played a key role in bands like The Clash, The Flowers of Romance, Public Image Ltd (PiL), and Cowboys International. In addition to his guitar skills, Keith was also involved in production, particularly contributing to PiL's early albums. Drawing from his teenage years working as a roadie for YES at the age of 15, Keith's journey took a turn around PiL's fourth album. Despite his work on what was then called *Commercial Zone*, eventually leading to a fallout with John Lydon, who then re-recorded the album entirely with session musicians after receiving the tapes from Richard Branson. The revamped album was released as *This Is What You Want... This Is What You Get*. One of Keith's lesser-known but noteworthy contributions was being a guitarist with Cowboys International, alongside members Ken Lockie (vocals), Jimmy Hughes (bass), Evan Charles (piano), and Terry Chimes (drums). Their debut album, *Original Sin*, is considered essential listening. Liver cancer took its toll, and Keith died November 1, 2022.

A BRIEF INTERVIEW WITH KEITH LEVENE
(The Clash, PiL, Cowboys International, Murder Global)

Questions by: Jason Gross of Perfect Sound Forever (PSF)

PSF: Weren't you working with Viv Albertine (Slits) before PiL?

Shit man, there's so much that I did in punk that I never got a word in! I formed the freaking Slits, man! It's all a bit much now.

PSF: It would be good to hear your perspective on this?

OK... I used to live in a squat with Vivianne and a friend named Q. All these magical moments... I really liked her. But we weren't having a scene or anything. I really fucking liked her! And she really liked me. She'd come to me for this and come to me for that. She's talking about how fucking interesting Johnny is and "*I wonder what it would be like to meet him*". And "*Oh, by the way Keith, could you teach me how to play guitar?*". And the next thing is that she's got a Les Paul Jr. and she can't play. A real punk rocker. So, I taught her how to play and I was great to her.

I see this drunk... It was me who named Paloma Palmolive. I basically just got it together. Nora (Forster Ari's mother) was managing them and the reason was 'cause every time they needed something, I'd say 'Nora, they need this or that.' Obviously, the link was that Ari Up was in the band.

Those bastards, fucking bitches man... I went up and did sound for them. Then they go get Dennis Bovell to produce them, which on a career level, I suppose made sense. But it was real cold. If I produced it, we'll never know now... I had a lot to do with the Slits. I went on a lot of gigs for them and did their sound. I fucking REALLY, REALLY helped them. Arianna really kept to herself and got on with it.

There's the Slits in a nutshell for you. It's more involved than that because Vivianne Albertine was having this scene with Mick (Jones). And she used to really torture him and give him hell. She lived in the same squat I lived in.

When we were in the Clash, Mick would come over and he'd always be yelling at me. When he found out that I was three years younger than him, actually this is a key point in me leaving the Clash... On my 18th birthday, he found out I was 18 (Mick was 21). Me with Mick standing at this bus-stop (laughs) and Vivianne said "*Oh, it's Keith's birthday*". He said "*Oh, I didn't know that. How old are you now?*" I told him and he went "*You're never 18*". Vivianne told him I was. When I was 14, I fell head over heels for Vivianne. So, this all goes back years.

So, I showed Mick my driver's license. Ever since that day, he was just this total fucking bitch, cunt to me after that. There wasn't a thing I could do that wasn't wrong. I was working one Saturday afternoon, and he goes "*WHY WEREN'T YOU AT REHEARSAL?!*". For a start, no official rehearsal had been planned and I was working! What's all this then? It carried on and carried on. And she (Vivianne) would come over and torture him and get into awful arguments at the squat. And I left the Clash through that, but I was still living at the squat. I was hanging out with my friends at Mill Hill and doing these other things. My home base was basically this place in Sheppard's Bush where we all lived.

After that, I bought a place because I did PiL. (laughs) It just all changed. By then, she was living in this place in Chelsea. So much shit just happened. It's no wonder that she doesn't talk about it that much.

PSF: Well, she did mention that she had played guitar with you.

Well, how sweet of her. That's a first. I never even heard her mention my fucking name, that I even exist.

(By permission)

◉ Paul Young was part of a huge explosion of pop and soul artists in the early 1980s. Alongside The Style Council, ABC, Level 42, and Aztec Camera, he was gaining a huge audience. His debut album, *No Parlez*, released in the UK on July 18, 1983, was filled with creative instrumentation, fashionable style, and polish. Influenced heavily by soul and Motown, his NEW WAVE sound had a lot of credibility thanks to tasteful covers of songs like 'Wherever I Lay My Hat', 'Love of The Common People', and Joy Division's 'Love Will Tear Us Apart'. *No Parlez* was an excellent first album, and Young's subsequent releases never quite matched its style and substance. A prime example of the genre and era, it still doesn't sound dated today, a true classic.

19

○ The first album, *Product Perfect*, from the band Fàshiön Music, was put out in 1979. Becoming just known as Fashion, they came from Birmingham and were very ahead of the trends. This record was a defining moment for them when lead singer and guitarist Luke Skyscraper, also known as Luke James, was in the group. The album had all the trademarks of POST-PUNK music - driving, repetitive drumbeats, freaky basslines, angular, ringing guitars and vocals reminiscent of David Byrne. Unfortunately, the album was overlooked by most record buyers, even without the freaky but great single 'Steady Eddie Steady' from 1978. *Product Perfect* proves Fàshiön could have been huge! At first very original and creative, seeming to take on a glamorous style, their sound later shifted into something much more radio friendly. There was a CD reissue of the album in 2008.

Fashion by Nigel Van Beek

○ Kevin Haskins, aka Kevin Michael Dompe, was born in 1960, in Northampton, England. Kevin, as the drummer, was a founding member of Bauhaus. He was also a member of Tones on Tail and Love and Rockets. Kevin has cited the drumming of Stephen Morris (Joy Division/New Order) and Kenny Morris (The Banshees) (no relation) as a major influence on him; the depth of their playing is evident on the sensational album release by Bauhaus, *In the Flat Field*. Few debut albums ever arrived so nearly perfectly timed & formed as was the case with *In the Flat Field*. Here Bauhaus practically single-handedly invented what remains for many the stereotype of goth music. Songs of tragedy, despair, and desolation, sung over dark, mysterious, and moody music. This record started off Kevin's and Bauhaus' careers with a near-perfect bang.

○ Robert (Bert) Hearn was born in Surry Hills, Sydney, Australia, in 1957. Bert grew up in Liverpool, in suburban Sydney and it was in his teens, the period of classic British rock bands, that he developed a love for artists like Hendrix and the prog-rock style from the era of Led Zeppelin to King Crimson. All this led to a wide-ranging taste of everything from The Allman Brothers to Kraftwerk. Bert picked up a guitar in his early teens and progressed to being one of the early exponents of the guitar synth in the early '80s. His first band was Echo 11, gigging throughout the suburban pub and inner-city club scene. In 1983-4 Bert was part of the Dropbears, who not only were a headline act of their own but also supported the likes of U2, The Cure and OMD. Ripple, Champagne Peasants, and The Hazards are among some of the other bands in his resumé. Bert has a lifelong passion for Gibson guitars and is often pursuing a new purchase of one. Away from music, Bert studied medical science and attained a degree in Ultra Sonography. He still plays guitar every day.

TAMING OF THE BEAST
ROBERT 'BERT" HEARN
(Actual Footage, Echo 11, The Dropbears et. al.)

I remember joining Dropbears around 1984. At the time I had a special association with Phil Hall, the bass player; we had met a few years earlier when his long-time partner, Lesley Pepper, was the bass player in the first band I had played in, called Actual Footage. Actual Footage was short-lived; we played a couple of times at the Sydney Trade Union Club and a couple of smaller venues before the band split, as was usually the case, due to musical differences.

This left me open to join Echo 11, and it also gave me the opportunity to exhibit the new to the market GR-300 Roland Guitar Synthesizer, just one of about 30 guitars I've owned over the years. It was the days before digital, and this analogue device was a beast to incorporate into songs, and in the hands of a novice, it could completely destroy a song! Fortune would have it that one night Echo 11 was playing the Manzil Room in Sydney's Kings Cross, and after that gig I was approached by Johnny Bachelor and Phil Hall and was asked to join Dropbears.

It was indeed an honour and a privilege to be asked to join a band that already had a solid reputation and fan base and had released several singles. I was not a particularly gifted player, but I could handle that beastly synth. As the newest member of Dropbears, I was invited to a Paddington studio for the "green screen" making of the video to accompany the recently recorded single 'Proud'. Dropbears exuded a high level of professionalism, and just after supporting the Psychedelic Furs, were in a great position commercially. Recording-wise I got to play on the minor hit single 'Shall We Go'. This song and the band made it onto the national prime time TV music program *Countdown*. Dropbears, mullets and all were adored and swooned at by the appreciative studio audience of 13–16-year-olds. Then there was the recording at Sound Level studios, Ultimo, for the video for the single 'Dancing Is Dead', which just so happened to have this book's author Michael Krilich, in the clip simulating the playing of a sax as a shadow projected onto a blank screen.

Undoubtedly the highlights of being in Dropbears were supporting The Cure at The Hordern Pavilion and U2 at the massive Sydney Entertainment Centre (SEC)! At the time I was supplementing my income doing building work and ushering at the SEC, so I went from being on the floor with the punters to being up there under lights. It was exciting to go back to the usher's prep room to see my fellow workmates to tell them "*I'm on stage tonight*!"

The gig held one more highlight when, at the afternoon pre-gig soundcheck, The Edge was intrigued by my guitar synth. I gave him a quick demonstration (but I like to remember it as 'a lesson'). Back in our Green Room there was a knock on the door, upon opening it was Bono offering us a bottle of Moet and wishing us "*all the best*!"

What a memory, eighties NEW WAVE was at its height, and I was in the thick of it!

⦿ Barton Price was born in 1962 in Palmerston North, New Zealand, and as the drummer for The Crocodiles, moved to Australia in 1981. The Crocodiles were fronted by the dynamic vocalist Jenny Morris and achieved top 20 status in NZ with the single Tears, but the move to OZ was a bit too much for them, and they soon dissolved. Barton went on to join Sardine v, a band described by legend Lobby Lloyd as "*Ian Rilen's artsy fartsy project*". Sardine v in its different forms, always packed venues whenever they played. In mid-1982 Barton joined Models, a band that has become regarded as one of Australia's best, so well respected they toured as support to David Bowie and, along with INXS, appeared at Rocking the Royals attended by Prince Charles and Princess Diana. Barton is no longer is part of Models but is a much sought after session player and in 2021 recorded as a member of Steve Kilbey

& The Winged Heels. 2025 sees Barton as a member of The Speed of Stars with Steve Kilbey, Hugo Race and Frank Kearns; their sophomore album is due in September 2025. Now, his main artistic focus is composition and painting. Through his most recent installations and performances, his musical notation is presented visually in a form whereby both the performer and the audience concurrently undertake the experience. To quote Barton, *"The score has become the work."*

LONG LIVE THE THREE PIECE
BARTON PRICE
(Crocodiles, Proteens, Sardine v, Models, Joan Jett, The Church, et. al.)

The following is kind of an abridged version of the story:

It was mid-1982, and I was playing with Sardine v, who supported Models (a 5-piece lineup at the time) at Paddington Town Hall in Sydney. We all got on very well, and I was asked to join the band. BUT…. when I told Ian Rilen I was leaving, he made a motion with a bottle in his hand, as if to say, *"cheers and good luck"*, but instead he said, *"no-one quits my bands!"* and then swung the bottle so hard that my glass broke in my hand. Regardless, Sardine v went down for shows in Melbourne, and we stayed at Macy's; coincidently it was where The Numbers were also staying, and I met siblings Chris & Annalisse (Annie) Morrow and their manager Keith Welsh. Sardine v returned to Sydney, but I stayed on in Melbourne to join Models. (Later in 1990 I would join The Morrows to form MPM, which evolved into the Maybe Dolls with my songs, but not me.)

Before the first Models rehearsals, guitarist John Rowel left the group (which was a pity because we were good buddies); Models were now down to a 4-piece. We only had one week to rehearse before an already booked national tour commenced. On the first day James Freud, Andrew Duffield and I turned up, but no Sean Kelly, so no rehearsals that day. On the second day we connected with Sean by the Yarra; he said he'd been to a fantastic party, which was still going, and we joined in, so no rehearsal that day. On the Wednesday we all caught up, but Andrew then announced he needed a break and wouldn't be touring, so, no rehearsal that day either. On the Thursday, Sean, James, and I decided to do it as a three-piece and rehearsed a bit - this was my first run-through of Models songs. On the Friday we had a full production rehearsal at the Seaview Ballroom, but everything took so long to get organised that I'm not sure that we even completed a full set!

Saturday came, and we started the tour. We were way underprepared and pretty much jamming live, just trying to cover the keyboard parts without Andrew (our keyboard player) with lots of long, extended, experimental passages, though that approach brought a great energy and vibrancy to the music.

The three-piece only lasted one tour, some people say it was a legendary moment, and some say it was atrocious. Personally, I loved it - a baptism by fire and the start of some lifelong friendships.

Long live the three-piece!

If anyone has any recordings, please let me know!

◉ The Southern Death Cult only released one album, the *self-titled* compilation in 1983. The set was made up of singles, B-sides, alternates, and live recordings. The highlights of the album would be the two tracks that comprised a single, 'Moya' b/w 'Fatman', along with 'All Glory' and 'Patriot'. Vocalist Ian Astbury was soon to drop the name after teaming up with ex-Theatre of Hate guitarist Billy Duffy, becoming Death Cult, and by late 1983, The Cult.

◉ Nikki Sudden, aka Adrian Nicholas Godfrey, was born in 1956, in London, England. In 1972 Nikki and his brother Kevin, aka Epic Soundtracks, founded Swell Maps; their early days cemented them as adventurous, arty, and experimental proto-punk. Swell Maps pushed the boundaries of sound and verged to musique-concréte with the use of all manner of found articles. There were two historic albums from them before breaking up; Nikki would go on to form Jacobites with Dave Kusworth, and Epic went on to be the drummer for Crime & the City Solution. On March 26, 2000, at 49 years of age, Nikki died from a heart attack after a performance in New York.

20

◉ In 1976, the influential punk rock band Buzzcocks played their first live concert, opening for the Sex Pistols and Slaughter & The Dogs at the Lesser Free Trade Hall in Manchester, England. This iconic show was witnessed by several musicians who would go on to achieve fame themselves, including Morrissey, Bernard Sumner and Peter Hook of the soon-to-be-formed Joy Division, Mark E. Smith of The Fall, and Mick Hucknall of Simply Red. Tickets to this historic punk event cost just £1 at the time. Though short-lived, Buzzcocks made a tremendous impact with their powerful live performances and are considered pioneers of the punk rock movement that transformed music in the late 1970s.

◉ Lee Harris was born in 1962 and raised in Essex, England. As the drummer, David was a founding member of Talk Talk in 1981, contributing to all the band's recordings until 1991. Talk Talk gained recognition as a top POST-PUNK/synthpop group, achieving success with the singles 'Talk Talk' in 1982 and 'It's My Life' in 1984. Seeking a more experimental direction beyond synthpop, they explored a unique fusion of rock, jazz, classical, and ambient music. Their 1988 album *Spirit of Eden* is widely acclaimed as a masterpiece of this innovative sound. When Talk Talk disbanded in 1992, he and fellow member Paul Webb created the experimental O.rang.

◉ Jim Irvin was born in London, England, in 1959. Jim is a British singer, songwriter, and music journalist. He was the lead vocalist, keyboard player and percussionist for the band Furniture, which was formed in 1979. Jim worked as an editor for Melody Maker and Mojo magazines, showcasing his writing talents. Furniture was first signed to Survival Records, an independent label, and released a single called 'Shaking Story' followed by an EP titled *When the Boom Was On*. In 1986, they signed with Stiff Records and released the single 'Brilliant Mind', which reached No.21 on the charts. That song came from their first full album, *The Wrong People*, which had a limited release in November 1986. It was Stiff Records' last hit single and has become viewed as an iconic '80s song. In 1989, Furniture signed to Arista Records and produced an album called *Food, Sex & Paranoia*.

◉ Norman Michael "Mick" MacNeil was born in 1958 on the Isle of Barra, Scotland. Mick was a former member/keyboardist for 12 years with Simple Minds, joining in 1978 at the time of the recording of the *Life in a Day* album. Mick also played on *Demons to Diamonds*, the last Visage album.

21

◉ In 1979, two months after Jerry Dammers started the 2 Tone Records label, the first date of the 2 Tone Tour happened at the Electric Ballroom, Camden Town, London. The concert event presented The Specials, Madness, The Selecter and Dexy's Midnight Runners. Tickets were 2 quid!

Jenny Tubbs

● Jenny (Tubbs) Barbato was born in Brisbane, Australia, on July 21, 1960. At a young age, Jenny was drawn to photography and music and studied piano and violin, attending the same high school along with future members of The Saints. Jenny's family had moved to the Gold Coast, and it was there in 1978 that she met and entered a relationship with Sunnyboys' Jeremy Oxley. It was this relationship that led to the inspiration for Jeremy's writing of the hits 'Alone with You' and 'Happy Man', among others. In 1980, Jeremy and Jenny moved to Sydney as Jeremy went to art school and Jenny began freelancing as a photographer for various music magazines, such as Stiletto. During this time, Jenny was asked by Troy Fenton to move to Melbourne to join The Fizzpops. The long-distance relationship was difficult, hence 'Happy Man'. Back in Melbourne in 1983, Jenny formed the bands Sophisticated Boom Boom with Vika and Linda Bull, Tanya Lee Davis, Kerri Simpson and Louise Taunt and The Whole Shebang, with Lisa Miller. Jenny managed, performed, and recorded in both bands. As a side to music locally and internationally, Jenny formed a Jive and Swing class in Melbourne and has taught Ballroom, Latin and Swing Dancing in London along with a workshop at the Edinburgh Fringe Festival. In 1995, while working on cruise ships in the Caribbean, Jenny met and married American jazz musician Artie Barbato, who, aside from studying and playing with many great American musicians, has also performed with Australia's Kim Salmon, and performed and recorded with Epic Records Boston band, O-Positive. He has also performed and recorded with Wreckless Eric, playing all brass on his last two albums, *Construction Time* and *Demolition and Transience*. Artie and Jenny now live in Lowell, Massachusetts, a canal town north of Boston steeped in history, including being the textile capital of the USA before the Industrial Revolution, the birthplace of Bette Davis, and the birth and burial town of Beat Writer, Jack Kerouac. Jenny continues to play music and dance every chance she gets.

NOT SO MIRACLE CURE
JENNY TUBBS-BARBATO
(Sophisticated Boom Boom)

Sophisticated Boom Boom was originally put together for a huge going-away party for friends of Louise Taunt and Caren Campbell. The evening of the party, us three girls thought it would be a good idea to loosen our vocal cords in preparation for our first gig by riding the roller coaster at Luna Park in St Kilda. There's nothing like 15 minutes of screaming on a roller coaster to get those vocal cords working. After the ride, we realised that may not have been the brightest idea and made a quick dash home to prepare a brew of lemons, ginger, garlic, and honey to soothe our now hoarse throats before heading to the gig. This seemed to do the trick! This brew would become a tradition for us before each gig as Sophisticated Boom Boom continued playing throughout the 1980s. One night while on tour in Adelaide, Louise was feeling a little run down and remembering our miracle pre-gig brew, though not having the honey and lemon, decided to chew on raw garlic cloves within minutes of going onstage. There were times we had to share microphones during certain harmonies, and I almost couldn't get a note out. She saw my face and realised what I was going through, and we both burst out laughing mid-song, on stage. The mood seemed to catch on in the audience though no one else knew what the laughing was all about. I look back fondly on Australia in the 1980s. What a decade. Anything was possible. Still is.

⦿ As important as CBGB was to NYC's punk, London had The Batcave Club for the Goth Scene, it had its opening on this day in 1982. The Batcave defined the new gothic attitude; it featured appearances by the likes of Bauhaus, Sex Gang Children, Virgin Prunes, Southern Death Cult, Alien Sex Fiend, and the opening night act and 'house-band' Specimen.

⦿ The Ocean Blue released their *self-titled* debut album in 1989. After a few years of hard slog gigging, they finally got committed to a studio, and what came out was quite a stylish performance. Lush, layered keyboards, carefully designed melodies and jangly guitar produce something akin to a hybrid of Cocteau Twins, R.E.M. and The Smiths.

⦿ *Can't Stand the Rezillos*, The Rezillos' debut album was released in 1978. It's refreshing when a band doesn't take themselves too seriously, and that was the case here. They were one big step ahead of most of their contemporaries with the pop-punk ideal. One could say this is basically the perfect pop-punk album, entertaining, somewhat quirky, infectious, and energetic, kind of a hybrid version of XTC and X-Ray Spex. Overall, a bunch of very smart, short, sharp, and vibrant songs that's a pleasure to revisit, anytime.

⦿ On this day in 1979 Tubeway Army went to No.1 on the British album charts with their sophomore album, *Replicas*. Released on April 4, here is a perfect chemistry of guitar and synthesizer mould into an absolute work of art. This Bowie without being Bowie, but soon Gary Numan would be recognised as a revolutionary figure of the electronic NEW WAVE movement, and comparisons to Bowie would soon be left long behind. It has been said that the band led by Numan was the first band of the POST-PUNK era to have a synthesiser-based hit, with their single 'Are Friends Electric'. The album also held the gems 'Down in The Park' & 'Me, I Disconnect from You'. Tubeway Army takes us to a dystopian future; it's cold, calculated, but a lot of fun.

22

⦿ In 1977, Elvis Costello unleashed his debut album, *My Aim Is True,* on Stiff Records in the UK. The record was produced by Nick Lowe, and the backing musicians were unnamed on the original release, apparently due to contractual issues with those artists. Rumor, has it the backing band consisted of members of Clover or The Shamrocks. *My Aim Is True* captures Elvis' raw energy in a way that was not fully replicated on subsequent records. The songs range from gentle country melodies to aggressive and passionate pieces, yet there is a peculiar unity to the album, thanks to its unpolished and hurried vibe. The set opens with two of the finest power-pop songs of all time: 'Welcome to the Working Week', a rousing call-to-action, and the infectious '(The Angels Wanna Wear My) Red Shoes'. The album then shifts gears, as he tenderly croons of naive love on 'Alison', only to defiantly espouse anti-conformity rhetoric just two tracks later on 'Less Than Zero'. Through this dynamic range, Elvis showcases both the mood and spirit that would come to define his influential early work. Despite being a studio album, Nick Lowe's production infuses *My Aim Is True* with the same immediacy and excitement as a live performance. Here, Elvis' raw passion shines through in a way not fully captured on subsequent records. The songs range from mellow country tones to furious tirades, yet a peculiar unity exists thanks to the rough, hurried feel. Though a studio album, Nick Lowe's production grants *My Aim Is True* the electricity of a live performance.

⊙ July 22, 1980, saw the release of the debut single 'I Belong to Nobody' b/w 'The Stranger' by Flaming Hands on the Phantom Records label (#PH-3). The core of the band was guitarist Jeff Sullivan & the sensational vocalist Julie Mostyn. Julie's vocal inflection has often been compared to that of Patti Smith; easy to see why- the mix of Flaming Hands' NEW WAVE/soul/psyche suited her perfectly, and it carried over into this Soul Inc. cover. The band always played to packed-out venues and did a highly acclaimed support of The Clash at Sydney's Capitol Theatre in 1982.

⊙ The debut EP from New York City's minimalist no-wave band 3 Teens Kill 4 was *No Motive*, released in 1983. The group took their name from a New York Post headline and were brought together by renowned artist and filmmaker David Wojnarowicz. The EP's six tracks are propelled chiefly by Korg and Casio drum machines, with a deliberate effort to avoid being "too musical". They succeeded, yet the pieces remain sufficiently intriguing to keep listeners engaged to the end. The varied gadgets, instruments, and machinery coupled with pre-recorded sounds make for very fascinating songs. The recording was deemed worthy of being re-released by the French label L'invitation au Suicide in 1984 and again on vinyl by Dark Entries Records in June 2017.

⊙ *Packet of Three* is the very first release by Squeeze; it was a three-track EP released July 22, 1977. Out on Deptford Fun City Records and produced by John Cale, this is a rare gem; it's a raw and aggressive Squeeze, quite musical and punkish. The talent here earned them a contract with A&M. While not a highlight of Squeeze's stunning discography, it remains one for completists.

⊙ Brothers Philippe and Hervé Lomprez, Denain, France, are Trisomie 21, aka T21. In 1984 they released their first full-length album *Passions Divisees (Divided Passions)*, a journey into atmospheric synthpop. The brothers flew under the radar internationally but earned a substantial local following from fans of the French Cold Wave movement. This set does not disappoint, at times vibrantly rhythmic and then meditatively thoughtful. The band's name, draws from Trisomy 21, relating to the extra chromosome resulting in Down syndrome.

23

⊙ The Passage's debut album, *Pindrop*, was recorded during the last week of July 1980. *Pindrop* is a mass of experimental sounds, dark and somewhat hazy. The atmosphere calls on that of Joy Division's *Unknown Pleasures* and incorporates a dungeon feel of NYC's Suicide. Nevertheless, it hosts great melody and rhythm. It's no wonder that NME reviewed it as being 'disciplined intellectual aggression, frantic emotions and powerful idiomatic musicality'. Essential.

⊙ The performance of the duo Strawberry Switchblade and their support cast on their dream-pop debut single 'Trees and Flowers' was very impressive. Roddy Frame from Aztec Camera, Madness' bassist Mark Bedford, oboist Kate St John and the production duo of Bill Drummond (KLF) and David Balfe (Teardrop Explodes) assisted Jill Bryson and Rose McDowall to create an exquisite piece that can be played as a loop over and over. Available in 1983, the song's subject matter was about Jill's agoraphobia anxiety disorder. Very tasty.

⊙ Martin Gore, born in 1961 in London, England, is renowned as a keyboardist and guitarist for the iconic band Depeche Mode. In 1984, their hit single 'People Are People' reached an impressive No.4 spot on the UK charts. Martin's talent shines through his dark and politically charged compositions, such as 'Policy of Truth' and 'Personal Jesus', which played a significant role in establishing Depeche Mode as one of the best-selling electronic acts of all time. It all began in 1980 when Martin crossed paths with Andy Fletcher at the Van Gogh club, a popular dance club. Impressed by Martin's musical prowess, Fletcher wasted no time in inviting him to join his band, Composition of Sound, which he had formed alongside Vince Clarke. The addition of Dave Gahan as the lead singer completed the lineup, and it was Gahan who suggested the name Depeche Mode. Together, they embarked on a musical journey that would leave an indelible mark on the world of electronic music.

Martin Gore - unknown

24

◉ Samy Birnbach was born in 1948, in Tel Aviv, Israel. Samy was a founding member and vocalist/lyricist with Minimal Compact, who formed in 1980. Minimal Compact had an initial solid performing period of 7 years before splitting, but there have been several reformations since and could turn up appearing near you at any time. To date they have released have 6 studio albums showcasing their unique style of Middle Eastern-flavoured dance/NEW WAVE electronica. Aside from the band, Samy is internationally known as DJ Morpheus, he has set DJ desks at festivals all over the world. Morpheus is famed and credited as the compiler of the *Freezone* series of ambient-chillout-downtempo sets, these albums have a perfect blend of electronica with ultra-rare tracks by the likes of David Byrne, Coldcut, Carl Craig, Kruder & Dorfmeister, Moby and Porcupine Tree being among them. Other projects by Samy include collaborations with luminaries such as Colin Newman, Hector Zazou and Steven Brown. In 2000, as DJ Morpheus, he received the Ibiza Award as Best Chillout DJ. And today, he also has had a radio show since the '90s on Radio Campus in Brussels and a monthly Chillout Program on FM4 for the Austrian Radio.

ONE NIGHT IN LIECHTENSTEIN
SAMY BIRNBACH aka DJ Morpheus
(Minimal Compact)

It was during a tour in 1986 or '87; Minimal Compact were in Liechtenstein. It had to be then, as we split in 1988 officially, even though the public never really let us split, every few years we kept doing reunions, especially in Israel, funnily enough.

Liechtenstein is a very small, peculiar place - really tiny, a principality; it thrives on banking and finance. It is almost like, on that side of the road, there is Austria, and on the other side, Switzerland. For this tour we actually took in Switzerland, just to make it worthwhile. But this night we were playing a hall; there were no clubs as such, so a hired hall by the promoter was the venue.

The public there are generally introverted, shy, and respectful, but unfortunately in the crowd that night were 3 or 4 Austrian 'yobbos', you know, crude, rude and drunk undesirables. They were doing their best to 'blow up' the gig; that was their idea of fun and a good night out! We were playing and doing our best to ignore their loud chanting sledges of "*silly boy, silly boy*" and the like. But the tipping point came when one of the yobbos threw a bottle of beer that landed on stage right near our recently bought synthesizer. This put Berry Sakharof, our guitarist, over the edge, and he lost his cool. Berry, normally the perfect gentleman and non-violent type, jumped off stage and started throttling the guy. The crowd cleared back with Berry over him, and he realized it was no use hitting him as he was so drunk, he was like a sack of rags! The rest of the audience did not interfere; they shied away and stood back, aghast! Berry stopped and returned to the stage, that didn't deter the yobbos from carrying on, but then in came the promoter and offered the yobbos a deal: "*I'll give you a crate of beer if you leave*". They accepted that and advanced outside, where he gave them the beer, then they proceeded to beat him up and disappeared into the night. That night sticks in the memory of a travelling rock band.

Samy Birnbach by Petra Gall

◉ Lynval Golding was born in 1951, in Saint Catherine, Jamaica. Lynval, as guitarist and vocalist, was a founding member of The Specials in 1977. He went on to form Fun Boy Three with Terry Hall and Neville Staple, who were active for 3 years from 1981; more recently, Lynval was touring with The Beat. In July 2023, Coventry University awarded Lynval an honorary degree, Doctor of The Arts.

◉ Robbie Grey was born July 24, 1957, and is best known as the frontman/vocalist for the band Modern English that formed in Colchester, England in 1979. Famed for the 1982 hit 'I Melt with You', they started out as The Lepers, but after a name change and a self-released single, they were then signed to 4AD. After four moderately successful albums, they split in 1987, reformed in 1990 for a couple of years, recorded the album *Pillow Lips* and then disbanded again. Since then, there have been several reformations, with Robbie being the one constant member. In 2013 the original members Grey, Mike Conroy, Gary McDowell, and Stephen Walker reunited: today Modern English still tour.

◉ Born Andonis Michaelides in 1958 in Nicosia, Cyprus, Mick Karn moved to the UK from Cyprus as a young child in the early 1960s. In London, he met the other founding members of the band Japan while attending school. Mick was a multi-instrumentalist but specialised playing bass guitar in a unique and original style that helped define Japan's distinctive sound. With his innovative bass techniques, Mick changed perceptions about bass guitar playing forever. Though mainly self-taught, his bass lines were instantly recognisable. After Japan disbanded, Mick explored many musical genres, including jazz, ambient, and progressive rock, both as a solo artist and by collaborating with other musicians such as Gary Numan, Midge Ure, Kate Bush, and former Japan bandmates. For a taste of Mick's solo work, check out his debut solo album, *Titles*, and the atmospheric Dalis Car project with Peter Murphy and Paul Lawford called *The Waking Hour*. Mick Karn passed away from cancer in London on January 4, 2011.

⦿ On this day in 1979 the debut single 'Dreamin' b/w 'Another Dream' by Brenda Ray was available. Lucious and delicious dub minimalism, it took us on a road missed by the greater population. Using a melodica at the forefront over Brenda's breathy vocals, what we get is a perfect piece of stark dub. Brenda Kenny was from Earlestown in the northwest of England near Manchester and was part of the outfit Naffi Sandwich, made up of Paul Catchpole, Gerry Kenny aka Freddie Viaduct and Brenda herself, who took on the guises of Polly Rithim & Brenda Ray. For more, seek out the reissue compilation *D'Ya Hear Me! Naffi Years 1979 – 83*.

⦿ In 1986, the album *Gift* by Sisterhood was available in stores. Following the split of Sisters of Mercy, an intense dispute arose among Andrew Eldritch, Wayne Hussey, and Craig Adams regarding ownership of the band's name. During this feud, Hussey & Adams performed under the moniker The Sisterhood. RCA Records further fuelled the conflict by offering 25,000 pounds to the first party to release new material. Eldritch, assisted by Lucas Fox, swiftly recorded and released *Gift* under the name Sisterhood, claiming the prize money and preventing Hussey & Adams from touring under that name. Eventually, Eldritch emerged victorious in the prolonged legal battle for control of The Sisters of Mercy name, while the others continued as The Mission.

⦿ On this date in 1993, U2 began a two-week reign at the summit of the American album charts with their release *Zooropa*. This record clearly demonstrates the band's inventiveness and creativity, perhaps even more so than their previous collaboration with Brian Eno, *Passengers*. One imagines Eno urging lead singer Bono to dial back his vocals and let the music shine through. On *Zooropa*, Bono's singing is more subdued, bolstered by harmonies and effects. Even guitarist The Edge ventures into new territory with 'Numb', one of the least characteristic U2 songs ever. His monotonic vocals and jagged guitar work create a singular mood unlike anything the band had done before. The disjointed guitar evokes Eno's early experimental work like 'Sky Saw'. Though odd, it is captivating. The haunting ballad 'Lemon' stands out as a highlight, mingling Eno's electronic touches, Talking Heads-esque harmonies, and shifting tempos. Bono's uncommon falsetto proves most pleasant. Legendary Johnny Cash lends his weathered voice to the finale, 'The Wanderer', grounding the preceding avant-garde pieces with warmth. U2 finish on a graceful note, clearly exhibiting Eno's influence that would soon be heard on his joint album with John Cale, Wrong Way Up. Deservedly, *Zooropa* earned U2 the 1994 Grammy for Best Alternative Music Album.

25

⦿ Liquid Liquid from New York City released the 4 track EP *Optimo* in 1983. The EP contained the track 'Cavern', which was used by Grandmaster Flash & Melle Mel on the massive hit 'White Lines (Don't Don't Do It)' later in 1983. 99 Records, the label that released 'Cavern', went broke through the costs of legal proceedings proving that the sensational bassline melody was straight lifted from Liquid Liquid's song. Even though the court found in favour of Liquid Liquid, Sugar Hill Records avoided any payment by claiming bankruptcy themselves!

⦿ Madonna's debut single 'Everybody' was put out by Sire Records and available July 25, 1982. The synthpop track was easy listening and straightforward NEW WAVE pop. There's an interesting story about Ms. Ciccone and this single. London's Blitz nightclub co-founder, Visage and Skids drummer Rusty Egan, was told about Madonna by her boyfriend Mark Kamins, who said Sire Records founder Seymour Stein was keen on signing her and wanted his opinion of this emerging performer. After meeting Madonna in New York, Rusty booked her for a club gig. Previously, after being given the master recording by Stein, Rusty had done a remix of 'Everybody', which Madonna reportedly said she hated (who was this young upstart criticising one of NEW WAVE's finest?), the single didn't catch on in the UK but sold over 250,000 copies in the US. After going on to sell 300 million albums, the young upstart seemed to have made it! From there, the mainstream pop path paved with gold was her route.

Thurston Moore by Petra Gallj

⦿ Thurston Moore, born in 1958 in Coral Gables, USA, has carved out a remarkable career for himself as the guitarist, vocalist, and songwriter of Sonic Youth since 1980. His immense talent and unique style have earned him a well-deserved spot in Rolling Stone's prestigious list of the 100 Greatest Guitarists of All Time. Sonic Youth's influence on the '80s generation cannot be denied. With their fearless experimentation, incorporating feedback, oblique tunings, and dissonance, they seamlessly merged POST-PUNK and avant-garde, pioneering what would later be known as 'indie-rock'.

⦿ Susan Ottaviano was born July 25 in Connecticut, USA, and was a founding member and the lead vocalist of Book of Love (BoL) out of New York City. In 1983, four friends who studied art and shared a passion for music came together to form BoL. The group was composed of Susan as the lead vocalist, Ted Ottaviano (no relation to Susan) as the principal songwriter, Jade Lee on keyboards, and Lauren Roselli also on keyboards. What made them unique was the lineup of three keyboardists, with Susan out front as vocalist. Signed to Sire Records, they released 4 albums before splitting in 1993. With a couple of singles to their credit, the synthpop quartet had a distinctly UK sound but went unnoticed until they released their *self-titled* debut album in 1986. Their entire collection of music showcases magnificent harmonies and shimmering synthesizers accompanied by richly orchestrated compositions. The seamless integration of their numerous keyboards produces a captivating sound that engrosses listeners from beginning to end. From their art student beginnings, BoL initiated their pop aesthetic by incorporating a range of culturally diverse reference points, from 'Modigliani (Lost in Your Eyes)' to 'I Touch Roses', these songs skilfully shift the focus of romance from the background to the forefront of our minds. Many say they don't know of BoL until they realise that they have heard them in the soundtracks of movies like *Planes, Trains and Automobiles, The Silence of the Lambs*, and *American Psycho*.

DEPECHE MODE'S GIRLFRIENDS?
SUSAN OTTAVIANO
(Book of Love)

When our first single, 'Boy', came out in the winter of 1985, it very quickly became a hit in dance clubs and on the American Billboard dance charts. Before we knew it, we were asked to open for Depeche Mode, and we were on a US stadium tour!

We had had very little live experience at the time and had probably never played for more than 200 people. We also had no time to prepare!

On the first night of the tour, the buttons on my bespoke cocktail dress started to come undone (our harried customer designer was as green as we were), and I spent much of the show with one hand on my back trying to button it back up, my first wardrobe malfunction! Hoots and hollers ensued!

This was not a good thing because, at this time in the '80s, there were very few women on the road touring, and we needed to be respected by the headliner's crew (which is do or die for an opener because we needed their help for our show to run smoothly).

The three girls in BOL were the sole women in an entourage of about 25 men. We were trying our best to hold our heads up high and act professional.

It was also customary for the crew of the headliners to do a little hazing on the openers. So, for us, it was spotlights on our boobs and a lot of other sexist stuff that we had to just deal with! Rock and roll!

A few nights later, when we were performing for an unruly crowd that wanted to see Depeche Mode and not Book of Love, I shouted out: *"We're Depeche Mode's girlfriends and if you're not nice to us, then they aren't coming out!!"* This immediately solved our problem, and the show went off without a hitch!

Later that night, Depeche Mode's tour manager came up to me and made it very clear that I was not to say that ever again! Oh well!

The next show, one of the guys in the Depeche crew asked me *"Whose girlfriend are you going to be tonight?"* So much for earning anyone's respect!

The band eventually heard about the incident, and Dave Gahan graciously gave me some pointers for managing a tough crowd, for which I am forever grateful.

◉ Play Dead's debut single 'Poison Takes A Hold' b/w 'Introduction' was in the racks June 25, 1981. It was a superb start of Goth/POST-PUNK for this band out of Oxford, England. Propelling funk that is dark and loaded with a solid rhythm section supports vocalist Rob Hickson's delivery. The sharp angular guitar by Re-vox is a highlight.

◉ Wire Train out of San Francisco had their debut album, *In a Chamber,* on the store shelves in 1983. Pretty simple jangle pop with a few excellent high points due to some clever songwriting, 'She's on Fire' and 'I'll Do You' are fine examples. 'Chamber of Hellos' gives a nod to The Cure's 'A Forest'. Altogether quite listenable and one that will always return to your turntable.

26

◉ On July 26, 1982, *Friend or Foe*, the debut solo album by Adam Ant, was released. To date it's his best-selling solo album, and arguably, aside from *Kings of the Wild Frontier*, this is the best album that Adam has made. Probably lacking the production values of later recordings, it has excellent songwriting, pop hooks and a great variety of instrumentation. The hit single 'Goody Two Shoes', 'Here Comes the Grump', 'Place in the Country' and the 'title track' prove his worth - all great songs-and confirm without a doubt Adam Ant is one of the integral personnel of British NEW WAVE.

⊙ On this day in 1977, Elvis Costello got arrested and was charged with 'illegally busking'. Elvis' first album, *My Aim is True*, had recently been released by independent UK label Stiff Records, who oddly had not yet secured a distribution deal in the USA. So, to remedy this, he decided he needed to be better known and subsequently set himself up outside the London Hilton Hotel, where a convention of CBS Records executives was under way. Elvis proceeded to play the whole album loudly to street listeners and those inside who could not avoid hearing him. He was soon arrested but not before being noticed by CBS executives, and they were indeed impressed; it led to a record deal with Columbia Records in the USA. He was fined 5 pounds.

⊙ Howard Devoto, the original frontman for The Buzzcocks and Magazine, released his only solo album, *Jerky Versions of the Dream*, in 1983, shortly after Magazine disbanded. The album showcases a departure from Magazine's music, with simple and uncomplicated tunes that have a more pop flavour. The production quality is notably high, reflecting Devoto's attention to detail. Knowing Devoto and his earlier demands of perfection, this album is remarkably unremarkable in its projection of being more NEW WAVE than POST-PUNK.

⊙ The Hunters & Collectors *self-titled* debut studio album, released on 26 July 1982, is EPIC; the sound here is exceptional! The album was wonderfully produced by the band along with Tony Cohen as audio engineer. Taking influence from CAN, "Hunnas" (as they were known to their legion of fans) provided rhythm and beat of the highest order. There were many bands sounding alike in the early '80s, not Hunters and Collectors; they stood out like a sore thumb! It was so refreshing to find something remarkably different, fresh, and unique. This debut single is inventive, infectious funk and so very tribal thanks to the guitar of Ray Tosti-Gueira and the insane percussionist Greg Perano. Delicious and a must for your library.

⊙ Ronald Stephen Valentine Peno aka Ron Peno was born in 1955 in Gosford Australia. Ron was the frontman vocalist for The Hellcats, Naked Lunch and famously for Died Pretty, for whom he was a founding member after his departure from The Screaming Tribesmen. Died Pretty were a staple of the Sydney inner city music scene, they soon earned a faithful following playing to packed audiences. Through to 2000 they released 8 studio albums and achieved several ARIA award nominations for their eclectic and distinctive output, taking influences from Velvet Underground, Bob Dylan, and Neil Young. When Died Pretty folded in 2003 Ron fronted Darling Downs with ex-Scientists & Beasts of Bourbon guitarist Kim Salmon and released several albums fronting Ron S. Peno and The Superstitions. Ron died 11 August 2023 after battling esophageal cancer.

⊙ Mark Seymour was born in 1956 in Benalla, Victoria, Australia. Mark was the frontman and songwriter of Hunters & Collectors. As a soloist he released several albums under his name and as Mark Seymour and The Undertow; his release *One Eyed Man* won Best Adult Contemporary Album at the ARIA Music Awards of 2001. Mark is the brother of Nick Seymour, bassist for Crowded House.

27

⊙ In 1985 Eurythmics went to No.1 on the UK singles chart with 'There Must Be an Angel (Playing with My Heart)'. The song shimmers and sparkles, thankfully, due to Annie

Lennox's stunning vocals. It was Eurythmics' only single to reach the top of the UK charts and has an added soul feel through the featured harmonica solo by Stevie Wonder.

Eurythmics Annie Lennox by Petra Gallj

● If you dig around, you might discover the striking first single called 'I Don't Want to Live with Monkeys' from The Higsons that came out on February 27, 1981. The band, named after lead singer Charlie 'Switch' Higson, started in Norwich, England. They produced an offbeat style of punk and funk music that was clearly influenced by Talking Heads. Robyn Hitchcock was so impressed with the band that he recorded a tribute song called 'Listening to the Higsons' in 1985. Earlier in 1981, two well-known songs by The Higsons, '(My Love Is) Bent (At Both Ends)' and 'We Will Never Grow Old', were included on the album *Welcome to Norwich-A Fine City*.

● Andy McMaster was born in 1941 in Glasgow, Scotland. He was a bassist, keyboardist, and vocalist for the power pop band The Motors. Along with Nick Garvey, he formed The Motors in London in 1977. The other original members were drummer Richard Wernham (aka Ricky Slaughter) and guitarist Rob Hendry, who was later replaced by Peter Bramall (aka Bram Tchaikovsky). Their song 'Airport', written by McMaster, was The Motors' biggest hit, reaching No.4 on the UK singles chart in 1978 and charting internationally. Their follow-up, 'Forget About You', also penned by McMaster, reached No.13. Both songs are now considered power pop classics. Their debut single, 'Dancing the Night Away', co-written by Garvey and McMaster, was released in September 1977 and peaked at No.42 in the UK. Formed in 1976, the band broke up in 1979. In 1980, Nick and Andy recorded the album *Tenement Steps*. The single 'Love and Loneliness reached No.58 in the UK and No.78 in the US. That album featured bassist Martin Ace and drummer Terry Williams, both formerly of the Welsh rock band Man.

● Conway Savage was born in 1960, in Fish Creek, Australia. Conway was a member of Nick Cave and The Bad Seeds, joining in mid-1990, with whom he played piano and organ and gave backing vocals with Nick Cave quoting him as "*The man with the golden voice*". As a solo recordist he released several critically acclaimed albums; *Nothing Broken* (2000), *Wrong Man's Hands* (2004) and the much sought-after compilation *Rare Songs & Performances* 1989–2004. Through the 1980s he was a member of a few bands, including Dust on the Bible, The Feral Dinosaurs and The Happy Orphans. His contributions to The Bad Seeds cannot be understated, being integral to the sound of their studio albums, including *Murder Ballads, The Boatman's Call* and *No More Shall We Part*, among others. In October 1995 Conway contributed lead vocals for 'The Willow Garden', a B-side of the single, 'Where the Wild Roses Grow'. In 2017 Conway was diagnosed with a brain tumor which he succumbed to, aged 58, on 2 September 2018.

28

⊙ Beate Bartel was born July 28, 1955, in West Berlin. Beate was an integral member of the groundbreaking bands Liaisons Dangereuses and Einstürzende Neubauten (EN) with whom she presented distinctive and adventurous aural design ideas. Beate came from a sound engineering role in public broadcasting and, in 1979, formed the all-female Mania D, which stood out as part of the Neue Deutsche Welle movement. In 1980 she was a founding member of EN, who established themselves as pioneers in avant-garde, industrial music. She would soon join up with D.A.F. member Chrislo Hass, releasing the series of CHBB cassettes in 1981; these four cassettes preceded the release of the Liaisons Dangereuses *self-titled* album, a highly regarded album for its inventive mix of minimal synth, dance beats and atmospherics. The album is considered essential listening for the period and genres. 2021 saw the release of *M-Dokumente*, a book concentrating on the visionary and innovative bands Mania D., Malaria! and Matador, the book is edited by Beate and fellow band members Bettina Köster and Gudrun Gut. This coincided with the release of the retrospective *M-Sessions* double CDs and/or vinyl box set, it contains rare originals and reworks by Monika Werkstatt. Translating to Monika Workshop, it is a collective of female, musicians, artists and producers based in Berlin Germany. The release was followed by an exhibition at Betonhalle, Berlin.

SO36 BERLIN
BEATE BARTEL
(Mania D, Einstürzende Neubauten, Liaisons Dangereuses)

Never look back – except on facts.

Is there anything to write that is not written or told before?

Where do I start?

Back then there was one place, the SO36.

Connected by a straight pathway through West Berlin as far as concerts were concerned, Kant Kino via Quasimodo to Quartier Latin, and in 1978 it extended right into SO36.

SO36 was sparse, square, smoky, functional. It was not a place to hang out, but was packed with intense experiences and friendships for life.

In November 1978 I saw and met Wire, the day of the hold up when the cashbox was stolen.

In June 1979, Alan Vega and Martin Rev from Suicide, whom I have met during a UK tour in July 1978 with The Clash and The Specials, were happy about the fact that the ceiling at Kippenbergers office, where they were staying, nearly collapsed on their heads.

In November 1980, Throbbing Gristle with their hefty audio frequencies that could make you feel like vomiting - a special, but not very pleasant experience and of course in 1979 - 1980 being on stage with my own band, Mania D. and with one of the first performances of Einstürzende Neubauten.

DAF, Fad Gadget, Daniel Miller and many more....

At the end of 1980 I left West-Berlin to set up something new with Chris Haas, Liaisons Dangereuses.

From Berlin, March 2024

⊙ On July 28th, 1979, the song 'I Don't Like Mondays' by The Boomtown Rats reached No.1 on the UK charts, where it remained for four weeks. The lyrics were inspired by the actions of 16-year-old Brenda Spencer, who opened fire at a school that Monday morning. Armed with a rifle, she killed two adults, including the principal, and injured nine children before retreating to her home. When questioned about her motive, Spencer simply replied, "*I just don't like Mondays. I did it for fun*". She had no other explanation for the seemingly random act of violence. Originally intended as a B-side, Bob Geldof and the band decided to feature 'I Don't Like Mondays' as a single after seeing it connect with audiences during their USA tour. The song captures the senseless tragedy of a school shooting carried out by a young girl who had no real reason behind the attack.

◉ Gerald Vincent "Jerry" Casale, born in 1948 in Ravenna, Ohio, USA, originally known as Gerald Vincent Pizzute, is a versatile artist. He is not only a singer but also a songwriter, composer, multi-instrumentalist, record producer, and music video director. Jerry is best known as a founding member of DEVO, a band that was formed in 1973. The group initially consisted of individuals from Kent and Akron, Ohio, including two sets of brothers: the Mothersbaughs (Mark and Bob) and the Casales (Gerald and Bob), along with Alan Myers. DEVO was a unique band that emerged from the punk rock scene, known for their unconventional style and artistic approach. Their core concept revolved around the idea of "De-evolution," suggesting that humanity has regressed rather than progressed. This concept was inspired by the dysfunction and herd mentality prevalent in American society, reflecting a decline in intelligence. Jerry has collaborated with renowned artists such as David Byrne, Debbie Harry, Brian Eno, Jermaine Jackson, David Bowie, and Neil Young, further establishing his reputation in the music industry.

◉ Malcolm Holmes was born in 1960 in Birkenhead, England, and was the original drummer with Orchestral Manoeuvres in the Dark (OMD). Malcom's first drumming sessions were for The Id, who included future members of OMD, and he joined OMD in 1980. He also played sessions for The Pale Fountains, Dalek I Love You & Lightning Seeds.

◉ The Payola$ out of Vancouver, Canada, released their debut album, *In a Place Like This*, in 1981. The band put together by British ex-pat Paul Hyde treats us to tidy '80s-flavoured power-pop loaded with some killer riffs and anthemic melodies best exhibited on the probably best-known track, 'China Boys'. Overall, today it's pretty dated and not quite reaching the quality of the 1983 Juno Award-winning song 'Eyes of a Stranger', that took out won Best Single of the Year in 1983.

29

◉ Virginia Astley released her first solo album, *From Gardens Where We Feel Secure*, in 1983. Virginia was the keyboardist with The Ravishing Beauties and The Victims of Pleasure. This album was far removed from the music of the aforementioned; it's a glorious piece of pastoral ambience, beautifully captivating and ever so subtle. Pure and perfect Sunday morning music.

◉ Martin McCarrick, born in 1962 in Luton, England, is a highly acclaimed music arranger/composer and classically trained cellist. Renowned for his exceptional talent, he was handpicked by Ivo Watts-Russell to lend his backing vocals and cello skills to the This Mortal Coil 4AD project. His contributions can be heard on the albums *It'll End in Tears*, *Filigree* and *Shadow*, and *Blood*. McCarrick's versatility as a musician is evident in his extensive body of work, which includes collaborations with esteemed artists such as Siouxsie and the Banshees, Bryan Ferry, Marc Almond, and Gary Numan, among many others.

◉ On July 29, 1980, the group consisting of Peter Hook, Stephen Morris, and Bernard Sumner made their initial appearance at the Beach Club night in the Oozits venue Manchester. It has been recorded that they performed under the name The No Names. The trio later evolved into New Order, adopting their name from an article titled 'The People's New Order of Kampuchea' proposed by the band's manager, Rob Gretton. It was not until October, when Gillian Gilbert joined as a keyboardist and guitarist, that they transitioned into a quartet. Her inaugural live performance with the band took place at The Squat in Manchester on October 25, 1980.

○ The Smithereens were heroes of college radio in the USA. Their brand of sixties-influenced power-pop was getting lapped up, and the band earned a huge following. The debut album, *Especially for You,* that was on the store shelves on this day in 1986 holds a bagful of catchy tunes, with grab you right away hooks, thanks to Pat DiNizio's superb songwriting. There's a distinct amalgam of hard rock power chords and Beatles-style pop here. This classic album of jangly guitar holds some excellent tracks; at the peak are 'Groovy Tuesday', 'Behind the Wall of Sleep' and 'Blood and Roses'

BAY CITY MORTAL COIL
MARTIN MCCARRICK
(Nick Cave, Dead Can Dance, The Glove, This Mortal Coil et.al.)

December 1985 - London

It's Sunday afternoon, and I am due to fly to Edinburgh early tomorrow morning with Ivo Watts-Russell from 4AD records to start work on the second This Mortal Coil album, *Filigree and Shadow.* With bag packed and cello at the ready, I wander out into the late afternoon drizzle, hopping on a bus to buy food for the evening.

Disaster strikes about an hour later when I have my wallet stolen in Sainsbury's, fleeced by a dirty East London pickpocket. I only find out when I try to pay at the checkout, and I have the indignity of having to leave the shop without my groceries, walking home in the rain because I no longer have money for the bus fare.

Back home I call Ivo and explain what has happened. I have no wallet, no money, no credit cards, no driving licence, and no way of getting to the airport the next morning. Ivo steps up, orders me a cab on the 4AD account, and offers to advance me £100 from the new album. I gratefully accept.

Once in Edinburgh we settle into Palladium Studios with owner and engineer John Turner. After the first day of recording, we eat dinner, then two of John's friends turn up, and the cards come out. We play poker, drink beer, and smoke cigarettes on repeat for the next few hours. An ebullient guy called Les who speaks with a broad Scottish accent wins nearly every game. This happens again the next evening, and then again, the next, until I am soon cleaned out of the £100 record advance that Ivo has loaned me. I throw my dud hand in for good. This Les guy is clearly a card shark of some kind. I sit quietly through the rest of the evening, sipping beer, watching suspiciously for marked cards or other indicators of cheating, but I turn up no evidence.

The next morning, I ask Ivo about Les. Who is he? Where is he from? Why does he turn up every night? Why does he look familiar?

"That's Les McKeown from the Bay City Rollers," Ivo explains.

The penny drops. The name is Les; he's Scottish and looks familiar – it could only be him.

For those who don't know, the Bay City Rollers are a Scottish tartan-clad pop group from the mid-1970s who had a string of hit records, their own TV show, and a fan base of screaming tartan-clad girls and boys who would become hysterical at the mere mention of their name.

This was not the first time the Bay City Rollers had interjected in my world. Back in the mid-1970s I was a young trampolining champion (don't ask), and I needed a light blue vest top for a competition. As a family, we had no money, but my ever-resourceful mother found me a near-perfect light blue vest from a bargain bin at the local market. The only issue, and it was a big one, was that it said Bay City Rollers in black capital letters across the chest. I must have washed that shirt 15 times, scrubbing at it to remove the name, but the print would not shift. I won the competition with an impressive half-twist crucifix into a front drop while wearing the vest inside out to obscure the print, but the fabric was so thin that the ink bled through, displaying the name SRELLOR YTIC YAB – *the* backwards version of the world-famous teen group.

Back in Edinburgh I chose not to divulge this story to Ivo for fear he might in turn tell Les when he appeared for his now nightly poker session. As it happened, Les turned up much earlier in the day this time, just as we were about to record some backing vocals, so Ivo asked Les to sing with me on a version of Gene Clarke's 'Strength of Strings'. If you listen to the This Mortal Coil version of the song, you will hear Les and I singing close harmony backing vocals throughout.

When Les died in 2021, I was reminded of those nights in Edinburgh and the inside-out vest incident and realised that Les had unknowingly played a role in my life, providing me with a story that linked my youth with my adulthood, two things both separate and connected, and this story has infinitely more value than the wallet I had stolen or the £100 I lost at poker. So, thanks, Les.
Bye Bye Baby.

30

◉ The creative and versatile Kate Bush, born Catherine Bush on July 30, 1958, in Bexleyheath, England, has never been one to be pigeonholed. She was just 19 years old when she had the No.1 hit song 'Wuthering Heights'. Her imaginative and experimental art-rock music, characterised by theatricality, textural innovation, and symbolic themes, makes her one of the most successful and influential female musicians ever. Bush's inventive pop sensibilities allowed her to seamlessly fit into the NEW WAVE genre. Her stunning 1985 No.1 album *Hounds of Love* spent a whole year on the charts. After a 35-year hiatus, Kate returned to the stage in 2014 for a series of 22 concert events featuring puppets, magicians, and dancers. She released a three disc live album of the shows titled *Before the Dawn* in 2016. Kate was appointed Commander of the Order of the British Empire (CBE) in 2013 in recognition of her contributions to music.

◉ Craig Gannon was born in 1966 in Manchester, England. Craig's career has a myriad of interesting twists and turns, especially through the 1980s. He first came to prominence with Aztec Camera and then with The Smiths after Andy Rourke was fired in 1986. Oddly, Rourke returned, and Craig took on the mantle as rhythm guitarist, becoming an official fifth member for live performances. Craig also had brief membership periods with The Bluebells, The Blue Orchids, The Adult Net and Colourfield. Today he is now a composer for film and television.

JIMMY'S SPIDERS
CRAIG GANNON
(Aztec Camera, The Smiths, The Colourfield, The Bluebells)

In 1989 I was recording the Adult Net album *The Honey Tangle* with Brix Smith. Craig Leon and Cassell Webb were producing, and the drummer was Clem Burke from Blondie. We used a few different studios, but we recorded a lot of the guitars at Led Zeppelin's Jimmy Page's house/studio in Cookham, Berkshire. It was a fantastic place with a river running right through the property. At that time, I didn't know much about Jimmy Page or Led Zeppelin but had heard about his interests in black magic and the occult.

I've recorded in a lot of residential studios over the years, and although I generally love working in them, the big downside for me is that they're usually in the countryside; hence, they're inundated with insects! I was (and still am) terrified of spiders, so I never really slept much in those studios, as I was too busy watching dark, furry patterns the size of my hand moving in the night and being on the verge of throwing up from fear. The first thing I'd do when arriving at a studio was to scan the whole bedroom. Under the bed, in the bed, in the pillows and everywhere in-between.

The living area of the place was a big cottage with two bedrooms; Brix had the upstairs bedroom, and I had the ground floor. We were shown to our bedroom. I opened the door to my room, and there they were, a million spiders clinging on to the outside of the windows, just waiting for me! (Incidentally, one of the tracks we were recording was called 'Spin This Web'). This was much more than I'd ever seen in one place before, studio or not, and although they were on the outside, I knew there'd be loads in the room. I went white but tried to keep calm. By that time Brix knew of my fear and looked at me and just laughed hysterically.

Brix was married to Mark E. Smith from The Fall at that time, and he'd come down a lot to visit her. After Mark named an eight-foot-long flower arrangement above the mixing desk 'Jimmy Page's Grave' and with a quick *"C'mon lads, let's go to the pub"*, we trotted up the country lane to the nearest local.

Anyway, once we'd settled into the house and studio, we soon found a huge witchcraft symbol on the patio. We thought there might be some weird vibes going around this house because of Jimmy Page's dabbling in the occult; that was although, apart from the spider situation, I only experienced one.

Each morning at dawn I'd get woken by a tapping sound as if someone was tapping their fingernails on glass, although as I was so worn out by the lack of sleep, I tried to ignore it. As the whole place was covered in ivy and foliage, I thought it must be a twig or something hanging over a window. After a few days of this happening around dawn each morning, I went to see what it was. I opened the bedroom door and went into the kitchen, and there at the glass door was a huge black crow tapping the glass with its beak. At the time it didn't really freak me out, so I walked up to the door to open it when the crow (which seemed to be well over a foot high) stopped tapping, looked me straight in the eye as if to say *"right, got the message now? let's just leave it at that!"* then just walked off slowly into the dawn mist. After that the tapping stopped, and I never saw or heard that crow again. I know because I was awake each and every night after that listening for it!

The recording of that album was a fantastic time for me, and it was a pleasure to work with everyone involved; unfortunately, I was completely knackered by the end because of the lack of sleep! As well as being a dream to work with, Craig Leon and Cassell Webb entertained us with jaw-dropping stories about Brian Wilson, Charles Manson, and others. The legendary Van Dyke Parks arranged the strings for one track. The album itself was a kind of mid-late '60s psychedelic, guitar-based power pop record with multi-layered West Coast harmonies. I still really like that album.

I heard Jimmy Page sold that house later, he was probably bullied out by the spiders!

● On July 30th, 1982, Bruce Foxton, former bassist of The Jam, achieved a No.23 UK single with his first release, 'Freak'. Although the song was likely purchased mostly by The Jam's fans, it did not meet the expectations of being a timeless classic; instead, it left them feeling underwhelmed and with Freak being somewhat forgetful.

● Gina X Performance first put out their debut album, *Nice Mover*, in 1978. Gina X's sound combined aspects of 1970s art rock, disco, and Kraftwerk-inspired electronic music. This style has been cited as an influence on Grace Jones and contemporary acts like Ladytron and

Goldfrapp. The stylish Euro disco songs on the album are captivating and unique, with Gina Kikoine's theatrical lead vocals taking centre stage. *Nice Mover*, with its detached, icy vocals, is reminiscent of The Flying Lizards. The irresistible 'No G.D.M.' was an instant hit in nightclubs, so it's surprising that 'Plastic Surprise Box' and 'Be a Boy' were not commercial successes. The latter song evokes Toyah and The Sugarcubes.

◉ Rat Scabies, aka Christopher John Millar, was born on 30th July in 1955, in Surrey, England. As the drummer, Rat was a founding member of The Damned in 1976. Over the years since The Damned, Mr. Scabies has played with all sorts of artists, including Donovan, Neville Staple, The Members, and The Mutants, and he formed a short-lived outfit called The Germans with Peter Coyne and Kris Dollimore, originally from The Godfathers.

31

◉ Craig Bloxom was born July 31, 1959, in Inglewood, Los Angeles, USA. Craig's earliest recollections of music were being introduced to Burt Bacharach by his mother and listening to Peter, Paul & Mary records. After the family migrated to Australia in 1965, Craig attended Nelson Bay High School; it was there he met his long-time musical partner, Michael Weiley. It was with Michael and Cliff Grigg he formed Spy v Spy in Sydney, and the 'Spys' would become one of the hardest-working bands of the burgeoning pub circuit. It was through these gigs and the airplay of their 1981 self-funded debut EP, *Four Fresh Lemons*, that they gained a faithful following and garnered support from many majors act like Midnight Oil. The Spy's album *A.O. Mod. TV. Vers.* earned Gold status, and internationally, Spys were gaining recognition, especially in Brazil, where they were regarded as a 'surf band', but they would soon splinter, with Cliff leaving in 1991 and then Craig also in the early 2000s when he took on an apprenticeship as a chef. 2023 saw Craig form ReggaeSPYS, which he describes as "mongrel reggae", presenting new versions of the material divorced from the Spys of old. In 2024 the ReggaeSPYS album *Unity Gain* went top ten on the Aria Album Charts, a peak that eluded Spy v Spy.

Craig Bloxom by permission

THAT NIGHT AT THE T.U.C.
CRAIG BLOXOM
(The RAF, Spy V's Spy, ReggaeSPYS)

Anyone who drank at the Trade Union Club would remember Animal, the doorman. He was stationed by the front door, and he had long greasy biker hair & beard with a menacing demeanour, he was placed there to enforce the 'No Work Boots' policy and discourage skinheads from coming up to the 3rd floor and causing trouble. Denis, the manager, was another intimidating character who paid all the bands from the safe in his office, and I'd seen him pull a .38 pistol from his drawer and rest it on his desk to intimidate you when the payment was over $1000 or so. I remember Denis being very proud of that revolver, and he let me play with it once.

They were indeed wild & exciting times, but having said that, both Denis & Animal were really nice blokes once you got to know them, and they had hearts of gold. Denis became Spy v Spy's benefactor on more than one occasion when one of us (Michael Weiley or me, because Cliff never got a driver's license) got locked up for non-payment of parking fines or speeding tickets. We were living in the squats of Glebe, spending all our money on drugs & alcohol, and if you didn't pay your fines, the local Glebe coppers would come by to haul us off to the station, where you had to pay off your fines off at $25 a day in Silverwater Prison. If we had a tour to Qld coming up and couldn't afford the gaol time we'd come to see Denis, cap in hand and he'd say: "*how much*?" then take a big wad of cash from his shirt pocket and give us $600 or so and say: "*I'll take it out of your next gig*". We played at the club every few months and Denis knew we were good for it. I did 2 stints in Silverwater for nonpayment of fines and both times were fucking terrifying but that's how it was back then until a kid got raped and killed at Long Bay Gaol for the same reason and NSW stopped it. So, one night after playing a gig somewhere circa 1983-84, I went the "Trades" and made my way past Animal up to the first floor for some heavy drinking. After a few hours and close to closing time, I thought I'd finish the night with a straight shot of vodka and be on my way down to the taxi rank and a cab home. A shot of vodka was $0.90 cents back then, and after skolling it, I made it to the top of the stairs heading home before that industrial strength vodka started coming back up again and I knew I was going to spew. I bolted to the handrail, leaned over & emptied my guts into the foyer below. Unfortunately, Animal was standing just underneath so coated him with vomit (and realizing with horror what I'd done) bolted down the stairs and out the front door running for my life. I remember him screaming "*you filthy c#nt I'm going to kill you*" as I ran down Foveaux Street screaming: "*SORRY Animal!*" I didn't return for about 3 months and when I did, he glared but didn't kill me so I'm still alive today due to Animal's kind and forgiving nature. Fuck me dead, those were the days, weren't they? That kind of shit could never happen today.

◉ On July 31 in 1976, Melody Maker magazine published an advertisement by one Stuart Goddard for musicians. The advert said: *Beat on a bass, with the B-Sides, interest in Them, The Kinks, own material, enthusiasm essential, excitement guaranteed. No kids or hard pros...* This was how he met Andy Warren, and they went on to form Adam and The Ants. In just under a year, The Ants would play their first paying gig on April 23, 1977, at the Roxy Club (Covent Garden). The Ants' first 'warm-up' to an audience was reportedly on April 7, in the packed bedroom of their soon-to-be-manager, Pamela Rooke, who was also known as Jordan Mooney, in Muswell Hill, North London. The line-up was Lester Square on guitar, Andy Warren on bass guitar, and Paul Flannagan drumming, and of course Adam. Andy soon left 'The Ants' to join up with ex-Ants guitarist Lester Square to form The Monochrome Set.

◉ Daniel Ash was born on 31 July, 1957 in Northampton, England. Daniel is best known as the guitarist for the iconic goth rock trailblazers Bauhaus. After nearly five years of epic recordings and performances, Bauhaus broke up, and the side project Ash had put together, Tones on Tail, with Bauhaus roadie Glenn Campling, became more of a working project. After releasing several EPs, a full-length album, *Pop*, and the club hit single 'Go!', the group mutated into the highly influential Love and Rockets in 1985. Daniel has released several solo albums, staying somewhat faithful to the goth mood yet somewhat brighter, with a level of pop about them.

◉ Gaylene Goudreau was born on July 31, 1958, in Chicago, USA. Gaylene, as guitarist, was a member of the predominantly 'all-girl' bands Lois Lain, SCAB, Bloodsister and the famed DA!. DA! was one of the seminal late '70s bands based in Chicago and came in to being in 1978. The initial four-piece of Gaylene, bassist Lorna Donley, drummer dawn Fisher and sole male David Thomas were famed for their incendiary performances, where the complimentary guitar playing of Thomas and Goodreau chimed in unison. Today, she works as an electrician and is a member of Revolt-Chix.

Gaylene Goodreau by permission

FIX YOUR OWN WALL!
GAYLENE GOUDREAU
(Lois Lane, Da!, SCAB, Bloodsister, Revolt-Chix)

I answered an ad that Lorna had put out in the Chicago Reader. I had just moved back to Chicago from Los Angeles, breaking it off with Lois Lain and was aching to get back into playing with people. They had a good drummer, and Lorna was a great bassist-singer; Evelyn, the other guitar player, played pretty much like a girl, constantly telling me to turn down! I wasn't having it and didn't get along with her at all, too mature and low-key for me. Lorna decided to let her go and keep me.

I went to St. Louis for a vacation and met David Thomas, great guitar player, and convinced him to come to Chicago and join Da! He completed our sound and off we went.

I loved David and the way we complemented each other's guitar riffs; we had an amazing cocktail of melodies and harmonies, and along with Lorna's bass, we just made magic happen for sure.

We went to Milwaukee to play with X, and I remember this show the most 'cause I simply was so not gonna be punked-out by the owner. We were literally 15 minutes late for soundcheck; we were dealing with traffic and such and the owner said, *"I'm not gonna pay you for this show now"*. I was like, *"Whatever, he isn't serious!"*.

So, during our set, I am not sure how I did this, but I split my finger open and was bleeding all over my white guitar and now struggled with blood and pain during my set. Anyway, so when this guy was telling us he isn't gonna pay us again. I was so pissed-off I went in the dressing room and kicked in all the walls. I then went out and told him, *"So you're not gonna pay us and now you'll have to pay to fix your walls"*. He screamed and yelled and stomped and said, *"You will never play here again"*. I was like… *"Damn straight we aren't!"*.

I was so empowered by that being in my early 20s. I needed that strength to get thru what was ahead of me in life for sure. Thanks for listening to my story.

● Denise Johnson was born in 1966 in Manchester, England. Denise was an early '90s member of Primal Scream and a contributing vocalist to A Certain Ratio, Electronic, Pet Shop Boys and Michael Hutchence. Denise's voice lent a soulful edge to anything she worked on, and she certainly stood out on the music of Primal Scream, most memorably on her first outing with them, the album *Screamadelic. Denise* passed away aged 52 on July 27, 2020, just prior to the release of her debut solo album, *Where Does It Go*.

◉ The Rock on Tyne Festival's second edition took place at Gateshead's International Stadium on July 31, 1982. The lineup included performances by The Police, U2, The Beat, Gang of Four, and Lords of The New Church.

◉ Malcolm Ross was born in 1960 in Blantyre, Malawi. His musical career started when he played guitar in the Scottish band Josef K and was part of the recording of the 1981 album, *The Only Fun in Town*, on Postcard Records. After the demise of Josef K, Ross joined Edwyn Collins in the group Orange Juice, playing and writing songs for both the *Rip it Up* and *Texas Fever* albums. After Orange Juice, in 1984 Ross joined Roddy Frame in Aztec Camera as second guitarist for a short while. He moved on to work with a wide array of artists like Dave Graney, Blancmange and Barry Adamson.

◉ The Times' debut album *Pop Goes Art!* was the introductory release on the Whaam Records label and was available in July 1982. An earlier album, *Go! With the Times*, had been recorded in 1980 but didn't get released until 1985. Born as a side project of Television Personalities, The Times gives us a way into the mod-revival movement. Dan Treacy and Ed Ball here swapped roles from the Television Personalities' duties to present a set of guitar-based songs, earning the mantle of being a retro classic. Some real gems to be found on this set, 'Miss London', the superb 'I Helped Patrick McGoohan Escape' and 'Biff! Bang! Pow!' stand out.

◉ Remember The Vapors? Yes, the band that made 'Turning Japanese'. But they were a bit more than that, and the debut album, *New Clear Days,* that was available July 31, 1980, proved that. *New Clear Days* did show that The Vapors stood up well against most from the ever-burgeoning NEW WAVE era. There are definite similarities to The Jam in their music, coincidentally it was The Jam's Bruce Foxton who was the one that 'discovered' them in a Surrey pub and gave them the support for The Jam's Setting Sons tour. Their songs were catchy, amusing and had all the desired hooks; 'Sixty Second Interval', 'Prisoners' and 'Letter from Hiro', are excellent, but rate only a 4-star billing when compared to the stunning 5-star 'Turning Japanese'

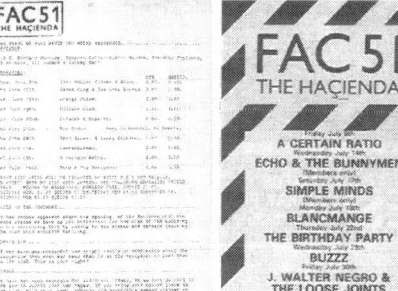

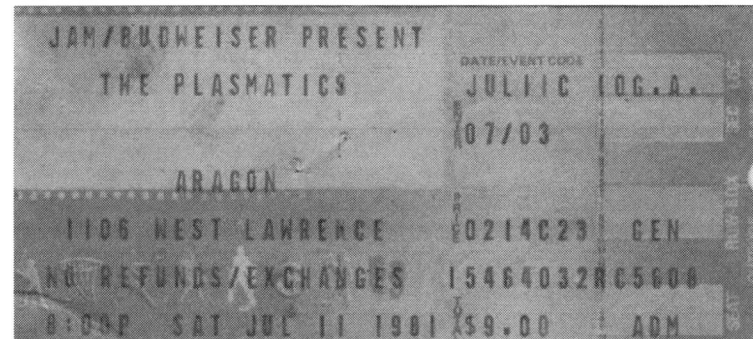

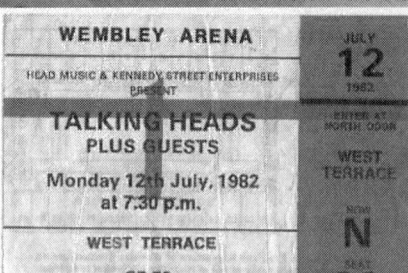

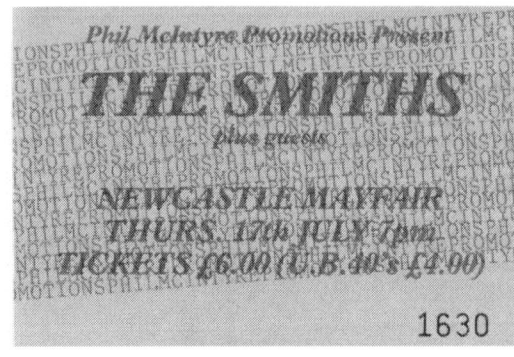

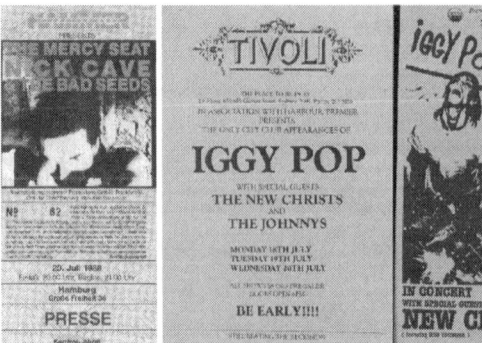

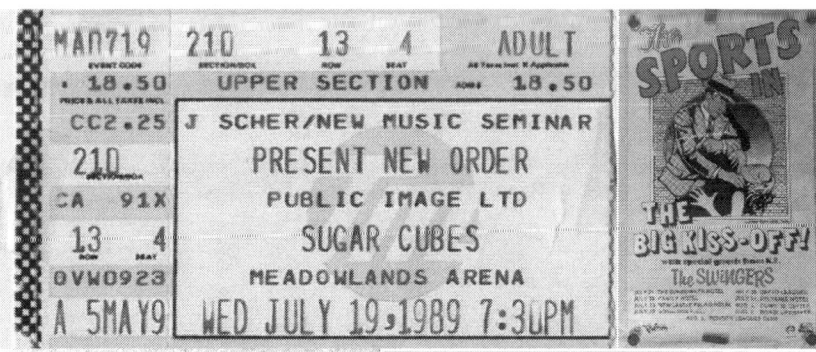

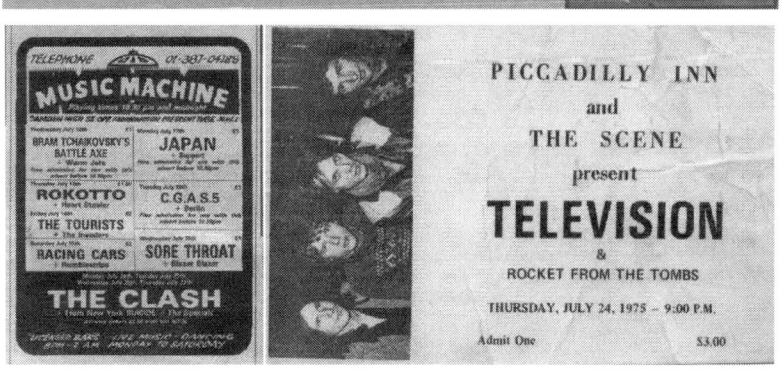

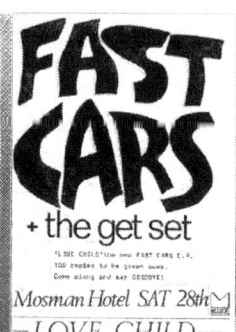

1

● The Associates dropped their opening record called *The Affectionate Punch* on this day in 1980. Right from the first song, you experience very ardent, theatrical, and impassioned yet straightforward tunes grounded in POST-PUNK. There's an extremely tense mood within the peculiar instrumentals, despite the work of the multi-talented Alan Rankine. Billy Mackenzie's singing is forceful and heartfelt; their gifts really come through with each play. When it first came out, the album was hailed as "*a sort of masterwork*" by Paul Morley, writer for NME and member of The Art of Noise.

● Crowded House released their stunning *self-titled* album on August 1, 1986. With the demise of Split Enz, Neil Finn and Paul Hester joined forces with bassist Nick Seymour, and what they ended up with was a worldwide acclaimed three-piece unit. *Crowded House* was a hybrid fusion of power pop, funk, and NEW WAVE. This first outing may not be essential Crowded House, but it's an album of songs with delicate feeling within intricate arrangements with infectious catchy hooks. Neil Finn's ability to write songs puts him in the upper echelon of songsters; his compositions 'Don't Dream It's Over', 'World Where You Live' and 'Something So Strong' are pure classics of musical prowess and lyrical sense.

● Kirlian Camera is an Italian electronic music group started by Angelo Bergamini back in 1979 and their first full-length album appeared in record stores in 1983. The album titled *It Doesn't Matter Now* come after the band had put out numerous EPs and singles. Bergamini has been the sole permanent member over the band's 40-year history, with many different musicians and singers passing through the changing lineups over the decades.

● Mick Medew was born in 1961. Mick's recording career began in 1979 when, as the lead guitarist, he formed a Detroit rock/Radio Birdman-inspired band called The 31st in Brisbane, Australia. In early 1981 he formed The Screaming Tribesmen, and in 1982 released a *self-titled* 7-inch EP to rave reviews. A relocation to Sydney in 1983 saw the release of the critically acclaimed single 'Igloo', which Mick co-wrote with Ron Peno, who would soon front Died Pretty. A new lineup in 1984 that included Mick, Chris Masuak on lead guitar, Bob Wackley on bass and drummer Michael Charles released the classic 12-inch EP *Date with a Vampyre*. The Tribesmen worked hard and gigged extensively nationally with tours to the USA and Europe. After many tours and lineup changes, they called it a day in 1996. A new outfit Mick Medew and The Rumours released a debut album, *For Your Love*, on I-94 Bar Records in 2009 and then toured the east coast of Australia in 2010. In 2011 the 'classic' line-up of the Screaming Tribesmen re-formed to play dates on the east coast of Australia and the Azkena festival in Spain. 2015 saw Mick's work acknowledged when he was awarded the prestigious GW McLennan Lifetime Achievement Award at the Queensland Music Awards. Since 2011, Mick's new project called Mick Medew and The Mesmerisers has released 2 albums on I-94 Bar Records. Mick also likes to fly solo sometimes, and during COVID's lockdown he recorded a solo album with his guitarist Brian Mann. Today he appears sporadically live and in online shows with his partner Ursula Collie.

THANKS, AND HERE'S YA BEER!
MICK MEDEW
(The Screaming Tribesmen)

1983, and here I was again behind the wheel of my 1974 Valiant Charger on that very familiar drive from Sydney's inner-city Surry Hills to The Royal Antler Hotel at North Narrabeen on the northern beaches, with my Screaming Tribesmen bandmates Janine Hall, who was also the bass player in The Saints, and Michael Charles, also the drummer for The Lipstick Killers.

"The Wolf Gang" was signed to the most elite booking agency in Sydney, Harbour Premier Artists Agency. We weren't on the guest list, but Janine knew people at "the agency", so we were in. At the time, my own band Screaming Tribesmen were enjoying having the No.1 indie single with 'Igloo' that year. It didn't help us though, not one little bit. "The people" decide which bands and artists become popular, and we were absent from that list.

We were on our way to The Royal Antler Hotel in North Narrabeen yet again, and we were not sure why. This time we were part of a 7- or 8-band bill that featured all Punk bands headlined by World War XXIV. When we finally arrived, we were told that we could not play because if we did, the Punks would riot. Screaming Tribesmen were not what you would call a hard-edged, righteous Punk rock group, and so promoter/manager Roger Grierson bought each of us a beer, said "*Thanks*", and sent us home.

⦿ MTV, the inaugural music channel on television, commenced its official broadcast on Saturday, August 1, 1981. The iconic phrase "*Ladies and gentlemen, rock and roll*", uttered by John Lack, accompanied by captivating visuals of the inaugural Space Shuttle launch, forever transformed the landscape of television. The initial complete airing of a music video was The Buggles' timeless hit, 'Video Killed the Radio Star'.

⦿ The Stockholm Monsters' debut album, *Alma Mater*, was released in August 1984. Produced by New Order's Peter Hook and released on the Factory label, the album was sadly missed by the buying public. There's no avoiding seeing the similarities to New Order, A Certain Ratio & Section 25. Mixing equal parts of arty POST- PUNK with synthpop and some jangly guitar, there are some superb tracks to be found, like 'Terror' and 'Your Uniform'. Many quote this album as a lost gem.

⦿ On this day in 1990, a case of 'reefer madness' unfolded when UB40 found themselves entangled in a web of unforeseen circumstances. Their trip to the Seychelles was abruptly cut short when local authorities stumbled upon the presence of marijuana within their hotel chambers. Consequently, the symphony of their melodies was silenced by being deported.

⦿ The debut album, *Burden of Mules*, was released by The Wolfgang Press in 1983 on the 4AD label. It is an interesting listen, with moments of cacophony, moodiness, mellowness, and ambiance. 'Complete and Utter' has a PiL-like approach, with distant Lydon-style vocals and prominent bass and drums. 'Slow as A Child' starts with dripping water sounds and features restrained guitar. The vocals are mixed low and are not easy to sing along with. Overall, it is fractured and inconsistent, but that adds to its interesting nature.

2

⦿ *Original Sin,* the first album by Cowboys International, was released in 1979. Led by Ken Lockie, Cowboys Int. delivered an excellent album of POST- PUNK / NEW WAVE. These guys were one of the neglected outfits with a classic album of the era. 'Thrash' is a track worthy of consideration for 'Song of the Year'. The album features smart use of keyboards and guitars to create wonderfully melodic NEW WAVE. Individually, the players do great; Lockie's voice is pleasurable, Terry Chimes drumming is tight, and Keith Levene's guitar contributions, as exemplified in the song 'Wish', are simply majestic. For lovers of POST- PUNK & NEW WAVE pop, *Original Sin* is essential listening.

⦿ Peter Farnan was born August 2, 1959. Peter is a composer, producer, performer, sound designer and teacher with experience ranging from theatre, film and TV to pop and rock music. He is best known as a founding member, guitarist, and songwriter for Boom Crash Opera and, before that, the POST- PUNK outfit Serious Young Insects. He has released three solo albums, the most recent titled *Home*. His 2017 album, *Pesky Bones Volume One*, featured well-known artists, including Deborah Conway, Paul Kelly, and Tim Rogers. In the theatre world, he has made sound designs and scores for Malthouse, MTC, Black Swan, QTC, Belvoir Company B and many independent companies. In 2013 he was musical director and composer for the feature film *The Boy Castaways,* where he worked with Megan Washington, Paul Capsis and Tim Rogers. His most recent composition commission has been the contemporary opera, *A Night At The Pink Poodle*, for Belloo Creative in Queensland. He has a Masters in Sound Design from the University of Melbourne and has taught songwriting and sound design at various higher education institutions. His occasional writing about music has appeared in the Daily Review, The Conversation, Rolling Stone and national street press.

WE WERE NOT 'ROCK'
PETER FARNAN
(Serious Young Insects, Boom Crash Opera)

By the time punk and post-punk had filtered down to Melbourne, Australia, in the '70s (which was relatively quick despite no social media), it was divorced from the social and economic conditions that gave rise to it. This wasn't depressed mid-to-late '70s Britain with garbage piling up, or crime-ridden pre-Giuliani New York. It was torpid, secure but dull, conformist Melbourne.

The scene around the Crystal Ballroom was therefore not inspired by grim economics but by stifling ordinariness. It had a flavour of playground nihilism and earnest experimentation. Most of us kids were middle-class types. Some were weirdos. Some wanted to be weirdos. There was much foolish risk-taking – the kind afforded by privilege and the innate knowledge that there was a secure fallback (see the movie *Dogs in Space*). For the rest, this was an experimental playground, not so much inspired by political revolution but by revolutions of style, genre, and form (inspired by the sounds and fashions from elsewhere). Where are the edges? What happens if we 'do this'? There was goth-posing, but there was also real experimentation. It was thriving, fired with energy and imagination, and it was authentic (whatever that word means).

To oversimplify and wildly and subjectively generalise, dark, wintery Melbourne glommed onto the more austere British version of post-punk ('it's grim up North'), while sunny Sydney (with some notable exceptions – SPK, Pel Mel) took to the American version (via Detroit – Iggy, MC5 et al.), largely dominated by the asteroid-like arrival and presence of Radio Birdman. I've generalised enough here to set fires blazing amongst protagonists and participants in both cities. And I've glossed over Brisbane and The Saints, thus inflaming a third city.

My band, Serious Young Insects, almost accidentally fell into the ballroom scene. Dolores San Miguel, punk promoter-célèbre, lived across the road from where we rehearsed – we seemed suitably short-haired and uptight. Put simply, we did not do Rock. We stumbled on the 3-piece format when we realised, we had more than enough ideas (3 writers, 3 singers) to fill the space. There was suspicion of our nerdy instrumental prowess in some quarters, but generally we were adopted for our quirky, disfigured pop shapes, predicated on a repudiation of '70s rockism (we didn't use the word 'gig', preferring the more austere 'job') and the absence of any trace of bluesy guitar solos. The rhythms were hyper-fast and jerky. Angularity was the order of the day (before it became a cliché). We hoovered up import singles and albums from the post-punk scene in Britain – Wire, Joy Division, Scrittti Politti, Teardrops, Bunnymen, Comsat Angels, and Swell Maps – and weaved these influences into our own antipodean configuration. A sentimental backward glance past the '70s to '60s pop, specifically The Zombies and The Beatles, was also considered acceptable.

Our twitchy, asexual schtick fit in and around bands like Models (who were big in this scene). We were not compadres of the Birthday Party and their ilk who projected threat and malice. But we recorded with their producer, the legendary Tony Cohen, so we felt like we were part of the same stew, and we were so excited to be in that stew. Within months of our first gig, we had opened for three of our heroes: The Cure, Magazine and XTC.

…and then we were sucked into the mainstream Australian pub rock industry. There were those that capitulated to this fate (Models – underneath the inner-city oppositional stance, who didn't want to be a rock star?); and there were those that genuinely eschewed this course and moved to England (The Birthday Party) for seemingly loftier reasons. There, they lived lives of penury and misery in dire squats. Back here we lived lives of penury and misery in Aussie beer barns and scungey motels.

In the pub rock space, bands had to have their own truck, lights, PA and crew. We played 6 nights a week. We toured the country nonstop. We had to keep moving to feed the beast. Where audiences expected an unrelenting four-on-the-floor thud – the perfect accompaniment to beer-slab culture – our nervy pop was too jerky, and our presentation too fresh and uncorrupted. Sydney bands like The Sunnyboys, with their rock guitars, fared better in this milieu. We did not do Rock. Five nights a week we met with indifference and the occasional hurled beer can or epithet. On the sixth night we played to enthusiastic, pogoing inner-city crowds who were 'our people'. This shot-in-the-arm propelled us into the next day's 12-hour drive, followed by another week of flying beer cans and abuse in the 'burbs of Sydney, Adelaide, Brisbane, and Perth before the relief of the next inner-city show.

We were signed to an indie label, but via a major (Epic/CBS). We were now playing that game. Already our music was losing its edge. Tony Cohen was out – 'sensible' producers were in. Our ferocious live fizz never made it to a record. We found ourselves appearing on the Australian equivalent of Top of The Pops, *Countdown*. We didn't fit in here either. We do not rock.

One improbable Friday evening we were to tape our appearance on *Countdown* at 6 pm, in Melbourne, and catch a plane at 7 pm to Sydney (the last plane!) in order to play a gig on the Central Coast (2 hours North of Sydney) that night. It was imperative we played this show in order to feed the beast (i.e., pay for the aforementioned weekly truck, lights, PA and crew expenses). To achieve this feat, we did our mimed performance at 6 pm, leapt into two awaiting vehicles and sped around the corner to a nearby park, where two helicopters flew us across greater Melbourne to the airport. On arrival at the airport, we disembarked in the middle of the airfield. Then we were driven across the tarmac and dumped on the apron with no idea which plane was ours.

Amidst roaring jet engines and taxiing planes, we implored a passing ground crew, "*Which of these planes is going to Sydney?*" "*That one,*" he said, indicating a staircase being retracted from a closing door. We ran up the stairs and banged on the door. Miraculously it opened, and, relieved, we flashed our boarding passes.

"*This plane is going to Hobart*", said the attendant. The door shut like a tomb, and we scuttled off the now moving staircase. Somehow, we got up to the concourse and found the right plane. Four hours later we played to 60 people in a venue that held 1600. The beast was fed.

Meanwhile the single stiffed. The accompanying album came and went. After The Police attended and vaguely approved of one of our gigs, we had some interest from the IRS in the

USA – this fizzled out. We were done. Our quirky, jerky, energised pop wasn't going to cut it. And we couldn't go back to the underground scene we had left behind. The Ballroom crowd, once all synth-elitist and anti-rock, had tilted towards 'rawk' guitars and Americana-gothic stylings – the Gun Club and the Cramps – not our cup of tea at all. After all, we did not do Rock.

Did I mention we hardly ever drank alcohol? We were tea drinkers.

O Peter Louis Vincent de Freitas was born in 1961 in Port of Spain, Trinidad and Tobago. Before joining Echo & The Bunnymen (ETB) in 1980, the band used a drum machine. Pete then became the steady replacement, contributing to their first five albums. In 1982, while still with ETB he showcased his talent under the name Louis Vincent on The Wild Swans' debut single, 'The Revolutionary Spirit'. Following the release of the album *Ocean Rain* in 1985, Pete briefly left the band while residing in the USA. ETB tested several drummers unsuccessfully before Pete returned for the rerecording of their *self-titled* fifth album. Music talent ran in the de Freitas family, as his two sisters were part of the band The Heart Throbs, and his brother Frank played bass for The Woodentops. Pete tragically passed away in a motorcycle accident on the A51 road in Longdon Green, Staffordshire, on June 14, 1989, at the age of 27.

O Steve Hillage was born in 1951, in Essex, England. Steve, a meticulous guitarist, was formerly a member of prog-rock act Gong and later earned a reputation as half of ambient/techno duo System 7 and as a frequent collaborator with The Orb. Steve is regarded as a virtuoso guitarist, where his work involves the use of effects, predominantly echo and reverb blended with synthesizers. He formed a solo band after Gong and entered session work and became much lauded as a pioneer in new age-ambient music before retiring from recording to concentrate on studio production. In the early 1980s, he entered the studio to work on the Simple Minds LP *Sons and Fascination*, Real Life's *Heartland* album and recordings by Nash the Slash and The Charlatans. Some years later he was in a club and heard The Orb had sampled his music; this led him to hook up with them, producing and playing on their classic 'Blue Room' with them. In 1990 he resurfaced in a duo with his long-time partner Miquette Giraudy to record as System 7.

O After the Visage project ended, Steve Strange formed a new band. However, the creative synthpop and technological style were gone. Overall, Strange Cruise's *self-titled* album is uninspired mainstream rock, lacking intensity and original ideas. The songs seem to follow a generic AOR formula, falling flat both lyrically and musically. This is disappointing given Steve Strange's previous creative moments.

3

O Born in 1959 in Coventry, England, Martin Atkins is a remarkably talented musician and best known by most as a drummer who has participated in numerous musical ventures. Martin has been a member of several bands over the years, including Public Image Ltd, Pigface, Brian Brain, Ministry, Nine Inch Nails, The Chicago Industrial League, and Killing Joke, among various others. His drumming was a defining element of PiL's 1981 album *Flowers of Romance*, and his contributions to the album have been cited as highly influential for POST- PUNK drummers of the time. In the late 1980s, Martin founded the record label Invisible Records, which released music by artists like Throbbing Gristle, Killing Joke and Genesis P-Orridge. Martin's solo album *Made in China* is an intriguing listen, combining found oriental sounds with electronica to create a truly one-of-a-kind sonic experience.

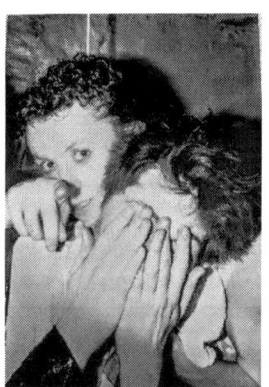

Pete Jones and Martin Atkins of Brian Brain

◉ Kirk Brandon, born on this day in 1956, in London, England, gained recognition as a vocalist-guitarist through his involvement with various bands such as The Pack, Spear of Destiny, Dead Man Walking, and Theatre of Hate. Kirk's rise to fame commenced in the early 1980s with Theatre of Hate, a NEW WAVE band, when their single 'Do You Believe in The Westworld' garnered extensive airplay and achieved a notable position of No.40 on the UK charts. Later, with Spear of Destiny, Kirk reached even greater heights on the charts, securing the No.14 spot with their single 'Never Take Me Alive'.

◉ It was in 1980 that The Dugites from Perth, Western Australia, released their *self-titled* LP. Fronted by the affable Lynda Nutter, some say they came across as a 'down-under Blondie', though they did not possess that US power-pop sensibility; their music was delicately crafted NEW WAVE. The songs are catchy, precisely played and loaded with memorable melodies. Keyboardist Peter Crosbie was the main songwriter; he ably latched onto a mix of '60s girl group feels and the NEW WAVE of the day. Lyrically topical, the songs were danceable and loaded with hooks and melody with a smattering of politics. This debut Deluxe label LP went top 20, attaining Gold status in Australia. It held three big-selling singles: 'In Your Car' b/w '13 Again', 'Goodbye' b/w 'No God, No Master', and 'South Pacific' b/w 'Gay Guys'.

◉ Members of Colourbox and A.R.Kane came together to create M|A|R|R|S. They had only one release, 'Anitina (The First Time I See She Dance)' b/w 'Pump Up the Volume', yet there were a myriad of remixes to move on to if one got tired of the earlier one. The initial release was out August 3, 1987, and not unlike anything by Colourbox, it is sample crazy; over 30 samples are used and uber cleverly arranged. Each version is vastly different according to the permission and timing of the samples being used on either side of the Atlantic. The original is not your basic cut-up toss in some samples track, there's a multitude of rhythm changes and swings. It would arguably become one of, if not the most influential tracks of nineties house music.

◉ On Sire Records, *Fear of Music*, the third studio album by Talking Heads, was released on August 3, 1979. It was recorded in New York City from April to May 1979 and served as the second instalment of the Brian Eno-produced trilogy. This album possesses an authentic live atmosphere, as if it were captured in the cosy setting of someone's living room (indeed, some of it, Tina's). The mixing aimed to replicate the energetic experience of a bass, guitar, drum, and keyboard ensemble. Talking Heads stripped down their production values, tone, texture, subject matter, and titles for this album. Eno's influence is apparent in the peculiar sounds and effects that permeate the record, with his eccentric studio additions showcased in 'Drugs', among others. Even today, the LP remains far from sounding outdated or gimmicky; the production retains its freshness and exhilaration. Lyrically, David Byrne delves into a realm of ultra-paranoia, exalting the mundane aspects of everyday life, such as paper, guitars, pets, and even air, which instills a profound sense of claustrophobia. This release showcases Talking Heads near the summit of their artistic prowess, encapsulating their trademark weirdness, quirkiness, mystery, and fragmented nature. It truly embarks the listener on a captivating sonic voyage.

4

◉ Techno monsters Age of Chance released their debut album in 1987. *One Thousand Years of Trouble* is an amalgam of samples, guitar, beats and pseudo-rap with huge production. This album was a pioneering precursor to the soon-to-explode genre of Grebo; the influence on Stereo MC's, Pop Can Eat Itself and Jesus Jones is clearly evident. Often fast-paced and frenetic, the grooves are indeed infectious, and go no further than 'Don't Get Mad, Get Even' to be infected!

◉ Ian Broudie was born in 1958, in Liverpool, England. Ian was a founding member/guitarist of Big In Japan, Care, and Original Mirrors and the producer of numerous bands such as Echo & the Bunnymen, the Fall, and Wall Of Voodoo. In 1989 Ian began recording alone under the name Lightning Seeds and on January 29,1990, released the debut *Cloudcuckooland*. The album comprising guest artists like Henry Priestman (Yachts), Andy McCluskey (OMD) & Ian McNabb (The Icicle Works) was often unfairly viewed as a second tier Britpop, but with the single 'Pure' it really proved to be a level above that. Across the album, even though Broudie's voice isn't forceful, it doesn't matter, because he constructs some excellent songs that come to fore for most of *Cloudcuckooland*; they are simple yet very enjoyable. Here, there are loads of catchy hooks, wrapped inside some very infectious, strong instrumentation.

◉ Vincent "Vini" Gerard Reilly was born in 1953 in Manchester, England. Vini was a founding member of The Durutti Column, a band that was Tony Wilson's first signing to Manchester's iconic label Factory Records. The name Durutti Column was inspired by the Spanish Civil War anarchist Buenaventura Durruti. The Durutti Column threw a curve to POST-PUNK. They took the era down another road; their method was one of being warm, ethereal, and atmospheric. The combination of guitarist Dave Rowbotham, drummer Chris Joyce, vocalist Phil Rainford, and bassist Tony Bowers were obviously like-minded to the final destination. Worth seeking is the EP *A Factory Sample*; it's an EP that also holds tracks by Joy Division & Cabaret Voltaire. In late 1979 Rowbotham, Joyce, and Bowers broke off to form the Moth Men, with Joyce and Bower ending up long-term members of Simply Red. With their departure, this left Durutti Column the sole province of Vini, becoming a prolific recorder.

◉ Paul Reynolds was born in August, 1962, in Liverpool, England. Paul was the guitarist and backing vocalist with A Flock of Seagulls. It was Reynolds' textural wash that was one of the main elements that made the band stand out. Contributing significantly to the group's sound, Paul was praised for his echo-laden, unique guitar style, which differentiated A Flock of Seagulls from many of the other synth-heavy bands of the period. Paul joined Flock in 1984 and has been part of the reformations in 2003, '04, '18 & '21.

5

◉ Pete Burns was born in 1959, in Port Sunlight, England. Pete founded the band Dead or Alive in 1980 and was the vocalist and songwriter. The band recorded 7 well received studio albums and had a booming hit with their 1985 single 'You Spin Me Round (Like a Record)', which was produced by the Stock Aitken Waterman team; it became their first No.1. In the mid-'90s Pete collaborated with the Italian electro/dance outfit Glam, releasing the single 'Sex Drive', and in 2004 he had moderate success with a single 'Jack and Jill Party', a collaboration with the Pet Shop Boys. Burns was known for his ever-changing, often androgynous appearance, for which he at one time accused fellow pop star Boy George of appropriating. Freely admitting that had been greatly modified by cosmetic surgery, he really has messed himself up with extensive polyacrylamide injections into his lips and cheek implants. Pete died from a cardiac arrest on 23 October 2016 at the age of 57.

◉ Climie Fisher was the synthpop duo of vocalist Simon Climie & Rob Fisher on keyboards. Fisher came from the remnants of Naked Eyes and Clime a respected session musician and songwriter. The successful single 'Love Changes (Everything)' was out in 1987. It appeared in the last throes of NEW WAVE, and thanks to a good chorus hook and an eager pop market, it reached No.2 in the UK.

◉ Litfiba, a band hailing from Florence, Italy, released their first EP, titled *Guerra*, in 1982. It's unfortunate that the majority of their music was in Italian, as they could have potentially achieved moderate success beyond Italy, especially in the UK, if they had English lyrics. This debut release showcases their inventiveness, atmospheric sound, and occasionally unsettling vibe, which proves that Italy was capable of producing POST-PUNK music on par with any other country. Litfiba's combination of angsty guitar, intense drumming, and desperate vocals offers a glimpse into the bleak times experienced by Italy and Europe as a whole.

◉ In early August of 1981, the Australian NEW WAVE band MEO 245 from Hobart, Tasmania, put out their sole record album, *Screen Memory*. The music was reminiscent of other iconic NEW WAVE acts and showed the influences of artists like Roxy Music and David Bowie, emphasising energetic synthesizers, a driving bassline, and catchy guitar riffs. The record peaked at No.69 on Australia's music charts. MEO 245 toured extensively to support the album but broke up just over a year after its release.

6

Bauhaus by Pedro Figueiredo

◉ In 1979, Bauhaus unveiled their impressive first single, 'Bela Lugosi's Dead', which some argue marked the emergence of a new genre known as gothic rock. This atmospheric and intense track, clocking in at approximately 10 minutes, showcased Peter Murphy's exceptional talent and is widely regarded as one of the greatest debut singles in the history of rock music. The inexplicably captivating connection between bassist David J and drummer Kevin Haskins in the rhythm section, along with Daniel Ash's occasionally frenzied guitar, created an eerie sensation reminiscent of a classic horror film from the 1960s. 5 stars.

◉ On August 6,1945, more than 200,000 civilians die from the explosion and/or radiation when an American B-29 bomber, the Enola Gay, drops an atomic bomb over the centre of Hiroshima, Japan. It was the first time an atomic bomb had been dropped over a populated place and the first time a nuclear weapon was used in warfare. The aftereffects of this WWII event are still felt today. From 1980, over the next year, following their glorious protest song 'Enola Gay', Orchestral Manoeuvres in the Dark would become very well known. The popularity of this classic song would be matched by 'Joan of Arc', 'Souvenir' and their biggest seller, 'Maid of Orleans'. 'Enola Gay' was included on the LP *Organisation*; it peaked at No.6 in the UK.

7

◉ Stephen Cummings, the former lead singer of Sports, released his first solo album, *Senso*, in 1984. The album showcased Cummings' talent and skill, proving that he was not solely reliant on his bandmates. Six out of the 11 songs on Senso were released as singles: 'We All Make Mistakes', 'Stuck on Love', 'Backstabbers', 'Another Kick in the Head', and the successful 'Gymnasium', which reached the top 30 on the Australian charts.

◉ Born on August 7, 1957, in Liverpool, England, Alexei David Sayle emerged onto the NEW WAVE comedy scene as a bold comedian and actor. His explosive and relentless humour captivated audiences, particularly in his portrayal of Jerzei Balowski, the eccentric landlord in *The Young Ones*. Originally released prior to *The Young Ones* in 1982, his single 'Ullo John Got a New Motor' reached No.15 on the UK charts after being reissued in 1984.

◉ The release of Toto Coelo's debut single, 'I Eat Cannibals', also known as Total Coelo in the USA, took place in 1982. These five peculiarly attired girls presented us with a delightful dose of disposable NEW WAVE pop. This single featured a catchy and repetitive chant that never ceases to captivate. Fun, quaint, disposable, and forgettable, though unforgettable for many.

◉ The Vanilla Chainsaws were world class POST-PUNK, and their debut single, released August 7, 1987, on Phantom Records #(PH-23) 'T.S. (Was It Really Me)' b/w 'Everything' is a prime example. The "T.S.". in the title refers to T.S. Elliot who gets namechecked in the complex guitar-based A-side. The single exhibits exactly what they were like live; tight, and intense.

8

◉ *Script of the Bridge*, the debut album by The Chameleons, was released on this day in 1983, on the record label Statik. This is an excellent album, one that stands high in ratings for the genre and period, and still, it holds up well with time. Shimmering guitars and a perfect rhythm section with delicate, atmospheric synth make for a great listen. Loaded with twelve great songs and very well produced, 'Second Skin', 'Monkeyland', 'Pleasure and Pain', 'Paper Tigers' and 'As High as You Can Go' really stand out, but 'View from a Hill', even though reminiscent of The Cure, is arguably the best piece from The Chameleons. You need this.

◉ Deborah Anne Conway was born in 1959 in Melbourne, Australia. Deborah is well known as a singer-songwriter and guitarist; she's worked as a model and actress and in 2023 Conway published her first book, *Book of Life*. Deborah was a founding member of Do-Ré-

Mi, and she was actor Tracy Mann's 'singing voice' in the hit TV series *Sweet & Sour*, in which she sang the theme song. To date, she has released a dozen solo and collaborative albums with her husband Willy Zygier, 2 with Do-Re-Mi and still does sell-out tours. After 30 years Do-Re-Mi reformed in 2018 with original members Helen Carter and Stephen Philip joining Deborah to play at the Australian Women in Music Awards, the response was such that Deborah and Helen decided to continue with more reunion dates bringing in new members creating an all-female line-up with Clio Renner on Keys, Bridie O'Brien on guitar and drummer Julia Day. On August 8, 2025, Deborah celebrated her 66th birthday with the release of a new album *Right Wing Propaganda*!

THE BEGINNING*
DEBORAH CONWAY
(The Benders, Do-Re-Mi)

"*Put an ad in the paper*" John said.
"*Really, that's how I should find a band?*"
"*Sure, 'singer wants band' with your phone number, put it in Juke and see what happens*".

I got two responses. One from a three-piece band led by guitarist Sai Ferran-Lucas, a stylish fellow, rake thin, dressed in black, of course, high cheek-boned, dark eyes, restless energy. He had plans, he wanted me to be part of them. I don't remember the audition, but he came over for a meeting in my bedroom of the large share house I was renting in Rockley Road, South Yarra. He paced around the room and pitched his spiel. It was good, he was an earnest young man with bags of ambition.

I was spoilt for choice. The other interested party was a guitar player called Greg Thomas from rock outfit The Benders, their singer had just departed. Greg had invited me to come down to sing with the band at a rehearsal studio in one of Melbourne's endless outer Eastern suburbs. I had carefully selected my wardrobe, a tight black jumper, emerald-green suede mini-skirt and blue tap shoes (without the taps). There was a queue of men in front of me, older than me, bearded and featuring some established beer guts amongst them. I had never met the previous singer, but it looked like he was the blueprint. I was the most colourful thing in and out of the room. I can't remember what I sang but I was getting enthusiastic vibes from the band. Clearly, they were looking for a different style of vocalist to the previous fellow. I got a call later that afternoon with an invitation to join.

At that point it got confusing. The drummer, a pale complexioned redhead called Dorland Bray, was dispatched to my Rockley Road house to persuade me that The Benders were a better option than Sai Ferran- Lucas's outfit. It was a tough choice but the redhead sitting on my bed making me laugh felt like my new best friend. I joined The Benders.

Patti Smith's Horses was a regular spin on my stereo and I wanted to her version of Van Morrison's 'Gloria', for the first gig. I rehearsed it along with the mountain of other pre-existing material. But after weeks perfecting my version of Patti's version of Van Morrison's version, I decided it wasn't a different enough version and therefore it was cabaret - basically the worst thing you could be at the dawn of the 19'80s.

We didn't need 'Gloria', the London Tavern was packed, oversold even, friends and family were in attendance to witness my debut which went off beyond anything I'd imagined. There were encores aplenty and a suitably sodden carpet attesting to a fine time. I loved it, being onstage was an incredible sensation, singing out front of that wall of sound but being entirely in control. I knew. This was for me. My abilities and my interests had just lined up. I was twenty.

We would play at the London Tavern a lot over the course of what would become our foreshortened lifespan. In fact, we played everywhere a lot for the next eight months. Barely a night off even though the crowds weren't there to justify us performing every Tuesday at The Market Hotel, Wednesdays at The Railway Hotel, Thursdays at The London Tavern, Fridays and Saturdays at Martini's or Macy's or wherever. No money had exchanged hands. Not that I was doing it for the money, I was modelling to pay the rent and it hadn't occurred to me yet that being in band might be a profit turning exercise. But I was craving a night in, especially over the long cold winter of 1980 when the audiences were all staying home to watch TV. I was becoming weary.

Many months and gigs later and I had started turning my back to the audience during the interminable guitar solos and pulling my singlet aside to flash my breasts at the drummer both for my amusement and to register my growing ennui. He never dropped a beat. And then we got a manager. A scientologist it turned out, I really have no idea from whence he came but he took over managing the band's funds and broke the news that despite our overactive gig diary we were in a considerable amount of debt largely due to a recording, 'Picnic at Oakleigh Rotunda', that had been made and released when the previous singer was behind the mic. Regardless of the fact that those financial obligations preceded my involvement, the manager informed me I would have to shoulder an equal percentage of what was owed. Which was considerable. Strangely, I didn't leave then. Nor did I leave after the night we performed at Billboard. This was supposed to be a gig where we would be paid… $25 each. I had been trying to find a carpark and had turned up fifteen minutes late, that is, 45 minutes before show time instead of an hour, to be informed by our new manager that for my infraction I would be docked $10!

My irritation with that injustice was subsumed by the breaking news that John Lennon had just been gunned down by Mark David Chapman outside his apartment block. December 8th, 1980.

Some weeks later Dorland told me he'd had enough of the band, and he was leaving. He didn't consult me before he decided but I knew that it was only him making this setup bearable. We'd shared our frustrations about the manager, the songs, the assembly line approach to gigs and talked endlessly of the musical influences we'd rather be exploring but which didn't overlap with the rest of our compadres. So, when he declared his intention to quit, I followed suit. We were going to move to Sydney to seek our fortune, to form a new band, to write our own songs, to play gigs as special events and to release records before stepping foot onto a stage. Our approach would be a paradigm shift away from everything I had experienced up to that point.

We packed our worldly possessions into my Honda Civic and drove north.

Excerpt from Book of Life by Deborah Conway, published by Allen & Unwin by permission.

◉ Caroline Crawley was born in Bournemouth, England, in 1963. Caroline had a distinctive voice and was one half of the duo Shelleyan Orphan; she also played a major part as vocalist on the Ivo Watts Russell 4AD. This Mortal Coil project album, *Blood*, was released in 1991. Shelleyan Orphan released four albums, and 1989's gorgeous *Century Flower* is arguably the highlight. Robert Smith was so taken by them that he asked Shelleyan Orphan to open for the Cure's 1989 tour. Caroline died on October 4, 2016.

◉ David Howell Evans, also known as The Edge, was born in 1961 in Barking, Essex, England, to parents from Wales. However, he was raised in Dublin, Ireland. He is most famously recognised as the lead guitarist, keyboardist, and backing vocalist of the renowned band U2. Apart from his work with U2, The Edge has collaborated with various other artists, including Johnny Cash, Jah Wobble, Ronnie Wood, and Tina Turner, among many others. Additionally, his brother Dik was one of the founding members of The Virgin Prunes. In

2011, Rolling Stone magazine ranked The Edge as the 38th greatest guitarist of all time in their prestigious list of 100.

⦿ Christopher John "Chris" Foreman, aka Chrissy Boy, was born in 1956 in London, England. Chris came to prominence in the late 1970s as the guitarist and founding member of Madness, along with keyboardist Mike Barson and saxophonist Lee Thompson in 1976. After Madness dissolved in 1986, he formed a new band, named The Madness, with Thompson, Suggs (Graham McPherson) and Chas Smash (Cathal Smyth); they soon broke up after releasing their debut album, *The Madness*. His next move was to form The Nutty Boys with Lee Thompson; they released the album *Crunch* in 1990.

⦿ *KooKoo*, the debut solo album by the then Blondie vocalist Deborah Harry, was available worldwide on this day in 1981. *KooKoo* was the result of Debbie and Chris Stein meeting and working with Chic's production maestros Nile Rodgers and Bernard Edwards. With such an unusual hybrid of styles and themes, we get an intriguing, compelling set, an album that went top 10 in the UK and No.25 in the US; it was certified gold for sales of over half a million copies. This is NOT Blondie; even though Chris Stein is present throughout, the instrumentation and structure are a world away. Go to *KooKoo* looking for Blondie, and you may be disappointed, yet it is an excellent fusion between Black funk and white pop. Blondie too was trying new things, and this was the case here; there's funk in 'Backfired', the reggae-infused 'Inner City Spillover' and the rap-laden 'Military Rap'. Debbie and Chris weren't going to be bogged down. Mention must be made of the outstanding graphics by H.R. Giger, designer of the ALIEN and ELP's *Brain Salad Surgery* cover.

⦿ Ali Score, aka Alister James Score, was born in 1951 in Yorkshire, England. Ali was the drummer and a formation member of Flock of Seagulls along with his brother Michael "Mike" Score on keyboards and vocals. He was an on-and-off member of the band from 1980 to 2004.

⦿ Peter Terrell was born in 1959, in Manchester, England. Peter was a founding member of A Certain Ratio (ACR), who formed in Manchester in 1977, taking their name from the lyrics of Brian Eno's song 'The True Wheel'. The early days of ACR saw them pushing the boundaries of POST-PUNK with a funky free jazz twist. Peter's contribution of jangly guitar and electronic noodling was integral to their early recordings. ACR's debut album release was a cassette entitled *The Graveyard and the Ballroom* on the Factory label in late 1979. The album is made up of one side being a collection of demos produced by Martin Hannett and the other, a live recording of ACR's October 1979 gig at the Electric Ballroom. This release is gold...and if you have one or can find one, you are extremely lucky!

BROKEN, BUT WITH GREAT MEMORIES
PETER TERRELL
(A Certain Ratio)

I am not sure what you people want to hear. I could tell you what it was like being a smack dealer in Hulme, Manchester, in the mid-80s. Or I could tell you how I escaped from Manchester to become a typesetter in the midlands for a while. Or I could tell you what it feels like to be a skint and broken old bloke with osteoporosis living in the arse-end of nowhere in the 2020s! Or I could tell you about how boring it could be at times to be in a band back then, on the cusp of the 80s. Don't get me wrong, being in A Certain Ratio was pretty great, that is, apart from being poor all the time. And yes, I feel lucky to have been around in Manchester in those days. And to have lived through it!

Ok, it's 2023, and ACR are about to start to promote their latest record, 1982. But that's the future, and it doesn't include me. So, I'm guessing you all want to hear about stuff that happened over 40 years ago. Ok. Erm, well, our soon-to-be manager and co-founder of Factory Records Tony Wilson was the first person I ever met who owned a Filofax, and he used it every day. Tony, who promoted us as 'The New Sex Pistols', was also known for being able to drive at top speed down the motorway in the middle of the night whilst rolling a spliff. Factory signed us and released our debut single, 'All Night Party', in 1979. That single was not only our debut but also the one for Factory Records as well; the 5,000 pressed sold out in no time flat!

Erm, in the USA, the Ratios almost got arrested for drinking whilst someone else was driving in New Jersey. We got away with it by claiming to be clueless English people, which really was precisely true! I must make mention of when we got threatened by the Mafia in Chicago cos we hadn't sold enough tickets!

Musically ... well, it was so different back then. Especially when you were about 20 years ahead of your time! The boredom came along cos of all the rehearsing we did, as well as playing gigs all over the place. We'd get sick of playing the same old songs, ha-ha. I guess that's a funny way of looking at it from an outsider's point of view, I suppose. When we played at Glastonbury, we did 3 encores, mainly cos the event's head honcho, Michael Eavis, was side stage and kept saying, Do another one. Well, it would have been rude not to, hey?

Also, we played quite a number of gigs with Joy Division, and it's hard to explain how good they were, them and us. I used to go to punk gigs a lot before ACR. In December 1977 I got to see The Sex Pistols, The Clash, Johnny Thunder's Heartbreakers and The Buzzcocks all on the same bill on a Sunday night at the Electric Circus in Manchester for an entry fee of £1.20! I also was fortunate enough to see JD at Rafters when they were called Warsaw, the last gig Buzzcocks did with Howard Devoto, and I even saw the first gig they did with Pete Shelley taking over vocals.

Oh, one time we were on with Was Not Was and the American soul and funk girl band The Brides of Funkenstein. That was a memorable gig.

By the way, I was being purely literal about being broken; I have had a broken leg and 3 broken arms over the last decade or so.

9

◉ If you looked on the record store shelves in 1981, you would have found *Fiction Tales*, the debut and only album by Modern Aeon. Here is one of those 'missed' recordings, dreamy, dark, brooding, and jangly. The pulsating bass and percussion on 'Playwright' sit perfectly behind the harmonised vocals; this is exercised in such a manner that it's the bass and drumming throughout that really give this album a cold wave aura. That's not to say there isn't a level of diversity in the songs; there certainly is. The record was immaculately produced, and the way the bleeps and swirls from the synthesizers sit with the textures is expertly done. You can file this near *Closer*, just along from *154*.

◉ *The Fugitive Kind*, the debut album by Swans Way, was available August 9, 1984. The initial releases on vinyl and cassette will only be found in second-hand bins, but fortunately the vinyl album has been re-released several times, and today, even the CD version is a rare find, as there was a limited release of about 100 copies pressed. In 1997 the album was re-released with extra tracks coming out as *The Best of Swans Way*. Reminiscent of The Fixx, *The Fugitive Kind* is atmospheric, jazzy, and rather sophisticated. 'The Anchor' is sax-laden and an equal of Pseudo Echo or Spandau Ballet, courtesy of Robert Shaw's rich voice and multi-tracked harmonies. A film noir soundtrack is called on with the mysterious 'The Blade', where Shaw's anguished vocal cries out to be heard. 'When The Wild Call's is an excellent song, and the trumpet playing is luscious. They had moderate success with the single 'Soul Train', so it surprising that they would fade into oblivion after this album. It's an album that should not be overlooked; it's interesting and wonderfully produced. It's out there, worth finding.

Swans Way by Paul Edmond

10

⦿ Thomas Temple Ellard, aka Tom Ellard, was born in Sydney, Australia, in 1962. Tom is the longest-surviving member of electronic music pioneers Severed Heads. Throughout the '70s to the 2020s, the band has challenged the music landscape with a wide blend of 'cut-up', 'industrial', and 'house' music. The band started one of the first online music websites, created interactive CD-ROMs and Blu-Rays, two computer games, and developed and toured live shows worldwide with extensive live video projection. In 2005 Severed Heads earned an ARIA award for Best Soundtrack for the movie *The Illustrated Family Doctor*. A new film is in development.

WE FITTED INTO NYC
TOM ELLARD
(Severed Heads)

Touring North America for the second time. It's 1990. This time we have a motorhome, a big thing, air-conditioned, couches. Half the party in a hotel room, half in the bunks, sneaking in for showers. Sometimes showers.

You get there, you find the locale, the street, the gig, you get the gear up the stairs, build it, drink the rider, go on-stage, and do the biz, slap backs and smile for the Birdie, pack it down, down the stairs, load the gear, and hit the road. It's already A.M., and it's day 20 or something.

City to city, always a few hundred miles yet to go. The rule is the driver has to have a buddy up the front to keep them entertained and alert. There was a young lady on the crew, she could do anything just as good as anyone, and she could do it more than. Anyway, thank you! As for me, well, I didn't trust people to be a buddy when I found one asleep up the front. I'll be the buddy, thank you!

So here we are on the road again. We're talking about Butterfingers. She loves Butterfingers more than any other bar. I never had one of those. *"Oh! You should try one in the next city"*, which was New York. We're just rolling into Brooklyn. I saw a sign 'Last Exit to Brooklyn', and I said, *"Oh! just like the book?"* *"What book?"* *"Last Exit to Brooklyn"*.

She didn't say anything. I didn't say anything. I was floating down the highway like a magic carpet. All the lights were fascinating.

There was another sign. It said, 'Clearance 10 ft. Large Vehicles Take Next Exit.' I thought about that for a while, and maybe I asked her, "*How tall is this motorhome?*" Maybe she answered, "*about 12 feet with the air-conditioning*". There was something wrong with that. Definitely something I was supposed to do...but I was too tired. So...I just slept.

A few seconds later we were in New York. It was a good gig.

◉ Rudi Esch was born Rudiger Esch in 1966 in Düsseldorf, Germany. Coming from several punk outfits of the early '80s, Rudi, as a bassist, was part of the second incarnation of the famed Dusseldorf band Die Krupps, who, along with Nitzer Ebb and Front 242, exemplified the industrial subgenre of E.B.M. (Electronic Body Music). Rudi is a published author of the book *ELECTRI_CITY: The Dusseldorf School of Electronic Music* delving into the history of the genre and its seminal bands such as Kraftwerk, NEU! and DAF. Rudi also co-authored the biographical DAS IST DAF with Miriam Spies and DAF members Robert Görl and Gabi Delgado. Using the title of his first book, Rudi has been organising the annual ELECTRI_CITY Conference in Düsseldorf since 2015, where lectures and concerts explore the history of electronic music and the cultural phenomenon of Punk. Participants included Andy McCluskey, Glen Matlock, Jah Wobble, John Foxx, Jean Michel Jarre, Daniel Miller and Marky Ramone. Today Rudi works as a music consultant and writes for Suhrkamp Publishing House and Omnibus Press in Berlin and London. He lives with his family in Graceland, in the southern part of Düsseldorf.

ALLES NEU! MACHT DER MAI
RUDI ESCH
(Die Krupps)

Only in hindsight can you really be sure about which are the pivotal moments in your own so-called musical career. A proper career is probably something very different. We were just happy to stick to our musical ideals and avoid day jobs. That was enough for the moment and way more than we could have hoped for. Punk and the POST-PUNK of the early eighties gave us a foundation for new ideas and line-ups. DIY was the expectation, and we started not only a new band but a label too.

Our record release party in January '87 in a youth club in the southern part of Dusseldorf attracted Klaus Dinger (KD), the self-acclaimed Gesamtkunstwerk (the complete artist), to stop by and say "*Hello*" to the band. We were in profound awe as we knew he was one of the founding members of Kraftwerk, even though these days he had nothing of the angular haircuts of his former bandmates. He looked like a hippie on acid and could have been the blueprint for Catweazle. We were not sure what to think of him but agreed to record our next E.P. at his studio Dingerland, in the northern part of Düsseldorf. It was right outside the airport, and when the planes were landing, you had to pause the tape. The more we worked on our material and tried to get it down on tape, the more the guitar player and I formed a close bond with Klaus. Klaus believed in astrology and only recorded when the moon was in the Seventh House. This affected studio work heavily. In other words, we were not getting that much work done. The band broke up, and the guitarist and I consequently formed a new band with the one and only KD. So far, so good.

One of the favoured sayings of Klaus used to be, "*Mutter, wie weit darf ich reisen?*", meaning, "*Mother, how far can I go?*" Like a shaman, he squeezed every drop of meaning out of these sayings and expanded our interpretation of them. He wanted us to leave any path of the unknown open to arrive with something brilliantly unique. It was a great concept, theoretically. Of course, to explore every meaning of this one saying, we were forced to smoke at least half as much as the shaman master smoked himself. And we did. Slowly we were getting more and more experienced but also getting nowhere. A regular day at the Klaus Dinger office would be a meeting between 11 and 12 in the morning, rolling some spliffs on a copy of Bowie's *Heroes* album, and finally getting ready for the studio work. This was followed by endless debates on what would be the right time to start recording. Finally, we'd make dinner plans, including magic mushrooms as a must-have ingredient! KD's most important rule was Alles neu macht der Mai, which roughly meant something like 'April showers bring May flowers'. In his own imagination and valued expertise, we had to wait until May to maybe get decent results from our recordings. But this was in November and probably the opposite of the Seventh House. I was slowly getting impatient. I was young, I had plans, and everything was just too slow and unbearable.

Now I know that he was a brilliant drummer, a visionary, and made music that was so futuristic that acceptance and honours only came decades later. Back then I had the feeling I was frozen in time. I made one last attempt to get some songs out of our collaboration. I played my very best bass riff to him and asked him to sit behind his drum kit. I named the song 'Germaniac', as that was the most Krautrock I could think of, and hoped he liked it. I played it purposefully and was expecting him to produce something that would evoke the feeling of the great Jaki Liebezeit of Can. But no, not this time. KD explained his time behind the drums is over, and he belongs to the front row. To the centre of the stage to be a singer and guitarist. Some weeks afterwards, I went to the studio and rehearsal space to collect my Ampeg B4 2x15 bass amp and the Fender P-Bass and hooked up with Ralf Dörper and Jürgen Engler to reform Die Krupps.

Alles NEU! macht der Mai by Rudi Esch in July 2023(c)

◉ Born in 1961 in Perth, Australia, Jon Farriss was the drummer for The Farriss Brothers, a band which later became INXS. In 1988, INXS reached the top of the American music charts with their hit song 'Need You Tonight'. Their 1987 album *Kick* sold over 10 million copies in the United States and included four singles that reached the top 10: 'Need You Tonight', 'Devil Inside', 'New Sensation', and 'Never Tear Us Apart'. Unexpectedly, in 2015, Jon teamed up with renowned West Indian cricketer Viv Richards, co-writing, producing, and playing drums on the catchy, soul-infused song 'Smokin' Joe'.

◉ On this day in 1985, Simon Le Bon from Duran Duran was air-lifted to safety when his boat 'Drum' overturned while racing off the English coast. Le Bon was trapped under the hull with five other crew members for twenty minutes until rescued by the Royal Navy.

Simon Le Bon by Roch Parisien

● Madness had arrived to the world with the release of their debut single 'The Prince' b/w 'Madness'. The song with that 'rock steady beat' was released August 10, 1979. Neither of them ended up as the album versions; this single was recorded by and released on 2-Tone. The *One Step Beyond* album versions released on the Stiff label produced by Clive Langer & Alan Winstanley somewhat lacked the immediacy of this landmark single.

● Don Martin, the bassist from the legendary Australian band Mi-Sex (aka MiSex), died on August 10, 2020, losing his battle with cancer; he was aged 61. New Zealand-born Don bravely fought cancer for several years but, knowing the battle was going to be tough, said an early goodbye to family and friends at a living wake in January 2020. Mi-Sex came together in New Zealand in 1978 with Murray Burns on keyboards, Steve Gilpin on vocals, Kevin Stanton on guitar and Don on bass. Mi-Sex were famed for their single 'Computer Games' that went to the top of the charts in October 1979 in Australia & No.5 in New Zealand. The debut album, *Graffiti Crimes*, which reached No.6 in New Zealand and the top 20 in Australia, was issued in July 1979 to coincide with their national tour supporting Talking Heads. The years have not been kind to Mi-Sex, with Gilpin killed in a car accident in 1992 and Stanton from cervical spondylosis in 2017. The band name was adapted from an Ultravox! track, 'My Sex', off their debut album, *Ultravox!*.

● Gareth Sager was born August 10, 1960, in Edinburgh, Scotland. Gareth is a multi-instrumentalist and classically trained pianist who was a founding member of The Pop Group, a band whose individualistic, often cacophonous sound that held broad elements of POST-PUNK, funk and dub are often quoted as inspirational and seminal. Their 1979 debut single 'She Is Beyond Good and Evil' is regarded as a classic of the time. The Pop Group split in 1981, with members going off to be part of the bands Pigbag and Maximum Joy, with Gareth forming Rip Rig & Panic, a band that included Neneh Cherry. 2010 saw Gareth, along with Mark Stewart and Bruce Smith, resurrect The Pop Group; they recorded two new albums and toured the world. Gareth's work can be found under several guises that include C.C. Sager, Pregnant, and Gareth Sager and The Hungry Ghosts.

● Thomas Schwebel was born on August 10, 1959, in Solingen, Germany. Thomas was a founding member of the bands S.Y.P.H. (1977), Mittagspause (1978), Fehlfarben (1979-84) and Trashmuseum (1984). Each of these bands are regarded as seminal units of the German punk, Neue Deutsche Welle and POST-PUNK movements. Of those mentioned, Fehlfarben had the most releases, with Thomas involved in up to one dozen albums. Thomas stayed active through the '80s and moved into writing screenplays and soundtracks. Thomas rejoined Fehlfarben for a tour in 2018 and the playing of their most successful album, *Monarchie and Alltag*,(*Monarchy and Everyday Life*) in its original form. Today Thomas is still working as a screenwriter.

FIRST TIMES
THOMAS SCHWEBEL
(*S.Y.P.H., Mittagspause. Fehlfarben, Trashmuseum*)

Remembering the early days of German punk and NEW WAVE for me means remembering lots of first times.

The first time hearing all the records that got us on our way, the likes of Ramones, The Damned, Patti Smith and The Sex Pistols. These were moments I cherish, and I will never forget.

The first gig, one of Germany's first punk festivals, was in June 78 in Düsseldorf with a lot of the bands who became the founding fathers of the scene: Male, Mittagspause (then called Charleys Girls), and the band I had started with a friend from my hometown, S.Y.P.H. Even though we couldn't really play any instruments, we started writing songs in German, and the first two of them later became classics, *Zurück zum Beton* and *Industriemädchen*. To this day, rumours exist that members of Kraftwerk were in the audience, and they were thrown out by punks in the crowd. I can't remember exactly if it's true or not, but I can't imagine it being true, as the whole audience consisted of the other musicians who were now not on stage.

Then, a first meeting of the great bands from Düsseldorf and Berlin was at the S.O.36. I was two months later; the next and even bigger festival took place in Berlin. It was in a cynical punk mode to commemorate the building of the Berlin Wall. Two nights of great fun and music. As two of the members of S.Y.P.H. were yet to arrive, I started a spontaneous band with Harry Rag, our singer, and some other likeminded musicians from Berlin who we had met just a few days earlier. And because we had no original songs for that lineup, we kind of invented a mashup. It consisted of some of the great hits of the bands we liked, such as Wire, Buzzcocks, etc.; it was three songs turned into one.

The whole weekend had everybody anxiously waiting for David Bowie and Iggy Pop to arrive; they were living in Berlin at that time. The organisers said that David was to do a live recording of that festival and then produce it! They didn't show up until 3 AM on the second night, arriving in a big Mercedes, being totally out of it on drugs, and then commencing holding court amid a crowd of dozens of admirers. Of course, we never heard from them again; the record came out ages after the event, and Bowie would later tell outrageous stories on American talk shows about the 'dangerous Berlin underground punk festival', which were all made up.

So, after having started the band only just a few weeks earlier, we had in our first handful of gigs with Kraftwerk, Bowie, and Iggy in the audience. It was meteoric and could only go downhill from there, but actually it didn't. It was only just beginning.

Two years later came the third and biggest festival of them all, the Vienna Festival in May, 1980. After Mittagspause had split up, our singer and I had started Fehlfarben at the end of 79. And in spring we got the invitation for the Vienna Festival; it was kind of a summit of the then-existing top bands of the German POST-PUNK scene. They had invited the major bands from Hannover, like Hansaplast, along with the bands from Düsseldorf, Male, Der Plan, S.Y.P.H., and Fehlfarben. A large coach was hired which came from Hannover down south to Düsseldorf, picked us up, and 60 musicians and friends drove to Vienna. A Magical Mystery Tour. Fehlfarben's first time playing abroad, and a splendid time was guaranteed for all.

For days we stayed in Vienna; we played at a museum as part of a programme of what became a very renowned and respected festival. Happy to keep playing, the end of our set came when the electricity was turned off by the Austrian organiser, just so that we would stop playing. I can't remember the trip back to Düsseldorf, but this weekend meant a sort of end of the first phase of this new scene. We signed with EMI after that to produce the album *Monarchie und Alltag*. Everybody else got contracts, money came in and…the rest is history.

38 years later, Fehlfarben were invited to the same festival, playing in the same venue, playing our first album in its entirety, and coming full circle.

⦿ Mark Stewart was born in 1960, in Bristol, England. As a 17-year-old, Mark was a founding member of The Pop Group with his friends John Waddington and Simon Underwood. The band sat outside pop music with a blend of jazz, funk, and noise. Their intense debut album, 1979's *Y*, was a bold, inventive piece of work that had a sound that soon would be rated by Nick Cave as highly influential in the POST-PUNK period. It challenged the norm of the day; was it a precursor to today's acid jazz? When The Pop Group split in

1981, Mark, along with Waddington and Ari Up, formed the dub-inflected New Age Steppers, who were pretty much pure dub, with their debut album inaugurating a new British dub record label, On-U Sound. Mark was soon to form Mark Stewart and the Maffia, aka Mark Stewart + Maffia, which included Steppers associate Adrian Sherwood releasing *Learning to Cope with Cowardice*, an album that remains unconventional, trippy, completely left field, but all the while compelling. Through to 2022, Mark released a further 6 albums, all absorbing recordings of intrigue. He also collaborated with Trent Reznor, Tricky, Massive Attack, Chicks on Speed, and Primal Scream. Mark died on April 21, 2023.

11

⦿ The debut single 'AEIOU Sometimes Y' by ĒBN-ŌZN was available August 11, 1983. The New York City duo of Ned "ĒBN" Liben (music computer programming, guitar) and Robert "ŌZN" Rosen (rap, lead vocals, vocal characterisations, organ) were pioneers of sampling. They had a foot in each of the worlds of European-influenced art-rock, NEW WAVE, POST-PUNK & the disco/pre-hip hop, rap & dance genres of the early '80s in NYC. Recorded in 1982, 'AEIOU', which went Top 20 on the Billboard Dance Chart in 1983, from the album *Feeling Cavalier*, made its mark in music history as the first commercially released US single to be produced with a music computer, the Australian music sampling computer Fairlight CMI. In June 2021, on Rick Rubin's Broken Record podcast, Moby spoke of 'AEIOU', saying ". . . *the strangest song in western pop music history. The lyrics are so phenomenal, and they make absolutely no sense – like a grad student thesis on semiotics while a guy is talking about trying to pick up a girl at a café.*" As much as ĒBN-ŌZN were remarkable audio artists, they were visual creators; their accompanying self-produced music video for 'AEIOU' is still featured on prime-time television programmes, and 'AEIOU' is still heard on alt-80s radio and satellite services like Sirius XM.

⦿ The Fall released their debut three-track EP recording *Bingo-Master's Break-Out!* in 1978 through the record label Step-Forward. Over the years The Fall had as many line-up changes as you've had breakfasts, and this is the only studio recording by the original The Fall line-up of Mark E. Smith, Martin Bramah, Tony Friel, Una Baines and Karl Burns. The EP was missed by the record-buying public, and it failed to make a showing on either the UK Singles Chart or the UK Indie Singles Chart! *Bingo-Master's Break-Out!* as a whole is pop-punk and as POST-PUNK as one could want. If The Fall never did another thing, this would satisfy. Legendary.

Joe Jackson by Roch Parisien

⦿ Joe Jackson was born David Ian Jackson, in Staffordshire, England, in 1954. In the late 1970s, NEW WAVE music was thriving, blending elements of punk, ska, electronic, techno, and pop. In early 1979, Jackson skilfully incorporated these diverse influences into his debut studio album, *Look Sharp!*, a concise 36-minute record. The album introduced Jackson's brilliant songwriting, and it became an immediate hit, propelled by the internationally charting single 'Is She Really Going Out with Him?'. *Look Sharp!* had a stylish cover featuring Jackson's trademark white shoes on a city sidewalk, reflecting his flawless sense of style. Later in 1979, Jackson released the almost equally successful *I'm The Man*, which contained the UK top 5 hit 'It's Different for Girls'. Other highlights in his prolific career include the 1982 album *Night and Day*, home to the US and UK top 10 single 'Steppin' Out'. To date, Jackson has recorded over 20 albums and continues to actively tour worldwide.

◉ Bob (Robert Leroy) Mothersbaugh was born in 1952 in Akron, Ohio. Bob is best known to us as the guitarist and occasional lead vocalist of DEVO. Still performing today, Devo has maintained a 'cult' following throughout its existence. He is the younger brother of co-founder and lead singer Mark Mothersbaugh. This Bob was known as Bob 1, while keyboardist Bob Casale was known as Bob 2.

◉ Dave Formula, aka David Tomlinson, was born in 1946 in Manchester, England. Dave played keyboards with Magazine, Visage, and the POST-PUNK / art-jazz outfit Ludus in the late '70s and early '80s. After his tenures with those renowned bands, Dave worked on independent film scores before pulling in his ex-Magazine compatriots Howard Devoto, John Doyle and Barry Adamson to assist him in the recording of the album *Satellite Sweetheart*. The album sat in the can for almost 2 years due to Magazine successfully reforming in 2009, and it was then released in 2010.

I WANTED TO PLAY JAZZ
DAVE FORMULA
(Magazine, Visage, Ludus)

I formed my first band in 1965 in Manchester - The St Louis Union. We had a hit record with 'Girl' in 1966 and were regarded as a premier Mod band.

The inspiration for the band developed from 1963, when in that year I went to see Duke Ellington, Count Basie, The Beatles, and The Kinks.

At the beginning of 1963 I wanted to become a jazz musician, but by the end of the year, a pop musician.

I did get a chance to play some jazz when I got the chance to play with Roland Kirk in Liverpool.

Jah Wobble by Petra Gall/ Brix Smith of The Fall by Petra Gall

◉ Jah Wobble, also known as John Joseph Wardle, was born in 1958 in London, England. He and John Lydon, his schoolmate, were part of a group of friends called The Four Johns, which also included John Grey and John Simon Ritchie, famously known as Sid Vicious. It is said that Sid Vicious mumbled a version of Wardle's name, which eventually became his stage name. Wobble decided to keep it because he believed it would be memorable to people. Although he gained public recognition as the original bass player for Public Image Ltd (PiL) in the late 1970s and early 1980s, he decided to leave the band after contributing to two albums. Since then, he has collaborated and released numerous albums with a wide range of artists, including Björk, Holger Czukay, Shara Nelson, Joolz Holland, Ginger Baker, Bill Laswell, Massive Attack, The Orb, Primal Scream, Brian Eno, and many others.

12

⦿ Simon Aldridge was born in London, England, in 1959. As a guitarist and backing vocalist, Simon has been a member of Kissing the Pink (KTP) since joining in 1982. KTP were formed in London in 1980, and though they have been through several changes, the line-up of today has been the longest serving and most stable. Through to 2003 KTP released four albums, with the debut LP *Naked* being the most successful in the UK. During 1986-7, releasing music as KTP, they peaked the US Dance charts with 'Certain Things Are Likely', and they also had Italy's biggest-selling 1985 single with 'One Step'. Simon remained with KTP until 1990, when he took the position of A&R Manager at ZTT Records and Perfect Songs Publishing. This was the start of an illustrious career in music industry management. He would become head of A & R at Sony/ATV and Columbia Records and would be integral in the signings of Seal, Gabrielle, All Saints & Wayne Hector, amongst a number of others. Today, Simon is a part owner of the independent music publishing company KTPM Ltd. He is in demand as a lecturer at universities and colleges across the UK.

AT HOME I'M A TOURIST!
SIMON ALDRIDGE
(Kissing the Pink {KTP})

At the end of 2005 we had a good number of demos, including the tunes 'One Step' and 'Certain Things Are Likely', which would make up half of our third LP, *Certain Things Are Likely*. We had finally decided that the brilliant record producer Pete Walsh was the man to take them into record form.

He had produced the single 'Love Last Forever' for us, which had not caught fire as the immediate release after 'The Last Film', but it had loads of radio play in the UK.

Pete had just come off making the brilliant LP *New Gold Dream* with Simple Minds, and together he and KTP felt it would be right for us to get together on these new songs and what was a new, more direct pop direction for us. I think it was Pete who suggested we go to Union Studios in Munich. It was a residential studio built in a beautiful old mansion in the south of the city in an area called Soln. It was right next door to what was reputedly Henrich Geobell's house in Munich, so it had some very spurious historical connections there.

We had a fantastic time recording, lots of live playing over sequenced synth patterns, and Pete got it all sounding big and powerful. He said, *"Right, let's get some female gospel on these"* & over to Munich flew the phenomenal singing trio of Ruby Turner, Mo Birch, and Jackie Graham! It's their voices that sing the *"Hey Mister"* hook on 'One Step', and there is no doubt that massive, memorable singalong hook helped make the single the huge hit it was in Italy.

Our preferred place to go out for a late-night drink after recording in Munich was a nightclub called The Pink Pussycat, and it was there we found ourselves suddenly drinking next to 3/4 of Queen, Brian May, John Deacon & Roger Taylor. Freddie was off elsewhere playing in the after-midnight underground life of Munich. I fell off my bar stool while talking guitar licks to Brian, and he helped me up while I still held onto my JD & Coke!

We recorded 4 songs in Union Studios over two weeks, while outside the snow fell and totally covered the beautiful Bavarian city.

The song 'One Step' became our biggest hit single from the third LP, holding onto the No.2 singles chart placing in Italy for what felt like weeks in 1986. We also had a massive No.1 Dance Chart hit in the USA with the PWL remixed version of 'Certain Things Are Likely', which incidentally held off Prince's 'When Doves Cry'!

We played all the summer festivals across Italy, and we performed (often in full mime) on many TV specials for things like Festival Barr, which was a free one-day festival often held in the various magnificent squares of the Italian cities, such as the famous Piazza Del Campo in Siena or the Piazza Maggiore in Bologna.

This was a special time for us as a band and so different from our life in the UK. We were so successful in Italy that we couldn't walk down the street without being accosted! We were asked for autographs everywhere we went. We were being driven in limousines to the gigs. AND… even being asked to all go into the cockpit of an Air Italy flight to Heathrow whilst in the air to get photos taken!

But upon coming home to London, we often didn't have enough money for the Tube & nobody recognised us at all.

Good life lessons right there!!!!

◉ Roy Hay was born August 12, 1961, in Southend, England. Roy is a classically trained, multi-platinum, Grammy award-winner and is best known as the guitarist, backing vocalist, keyboardist, and musical arranger with Culture Club. Culture Club were associated with London's Blitz Club and the 'New Romantic' trend becoming hugely successful worldwide, selling over 50 million records. Roy was integral to the songwriting of all their major hits that included 'Do You Really Want to Hurt Me?', 'Karma Chameleon', 'Time', 'The War Song' and numerous others; his musicianship gave much to the quality of the finished songs. Over an on-off five-reformation period spanning almost 40 years, Culture Club released 6 albums, all to critical acclaim, leading frontperson Boy George to become internationally famous. After Culture Club 'version 1', Roy formed This Way Up, releasing a handful of singles and one album. A move to L.A. in 1989 saw Roy being involved in production and screen soundtrack work, giving time to his own company, Haywired Music. Roy's musical prowess and technical abilities were brought to the attention of Hans Zimmer, who brought him into the fold of his media company, Media Ventures. A reformation of Culture Club saw several tours with over 100 performances that included sell-outs at the Hollywood Bowl supported by the LA Philharmonic. Today Roy remains active with Haywired Music, working out of his home studio.

AN INTERVIEW WITH ROY HAY
(Culture Club, This Way Up, Producer)

Hi Roy, good morning, and thanks to Nico Golfar for making this happen. How did you fare in those horrible wildfires?

Well, I'm in Tarzana, you go straight over the hill, and there's The Palisades, the fires stopped about 2 miles away. I wasn't really concerned for my safety as the prevailing wind blows the other way. It's devastating, The Palisades is gorgeous man, the place you just want to live, and now it's gone!

Let's go back to the start. What sparked your interest in music? What instrument did you start with, and at what age?

I grew up in a very musical house, we had a piano, and my older brother had a drumkit. My father played all the standards, and he was very popular down the pub. Dad couldn't read music, so he prompted me to have music lessons and study music. I started with piano; music was at home all the time.

In your growing years what did you listen to, and what became your greatest influences?

Growing up in seventies there was exposure to so much great music. Everything from Bowie to Motown to Zeppelin, a lot of soul, a lot of rock, and progressive too, and then there was great pop. The Marc Bolans and Slades of the world were just great, inspiring. I have been revisiting a lot of that stuff recently, Wizzard and the like. From a songwriting point of view, they were really terrific, Roy Wood was an incredible talent. London and southeast England were such a melting pot, glam and obviously the West Indian influence, there was a lot of reggae, ska, and all this was linked to fashion. The diversity of music in the top 40 in 1974 was incredible. That does not exist today.

You were about 20 years old when you joined Culture Club. Obviously, hair, style and image were important in that era. How comfortable were you with that? What were you doing before that. I have read that you are a qualified hairdresser, do you still do people's hair?

There was a combination of music and fashion, there has always been a connection between the two and we were on the cutting edge of that. It was exciting, very exciting. Particularly in the early days of Culture Club, we made our mark. I do maintain though, that it wasn't all about our image, our music was enough really to have us known. Yeah, I was a hairdresser, and I even worked in the city, in finance. That really wasn't my destiny though. One day, I went to my boss and said, "*I'm much more interested in music, I think I'm going to go find that world*". "*Well, off you go, go find your world Roy!*" No, I haven't cut hair for 40 odd years. Ha Ha!

Would you say the The Blitz Club was the big break that Culture Club needed to become known? What was that like, what was it like working with Rusty Egan and Steve Strange.

The Blitz was a big step for George becoming 'a face'. There was something about those kids there then, they just wanted to get noticed. Of course, there are certain people that were there that were 'faces', Steve Strange, George and the like. Some went off into fashion, the media, and some into music. The Spandau boys were obviously there, but it was there that George established himself as a 'face'. I liked hanging out with those guys, Rusty was a very amusing chap, he was really into music, nobody was into music like Rusty, he had and still has incredible energy. It was a very exciting time in late '70s, punk was exciting, it changed everything, we went from listening to prog-rock like Genesis and Yes, who are my favourite, to this new release.

Culture Club had a few singles that really didn't figure, then 'Do You Really Want to Hurt Me' was a worldwide SMASH. The change was meteoric, how did that affect you and those around you?

Before that came out, we were one of the 'cool' bands in London, playing all the clubs. We were on a club tour when the song came out, it was one of those records that had its own destiny, it really did, nothing could stop that song. George even tried to stop it being a single, as it really wasn't representative of the band in that time. In fact, when we did a tour of the UK playing the first two albums that song stood out on its own. You see, we were much more drums, bass and guitar driven, kind of an Adam and the Ants meets soul kind of a way, I don't know how to describe it! Much to our disdain, because we were the coolest band in London, the song was picked up by David Hamilton, a housewife DJ in the afternoon on Radio 2, and he made it his record of the week! That was not the image we were after, but they were the ones that started buying it. We wanted to get on Top of the Pops but missed it by one spot. But luckily Shakin Stevens got sick, and we were next on the list, so we got the gig, and rest is, as you say, history. People were struck by our image, and of course George. They loved him. We went from 37 on the chart to No.1! The tour then was playing to just 200 to 300 kids, and suddenly we went to having 1000 waiting outside. So, the promotors upgraded us to larger theatres, still with screaming kids outside wanting to get in. We went from this cool band going around crammed in a transit van as young bands do, earning 100 quid a night, then propelled with momentum taking us all over the world! I still get goosebumps when I hear that song intro on the radio. It was special, a real amazing experience to go through, we were so young. George and me were only 21.

That and 'Karma Chameleon' were as close to perfect pop tunes as one could get. Sure, the band was all involved in writing them. How did you go about structuring those songs? The idea started somewhere, was it your music or George's lyrics, or what?

'Karma Chameleon' was a very interesting song. *Colour by Numbers*, as a whole makes sense except for 'Karma Chameleon'. The rest of the album is soulful and musical, it's kind of like Elvis Presley meets Bow Wow Wow, I don't know. Due to it being so anthemic, it's hard to deny it. When we play it live, we play it at the end the show, and we don't have to ever sing a word, the crowd does that! I probably wouldn't have bought 'Karma Chameleon', even though I made it. I was the music guy, George was always pretty much the lyric's guy, he had a lot to say, still does. HAHA! It was born out of a jam of sorts, all revealed in an in-depth Culture Club documentary to be released in May.

After Culture Club you moved to the USA and got into production and film scores. You formed Haywired, what is Haywired involved in presently?

The band never really split up, it just fizzled, we sort of drifted apart, just had a break, we had a lot of breaks…HA!. I had time and was looking at songwriting and came to LA in that period. I love the Hollywood hills; the parties are glamorous and great. I created Haywire in 1989 and got into producing, but it dissolved about 5 years later. Hammersound is my latest venture, the name born from being a fan of West Ham United. We are involved in film and television commercial production. It's a painful existence being a West Ham fan, yet when it's in you, you can't get rid of it! HA HA HA!

You have been associated with many artists over the years, who is the ONE that made you think wow, or he or she is ahead of the game?

Right now. I was so impressed with Howard Jones last week, such an incredible talent that man. If you get a chance don't miss him. I got to meet so many, Prince was exceptional, he was a big fan of Culture Club. My favourite guy that I met, and I spent an evening with, was Chris Squire, the bass player from YES. I met all those guys, Steve Howe, Rick Wakeman, very special people. Give a listen to the audio book with Phil Collins, brilliant.

OK so away from music, you play golf, is that right? Got a handicap? Where are some of the places you have played?

Yeah, I love to play golf and play all over. I have a membership at the New Course, St. Andrews in Scotland. I have lot of buddies that play, and I played with them when over your way in Australia. I really liked The Australian Golf Club, and the one at La Perouse, the

New South Wales Golf Club, out on the point, it's a really great course, sensational I recently played at Palm Springs, both Big Horn and The Vintage were amazing! and I got my handicap down to as low as 7, but today I'm about a 12.

So, what music relaxes Roy Hay list? What excites you?

For relaxation I'm into either listening to classical or choral music, firstly. I do get excited when cooking or when I'm driving, listening to classic rock or soul. I don't like most pop these days, the lack of bands is depressing. I like Kendrick Lamar and I loved his Super Bowl performance.

Thanks Roy!
Keep it in the short grass buddy!

⦿ On this day in 1982 Phantom Records released the historic single 'Leilani' (PH-15). It was the debut release from the Australian garage/psych/power-pop outfit, who at that time carried the moniker of Le Hoodoo Gurus, but soon they were to become The Hoodoo Gurus. The band consisted of Dave Faulkner (guitars & vox) and James Baker (drums), Roddy Radalj, aka Roddy Ray'da (guitars), & Kimble Rendall (guitars), a unique line-up, as there was no bass player. This guitar sound reinforced the carried sound of jangly garage rock, rocking power pop, and twangy surf music, while holding together some sweet melodies and grabbing hooks. Ray'da and Rendall departed in late '82 and were ably replaced by the ex-Hitmen bassist Clyde Bramley and ex-The Fun Things guitarist Brad Shepherd. The song was re-recorded for their sensational 1983 debut album *Stoneage Romeos*. Brad remains with The Gurus to this day!

⦿ Ron Mael was born in 1945 in Culver City, California, USA. Ron and his brother Russell were the creators of the US undefinable band Sparks. Ron has always been the main songwriter/lyricist, and as a live performer, he is generally inactive, playing keyboards and synthesizers which was in stark contrast to the energetic Russell. Artists such as New Order and Duran Duran have cited Sparks as being influential in their output.

⦿ Ian Rilen was born on in Bendigo, Australia, in 1947. Ian is a legend of Australian rock music. In Ian's early days he was a member of Band of Light, Blackfeather, the legendary Rose Tattoo (the Tatts), and quite a few other outfits. Ian earned a reputation as a hard-living, hard-playing man. As the bass guitarist and main songwriter with the Tatt's he wrote their biggest hit, the top 20 single, 'Bad Boy for Love'. During the '80s he was with the celebrated X, with whom he played bass guitar, though he did play rhythm guitar on the recording of 'Sad Days Girl'. Then there was Sardine v, described by Lobby Lloyd as "*Ian's arty-farty band*" where he was vocalist and guitarist, along with wife Stephanie Falconer and an ever-changing line-up that included Phil Hall, Barton Price, Michael Skinner, Johanna Piggott & Greg Skehill; they packed out every gig they played. Ian recorded one solo album *Love is Murder,* released in February 2001. His fast living caught up with him when he died on 30 October 2006, aged 59.

13

⦿ On August 13, 2002, Stuart Goddard, aka Adam Ant, pleaded guilty to threatening drinkers at The Prince of Wales Pub in London earlier in January. The former 1980s pop star had returned to the bar with a starting pistol after being refused entry. He had also thrown a car alternator through the window of the pub; it was unknown where he acquired the alternator.

⦿ Michael "Mickey" Bradley was born in 1959 in Derry, Northern Ireland. Mickey is the bassist for the Northern Irish band The Undertones. Mickey is a radio announcer on Northern Ireland's BBC and has the programme The Mickey Bradley Record Show. Mickey has written a book, *Teenage Kicks: My Life as an Undertone;* of it, he says, "*My older brother Martin has read it and gives it his approva*l." During 2018 and 2019 The Undertones were back on the road, playing dates in Northern Ireland, Scotland, England, the USA, and Australia.

Feargal Sharkey by Roch Parisien

⦿ Another original Undertone has a birthday today as well as Mickey Bradley. Seán Feargal Sharkey was born on 13th August, but a year earlier in 1958 than Mickey in Derry, Northern Ireland. Feargal was the lead vocalist for The Undertones in the 1970s and 1980s. He went on to have a moderately successful solo career; his single, 'A Good Heart', was an international hit.

14

⦿ On 14th August 1983, *The Batcave: Young Limbs and Numb Hymns* compilation album was available on London Records. Today, extremely rare, the album was a sampler of the acts that appeared at the seminal London Goth venue The Batcave. Bands included on the album are Specimen, Sexbeat, Test Dept., Patti Palladin, James T. Pursey, Meat of Youth, Brilliant, Alien Sex Fiend and The Venomettes. From the liner notes: 'Look past the slow black rain of a chill night in Soho, ignore the lures of a thousand neon fire-flies, fall deft to the sighs of street corner sirens, come walk with me between heaven and hell. Here there is a club lost in its own feverish limbo, where sin becomes salvation and only the dark angels tread. For here is a BATCAVE. This screaming legend of blasphemy, lechery, and blood persists in the face of adversity. For some The Batcave has become an icon, but for those that know it is an iconoclast, it is the avenging spirit of nightlife's badlands, its shadow looms large over London's demi-Monde: It is a challenge to the false Idol. It will endure'.

⦿ Reg Mombassa, aka Chris O'Doherty, was born in 1951 in Auckland, New Zealand. Reg, as guitarist/vocalist, was a founding member of Mental as Anything and played solid with them from 1976 until departing in 2000 to concentrate more on his art. As part of 'The Mentals', Reg's composition and style of playing were integral to their wide-ranging sound; his contribution to their early success cannot be overstated. As a side project to The Mentals, Reg was part of The Stetsons, an outfit playing country and western rock; the band had a host of members, including Reg's brother Peter and Martin Plaza from The Mentals, Chris Bailey, and "Buzz" Bidstrup from The Angels and GANGgajang. In 1991, Reg, along with brother Peter, formed the band Dog Trumpet, which has been Reg's primary musical project after The Mentals. Through to 2025 Dog Trumpet has released 8 albums, with another in the offing. As an accomplished artist, Reg's artwork is famed for its very eccentric individualist design and look at society. His artwork has been exhibited multiple times in Australia and in his homeland, New Zealand, as well as France, Italy, China, the USA, Thailand, and the UK. Some of Reg's works are included in the permanent collections of the National Art Gallery Canberra, the Art Gallery of New South Wales, and Powerhouse Museum. Hardly a day can go by in summer without seeing one of Reg's designs on a Mambo T-shirt or pair of shorts. His work on record album cover art is renowned, having done covers for Crowded House, Paul Kelly, Mondo Rock and PiL.

INNER CITY MUSIC (LATE 1970s)
REG MOMBASSA
(Mental as Anything, The Stetsons, Dog Trumpet)

From 1970 to around 1977 I lived in inner-city Sydney share houses near Taylor Square in Darlinghurst, Surry Hills, and Paddington. I was either working in a succession of menial full- and part-time jobs or studying art at the National Art School, as well as playing in several bands. There were a lot of pubs, bars and community halls in the area where bands could play.

Even before the explosion of bands and venues that occurred after the rise of punk and NEW WAVE music in 1976, the area had a healthy live music scene. The first venue I attended in 1970 was Witties Wine Bar on Taylor Square, where I saw the Original Battersea Heroes; they were a popular jug band at the time. French's Wine Bar a little further down Oxford Street featured blues and rockabilly bands like The Four Day Riders, The Goldtops, The Hawaiian Housewreckers and The Mangrove Boogie Kings. It was there that I saw The Pelaco Brothers play around 1977; that band featured Steve Cummings, Joe Camilleri and Peter Lilley. I saw the legendary slide guitarist Hound Dog Taylor and his House Rockers play in 1976 or 1977.

Martin Plaza and I started Mental as Anything in 1976 with fellow art students from the National Art School. We began rehearsing in the lounge room of the share house I was living in on Oxford Street near Taylor Square. We had our first residency in the back bar of the Unicorn Hotel a little further up Oxford Street in 1977 and did our first gig with my brother Peter on bass a few days after Elvis died in 1977. After 1976 bands played in just about every hotel and bar on Oxford Street as well as local community halls like Heffron Hall, where I saw X play, and the Anthony Doherty Hall in Surry Hills, where The Mentals did some early gigs. The Paddington Town Hall and the Cellblock Theatre in the art school also hosted some memorable gigs at the time. It was an exciting and creative time and place with a very healthy live music scene and heaps of available venues. New bands played with few restrictions or regulations, and there was plenty of inexpensive rental housing for students and aspiring musicians.

◉ Bruce Thomas was born on 14th August, in Stockton-on-Tees, England. Bruce was the bassist for Elvis Costello and The Attractions from 1977 to 1994. As a session player, Bruce has recorded with the likes of Billy Bragg, Madness, Paul McCartney, The Pretenders, and Suzanne Vega on over 150 albums. After his favourite bass guitar was stolen and unable to find a satisfactory replacement, he decided to develop his own design in conjunction with London's Bass Centre, and the 'Profile Bass' was born. In 1991, Bruce published the award-nominated The Big Wheel, detailing his time with the band. That was followed by the more revealing and detailed books *Rough Notes* and *The Open Road*. He trained in Kung Fu with

Master Derek Jones and is also known for his definitive and best-selling biography of Bruce Lee, Fighting Spirit.

MACA'S BASS
BRUCE THOMAS
(The Attractions)

Now here's a thing! Drummer Peter Thomas (who is no relation, by the way) and I were doing a recording session at Abbey Road Studios -- (not with Elvis Costello and the Attractions), possibly for some Japanese pop singer whose name escapes me. We were on a break and wandering the corridors in the basement, idling about. For some reason, PT opened a janitor's cupboard – the kind where brooms and mops and buckets are kept. As he did, I saw his jaw drop and his face blanch. *"What the f**k!!"* he whispered. *"Look at this"*. He held the door ajar for me to peep in. And there among the brooms and mops, leaning up in a dark corner, was a Hofner 500/1 Violin Bass. *"But look at this!"* I said. Because taped along the top side of this bass was a set list of the songs. It was the same set list from the Beatles' last live show on 25th August 1966, at Candlestick Park, San Francisco.

The tape said: 'Rock and Roll Music', 'She's A Woman', 'If I Needed Someone', 'Day Tripper', 'Baby's in Black', 'I Feel Fine', 'Yesterday', 'I Wanna Be Your Man', 'Nowhere Man', 'Paperback Writer' and 'Long Tall Sally'.

Obviously, my first thought was how we might smuggle it out of Abbey Road, but at the same time there were several equally obvious realisations. Which one would keep it? You couldn't tell anyone about it. And you certainly couldn't try to sell it. It would be worth millions -- more than Hendrix's white Strat – more than any other guitar in the world! You could only ever look at it, hanging on your bedroom wall. And whichever one of us had it would certainly be vulnerable to blackmail by the other!

I'd always assumed that the Beatle bass Macca has been using on recent tours was 'the bass from the cupboard'. But apparently not. Now, if this little anecdote helps in any way to track the original down eventually, then good. But we definitely saw it, maybe sometime in the mid-90s. (Note: I'd be quite happy to share the reward).

ED: Paul McCartney's violin-shaped Höfner 500/1 bass was stolen from the back of a van during the night of 10th October 1972, in the Notting Hill area of London. Ronald Guest, the landlord of the Admiral Blake pub in Ladbroke Grove, bought the guitar unaware that the bass was 'stolen property'. On September 2, 2023, a newspaper article was published in London's Sunday Telegraph about the missing bass attracting worldwide interest. Lost for over 50 years, Guest's grandson Ruahadri returned the guitar on February 15, 2024.

15

● Matt Johnson was born in London, England, in 1961. As a singer-songwriter, he is most well-known for being the lead singer and only constant member of his band, The The. In 1979, Matt put an ad in the New Musical Express looking for people who were fans of bands like the Velvet Underground, the Residents, and Throbbing Gristle to start a band with him. The The began as just Matt and one other person, then expanded to four members and eventually became Matt as the only permanent member with a rotating cast of other musicians joining him. These musicians have included Johnny Marr, Simon Fisher Turner, and Gail Ann Dorsey. The band achieved commercial success with their song 'Uncertain Smile', which reached No.68 on the charts in 1982. The song was from their album *Soul Mining* and became a classic largely thanks to an extended piano outro played by Jools Holland.

● Debbion Currie was born August 13, 1963, in southeast London, England. Debbion was the formation vocalist with Colourbox in 1981. Colourbox were signed to 4AD, and Debbion recorded the double-sided single 'Breakdown' b/w 'Tarantula' with them. She parted ways with Colourbox in 1983 and soon would be recording with Viv Albertine, who had recently left The Slits. Always interested in dance, Debbion worked with Malcolm McLaren, eventually leaving London to study dance at Leicester Polytechnic. In recent times Debbion has been operating a quirky little preloved vintage shop called 'Secret Love'; she sometimes DJs and is a mum to four creative award winners.

THE RIGHT PLACE AT THE RIGHT TIME
DEBBION CURRIE
(Colourbox 1981-1983)

Believe it or not, I had never considered myself a singer before this time. The boyfriend I had at the time, Michael, had gone to school with Martyn Young and Robs (Ian Robbins), and they had always messed around musically. When I met Michael, they were a band called Baby Patrol and were about to release a single called 'Fun Fusion', described on Discogs as synthpop &/or power-pop.

It was a big deal because he had borrowed the money to buy a synthesizer that was used to make the record. Anyway, as they had all known each other from school, I never really understood their relationship with each other except that he wasn't actually on the record. I can't remember how it came about, but I was just getting into jazz voices like Sarah Vaughan and Ella Fitzgerald. As I discovered new tracks, I would sing along with them with my boyfriend, not really thinking that he was listening to me.

Long story short, he told the boys that he had a girlfriend that could "*sing!*"

I was working for the now-famous Pineapple Dance Centre at the time, as that was what I wanted to be: a dancer. Being a singer never occurred to me, and before I knew it, I was whisked up to an address in Notting Hill to meet Robs and Martyn, had a microphone stuck in front of my face and was asked to sing the Irving Berlin song 'Putting on The Ritz'. I absolutely loved this mash-up of electronic music to an old jazz number, which I knew due to my love of old musicals and dance scenes.

I think the then manager of Modern English, Ray Conroy, must have played it to the heads of the 4AD Records label at the time; I remember going upstairs to a really small office space in Earl's Court where I was to meet Ivo Watts-Russel and his then 4AD partner Peter Kent. Everything happened really quickly then, and before I knew it, we were recording a double A-side single, 'Breakdown' b/w 'Tarantula'.

It was wild, as it was not seen at the time as what the die-hard 4AD fans saw as something the label should be doing. Perhaps it was too commercial-sounding. The single really put Colourbox on the map. We soon had sessions on the radio, music paper interviews and articles in fanzines.

The song 'Tarantula', which was a joint writing project by today's standards, was later re-recorded by This Mortal Coil and again by Beck for a movie. Nowadays, I would probably have been credited as a writer as I formed all my own melodies and changed the words as I saw fit, but it was the '80s, and I was a naive female. For some reason the label wanted to re-record the songs again with a producer called Mick Glossop; these were faster and punchier but not necessarily better. Anyway, it was re-released as that.

After this I left the band, and the singer Lorita Graham took over and recorded everything else that is now known as Colourbox.

Interestingly enough, this has created an important and satisfying thread throughout my life, an achievement, I suppose, and I'm often surprised when people still talk about the band and those singles that I recorded. For years my name was spelt incorrectly on everything, and Lorita's real name was Debbie, so you can imagine the confusion.

My best memories of the whole episode are of working with Vaughan Oliver of the graphic designers 23 Envelope; they did all the artwork for 4AD. He sadly passed away in 2019. Working with, and becoming friends with, Ivo Watts-Russell and sitting around the 4AD office with other bands like Cocteau Twins and Xmal Deutschland, I felt at home, and they felt like family. Even though I was the odd one out, I never felt uncomfortable.

Colourbox had many incarnations, with the band eventually becoming Martyn and his brother Steve. The Colourbox/A.R.Kane collaboration MARRS had a hit with 'Pump Up The Volume'; it was a huge success but seemed to bring with it huge chaos, disruption, and bad feelings. However, by now I was well out of it.

I soon started to work with a musician called Steve Beresford and my then friend Viv Albertine, who had recently left The Slits. There was some recording with Dennis Bovel and work on an album by a band called Dubset with the amazing award-winning film music composer, Nigel Holland. I also danced for Malcolm McLaren; nothing massive, really.

I got married and had 4 children, all creative, and continued to write and perform with their father, who himself was a singer-songwriter and toured extensively with Erasure as a backing singer. Having embarked on a degree in dance at Leicester Poly, I never returned to London. My kids are now heavily into music themselves, with my daughter signing a contract with Asylum/Warner at 14 years of age. My experience in the business was very helpful with this process, though I found that the whole industry was so different from the one I was involved with, a true indie label at the right time. Could the same story happen now? I'm not so sure… but it was A BLAST!

◉ In 1981, the masterpiece album *Pretenders II* was released. Pretenders had attained a big following, and soon this, their second album, soared to the No.10 position on the Billboard 200 chart. The LP delivered the allure of 'The Adulteress', a captivating melodic hit single. Moreover, this recording showcased other signature classics, each a testament to their unrivalled artistry. From the soul-stirring 'Message of Love' to the fascinating 'Talk of the Town', and from the vibrant 'Pack It Up' to the ethereal rendition of a Ray Davies composition, 'I Go to Sleep'.

16

◉ *Press Colour,* the debut studio album by Lizzy Mercier Descloux, aka Martine-Elisabeth Mercier Descloux, was on the shelves on this day in 1979. This is possibly the shortest full-length album of all time, running just a smidge over 22 minutes. She's French, which is exhibited by a level of French elegance and French sophistication. Her reworkings of Arthur Brown's 'Fire' and the 'Mission Impossible' theme are now her own. The chic turning 'Fever' into 'Tumor' was very cheeky. It's far from a great album, yet for '79 and the style applied, it stood out. Still does today, interesting. Lizzy died of cancer at age 47 on 20 April 2004 in Saint-Florent, France.

◉ Marc Moulin was born in 1942, in Brussels, Belgium. Coming out of the field of jazz from the band Placebo, Marc was a founding member of Telex. Along with Michael Moers and Dan Lacksman, they were forerunners of synthpop driven Eurodisco. Leaving guitar out of the instrumentation, they achieved moderate success with their 1979 debut album, *Looking for St. Tropez*, which held the dance floor smash hit single 'Moskow Diskow'. Marc died of throat cancer on 26 September 2008.

17

● Belinda Carlisle, aka Belinda Jo Carlisle (birth name), aka Belinda Jo Kerzcheski, aka Belinda Kurczeski, aka Dottie Danger, was born in 1958, in Hollywood, California. Belinda's musical career began in 1977 when she was the drummer with The Germs, a punk outfit from Los Angeles. But fame came her way as the lead vocalist, Belinda, and formation member of The Go-Go's. In the mid-80s, their brand of NEW WAVE-surf rock-pop made them worldwide superstars with songs like 'We Got the Beat', 'Our Lips Are Sealed' and 'Head Over Heels'. As a soloist, Belinda's music leant more toward emotionally charged epic pop ballads. It was with her solo releases that she continued to earn much respect from critics and the public alike. Her 1989 album *Runaway Horses* went to the top 5 worldwide, but it could not eclipse the No.1 selling single of 1987, 'Heaven Is a Place on Earth'.

● Stephan Eicher was born in 1960, in Munchenbuchsee, Switzerland. In 1980, with his brother Martin performing as Grauzone, they released their debut single, 'Eisbär'; it achieved minor chart success in Austria and Germany. Grauzone were largely unknown outside Europe but were well known to followers of Neue Deutsche Welle (New German Wave). Stephen's songs with Grauzone and from his numerous solo albums were sung in a variety of languages, including Swiss, German, French, German, English, and Italian; he even uses different languages in the same piece.

● On this day in 1977 the 'classic' line-up of Mental as Anything (which lasted from 1977 to 1999) played for the first time at Cell Block Theatre in Sydney. The band consisted of Martin Plaza, aka Martin Murphy, on vocals & guitar; Reg Mombassa, aka Chris O'Doherty, on vocals & lead guitar; Peter O'Doherty (brother to Reg) on bass guitar & vocals; Wayne de Lisle, aka David Twohill, on drums; and Greedy Smith, aka Andrew Smith, on vocals, keyboards & harmonica.

Colin Moulding by Roch Parisien

● Colin Moulding was born in Swindon, England, in 1955. Colin played bass in the fantastic XTC, one of the smartest and indeed catchiest British pop bands to emerge from the punk and new wave explosion of the late '70s and early '80s. Their songs were quirky & jerky, sharp & precise. XTC's meticulous hook & melody-laden songs soon proved that the songwriting team of guitarist Andy Partridge and Colin was to be one of the best of the era. Major success though somewhat eluded them in both Britain and America, yet they did develop a devoted cult following worldwide; they remain loyal to this day. In 2017 Colin teamed up once again with the original XTC drummer Terry Chambers to form TC&I, and they released the EP *Great Aspirations*.

◉ Kevin Rowland was born on this day in 1953. He is an English singer and songwriter from Wolverhampton, with Irish roots. Before forming Dexys Midnight Runners, Kevin was part of an art-rock band called Lucy and The Lovers. They took inspiration from Deaf School, the famed Liverpool art-rock band. Later, they transformed into the punk group The Killjoys. Dexys Midnight Runners achieved global success with their hit single 'Come on Eileen'.

18

◉ Nigel Griggs was born in 1949 in Hatfield, England. Nigel was the bass guitarist for Split Enz from 1977 to 1985, when they disbanded. After Split Enz split, Nigel joined Enz drummer Noel Crombie, Enz founding member Phil Judd and the guitarist Michael den Elzen in the band Schnell Fenster, which lasted about 6 years. Nigel has been a faithful re-joiner of the numerous Enz reunions. In 2002 he released a solo album, *Sleeper*.

◉ On this day in 1977, The Police played as a three-piece band for the second time. That line up was Stewart Copeland, Sting and Andy Summers. The gig was at Rebecca's Birmingham, in the West Midlands, England. They were criticised by punk bands for not being authentic and lacking 'street cred'. What the Police did perhaps was to take from punk the brand of nervous, energetic disillusion soaking in 1970s Britain. The original guitarist Henry Padovani played his last gig with the band on August 5; he went on to be part of Wayne County.

◉ In 1986, Recoil, the solo project of Alan Wilder, who was still a member of Depeche Mode at the time, released his first album, *1+2*. Consisting of only two tracks and coming in at almost 33 minutes, the album features a combination of Depeche Mode samples and original sounds utilised in their recordings, along with samples from Duet Emmo and Kraftwerk, all woven together to create a captivating, industrial-style electronica experience that is a must-have for any collector of the genre.

◉ On August 18, 1978, 'Hong Kong Garden', the debut record release by Siouxsie and the Banshees, was released. It peaked at No.7 and was their second highest UK charter, behind 1983's 'Dear Prudence' (No.3). The song was named after the Hong Kong Garden Chinese Restaurant in Chiselhurst's High Street. Siouxsie Sioux was quoted, "*Me and my friend were really upset that we used to go there, and, like, occasionally when the skinheads would turn up, it would really turn really ugly. These gits would just go in en masse and just terrorise these Chinese people who were working there. We'd try and say, 'Leave them alone', you know. It was a kind of tribute*".

◉ Wall Of Voodoo's debut album, *Dark Continent*, was released in 1981 on IRS Records. It achieved moderate sales and reached No.17 on the US album charts. Some argue that it is WOV's best album, even surpassing the success of *Call of The West*, which features the hit song 'Mexican Radio'. The strength of lies in Stan Ridgway's songwriting, which is what he is best known for. Musically, WOV delivers nothing short of excellence. The album has a touch of NEW WAVE with layered keyboards, complemented by unique percussion and jangly guitars. Ridgway's monotone vocal delivery adds to its beauty. A must-have for any music lover.

19

◉ Mark Wilson Cline was born in 1959 in Atlanta, Georgia. In 1979, Mark, along with fellow art students at the University of Georgia, Armistead Wellford and Mike Richmond, founded the seminal Athens, Georgia, band Love Tractor. Love Tractor has long been regarded along with The B-52's, Pylon, and R.E.M. as the founders of the Athens music scene. Mark, a multi-instrumentalist, plays guitar, synths, and bass, and his talents led him to being an essential part of the six albums recorded and released by Love Tractor. Love Tractor toured extensively from 1980 to 1993, cutting their teeth touring with the likes of New Order, The B-52's, and The Psychedelic Furs. While in Love Tractor, Mark has had the opportunity to work with musicians like Joe Rowe and Doug Stanley of The Glands, Bill Berry of R.E.M., Kit Swartz, and Andrew Carter. Although they are no longer a touring band, Mark continues to write and record with Love Tractor.

Mark Cline fronting Love Tractor by Lynne Harty Siler

THE HISTORY OF LOVE TRACTOR
MARK CLINE
(Love Tractor)

It is no act of misguided hyperbole to declare that Love Tractor has always been genre-bending, art rock pioneers. We just happened to be inadvertent architects of the Athens, Georgia, scene and sound; our melodic, textured and disco-driven rock is still claimed as a huge influence on subsequent generations. Love Tractor strived to always stand out as artistically brave — with a willingness to fail and to succeed.

Love Tractor was founded in 1979 by me and my art student friends Armistead Wellford and Mike Richmond; it was simply a vehicle to entertain our art school pals and apply some of the conceptual thinking we were studying in art school—in the then backwater college town of Athens. We played our first gig at a house party in 1980 at the infamous "Pylon Park", a rambling and decrepit Victorian house lurking on the back two acres of overgrown land and inhabited by members of the seminal band Pylon, as well as me and Kit Swartz. Rocking, drunken, drugged house parties were par for the course with Athens' art students and fitted nicely with the conceptual art movement popular at the time. Kit Swartz (the Side Effects) and Bill Berry (R.E.M.) shared drumming duties.

Our debut, *self-titled* album was released in 1981—while we were all still in college. The album was 100% instrumental, and it received critical acclaim from music journalists, describing it as *"a unique blend of rock, post-punk, disco, and art-rock"*. Danny Beard, owner of DB Records, brought in Alfredo Villar, of the seminal Atlanta band The Fans, to add synths, pianos, and string arrangements. The album's mix of angular guitar riffs, hypnotic rhythms, and funky bass lines, coupled with the band's art-school sensibility, established us as '*the band to watch*'. The album featured the classic tracks 'Buy Me A Million Dollars', 'Sixty Degrees Below', and 'Fun to Be Happy'. Kit Swartz was the drummer for this and the next album (after Bill Berry left for R.E.M.). R.E.M.'s Mike Mills cited our first album, *Love Tractor,* as "*a go-to for me when I need to be reminded that there is a reason to listen to music*".

In 1983, our second album, *Around the Bend,* ironically a far more experimental record, contained one commercial(ish) song, 'Spin Your Partner', which had an accompanying video that received significant rotation on MTV. The album showcased our growth and evolution; we incorporated vocals on three tracks and other experimentations, enhancing the overall sound. Again, Alfredo Villar joined us to add synths, pianos, and string arrangements. *Around the Bend* was well-received both critically and commercially; it topped the college charts and solidified Love Tractor's place in the alternative music landscape. It was now we began 10-plus years of dedicated touring; gone were the days of one-off shows and mini tours.

In 1984, we released the '*Til the Cows Come Home* EP; it featured the alternative charts-topping song 'Neon Lights'. This EP exhibited our ability to create catchy, danceable tracks that were still rooted in their post-punk and art-rock sensibilities. Famed rock critic Robert Christgau listed it as the #3 best EP of the year in his Pazz-Jop Critics Poll. The song 'Neon Lights' was a radio breakthrough, garnering the band international attention. Andrew Carter took over on drums when Kit Swartz left for grad school.

This Ain't No Outer Spaceship, produced by Pat Irwin (Eyed Spy, The Raybeats, The B-52's), was our first fully vocal album; it was released in 1986 on Bigtime/RCA records. The album marked a departure from our earlier experimental sound; we refocused our efforts on songcraft, and this was evident on the popular tracks 'Beatle Boots', 'Small Town' and 'Cartoon Kiddies'. Critics saw that we were determined to evolve and incorporate new influences, such as R&B, folk and narrative-driven lyrics. The album's rave reviews helped cement Love Tractor's status as one of the pioneers of the Athens music scene.

We are proud that Love Tractor was featured in the 1986 documentary film *Athens, GA: Inside/Out*, a film that has been described as "*the definitive portrait of the city's world-renowned music scene*".

Well received critically and commercially, Love Tractor's fifth album, 1988's *Themes from Venus,* was produced by the famed producer and the Let's Active frontman Mitch Easter. This release gave us the hits 'Venice', 'I Broke My Saw', and 'Crash'. Diverse and multi-layered, we integrated complex arrangements and imaginative instrumentation with a move towards symbolic lyricism. *Themes from Venus* was a sonic tribute of sorts to the band members' childhood musical crushes: T. Rex, Bowie, Roxy Music, Pink Floyd, NEU!, early Brian Eno and progressive rock. Music writer and critic Annie Zaleski stated, "*Themes from Venus presaged the future: Tame Impala's blissed-out electro, thrumming '90s post-rock, and the success of freewheeling pop merchants such as The Pixies*." To say the album was ahead of its time is an understatement. We supported *Themes from Venus* with an extensive 60-date stint on the B-52's *Cosmic Thing* tour.

In 1995, the band emerged from a three-year touring hiatus and embarked on creating *The Sky at Night*. Like a Proustian madeleine, this album became a means of rekindling memories and refining our signature sound. The project quickly expanded far beyond its original scope and became a long and fruitful journey of rediscovery. Doug Stanley from The Glands joined the fold in 1995.

After numerous revisions, *The Sky at Night* was finally released in 2001 on Razor and Tie. This self-produced album exemplifies our continued relevance in the alternative music scene, yet with a more refined sound. Recorded in a 16-track studio (Elixir Sound), this limitation created a forced minimalism and deep decision-making regarding the song arrangements — critics and fans say it is our finest 'sounding' album to date. This hard-won, future-facing album provided a satisfying yet strangely nostalgic experience for fans, while also serving as a testament to our evolution as a band.

Love Tractor has played live sporadically since 2016 with Andrew Carter and Joe Rowe (The Glands) on drums and Bill Berry playing keyboards and acoustic guitar on a few songs. In January 2023, we rejoined our Athens, Georgia, pals The B-52's for the final show of their last world tour, in, of course, Athens. We have returned to the studio and are currently at work on an album of new material and are amid rereleasing our back catalogue.

◉ Stephen Huss, born in 1967 in Ontario, Canada. He embarked on a musical journey alongside his brother Darrin when they established Psyche in 1982, delving into the depths of synthpop with a haunting twist. In 1985, the duo unveiled their triumphant debut album, *Insomnia Theatre*, under their very own record label, Malignant Records. Stephen, as a solo artist, crafted an extensive collection of instrumental ambient soundscapes, which have been meticulously compiled and released over the course of several decades. Despite his battle with schizophrenia, Stephen's musical genius persisted. Tragically, on August 4, 2015, Darrin Huss shared the heartbreaking news of his brother's passing on Facebook, stating, "*My beautiful genius little brother Stephen Huss played his last melody over the weekend. Leaving us behind in this life*". Nevertheless, Stephen's legacy with Psyche and his vast array of electronic masterpieces continue to resonate.

Psyche – Darrin & Stephen Huss by Alain Duplantier

◉ On this day in 1986, Lowlife released their first album, *Permanent Sleep*. Shortly after his departure from Cocteau Twins, bass player Will Heggie joined forces with Craig Lorentson (vocalist), Stuart Everest (guitarist), and Grant McDowell (drummer) to create a deeply sombre and dark record. The influence of The Cocteaus is evident with the reverb-drenched guitar, funeral-like techniques, and an utterly suffocating atmosphere, all of which are distinctive characteristics of POST-PUNK in the mid-1980s. It is a captivating blend of ethereal pop and haunting dreams.

◉ August 19, 1981, marked a momentous occasion when Neil Tennant crossed paths with Chris Lowe at the electronics store where Chris was employed. Once they connected intellectually, they embarked on a collaborative journey, composing music with a focus on dance. Initially, they contemplated naming themselves West End but eventually settled on the moniker Pet Shop Boys, inspired by acquaintances who worked at a pet store in Ealing. This decision proved to be extraordinarily fruitful as Pet Shop Boys achieved tremendous success, reaching the top spot on the UK and US charts in 1986 with their hit single 'West End Girls'. They went on to secure three more UK No.1 singles, including 'It's A Sin', 'Always on My Mind', and 'Heart'. In addition to his musical pursuits, Neil played a pivotal role as an editor and critic for the music magazine Smash Hits. AND the Pet Shop Boys made lots of money.

⦿ In 1979, Open Eye Records released *Street to Street*, a compilation album. This album, the first of a two-volume set, consists of twelve tracks that were recorded at Open Eye's 4-track studio over a span of 12 months starting from May 1978. It showcases songs by notable artists such as The Id (later known as Orchestral Manoeuvres in the Dark), Modern Eon, Big In Japan (Bill Drummond & Ian Broudie), and Echo & The Bunnymen.

20

⦿ The debut single, 'Ignore the Machine' by Alien Sex Fiend, was out in 1983. Oddly, and even though it opens with lines from a Rolf Harris song, 'Ignore the Machine' is electro-goth personified. ASF was a vehicle for Nick Wade, aka Nik Fiend, whose band was a house feature of Soho's The Batcave Club. The single is relentlessly intense, with a backbeat that just persists, and it's hard not to see the influence of Alice Cooper here. Classic of genre.

⦿ There's an intriguing history behind the song 'Ça Plane Pour Moi', which was recorded on August 20, 1977, in London's Morgan Studios. The song was adapted from Jet Boy, Jet Girl, written by Alan Ward, who was part of the band Elton Motello. 'Ça Plane Pour Moi' was credited to Belgian Plastic Bertrand, but it was in reality sung by Lou Deprijck. Looking for a face to present the song publicly, Lou chose fellow Belgian 23-year-old Roger Jouret, and it came to be that Plastic Bertrand would make his first TV appearance on the show Rendezvous Sunday on November 6th, 1977. The single backed with 'Pogo Pogo' would go on to sell over eight million copies worldwide, going to the top of the charts in Australia, Belgium, France, Japan, Germany, and Italy. Plastic achieved celebrity status and toured the world on the strength of the song. Deprijck took the case to a Belgian court in an attempt to get credit for his epic tune, but the court ruled that Plastic would remain the "legal performer". Oddly, the decision was not made on comments by a noted linguistics expert but rather on administrative documents, including contracts, and Plastic's presentation on the record covers. But in July 2010, to end the folly, Plastic Bertrand said, "*It was time to stop pretending*" and confessed that he had nothing to do with the recording of the single. He quoted to Belgian newspaper Le Soir, "*I don't mind saying it was not my voice; I wanted to sing, but Lou would not let me into the studio. I am the victim.*" A few months before the vocals for 'Ça plane pour moi' were recorded, the record firm used the same backing track with the same musicians to release 'Jet Boy, Jet Girl' by Elton Motello.

⦿ Doug Fieger was born in 1952, in Detroit, USA. It was one song that gave Doug and his band, The Knack, celebrity status; that song was 'My Sharona'. The song became the best-selling single of 1979, spending six weeks at No.1 on the Billboard chart, and the band's debut album, *Get the Knack*, was a huge success as well, spending five straight weeks at No.1. It's fair to say that even though they had that dual success, The Knack qualifies as 'One Hit Wonders'! Doug wrote the song for Sharona Alperin, who ended up appearing on the single's cover sleeve; they would become a couple even though Sharona was not his girlfriend at the time. The song not only made The Knack overnight sensations, but it also proved a boon for Weird Al Yankovic, whose parody called 'My Bologna' gave him his first hit single and put him on the road to stardom. On February 14, 2010, Doug died after a long battle with cancer.

⦿ Ralf Hutter was born on August 20 in 1946 in Krefeld, part of what was the Allied-occupied Germany. Ralf, along with Florian Schneider, in 1969 was a founding member of Kraftwerk in Düsseldorf. He was a classically trained pianist but found it boring, unnatural, and irrelevant to modern man, so he ventured into jazz-rock and experimentalism. It was with the improvisational ensemble Organisation that he met Florian, and after the release of one album, *Tone Float*, they split to form the band that would become the dominant pioneers of electronic pop music. Kraftwerk's influence on modern music cannot be overstated. Their sound is visionary; it combines driving, repetitive rhythms with catchy melodies with a minimalistic and strictly electronic instrumentation. Ralf is a keen cyclist and fan of competitive racing and was once involved in a serious cycling accident that left him in a coma. When he awoke, his first words were, *"Where is my bicycle?"*. In 1993 Kraftwerk provided the theme for the Tour de France; it incorporated the sounds of bicycle chains, gear mechanisms and the breathing of the cyclist. Today, they tour the world and are known for their spectacular 3D performances to packed audiences.

◉ Matthew David Moffitt was born in Sydney, Australia, in 1956. Matt was the frontman-vocalist of Matt Finish, a hard touring band, and gathered a very faithful following, especially on Australia's eastern seaboard. The band's debut album, *Short Note* of 1981, peaked at No.14 nationally, with the title track single also going top 20, but the success was short-lived, with the band splitting by year's end. A reformation in 1983 and a new album, *Word of Mouth*, kept them on the road for another year until another split. Moffitt went solo, releasing the album *As Little as A Look* in 1986; it held the very well-received single, 'Miss This Tonight', going top 30. Yet another reformation of Matt Finish saw them together for their longest period of 13 years, until Matt's passing on 13th August 2003.

◉ UB40 released their debut album *Signing Off* in 1980. UB40 were at the forefront of the new dub/reggae insurgence; here they came to us with a very strong offering, and for sure the band could be accused of a few banal releases, but not here with *Signing Off*. The album is full of finesse musically, but it also is rich in social and political statements, a testament to the real anger toward the ever-present racism and poverty that was Thatcher's Britain. The combination of pop and reggae here was a success for UB40; the keyboards are smooth, and the horns are excellent, the standout being Brian Travers' sax. The band's main stamp was Ali Campbell's rich, appealing vocal delivery, *"I'm a British subject not proud of it, while I carry the burden of shame"*. Says a lot.

◉ *Upstairs at Eric's* by Yazoo (known as Yaz in the USA) was released in 1982. Was this the ultimate Eighties synthpop manifesto? Here we have Alison Moyet, a brash girl singer with a stellar, soulful voice, and Vince Clarke, who was the keyboard geek punching the buttons. This album verges on synthpop perfection via Vince's brilliance as a pop music creator, producer, composer, and musician. But it was together that they made an album full of club classics like 'Situation', 'Too Pieces' and 'Don't Go', along with 'Midnight', a torch ballad Smokey Robinson could have written for Dusty Springfield. Clarke had already tasted fame with Depeche Mode; he famously quit them after they rejected 'Only You', which became Yazoo's first hit! In mid-1983, way too soon for their adoring public, the duo called it quits; Vince moved on to Erasure, and Alison to solo hits, but their short-lived partnership was the essence of a sideways-haircut romance. The great thing about synthpop in this era is that it always kind of feels experimental by default; *Upstairs at Eric's* is no exception. Clever music.

21

◉ Mark "Cal' Callaghan was born in Aldershot, England, in 1957. Mark is probably best known to most as a founding member of GANGgajang, coming together in 1984 with ex-Angles members drummer Graham 'Buzz' Bidstrup and bass player Chris Bailey. Prior to GANGgajang, Mark earned an honoured reputation as a singer-songwriter frontman with

The Riptides. They had a brand of sixties-styled pop-surf-rock that garnered a faithful following, especially by the new mod revivalists. The Riptides dissolved in 1983, but Mark rebirthed them in the late eighties, recorded an album, *Wave Rock*, and toured to eager, packed audiences. From 1985 to 2002, GANGgajang recorded four very well-received albums mostly containing Mark's intelligent songwriting; the *self-titled* debut album sold over 120,000 copies. The single 'Sounds of Then (This Is Australia)' lifted from the album is a prime example of Mark's ability to capture mood and portray a vision.

◉ Budgie, born Peter Edward Clarke in 1957 in St Helens, England, replaced Palmolive as the drummer for The Slits in 1979, coming from Bill Drummond's band Big in Japan. His time with The Slits was brief before he joined Siouxsie and the Banshees as their new drummer, taking over for Kenny Morris. It was while playing with Siouxsie Sioux in The Banshees that they formed the side project The Creatures, which coexisted alongside The Banshees and even continued after The Banshees split up. Budgie and Siouxsie married in 1991 but divorced in 2007. Following the breakup of The Banshees in 1996, Budgie worked with many different artists and started an experimental percussion group called The Butterfly Effect with 3 drummers and a guitarist. More recently, he has been a member of John Grant's studio and touring band and began a new collaboration with Lol Tolhurst and Jacknife Lee, releasing an album titled *Los Angeles*. In early 2025 Budgie released his book *The Absence*, taking the reader through Budgie's passage of the late '70s and early '80s British post-punk scene. A press release quoted Budgie as saying, *"Damned if you do, denied if you don't. I present my mistakes that I may learn and others may avoid"*.

◉ Robert Hazard was born Robert Rimato on August 21, 1948, in Philadelphia, USA. Coming from a musical family, his father was a tenor opera singer with the Philadelphia Opera Company. In 1979, Hazard recorded a demo of his composition 'Girls Just Want to Have Fun' with his band Robert Hazard and the Heroes. The demo was picked up by Cyndi Lauper, and the song became her biggest seller, reaching No.1 worldwide. The Heroes had a minor hit in 1983 with 'Escalator of Life', which peaked at No.58 in the USA. Over his career, Hazard recorded six moderately received albums before passing away on August 8, 2008, from pancreatic cancer.

Joe Strummer - Unknown

◉ Joe Strummer, aka John Mellor, was born in 1952, in Broomfield, England. Joe was co-founder, lyricist, rhythm guitarist and lead vocalist of The Clash, The Mescaleros, the 101ers, Latino Rockabilly War, and the Pogues, as well as a successful solo career. Formed in 1976, The Clash were part of those bands that established British punk. Initially raw and thrashy, they were creative enough, though, to later encompass elements of reggae, ska, rockabilly & funk. In 1979, worldwide acclaim followed the release of *London Calling*, arguably the best album released that year; it was The Clash's magnum opus and all the better for the fact that it transcended punk. Here, ska, rockabilly, and jazz all sat effortlessly alongside the prescribed three chords on this double album. Worth it for the title track alone, *London Calling* is studded with gems throughout; nonetheless, in 1982, Combat Rock became their biggest seller. In 1989 he released a solo album, *Earthquake Weather*, which was panned by critics and missed any commercial success. He contributed to several film soundtracks, including those for *Sid and Nancy* (1986) and *Grosse Pointe Blank* (1997). In 1999 he formed a new band, Joe Strummer & the Mescaleros, releasing a handful of recordings. Over the years he appeared in several movies; a must-see is Strummer's role in the Jim Jarmusch film *Mystery Train*. Joe died from a heart attack on 22nd December 2002.

◉ On this day in 1978, Yukihiro Takahashi, the drummer/percussionist and vocalist with Yellow Magic Orchestra, released his debut album, *Saravah!*. This album is sophisticated and has a lounge mood; it's styled on French pop predominantly created by traditional instrumentation holding a collection of standards and original easy listening tracks beautifully arranged and produced. Even though supported by his YMO bandmates, the music is far removed from what they are famed for; Yuki was soon to venture into computers and electronics and break new ground in the soon-to-surface technopop genre. Delicious martini and dinner music.

◉ 'In The End' b/w 'Undecided' and 'Big Words', the debut single by The Reasons Why, was released in 1987 on Phantom Records (PH-21). Jangly, infectious, and harmonious is how this could be described. There's much that could be compared to The Only Ones, The Jam or The Monkees. Much to love here.

22

◉ Michael Aston was born August 22, 1957, in Bridgend, South Wales. With Michael on guitar, his brother John, aka Jay, as vocalist, along with lead guitarist Ian Hudson, they formed the original working title of Slavaryan. After a move to London in 1981, they adopted the now well-known moniker Gene Loves Jezebel, the band that's become highly regarded in the Goth & POST-PUNK genres. GLJ recorded four albums before Michael departed for a solo career and to also form Immigrants, to be renamed as Edith Grove; they released the album *Why Me, Why This, Why Now* in 1995. After much legal wrangling about use of the name Gene Loves Jezebel, founding member Michael Aston now owns the rights to the band name in the United States and continues to record and tour worldwide. Jay has limited rights to the name in the UK.

AN INTERVIEW WITH MICHAEL ASTON
(Gene Love Jezabel)

Hi Michael, where are you living these days? I understand that you grew up in Wales, correct? Did you grow up in a musical household? What prompted the move to the USA?

I've lived in Los Angeles, California for the past 34 years with my gorgeous wife and our fabulous five children. I grew up in industrial South Wales, a place called North Cornelly, a small village, which was a magical place to grow up as we had every body of water: river, lake, and sea, and forest, mountain, and vale.

You formed Gene Loves Jezebel in 1980 with your brother John, where does the band's name actually come from? I've read it relates a Gene Vincent song and that it was taken from graffiti, so let's nail this down! And what's with Slavaryan?

I moved to Porthcawl, South Wales, in 1976 when I was 18 with my ex-wife: it was a "shotgun" wedding. My musical journey began in 1978 or 79 when I was approached by local guitar player Ian Hudson, who asked if he could join my band. My band at the time consisted of me and was called Slavaryan. We started rehearsing together and played a few shows, most notably opening for Crass. Around 1980, I was made redundant from the steel mill and used the funds to move to London to become a rock and roll star. My ex-wife had been accepted to St Martin's School of Art. That's really where my life really began as an artist. After moving to London, I put an ad in the N.M.E. for a guitar, drums, and bass. I met the original drummer, James Chatter, and after a few months of rehearsal with various players, I moved to Pimlico and asked my brother, John (Jay), to move to London and join my band with Ian Hudson – both were still in Wales. I paid for a demo. We improvised and dropped the songs at various labels. Situation Two picked us up, and the demo actually made it to the first EP and got rave reviews. The EP was called *Shaving My Neck*. Julianne Regan, who eventually formed All About Eve, played the bass on the EP. Actually, Gene Loves Jezebel was a name change that occurred after our first big show at the ICA in London. An art student at a party we had gone to asked my brother and me what our names were. Jay said, for some reason, that my name was "Gene" and his name was "Jezebel". The student asked, *"Does Gene Loves Jezebel?"* And there it was. Jay later claimed that I was named after Gene Vincent because I had severely broken my leg playing soccer as a child. As to Slavaryan, I came up with the name recalling a history lesson from secondary school about the Battle of Stalingrad. I recalled that the Nazis despised the Slavs and regarded them as inferior and thought the Aryan race superior, but as the Russians repelled the Germans and essentially won the war, I remember quipping to the teacher, *"I guess the Slavs were the superior race!"* I decided to discontinue the name, as I didn't want to explain this every time I did an interview. Ha!

Who and what were your musical influences growing up? You worked with John Cale and Velvet Underground members, how did that come about and how did that affect you being around such legendary artists?

I would say the Velvet Underground, Public Image, Japan, Echo and the Bunnymen, Budgie, Neil Young both acoustically and electrically, Led Zeppelin, Steve Marriott, Terry Reid, and Burke Shelley, singers mostly, so many singers I loved, including the Ronettes – I was a huge Phil Spector fan. We did work with John Cale – it was a wonderful experience. Sadly, the recordings were never released and were lost.

'Desire' made the soundtrack to the movie 'She's Having A Baby' Pretty good cast on that soundtrack-wise. How did that come about? You have a cameo in that movie.. what!.. how!.. why?

Yes, I did have a cameo in the John Hughes movie, *She's Having a Baby*. I was the only one who woke up early enough in the morning and made my way down to Paramount Studios to film it. The cameo amounted to naming the baby in the film, so I tried to think of the most original name I could to make sure it didn't end up on the cutting room floor. I choose "Winthrop".

And in the studio, what recordings are you most proud of and why?

Well, the first two records, by far, *Promise* and *Immigrant*. I think the best of Gene Loves Jezebel ended with Ian Hudson's nervous breakdown and departure. The best work we did was when he was at the helm. Interesting fact, Gene Loves Jezebel's lineup changed on every recording. It was essentially, a duo, "Gene" and "Jezebel".

Through the '80s what was your most exciting gig and/or memorable event? Did you ever have a scary moment touring?

The most exciting gig was Buenos Aires, Argentina; this was the first time we travelled to South America. Apparently, we were the first European band to play there. It was interesting because it was right after the Falklands War, and everyone was worried about how we would be treated. We were embraced and welcomed beyond our wildest imaginations.

Scary? Maybe the 1986 Street Scene Festival in Los Angeles – there must have been 100K people there. On the Saturday, the Ramones were supposed to play, and for whatever reason, they did not show up, and the crowd got a little testy, and they started to tear up the stage, and in the melee, police were injured. On the Sunday there was a shooting and four stabbings; it was the last Street Scene Fest ever.

OK.. you met and worked with John Cale, but who else did you meet and had to pinch yourself and say,"is this really happening?"

I've met with just about every legend you can imagine but beyond a "hello", I just don't want to know my heroes, so I don't engage.

Primarily you are known as a vocalist, so who are your top five favourite singers of all time? I heard you once mention Astral Weeks, it's in my top 10 albums of all time, is Van Morrison one of the five?

Yes, *Astral Weeks* is one of my all-time favorite records. Yes, "Sweet Thing" is quite wonderful.

You performed on a cruise ship; how does that work? You would be at pretty close quarters with the punters the whole time, it's not like you can go home, like walking the deck you'd bump into fans surely. Is there privacy there apart from locking yourself in your cabin?

The cruise ship was an absolute joy. I've always enjoyed meeting "the punters". As far as privacy, my wife and I had our own suite and porter, and ate all meals in a white-glove service private dining area with the other musicians. It was great to spend hours chatting with Master G, from The Sugarhill Gang and so many of my contemporaries that I had not seen in decades. It was a wonderful experience.

Aside from the aforementioned what have you been up to recently music-wise, recordings and any live performances?

I am currently recording what I regard as a totally new direction and quite possibly the best work I have ever done so I am very excited. I've spent the last 28 years raising five children and I'm very proud of that.

What's on your turntable at the moment?

Roy Buchanan is my current fix, but I do love to look back, there is so much music to discover.

Thanks very much Michael.

You are more than welcome; it has been my pleasure.

◉ Roland Orzabal, aka Raoul Jaime Orzabal de la Quintana, was born in 1961 in Portsmouth, England. Roland is the singer, songwriter, and guitarist of Tears for Fears (TFF). One of their biggest hits was the 1985 US No.1 and UK No.2 single, 'Everybody Wants to Rule the World'. Before forming TFF in 1978, Roland and his TFF bandmate Curt Smith created the mod/ska-orientated band called Graduate. They released one album titled *Acting My Age* before disbanding. In 1986, Roland received an Ivor Novello award for Songwriter of the Year, thanks to the success of TFF's album *Songs from the Big Chair*. In 2014, he gained critical acclaim for his romantic comedy novel, *Sex, Drugs & Opera*. In 1991, TFF split with Smith leaving the band, but Roland continued to keep the name alive and achieved great success with the single 'Laid So Low (Tears Roll Down)'. Roland and Curt reunited in 2000 and have been touring together ever since.

◉ Debbie Peterson was born in 1961, in Los Angeles, USA. Debbie played drums with the NEW WAVE popsters, The Bangles, but also sang lead vocals on two of the band's released singles, 'Going Down to Liverpool' (1984) and 'Be with You' (1989). She is the younger sister of fellow Bangles member Vicki Peterson. The Bangles' singles, Prince's 'Manic Monday' and 'Walk Like an Egyptian', both went top 3 in the UK & US, the latter was a million-selling single and became Billboard's No.1 song of 1987!

◉ The exceptional guitarist Masami Tsuchiya was born in 1952, in Shizuoka, Japan. Masami was the vocalist/guitarist with Ippu-Do, who were all but superstars in their homeland, recording four studio albums between 1979 and 1983 with massive sales. A live set, *Live and Zen* in 1984, featured Japan members drummer Steve Jansen and keyboardist Richard Barbieri and the astounding bassist Percy Jones. Between 1982 and 2013 he recorded 8 albums to critical acclaim, with the debut album *Rice Music* viewed as a hybrid Nippon-Western classic. Masami was always in demand as a session/live player, contributing to works with Bill Nelson, Ryuichi Sakamoto, Japan, and the Duran Duran side project Arcadia.

I PRETEND COOL
MASAMI TSUCHIYA
(The Plastics, Melon, Ippu-Do, Japan)

At the end of 1981, the band Melon, who I worked with for one of their recordings in New York, were performing at a disco called 'Tsubaki House' in Shinjuku near Tokyo, and the members of Japan, Mick Karn, Steve Jansen, and Richard Barbieri, were in the audience. I was aware that they liked my band Plastics and Melon, but the fact that Melon's bassist at that time was Percy Jones was the biggest reason why they came to see them live.

Of course, I knew they were members of Japan, and they knew me too. Around that time, I was recording my solo album *Rice Music* and talking with Mick and Steve; they promised me they would participate in the recording, and they did so accordingly, and their contributions were remarkable. During the recording with the three of us at Air Studios in London, David Sylvian came to the studio by himself and said, "*Actually, we'll have our last live tour in fall or winter of this year, but there's no guitarist, so would you like to participate?*" I really wanted to agree immediately, but I deliberately pretended to think a little and answered, "*Ah, yeah...Okay, I'll think about it*". I was young, so I pretended to be cool.

Air Studio was in a bit of an uproar because David wasn't the type to do something like that alone; I am unsure that neither Mick nor Steve knew he was coming.

Joining the band was very smooth, and everyone was really kind to me even though I didn't speak much English at that time. During this last tour, Japan was going through a difficult time as a band, but I think it was a very special and precious time for us all. It was September 1982, and my band Ippu-Do's single 'Sumire September Love' was released, becoming a huge hit in Japan. It drew a lot of attention back home, so Japanese TV crews chased us fervently to the tour destinations. The image of me singing with the members of Japan was relayed and became a hot topic because at that time, it was still rare for a Japanese artist to go abroad and work with bands. I think that the style of my appearance in the media gave the Japanese audience a strong impression of the relationship between my home country and the UK music scene.

I've never asked the reason why they named the band JAPAN, but it seems that the symbolic band name reflected the fact that the members were inspired by Orientalism. And I intuitively understood what they expected of me.

Even now, young musicians ask me. *"How on earth did you join Japan?"* At such times, I still pretend to be cool and say, *"I didn't try anything special; we were destined to do it together"*.

23

◉ Edwyn Collins was born in Edinburgh, Scotland, in 1959. He is best known as a producer, record label owner, and lead singer of the band Orange Juice. In 1976, Edwyn formed the band Nu-Sonics, which later evolved into Orange Juice. Along with other Scottish bands on the Postcard record label like Josef K and Aztec Camera, Orange Juice was considered part of the musical movement called 'The Sound of Young Scotland'. With their single 'Rip It Up', Orange Juice transitioned away from the POST-PUNK guitar sound they were previously known for, instead using synthesizers to create an infectious top 10 hit song in the UK. Historically, this was the first major hit song to feature the Roland TB-303 bass synthesizer. As a solo artist, Edwyn had another hit in 1994 with the song 'A Girl Like You'.

Do Re Mi by Brett Hilder

◉ August 23, 1985, was the release date for the Australian band Do-Ré-Mi's debut album. Following on from the success a few months earlier of the two singles 'Man Overboard' and 'Idiot Grin', the album *Domestic Harmony* received critical and public acclaim. This recording is loaded with smart social and political comments; nevertheless, the album is fun musically and perfectly constructed. Song after song we find infectious guitar riffs from Stephen Philip, and the rhythm section of Helen Carter and Dorland Bray add an artistic touch of their own. Deborah Conway's delivery doesn't leave the listener guessing with in-your-face lines relating to anal humour, penis envy and pubic hair. The song 'Man Overboard' is nothing short of sensational; 'Theme from Jungle Jim', 'Big Accidents' & 'Warnings Moving Clockwise' are just sublime tunes. Essential listening.

◉ Robert Smith (keyboards, vocals, strings), Steven Severin (bass, keyboards), Jeanette Landray (vocals), and Andy Anderson (drums) formed The Glove and released the album *Blue Sunshine* in 1983. The band comprised members from The Banshees and both present and future members of The Cure. Jeanette Landray, a lesser-known figure, collaborated for this unique psychedelic project. Noteworthy tracks from the album include 'Like an Animal', 'Sex-Eye-Make Up', 'This Green City', and 'Orgy'. Robert Smith is featured as a vocalist in two tracks, 'Mr. Alphabet Says' and 'Perfect Murder', with Jeanette handling the vocals for the remaining songs. *Blue Sunshine* was recorded between 1981 and early 1983, showcasing a distinctive sound that diverges from the styles of The Banshees and The Cure, making it a valuable addition for fans of either band.

◉ The 1980 Heatwave Festival was held at Mosport Park Toronto, Canada. The event was highly successful, with over 85,000 music fans attending. The Clash, who were originally booked to play, cancelled, as they had difficulty getting past customs. Other bands appearing included Talking Heads, The B-52's, The Pretenders, The Rumour (without Graham Parker) and Elvis Costello and the Attractions, and Rockpile with Nick Lowe & Dave Edmunds.

◉ Shaun Ryder was born in 1962, in Little Hulton, Lancashire, England. Shaun is best known as a founding member of and frontman for Happy Mondays, who formed in 1980. The band was one of the leading lights of what was known as the Madchester scene that came to the fore in the 1980s-'90s. Going through several splits and reformations, through to 2007 they released five moderately selling albums, with *Pills 'n' Thrills* and *Bellyaches* of 1990 being their most successful. Prior to the first split Shaun formed Black Grape, which has that same on/off existence today as Happy Mondays. Another project of Shaun's was the 'supergroup' Mantra of the Cosmos coming together in 2023, consisting of Shaun, former Oasis bassist Andy Bell, drummer Zak Starkey and Happy Mondays percussionist Bez, aka Mark Berry.

24

◉ Mark Bedford was born in London, England, in 1961. Mark was the on-again /off-again bassist for Madness. He initially joined in 1978, when Madness had a split in 1986, and Mark went to play bass with Voice of the Beehive, returning in 1992, then left again in '94 for a couple of years after the rebirth of the band then and left again in 2010 for a couple of years. He now is a fixture of the present touring outfit. Since 2011, he has also been part of The Lee Thompson Ska Orchestra, a band he put together with Madness saxophonist Lee Thompson.

◉ Zeus B. Held was born in 1950. Zeus is a German producer and musician, known for his part in Gina X Performance (GXP). Zeus has also been involved with quite a few other artists out of the krautrock, techno, and NEW WAVE eras. He produced Men Without Hats on their successful album *Pop Goes the World*. Others he has collaborated with or produced are the likes of Dead or Alive, John Foxx, Fashion, and, of course, GXP. GXP were electro pioneers who formed in 1978 as a collaboration between Zeus and charismatic singer-songwriter Gina Kikoine. They hailed from Cologne and mixed cool Euro-disco synth pop with an arthouse performance sensibility, as well as sexually provocative imagery. Largely unheralded, the GXP singles 'No G.D.M.' and 'Nice Mover' are pure gems, delivering sounds and beats that would go on to influence many artists for decades afterwards.

HOW I MET HEINZ FUNK AND FELL IN LOVE WITH THE VSM201
ZEUS B. HELD
(Gina X Performance, Birth Control)

1977 was my fourth year as Birth Control's keyboardist, and I became increasingly interested in music off the Rock Trail.

I bought my first Mini Moog at Kuttney's Musikladen in the Altstadt Cologne in 1974. I modified it for my live needs at the Matten & Wiechers Synthesizer studio in Bonn.

At that time I heard about this new "vox synthesiser" from Sennheiser. Apparently, it was an expensive and pretty complex tool to operate. I was curious and eventually found out that one could book a session at Hamburg's Studio Funk to use this device. So, I booked a studio date, took a few recordings of song sketches with me, and drove up to Hamburg to try out some ideas with this new "vocoder".

At the studio I was greeted by the Tonmeister and an assistant engineer. Once we transferred my 4-track tapes onto the 16-track two-inch, we were joined by Heinz Funk, owner, musician, sound magician, creative entrepreneur, and entertainer. I found him to be a very charming person.

We worked on the vocoder sounds for each track, and Heinz pretty much showed me the tricks of how to "vocode", how the voice modulation works, and how to fine-tune the frequency and filter dividers. He also demonstrated various sound combinations between vocoder and acoustic instruments. By using different filters and compressors, you could create a variety of sounds in an analogue fashion, many of which foreshadowed the spectrum of filter modulation and envelope manipulation in the digital age still to come. He also had one of the biggest Moog modular setups with a massive ribbon controller and an eight-voice analogue step sequencer.

My breakthrough moment was understanding the way the Sennheiser VSM201 works with the Mini and the Polymoog as "replacement signals". It was a long and amazing day, and I managed to record four tracks, which are all on my first solo album, *Zeus' Amusement*.

After working with Mr. Funk and this new electronic box, I knew I needed to get my own VSM to write music and create new sounds with. It reminded me of the feeling I had when I first played on a Wurlitzer e-piano or a Hammond – a sound which asks for a specific way to play and make music. So, upon my return to Cologne, I went to my bank for a loan.

The VSM cost 16,000 Deutschmark, which was about the price of a new Steinway grand piano. My bank manager asked me to provide a guarantor, as he could not see any economic sense in investing in such a device. Luckily, I found an affluent friend of a friend, and about six weeks later I had the magic box. It has the serial No.14!

After recording the vocoded vocals of 'On the Road Again' in Decca Records Paris studio with French space rock band Rockets, I went underground and spent days and nights in Cologne's Studio am Dom, later called Sound Experience, where I laid the foundations for the Gina X Performance album *Nice Mover*.

The intro of the title track is an especially unique example of polyphonic vocoding with the VSM, using a Polymoog replacement signal with a ribbon controller for the glissando. In my mind it was a whole choir shifting up and down parallel scales. With this polyphonic electronic entrance, the album starts and takes you through a great journey of new sounds closely intertwined with great lyrics performed in dialogue between Gina Kikoine's cool androgynous vocals and vocoder lines.

● Jean-Michel Jarre was born in 1948, in Lyon, France. J-M J is arguably one of, if not the, best-known artists from the European electronic music community. His work elevated the synthesizer to new peaks of popularity during the '70s. Highly regarded as a pioneer in the electronic, synthpop, ambient and new age genres, he is also renowned for his exceedingly visual, dazzling concert spectacles consisting of lasers and fireworks. He was the first Western musician officially invited to perform in China and holds the world record for the largest-ever audience at an outdoor event, playing before 3.5 million in Moscow! He is the son of the famed film composer Maurice Jarre and was once married to actress Charlotte Rampling and even has the minor planet No.4422, named "Jarre", in honour of him. 1984 saw Jean release the sampling-loaded album *Zoolook*, an album that was groundbreaking in its aural design. On the track 'Diva', he samples Laurie Anderson's voice to provide a wonderfully bizarre piece. Throughout, vocal samples from all over the world are majestically intertwined with a bewildering array of sounds, taking us into an as-yet unexplored territory showing new sonic possibilities.

◉ Michael 'Snapper &/or Snap' Knapp was born in 1956. From Hamilton, New Zealand, Michael is best known as the drummer for the band Dropbears, who were based in Sydney, Australia, and were originally formed by fellow Kiwi singer-guitarist Johnny Bachelor. Dropbears had minor successes with the 1984 singles 'Shall We Go' & 'Proud' and 1985's 'In Your Eyes'. The band amassed a faithful following, playing to a full house wherever and whenever they played. After Dropbears split, Snapper went on to be part of (Curious) Yellow with ex-Dropbears member Phil Hall and then toured with Dave Dobbyn and The Stone People before settling back in New Zealand, working with The Academy of Performing Arts. Snapper passed away on July 15, 2022.

◉ The son of a Dutch mother and Polish father, David Marx was born in Swindon, England, on August 24th, 1959. He was influenced by The Beatles and Jimi Hendrix, and this led him to start playing guitar as a ten-year-old, and by the time he was 17, he had formed Swindon's first punk band, The Aggravators, who would support The Clash during the White Riot Tour; Joe Strummer would dedicate their song 'Garageland' to them. After a stint with Steve Baker in The Humans, he began working and recording with XTC's Barry Andrews, who had just left the band after the release of their second album, *Go 2*, and played on Barry's debut release, the *Town and Country* EP. It was with Andrews that he formed Restaurant for Dogs and toured with Robert Fripp's League of Gentlemen. Through the eighties David progressed as a singer, songwriter, performer and producer, and while living in New York he attained session work with the likes of Shriekback, Johnny Thunders, Sylvain Sylvain, Holly & The Italians and Jimmy Pursey. Over the years to date, David has released four albums on his own Revolver label. In 2000, as a tribute to the recently deceased drummer Kevin Wilkinson, David compiled the 43-track double album, *Green Indians*, that featured a huge cast, with tracks by Marx, Robert Fripp, Howard Jones, John Otway, Midge Ure and the bands China Crisis, Squeeze, Simple Minds, Shriekback, and The Waterboys, among a host of others.

UPON REFLECTION: RESTAURANT FOR DOGS
DAVID MARX
(The Aggravators, Restaurant for Dogs)

The story goes that The Beatles were really tight.

So tight that they'd spend many an hour sleeping one on top of another, just to stay warm, especially during the many hours driving back to Liverpool in their frozen van. They'd apparently take it in turns to manoeuvre whichever Beatle was on top, to the bottom – where most of the band's collective body heat was to be found.

I wouldn't say Restaurant For Dogs, the band I was in with Barry Andrews, Bruce McRae and Kevin Wilkinson, was quite as tight, but we weren't far off.

The very day Barry announced that he was leaving XTC, he and I immediately went for beer and conversation. Well, I say beer. I didn't really start drinking until my mid-twenties, but you hopefully get my quintessential drift. Two days later, while I was playing guitar in a local Swindon country band (Cimmeron) at a place called The Rodbourne Arms – XTC's drummer, Terry Chambers' local – he asked me to form/join his next band.

This essentially entailed the two of us and a drummer with a very suspect moustache from Marlborough by the name of Rob Wilford sharing XTC's rehearsal space beneath The Affair nightclub in the centre of town. Perhaps a month or so later, we recorded an EP called *Town and Country* (released by Virgin in May 1979) at London's Townhouse.

Produced by the marvellous Martin Rushent (The Human League, The Stranglers, The Buzzcocks) and engineered by a very young, softly spoken Hugh Padgham (Paul McCartney, Peter Gabriel, Elton John, The Police, XTC), said recording was immediately followed by a barrage of mediocre press and a short British tour under the (highly non-inventive) moniker of The Barry Andrews Band.

After a rather inflammatory final gig at London's Hope and Anchor, Rob was dismissed, and Barry and I moved to London – where we literally shared a mattress and a dodgy duvet on the floor of a Kings Cross squat for the best part of six months.

To be sure, squatting was all the rage in London during the late seventies and early eighties. Just ask Joe Strummer. To substantiate as much: we were on the second floor of Hastings House, while most of the band Madness were on the first (and rumour had it, they had heating!).

Shortly thereafter, we started auditioning drummers and guitar players (although I played both guitar and bass on the aforementioned EP), Barry wanted me to primarily play bass live. So, into the fray entered Messrs Wilkinson and McRae, after, we briefly returned to the comfy slipper of Swindon, in search of warmth and comfort.

Decamping to a damp Marlborough rehearsal room, it was immediately obvious that Kevin (who played on my first three albums as well as with The Waterboys, The Proclaimers, Robert Fripp, Squeeze and Howard Jones) was probably the finest drummer either of us had ever encountered.

While Bruce was probably – and surely still is – the most hilarious human being this side of Robin Williams. Nigh guaranteed to still make me howl like the perennial big girl's blouse within a mere twenty seconds of meeting. Said combination of passion, talent, wit and hilarity ensured the four of us stayed super tight as friends for many, many years after Restaurant For Dogs had invariably dissolved. Each going their own separate way. Each remaining unsurprisingly loyal to an unspoken love.

In fact, whilst living in New York, I always remember one occasion when Kev picked me up at Swindon train station, and on the drive to his house, we stopped to speak to Barry, who just happened to be walking across the Co-Op car park in Old Town.

I hadn't seen Barry in almost a year, though we immediately carried on from where we'd left off – amid a high-octane splatter of surreal jocularity and lightning wordplay.

Immediately thereafter, Kev said, *"You two speak to each other in such a way that literally no one else will ever have a chance of remotely understanding. It's amazing how you can both even exist, let alone live without each other"*.

25

● Willy DeVille, aka William Paul Borsey Jr, was born in 1950 in Stamford, Connecticut, USA. He formed Mink Deville; when carrying the moniker Billy Borsay in 1974, the band cemented themselves as New York City legends when they were the house band at the renowned CBGB's night-club. Their debut single 'Spanish Stroll' from 1977 was the band's and Willy's greatest success, peaking at No.20 in the UK and No.4 in New Zealand. Willy died aged 58 following a battle with pancreatic cancer.

◉ Elvis Costello, aka Declan Patrick MacManus, was born in London, England. on August 25, 1954. After resigning from his position in the offices of Elizabeth Arden, he became a significant figure in London's pub rock scene and played a crucial role in the emergence of the British punk and NEW WAVE movement during the mid-to-late 1970s. Elvis is an incredibly productive musician and composer, having recorded more than 20 albums and published over 600 titles. Many of his compositions have been performed by renowned artists such as Johnny Cash, Roy Orbison, Dusty Springfield, and Bjork. Throughout his career, he has collaborated with numerous notable musicians, including Paul McCartney, Burt Bacharach, T-Bone Burnett, and his wife, Diana Krall. Elvis's body of work is consistently captivating, with his first three albums, namely *My Aim Is True*, *This Year's Model*, and *Armed Forces*, being considered essential listening for NEW WAVE and POST-PUNK music enthusiasts.

Willy Deville by Petra Gall/Elvis Costello by Kristan James Melik

◉ Geoffrey Downes, born in 1952, embarked on his musical journey by forming The Buggles in 1977 alongside Trevor Horn and Bruce Wooley. Notably, it was Bruce Wooley's composition, 'Video Killed The Radio Star', that catapulted them to fame, despite his departure from The Buggles. Wooley went on to release the song with The Camera Club, a band that featured Thomas Dolby. Following this success, Downes joined forces with Trevor Horn to collaborate with the prog-rock monsters YES on their album *Drama*. Additionally, he teamed up with YES guitarist Steve Howe to form the highly acclaimed "supergroup" Asia.

◉ Vivien Goldman was born in 1954, in London, England. Vivien is a British journalist and writer and, as a musician, was a member of The Flying Lizards. She was a contributor to the music magazines Sounds, NME and Melody Maker, writing about dub, reggae and POST-PUNK occurrences and influences of the day. Living in Paris during the early '80s, Viv was a member of a NEW WAVE duo called Chantage who had small successes, but really, only in France. 1981 saw the release of her EP *Dirty Washing*, which was partly produced by John Lydon. Later in 1981 two of the tracks from the EP, 'Launderette' and 'Private Armies', were issued as a 7" single in the UK. Vivien also contributed vocals to a dub version of 'Private Armies' that was included in the New Age Steppers' *self-titled* debut.

● On August 25, 1979, The Knack went to No.1 on the US singles chart with 'My Sharona', it would become the best-selling single of the year. This was the band's only chart topper, going No.1 in Australia and No.6 in the UK. It surfaced again in 2009 and went to No.59 through its use in the Oatibix cereal advert.

● John Alexander McGeoch was born in 1955 in Greenock, Scotland. John was listed by Mojo magazine in their top 100 Greatest Guitarists of All Time. His playing as a member of Magazine, Siouxsie and the Banshees, Visage, Public Image Ltd, and Armoury Show earned accolades from his contemporaries worldwide, with the '80s generation of guitarists labelling him as "the NEW WAVE Jimmy Page", through his highly influential playing. He executed rare, complex techniques that bewildered his peers; his work on the Siouxsie and The Banshees song 'Spellbound' was touted as arguably his best performance. John Frusciante, guitarist of Red Hot Chili Peppers, is quoted as saying, "*I taught myself to play by learning all John's stuff in Magazine and Siouxsie and the Banshees*". On March 4, 2004, John died in his sleep, aged 48.

● James Warren was born in 1951, in Bristol, England. James quickly made a name for himself as a guitar and bass player when he joined his first band as a 17-year-old in his hometown of Bristol. Just a year later, he was invited to defect to what James calls 'an intriguing group bearing the mysterious name Stackridge'. Stackridge's style was eccentric and wildly eclectic prog rock, but even though they appeared to lack commercial potential, Beatles producer George Martin was sufficiently impressed to produce their 1973 album *The Man in the Bowler Hat*. Sticking it out with Stackridge until 1978 with a lot of new sounds in the air, James and fellow band member Andy Davis decided to try something completely different, The Korgis. The mantra was '3-minute radio-friendly pop with quirky lyrics', and their first three albums met their aspirations successfully. The 1979 single 'If I Had You' peaked at No.13 in the UK, and 'Everybody's Got to Learn Sometime' was a hit worldwide! The song has continued to have a life of its own, with over fifty cover versions to its credit. James' career path from the '80s to today has led him into songwriting, production, and even the occasional reformation and touring with Stackridge or The Korgis and even twelve years of session singing in Brussels for Reader's Digest! James has also been involved with a 21st-century Korgis project alongside brilliant Aussie multi-instrumentalist, songwriter, and producer Al Steele and fellow early Korgi vocalist-guitarist John Baker. Their 2021 album *Kartoon World* received ecstatic reviews from the UK music press.

IT WAS FAR FROM JUNK MAIL!
JAMES WARREN
(Stackridge, The Korgis)

In 1977 I moved to the historic city of Bath in the Southwest of England, it is famous for its Roman remains and beautiful Georgian architecture, and one day I was intrigued by a card slotted next to a doorbell simply stating 'David Lord: Sound Recording Services'.

Having spent most of the decade until that point touring with Stackridge I was up for trying a new venture and had a few song ideas I was keen to develop. I rang the bell and met David, a classical composer who recorded local folk musicians as a hobby. What a fortuitous encounter! Neither of us could have imagined at the time what an amazing few years that would lay ahead of us.

David was a phenomenal musician and sound recordist, as well as an absolutely lovely chap, and the demos we produced tempted my erstwhile Stackridge companion Andy Davis to quit London and join me in Bath, developing a new project under David's expert guidance. The Korgis were born!

At this time David Lord rented a top-floor apartment in a lovely Georgian crescent, and the first *self-titled* Korgis album featuring the hit 'If I Had You' was joyously recorded there, often to the annoyance and complaints of the neighbours living below, who for a six-month period often had to cope with an incessant bombardment of drums and electric guitars well into the early hours of the morning. We tried every room in the apartment to obtain the required vocal sound, including the bathroom, and I'm still amazed we managed to produce a home-made single that took UK radio by storm. The flagship BBC-TV pop show from that period, *Top of the Pops*, is still often repeated to this day, and only last week the episode featuring The Korgis singing 'If I Had You' was aired again!

The success of the initial Korgis' recordings enabled David Lord to house his audio equipment in new premises, and there at Crescent Studios we produced 'Everybody's Got to Learn Sometime' and Peter Gabriel his fourth solo album, often called *Security*. David worked with a whole host of artists thereafter from every musical genre, as well as two more albums by The Korgis, and thus throughout the 1980s the little city of Bath unexpectedly became an essential place to rock up to in order to realise your pop music dreams. Who would have thought it?

26

● Jet Black, aka Brian John Duffy, was born in Ilford, England, in 1938. Jet was a founding member of The Stranglers, but due to health complications, Jet stopped touring as a player in 2015 and then officially retired in 2019. Before forming The Stranglers, he was a successful businessman owning a fleet of ice cream vans. Jet has had no contact with former Stranglers singer Hugh Cornwell since he left the band in 1990. According to Cornwell's 2004 autobiography, when he telephoned Black to announce his resignation, Jet's response was simply "*OK, fine!*" Jet died at his home in Wales on 6 December 2022, at the age of 84. Stranglers' bass player Jean-Jacques Burnel said on the passing of Jet, "*The welcoming committee has doubled!*", referring to the passing of their 71-year-old keyboard player Dave Greenfield, who died from COVID-19 complications in 2020.

Jet Black by Roch Parisien / Glen Matlock by Roch Parisien

● Ian Dury & The Blockheads released their rousing debut single 'Sex & Drugs & Rock & Roll' in 1977. Out on the Stiff label, the song was written by Ian Dury and Chaz Jankel, and it became a youth anthem and the title a new phrase in the English vernacular. Surprisingly, the single charted poorly but fared well on the independent charts.

● Machinations' debut single, 'Average Inadequacy' b/w 'Arabia', was a great kickstart for this very different sounding band. Released in 1981 on the Phantom Records label (PH-12), it received high-rotation play, and from here it was up, up, and away for this young band. They sounded somewhat electronic due to being driven by a drum machine and a couple of synths but in time were to become more guitar-based funk. This single is minimalistic but very danceable, in the day, it always had the club dancefloors heaving.

⦿ The debut single 'Anyway' by Oto was released on this day in 1984. Oto is a French Cold Wave trio that formed in Nancy in 1982. The song is a fantastic example of dark electro, with pulsing beats that rival the best in the genre. If you're interested, you can find it at boomkat.com.

27

⦿ Glen Matlock was born in 1956, in London, England. Glen played bass and was a formation member with The Sex Pistols until he left in February 1977 and was replaced by Sid Vicious. Glen would later play with Sid in Vicious White Kids in 1978 and was quoted in saying "*Sid has as much talent as a breadboard*". Glen went on to form Rich Kids with himself as bass guitarist & vocalist, Midge Ure on guitar & vocals, Steve New on guitar and vocals and drummer Rusty Egan. The Rich Kids had a top 40 single with 'Rich Kids'. Glen also played bass on the Iggy Pop album *Soldier* and The Damned album *Not of This Earth*. He even joined a reformed Faces, playing at the Vintage at Goodwood festival near Chichester in August 2010. In late 2011, Matlock joined Clem Burke, James Stevenson, and Gary Twinn as part of a "punk supergroup" known as The International Swingers, who were based in Los Angeles & toured Australia and USA.

⦿ The mid-1970s saw the emergence of a few proto-punk and POST-PUNK albums and artists that foreshadowed the music to come in the second half of the decade. One notable example is the *self-titled* debut album by Jonathan Richman's band The Modern Lovers, released in August 1976. Featuring Jerry Harrison on keyboards, Ernie Brooks on bass, and David Robinson on drums, The Modern Lovers' sound was heavily influenced by The Velvet Underground and included the seminal tracks 'Roadrunner' and 'Pablo Picasso', both of which were produced by John Cale and have since become timeless classics. If you haven't heard this recording, seek out the re-release that includes the brilliant 'I'm Straight'. It's a must-listen and comes highly recommended with 5 stars.

⦿ Soda Stereo, hailing from Buenos Aires, Argentina, unveiled their *self-titled* album in 1984. While they were highly regarded in their homeland, like many other Latin American NEW WAVE bands, they remained relatively unknown on the international stage. The album presents a delightful and effective fusion of NEW WAVE elements with ska influences, as well as dashes of '80s Euro funk. Frontman Gustavo Cerati skilfully leads the band, skillfully blending rhythmic dynamics with precise guitar and keyboard accents. Notably, tracks like 'Tele-Ka' and 'Why Can't I Be the Jet Set?' showcase Cerati's clever vocal performances.

⦿ The debut release by The Visitors was a 4-track *self-titled* EP and was released in 1980 by Australia's Phantom Records. The Visitors were a Sydney 'inner city super-group" of sorts, putting out a sound not too far removed from that of The Doors. This hybrid of POST-PUNK, power pop and garage psyche was nothing short of sensational at the time and still stands the test of time today. The highlight of the EP is the crunching 'Brother John'.

28

⦿ 'Golden Brown', 'Strange Little Girl', 'Always the Sun', 'Peaches', 'No More Heroes', 'Nice & Sleazy'...Sound familiar? All big hits, all great songs, all written and sung by Hugh

Cornwell, the songwriter behind The Stranglers, who was born August 28, 1949. When future historians of music draw up a list of the movers and shakers who changed the modern musical landscape, there will be no doubt that Hugh Cornwell's name will be prominent amongst them. As a pioneering musician, songwriter, and performer, his pervasive influence persists in the record collections of music aficionados, across this spinning globe's radio waves, and on stages around the world. Hugh's presence is unquestionable. As leader of The Stranglers, Hugh was the main songwriter of all the band's most memorable songs across ten stellar albums. After their 1977 debut, *Rattus Norvegicus*, follow-up albums *No More Heroes, Black and White, The Raven* and *The Gospel According to The Meninblack* consolidated Cornwell's stature as a unique songwriter and musician. His lyrics to 'Golden Brown', from the *La Folie* album, and their multiple meanings, is a songwriting masterclass. Fast forward to 2024, and Hugh's latest studio album, *Moments of Madness*, is an album of acute, pithy, and witty observations which has received widespread critical acclaim. Hugh is still touring with a full band internationally to sell-out crowds, exciting the fans with iconic Stranglers hits and his own extensive classic back catalogue.

Hugh Cornwell by Petra Gall/ Hugh Cornwell by Roch Parisien

GOALLLLLLLLLL
HUGH CORNWELL
(Original Singer, Guitarist and Songwriter from The Stranglers)

When I was signed to A&M records in America, they had access to the owner's box of New York Cosmos football team. I was invited to a game one day and travelled out by limo to the Yankee Stadium in the Bronx. We were going to be late for the start of the game, but I was told: *"Don't worry, Pele won't score until we get there"*.

We arrived and took our seats in the owner's box, which is very prominent in the stadium.

Pele looked up, saw that the owner's box had filled up, and promptly scored immediately!

○ DEVO came to the world on August 28, 1978. This was via the debut album release *Q: Are We Not Men? A: We Are Devo!*. This album is quite simply STUNNING. It'll make you laugh; it'll make you think, and it makes you want to dance like Elaine Benes. This was the start of 'Devolution', a package containing everything from the NEW WAVE of 'Sloppy' and 'Satisfaction' to the punk of 'Uncontrollable Urge' and 'Too Much Paranoias'. There's even a return to '60s-style pop with 'Come Back Jonee'. though a bit more frenetic. The album highlight tracks are what amounts to Devo's manifesto: the tune 'Jocko Homo' and, of course 'Mongoloid', the story of a mentally handicapped man who fits in so well with society that nobody is aware of his condition. Majorly produced by Brian Eno and to a lesser degree by David Bowie, the album is a landmark in rock music. Constructed around the use of synthesizers it's fair to say it was seminal in the development of NEW WAVE in the USA and synthpop internationally. Quirky, off-beat, strange and at times brash, DEVO were able to garner a huge following through being 'alternate'. Can it be categorised? Not likely. Eno's production value showed how DEVO used synthesizers as an important textural element; this innovation began to lay the groundwork for the synthpop explosion that would follow very shortly. Eno was able, through high-level production, to give the album a lo-fi sound, all the while maintaining an irreverent, infectious quality. There was an almost excruciating tension in the speed of their jerky, jumpy rhythms, outstripping Talking Heads or XTC and other similarly quirky NEW WAVErs of the time. *Q: Are We Not Men? A: We Are Devo!* revived the absurdist social satire of Frank Zappa & The Mothers of Invention; the album didn't grab everybody, but Devo's appeal became broader a couple of years later with the release of *Freedom of Choice*. Loopy and weird, it's an album that goes beyond musical enjoyment to an experience of enlightenment. This is the kind of music that transcends entertainment and becomes a lifestyle. The stuff legends are made from!

⦿ You could not complain on August 28, 1978! Why? Because The Rich Kids one and only album, *Ghosts of Princes in Towers*, was available! Leaving the Sex Pistols was a great career move for Glen Matlock, contrary to Malcolm McLaren's claim that he was sacked because he liked The Beatles, Glen explained he'd had enough of the "*shit from John (Lydon)*". This led to the line-up of Matlock, Midge Ure, Rusty Egan and Steve New for an album produced by Mick Ronson that is power-pop of the highest order. Go no further than 'Rich Kids', 'Put You in the Picture' and Midge's glorious anthem 'Marching Men' when looking for highlights. Rich Kids were largely missed back in 1978; nonetheless this album ensures they won't be forgotten.

⦿ Roaring Boys released their *self-titled* first album in 1986. The band originated from Cambridge University, England, and was guided by Billy Gaffy, manager of Rod Stewart. Signed to CBS Records, they launched their sole album featuring two singles, 'Every Second of the Day' and the popular 'House of Stone', influenced by Roxy and Icehouse. While showcasing potential in new romantic synthpop, some songs veered into mainstream rock, lacking overall consistency.

29

⦿ The first full-length album, *One Afternoon in a Hot Air Balloon*, by the Sheffield POST-PUNK unit Artery, was available in 1983. It was a follow-up to the well-received mini-LP *Oceans* of 1982. Overall, here the sound is markedly different from the dark, moody output they were known for. The album had a broad spectrum of feels, and that can be attributed to the fact that all the music is composed by the creative keyboardist Christopher Hendrick, who reportedly was only a member during the recording of this album.

⦿ This day in 1980 saw the release of the debut single 'I Belong to Nobody' b/w 'The Stranger' by Flaming Hands on the Phantom Records label. The core of the band was songwriter and guitarist Jeff Sullivan and the sensational vocalist Julie Mostyn. Julie's vocal inflection has often been compared to that of Patti Smith; easy to see why - the mix of Flaming Hands' NEW WAVE/soul/psyche suited her perfectly. The band always played to packed out venues and played support of The Clash for the highly acclaimed seven-night stint at Sydney's Capitol Theatre in 1982.

⦿ Elizabeth Fraser, referred to by many as Liz, was born in 1963 in Grangemouth, Scotland. She is best known as the ethereal vocalist for Cocteau Twins, a band where her voice took centre stage, creating a mesmerizing texture that transcended the lyrics. Liz's songwriting for The Cocteau's varied from straightforward English to the enchanting sounds of glossolalia or abstract mouth music. Interestingly, Liz admitted to using foreign words without fully understanding their meaning, finding their significance only as she sang them. Her voice was not just an instrument but a force that required immense physical exertion, as she sang against the wall of sound in many Cocteau Twins songs, describing it as an "*endurance test*". It was at a local club called the Nash where Liz's path crossed with Robin Guthrie. One night in 1980, Guthrie spotted the 17-year-old Fraser dancing on the floor and invited her to join the band he had formed with his friend Will Heggie. Accepting his offer, Liz found not only a bandmate but also a kindred spirit. She looked up to Guthrie and credited him as an essential part of her journey, saying, "*I could never have done it without him*". The unique sound they developed together was a result of their chemistry, which became even more potent when Simon Raymonde, a Londoner, replaced Heggie. Throughout her career, Liz has collaborated with various artists, including Ian McCulloch, Massive Attack, and Peter Gabriel. She even lent her vocals to two pieces featured in the first two *Lord of the Rings* movies. Her meticulous approach to production techniques and the layering of vocals added a majestic texture to all of Cocteau Twins' recordings. Liz possesses a voice and style that are simply unparalleled. In 2022, Elizabeth embarked on her latest project, a collaboration *self-titled* EP with Damon Reece under the name Sun's Signature. This showcases her ongoing creativity and dedication to her craft.

Liz Fraser by Petra Gall

● Michael John "Mick" Harvey was born in 1958 in Rochester, Australia. Mick is a founding member of The Boys Next Door, The Birthday Party and Nick Cave and the Bad Seeds. He was also a member of Crime and The City Solution on and off from 1985 to 1991. From 1995 to date, he has released 9 solo albums and contributed to over a dozen soundtracks and produced numerous albums by a multitude of artists. A very talented musician, he has been listed as playing guitar, bass, piano, organ, synthesizer, xylophone, glockenspiel, harmonica, and drums/percussion, as well as being a vocalist. In early 1988 Nick Cave asked each of the Bad Seeds, past and present, to choose their favourite tracks from the ten studio albums, and then their lists would be discussed until a final list was produced. Only Mick responded, and it is his listing, unchanged, that makes up *The Best of Nick Cave & The Bad Seeds*.

ATHENS - SEPTEMBER 1982
MICK HARVEY
(The Boys Next Door-The Birthday Party, Nick Cave & The Bad Seeds)

Shortly before recording *The Bad Seed* EP, we were to play our first show as a 4-piece. An offer had come from Athens to be part of a 3-day event, with The Birthday Party, The Fall and New Order to be featured on consecutive nights with a local support band.

At the time, it was a very exotic place to play, Athens. Perhaps it still is. The dictatorship had finished in 1974, but the country was still coming out of its shell. Before this 3-day event, the only "NEW WAVE" bands to have visited Greece were The Police and Talking Heads – both of whom were already pretty much mainstream. So, this was to be a watershed moment for the Greeks – and us!!

We flew in from East Berlin via Budapest on Malev Airlines. An arduous journey which first required one to transit a short stretch of East Germany from Rudow to Schönefeld Airport in East Berlin and then connect through Budapest. By the time we arrived, we were all pretty wiped out, and Nick had an escort of a couple of German girls he'd been talking to on the plane. I don't think they had any idea who he was, nor did they have any real interest in him; they just thought they could blag a free place to stay for the night. We checked into the aptly named Xenophon Hotel. Some kind of argument ensued, as someone was probably meant to be sharing Nick's room (as was still the custom in those days), and someone might have called him a c%$†. It might have been me. Or it might have been Tracy. I really don't remember. Whoever it was, Nick became very angry and stormed off into the night; it hardly needs to be said that he was already quite drunk.

Sometime in the early morning we were woken to be informed that Nick had spent some of the previous night in an Athens jail. They had let him out after he sobered up a bit. At least, this is the way I remember it. Nick had become so disoriented by his night on the tiles that he was convinced he was still in Berlin and had persisted in asking the police and then anyone he met (Greeks with no English, no doubt) how to get to the U-Bahn station in Kreuzberg called Kottbusser Tor. By pure luck he found himself sitting on a bench at Katopatissia Station as the dawn broke. He looked up to see the sign for Xenophon Hotel and stumbled home.

News of Nick's night out reached the Athens newspapers, and from all the feedback we received, the firm opinion had been reached that our show was to be the wild one of the three. We were deemed to be the "punk" energy and anger release event of the extended weekend. And our show was the first night.

And so, it came to pass. We had never played to 5,000 people at our own headline show before, but that's what was about to happen, and, in the lead-up to going on stage, it was like a Rolling Stones show. The crowd were chanting and clapping, and to be honest, the whole atmosphere was quite alien to us. Despite being used to high levels of enthusiasm from our audiences, we were not used to being treated like rock stars – quite the contrary, in fact. I'm sure the others were "ready for action" as usual, but for me it was my first full show playing drums, ever, and it was also our first show in months AND much of the material was new.

It mattered little. The crowd simply erupted every time we started an even moderately fast number, and between songs there was just non-stop yelling and screaming. Somewhere towards the middle of the show, the security became heavy-handed with the unruly enthusiasts at the front, which led to the inevitable intervention from Nick, followed by the security's inevitable abandonment of their duties. And, of course, on seeing this intervention, the audience went nuts and instigated the inevitable stage invasion. It must have been near the end of the set, actually, as we could not have continued like that for long.

Some short time later we left the stage and were called back for an encore. We really didn't have anything up our sleeves, so we did a pretty much unrehearsed version of 'Funhouse' while Jim Thirlwell (Foetus) joined us on saxophone. I'm still unsure as to whether or not he can play saxophone. Of course, that particular piece could go on for some time, as it is a linear song with no chord changes. A version recorded to a cassette at the mixing desk made it onto the live album, which was released in the 90s. During the start of this song, the side doors of the basketball arena were pushed open, and another thousand or so people forced their way into the concert. The stage was reinvaded. The whole night was some kind of delirious, ecstatic outpouring for the Athenians.

Members of The Fall and New Order were apparently watching from the back of the room. We were told the latter were terrified by what they saw. I can only imagine The Fall would have been laughing their heads off.

The next 2 nights were much less out of control, but on the last night there was one more memorable incident at the end of the New Order set. Seemingly frustrated or bored or simply having a psychotic incident, lead singer Bernard Albrecht took hold of his melodica, lined up the head height of the audience and hurled it underarm into the crowd as hard as he could. He then turned and walked off the stage. 30 seconds later, a man was escorted from the crowd about 20 metres from the stage past where I was sitting in the wings, bleeding profusely from his head as the band played on. It was hard to tell exactly where he was bleeding from as he passed me in the front row of the side stalls; there was blood everywhere. I had seen Mr. Albrecht in May the previous year at a show in London bashing his head repeatedly with his melodica as some kind of finale to their show. Perhaps he should have persisted with meaninglessly harming himself instead of tonight's utilization of the melodica as an implement to inflict injury on an innocent member of the audience. This was one of the most callous, pointless, and stupid acts I've ever seen by a member of a band. Maybe THE most pointless and stupid, and I can assure you, I've seen plenty of dumb things over the years.

◉ The inaugural Rock On Tyne festival took place on August 29, 1981, at the esteemed Gateshead International Stadium. The lineup for this momentous event included renowned acts such as U2, Ian Dury & The Blockheads, Huang Chung, The Polecats, Doll by Doll, Pauline Murray, and Elvis Costello & The Attractions.

◉ Jim Skafish is a Chicago, USA, resident born in East Chicago, Indiana, on August 29 in 1956. Jim is best known as the frontman for the punk/new wave outfit that bore his name. Jim formed Skafish in January 1976, presenting influences of Bowie and the New York Dolls, yet with substance that belied categorisation. At that time in Chicago, Skafish were breaking new ground and earned a reputation for spellbinding performances. Jim was classically trained and, in his youth, was viewed as somewhat of a protégé, venturing into jazz and forming a trio when only 16 years of age. Over the years, Skafish has been an enduring headline act and opened for the likes of Iggy Pop and the Stranglers. With 6 albums to date, Jim has recently rereleased an expanded set of Skafish's second album, *Conversation*, that was originally out on I.R.S.

BATHING SUITS, BEER BOTTLES, A GUN: THE BIRTH OF CHICAGO PUNK
JIM SKAFISH
(Skafish)

A year after I graduated high school, I was added as the keyboardist to the hard rock power trio White Lightnin' in 1975. The band consisted of guitarist/vocalist Donald Kinsey, who had played lead guitar for Bob Marley and Peter Tosh; bassist/vocalist Busta Cherry Jones, who had been in UK Sharks (and later went on to play with the expanded live Talking Heads lineup, as well as Eno); and drummer/vocalist Woody Kinsey, who had drummed for blues great Albert King.

We were preparing to record the group's second album at Bob Marley's studio in Jamaica but ended up cutting tracks at Chicago Recording Company (CRC Studios). Midway through the sessions, the band's label, Island Records, halted the project, and White Lightnin' ended up disbanding, never to reform.

In addition to the White Lightnin' project, I enrolled at the American Conservatory of Music in Chicago to get a music degree in the fall of 1975. A few years prior, I studied jazz piano there with international jazz legend Willie Pickens while I was still in high school. Since I had been classically trained from age 6, I was torn between getting a proper music degree and my all-consuming desire to create my own music. Attending music school was no fun for me because it was far too conservative and restrictive. So, I left the American Conservatory of Music after only two weeks of attendance.

Everything seemed up in the air nearing the end of 1975, except that I felt an obsessive, unshakeable passion to form my own band. I was hell-bent on creating music I believed would change everything, and no one could convince me otherwise.

At that time, the Chicago scene was staid, conservative, and safe, dominated by singer-songwriters, folk music, jazz, blues, and rock music. When I decided to form my own group, I intended to drop a metaphorical atom bomb on Chicago. However, I was in no way prepared for the events that would follow.

I was 19 when I formed the first incarnation of my band in January 1976. A month later, we debuted when we crashed an audition night at Club B'Ginnings, a well-known music venue in the Chicagoland area.

Chicago-based journalist/author Bob Kurson captured the moment in his story, Spirit Lives On For Chicago Punk Pioneers, that appeared in the Chicago Sun-Times years later. His perspective really helped to shed light on what happened back in the day.

Kurson wrote, 'Jimmy Skafish broke Punk in Chicago in 1976 during an audition night at the now-defunct B'Ginnings nightclub in Schaumburg. Wearing an old lady's one-piece bathing suit and a purple page-boy haircut, Skafish sprinkled the crowd with holy water while spewing bilious, fury-driven songs that terrified the entirely unsuspecting crowd. It was the first of countless performances at which the audience would literally desire to kill the outrageous singer, but it was also the birth of punk in Chicago'.

After our first gig, we did another show and embarked on an intense rehearsal schedule, and I continued to compose. We went into the studio and cut four songs that summer, which some considered to be the first punk, NEW WAVE, and alternative recordings by a Chicago artist. In part, those tracks helped me to get management, which I desperately wanted and needed. Scott Cameron, who managed Muddy Waters, Willie Dixon, Stan Kenton, and Mighty Joe Young, came to my basement to see my band play. He later recalled that he was taken aback and intrigued by what he heard and saw. Scott also had a copy of the tapes we recently recorded, and by early fall, he decided to take on the task of managing me.

The first order of business was to put a Chicago area tour together. The tour, which went from November through December 1976, opened on November 7th, again at Club B'Ginnings. Cheap Trick were in attendance, and to my absolute surprise, they immediately became fans and supporters of my band.

During that tour, there were many violent reactions from the audience. In addition to my appearance, I was singing about such topics as gay bashing, being a societal and family misfit, graphic bullying, fat shaming, gender confusion, paedophilia, and attacking/satirising organised religion. Needless to say, this didn't always go over too well.

But one show of that tour really stands out. We played a club in Rockford, Illinois, the hometown of Cheap Trick, and guitarist Rick Nielsen was there to see us. During our performance, the audience's hatred was about to volcanically erupt.

As the audience locked arms and began approaching the stage as a singularly focused mob in lockstep to attack my band, Rick Nielsen, wearing a fur coat and a baseball cap, stood with his back at the front of the stage, eye to eye with the mob. He was holding a beer bottle firmly above his head, ready to strike the audience if they didn't retreat. Surprisingly and luckily, the audience did back off. I'm certain it wasn't due to Rick's intimidating physicality but his celebrity status. And we made it out of Rockford alive that night.

Since Cheap Trick were at so many of my early shows, they had a clear, accurate perspective of what happened back in the day. They talked about those recollections when they wrote the liner notes for my 2008 retrospective, *What's This? 1976-1979*, saying, *"Unpredictable, over the top, with life-or-death conviction and reckless abandon, Skafish created punk, new wave, and alternative rock in Chicago"*.

By the end of our 1976 tour, we had started to develop an audience (even in the midst of all the violence directed against us), and we were getting local press in Chicago. There were no other punk bands or anything like us on the scene at the time. We were flying solo.

On February 4th, 1977, we were booked to open for the 1950s nostalgia act Sha Na Na at the Arie Crown Theatre in Chicago. On the day of the show, there was a full moon, one of the Chicago "L" trains crashed, and I could feel a sense of morbidity in the air.

During our set, the audience of 6000 were hurling things at the stage, giving us the middle finger, and screaming obscenities while mothers covered their children's eyes.

The climax of our set came when I was stripping down to an old lady's old-fashioned one-piece bathing suit with a babushka and applying lipstick to my face. My band was jamming an atonal onslaught that sounded like Sun Ra meets Ornette Coleman. As I lumbered back up on my feet after completing my strip, we were preparing to launch into 'Sign of the Cross', one of the first blatantly blasphemous rock songs, which I wrote in 1976.

As the tension built, the audience was starting to break into a full out-and-out riot while rushing toward the stage to attack my band. Right as the audience was climbing on stage, the Chicago Police rushed on stage and immediately stopped the show.

This may have been luckier than I thought in the adrenaline rush of that moment. That's because my friend and filmmaker, Dan Winner, who was filming part of the show from the audience, saw someone right behind him pointing a gun at me on stage preparing to pull the trigger at the moment the Chicago Police halted the show! After the show, I remember feeling completely "out of it" for about a week. Billboard magazine was there to review our performance and later that month, gave us our first national press.

Two months after the Sha Na Na show, we were the first Chicago punk band to perform at CBGB in New York when we played with The Mumps on April 12 & 13. Those shows went well, except for a nasty review in Variety. CBGB owner Hilly Kristal was warm, down-to-earth, and welcoming toward me, which I appreciated. The Ramones were in attendance at the shows, and that's when I first met Joey Ramone. Subsequently, my band ended up doing two shows with the Ramones in Chicago.

When we got back to Chicago, the kids were rioting at our shows that summer – but this time, in a celebratory way. My audience size increased, and they got what I was saying. They saw themselves in me, and I saw myself in them. This was a fan base somewhat made up of misfits, family rejects, and queer and transgender people who did not fit into the rigid confines of conformist society. Some of the audience came from La Mere Vipere, Chicago's first punk dance club, which converted from being a gay bar that May.

My band's shows were providing an outlet and cathartic release for members of the audience. A perfect example of this was when a group of kids dressed as nuns and priests rushed the stage during 'Sign of the Cross' and staged a mock orgy. I loved it!

That summer reached its pinnacle when I did my 21st birthday show on August 29 at Ratso's in Chicago, just four weeks after having emergency knee surgery from a dancing accident. The audience was fanatically frenzied and even tried to bust down the dressing room door after the show.

Looking back, I'm grateful that I had the vision, courage, musicians, management, and the force of personality to make this happen. I could use many words to describe the experience: 'obsessive', 'all-consuming', 'perilous', 'life-threatening', 'exhilarating', 'depressing', and the list could go on. Certainly, it was an incredibly turbulent ride going through it all – and it's still emotional for me to recall those days.

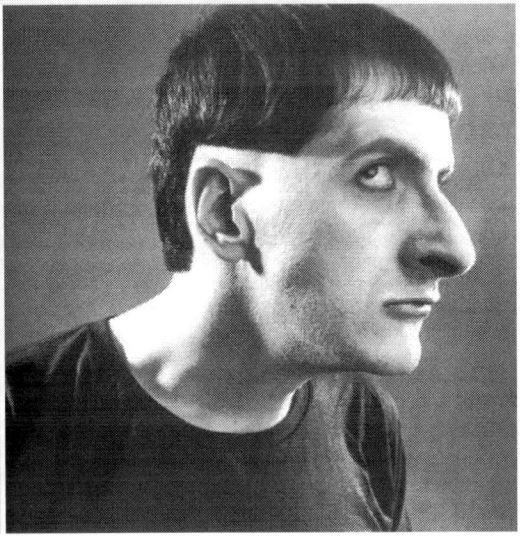

Jim Skafish by permission

30

● Graham 'Buzz' Bidstrup was born in Adelaide, Australia in 1952. Highly regarded as a drummer, Buzz is also well known as a producer, manager, and songwriter, one of whom being The Angels' chart-topper 'No Secrets'. Buzz's musical pedigree is that of Australian rock 'royalty', having worked with The Angels, GANGgajang, Jimmy Barnes, The Party Boys, Richard Clapton & Australian Crawl, among a host of others. Putting those aside, he's also produced albums for the likes of The Riptides, The Numbers, The Stetsons, Nathan Cavaleri and Diana Anaid. In 1999 he began managing renowned Australian Indigenous performer Jimmy Little, co-creating The Jimmy Little Foundation & Uncle Jimmy's Thumbs Up. Buzz has been CEO of both charities for over 20 years, providing preventative health programs for Indigenous Australians in remote and regional areas.

AN INTERVIEW WITH GRAHAM "BUZZ" BIDSTRUP
(The Angels, GANGgajang)

Hey Buzz, You were born and grew up in Adelaide, South Australia is that right and joined The Angels in mid-1976, what were you doing before The Angels?

Yes, born and bred in SA and started playing in bands when I was 12. I learned a bit of piano and also played a right-handed guitar upside down (as I'm a lefty)… At 14 I was asked to join Fahrenheit 451 a band of older guys who were 18 – 20. They were all UK migrants so they had heaps of relatives who kept arriving in Adelaide with clothes and music from the UK, so we played lots of Beatles, Stones, Hollies and Top 40 hits of the time. We played 4-

5 nights a week from 8pm – 12pm, so we knew over 100 songs…We wrote a few of our own songs and used to play them saying they were covers as the venues did not want original music. I went to the UK in 1974 and got too stoned to do too much except I did jam with a band called Diversions…. the singer was Lene Lovich who had a big hit a couple of years later with Lucky Number. Missed that one!

On the first album 'The Angels' you are listed as Buzz Throckman, were you hiding from the law?

It was a joke name dreamed up in a hotel room in Copenhagen. I used it because I wasn't sure how long I'd stay with 'The Keystone Angels' who had a bit of a joke reputation in some Adelaide music circles, especially the ones Chris Bailey hung out in.

The Angels soon grew to be one of Australia's major acts and you departed in 1981 before the release of the 5th album 'Night Attack'. What drove you leave when they were at their peak? Did the extensive USA tour and touring in general take its toll?

Well, it was the culmination of a few things. I became very aware that all the advances for our touring and recording were being repaid only from the sales of records, so while the band had a debt of half a million, the songwriting royalties were paid through without any deductions. A lot of the songs were created in a group effort, and despite trying to get some kind of compensation for the time and effort non-writers put in to create them, all requests were denied. As soon as I knew it was not going to happen, I looked for something to do that would be more equitable. In the end I got a better deal put in front of me.

So, you got into production work, to date attaining a vast resume at the controls for the likes of Smokey Dawson, Nathan Cavaleri, Diana Anaid and The Riptides and you've also been associated with several movies and TV drama, 'Sweet and Sour' was a cracker, what work in that regard are you most proud of?

I did a lot of work with film composer Cameron Allan, writing and producing film soundtracks, and that led me to the ABC series *Sweet and Sour*. I've been involved in the production of about 60 albums; I mixed the Hoodoo Gurus' debut single 'Leilani' and recorded and mixed a Tiny Tim record!

I read that you learnt your way around the studio under the wings of Harry Vanda & George Young, they aren't just music legends in Australia but world-wide. What was that like? Did you have pinch yourself to see that it was really happening?

Yes, I was very fortunate to be signed to Alberts and be mentored by George and Harry. They were wonderful to the band, and George was especially interested in my desire to learn to engineer and produce. I just watched and asked questions, and when there was downtime in Studio 2 (which was always empty at night), Mark Opitz, the engineer for Face to Face and No Exit, would set me up there with a synth, a guitar and a mic, and that is how I learnt to operate the board and record in the studio. Later, when George knew I could power it up and down safely, he gave me a key to the studio so I could go in there any time it was free. I recorded lots of demos, including 5 tracks for Flowers that got them their deal, and many other tracks, including some with the guys from Mi-Sex. After I left The Angels, I worked pretty much exclusively at EMI Studios 301 for three years and further honed my recording skills. I also worked on Paradise, Festival and my favourite, Rhinoceros, where we mixed GANGgajang's debut album.

Back into live work. In the '80s you were a member of The Party Boys, The Numbers and GANGgajang among others. The '80s was such a vibrant time in Australia, is there a venue, gig or event that stands out for you then and why?

Many venues bring back memories: The Flix at Manly, run by Larry Danielson, who would go on to fame as the "Woolworths Bomber"; the Comb and Cutter (blood in the gutter); and that pub on Canterbury Road run by Lady Humphries. There she would be at the end of the night in the middle of the room in her twin set and pearls, standing in all the broken glass, beer and vomit that 1000 Angels patrons had just created.

We know you as a drummer but are you proficient with other instruments? As drummers go who is your favourite and why?

Yes, I play some guitar (I'm left-handed, so I play it upside down) and keys. I taught myself about programming synthesizers and computers in the early-'80s. For favourite drummers I can't go past Ringo, Charlie, Bonzo and Joe Morello from Dave Brubeck. There are heaps of engineers, musicians, producers and bands I admire, including Daniel Lanois, George Martin, Rick Rubin and heaps more!

There was a departure from 'rock' and you became the manager for Jimmy Little, and the CEO of the 'Uncle Jimmy - Thumbs Up Organization', how did that come about and what is the aim of the organization?

It came about through my association with Mark Callaghan, who is the singer of GANGgajang, and at the time of the release of Jimmy's 1999 record *Messenger*, he was the A&R manager of Festival Records. I was asked to help look after Jimmy during the release of that record, and it grew into a wonderful friendship that grew exponentially into the Jimmy Little Foundation and Thumbs Up! Basically, we use music and video to engage school children, and residents in remote Indigenous communities to deliver nutrition and healthy lifestyle education. Our motto is 'Good Tucker – Long Life'. I was part of a team that devised the Good Tucker App, a simple way to pick healthy foods and drinks by reading bar codes. We have worked in over 50 communities all across the top end over the past 20 years.

The world is in the grip of COVID-19 and the whole music industry has been turned upside-down; touring is almost a forgotten concept. What is Buzz doing to keep his hand in music?

I'm very lucky because I have a studio at home and all the instruments I need to make music, so that is always going on. I also run Thumbs Up! from a home office, so that is something I work on pretty much every day. I taught myself how to edit on Final Cut and that is a skill I love using. I've been making little films, and my wife and fellow GANG founding member Kayellen Bee are always being creative in music and written word.

Away from 'Thumbs Up' and the music industry, what do you do to keep your juices flowing. And lastly, if I was to come to your place to have a cuppa what music would you turning me onto?

I enjoy gardening; it is quite therapeutic and a great way to get a bit of exercise. I like eating fresh vegetables I've grown myself, and my citrus is pretty good too. We would listen to a range of music; it really depends on what kind of mood I'm in, but it is always good to play new material to music fans and get some feedback.

Interesting stuff, thanks so much Buzz. It's a pleasure to have you part of this.

◉ Martin Jackson was born in 1955, in Manchester, England. As a drummer, he has played with several bands from Manchester, and arguably his most successful stint was with Magazine in 1978 as a formation member. He played on Magazine's debut *Real Life* album and Swing Out Sister's 1986 hit 'Breakout'. Martin also has stints with The Freshies, The Chameleons, Broken Glass, Design 9, and The Durutti Column.

⊙ In 1985, the underrated jangle pop band One Thousand Violins formed in Sheffield, England, and released their first single, 'Halcyon Days', on August 30. The band took their name from an Orange Juice lyric. While the A-side 'Halcyon Days' was joyful pop, it was the melancholic B-side 'Like One Thousand Violins' that listeners voted into John Peel's BBC Radio 1 top 50 songs of 1985. One Thousand Violins had a brief 4-year lifespan, represented on the Cherry Red compilation *Halcyon Days: Complete Recordings 1985-1987*.

⊙ Our Daughter's Wedding, aka ODW, had their debut single 'Nightlife' b/w 'Raincoats & Silverwear' available in 1980. ODW got their name from the section divider in a greeting-card display stand; they were out of New York City and were forerunners in American synthpop. ODW became famed for their next single, 'Lawnchairs', and were clearly influenced by the likes of Kraftwerk, UNITS and OMD. ODW are an interesting listen but not essential

⊙ Section 25 released their debut album, *Always Now*, in 1981 through Factory Records (Cat. Number FACT 45). Not quite up there with their famous labelmates and friends Joy Division, but it's still one of the important albums of POST-PUNK. The production team of Martin Hannett and Ian Curtis bring to the fore the atmospheric and unnerving edginess of Section 25. This first outing highlights an incredibly powerful rhythm section; the crisp, clear drum sound provided by Vin Cassidy and bass by his brother Larry was fresh in a world that had had a myriad of Joy Division clones. It's fair to say that Section 25 existed in some weird space between Joy Division and bass-laden Wire. If you're looking for a companion outing from the Factory stable and one of the lesser-known bands POST-PUNK bands, then Section 25 is sure to satisfy. One must make mention of the artwork and packaging of the original release; it's one of the most exquisitely designed sleeves ever, with ornate marble printing elegantly hiding within a solid yellow folding envelope. 'New Horizon' and 'Babies in the Bardo' provide immense aural pleasure through their atmospherics.

⊙ Lynda Nutter was born in 1955, in Henley, England. As a child with her father as a bricklayer, Lynda immigrated to Australia on the '10 Pound Pom scheme'. Growing up in Perth, aged 23ish, Lynda's first band was Johnnie Natural and the All-Star Rhythm Aces featuring The Naturalettes, but Lynda first became known to a wider audience as the vocalist and sometime percussionist with The Dugites out of Perth, Western Australia. The Dugites (a dugite is a venomous Western Australian snake) formed in 1978, becoming hugely successful on the strength of some great songs written mainly by keyboardist Peter Crosbie. The *self-titled* debut album produced by Bob Andrews went gold in Australia, reaching No.22 on the charts. It held the song 'Gay Guys', oddly banned by commercial radio but the first song played on the new national youth radio station 2JJJ, aka Triple Jay. After three albums and a handful of excellent singles and as a tour support to Elton John, The Dugites folded in 1984. Today Lynda is an advocate for indigenous people's issues.

⊙ John Peel, aka John Robert Parker Ravenscroft, OBE, was born August 30, 1939, in Heswall, England. John was an English disc jockey, radio presenter, record producer and journalist who won numerous broadcasting awards. His greatest attribute was bringing unknown and often unsigned bands to the public via his radio programme and through his pre-recorded Peel Sessions performances. He was quite often the first person to play new releases and became one of the very few DJs around the globe that left a mark. Peel gave new, upcoming independent bands a spin when no one else would; in this manner, he introduced hundreds of artists that would never be heard. John was also the longest-serving of the original BBC Radio 1 DJs; he broadcast regularly from 1967 until his passing on October 25, 2004.

31

● Deaf School's debut album, *2nd Honeymoon*, was on the shelves August 31, 1976. Proto-POST-PUNK and NEW WAVE & prior to punk, these darlings of the Liverpool music scene had elements of the day's glam and art rock. Many say they were ahead of their time; echoing Roxy Music, they have been quoted by many as influential, most notably by Suggs from Madness. The tunes in this set remain attractive through their quirky, catchy design. Check it out to see what many felt filled a gap in Liverpool between The Beatles and early POST-PUNK NEW WAVers. Many state that the only bands that mattered out of Liverpool were The Beatles and Deaf School.

● The Happy Mondays' first single release, 'Freaky Dancin'', b/w 'The Egg', was on the store shelves on this day in 1986. The A-side just bounces along; it's very bright and the band is very tight, a far removal from the *Forty Five* EP of 1985, where, like many of their contemporaries, they had that Joy Division influence. To the B-Side, and here they are that little bit atmospheric and melodic. Together they are both quite infectious; the groove certainly is dancefloor orientated.

● On this day in 1981 you'd find Level 42's *self-titled* debut album on record store shelves. "*NEW WAVE-fusion-jazz-funk*" is how bass-playing vocalist Mark King once described the band, and he wasn't far wrong. Arguably, this is the best set by this band, more musical than vocal; here they had a rather unique sound at the time. Listen close, and King's slap-bass skills shine through. The blend of bass, sparkling keyboards and ever so subtle guitar makes for a really smooth album. From here, Level 42 became very synth-driven and won another audience altogether.

● Gina Schock was born in 1957 in Baltimore, Maryland, USA. Best known as the drummer for the Go-Go's, Gina also appeared occasionally with the Norwegian band A-ha. With the Go-Go's, Gina was a driving force behind the band's musical creativity, urging them to "push boundaries". Gina took out a lawsuit against the other members for unpaid royalties, and after two years of court wrangling, there was a settlement in 1999. During the court battle, Gina formed the band House of Schock, releasing a *self-titled* album in 1988. Differences were overcome, and Gina was part of subsequent reformations and farewell tours.

● Glenn Tilbrook was born in London, England, in 1957. Glenn teamed with co-lyricist/guitarist Chris Difford to lead Squeeze (known as UK Squeeze in Australia). These two guys are often quoted as being the 'Lennon and McCartney of the '80s'. They generated a smart, sophisticated brand of pop but sadly never achieved commercial success commensurate with the accolades bestowed upon them. John Cale co-produced the debut LP *Cool for Cats* with the band, which was released in 1978; it held a minor hit, 'Take Me, I'm Yours', but it was 1979's 'Cool for Cats', the album's title track, that was Squeeze's UK and international breakthrough. Their songs, 'Cool for Cats', 'Pulling Mussels (From the Shell)', 'Tempted', and 'Black Coffee in Bed', remain timeless classics.

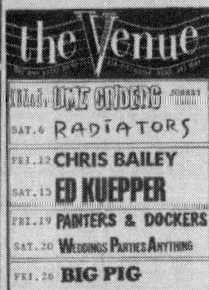

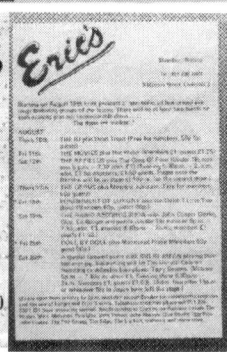

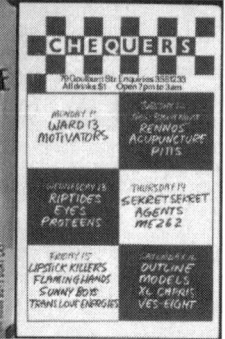

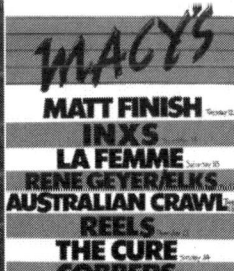

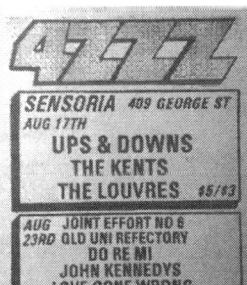

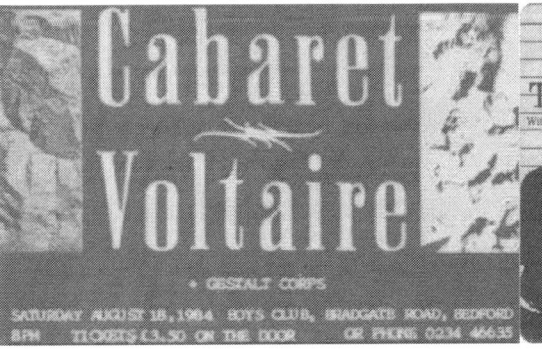
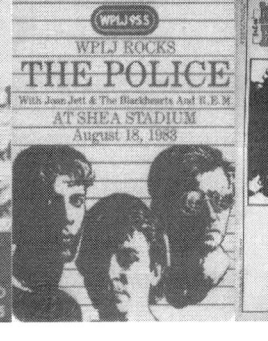

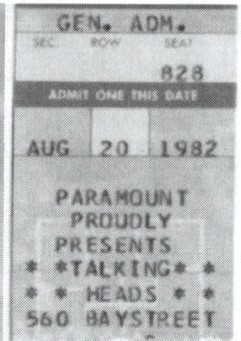

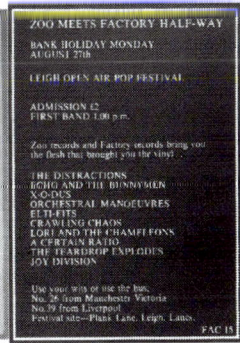

1

◉ Glenn Campling was born in 1957. Glenn's musical origins stem from a grand vintage, he was a teenage fan of Bowie, T Rex, and Roxy Music. Glenn attended Northampton Art College where he befriended Daniel Ash. Not actually a musician, he became the backline engineer and roadie of Bauhaus, starting with lugging the band's gear in his Morris Minor! After tinkering with sounds and ideas it was in late 1981 Daniel suggested that they form Tones On Tail. Glenn's part in this seminal band should not be underrated and neither should their impact or influence. Their huge dance-floor club hit 'Go!' for example, was created around Glenn's killer bass line, later sampled by Moby for his top ten smash of the same name. Tones disbanded in late 1984 with Ash and Kevin Haskins forming Love and Rockets with former Bauhaus bassist David J. After a lengthy hiatus from music, Glenn re-surfaced in 2008 with the previously unreleased set Black and Whole. In 2011 Glenn teamed up with solo artist Mark Garner to form Lone Station who with a unique style and sound released the debut album *Dark Matter*. Their 2nd album *Machine* was released as a download only in 2018. Then in 2021 there was the very limited-edition remix vinyl album titled *Altered State*.

FUN, FUN, FUN....
GLENN CAMPLING
(Tones On Tail, Bauhaus roadie)

Tones On Tail began as a Daniel Ash solo project at a time when he felt a need for release from the confines of the well-established gothic band Bauhaus. He invited me to contribute, simply because I owned a magnificent Dr. Rhythm drum machine. I've always loved drum and bass, so it was with that we found something, a new toy to play with.

Our first 4 track EP was *self-titled* and released on 4AD in 1982. To our amazement we hit somewhere in the top 100 of the NME alternative chart, so we carried on having fun in between Bauhaus tours.

My fun moment was during a Bauhaus mini tour in Japan when a bunch of kids came up to me, knowing only I was crew, asked me for band autographs. On telling them my contact name, I found myself surrounded by Japanese fans asking for MY autograph.

Blessed were the Eighties. Fun, fun, fun....

◉ In 1990, The Cure came up with an unconventional method to premiere their newly reimagined album *Mixed Up*. Along with DJs Mike Halloran and Lewis Largent, the band hijacked the airwaves by setting up their own makeshift radio station within the Fiction Records headquarters. For one night only, they took over the playlist, spinning an eclectic mix of tunes from the likes of The Human League, De La Soul, Dinosaur Jr., Jimi Hendrix, and of course their own remixed tracks from Mixed Up, giving listeners a taste of what was to come from their revamped record. It was an ingenious guerrilla marketing tactic that allowed The Cure to creatively subvert the traditional album rollout.

◉ Bruce Foxton, born in Woking, England in 1955, was a member of The Jam where he played bass and occasionally sang lead vocals. He took the spotlight on tracks such as 'News of the World' & 'David Watts'. In 1983, he achieved success with his own hit single, 'Freak'. Later, in mid-'91, he received a call from Jake Burns of Stiff Little Fingers, which led to him playing bass with them for the next fifteen years. Simultaneously, Bruce engaged in various other projects, including Sharp, where he teamed up once again with former Jam drummer Rick Buckler for a single called 'Entertain Me'. In 2006, Foxton left Stiff Little Fingers and joined Casbah Club, alongside Simon Townshend (brother of Pete Townshend) and Mark Brzezicki and Bruce Watson of Big Country. They embarked on a tour supporting The Who in the UK the following year, which planted the seeds for the formation of From The Jam. Presently, Bruce continues to tour with From The Jam, consistently receiving rave reviews at every performance.

● September 1, 1979, saw the debut release, the single 'Back to Nature' by Fad Gadget aka Frank Tovey. Minimalist synthesis made for what was rather distinctive music at the time. Fad Gadget was at the forefront of synthpop, and as live performer at the time Tovey had a high degree of shock value. The early performances were quite outrageous, wild, and unique, he was well known for covering his naked body in shaving cream, and often ending with the man injuring himself.

Fad Gadget aka Frank Tovey by Petra Gall

Kukl by Petra Gall

● Kukl from Iceland released their debut LP, *The Eye*, on September 1, 1984. Released on One Little Indian and Crass Records, this lineup was an excellent vehicle for Björk's striking and instantly recognisable vocal delivery. Bjork slots in perfectly with the band; they are primal, haunting, dark, and adventurous. It is plainly evident that they have been listening to The Banshees; it's not easy listening, but rewarding for those with an open ear to *The Eye*.

● On September 1, 1983, Mick Jones, the lead guitarist with The Clash, was sacked! His band partners Joe Strummer and Paul Simonon believed Mick had 'drifted apart' from the original idea of the group (whatever that was)! Mick went on to form General Public with Ranking Roger and Dave Wakeling of The Beat and then formed Big Audio Dynamite, which became later known as Big Audio Dynamite II, and then Big Audio, and/or even often abbreviated to BAD.

● David Lawrence "Dave" Mason was born in 1954, in Dubbo, Australia. Dave was/is the founding mainstay/frontman of the new-wave pop group, The Reels. Dave wrote and sang their hit singles, 'Love Will Find a Way', 'Prefab Heart', 'After the News', 'Shout and

Deliver' and 'Quasimodo's Dream'. 'Quasimodo's Dream' has been listed by APRA at No.10 of their Top 30 Australian songs of all time!

⊙ Lindy Green was born September 1, 1960, in Sydney, Australia. Always a fervent follower of Sydney's inner-city music scene, through the '80s and '90s, she was the lead and backing vocalist of numerous bands, rubbing shoulders on stage and in the studio with some of Australia's seminal musicians. Lindy fronted The Siberian Allstars alongside Richard Burgman (The Sunnyboys, The Saints), Phil Hall (Dropbears, Sardine v, Lime Spiders), Michael Knapp (Dropbears) and Carol Anderson (The Girlfriends, Box of Fish).

MY CITY OF SYDNEY
LINDY GREEN
(Amazing Woolloomooloosers, Siberian Allstars et.al)

I have always loved music. I remember watching Uptight in '67, Happening '68 and Happening '69. I used to write down, memorise and sing along to every pop song I liked. The first single I ever bought (at age 8) was The Beatles' 'Hey Jude', but I ultimately preferred the rockier B-side, 'Revolution'. I still have it!

One of my first crushes was Jim Keays of The Masters Apprentices. By 1970 (age 10), I was doing my own, singing-into-my-hairbrush version of 'Turn Up Your Radio'. The '70s was a kind of awakening for me. Having left the insular Eastern Suburbs to attend Sydney Girls High, my friend group broadened beyond anything I might've expected or recognised. It was a time when Sharpies were at every concert and "Becca loves Chook" was graffitied on every bus. These Sharpie chicks were at SGHS along with hippies and surfy chicks. I somehow managed to befriend them all.

I started going to Bondi Lifesaver at the tender age of 13. It was easy to change the three to an eight on my school bus pass, which is what we used as ID. I saw AC/DC, XL Capris, Skyhooks, Split Enz, Mother Goose, The La De Da's, Buffalo, Rose Tattoo, Finch, Band of Light and literally hundreds of both local and OS touring bands there.

By the late '70s there was an eruption in the local music scene, a real shift towards something new; it felt like we were pioneers venturing into an intoxicating (pun intended) new world. Venues were sprouting up all over in the inner city and surrounds, and live bands played every single night of the week, often 4 or 5 at a single venue. The first influx of Kiwis was arriving, and they brought with them their own particular brand of alternative music. Toy Love was a stand-out.

I became entrenched in this scene, seeing bands every night, a different band every night. The Civic Hotel hosted Radio Birdman, Lipstick Killers and early Mental as Anything had a regular weekly residency. French's Tavern – Thought Criminals, Bedhogs, Sekret Sekret. The Heritage Kings Cross - X, Socket Set. Sydney Trade Union Club – Craven Fops, Flaming Hands, Dropbears and oh so many more bands and venues thrived in the period. These bands/people became my tribe.

Between leaving school in '77 and exploring the globe in '79, I worked in a then-renowned Mr Christian shoe store in Bondi Junction. I sang and listened to music all day in the shop, often visited by my musician friends. One particular day, I was singing away as usual, and a man came in, looked at shoes for a while and then introduced himself to me as Chris Gilbey and asked if I'd like to record a pop song? Without hesitation, there was an enthusiastic reply of *"YES!"*

There was an arranged studio time for the following evening after I finished work. I was excited and nervous at the same time and asked my friend and workmate Edith to accompany me.

We arrived at the studio, and Chris played me the song. I must admit, I didn't love it, I entered the vocal booth and recorded a take anyway. In hindsight it was recorded incredibly quickly, with only a few overdubs and drop-ins until he seemed happy with the result. Edith watched on.

We then talked about image, release dates and possible tours. It was at that point that I became uncomfortable with his vision for me. I already had an alternative and edgy self-image. We were pretty much heading in opposite directions; he saw pink, fluffy and fairy wings.... I saw black, tartan and piercings. It soon became apparent that I was unwilling to wear the pink dress and was entrenched in another, less mainstream, indie scene.

Chris seemed frustrated and turned to Edith and asked her if she'd be willing to "*have a go*". She asked me if I minded. I said, "*Go for it*," and she did. The song key was changed, and Edith Bliss, who was already wearing a pink dress and had magnificent blonde curls, successfully recorded and released 'If It's Love You Want'. In 1979 the single peaked at No.24 on the Australian chart! Edith went on to have two more top 100 singles and a career as a TV presenter. Sadly, Edith passed away in 2012.

O Douglas McCarthy was born in 1966 in London, England. Douglas is best known as the vocalist-guitarist and keyboardist with Nitzer Ebb. Born in Barking, Douglas has gone by many names as part of a wide array of recording and live performance outfits, such as Fixmer/McCarthy, Nitzer Ebb Produkt, Homotronic, Sunz of Ishen, and DJMREX. Nitzer Ebb was established in 1982 in Chelmsford, Essex; they were the grittier cousins of label-mates and touring partners Depeche Mode, and they harnessed pulsing rhythms and synths. Nitzer Ebb went to sell over 100,000 units in the USA and, after releasing 6 albums, folded in 1995. They undertook a reunion in 2006 and, through to 2023, have been appearing sporadically.

O The debut *self-titled* album by Sunnyboys was released in 1981. During the early '80s Sunnyboys were arguably Australia's premier power pop/POST-PUNK band. The Oxley brothers Jeremy (vocals-guitar) and Peter (vocals-bass), Richard Burgman (vocals-guitar), and Bil Bilson (drums) went into the studio with producer, the legendary Lobby Loyde, to create one of the great Australian albums. They successfully combined the NEW WAVE energy of the early '80s with the guitar sounds of the '60s, a sound that was faithful to that of The Remains or The Sonics. The music is uncomplicated, yet sophisticated, pure and simple guitar based, yet each song is catchy, infectious, and oozing with energy. 'Alone With You', 'I Can't Talk To You' and 'Happy Man' sit as classic power-pop tunes.

O The album *Gone to Earth*, which is often claimed as David Sylvian's pinnacle, was released in 1986. This piece of atmospheric pop-chic all but defies description. The songs here are stunning, of rare beauty, and tied up with emotion in the playing. Sylvian seems to reach inside himself to such great depths of thought and creativity. Rarely does one find music of such emotional grace and delicate power. Superbly produced by David and Steve Nye, every note by Robert Fripp, Bill Nelson, Kenny Wheeler, Mel Collins, and fellow musicians are meticulously placed. It's easy to see the design was to remain subdued and understated; the music itself complements this, shifting atmospheres seamlessly moving from jazz to ambient to avant-garde to meditative rock, and all around, always perfectly setting and setting off Sylvian's lyrics. The moods evoked here are done to perfection, and the songs here are ones which are true landmarks. Sublime.

O September 1, 1979, and Talking Heads appeared at the Edinburgh Rock Festival. Also, on the bill were Squeeze, The Undertones, Van Morrison and Steel Pulse. The Talking Heads set list was 'Artists Only', 'Stay Hungry', 'Cities', 'Paper', 'Mind', 'Heaven', 'The Book I Read', 'Air', 'Warning Sign', 'Memories Can't Wait' and 'Psycho Killer'.

2

◉ Front 242 released their debut album *Geography* in 1982. This album kicked off a career for one of the most consistent industrial bands of the 1980s; more electronically based than their contemporaries, Front 242 were a premier exponent of industrial or EBM. The songs on *Geography* are rather short and have a much coarser, edgier, more dynamic sound than later releases. There are layers of analogue synth beeps, beats and tinkly bonks and what must have been painstaking production work. The track 'Art & Strategy' calls Throbbing Gristle or early Human League. 'GVDT', a song reminiscent of Kraftwerk, is almost synthpop, with some great vocal production loops and sampling. Overall, comparisons to Depeche Mode or Cabaret Voltaire are unavoidable; nonetheless, it remains very engaging listening. There's a lot of variation throughout and some very inventive ideas laid down. These guys spent a lot of time melding together a very innovative and largely missed album.

◉ Grauzone released their influential *self-titled* debut album in 1981, featuring the track 'Eisbar' (polar bear). The album blends NEW WAVE, techno, electronica and is reminiscent of John Foxx. Even though they hailed from Bern, Switzerland, Grauzone was a key player in the early Neue Deutsche Welle (New German Wave) movement. The band, led by the Eicher brothers Martin and Stephan, along with Marco Repetto on drums and GT on bass, garnered a significant following despite only performing ten live shows. For fans of unconventional electronica, this album is a must-have, showcasing a timeless appeal.

◉ Michael Rother was born in Hamburg, West Germany, in 1950. Michael is an electronica expert and the mastermind behind acts like Harmonia and Neu!. A little-known fact is that he added guitar to Kraftwerk in the early '70s. Michael was instrumental in bringing to the fore art-rock, Krautrock, and experimental electronica through the '70s; his work with trance, electro-pop, and experimental art-rock is largely unheralded but nonetheless legendary. He pioneered hypnotic and intense beats, as well as spacious, avant-garde sounds that characterised the work of Neu!, a band that was a major inspiration for techno & synthpop artists of the NEW WAVE. OMD, Depeche Mode and Human League have all quoted him as an influence.

◉ In 1981, Slow Children, a synthpop pair consisting of Pal Shazar on vocals and Andrew Chinich on guitar, made their debut with the release of the *self-titled* album. The album features a delightful mix of power pop guitar infused with drum machine, sequencers, and synths, all set to an unrelenting tempo. Although the track listings for the album in both the UK and the USA were slightly different, 'President I Am' on both records starts with a Devo-like sound before transitioning to something reminiscent of Lene Lovich or Clare Grogan. The music on this album is cleverly crafted and sure to appeal to those with a discerning ear.

3

◉ Captain Sensible, aka Raymond Burns, released his debut solo album, *Women and Captains First*, in 1982 through A&M Records. It's been said that the bassline from the song 'Wot' is worth the price for this album alone! Well, not quite. With the help of the producer, New Musik's Tony Mansfield, the Captain put out an album of definitely likeable and very well-arranged collection of pop songs. In 1982 he reached No.1 in the UK with a cover of Rogers and Hammerstein's 'Happy Talk', a song from the musical *South Pacific*; it is included on this LP. The record was somewhat a vast departure from the music of The Damned, the band he was presently with. His exploration into pop was delectable; through MOR concepts ranging from country western to cabaret, we got a very entertaining set. Fun.

Sept 3 Susanne Freytag by Petra Gall

○ Susanne Freytag was born in Düsseldorf, West Germany, in 1957. She played a crucial role as an original member of Propaganda and has remained a part of the group through its Channel's various reformations. Initially, the lineup consisted of Susanne Freytag, Ralf Dörper, and Andreas Thein, and later Claudia Brücken joined in 1983. However, it wasn't until 1985, after Thein's departure, that Michael Mertens joined the band, solidifying the lineup and leading to the release of their remarkable debut single, 'Dr Mabuse'. Presently, Susanne occasionally appears in X-Propaganda alongside Claudia Brücken while also pursuing a career as a counsellor and psychotherapist. She holds a diploma in psychotherapeutic counselling and a clinical diploma in transactional analysis psychotherapy from the Metanoia Institute in London. Susanne's passion for learning is evident in her dedication to her studies.

○ Andy Griffith, aka Griff, was born in 1961 in Melbourne, Australia. Andy grew up with musical heroes like Alice Cooper and David Bowie, with a passion for their theatrics. Andy took inspiration from those theatrics when at high school, even though he was not able to play an instrument, and turned on the thrash of 'punk' and formed Gothic Farmyard with schoolmates. The band had a manifesto: 'To create the greatest rock concert in the world.' He drew people's attention 'by yelling at them'. The band moved from school to Melbourne's pub/club scene in the early '80s. The movement brought in experimentalism and a D.I.Y. attitude whereby they released and distributed cassette tapes themselves. Years later Andy became the multi-award-winning author of the Treehouse series of books, selling over 10 million copies in Australia alone!

THE BIRTHDAY PARTY
ANDY GRIFFITH
(Gothic Farmyard & Author)

If anybody ever asks me, "*What's the best gig you ever went to?*", I don't need any time to think about it. I go straight back to a hot summer's night at the Astor Theatre in 1982, where my friends and I have come to see a dream lineup featuring The Go-Betweens, The Laughing Clowns and our local heroes, who had recently returned from a gruelling but ultimately triumphant stint in the UK, The Birthday Party.

The art deco opulence of the Astor is a perfect venue for this gathering of Australian POST-PUNK rock royalty. We are happy to trade the blinding heat of the late-afternoon sun for the relative dark and cool of the theatre and, armed with plastic pots of beer, position ourselves in front of the stage.

The Go-Betweens open the night with a solid show of brilliant idiosyncratic pop. They are followed by Ed Kuepper, who leads his post-Saints outfit, The Laughing Clowns, through a jazzy horn-drenched wig-out. By the time the Laughing Clowns has finished, the theatre is packed and hot, but we do our best to keep our fluids up by skolling as many plastic pots of beer as we can manage before The Birthday Party stagger and stumble onto the stage.

The laconic Phil Calvert takes his place on drums. Next to him, guitarist Mick Harvey watches proceedings like a hawk. Tracy Pew, in full cowboy gear and a ten-gallon hat, starts playing a menacingly slow and ominous bass line from his low-slung guitar. The audience holds its collective breath as Nick Cave, sporting an impossibly large mane of spiky jet-black hair, shuffles forward and snarls, *"King Ink strolls into town; he sniffs around ..."*

And then, right on cue, the elegantly wasted Roland Howard, looking like a Kafkaesque half-man, half-insect, rends the air with a dramatic blast of atonal guitar. We are instantly mesmerised and, as one, push closer to the front in a hot, seething mass. There's a thrilling primal energy in the air, as if they've opened a portal to another dimension, and nobody, especially not the band, is quite sure what might come out or what might happen next.

Nick stalks the stage, grunting, howling, and ranting like a deranged preacher. It's more like an exorcism than a concert. Rowland's vampiric face is shrouded in smoke from the ever-present cigarette dangling from his lip as he coaxes ever more unearthly sounds from his guitar. Tracy Pew contorts himself into a backbend and thrusts his bass to the roof as 'King Ink' gives way to the crazed jungle beat of 'Zoo Music Girl', the hilariously over-the-top violence of 'Scrapyard' and the fiery chaos of 'Blast Off'. And that was just the beginning! At one point Nick leans out from the stage over the audience supported by the heaving mass of bodies, grasps my outstretched hand, looks into my eyes and screams directly into my face. When my daughter recently asked me for the top five greatest moments of my life, she was a little put out to discover that this moment made the list but her birth didn't.

After bludgeoning the audience into blissful submission one last time with a cacophonous encore of 'Dead Joe', they leave the stage, and we all stagger out, dazed and exhilarated, and congregate in large groups in the middle of Chapel Street. At least I think it was at Chapel Street. The world didn't seem quite the same anymore. And neither were we!

⊙ Paul Haig was born in 1960, in Edinburgh, Scotland. Paul is best known as a singer-songwriter who was originally a member of the 1980s POST-PUNK band Josef K. Between 1979 and 1981, Josef K recorded five singles and one album, *The Only Fun in Town*, with Haig being the lead vocalist, before splitting in August 1982. Paul signed with Belgian independent label Les Disques Du Crépuscule, launching a solo career and releasing a few albums with them before, in 1999, taking on the name Rhythm of Life Organisation and creating his own record label, Rhythm of Life, on which he released seven albums. Through the '80s, Haig went on to work with such talents as Alan Rankine, Billy Mackenzie, Cabaret Voltaire, among others.

⊙ Alan Hempsall was born in 1960 in Levenshulme, Manchester. In late 1977 Alan was a founding member of Crispy Ambulance; his band members comprised guitarist Robert Davenport, Keith Darbyshire (bass) and Gary Madeley (drums). They self-released their first single, 'From the Cradle to the Grave', in April 1980; this led them to signing with Factory Records and releasing the 10" single 'Unsightly and Serene'. During this time Alan famously stood in for Joy Division's Ian Curtis, who was recovering from a suicide attempt; the unexpected performance was not appreciated by the punters, and they rioted. They followed up with an album and two 12" singles on Factory/Benelux before disbanding in October 1982. The four members augmented their lineup with an extra guitarist and percussionist and reemerged under the new name Ram Ram Kino, releasing one 12" on PTV's Temple

Records Ram Ram Kino disbanded in autumn 1987, and it was at this time that Alan spent a short time playing Brazilian street music in Inner Sense Percussion, a large informal samba ensemble. Alan left Inner Sense in 1990 to pursue a professional career and bring up a family. He spent many years in advertising sales. In 2016 Alan joined forces with solo electronic music composer Dave Clarkson to form Scissorgun, a two-piece electronic group with Alan on vocals and guitar and Dave Clarkson taking on synths and rhythms. To date they have released three albums. Alan also plays guitar in a three-piece improv rock group called Karpadia, which occasionally plays at small venues in Manchester.

AMBULANCE TO HOLLAND
ALAN HEMPSALL
(Crispy Ambulance)

My moment of clarity came at a relatively early age. Not everyone has them, admittedly, but mine happened in summer 1972. The Alice Cooper Band had just reached No.1 with 'School's Out', and the moment I saw them on Top of the Pops was when I realised that this was the game for me. It wasn't just the image; it was the sound of the guitars, the sheer chutzpah. From then on, I obsessed about music in general and forming bands in particular.

After several half-baked projects and false starts, I was older, and once school was done with, I had the time to form Crispy Ambulance in autumn 1977 with Robert Davenport, an old school friend who I'd known since late primary school. Robert had picked up a cheap Woolworth's guitar, so we just needed bass and drums. Keith Darbyshire had been another school friend who had recently bought a Fender Precision bass, perhaps with half an eye on what me and Rob were doing. Keith joined in February 1978, whereupon we embarked on a flurry of gigs in local venues with a series of temporary drummers. It was during this nascent period that we played a very messy gig at Band on the Wall. Unbeknownst to us, Rob Gretton and Joy Division were in the audience. They'd just popped in off spec after a rehearsal. They liked us and made a note of the name.

Gary Madeley joined on drums in January 1979, and the line-up was finally stable. Shortly after this I had a chance meeting with Bernard Sumner (Joy Division guitarist), during which it became apparent that they'd all seen us and enjoyed it and that we should come along and meet the others. This was how the Factory Records connection happened – pure serendipity.

Within a few weeks we supported Joy Division at The Factory, and Rob Gretton took us under his wing, giving advice on releasing your own single and suchlike.

So, we followed the formula, borrowed money, got the job done, got Rough Trade distribution on board, John Peel, etc. Once that was done, I remembered a soft approach from 4AD which I was excited about. Within about 3 days of telling Bernard, suddenly we were being offered a deal on Factory. We took the deal with Factory. Famously, Factory deals were usually done on no more than a handshake anyway, so to my mind that fluidity cut both ways.

Looking back on it now, it's clear what Rob Gretton and the band were doing. When they were just starting out and struggling, they were helped and advised by Pete Shelley and Richard Boon of New Hormones and The Beach Club. They were merely doing as they'd been done to, so to speak. That trickle-down philosophy is one of the reasons the Factory Records story is one that people keep coming back to, notwithstanding the fact that it's just a bloody funny story.

Factory Records used to regularly have bands on tour together doing Factory nights all over Europe and even the USA. It was on one such European jaunt that Crispy Ambulance were pitched in with Section 25 for a string of around ten gigs in Holland and Belgium, with one in Bochum, Germany. Section 25 consisted of brothers Larry and Vin Cassidy on bass and drums, respectively. There was a new percussionist called John who'd been parachuted in after the recent sudden departure of long-standing guitarist Paul Wiggin. Also with the section was their perennial sound engineer, Jon Hirst. Jon and I had bonded over a mutual love of hash, so I knew I'd be in good company with him in tow. Section 25 had been on Factory a little longer than us and took charge of the transport hire, a 12-seater minibus with the back row of seats removed to carry our amps and guitars. A ferry from Harwich to Hook of Holland had been booked for eleven at night. Rather oddly, despite having been in what was then called the Common Market for some years, we still needed to have all the paperwork required for the dreaded carnet. These documents had all the records for our equipment, as was necessary to come into and out of various places, serial numbers, dates of purchase, etc. It all needed verifying and stamping along the way.

During the drive to the ferry terminal, it became apparent that we'd underestimated the amount of time the journey was going to take, and as the daylight dimmed gradually outside, so the mood inside the van did likewise. With Vin behind the wheel and Larry riding next to him up front, Vin was ideally placed to bear the brunt of his elder sibling's mounting anger. If we missed this ferry, then whilst some of the tour might be salvageable, the first couple of dates would be down the pan. All very embarrassing and not what we want at all.

Arriving at Harwich Ferry Terminal a few minutes before 11pm to find the parking area empty with large sections in darkness, we drove straight up to the customs and passports offices to find them closed. Larry was now in a blind screaming panic, whilst I and the rest of the Crispies were sat glumly in the back and more than a little resigned to our seemingly inevitable fate. Vin jumped out of the van and ran toward a side gate which was closed but unlocked and swung it open. We drove through the barrier and onto the main concourse, again empty aside from a lot of large rubber cones arranged in a zigzag, which Vin proceeded to drive through, scattering them like bouncy skittles, on towards the far side and what we assumed would be the water's edge. Suddenly a large barrier with fencing on either side appeared in front of us, and things, again, looked very bleak indeed. Then out of the darkness, a man in a uniform came running over to apprehend us. It was way too dark to tell what kind of uniform he was wearing, but surely now we were screwed. Then, to our collective astonishment, he simply unlocked the barrier and let us through with a cheery wave. "*Bloody customs hold you up, did they?*" he asked. "*You know it*", fired back Vin.

As we rounded the last bend, we could see the silhouette of our lone departing ferry around three hundred yards away. To our horror, the tailgate was in the early stages of rising up to close. Vin floored the throttle whilst Larry bawled, "*BIB YOUR FOOKIN' 'ORN!*" Pointless, surely? Vin thumped the horn repeatedly, whereupon the tailgate simply stopped and then slowly lowered back down to let us on board.

Once we'd boarded, we got out of the van in stunned disbelief at the events of the last five minutes and headed straight for the bar where a scene from the last days of Rome was playing out. In no time the drink was flowing, and having bought some whisky from duty free, we repaired to our bunk cabins and fired up Jon's pipe. We'd picked up a hairy hippy bloke from Northern Ireland at the bar. We were so smashed we didn't even mind when he produced a penny whistle from somewhere. We fell asleep to the sound of old Irish rebel songs.

We disembarked in Holland the next morning, and our first port of call was to be Rotterdam. We weren't supposed to be there, but that was where we were going. Our first gig was in Eindhoven, but Jon had a friend in Rotterdam who dealt in cocaine. The idea was to collect a couple of bags for the duration. That's how we found ourselves in a swanky downtown apartment with picture windows, art on the walls and a view of the city. We were entertained by a casual, urbane but rather shadowy individual. It all reminded me a bit of Turner's flat in Performance.

The rest of the tour went like clockwork, albeit in a bit of a blur. Section 25's new recruit, John, hadn't taken well to tour life at all, and by day three we had no option but to get him on the first plane out of there. I'd spoken with him the day before, and he seemed to be a nervous wreck, disconsolate. Gary stood in on percussion for the remainder of the tour. Aside from this setback, there were the usual tour high jinks: getting thrown out of nightclubs, getting snowed in, beer for breakfast, spliffs all afternoon, and gak all night. Wally from the Minny Pops, who was acting as Factory's Benelux Mr Fix-It, had kindly strung all the dates together and was probably super patient looking back. The major plus was that despite being pumped full of drugs, both bands were at the top of their game, and the music is what we're all there for, after all. Lucky, really. Thankfully the tour was recorded extensively with a direct feed from the mixing desk, and there are several examples of this on Crispy Ambulance's live compilation Fin.

The most amazing part was even though we passed through multiple borders on the tour and had our carnet (goods passport) checked every time, nobody noticed or questioned the empty space where our departure stamps and signatures should have been. Not even once.

● On this day in 1981 we saw GOD. *God* was the first album (a double) by Rip Rig + Panic. Essentially not having lead-vocalist to call on, the band recruited Neneh Cherry and Ari Up, and the ladies did great! *God* is a powerful combination of jazz-funk, free-jazz, POST-PUNK, and avant-garde. The melting pot result is bewildering; on what is overall an instrumental album, it's evident that much of the music was improvised around preconceived ideas. It can be compared somewhat to The Pop Group's *Y* album, though much jazzier. Takes a few listens but is well worthwhile.

● In 1982, Scritti Politti made their debut in the music scene with *Songs to Remember*, an album that stood out among others due to its distinctive blend of NEW WAVE, pop, reggae, funk, soul, and jazz, accompanied by thought-provoking lyrics deeply rooted in political philosophy. What sets this album apart is its ability to succeed where many others have fallen short, thanks to the impeccable production and the seamless fusion of genres, resulting in an extraordinary collection of songs. The synergy among the different elements simply clicks.

● The Wake's debut album, *Harmony*, was released in 1982 on the Factory label, number Fact 60. The band, formed in Glasgow, Scotland, in 1981, was a perfect fit for Factory Records, known for their dark, gloomy POST-PUNK sound. However, they later transitioned to a brighter dream-pop style. Drawing comparisons to New Order circa *Movement*, especially with the track 'The Old Men', The Wake's music features multiple elaborate guitar riffs, metronomic drumming, and understated dreamy melodies. They are one of the lesser-known Factory stablemates, but their music is worth a listen.

4

● Martin Chambers was born in 1951 in Hereford, England. Martin was a founding member and the drummer of The Pretenders. He wrote and sang backing vocals and lead vocals on the song 'Fast or Slow (The Law's the Law)', which was the B-side of both the singles '2000 Miles' and 'Show Me'. In addition to Martin, the original band line-up was Chrissie Hynde (vocals/guitar), James Honeyman-Scott (guitar/vocals/keyboards), and Pete Farndon (bass guitar/vocals). Hynde and Chambers are the only two surviving original members; he has served two separate tenures with the group. His last recording with them was the 2020 album *Hate for Sale*.

⦿ Mike Joyce, the drummer of The Smiths, left the band in 1987, stating that his role in the group had been fulfilled. Following his departure, Joyce sued Johnny Marr and Morrissey for an equal portion of performance and recording royalties. He successfully won the case and received approximately £1,000,000 in compensation.

⦿ Sydney band The Sparklers through Phantom Records, released their debut single 'Overworking' b/w 'Baby Baby' in 1986. The Sparklers came together after the dissolution of Sunnyboys, when ex-embers Peter Oxley (bass) and Bil Bilson (drums) teamed with Peter's sister Melanie (vox) and Lime Spiders member Gerard Corben (guitar) & Chris Abrahams to produce some superb infectious NEW WAVE pop.

5

⦿ The debut album by the Comsat Angels, *Waiting for A Miracle*, was released in 1980. Recorded in under 2 weeks, this is an impressive opener for a little heralded band. The Comsats should be mentioned alongside Echo and the Bunnymen, Teardrop Explodes, and Psychedelic Furs at every turn. Always somewhat moody and dramatic in the Joy Division vein, one can't help seeing a little of U2 in them, a band that they toured with prior to the album's release. The music is far from complicated yet has an infectious melodic quality. 'Independence Day' gave the band its greatest commercial success, a truly great POST-PUNK song and by far the best track on the album. It holds a hook that's far away from the minimalist feel of the rest of the tracks and that customary Comsat style chant. Value.

⦿ Sal Solo, aka Christopher Scott Stevens, was born in 1961 in Hatfield, Hertfordshire, England. As a vocalist, he started his career with an obscure band called The News, who only released one 7" single on GTO Records. In 1979 Sal fronted Classix Nouveaux, who released three albums. In 1984 he gained respect as the singer for the French space rock group Roketz, who were one of the most popular bands in Italy.

THAT'S PRETTY MUCH THE STORY
SAL SOLO
(Classix Nouveaux)

It was 1977, and my band at that time, The News, had a record deal with the guy responsible for the Bay City Rollers. He didn't like that I started to employ distorted guitars and talked about punk. While in the studio with Jonathon King producing, he said, "*You haven't given up your day jobs, have you?*" And sure enough, we were soon dumped from the label.

I decided I'd had enough with my own band, so I should join someone else's. After scanning the Melody Maker ads, I ended up at auditions with some punk band who had the original Police guitarist, Henry Padovani, and then X-Ray Spex, sans the recently departed Poly Styrene. Half of Spex wanted another guy, and half wanted me. That day the drummer, BP (Paul Hurding), said, "*I want to form a band with you,*" and so it was. Two Spex and two News. Our first gig in 1979, at the Music Machine in Camden, was billed Classix Nouveaux 'ex X-Ray Spex'. Punk was kind of on the way out in London at that point, but an army of punks soon became our dedicated following. However, on the social scene, we were attending clubs where people dressed as peacocks, and George O'Dowd, Marilyn, and others who later became Haysi Fantayzee and Sigue Sigue Sputnik could be seen any night. One time, the future Boy George told me he could sing and proceeded to offer a spontaneous a cappella. Another time, he told me that a theatrical place in Covent Garden was closing down, so I should get over there quick. The Dracula cloak and 'King And I' pants in our first video were the result.

I think the band were together about a year when a music paper had a letter mentioning New Romantics as the new thing and naming the bands Ultravox, Japan, and Classix Nouveaux. Soon new bands from Birmingham, Liverpool, and all over wanted to be in on this London movement. The New Romantic thing was mostly about looks and not so much a specific sound. In the clubs, electronic music (such as it was at the time) with a generous helping of Bowie, the typical diet was – The Human League, Kraftwerk & OMD et al. We did a few gigs opening for Ultravox, and I have to say they deserve the title of originators of that musical genre more than anyone else. We also did a couple of gigs opening for Gary Glitter at his low point, and the audience were spitting at him and hurling insults. One time at The Lyceum, Boy George was in our dressing room, and he wanted one of us to go with him to knock on Gary Glitter's door. George was not yet famous but still just as flamboyant.

Our manager was most interested in seeing the world, so we ended up touring places like Bangkok, Finland and India. Lots of alcoholism in Scandinavia. Once in Finland, an audience member climbed up the stage to present me with a sausage; I was never sure about the meaning of that!

Our biggest success came in Poland. It was still communist, and the government decided that some Western music might keep the youth happy. I guess nobody else was home at EMI that day, so we got the gig. Usually when you arrive in a country for the first time, you must work at becoming known. But we arrived at Warsaw airport to screaming crowds. We looked back to see if someone famous was on our plane! In Communist times, the government controlled the only TV, radio, and magazines, so when they decided to bring us, they made sure we were plastered everywhere. To this day, we still have a dedicated Polish following.

With all the foreign tours, maybe we neglected our native UK a little. Our first chart single, 'Guilty', reached the mid-40s, then the BBC had an electricians' strike, and with no Top of the Pops for 6 weeks, we didn't get the extra push needed to propel it further. On our second album, *La Verite*, EMI decided to take us under their wing and devise a special promotional campaign. They saw us as aliens, and so indeed, the next video had us floating about in space with props from the movie Alien. Our drummer cried when he saw it, as it was so awful! After that they almost gave up on us, but there was a live Saturday night TV show with Chris Tarrant and Lenny Henry. Slade didn't want to sing live, so I said I would. I guess the vision of a screaming Nosferatu caught the imagination of the public, and the next thing, we were in the Top 20.

By this time, the New Romantic thing had more or less died. Culture Club and Duran were doing happy pop songs, Spandau were white soul boys, and Japan had gone a more ambient route. For our third album, *Secret*, we wanted to get a good producer, and so it was between David Lord, who had worked with Peter Gabriel, and the guy who did The Thompson Twins. The latter won out, and we got super American producer Alex Sadkin, who is to this day the best producer I ever worked with. About 6 weeks into the project, EMI said we'd already blown the whole budget. Alex said he was never given a budget; otherwise, he would not have agreed. So, EMI used the promotions budget on the recording and dumped us as soon as the album was released with no promotion.

That's pretty much the story of Classix Nouveaux in the '80s!

◉ Released On September 5, 1982, *Zimmerkampf* was the debut album from Canadian synthpop outfit Moev. The vocals of Madeline Morris are reminiscent of Toyah, and the scratchy guitar that of the Factory label bands, but mostly competent synthpop. There's a lot of tinkly bonk going on here, but not that much that would remain solid in one's memory. The fragile 'Cracked Mirror', with its minimalist naive feel, sits as one of the better tracks, bubbly techno with a degree of elegance.

6

◉ *Happy Birthday*, the debut album and the single of the same name by Scots Altered Images, were released a month apart in 1981. The single from August went to No.2 in the UK, and the September-released album went to No.26. Clare Grogan & Co. were all that a NEW WAVE outfit should be; they had an irreverent attitude, where they seemed to cross bubblegum pop with a goth-tinged POST-PUNK. Aside from the single, vocally, comparisons can be drawn to Yoko Ono; musically, there's a high degree of ingenious adventure.

◉ On September 6, 1980, The Jam reached the top spot on the UK singles chart with 'Start!' b/w 'Liza Radley'. This was their second No.1 hit, following 'Going Underground' b/w 'Dreams of Children'. The song was taken from their fifth album, *Sound Affects*. Instead of just covering The Beatles like they did with The Kinks, The Jam borrowed directly. Everything from the bassline to the stereo mix was reminiscent of The Beatles' song 'Taxman'. It was a bold move, but a tribute to one of their biggest influences. Interestingly, George Harrison didn't take legal action against them, despite having previously lost a plagiarism case with his 'My Sweet Lord' versus The Chiffons' 'He's So Fine'.

◉ Here's a song that represents the height of NEW WAVE pop music. Cyndi Lauper's rendition of 'Girls Just Wanna Have Fun' is on par with hits by other leading NEW WAVE acts like The Go-Go's and Bananarama. Lauper embodied the energy, vibrancy, and playfulness of 1980s pop culture. She had an endearing personality, a powerful singing voice, and the ability to thrill audiences. When she released this debut cover of Robert Hazard's song in 1983, Lauper was prepared to showcase her uniqueness. The tune became an international smash, reaching No.2 on both sides of the Atlantic. Lauper showed she was no ordinary pop star.

◉ The electronic music group Vice Versa released their first EP record called *Music 4* in 1979 on Neutron Records. Vice Versa was formed in 1977 by Stephen Singleton, Mark White, Ian Garth, and David Sydenham. Singleton and Sydenham played synthesizers, Garth played guitar and some synthesizers, and later White became the vocalist. Singleton is also recognised for playing saxophone on early recordings by the band ABC.

7

◉ The smash hit 'Video Killed the Radio Star' was released in 1979. The video clip of that song was the first shown on the debut broadcast of MTV when the US channel started broadcasting at 12:01 AM on August 1, 1981. The single went No.1 in over a dozen countries. The Buggles were English studio maestros Trevor Horn and Geoff Downes and at the time also included Bruce Woolley, who co-wrote the hit song.

◉ Benjamin Bossi was born in San Francisco, California, in 1953. Benjamin was the saxophonist of Romeo Void and an integral component in the band's biggest singles. His driving sax solos, influenced by jazz and funk, were what made the songs 'A Girl in Trouble (Is a Temporary Thing)' and the 1982 hit 'Never Say Never' stand out. Romeo Void disbanded in February of 1985 after a European tour, and by that time, Benjamin was experiencing the beginnings of tinnitus, which troubled him for the rest of his life. He continued to play with a variety of musicians in the Bay Area, moved to NYC, living in Manhattan and working at what was then called the Museum of Radio and Television and playing in music projects there. Benjamin died on December 13, 2022, due to complications from Alzheimer's disease.

O Christine Ellen Hynde was born in 1951 in Akron, Ohio, USA. In 1973, Chrissie moved to London, where she worked at Malcolm McLaren and Vivienne Westwood's punk-themed clothing boutique called SEX. She also worked as a house cleaner and even did the cleaning in Keith Richards' home. In 1978, along with Pete Farndon, James Honeyman-Scott, and Martin Chambers, she formed the band The Pretenders. Together with Honeyman-Scott, she wrote the group's first hit song, 'Brass in Pocket'. For four years, Hynde had a relationship with Ray Davies of The Kinks, with whom she had a child. After that relationship ended, she married Jim Kerr of Simple Minds, and she had another daughter. Throughout her career, Hynde has continued to tour and record. She has released a dozen albums with The Pretenders and three solo albums. Now in her sixties, Hynde continues to perform and create music. Her gritty, distinctive voice and songwriting have endured and influenced generations. As if you didn't know, she is considered an icon of rock music.

O Hamilton Lee, aka Hamid Mantu, was born in 1958 in London, England. As Hamilton Lee, he was the drummer of Furniture, who had the UK chart hit 'Brilliant Mind'. As well as drums, he also played occasional keyboards for Furniture throughout the band's existence between 1979 and 1991 and played on all the band's recordings. Known to be rather innovative, he helped to bring in relatively unusual instrumentation such as the tongue drum. Since he has been part of Natacha Atlas, The Transmitters, Lunar Dunes, Solus 3, Ghost Shirt, Xangbetos and the Flavel Bambi Septet, as well as various session appearances.

O Judy McGee was born September 7. Jude played sax/keys and was the vocalist for Pel Mel, who came together in Newcastle, Australia, in 1979. In the mid-1980s, to be where the 'action' was, the band moved to Sydney and became one of the hard-working units of the vibrant inner-city pub/club scene. The early lineup was made up of Graeme Dunne (guitar & vocals), Glenn Hill (bass), Dave Weston (drums) and Jude's sister Jane on guitar. Pel Mel's version of POST-PUNK funk earned them a faithful national following, and they went on to record two critically acclaimed albums, *Out of Reason* in 1982 and Persuasion in 1983. The band split in 1984, but a reformation as Pel Mel Organisation in 2012 saw them play some well-received sporadic live dates. In 2017 Jude and partner Dermot Browne, as Jude McGee and the Soft Touch, released the album *The Household Guide to Heartbreak* on Blue Jube. There aren't enough O's in smooth to describe this recording. The scene is set from the opening with a whistle reminiscent of an Ennio Morricone soundtrack, a great touch, a soft touch. The instrumentation never overwhelms Jude's vocals, which throughout are gentle, melodic & mesmerising. Concrete Boat drifts like a Beach Boys classic summer tune. The title track, jazzy with a laid-back lounge feel, presents the smoothness of Ronny Jordan or Lee Ritenour, though not so guitar laden. The textures laid out by simple, yet artistic, keyboards, guitars and saxophones are never demanding of the listener, but it's hard not to pay full attention. Overall, it is beautifully written and produced; Jude & Dermot have excelled here.

O Palais Schaumburg released their *self-titled* debut album in 1981. This album is considered a standout in the German NEW WAVE genre, featuring a mix of dance tracks and primitive chanting with unexpected bursts of free jazz. The ethos behind the album seems to be one of fearless experimentation, with a variety of vocal effects and instruments such as trumpet, xylophone, percussion, and keyboards. The overall sound is delightfully strange and unique.

O The Revillos released their first single, 'Where's The Boy for Me?', in 1979. Labelled as DIN 1, it was the inaugural release on DinDisc, an offshoot of Virgin Records that operated somewhat independently. DinDisc lasted until early 1982. The Revillos emerged from the breakup of the punkier Rezillos. The recording of this single was by Eugene Reynolds (whose real name was Alan Forbes), Fay Fife (Sheilagh Hynd), Rocky Rhythm (Reynolds' brother Nicky), Felix on bass, Babs and Cherie Revette as backup singers, and original Rezillos member Hi Fi Harris (Mark Sinclair) on guitar. The Revillos, which went through many lineup changes until the late 1990s, would make two albums and release about a dozen singles.

⊙ On September 7, 1979, The Slits released their LP *Cut*. It moved away from punk, combining their passion and love for reggae/dub with punk's DIY spirit. With producer Dennis Bovell, they created a POST-PUNK album that was subtly stunning. Ari's singing may be an acquired taste, but the bouncy, thick music is delectable and contagious. The dub/reggae beat makes for foot-tapping sing-a-longs with hypnotic rhythms and tasty vocals. The tracks are primitive yet clean and clear. *Cut* showcased the band's capabilities, with songs like 'Instant Hit', 'So Tough', 'Ping Pong Affair', and 'Love and Romance'. 'Spend Spend Spend' and 'Shoplifting' target consumerism with humour. 'Typical Girls' and their unique take on 'I Heard It Through the Grapevine' make the album catchy, memorable, and essential.

⊙ 'Tar' b/w 'Frequency 7', the debut single by the 'supergroup' Visage, was released in 1979. Some might argue that it was the second release, after 'In the Year 2525' from 1978. That single-sided, unmarked white label came in a no-frills white sleeve, with stamp printing labelled 'Steve Strange Project – James Ure, Rusty Egan, Steve Harrington'. Visage was not mentioned. Moving on to 'Tar', *Remember, health warning!* exclaims Steve Strange. From here, Rusty Egan's and Barry Adamson's rhythm section excels with stunningly tight drumming and bass. The swirling, snarling synths by Billy Currie, Midge Ure and Dave Formula are an absolute joy that leaves John McGeoch's saxophone wailing and simply sublime. A great single and a highlight of the debut LP *Visage*.

8

⊙ In the early 1980s, along with bands like Teardrop Explodes and Echo and The Bunnymen, Afraid of Mice emerged as part of the Liverpool music scene. Despite gaining recognition for their live performances, it's surprising that their *self-titled* debut album, released early to mid-September 1981, went unnoticed by the public. The album features clever, catchy, and powerful songs that strike a perfect balance between dark POST-PUNK energy and unique instrumental variations, leaving no doubt about Afraid of Mice's musical identity.

⊙ Mark Gable (Mark Dixon Kitchen) was born in 1950 in Captains Flat, Australia. Mark is best known as the frontman/vocalist and mainstay of The Choirboys, who came together in 1978 on the northern beaches of Sydney. The band has always sat on the fringe of POST-PUNK with hard rock leanings; they have recorded eight albums and released numerous singles. Their 1987 single 'Run to Paradise' is regarded as an antipodean seminal rock anthem which still garners much airplay. Mark has also ventured into radio hosting programs based around eighties music.

RADIO BIRDMAN
MARK GABLE
(Choirboys)

Radio Birdman was my introduction to what was to come in the world of modern music. Now, we are talking something like 45-plus years ago, and I was in a band from the Northern Beaches of Sydney called Vella. The year was 1976, I think; the place was St Leonards Park,

Music Shell, the reason was a band comp. I don't remember performing at the event; I only remember Radio Birdman and for 3 reasons:

1. I had never seen or heard anything like them on stage before this day; they represented the end of self indulgent wankery that had reigned supreme in the 70s, and I could not tell you why in logical terms; I just felt it.

2. Deniz Tek tuned his guitar at full volume on stage between songs. I have never seen such strong self-expression from anyone onstage or, for that matter, anywhere else.

3. After their performance, we went backstage, and there was, of course, Radio Birdman; two of them had decided to do 'the spin one dude around while the other dude tries to hold on'.

Once again, I was shocked and excited as the two (and I don't remember which two) proceeded to trash the place. This was the predecessor to the punk movement, and I was in love!

You see, Radio Birdman had made it possible for the everyman/woman to play Rock 'n' Roll again, and that was a very beautiful thing. They had said to me, "*It is OK just to be you, and if someone does not like it, they can FUCK OFF.*"

By the way, I think they won the band comp that day, and even if they didn't, they did!

○ Aimee Elizabeth Mann, born in 1960 in Richmond, Virginia, USA, has enjoyed a remarkable career spanning over four decades. Her exceptional talent for songwriting has earned her a spot among National Public Radio's Top 10 Best Living Songwriters. Aimee's musical journey began as a bass player with the band Young Snakes from Boston, but it was with 'Til Tuesday that she gained widespread recognition. Leading 'Til Tuesday until 1989, Aimee and the band released three albums, including the highly successful single 'Voices Carry', which achieved top ten status in the US and garnered international acclaim. Following the band's disbandment, Aimee embarked on a solo career, earning multiple Grammy nominations, winning two, and even receiving an Academy Award nomination for her contribution to the Magnolia soundtrack.

○ Benjamin Orr, aka Orzechowski, was born on this day in 1947. Along with Ric Ocasek, they were lead vocalists for The Cars. Orr was the bass player, and even though he wrote excellent songs for his solo work, he was never credited as a songwriter with the band. He had the lead vocal mantle for some of their best-known songs, including 'Candy-O', 'Just What I Needed', 'Let's Go', and 'Drive'. In 1986 Orr released the solo album *The Lace* to moderate sales and, reaching the top 30 in the US, the single 'Stay the Night' claimed high rotation. Benjamin died of cancer on 3rd October 2000.

○ Frank Tovey, who was born in London in 1956, went on to become the legendary avant-garde synth artist behind the project Fad Gadget in 1980. That same year, he sent a demo tape to Mute Records founder Daniel Miller, who had just made waves with his own synth project The Normal and its hit 'Warm Leatherette'. Through their friendship, Tovey essentially became the face of The Normal during live shows. Tovey's own live performances in the early '80s were wild - he was known for covering himself in shaving cream, playing instruments with his head, and often injuring himself on stage. After one show in 1980, he had to go to the emergency room after splitting his head open while using it to play drums. Following the 1984 album *Gag*, he dropped the Fad Gadget moniker and began recording under his real name. Tovey had several other music projects over the years, including the industrial-dance MKultra, Mr Tovey and the Pyros, and the minimalist noise song project The Frank Tovey Acoustic Concept. He wasn't afraid to experiment with unusual instruments and sounds. *The Best of Fad Gadget* compilation in 2001 and touring with Depeche Mode seemed to revive interest in his Fad Gadget work, but sadly he died of a heart attack at home in London in 2002 at age 45.

◉ On the weekend of September 8-9, 1979, the event billed as 'FUTURAMA 1979 – The World's First Science Fiction Festival' was held at Queens Hall, Leeds. Many of the acts that performed were as yet unrecorded; some of the bands that appeared were Cabaret Voltaire, Echo & The Bunnymen, The Fall, Joy Division, Orchestral Manoeuvres in the Dark, PiL and The Teardrop Explodes. Entry was £5.00 a day.

9

◉ Robert Davis Edmonds, aka Lu Edmonds, was born in Welwyn Garden City in 1957. Lu, best known for his guitar work, is also a multi-instrumentalist with exemplary prowess on an array of 'left field' instruments, such as the saz, bouzouki and the cumbus. Lu certainly has been around, having played with The Damned, The Spizzles, The Mekons, Shriekback and was even a Bloke in Billy Bragg & the Blokes. In the studio Lu has added to the works of The Waterboys and Kirsty MacColl. And since 1986 has been an on-off member of PiL.

IS NEW WAVE OLD WAVE?
LU EDMONDS
(The Damned, The Mekons, PiL, Shriekback, et.al)

NEW WAVE is now so old it's no longer actually that new, and anyway, whatever emerged post-Punk hasn't exactly stood still. As I remember it, NEW WAVE was maybe more about the 'wave' bit than the 'new' bit – a crazed surge, a reckless leap into the unknown, wild & disobedient. And fairly hilarious at times. Looking back from 1977, counting 45 years ago would land you in 1932 – bang in the middle of the Depression and the heyday of all that jazz. At the dawn of POST-PUNK, in the midst of the Winter of Discontent, the august and highly respected BBC saw off the last of 'The Black & White Minstrel Show' (yep! blackface, the whole shebang). The world moves on.

If you look forward from 1977, counting 45 years lands you in 2024 – are we there yet? Seems not, with all these great POST-PUNK festivals, tours, and reunion tours. But what I really like is that musicians from all corners of the planet, not just from the so-called First World and not just from the POST-PUNK genre, are making music that is possibly as wild, insanely raucous or controversial as anything that got dreamed up in 1977 by some 'Golden Billion' rebels from London and New York and other places. The world moves on a bit more.

Pick a date: OK, let's try 5th August 1977. I had just turned 20; it was my first ever gig as the newest (and youngest) member of The Damned at the legendary Mont-de-Marsan Punk Festival near Biarritz, south of France. I recall long chopped-out white lines of something (I believe it was military-grade Pervitin) being carried aloft backstage on mirrors by traditionally besuited drug waiters, fuelling the next band up onstage into acts of brazen punk outrage; stink bombs let off during the Clash's mesmeric set (Capt. Sensible & Rat Scabies, it was them) and everyone generally acting out like it's going to be the end of the world at any minute. I was lost in it all, the end of my teenage years.

Later wanderings over Asia, Africa and the Middle East were also lucky, with so much music to hear and so many great people to play with, including those who liked this NEW WAVE and POST-PUNK thing and those who had no idea whatsoever what this 1977 was all about. Now officially designated a true cultural moment, the year 1977 has its luminaries & visionaries (e.g., Marc Zermati, who produced the legendary Mont-de-Marsan festivals, or John Lydon, who wrote and sang the words to all those songs). On the other side, you had chancers and bystanders like me who got caught up in the mayhem but kept going, made friends, and somehow learnt just enough basic craft to make a living (almost) at it and survive.

The old adage goes something like this: if you can remember anything, you likely weren't really there. Me, I'm still just trying to be here, with my dream intact to play on every continent (Antarctica currently missing) and hoping that one day all musicians from everywhere will be able to do the same. That might make for a better world.

⦿ Robert Palmer's album *Clues*, released on September 9, 1980, marked a departure from his usual rock sound into the realm of synthpop. Featuring a talented lineup of musicians such as Gary Numan, Chris Franz, Andy Fraser, and Alan Mansfield, the album offers a unique blend of sounds and genres. While some may argue that *Clues* falls slightly short of Palmer's usual standard, tracks like the classic single 'Johnny and Mary' and the gem 'Woke Up Laughing' showcase his undeniable talent. Give this album a listen and discover the intriguing and diverse musical world of Robert Palmer.

Dave Stewart by Petra Gall

⦿ David A. Stewart was born in 1952 in Sunderland, England. He is also known as Dave Stewart, the guitarist, songwriter, producer & member of Longdancer, The Tourists & Eurythmics. When the Tourists came to a halt in late 1980, a romantic relationship between Dave and Annie Lennox ended as well, but they did agree to collaborate, and Eurythmics was born. They had an infective, soulful synthpop sound, and through Dave's technological mastery and Annie's commanding vocals, they created one of the great 'bi-sexual' duos of all time. The title track of 1983's *Sweet Dreams (Are Made of This)* album became an international smash, and the hits kept coming: in 1984, 'Here Comes the Rain Again'; in 1985, 'Would I Lie to You?'; and in 1986, 'Missionary Man' were perfect examples. Were they good? YES... Doubleplusgood!

⦿ On this day in 2014, there was a hullabaloo when half a billion iTunes accounts were spammed with U2's latest album, *Songs of Innocence*. It was free and embedded into their personal music libraries. Like it or not, if you have iTunes, you have it!

10

⦿ It's September 10, 1985, and LOOK! On the shelf! It's that debut from The Dentists, 'Strawberries Are Growing in My Garden (And It's Wintertime)' b/w 'Burning the Thoughts from My Skin & Doreen'. One would be excused for immediately thinking, 'Is this The Byrds or The Who or maybe The Smiths?' Such is how it is tinged with '60s psych and modern POST-PUNK. This is lovely stuff; shiny, brilliant tunes, the A-side is to die for.

⦿ Johnnie Fingers was born John Peter Moylett in Dublin, Ireland, in 1956. Johnnie was known for his flamboyant style and often performed in striped pyjamas. As an original member of The Boomtown Rats, he played keyboards for the band from 1975 to 1986, but he did not join the reformed version of the group in 2013. After The Boomtown Rats disbanded in 1986, Moylett and drummer Simon Crowe created a trio called Gung-Ho. Crowe was the lead singer along with Moylett's wife, Yoko (not Yoko Ono). Moylett has worked in the music industry in Japan for nearly 20 years. He is part of the team that organises Fuji Rock, Asia's biggest live music festival. The festival featured major acts like Rage Against the Machine, Coldplay, The Chemical Brothers, Oasis, Roxy Music, and Thom Yorke.

11

◉ Stuart Coupe was born in 1956 and grew up in Launceston, Tasmania. Stuart, who provided the foreword for this book (see Part One), has worked as a journalist, author, editor, manager, record label director, radio presenter, publicist, and tour promoter. One of Stuart's landmark projects was being co-founder of the Adelaide-based *Roadrunner* magazine, which led him to be one of the major writers for *Rock Australia Magazine* (RAM), among numerous other publications. In the very early '80s with Roger Grierson (see June 25), Stuart established GREEN Records, a label that was the stepping stone in recording for the likes of up-and-coming Australian bands like Tactics, Do-Re-Mi and The Allniters. As a band manager, he held the reins for many bands, including The Hoodoo Gurus, Paul Kelly, Dropbears and The Flaming Hands; members of all these bands have contributed to this book in one way or another. Highly regarded as an author, Stuart has written or co-written many books, such as *The New Music, The New Rock'n'Roll* with Australian rock writer and historian Glenn A. Baker, and *The Internet Music Guide* with Richard Kingsmill. More recently he has written the highly acclaimed page-turner *Roadies*, a biography of Paul Kelly, and his memoir *Shake Some Action*. These days Stuart also runs Stuart Coupe Publicity, where he handles the publicity for numerous independent artists within a myriad of genres, from jazz to folk to Americana and blues.

◉ Peter Gabriel entered the history books at the MTV Video Music Awards on September 11th, 1987, with his influential video 'Sledgehammer'. The former Genesis frontman's song from the album *So* was a worldwide hit, going No.1 in several countries. At the MTV Awards it scooped nine awards, including Best Video, making it the most successful single video. The video clip was created by stop-motion animation using Plasticine; it became No.4 in MTV's 100 Greatest Music Videos Ever Made.

◉ Michael "Mick" Talbot was born in 1958, in London, England. Mick, as a keyboardist, was a founding member of The Style Council along with Paul Weller. Prior to the Style Council, he had stints playing keyboards with Dexys Midnight Runners, The Merton Parkas, Soundscape, The Bureau and venturing into acid-jazz with Players, Galliano, and Young Disciples. He has also released albums with fellow former Style Council member Steve White under the name Talbot/White.

◉ Neal X, aka Neal Whitmore, was born in 1960, in Henley-on-Thames, England. Neal was the guitarist with Sigue Sigue Sputnik (SSS, a Russian term supposedly meaning "burn, burn satellite"), who were created & led by former Generation X member Tony James. The concept behind SSS was simple: the band portrayed a postmodern, comical/ironic style and sound, totally over the top in appearance and marketing. They saturated the media with slogans and interviews. When he recruited Neal X, Martin Degville, Chris Cavanagh, and Ray Mayhew, it was partially because they lacked extensive musical experience. To Tony James' delight and surprise, they had a No.3 hit single in the UK with 'Love Missile F1-11' in 1986. Neal X has also collaborated with Adam Ant and Marc Almond. In 2012, Neal formed a new band known as The Montecristos.

12

⊙ Barry Andrews was born in London, England, in 1956. Barry was the second keyboard player with XTC, joining circa 1976 after the departure of Johnathan Perkins. Barry was part of the recordings for the XTC albums *White Music* and *Go 2*, leaving in 1978 after multiple disagreements with Andy Partridge. Fortunately, this led him to team up with Robert Fripp in the creation of The League of Gentlemen, with whom he recorded one *self-titled* album in 1980. Through the early '80s Barry collaborated with several renowned artists, most notably Brian Eno, Iggy Pop, and David Bowie. In 1981 Barry, along with Dave Allen and Carl Marsh, formed Shriekback and has since released well over twenty studio and live recordings with a revolving door of personnel. As a solo artist, Barry has recorded critically acclaimed solo albums. Apparently in his spare time Barry puts his hands to carpentry, making furniture.

WITHOUT REAL STRING OR FISH (AT THE END OF IT ALL)
BARRY ANDREWS
(XTC, League of Gentlemen, Shriekback)

I often think about whatever alchemy of mind and circumstance it is that produces that elusive last track, you know… the one that appears when the album seems to be over. When you think you've mined whatever seam of compressed life experience, obsession and influence cluster it is that songs come from, and you're not exactly content but applying a sort of willed gratitude that, at least, it's not all total shite, and – a baby miracle – another tune comes into being that you really didn't expect and that seems to have, more than the others, a character that didn't seem to have much to do with you (a bit like your children).

I find these are the ones I tend to listen to for fun the most. They're more like someone else did them. Past examples include 'Coelacanth' (from *Oil and Gold*), 'Sticky Jazz' (off *Big Night Music*), 'Exquisite Corpse' (part of *Sacred City*) and 'Hubris' (appearing on *Jam Science*). On the album *Without Real String or Fish* we have two, 'Beyond Metropolis' and 'Soft Estate'. Both voyaging into new territory, with 'B M' an alt-funk anthem in an aircraft hangar with shards of space junk flying out of the darkness at you. The chorus being a Bowie-esque, aching sunset of chords encroaching word clusters of outrageous audacity. There is – gasp – even a key change (yeah, we can do that muso shit if we want!) and a key change back too. The groove upon which it was built was a thing I wrote a couple of years back; I had sent it to Carl, but he hadn't – as of last summer, when my 'we are now finishing this fucking record if it kills me' protocol was in full effect – come up with anything for it.

I had booked Stuart Rowe for the mixing; we had enough tunes, Carl had 3 songs on the album, God was in his heaven, and the sun was sporting a roguish titfer. Then, in his fearful aspect as the demiurge of deadline bending, Carl sent a roughie I couldn't refuse. At a stroke, the mixing (which was to have been a stately affair of considered tweaking and contemplative strolls around the elegant parterres and formal gardens of the Lighterthief estate) turned into the usual Shriekback panicked scramble as we struggled to bring the prodigal 'Beyond Metropolis' to the same stage of development as its siblings.
Not to do so would have been unthinkable; of course, it had the word 'Enchromosoniradiopolis', for crissakes. The heart bows down.

◉ Juan Atkins was born in Detroit, Michigan, in 1962. Juan is a DJ, producer and innovator bestowed with the mantle of 'The Pioneer of Detroit Techno'. Inspired by the likes of Kraftwerk and YMO, in 1980 Juan was a founding member of both The Belleville Three and Cybotron, who led the way with their electronic dance beats. Cybotron's 1983 album *Enter*, holding the single 'Clear', broke ground in the USA, recently explored only by the likes of Herbie Hancock, Afrika Bambaataa, Units and DEVO, and yes, a very limited number of others.

◉ Renowned drummer, producer and journalist Will Birch was born in London, England, on September 12, 1948. Will paid his dues with various bands as a drummer prior to being part of The Kursaal Flyers, who had the top 20 single 'Little Does She Know' in 1976. After the Kursaal Flyers dissolved, Will formed The Records. It was 1978 when they released the sensational power pop song 'Starry Eyes'; it was co-written by Will and was included on the debut album *Shades in Bed*. With the split of The Records, Will moved into production, working with the likes of Dr. Feelgood, The Long Ryders and Yachts. Will attained high respect in the industry for his journalism exploits, where his exposés delved into the UK music scene. Highlights of his writing skills are *Ian Dury: The Definitive Biography*; *Cruel to Be Kind: The Life and Music of Nick Lowe*; and *No Sleep Till Canvey Island – The Great Pub Rock Revolution*.

WAITING FOR PUB ROCK TO BITE
WILL BIRCH
(The Kursaal Flyers, The Records, Producer)

Inspired by Elvis, Lonnie, and The Beatles, I wanted to be a pop musician.

I played basic banjo and sung badly in a school skiffle group aged 11, then around 1963 I started building my first drum set. Encouraged by schoolfriend Dave Mattacks (later of Fairport Convention), many a Saturday was spent touring the London drum shops where Dave seemed to know everyone. Once equipped, I worked my way through various groups from the Southend, Essex area, starting with The Tradewinds in 1965. We played 'R&B' in the town's youth club, and that year appeared in a BBC TV documentary about sex and teenagers entitled 'The Young Adults'. My next group was The Flowerpots, who were joined in 1966 by John Wilkinson, whom, I'm told by his brother Malcom, I christened 'Wilk Johnson'. An 'o' was added to 'Wilk' by the recipient during the early days of Dr Feelgood.

Throughout the late 60s/early 70s, there followed a series of 'progressive' bands. I had an office job in London where the weekly music papers were available on a Wednesday, 24 hours ahead of the provinces. As well as learning about upcoming concerts and securing tickets immediately, this gave one the advantage of answering 'musicians wanted' ads in the Melody Maker ahead of the masses. I confess I answered quite a few (only to fail every audition). But via a 'group wanted' ad, our then-current combo, known as Surly Bird, became 'managed' by former Who mentor Peter Meaden and his then-business boss Tony Hall. We recorded some demos, and Peter got us a few gigs as 'Glory', but after 12 months, the experiment had run its course.

Surly Bird ('catches the germ') opened for acts including The Edgar Broughton Band, Status Quo, and on the bill at a Southend benefit concert for Shelter, David Bowie. Our group had at various times featured singer Paul Shuttleworth and guitarist Graeme Douglas, and in early 1974 we started playing a local pub as the Kursaal Flyers. There was a very brief period during which I disappeared to drum for Charlie and the Wide Boys via their agent Dai Davies, but I clearly wasn't up to it and quickly returned to 'the Kursaals'.

A year or so earlier, via Wilko, I had become pals with 'the Feelgoods' and once or twice deputised for their drummer, the Big Figure. In 1973, through a friend named Kevin Percy, I helped to get the Feelgoods their first date on the London pub rock circuit, a favour they returned the following year. This saw the Kursaals appearing at The Kensington, a top pub venue where we were spotted – via Chilli Willi drummer Pete Thomas and his manager Jake Riviera – by agent Paul Conroy. Our music was essentially country rock, inspired by Paul's love of the Flying Burrito Brothers, but we also covered The Monkees hit 'I'm A Believer' plus lots of Eddie Cochran.

Graeme and I soon started writing songs for the Kursaals, such as 'Hit Records' and 'Pocket Money', and with Paul's frontman humour and charm, we started to enjoy favourable reviews in the music press. In late '74, with Conroy as manager, we decided to 'go pro'. This was risky, but by April 1975 we had secured a deal with Jonathan King's UK Records and were booked to support those Flying Burrito Brothers on a six-week European tour. This was extremely exciting. Later that year we became the subject of a BBC TV documentary entitled *So You Want to Be a Rock'n'Roll Star* directed by Mark Kidel. In 1976 we signed to CBS and enjoyed our hit record 'Little Does She Know', produced by Mike Batt. My father – who a couple of years earlier had shouted, 'When are you going to give up all that pop music nonsense?' as I left the house for a Stephen Stills concert – was now saying to his friends, "*Did you see my son on Top of The Pops?*"

Over a decade's worth of dreams had come true. But the point here is that beyond drive, ambition, and perhaps some entertaining songs, our moment of success can be attributed completely to the existence of the London pub rock scene. Prior to that, with very few exceptions, you could only get meaningful live work if you had an agent, and you could only get one of those if you had a record deal (to echo music scene guru Dave Robinson). But pub rock changed all that. And for several influential acts, including Kilburn and the High Roads featuring Ian Dury, Dr Feelgood, and Eddie and the Hot Rods, it provided a springboard to success and led organically to the UK punk rock phenomenon. Punk's commercial appeal was brief, but its influence on popular music would be felt throughout the decades that followed.

Will Birch - February 2025

● In 1980, David Bowie, the ever-changing chameleon, dove headfirst into the NEW WAVE genre with his album *Scary Monsters (and Super Creeps)*. With this record, Bowie departed from his experimental trilogy with Brian Eno - *Low*, *Heroes*, and *Lodger* - though he still surrounded himself with talented musicians like producer Tony Visconti. Scary Monsters showed Bowie melding glam rock themes with avant-garde synthesizers to create highly accessible yet dark and introspective art. The cornerstone track 'Ashes to Ashes' was essentially a sequel to his classic 'Space Oddity', with Bowie offering explicit self-criticism by labeling Major Tom a space-bound junkie, pathetically clinging to fantasies that he'll "stay clean tonight". While not necessarily breaking new ground, Bowie delivered track after track of instant classics on the album. It kicked off powerfully with the compelling 'It's No Game', before unleashing other gems like 'Up the Hill Backwards', the title track 'Scary Monsters (And Super Creeps)', 'Fashion', 'Kingdom Come', and 'Because They're Young'. With sublime guitar work from legends like Fripp, Townshend, Hammer, and Alomar, combined with Bowie's brilliant songwriting and vocals, Scary Monsters affirmed Bowie's rightful status as a legend.

● Clyde Bramley was born on September 12, 1954, in Fremantle, Western Australia. Clyde played bass for the Hoodoo Gurus 1982-88. After seeing The Easybeats play at the Regent Theatre in Townsville, Clyde went and bought his first bass, a Maton Lute, just like the one Dick Diamonde used. Clyde has also been a member of Johnny and the Hitmen (1978), The

Other Side (78-79), The New Christs (1980), The Angie Pepper Band (1981), The Stepfords in the 1990s and a reformation in 2015. He even played keys on the single Teenage Blues by Sydney band Naked Lunch. More recently Clyde has been playing bass with The On and Ons (2015- present).

AN INTERVIEW WITH CLYDE BRAMLEY
(Hitmen, New Christs, Angie Pepper, Hoodoo Gurus et.al.)

Hi Clyde, I understand you grew up in North Queensland; is that right? It's a pretty remote part of the musical world. What's your first memorable musical moment?

The summer of '67/68 was when rock and roll happened for me, and the song that did it was 'Itchycoo Park' by The Small Faces. Then The Monkees and Bubblegum followed soon after. I went to high school in Townsville, and the city's geographical isolation meant that very few touring acts made it there, although we did get The Johnny Farnham Show rolling through a couple of times a year. You got half a dozen singers like Ronnie Burns, Jon Blanchfield, Marty Rhone, and Mike Furber, as well as Johnny, all backed by Brisbane band Hands Down. Because of Townsville's isolation, it had a very strong local scene, and one of the first bands I saw at our school dance was called M.I.5. Little did I know that the organ player was Charlie Georgees, who would go on to be the fantastic lead guitar player in The Hellcats, The Hitmen and The Other Side! The first international act I saw at the suburban Regent Theatre/Roller Rink in Hermit Park (Townsville has such great suburb names… Hermit Park, Belgian Gardens, Rising Sun!) was The Easybeats – a life-changing event, as a couple of months later I would go to Palings and purchase a teardrop-shaped Maton Lute bass guitar, just the same as The Easybeats' Dick Diamonde played!

Winding back to your teens, were you part of any bands back then? And what were you listening to that influenced your future direction?

In 1970 my first band was Heavy Blanket, playing bad versions of Black Sabbath, Led Zeppelin, Creedence, etc. We did a number of gigs around Townsville for a few months, and then my parents said I had to concentrate on schoolwork. In '72 my family moved to the Darling Downs, where I played in local bands and did a creative arts course at the Darling Downs Institute of Advanced Education, now Uni of Southern Qld. In '76 my bandmates and I made a trip to Sydney, and my life changed once again by seeing Radio Birdman at the Oxford Funhouse. We returned to Toowoomba and became Streetlife, a punk/garage covers band. We were invited to play with The Saints at their house/club/gig Club 76 in Brisbane just after 'I'm Stranded' came out, and they were amazing. I was mesmerised! We moved to Brisbane for a short time, Jeff Wegener joined on drums, and we did a few gigs with Jim Dickson's Survivors. Then we broke up in mid '77, and most of us drifted down to Sydney to start a new life.

In 1978, after a stint with The Hitmen, you were part of The Other Side, which had Rob Younger as vocalist; they were short-lived, and you were soon to become a member of The New Christs and then The Angie Pepper Band. What was it like being in such line-ups, especially with legendary ex-Radio Birdman member and a singer like Angie Pepper?

Rob Younger was something of a mentor to me in my early days in Sydney. We used to hang out, go to gigs, play records, drink beer… that kind of stuff. Through that association I ended up in Johnny and The Hitmen for a short time with Charlie Georgees, Angie Pepper, and Steve Harris. Rob recruited Charlie and me, plus Mark Kingsmill, for The Other Side after Birdman split. Sadly, the band never recorded, although Rob was starting to write some great songs, many of which ended up in The New Christs repertoire. Mark left after a while to join a rejuvenated Hitmen with Chris Masuak and Brad Shepherd, and Ron Keeley – former Birdman drummer – came in to replace him in The Other Side. Ron ended up moving to the UK, and Charlie decided to head back to North Queensland, and that was it for The Other Side. Rob and I were looking to get another live band happening, but, in the meantime, we joined forces with Bruce "Cub" Callaway, John Hoey, and Ken Doyle for a recording project that became The New Christs' (and my own) first record, 'To Face A New God' b/w 'Waiting World' on Green Records. That line-up, however, did not play live. Not long after I got an offer I couldn't refuse from Angie and Deniz Tek to play with them and Steve Harris and Ivor Hay (ex-The Saints) in The Angie Pepper Band. We gigged around at places like The Paddington Green and recorded an album's worth of demos at Trafalgar Studio with Charles Fisher producing/engineering. The single 'Frozen World' b/w 'Miss You Too Much' was the only thing released at the time, doing very well on the indie charts. Angie was a great frontwoman with a load of sex appeal and personality, and combined with Deniz's blistering guitar and Steve Harris' amazing keyboard work, the band could have been a real contender. Deniz and Angie married and moved to the USA for Deniz to follow his medical career. A CD of the demos plus some Passengers recordings was released a few years back.

In 1982 you joined The Hoodoo Gurus as a bassist after the departure of the guitarists Roddy Radalj & Kimble Rendall. With the addition of Brad Shepherd joining Dave Faulkner and James Baker, you recorded the album Stoneage Romeos; this is seen as an epic '80s, indeed Australian, recording. How does this sit with you in your recording career?

Brad and I were playing in Super K, a Bubblegum band that recorded a single 'Go Go' b/w 'Recurring Nightmare' for Green Records, when I was approached to join Hoodoo Gurus, I think at James Baker's suggestion, as I had met him when The Scientists played at French's. Or it could have been at the behest of Stuart Coupe, then managing The Gurus, who had put out the Super K single. Subsequently, when Rod decided, he was going to leave, I suggested Brad would be the perfect replacement. And he was! *Stoneage Romeos* was recorded at Trafalgar Studios in Annandale with Alan Thorne engineering and producing. It was a great experience recording that album and hearing those songs come together in the way they did. It remains one of the favourite recordings that I played on.

It was a five-year stint with The Hoodoo Gurus; they were flying high. Why the move?

In early 1988, after five years of fairly relentless gigging, I was suffering from tour fatigue, my private life was unravelling somewhat, and I had become a not-so-nice-to-be-around person. It was best for all concerned that I left when I did. Consequently, I was able to bounce back quickly and move on to new adventures. I don't regret that decision at all, though I must admit to the occasional wistful feeling! After the decision was made, I had two great gigs to go out on, the final being at Expo '88 in Brisbane in front of 15,000 people. We were picked up by motor launch from our hotel on one side of the Brisbane River and whisked across to the Expo stage, which sat over the water on the other side. Very James Bond! Standing on stage, it was difficult to believe that this would be my last ever gig with the band, and as it turned out, it wasn't! 26 years later I was able to join in a short tour billed Be My Guru – The Evolution Revolution, featuring all past and present members of Hoodoo Gurus.

So many bands and so many venues and tours. Do you have one that is a favourite that sits strong in your memory?

Before that Expo gig, the Gurus did a 3-set, unannounced, afternoon warm-up show at The Hopetoun in our home base, Surry Hills. The Hoey had a pretty good crowd for the first set, was full for the second, and sardine-packed for the third! We played just about everything we knew from the band's career at that time and had a thoroughly enjoyable gig. The Gurus did two tours with The Bangles, and they were a joy to behold every night. In 1990 I was both honoured and cursed to play in P.J. Proby's band. That is an epic tale in itself and will be the subject of a forthcoming book by Mark Cornwall and Brett Stevenson.

With Naked Lunch you recorded 'Teenage Blues' playing keyboards; how did that come about, and do you think you are a proficient keyboardist?

As a child I was "required" to have piano and music theory lessons (not to mention elocution – would you believe?) and I hated it! But, of course, in retrospect, I'm glad I had that background when I was bitten by the rock and roll bug. I am a very, very ordinary keyboard player, but I know chords and can pick out a melody – usually one hand at a time. Tony Robertson is a long-time friend, and out of the blue, he called me up and asked me to play on The Naked Lunch recording. To this day, I have no idea why.

Of all the bands you have been with, which do you feel was the most rewarding musically?

Not being much of a songwriter myself, I tend to gravitate toward people who do write great songs. And I have been extremely fortunate in that regard. Dave, of course, in the Gurus, and before that Rob and Deniz, then Wayne Tritton in The Madisons, Miss Monica and the boys of The Stepfords, and Jed Brown of The Rainy Season – all good bands that I have made albums with. I must mention too, The Wetsuits, the only band that has let me play six-string guitar – we played a lot of weird and wonderful gigs that only a surf instrumental band could – and made an album that I'm quite proud of. Since 2015, I've been working with Glenn and Brain Morris in The On and Ons. We've recorded 3 albums released on Citadel, with whom I have had a long association. Glenn is the most prolific and humble musician I've worked with, and he continues to challenge me with a never-ending repertoire of new songs.

Your latest outfit, The On & Ons, have been gigging regularly. With five albums in the can, how fulfilling has The On and Ons been for you?

During 2023, The On and Ons released the album *Let Ya Hair Down*, and as the promo says, 'it's hook-laden songwriting, lockstep playing with uplifting harmonies'. I get to be engineer and co-producer on our recordings, so every piece of audio recorded goes through my hands, which is incredibly fulfilling. We look forward to playing live again in the very near future.

When not playing music, what are your main interests? Have you got a sport you follow?

These days my sporting passion is NASCAR, American motor racing, and a couple of years ago I was able to go to a couple of races in Michigan. I've been a bit of a closet rev-head since the seventies when I used to go to the speedway in Toowoomba. I'm hoping that in the not-too-distant future I'll be able to get back to the US for a couple more races. I'm pleased to say that NASCAR has come out strongly in support of the BLM movement.

◉ Japanese experimentalist and electronic musician PHEW, aka Hiromi Moritani, was born in 1959 in Osaka, Japan. When her punk band Aunt Sally dissolved, Hiromi ventured to Europe with ideas of her own for new Japanese-influenced electronica. January 1981 saw her meeting up with Can members Holger Czukay & Jaki Liebezeit; they spent time in Conny Plank's studio, and the result was the album *Phew*. The whole thing is very Can-like; it's daring, loaded with great percussion and synthesizers. Hiromi vocalizes in Japanese, detachedly, emotively and in desperation to end up with a recording that intrigues. Missed by many, this album is historically valuable and a compelling listen.

June Miles-Kingston by permission

● June Miles-Kingston was born in East London, England, in 1955. She met the guitarist Kate Korus while working on the set of the Sex Pistols' film *The Great Rock 'n' Roll Swindle*. Along with bass player Jane Crockford, vocalist Ramona Carlier, and June as the drummer, the Bomberettes were born. With a name change, The Mo-dettes signed to Rough Trade and released their first single, 'White Mice', in December 1979. From here, before they split in late 1982, there were a handful of singles released and only one album, an anthology of sorts, *The Story So Far*. June, who bought her first drumkit from The Sex Pistols' Paul Cook, would go on to be part of The Communards, Fun Boy Three and Everything but The Girl, and is still a session singer for numerous bands. June has become a highly regarded filmmaker, most notably with her award-winning production *Dear Miss Bassey*. She is currently working on a film about her life as a drummer.

ATTITUDE AND ETHIC IS ALL YOU NEED
JUNE MILES-KINGSTON
(The Mo-dettes, Funboy 3, Everything but the Girl, Communards, et.al)

I was brought up in the wilds of East London, where you had to have an attitude to survive, so punk was the perfect fit for me. It was all about attitude. During my stint at art school, I worked as an assistant on The Great Rock 'n' Roll Swindle with director Julian Temple, where one of my jobs was to get Sid and Nancy off their mattress and on to the film set each day. Not easy! Steve Jones and Paul Cook were great; Steve was a comedian; he kept us all amused. Paul showed me how to set up a kit I'd bought from him, and I jammed with Steve and Joe Strummer in the carpet-lined basement of our Marylebone squat. Within a few months the Mo-dettes were supporting the Clash, Siouxsie, the Specials, Madness... we had no idea what we were doing!

But that was the punk. No-one questioned the fact that we were all girls or that we weren't professional musicians. If you could make a noise, you got the gig. It was a short-lived era, but it had a profound effect on me and other women musicians. I don't think we'd have had that opportunity without Punk. It was political as much as musical. It definitely changed the playing field for us girls, and every band I've worked with since has resonated with that punk ethic of equality and inclusivity. We had no idea; it was attitude and ethic.

● In 1981, Simple Minds released their fourth album titled *Sons and Fascination/Sister Feelings Call*, which was a unique marketing strategy that offered both a double album and two separate single albums depending on the location and time of purchase. It was an unusual move to have *Sister Feelings Call* as a bonus LP initially included in the first pressings of

Sons and Fascination, then later distributed separately at a discounted rate. This album showcases the band approaching their best, featuring a collection of electrifying dance anthems that dominated the NEW WAVE modern sound and filled dance club floors. Some of the notable tracks include 'Love Song', 'In Trance as Mission', 'Sweat in Bullet', 'The American', and 'Theme for Great Cities', which are now considered staples of a definitive Simple Minds 'best of'. Simple Minds played a pivotal role in shaping the NEW WAVE rock era and are a must-have in any music library that celebrates this genre. The band's sound has evolved from being Roxy Music/Bowie imitators to becoming proficient in synthesizer technology.

⦿ Released one year to the day of *Sons and Fascination/Sister Feelings Call* in 1982, *New Gold Dream (81-82-83-84)* captured the Scottish outfit Simple Minds at the pinnacle of their experimental, avant-garde NEW WAVE period. Before transitioning to a more grandiose arena rock sound, this album highlights the band's knack for sophisticated production and rich, electronic-psychedelic textures. Though understated, *New Gold Dream* shimmers with artistry and stands as Simple Minds' definitive work. While later renowned for stadium anthems, this album showcases the band channelling an uplifting, romantic vibe on funk-infused hits like 'Promised You a Miracle' and moody gems like 'Colours Fly and Catherine Wheel'. Devoid of any filler tracks, *New Gold Dream* encapsulates Simple Minds' versatility and mastery of the '80s new wave genre. It remains an essential listen for NEW WAVE fans seeking the creative peak of a seminal NEW WAVE band.

⦿ Born in Frankfurt, Germany, in 1957, Hans Zimmer is a well-known composer and record producer of film scores, having created the music for over 150 movies. His extensive repertoire includes soundtracks for blockbusters like *The Lion King, Pirates of the Caribbean, Gladiator, The Last Samurai*, and many other major motion pictures. However, few people realise that before becoming a renowned Hollywood composer, Zimmer played keyboards and synthesizers and produced music for various bands in the 1970s and 1980s. He gained recognition as a member of the group Krakatoa and worked with The Buggles, even making a brief cameo in their famed 1979 'Video Killed the Radio Star' music video. Zimmer was also part of the avant-garde Italian synthpop outfit Krisma and collaborated with Ultravox's Warren Cann in the group Helden. Additionally, he contributed to the Shriekback album *Oil & Gold* and produced the single 'History of the World, Part 1' for The Damned, which was described as 'Over-Produced by Hans Zimmer' in the liner notes on their 1980 record *The Black Album*. Though known today for his film scores, Zimmer had a robust career as a producer and musician long before entering the cinematic realm.

13

⦿ Stephen Cummings was born in 1954 in Melbourne, Australia. Stephen's career began as part of The Pelaco Brothers in the '70s, and he became an extremely well-regarded solo artist known for his story-telling lyricism. Nationally, Stephen became first known as the frontman vocalist with The Sports, a highly successful band that was active from 1976 to 1981. The sports' popularity rocketed through 1979-80 with the singles 'Who Listens to the Radio?', 'Don't Throw Stones', 'Strangers on a Train', and 'How Come'. The critically acclaimed 1984 debut solo album *Senso* had moderate sales, riding on the back of the high-charting single 'Gymnasium'. His album of 1989, *A New Kind of Blue*, won an ARIA award for Best Contemporary Adult Album. In 2020 Stephen suffered a stroke, and he announced his retirement. But you can't keep a good man down; in 2023 he released his 21st album, *100 Years from Now*.

AN INTERVIEW WITH STEPHEN CUMMINGS
(The Sports, Solo)

Hi Stephen, You grew up in the sixties; what do you remember sparked your interest in music, like many? Was it The Beatles, Elvis or...?

It was Elvis in the beginning. Our neighbours would occasionally take me to the football, and they were a family of rockers, and I just loved the mayhem of early rock n' roll. My taste quickly evolved to pop music, and I was enthralled with the Rolling Stones, Cream and Velvet Underground. I caught the first tours in Australia by Roxy Music, Pink Floyd, Little Feat, Lou Reed, etc., but interestingly, I was a fan of Australian groups and saw most of the important groups of the 60s and early 70s play live on many occasions. Standoutswere The Loved Ones, The Wild Cherries, The Easybeats, The Dingos and Spectrum.

You are pretty much regarded as a vocalist; do you play any instruments? Your history talks of your time with The Pelaco Brothers and, before that, Ewe and The Merinos (chuckles.) Was that the first band that you were ever part of? Tell us a bit about them.

Basically, Johnny Topper and I started The Pelaco Brothers with Peter Lillie. Peter and Topper were well-known performers as humourists and 'comix' artists at the Much More Ballroom in Fitzroy, where they had the first 'Head' gig in Melbourne, possibly Tully or Mackenzie Theory. Peter taught Topper and me to play bass and guitar. As our hopes expanded, we added other instruments and musicians to the group, and I was relieved of my guitar duties, as I was a beginner. We mixed country, rock and roll, western swing, rockabilly, and jump blues together to be the ultimate basic party band with an over-the-top Australiana awareness. Our first gig was at the Tower building attached to the Pram factory in Carlton.

The Sports formed in 1976. I remember seeing the band in the early days, and you were doing some great R & B standards covers and even Graham Parker. The Sports supported Graham Parker & The Rumour on a late '70s tour; did he know that you covered his songs?

When we first formed, we were really into Little Feat and Ry Cooder, and our aim was just to play every week. We were a bit like Brinsley Schwarz, a 1970s English pub rock band named after their guitarist Brinsley Schwarz, with Nick Lowe on bass and vocals, keyboardist Bob Andrews and drummer Billy Rankin. The band evolved from the 1960s pop band Kippington Lodge and Dr Feelgood, who mixed their own songs with R&B rarities to keep the audience dancing. They saw us live, so they knew what we did. Graham Parker's manager was Dave Robinson, one of the founders of Stiff Records, which is why we ended up at Stiff; we also had one album on Sire Records in London.

The Sports were signed to Stiff Records; you were now stablemates with Ian Dury, Elvis Costello, and Nick Lowe. That must have been seen as a crowning achievement for the band. Stiff released 'Who Listens To The Radio?', and it sold pretty well here and even better in the States, even finding its way on prime-time TV. Did you guys follow that up with a tour?

Well, we got a good deal with Clive Davis at Arista Records in New York and toured some clubs. We played the Palladium in New York with The Buzzcocks and The Fall and later some concerts with The Motels and a bunch of guitar power pop groups with stripy shirts and Rickenbacker guitars. The whole thing about getting overseas deals and releases was very vague. I don't think I understood we had a deal overseas till we were on the plane to America. Nobody at the record label really explained what a big deal it was, and eventually

Michael Gudinski started managing us because his dream was to have a successful group in America, and he thought we could be it.

1979-81, it seemed that nearly every other week you were on ABC-TV's music program Countdown. Later, your solo work was very well represented too. Ian 'Molly' Meldrum must have thought highly of you personally. Molly had a big influence here and seemed like a very likeable guy. What are your thoughts on Countdown and Molly?

Obviously, it was an important show for enlarging your fan base, but there was always some drama about getting on or not. Basically, the new groups had to get there at nine in the morning, which was difficult after playing the night before at a hotel or club till after midnight. The bigger groups like Sherbet and Skyhooks didn't have to turn up till later. Molly was routinely late because he was always going to watch St Kilda play in the Aussie Rules football. We were never particularly close to Molly, as we were shy and more worried about how we looked to fellow rock musicians.

The Sports folded in 1981, not long after the single 'How Come?' and the album Sondra were highly successful. What led to that demise?

The way that music works is groups can become successful very quickly, and they likewise become out of print and forgotten equally as quickly. This was something that ran through our collective thoughts. We understood we couldn't go on rejigging what we were; better just to start again. Martin, Andrew, and I were the songwriters, and we had other things we wanted to do.

Stephen Cummings is now a soloist, and your debut album Senso fared terrifically commercially. It held some great songs, with the 'Gymnasium' single peaking at No.27 nationally; there was even an extended dancefloor mix. The song was very techno; you were now venturing down a whole new path. Who drove that production and instrumentation?

It was a result of what I was listening to, which was mainly funk and progressive pop music, and it also coincided with the rise in home recording and drum machines.

You've played with and been in the studio with many great musicians; who has impressed you most with their level of creativity?

I have been lucky to play with many good musicians. Joe Camilleri and Martin Armiger are standouts, but also Steve Kilbey, Robert Goodge, Chris Abrahams, and Billy Miller, who were important later in my solo career.

Not long after announcing your retirement from music in 2019, you suffered a stroke. These things make you sit back and take stock. How is the rehabilitation coming from that?

My rehabilitation is going well but slowly; basically, I can't play guitar anymore, which has been a shock, but fortunately this has happened at the end of my career. I made a new album in 2023, *100 Years From Now*, with my friend Robert Goodge, who is a great guitarist and producer who was in I'm Talking and played a handful of gigs, which was great but taxing, but I have played and made music with Robert for over twenty-five years; we can always have a laugh, which is important.

You've written three books; would you call them successful? Were they long in the making like this one of mine (10 years+), or does writing come easy to you? Do you think you'll be writing more?

As a pretty big reader, I feel good about my writing. I especially liked writing book reviews for 'The Age' for a couple of years. I have another novel worked out, but I have no idea if I will complete it.

What's next for Stephen Cummings?

I still have a passion for music, but the direction the arts has moved in pandemic times has made me wonder if there is a place for me in it. I connect with a lot of interesting people and fans on my Facebook page, where I have a lot of followers. I post art images, photos or book or film reviews. It keeps me entertained and connected. I might make an EP of some favourite covers this year; we'll see.

What does Stephen Cummings listen to on a Sunday morning or just when relaxing?

I might play some Southern soul music collections or Kevin Ayers or Laura Nyro. I also like to keep up with new Australian acts, and I like Sweet Whirl, Scott and Charlene's Wedding, and New Estate and Crow, among others.

THANKS, STEPHEN.

◉ Steve Kilbey was born in Welwyn Garden City, England, in 1954. Steve is the lead singer-songwriter and bass guitarist with The Church. He moved from being just another muso to being a pop star when 'Under the Milky Way', the lead single from The Church's album *Starfish*, became a worldwide hit in 1988. A prolific composer, Steve has over 750 registered compositions with the Australian copyright agency APRA and is an inductee to the Australian Songwriters Hall of Fame. Steve has been part of numerous solo and collaborative recordings with artists such as Gareth Koch, Martin Kennedy, Stephen Cummings, Grant McLennan and Ricky Maymi as a vocalist, musician, writer and/or producer, but it is his music with The Church that is the most enduring. 2021 saw Steve collaborate with Roger Mason, Gareth Koch and Barton Price on the project named Steve Kilbey and The Winged Heels and with Martin Kennedy for the album release of *Jupiter*.

14

◉ Born on September 14th, 1959, in Kongsberg, Norway, Morten Harket is best known for being a founding member, lead singer, and songwriter of the pop band A-Ha. Their hit 1985 song 'Take On Me' propelled them to No.1 in the USA, making A-Ha the first Norwegian group to achieve such success. At the 1986 MTV Video Music Awards, A-Ha won six awards for the innovative music video for 'Take on Me', which featured the band members in a live-action pencil-sketched animation sequence. As a solo artist, Morten Harket has released six albums, four of which reached the top of the charts in Norway.

◉ In 1979 The Slits released their debut single 'Typical Girls' b/w 'I Heard It Through the Grapevine'. These girls were adorable, somewhat punky, but adorable, nonetheless. The A-side, simple and minimalist, the pumping piano leads us into the reggaeish vocal plane, hard not to tap your foot to. BUT it's the B-side, it's the side where they make a classic song their own, Ari Up's vocals searching and exclaiming. The groove is simply a killer; it's going to be a song that is never going to age. Could have come out yesterday or even tomorrow.

15

◉ David Knopov was born in Liverpool, England, in 1958. 1976 saw David form his first band, The O'Boogie Brothers, named after Dr Winston O'Boogie, aka John Lennon. This nine-piece combo included Ian Broudie (Big in Japan); a highlight was supporting Deaf School at Eric's on Christmas Eve 1976. David went on to form Ded Byrds in 1978. The band supported The Undertones, The Pretenders, Ultravox, 999 and Joy Division. After signing to Sire Records, the company insisted that the band change their name, and David left. This enabled David to study for his BA in fine art. His skills led him on to a successful career designing for Factory Records, The Hacienda, Elle Magazine, MPL, Virgin and Malcom McLaren. David is still working today on his well-reserved artwork. The other string to David's bow is that his voice resembles Frank Sinatra, and for over 30 years David has entertained a global audience with his Sinatra act Perfectly Frank. Dawn French is quoted as saying, *"When David is up there, he is Frank!"* David has had the pleasure of performing for H.R.H. Queen Elizabeth during the Golden Jubilee celebrations and the King of Greece for his 70th birthday. David still performs with his 11-piece ska band named … wait for it … Baked A La Ska. Since 2008 the band have recorded five albums on their own label, Lime Field, and have played countless festivals and gigs. As David puts it, *"I'll never retire; I have nothing to retire from. That's for people who have jobs. I don't have a job; I have a life."*

David Knopov on left by Janette Beckman

MY AIM WAS TRUE
DAVID KNOPOV
(Ded Byrds, Photographer, Actor)

In the hot summer of '77 I had a job photographing street parties to celebrate the Queen's Silver Jubilee. I was hired by Liverpool Council to make a community record of the event.

After a week I realised that one of these parties looks the same as the other, so I would photograph these celebratory parties from every conceivable angle to cover me for the week.

Then on Thursday and Friday I would go to Eric's, the punk/NEW WAVE club, to shoot the sound checks of artists who were performing that evening.

I was in luck; one Friday afternoon at Eric's, there was this very skinny chap in a cheap suit wearing Buddy Holly glasses. I asked if it was okay to photograph him while he was rehearsing. While I was shooting away inside Eric's, little did I know the whole of Matthew Street was being plastered with life-size black and white posters of the same chap. When I stepped outside, there were hundreds of that 'four-eyed' guy staring right back at me.

I asked if he would come outside and pose next to his wall of images; he obliged. I rushed back to the dark room to process my film and print plenty of 10x8 photos to sell at the concert. The photos flew out, selling like hotcakes, and I made oodles of cash (at fifty pennies a photo, I made £40, which in those days was oodles of cash).

Monday morning the boss of the Jubilee project went into the dark room. I strolled in late as usual, and he called me to one side, holding up a row of negatives.

"I didn't know Elvis Costello played at a Silver Jubilee street party!" the boss said.

"He would have done, but he hates the Royal Family," I replied. I was sacked on the spot.

⦿ Tim Whelan was born in 1958, in London, England. Tim is a singer/multi-instrumentalist, at one time a member of Missing Presumed Dead and a founding member of Furniture, who formed in 1979 in West London. Furniture released their first single, 'Shaking Story', in 1981. Initially they were signed to indie label Survival, releasing singles and a mini-album, *When the Boom Was On*, in 1983. They were augmented occasionally by his brother Larry Whelan on saxophone, and in 1986 they signed to Stiff and released the single 'Brilliant Mind', which went to No.21 in the charts. It was the Stiff label's last hit and has come to be regarded as something of an '80s classic. Mid-1986 saw Furniture go into the studio to record their debut album, *The Wrong People*; it had a limited release in September of 1986. The album followed the June release of *The Lovemongers* in Japan. It contained singles and demos that were held by the band's previous label, Premonition Records. In 1989 they signed to Arista Records and made an album called *Food, Sex & Paranoia* before splitting in 1990. Tim briefly sang with west London post-punk band Transmitters before becoming a found member of world-beat electronica collective Transglobal Underground, who he continues with to this day.

WEST LONDON VENUES
TIM WHELAN
(Missing Presumed Dead, Furniture)

You could smell the old beer and cigarettes as you walked through the door! It was the old pub law 'to have a nice sticky floor'.

The Magic Sponge: "Older by the Minute" What gave the early '80s its particularly malodorous flavour was the feeling of living in the aftermath of one age in the limbo before the next. Post-docker pre-yuppy, you could say. We had no idea what horrors were coming for us and were all the happier about it. Although we tried hard not to be happy. After 1977 the revolution hadn't happened, the 2 sevens hadn't so much clashed as belched, and there was an inevitable feeling of "WTF just happened?" Many people wore grey. I know I did, but that's because I used to put the black stuff in with the white stuff in the launderette; it saved money.

The Clarendon was a ballroom in the middle of old Hammersmith, a functional place with an enjoyably dysfunctional basement. At lunchtimes it was a strip club; in the evening it was a home for homeless music that no one else would give a roof to, psychobilly, avant-garde, early alternative comedy and that strange, grey-clad space in between goth and '80s pop that bands like Furniture wandered through.

The Trafalgar was a grim, joyless, keg-bitter-infested building in the grim, dreary Shepherd's Bush shopping centre (long since tarted up). It was a perfect place to play daft music, as even the local skinheads found the place too depressing to work up the energy to beat anyone up in it, and no one in their right mind would walk in there for a relaxed pint. The Transmitters had split into 2 bands, Transmitters and Missing Presumed Dead, who would meet up at the pub, become the Transmitters Presumed Dead and play either free jazz or ska, depending on the mood.

The White Hart in Acton was once described in some music magazine as 'the last bastion of civilisation before the baleful jungle of downtown Ealing'. The pub was so pleased with this that it adopted 'Last Bastion' as its nickname, probably just to remind anyone from Ealing of what they thought of them.

The Kings Head, just up the road, was my regular haunt, which did them no good at all, as I started doing the sound at the place, and I was bloody useless at it. The Birthday Party suffered at my hands, but some of them hadn't even turned up (maybe they'd been warned). Eventually, when I got feedback from one bloke with an acoustic guitar, I sacked myself, and the venue did rather better. The live room was meant to be haunted... I never saw any proof of this.

The Kensington was in Kensington and was kept remarkably clean by the standards of the day. People did interesting things there, like play in time... This made me uneasy, although I eventually sold out and learnt to play in time myself. Honest!

16

⦿ *Untitled*, the debut LP by Marc and The Mambas, was for sale September 16, 1982. With Marc Almond, here were The Mambas, made from the record label Some Bizzare's personnel Matt Johnson (later of The The), Ann Hogan and Cindy Ecstasy. Almost lounge or cabaret in presentation, it displays Marc's main influences and exhibits the quality of his vocal abilities. To dismiss him because of cover versions is missing the point; Scott Walker's 'Big Louise' is simply atmospherically sublime, and the melodrama created in Lou Reed's 'Caroline Says' is subtle and pleasurable. A must for Marc Almond lovers.

⦿ Colin Newman was born in 1954, in Salisbury, England. Colin, as the up-front vocalist, guitarist and songwriter, was a formation member of Wire. As a solo artist he has released six critically acclaimed solo albums, but it's with Wire that he has displayed a high level of originality. There's no denying that Wire stands as a band that commands attention for the output of the last 45+ years. As an individual, aside from his solo efforts, he delved into production and arrangement, working with the likes of The Virgin Prunes, Minimal Compact and Hawkwind. On his return from a sojourn in India, he brought in a new direction for Wire, an innovative electronic approach. This saw the band find a new market both internationally and locally with a generation acceptant of '80s synthpop. His collaboration *Commercial Suicide* with his wife, Malka Spigel, is an absorbing listen, respect.

⦿ On this day in 1978 The Stranglers headlined an open-air event at Battersea Park, London. It was the first time strippers had appeared with the band, taking the stage during 'Nice and Sleazy'. There was a special guest appearance by Peter Gabriel.

Talking Heads by Robert Mapplethorpe

⦿ In 1977, Talking Heads released their first album, *Talking Heads:77*, which quickly garnered critical acclaim for this fledgling New York City band. While the album didn't make an impact on the US charts, it reached No.60 in the UK. Despite its modest local success, one of its singles, 'Psycho Killer', peaked at No.92 on the Billboard Hot 100, introducing Talking Heads to a wider audience. The band's unique style and innovative sound set them apart, showcasing a blend of creativity, intelligence, and simplicity. The album features a mix of complex rhythms, unexpected tempo shifts, unconventional guitar tunings, and distinctive single-note patterns. David Byrne's exceptional songwriting and vocal abilities shine throughout the record. Few debut albums rival the inventiveness of *Talking Heads:77*, placing it alongside classics like Television's *Marquee Moon*. Arguably, until the release of *Remain in Light*, Talking Heads' subsequent albums struggled to surpass the groundbreaking impact of their debut.

17

◉ Like a call across the valleys, Big Country's debut single 'Harvest Home', released in 1982, was a call to say they had arrived. The anthemic address was typical of Big County's Celtic exclamation. The single failed to chart, but they earned enough respect to be clutched by The Jam as support for their last tour. Good exposure indeed.

◉ Australian singer Scott Carne was born in 1963. Scott is best known as the frontman for Kids in the Kitchen, which formed in Melbourne, Australia, in 1983. Late '83 and '84 saw his band attain two top 20 singles on the Australian national charts when 'Change in Mood' peaked at No.10 and 'Bitter Desire' made it to No.17. On the debut LP *Shine* Kids in the Kitchen exhibited a brand of NEW WAVE that sat squarely in the New Romantic genre and had a quality of complex dancefloor funk that equaled their international contemporaries such as Spandau Ballet or Ultravox. With commercial interest in the genre waning, 1987's album *Terrain*, albeit excellent in output, the band could not duplicate their earlier success and folded in 1988. Today Scott is the driving force behind 'The Absolutely '80s' spectacular, shows that feature icons of Australian NEW WAVE.

◉ In 1977 DEVO released their second single, a cover version of The Rolling Stones' '(I Can't Get No) Satisfaction' on Booji Boy Records. Later in 1978 that original version was part of a 5-track EP named *B Stiff* compiled from previously released singles, including their first outing, 'Mongoloid'. A Brian Eno-produced version appeared on the album *Q: Are We Not Men? A: We Are Devo!*. Of that recording Bob Mothersbaugh said, "*It was our goal to be as faithful to what we were doing as we could. But Brian and David (Bowie) added extra harmony vocals and some synthesizer parts. When we weren't in the studio, Eno would go in on his own and add extra parts over the top of our songs. Most always, we took all the stuff out that they did*". In the end, the song basically emerged unchanged from Devo's prior recording; 'Satisfaction' was only released after Mick Jagger approved it. The song was The Stones' first No.1 single in the US.

◉ Ian McCulloch's debut solo album, *Candleland*, was released in 1989, showcasing his undeniable talent and proving that he was more than just a member of Echo & the Bunnymen. The inclusion of Elizabeth Fraser from Cocteau Twins on the title track adds an extra layer of brilliance to the album. With his clear musical vision and atmospheric creations, Ian's presentation is cohesive and subtle. *Candleland*, produced by Ray Shulman of Gentle Giant, reached No.18 on the UK Albums Chart.

◉ The Motels led the way for NEW WAVE bands from the United States. There were many others, such as Berlin, Quarterflash, and 'Til Tuesday, but The Motels were the pioneers of this movement. Their *self-titled* debut album, which was released on this very day in 1979, is exceptional. The standout track, 'Total Control', is incredibly captivating, just like the rest of the album. If you're a fan of NEW WAVE music, it is worth your time to seek out this album. Additionally, if you enjoy The Motels, their compilation album *No Reservations*, also known as *No Vacancy*, is a meticulously curated collection that is packed with fantastic songs.

18

◉ Martin Bramah was born in Manchester, England, in 1957. Martin was a founding member of The Fall, The Teardrops, Thirst and Blue Orchids. The Fall came together in Manchester in 1976 when Martin teamed up with Mark E. Smith, Una Baines, and Tony Friel. Such was their output over more than 40 years. The Fall earned the label as 'the most prolific band of the British POST-PUNK movement'. Martin's first tenure with the band lasted about 3 years, departing in April 1979, not long after the release of their debut album, the astounding *Live at the Witch Trials*. He returned in 1990 for the *Extricate* album, leaving while on tour in Australia later that year. Arguably, Martin's work with Blue Orchids is his crowning glory, releasing 7 albums to date to critical acclaim. In 2022 he reunited in a collaboration with ex-Fall members Simon Wolstencroft, Steve Hanley, and Pete Greenway as House of All.

◉ Joanne Catherall was born September 18, 1962, in Sheffield, England. She is one of the two female vocalists for The Human League. The story of how Joanne & Susan Sulley came to join The Human League remains firmly embedded in pop legend. Although verified by all involved, it was questioned at the time in some quarters as a modern Cinderella story or a deliberate publicity stunt. The story goes that Phil Oakey spotted two teenage girls dancing at the Crazy Daisy Nightclub, with what he considered unique dance moves, immaculate make-up, and an ultra-feminine dress style. Phil felt they would be ideal, and both were invited to join the tour. Catherall and Sulley accepted the offer, but then he had to convince their parents. Fears were laid to rest when Oakey visited the girls' parents to assure them that, in Oakey's words, *"This isn't a heinous plan to take the girls abroad and sell them; they will come to no harm."*

◉ In 1982, Cocteau Twins released their first EP, *Lullabies*. The EP followed on from their dazzling debut album *Garlands* a few weeks earlier. Here there's a more minimalist, sparse sound than the goth layers of *Garlands*; the drum machine programming is more interesting, and the songs are overall more melodic. Elizabeth Fraser's vocals seem to be finding a greater level of confidence here; coupled with Robin Guthrie's guitar style, we are given a blueprint of what is to become The Cocteaus. *Lullabies* certainly aren't anywhere near their peak but did show Cocteau Twins were headed in the right direction.

◉ Dee Dee Ramone, aka Douglas Colvin, was born in 1951, in Prince George County, Virginia, USA. Dee Dee played bass with the Ramones. History shows that Dee Dee was the archetypical 'live hard – die young' rocker. He was a male prostitute, a convicted mugger, a heroin user and dealer, an accomplice to armed robbery and acclaimed as a genius poet who was always headed for an early grave. Dee Dee was the group's primary songwriter, putting his talents to Ramones classics like 'Rockaway Beach', '53rd & 3rd', and 'Poison Heart'. Dee Dee appeared on a dozen albums, played countless live dates and was with the Ramones through several line-up changes but departed in 1990. Surprisingly, after parting ways with the Ramones, he embarked on a brief, unsuccessful career as a hip-hop rapper, taking the name Dee Dee King. He recorded 5 solo albums, the last in 2000 being reworkings of Ramones songs and a couple of covers. It was Dee Dee that came up with the name The Ramones; it was a reworking of Paul McCartney's hotel check-in name of Paul Ramon. Dee Dee died of a drug overdose on 5th June, 2002, and was buried at the Hollywood Forever Cemetery in Hollywood, California, not far from the cenotaph of his former Ramones 'bandmate, Johnny Ramone.

◉ Heaven 17 released their first LP, *Penthouse and Pavement*, in 1981 on the Virgin label. As a brilliant album should, it was certified gold in the UK and held some great singles. '(We

Don't Need This) Fascist Groove Thang' and 'Play to Win' were both on high radio rotation and immediate dance floor hits. Much of the NEW WAVE and electronic music of the late 1970s and early 1980s can sound a bit dated all these years later, but this landmark album still sounds fresh and funky over 40 years after it was recorded. It's hard to deny that this is one of the best synthpop albums ever; precise keyboards, political-social comment, funky dance rhythms, pop hooks, and distinctive vocals are all firmly in place – truly the signs of a classic album. What more could you ask for? Except for a few tracks, this album is perfect Reagan/Thatcher-era '80s NEW WAVE dance music. The trio of Martin Ware, Glenn Gregory and Ian Craig Marsh that was Heaven 17 were now paving the way as a big influence on the future direction of synthpop. Often somewhat cold and clinical but all the while charming, witty, entertaining, and thought provoking. Essential.

◉ The Passions, hailing from Shepherd's Bush, England, released their second album, *Thirty Thousand Feet Over China*, in 1981. Highlighting Barbara Gogan's vocals, the album includes the captivating track 'I'm In Love with A German Film Star'. Contrasting their previous darker post-punk sound, the record leans more towards pop. Despite being overlooked, this album deserves a second listen. Standout tracks like 'The Swimmer' and 'Bachelor Girls' further showcase the band's talent.

◉ On Monday, September 18, 1978, just nine days after they'd first met, Yello played their first performance at a fashion show at the Cinema Forum in Zurich, Switzerland. The event was a showcase for the winter collection by dressmaker-designer Ursula Rodel, who created clothes for movie stars like Maria Schneider and Catherine Deneuve.

19

◉ Big Dish from Airdrie, Scotland, released their debut album, *Swimmer*, in 1986. With comparisons to Aztec Camera & Blue Nile, they indeed had a level of sophistication and style about them. *Swimmer* is a pleasurable listen, with some tasty melodies and harmonies based around Steven Lindsay's smooth vocals. The album opens beautifully with two excellent pieces in 'Prospect Street' and 'Christina's World' and carries on well, through to and beyond the atmospheric title track.

◉ Daniel Lanois was born in 1951, in Quebec, Canada. Daniel is highly talented as a musician but possibly best known for his massive list of production work, which includes the U2 albums *The Joshua Tree* and *Achtung Baby* and Bob Dylan's *Oh Mercy*, as well as Dylan's award-winning *Time Out of Mind*. He has entered quite a few collaborations with the likes of Peter Gabriel (*Birdy*) and Brian Eno (*Apollo*). As a solo recording artist, Daniel has released several albums, most notably his debut, *Arcadie*, in 1989.

◉ Rusty Egan, born Peter Anselm Egan, the son of Irish showband leaders, was born in 1957, in London, England. In 1977 Rusty was a founding member and the drummer for The Rich Kids up until 1979 and then with Midge Ure, Billy Currie, John McGeoch, Dave Formula, and Barry Adamson formed Visage with Steve Strange as vocalist. Visage went to the top 10 in the UK with their second single, 'Fade to Grey'. It was during this period that Rusty and Strange created The Blitz Club in Covent Garden, where Rusty was the DJ while the ever-flamboyant Steve Strange was on the door. Opening in October 1980, it was arguably the most influential New Romantic nightclub in London. From The Blitz, Rusty and Steve embarked on several other club ventures, including the Camden Palace, which was regarded as London's biggest and most adventurous club. It was here Rusty was integral in promoting electronic music in London, and it was here that Madonna made her British debut after Rusty brought her from the USA! Rusty owned Trident Studios and formed a music publishing company, signing Soft Cell, B-Movie, Johnny Hates Jazz, and Specimen.

Rusty was also working as a producer for Spear of Destiny and Shock the Senate and made many one-offs. In 2017 he released the album *Welcome to the Dancefloor*, featuring Tony Hadley, Peter Hook, Midge Ure, and others. Rusty now releases records he has produced through his own label Future Music via Universal and Blitzed, including *Blitzed*, the album for the soundtrack he wrote and recorded for the TV documentary of the same name. In 2023/4 Rusty toured with Heaven 17 and supported Marc Almond and others as guest DJ. Later this year, Demon Records are releasing a 100-track box set of tracks that Rusty played at the Blitz, which he personally curated, with Rusty's next multi-artist album, *Romantic*, due for release in 2025.

THANK YOU!
RUSTY A EGAN
(Rich Kids, Visage, Blitz nightclub)

In 2017 I released *Welcome to the Dancefloor*; it was an album that was meant to be a Visage album, but I was told, "*Steve Strange is Visage; he does not need you or the band*," so I made it my own album. To close out the album, I said "*THANK YOU*" by the track of the same name. I thanked as many inspirational artists as I could, from the members of Kraftwerk to Jean-Michel Jarre to Moby, among a host of others. When I made Welcome to the Remix, I asked Kretz if they would remix 'Thank You' and suggested a whole other list of inspirational people. It's sad to say that many of the artists didn't seem to think that it was important. So now, I should make a new track and list of all those who have said "*thank you*" and have even better actually asked if I am, OK? I know I would do the same.

I could say in most stories there is a light bulb moment, like with 'We Will Rock You', the 'include the audience' idea from Brian May, which was such a game changer, or clothes, or haircuts, or the addition of a synth. There's playing an album to a band and saying, "*Guys, you need to change directions. Here's a producer; meet Flood*", or maybe even introducing Martin Rushent to the synth and SMPTE code. It's whatever inspires or sets them off in a new direction. Then there are DJs who had no idea about a small emerging genre or how to play out things in a certain style. One may unwittingly give away the 'golden nugget', and they, the recipients and users of said nugget, never give that 'thank you' because it means it was not their idea.

In 2019 I made a few comments on social media relating to my being a founder of The Batcave Club that all these years later seem to be cited as the onset of the musical term Goth Music. I was pointed to an American, Donny "Doktor" Sanders, host of Gothcast, who had made a short documentary called History of The Batcave Club. This documentary on YouTube is a must for a look into that time and its impact on goth culture today.

We'll now travel in time for some goth history! I hope you enjoy this snippet view from 'The Batcave'.

Well, I had not given much thought to this period until I corresponded with Jon Klein, the guitarist from The Batcave 'house band' Specimen. Through an interview of sorts, Jon kind of summed up very simply my role in the team that created the club and how Specimen moved into the industry. Once The Batcave was up and running, Kevin Millins and I were on to the next idea; for me, that was Yello, then to New York with Celluloid Records.

Here is my chat with Jon :- 20/01/2016

Jon…

Hi Rusty, I hope you are well!!! I was going to reply to you on the Specimen site but thought it might be better for you to come direct. I'm working on a project about the Batcave story, so it would be great to do a chat/interview if you have time.

Rusty A…

OK, but I am not really a part of the story. I did not run The Batcave; I did not even DJ, but I did spend a fortune financing it.

Jon…

Yes, you put your money where your mouth is big time; I do recall that you also drummed for us on our first Trident session and hassled us to straighten and toughen our rhythms, a bit of a Godfather really (except that makes you sound too old!). For me, it was a massive difference you made!

Rusty A…

That's cool; I did mentor you. I was the first person to book you, get you in the studio and then introduce you to Seymour Stein from Sire Records and London Records.

Jon…

Yes, you got us signed to Metropolis and also met Final Solution at your Trident Studios, and that led to the idea of the Batcave. London Records came to the Batcave to check out Specimen, got interested, then we all got together and organised the *Batcave* album, which I recall was Flood's first proper production job. Is that the way I remember it? – Probably your idea!? Seymour Stein heard about us via the two Danceteria shows we did in NYC, where we totally set designed 2 floors of the club and created a bit of a stir. It must have been around that time that you and Steve Strange opened Camden Palace; that was a pretty major happening! Thank you.

Rusty A…

Let's get together one of these days; it's great to hear from you!

If I ever get to write my book, it will have a load of people exclaiming, *"NO, that's a lie!"* because they have lived with it for over forty years, as I was 'The Invisible Man'. If they are cool, they will confirm that yes, that did happen, there will be a 'thank you', and yes, Rusty was in the room!

◉ The debut single by Yachts 'Suffice to Say' was in the racks on this day in 1979. Released on the Stiff label, these power poppers penned a clever song where they sing about the song itself. It's fun, catchy, and somewhat irreverent. The highlights here are the harmonies and the keyboards of Henry Priestman, very reminiscent of The Stranglers' Dave Greenfield.

20

◉ Sweet Pea Atkinson, aka Hillard Atkinson, was born in 1945, in Oberlin, Ohio, USA. Sweet Pea was a lead vocalist with WAS (NOT WAS) along with Harry Bowens and appeared on all five studio albums. Sweet Pea recorded two solo albums; the first, *Don't Walk Away* from 1982, was what could be regarded as 'the great lost Was (Not Was) album', a recording not so left-stream as WAS. It's an album of modern soul with great grooves for dancing. Sweet Pea was in high demand as a support session vocalist for his smoky blues-soul voice; he worked with the likes of Iggy Pop, Bob Dylan, and Brian Wilson, among a host of others. Sweet Pea died after suffering a heart attack on May 5, 2020, aged 74.

◉ Alannah Joy Currie was born in 1957, in Auckland, New Zealand. She was the lyricist, percussionist, vocalist, and saxophone player with the Thompson Twins. The band name was adopted from the character detectives Thompson & Thompson from The Adventures of Tintin comics. In 1981 Alannah joined what was then a 7-piece unit as a part-time sax player. By 1983 the line-up had been pared down to just three members. Tom Bailey, Joe Leeway and Alannah, who together created a dance-heavy synthpop band. Through '83 they figured dominantly on the singles charts worldwide with 'Lies', 'Love on Your Side' and their most successful tune, 'Hold Me Now'. 1984 saw the album *Into the Gap* sell over 5 million units worldwide; the Twins were HUGE! Leeway departed in 1986, and the Twins continued as a duo. With the dissolve of The Thompson Twins in 1992, Currie and Bailey teamed up with Keith Fernley to form Babble, a 3-year-long project that had a sound of dub-influenced chill-out. Since leaving the music business in 1996, Alannah has continued working as a visual artist in London and New Zealand. She works with both glass and soft sculpture and continues to write. She uses various pseudonyms, including Miss Pokeno, the Sisters of Perpetual Resistance and the Armchair Destructivists.

Alannah Currie by Gavin Evans

IN THE BEGINNING
ALANNAH CURRIE
(Thompson Twins, Babble)

In 1968 I was given a transistor radio for my eleventh birthday. Turquoise plastic with a silver mesh front. Fancy. It was my own personal direct line to pop music and saw me through many a heartbroken teenage romance. I discovered early on that if I rested that transistor on the window ledge in the bathroom and then lay in the bath, submerging my ears under water, I could dub out the vocals of whatever track was playing and sing along with my own invented lyrics. I didn't know it then, but that was the beginning of my songwriting career. I dreamed of being a poet, but that was never going to happen in the State House suburb of Auckland I was raised in. Girls got married early and weren't encouraged to have ambition for much else.

At 19 I ran away to London. It was 1977, and I found myself in Brixton. It was not the scene from Mary Poppins I had visualised. The place was a dump. There were still bomb sites full of rubble, buildings black with centuries of soot and everywhere empty houses with boarded-up windows because the councils had run out of money to repair them. But it was full of possibility and excitement. Reggae music and dub sound systems blasted the streets. I moved straight into one of those empty council house squats, bought myself a pair of red rubber boots with pointy toes and a big Chinese-style hat and started going to gigs. Already a young feminist, I was fuelled by punk attitude and inspired by the Slits, the Raincoats, the Mo-dettes, and the Au Pairs. I started my own loud experimental band called the Unfuckables with a girl across the street. We were pretty bad. It was not pop music. But it was a lot of fun.

Some boys from Sheffield moved in across the street and had a band called the Thompson Twins. At first I thought they were sort of lame, but then I saw them play at the 101 Club on St Johns Hill and realised they knew how to write fierce pop songs. Ones like 'Squares and Triangles' and 'Politics'. I became friends with Tom, who was a really good musician and knew about harmonies and chords and all the stuff I didn't know about. He kept pestering me to join their band because he liked my wildness and dirty improvised saxophone playing. I didn't want to be in that band, though. Too many boys. I wanted to be in one of my own.

It took a while, but eventually I did rob that band of their two best men… Tom and Joe. And in 1982 we started our own band writing synthpop songs. I was in heaven then. It was a truly glorious time. 'Fuck politics, let's dance' was our mantra. The three of us would spend hours and hours in the front room of my squat with an eight-track Teac and an Ob-Xa synth and various percussion instruments writing and recording songs. Tom made up killer melodies and horn riffs, and I'd write the words, and together we'd all make up rhythm tracks…loop them…then overdub more beats…pickpocketing from the best. We traded ideas and learnt from each other. Nothing was out of bounds...nothing was prescriptive... We just made it all up as we went along. We sent four of these rough songs on a cassette to Alex Sadkin, who had just produced Grace Jones' *Nightclubbing* album, and a few weeks later we were on a flight to the Bahamas to work at Compass Point Studios with him. It was that fast. Mad and hugely exciting! We arrived on that tropical island, all squat, smelly of cigarettes and dirty leather jackets, and sat nervously waiting to meet Alex in the studio reception.

He was late, but eventually a taxi pulled up, and in walked Grace. She pauses at the door and scans the room … She fixes her gaze on me and Tom, then points one long beautiful brown arm at us and says, "*tak…take my bags to my room!*" Blindsided with adoration for her, we do as she bids without question. And so began the best adventure in music-making three ragged kids from South London could have ever hoped for.

⊙ On September 20, 1978, Joy Division made their television debut playing 'Shadowplay' when they appeared on the Manchester TV programme *Granada Reports*, in the Tony Wilson-hosted segment What's On.

⊙ The collaboration set *The Bridge* recorded by Thomas Leer and Robert Rental was in the public's hands on this day in 1979. Two vastly different sides of experimental synthpop and Enoesque music that are thoroughly absorbing. A fine first from these two guys. It's easy to see that they were influenced by German industrial and minimal synth, and of course Brian Eno's work. It was recorded at home; it's lo-fi and rather ahead of its time; you can file it next to any Throbbing Gristle and Cabaret Voltaire release. That said, they exhibit more variation; side one is the earliest of what we came to know as synthpop, with flavours of Kraftwerk, The Human League and Depeche Mode. Side two, stimulating and indeed enjoyable, features dark drone ambience and oblique musical sketches that are easily revisited by the listener.

⊙ Born on September 20, 1951, in Islington, London, Joe Leeway was an integral member of the classic Thompson Twins lineup alongside Tom Bailey and Alannah Currie. As one of the band's backup vocalists and multi-instrumentalists in the 1980s, Leeway helped shape the Thompson Twins' signature sound and image. After starting with the band as a roadie, Leeway officially joined as a member in 1980 and remained until 1986, contributing to albums like *Here's to Future Days*. Arguably, Leeway's greatest musical achievement was co-creating 1983's *Quick Step & Side Kick*, the Thompson Twins' breakthrough album that peaked at No.2 in the UK. With its blend of infectious harmonies, cutting-edge synths, and danceable beats, the album exemplified the band's warm yet innovative NEW WAVE/pop style; it had a sense of warmth and playfulness, something that contemporaries like The Human League didn't have. *Quick Step & Side Kick* yielded hit singles like 'Lies', 'Love on Your Side', and 'We Are Detective' that still hold up decades later as classics of the era.

⊙ John Lever, drummer with The Chameleons was born in Manchester in 1962. Coming in from The Politicians, John joined when Brian Schofield departed, and he went on to play on each of The Chameleons' four albums. After the split in 1987, John was part of The Sun and the Moon with ex-Chameleon Mark Burgess and the Red-Sided Garter Snakes with Dave

Fielding, also a Chameleon member. He also joined Burgess to play the band's back catalogue in ChameleonsVox. John died on March 13, 2017.

⦿ Though destined to become a highly impactful band, The Stone Roses had very modest origins. Their first single in 1985, 'So Young' b/w 'Tell Me', comes across as rather ordinary and gave no hint of the sound they would perfect by the time of their *self-titled* debut album four years later. Over that period, the quality of their songwriting and image underwent major improvements. The debut single is one mainly for die-hard fans seeking completeness.

21

⦿ Before they were Faith No More, they were Faith No Man, and it was Faith No Man that released the one and only single 'Quiet in Heaven' b/w 'Song of Liberty' in 1983. The vocals that are in the background by Mike "The Man" Morris are overshadowed by an aural onslaught of ultra-percussive bass and drumming that gives a nod to PiL.

⦿ Mylène Farmer, aka Mylène Jeanne Gautier, was born in 1961, in Pierrefonds, Canada. Mylene, a singer, actor, writer and illustrator, is huge in France and Europe. Having sold over 30 million units of her dozen or so albums worldwide, she has become an icon of French music. Much of her success can be attributed to the extraordinary talent featured in the extravagant and brilliantly produced Laurent Boutonnat film clips that come across as mini-films, which, all the time, engage, and exhibit subject matters of death, the occult, romance, and violence. Mylene is the only artist that has had over 20 songs make it to the top position on the charts, as well as being the only French artist to twice fill the Stade de France (Stadium of France). Her 1986 *Cendres de Lune* (*Ashes of The Moon*) album is a daring and expressive outing; from this, she was tagged as 'The French Madonna', but with her level of creativity and panache, she's more like 'The French Kate Bush'. As a vocalist, Mylene is always melodic, intriguingly seductive, and mysterious. Her range of methods is difficult to pigeonhole; she branches from synthpop to café to pastoral to ethereal.

⦿ Dave Gregory, aka Lord Cornelius Plum (Dukes of The Stratosphear), was born in 1952 in Swindon, England. Dave is best known as the guitarist/keyboardist for XTC and was an integral member through their golden recording era of the '80s into the '90s. In 1999, in the middle of recording Apple Venus, Dave left XTC, citing "*In recording everything went wrong*" and that Andy (Partridge) was "*not interested in what he had to say*". Staying as part of XTC became untenable for Dave; the growth of bitterness within him due to the 'attitude and lack of respect', meant he had to leave. His departure led him to the studio to record solo works and become a highly sought-after session player, and with that record, he performed under various guises such as R. Gregsy Moore, David Dreams, Jet Pastorius, Bongo & The Proteus Orchestra. In 2012 he was part of Big Big Train and Tin Spirits.

⦿ British producer and songwriter Rupert Hine was born in London, England, in 1947. Rupert had an extensive catalogue of production credits with the likes of The Fixx, The Members, Bob Geldof, Thompson Twins, among a host of others. His greatest success came in 1984, when he topped the UK Albums Chart with Howard Jones' debut album, *Human's Lib*. Rupert released 6 solo albums before he died on June 5, 2020.

⦿ In 2011 R.E.M. announced that they were calling it a day as a band and were splitting. The decision didn't come lightly; the trio had been discussing the possibility of breaking up for several years, and the decision was made easier by the lacklustre critical and commercial response to their latest releases. A publicity release quoted: "*All things must end, and we wanted to do it right, to do it our way. We walk away with a great sense of gratitude, of finally, and of astonishment at all we have accomplished. To anyone who ever felt touched by our music, our deepest thanks for listening."*

○ On September 20, 1979, Pennie Smith took the classic *London Calling* album cover photograph. It is one of the most famous photographs in the history of rock 'n' roll. The photograph shows Paul Simonon about to smash up his bass guitar during a show at The Palladium, New York City.

○ The debut album by 10,000 Maniacs was released in September 1983; however, it did not receive much recognition. The melodic NEW WAVE sound of *Secrets of the I Ching* is quite enjoyable and should have garnered more attention. Natalie Merchant's unique and appealing vocal style is noteworthy, but the standout feature is undeniably Robert Buck's skilful guitar work. The album offers a diverse range of musical styles, incorporating elements of jazz, NEW WAVE, and folk. Tracks like 'Pit Viper' and 'Daktari' are particularly strong, making it surprising that the album did not achieve greater success.

22

○ *Friends*, the first full-length album by The Bolshoi, was released in 1986. Call it NEW WAVE, gothic rock, or POST-PUNK; The Bolshoi is quite undefinable; only the listener can be the judge. There are flavours of Sad Lovers & Giants, Echo & The Bunnymen and even Bauhaus, at times bright, at times melancholy, but nonetheless engaging. The production is neat, crisp, and clear, with the standout tracks being 'Away' and 'Sunday Morning'. Very much capturing the zeitgeist, and today it remains an intriguing listen.

Nick Cave by Petra Gall

○ Nick Cave was born in Warracknabeal, Victoria, in 1957. Nick Cave's mind is a deep spring of dark beauty and improbable inspirations. He is a restless, relentless creator, bouncing carelessly across genres and forms, from music and literature to screenwriting, acting, and even theatre. After cutting his teeth in the late '70s and early '80s with the bombastic Birthday Party, Cave assembled the seminal POST-PUNK outfit the Bad Seeds in 1983, refining his music's mix of blues, gospel, and experimental elements. Charting successes have mostly eluded Nick's work, but in 1995 with Kylie Minogue, he had a top 10 hit with 'Where the Wild Roses Grow', & in 1996 a UK No.36 charter with PJ Harvey 'Henry Lee'.

○ Herman de Tollenaere was born September 22, in Leiden, The Netherlands. Herman, who holds a PhD in history, was a co-founder of the band Vipers and well known as the frontman-vocalist for Cheap 'n' Nasty. From 1978 he was the editor of Pin (then the only non-Amsterdam Dutch punkzine) and the founder of Rock Against Racism Netherlands. In Pin, he wrote the earliest Dutch punk comic strip and published the first Dutch interviews with Poison Girls, The Raincoats, and the new band of Brian James, ex-Damned. Cheap 'n' Nasty's first concert was with Crass in 1980, at Crass headquarters. In 1981 they recorded and released the EP Covergirl on their own label; it featured Herman on vocals/toy saxophone and became the only early Dutch punk band with a positive record review: "*The four songs on this record are very original and well played. I feel like cheering*".

OPENING FOR U.K. SUBS
HERMAN de TOLLENAERE
(CHEAP 'N' NASTY)

In early 1980, the U.K. Subs played in Rotterdam, the Netherlands.

Terry, my Cheap 'n' Nasty bass/female lead vocals bandmate, and I interviewed them for our fanzine Pin. Subs singer Charlie Harper said, "*You are a band as well. Later this year, we will play in Venlo. Do you want to open for us?*"

Of course! We contacted the promoters of that concert in the Ons Huis venue in Venlo, Bureau Pinkpop (also organisers of the big open-air music festival of that name). Bureau Pinkpop said, "*We will not pay anything for a support band.*"

Then, Charlie Harper stepped in. He paid for petrol to get from the western Netherlands to southeastern Netherlands Venlo. First with Terry's tiny red Fiat from Delft to Zwijndrecht, and next with Terry's brother's car to Venlo.

At least Bureau Pinkpop provided fruit for us to eat.

Almost nobody in Venlo knew we would play, except the only Venlo Pin subscriber, Karin, and a pen pal of Terry, who travelled from Helmond to Venlo especially to see us. Still, we had to play an encore. Big audience, surely more than a thousand. Later it was written that Party for Freedom (PVV) party politician Geert Wilders, then 14, was one of them.

After playing, I thanked the audience from the stage, saying, "*You have shown tonight that there is something better in Limburg province than Catholic bishop Gijsen*" (an extremist conservative; later denounced by his own diocese for his paedophilia).

Charlie Harper said, "*Come back to play with us anytime!*" We did. In March 1981, in Eindhoven, when Cheap 'n' Nasty opened for the U.K. Subs again, Alvin Gibbs, their bassist, bought the first copy of our Covergirl EP. He still has it.

◉ Peter Hartinger, aka Jan Cux, was born in Duisburg, Germany, on September 22, 1959. Peter is a highly respected music journalist and photographer who socialised with British glam rock in the early seventies. The bombast rock of the seventies increasingly alienated him, so the punk revolution acted as a liberation for him. By the beginning of the eighties, Peter saw that punk had reached a point where its musical and social innovative power seemed to be waning; pure 1-2-3 punk rock had and what it had become was now a bore musically! For him, the new magic words were 'POST-PUNK' and 'indie'. "Good" were the small independent labels, fanzines, the small clubs, the small record stores, and independent distribution channels; "Evil" were the major record companies, like EMI and indeed the big concert arenas. The worst was commercialism! In 2021 he published the book *Der Lärm der Nacht - POST-PUNK im Westen (The Noise of the Night - POST-PUNK in the West),* which makes concert photos from the POST-PUNK era accessible again. It features pictures of Einstürzende Neubauten, Chameleons, The Fall, Siouxsie & the Banshees, Alien Sex Fiend, Tuxedomoon, Portion Control, Sonic Youth and many other bands. In summer 2024, Peter's photographs were exhibited at the 'rock'n'pop museum' in Gronau, Germany.

OBSERVATIONS OF NEUE DETSCHE WELLE AND POST-PUNK

PETER HARTINGER
(Journalist, photographer)

THE EVENT RELECTIONS

In 1981, NEW WAVE had really taken off in Germany under the trademark "Neue Deutsche Welle" (NDW). Many bands from the underground had suddenly become interesting for the big record companies. The scene was seething; there was talk of selling out. First and foremost, it was Fehlfarben who had made their breakthrough with their album *Monarchie und Alltag (Monarchy and Everyday Life)*. Their song 'Es geht voran' became the anthem of a whole generation. Just at the peak of success, the charismatic singer Peter Hein left the band. The outcry was great when immediately before the first big festival of the NDW in the Philipshalle in Düsseldorf on June 17, 1981, it leaked out that Janie Jones, as Peter Hein liked to be called, would not be on stage but only in front of it. What had happened? Fehlfarben was heavily criticised in the scene beforehand because she had signed with EMI. The band Rotzkotz even made a song about it, 'Tante EMI'. Against this background, Hein decided for his job at Rank Xerox and against the career with Fehlfarben. The concert of Fehlfarben without their frontman turned into a fiasco. Guitarist Thomas Schwebel could not inspire the audience. The audience reacted disappointedly, even a little aggressively. Very German, very "kraut" and experimental were the Wirtschaftswunder. The band around the eccentric singer Angelo Galizia belonged to the quartet of the top bands of the NDW that performed in Düsseldorf. They had had a small underground hit with 'Der Kommissar', which humorously took a German crime series for a ride. Just like the avant-garde Palais Schaumburg, the Wirtschaftswunder didn't hit the nerve of the masses in front of the stage that day. Palais Schaumburg were the darlings of the feuilleton with their atonal stumbling funk. Some claimed they had listened to too much Residents. The pointed lyrics of singer Holger Hiller paired with dissonant sounds catered to intellectual audiences and didn't go down well that night, also because of the bad sound. The music of Palais Schaumburg was just too top-heavy for the audience on this national holiday. This changed only when DAF (Deutsch-Amerikanische Freundschaft) went on stage. The raging mob had been waiting for them. With hard beats and synthetic pogo sound, the audience went wild. When DAF played their hit "Der Mussolini" towards the end of the evening, all dams broke, and the crowd surged up to the stage. Robert Görl, Gabi Delgado and all of us sank into the "All against all" chaos of pogo. Unforgotten.

THE OPENING OF THE LEGENDARY ZECHE CLUB IN BOCHUM

November 7, 1981, the Zeche in Bochum venue (West Germany) is opened. In a former industrial wasteland, in a building formerly used as a locksmith's shop of the coal mine "Prinz Regent", which opened in the early eighties, is the concert venue that has long since become a myth, simply called Zeche (Mine). The concert venue, which was initially funded with public money, was always a first-class address for NEW WAVE and POST-PUNK bands from Germany and abroad. Everybody has been here! - They've all played here: Cabaret Voltaire, Wire, Sister of Mercy, The Fall, and Depeche Mode, just to name a few.

After more than 4,000 concerts, the Zeche is still a fixed address for club tours, especially for bands that don't (yet) fill the really big halls. In that November 1981 opening event, Croox, the band from Düsseldorf, fit perfectly into the ambience of the Zeche; with its pipes and scaffolding on the walls and under the ceiling, they made an industrial, yet lively, impression. Croox played hectic synth-electronics, mainly leaning on their only female member, Bine. They provided a chaotic, sometimes dissonant NEW WAVE sound with German lyrics. Their second album, *Geld Her!*, had just been released with new music that was fresh and distinctive. Next, the local band Vorgruppe played. The 3-man band put their accents, similar to Croox, on electronics, a little less experimental. Surprisingly, one or other punk piece was also played; all in all, the music felt more honest. The band from Herne had released a small underground hit with their debut album *Im Herzen von Nielsen 2*. Their music was playful to unconventional with German "Sprechgesang", a typical characteristic of the German variety of NEW WAVE. Hass (Hate) performed the last gig of the night. Monotonous punk to which not much could be said. Hass were on the legendary Soundtracks zum Untergang punk sampler and therefore known to some people who had come just for them. For the punks now was the opportunity to dance pogo – the musicians seemed to be honestly bored. The show became more interesting in the end when a singer was taken from the audience – of course planned. Late at night I drove home, not knowing how often I should return to this magical place.

GARAGELAND & A BEER WITH JOHN PEEL

Sometimes it's the encounters with unique people, places with a special fascination or bands that leave a lasting mark on a person's life. In my case it is the Garageland, a record store that changed my life. The famous cult store, which was to become famous beyond Germany's borders, opened on November 2, 1983, near the university in Duisburg, a rather dreary working-class town in the Ruhr area. For me it was soon clear; a side job in this store had to come. Which then also became true. As unsexy as Duisburg was, so hipper was Garageland with its trendsetting assortment for all of West Germany. The founders, Rolf and Lothar, offered a two-pronged assortment. Reggae on the one hand, NEW WAVE/POST-PUNK on the other. They liked to orientate themselves on what the icon John Peel sent into the ether week after week in his radio show. Eventually, the music that Peel broadcast via BFBS (British Forces Broadcasting Service) was also available in West Germany. Lothar Röse, the specialist for the rock section, was a music enthusiast. It is said that he was responsible for the first airplay of the in Germany-famous Toten Hosen via John Peel. Allegedly, he sent a single from his range to the BBC. On the occasion of record purchases in London, it came to the first personal contact with our Garageland posse. In an article in the Independent of October 2, 1993, Peel describes the first meeting: "*I do these programmes for British Forces Broadcasting [BFBS], and although there doesn't seem to be a lot of forces listening, they are obviously very popular with the Germans. Tullus and his mates turned up at the BBC one day... and phoned up from reception to ask if I had time for a beer.*" Looking back, Lothar said, "*Peel had always asked his listeners to come over, and we just took him at his word*". From then on, whenever he had business on the continent, he came to visit Duisburg whenever possible and then occasionally to Garageland (although I don't think he got to see much that was new since we had orientated ourselves quite strictly to the Peel repertoire).

From 1984 on, Garageland organised an incomparable concert series in the Ruhr area. Lothar made a mixtape of exciting music and rattled off possible concert organisers. That's how the unique concert series with bands like Test Department, Laibach, Sonic Youth, Mark Stewart & the Maffia, etc., started in Oberhausen in the eighties. The extraordinary store remained a pulse generator and mecca for music fans in West Germany until the mid-nineties.

EINSTÜRZENDE NEUBAUTEN or
HOW F.M. EINHEIT MADE MY GIRLFRIEND PUKE

October 9, 1985. In the record store. For the first time, the freshly pressed LP *1/2 Mensch* is on the novelty shelf with a whopping number of copies. Every second customer fiddles with the work. Bestseller. Einstürzende Neubauten at the height of their fame.

The Wuppertal Börse venue is packed when Blixa Bargeld comes on stage with a necessary delay. A cassette moves into the player, which should be observed more often that evening (and not only on stage). The audience stands motionless; nothing happens on stage, while 1/2 Mensch wobbles noisily out of the speakers. Then Einstürzende Neubauten begin to beat rhythmically. A shopping cart, steel beams, and metal sheets are worked on with a hammer and metal pipe. F.M. Einheit elicits dull, wobbling vibrations from thick steel springs. My girlfriend suddenly feels totally sick ... She has to get out of the hall into the fresh air. I have to remember that the US Army is said to have experimented with subsonic basses as a weapon.... You should try contacting F.M. Einheit!

The show is visually very unusual. On stage there is no conventional rock band with guitar, bass and drums; the metal objects on which they bang around create very special sounds. Blixa Bargeld's stage presence is extraordinary, but the noise, on the other hand, can't really inspire me. The visitors, on the other hand, waited spellbound – or were they bored? Nobody wanted to demand the encore, which is usual in the schedule... It was embarrassing that the Neubauten came again anyway. Einstürzende Neubauten had just taken off! Their new LP sold magnificently; there was talk of 30,000 copies. 1/2 Mensch even inspired the Japanese Sogo Ishii to make a documentary film about the band. As a result, Einstürzende Neubauten became more and more interesting for the establishment, the art business and important cultural figures. Commercially, it seemed to be the right way to open up and make the industrial noise of the early phase (Kollaps,1981) more audible through more song structures. A milestone on the threshold of commercialism. For the band, the beginning of a great career that culminated in banal kitsch with Alles in Allem in 2020 at the latest.

◉ Pete R Jones, aka 'Joyless' the bassist, was born in 1957 near Watford, Hertfordshire, England. Pete started his first band at 15 and learnt his craft listening to classic rock players like Geezer Butler, Jack Bruce and especially Chris Squire from YES: "*I loved his crunchy Rickenbacker.*" Pete's first recording venture was as a 17-year-old amateur with Bogart but went "professional" being part of Cowboys International in 1980 and got to go on tour. From there, Brian Brain toured internationally with drummer friend Martin Atkins, who was fresh out of PiL. Soon through Martin's recommendation, Pete was a member of PiL; "*I couldn't stand PiL's music.*" Understandably, it was a brief tenure; that was in 1982/3. "*Atkins and I wrote Solitaire, but after I left, they couldn't be arsed to give me credit for it.*" Pete moved away from music for a few years, coming back to release the *Twisted* album in 2000, then 2005's Neurotechnic. Soon to come were releases with Department S, solo and collaborative works and many guest appearances. Late 2024 saw Pete release *The Pete Jones Compendium of Nonsense*, a 49-track compilation of Pete's work. It holds work by him as Joyless Jones and a number of collaborations, including his recordings with Department S, The Creepy Dolls and Fever Creature. Mid-2025 saw Pete release excellent covers of Cowboys International's 'Thrash' and Kraftwerk's 'Calculator'.

ONE OF THE COOLEST BANDS ON THE PLANET
PETE R. JONES
(Cowboys International, PiL, Department S)

The period from 1979 to 1983 was just a great time to be making music in the UK, though I never realised the significance of this at the time. I was in my early twenties, with no money, living at my mum's house and playing bass for Brian Brain. The 1980 tour with Cowboys International had come to nothing, and I was feeling pretty downbeat about it all. We had managed to do a couple of short USA tours with Brian Brain that lifted the gloom, but this was short-lived.

August 24, 1982. I was sitting at my mum's house doing fuck all and twiddling my thumbs as per usual. The phone rang. Martin Atkins was calling from New York. He was still in the USA following our last Brian Brain tour. He managed somehow to ingratiate himself back into the PiL camp, made his peace with Keith Levene and started recording some new songs with them. The problem was the band was running short of money, and none of it was forthcoming from a record company of any sort, least of all Virgin Records. It was all a mess. John Lydon was just finishing filming a movie in Italy along with Harvey Keitel and had been paid very well for doing so; that money was helping to keep the band afloat. The only way to get out of the financial mess was to play some gigs, but nobody seemed very keen to do so. The last PiL gig was the infamous riot show at the Ritz in May 1981, and some promoters were nervous about what might happen if they booked the band. PiL tried to find a bass player to fill the vacated Jah Wobble slot but hadn't unearthed anyone in the USA they thought would be suitable (or willing). Finding Bill Laswell too expensive, they needed a cheaper option, so Martin suggested getting me over to step in, hence the call. I didn't say yes straight away, though. I had a real problem on two counts, one being that I couldn't stand the band. I always considered PiL to be mediocre at best. I liked a few of their early songs, but to me, the rest was just self-indulgent crap. You know what they say about experimentation often being the domain of the talentless, right? Secondly, I thought John was a complete arse!

I really couldn't tolerate Lydon; my previous meetings with him hadn't exactly been full of grace and charm, so I thought playing in the same band might be difficult. On top of all this, my old Cowboys International buddy Ken Lockie was now involved, as he was an old friend of Keith Levene and also living in NYC. He was ostensibly there to play live keyboards with the band. This wasn't looking too good. Martin previously told me how difficult Keith was during the 1980 tour and that there were often a lot of drugs around; well, there's always a bright side! I was finding it hard to put a positive spin on it. I'd already been to America coast to coast with Brian Brain four times, so I didn't feel a burning need to go there again in a rush. I had a feeling if I went, it might be for some considerable time away from my friends and family. It wasn't just going to be for a few dates. On the upside, I assumed that money wouldn't be an issue. As far as I knew, the PiL finances were in good order, as they were still officially signed to Virgin Records, and I was expecting to be well paid for the honour of playing. On that score, I was perhaps a little naïve!

I said to Martin that I would think about it, and I asked him to call me back the next day. An obviously irritated Keith then got on the phone and was banging on about how great PiL were and that I did realise I was being offered the chance to join the best band on the planet and why was I hesitating? He said I should just get on a plane to NYC there and then. "*Yes, Keith, OK,*" I told him I'd think about it. I could tell he was none too pleased, but I was genuinely not overly impressed at the thought of joining them. But there was no alternative. Despite my better judgement, the next day I told Keith I would do it, and by the second week in September, I was waiting for the necessary work visa and plane ticket to arrive.

I went out and bought all the available PiL albums to learn the old songs. It didn't take long. Wobble's bass lines weren't exactly the most challenging. I learnt them all in one afternoon. Wow, this is going to be easy! I couldn't believe how bad some of the songs were, though. Apart from the odd tune, most of their stuff sounded like a complete dirge to me, tuneless drivel, particularly most of *Metal Box*. *Flowers of Romance* was OK even though it didn't have many bass parts on it. I was there at Manor Studios while it was being recorded and saw first-hand just how much dithering about was involved. Otherwise, I felt I could easily deal with any childlike antics of Messrs. Lydon, Levene and Lockie on a personal level didn't frighten me one bit, and at least I had an ally in Martin Atkins. We were mates, so I was sure we'd be able to watch each other's backs if things got difficult.

I eventually decided to suck it up, and after waiting a while for the work visa to come through, off I went. I gave no thought to contracts or my terms and conditions. As I said, I thought money wasn't going to be a problem, especially once we were touring. I didn't think to ask for a contract; it just wasn't the done thing.

The first PiL gig was planned for September 28, 1982, so there was plenty of time. I thought I'd have a few days to get rid of the jet lag before we set to work, you know, get settled in my room at the Iroquois Hotel, have some fun, see the sights again and see who was knocking about. But on that score, I was very much mistaken.

When I landed at JFK airport, Martin came out to meet me. I thought that was a bit odd, as I knew full well how to get to Manhattan from JFK using public transport, and I didn't have a lot of stuff with me, not even a guitar. Martin was looking a bit red-faced and flustered, and after saying a quick hello, rushed me out to the taxi rank. *"They're waiting for you at the studio for you to put a bass part down." "What? Who? PiL? Are you fucking serious? I'm fucking shattered after the flight, and I could really do with a shower and a lie down."*

Well, he was serious. PiL were recording at Park South Studios on West 58th Street, and they were indeed waiting for me, holding their studio session open and thus keeping another band, who were there for an evening session, waiting. When I asked Martin what we were supposed to be recording, he tried singing the song to me in the back of the cab. He wasn't famed for his tunefulness, bless him, and the notes he was singing all sounded the same, as if sung through a sock by a man with a severe sinus problem. I couldn't make out what the tune was.

'*It's OK, Martin, I'll work it out when I get there, for fuck's sake.*'

I really was pissed off with them putting me on the spot like that; it was a bit inconsiderate. No thought at all for how I was feeling or what state I was in. As it happens, I'd been knocking back large vodka and tonics throughout the flight and was half-pissed, but I knew sympathy wasn't going to be featuring much in this band.

When we arrived at the studio, I swept in, past a gaggle of really pissed-off musicians from the waiting band who were sitting with their gear in the studio foyer. Their eyes followed me like daggers into the control room. I felt quite sorry for them. I'm thinking, *"Go home, boys; I think it's going to be a long night."*

In the control room it was a full house. There sat Keith Levene, Ken Lockie, the new PiL manager Bob Tullipan and his girlfriend Maureen Baker, plus Bob Miller, who was the engineer for both the studio and live sessions. Quite an audience, I thought. After saying a quick hello, I sat down and was given a Fender bass to play, and it was plugged straight into the desk. A track was played, and Keith said, *"Have a listen to this and play along"*. It was a song called 'Mad Max', a simple disco ditty in G minor that I soon worked out a bass line for, and off we went.

Take after take, after take, after take, on and on it went, late into the night like death itself; I thought it was never going to end. This was certainly being thrown in at the deep end, and I wasn't sure if it was some sort of endurance test. Normally, I would have expected to record in the main room of the studio with a full bass rig rather than stand in front of a load of strangers in the control room. I soon realised that it was just typical PiL, pure chaos. I felt totally unfazed by it all; I was confident in my ability, and the bass line I was being asked to play wasn't very taxing. Nobody said much; polite conversation wasn't the order of the day, but as the hours slipped by, I was getting more and more tired. I declined the offer of 'something to help me stay awake' from someone, and I just plodded on. Ken Lockie was the same as he ever was; he said very little about lots.

After an hour or so, John Lydon suddenly popped up from behind the mixing desk like a gnarly old jack-in-the-box! Nobody told me he was there. He always had to make an entrance, that boy; he couldn't even make the effort and show some basic social skills or respect when I turned up, just to say "*hello*" and "*how are you?*" The session went on until God knows what time; the last take was no better than the first, and we seemed to have spent most of the night watching Keith twiddle knobs on the mixing desk and talking bullshit. What a start! I was again offered various powdered substances to help with the jetlag, but I preferred to work with a straight head in the studio. I learnt from the quality of the early Brian Brain recordings that drugs and studios aren't a good mix.

Martin and I eventually retired to the Iroquois Hotel and grabbed a quick couple of beers and some welcome sleep. This is going to be a challenge, I thought. The 'Mad Max' song we worked on sounded average until I beefed it up a bit. Martin's drums were solid, which was to be expected. There were some poorly played bass and synth parts on it from Keith, not much guitar. There was what I assumed was a guide vocal from John. It nearly made me laugh out loud when I first heard it. For some reason, he was singing in a really high register, and it sounded dreadful. I'm pretty sure everyone else thought so too, but no one had the audacity or the guts to say anything to John about it. It was a bit like the emperor's new clothes story, and here was the emperor, standing stark-bollock naked for the world to see, and no one said a word. I wasn't going to speak out, that's for sure.

After a couple of days, the focus quickly shifted to the live set, and our first rehearsal was planned at a Manhattan studio space, Blondie's old hangout. It was good to be playing with Martin again. We were a tight rhythm section, worked on and cemented over a number of years. The PiL tunes sounded great on that score.

We ran through some of the old material from *First Issue* and *Metal Box*. It was a piece of piss to play those simple wobble basslines, but I wanted to make my own mark on the bass tone and add a bit of grunt, rather than just parody. The wobble sound was very fat and heavy on the bottom end. Our engineer Bob Miller had never heard *Metal Box*, so he didn't really know or understand what that original PiL sound was all about. I could have just copied that, rolling all the mid and top ends of the bass, but I was keen to make my own, distinct noise. What I played seemed to go down all right with the others; nobody said anything to the contrary, so we soldiered on and knocked a semblance of a set into shape.

I was given some cash to go out with the roadie to buy another Fender bass, which I thought was cool. There seemed to be loads of cash floating around. It reinforced my belief that there was plenty of money; there always seemed to be enough for pharmaceuticals and beer.

In between rehearsals and much hanging around, more time was spent at Park South studios. We were recording a new PiL album, and it was to be called *Commercial Zone*. A lot of tracks were already recorded by the time I arrived on the scene, but I went in and overdubbed the bass parts. Keith had already put some bass tracks down, but most of it was sloppy playing and not very dynamic. Keith was quite an innovative guitarist at times, but in my view, he wasn't such a great bass player. Most of the songs were partly done, just ideas that needed finishing and vocals added. John would be there most days, usually lying down in the studio room, listening and working on lyrics, occasionally wailing along. His voice carried on like a high-pitched engine, about an octave higher than I'd heard him sing previously, very irritating and not easy to listen to.

We worked on a track called 'This is Not a Love Song', probably the best of the bunch. But it sounded very bare back then, as it didn't have any guitars on it; they were all added much later. I had not the faintest idea it would be a worldwide hit further down the line. Martin Atkins hated the song and still does. The recordings followed the same pattern. Keith was running the show with Bob Miller recording take after take after take until my fingers all but fell off. Then Keith did a bit of twiddling with things, and we would all sit around talking. Sometimes, I couldn't understand what Keith was saying or what he wanted. There was often a heavy atmosphere in the studio, really depressing, and it suffocated any creativity on my part. The sound of laughter was anathema to PiL, it seemed.

The first gig at Roseland NYC was fast approaching, and we booked a soundstage rehearsal space with a full stage, sound, and lighting in place. It was looking really good. Black and white tile effect scenery that went up and over our heads made by a company called See Factor. It reminded me a bit of the tiles you get in a public toilet, but under the lights it was cool. Very stark, which suited the sombre tone of the music. We put a row of bright white spotlights above the drums facing the crowd, which could be used to good effect. Blasting the audience with bright, white lights is something you see a lot these days, and very effective it is too, in giving people a headache! We used sub-bass speakers on the PA that produced very low frequencies. You can only use these for short periods; otherwise, the audience will start losing control of their bowels. Roseland has a lot of history and was an interesting choice for our first venue. It was a converted ice-skating rink in New York's theatre district on West 52nd Street built in 1932, with a 2,500 capacity plus 300 upstairs if required. Of course, for our opening show it was sold out.

Bob Tullipan put the Roseland show together with the help of NYC promoter Ron Delsner, who helped find the cash to put the show on. For my part, I had no idea that PiL were so cash-strapped; it never occurred to me. Nobody told me or discussed it, and we never talked about money in the contractual sense. John got around £10,000 from making the film *Cop Killer* in Italy with Harvey Keitel, so he was all right for a bit. Virgin Records effectively financially dumped PiL like a hot potato, which again I knew nothing about. I thought they were financing the new album.

I was so green about all the business side of things; I really was, and in some ways, I never felt it was my place to ask. Virgin still had a contractual hold over the band, so we were unable to negotiate a separate distribution deal in America or anywhere else. There was an interest in the new album from Stiff Records America, who were keen to put it out, but as soon as they realised the contractual problems with Virgin, they weren't interested. We were effectively without a record company, and the only way Virgin would release anything was if we paid the recording costs ourselves and delivered to them a finished album.

September 28, 1982, 6 days after my 25th birthday, the day of the first gig soon came, and we were all on edge. We were under-rehearsed, but with the PiL material that didn't really matter, and nobody seemed too bothered about it. Even still, nerves were jangling. There was a lot of tension, and everyone was quiet, especially John. I got the impression that he felt there was a lot riding on these gigs, which indeed there was. We couldn't afford another debacle like the Ritz show; otherwise, promoters wouldn't touch us. It had to be a success. USA TV came in to interview the band, and they filmed part of the soundcheck; this was shown on the national news.

There was an awful lot of cocaine going around the band at the time. I can't say who took it all, but there was never any left by the end of the night. It was being sucked up by the nose-full with gay abandon, and I was doing my bit by hoovering up as much as I could. Somebody in the band was smoking it too, allegedly, and he became a right fucking mess.

The idea of the live shows was that each one was going to be an 'event', and we made up posters that said 'You are now entering a Commercial Zone', which we put in the foyer of the Roseland theatre. I only remember seeing them the once.

Bob Tullipan preferred to arrange gigs with various independent promoters across the USA. Instead of going with the well-known and established big names, there were some interesting venues lined up, like the Galleria in San Francisco and the Showbox in Seattle. The graffiti artist Futura 2000 was a friend of the band – lovely bloke – and I think the idea was to get him to do some art similar to what he did with the Clash live on stage in 1981, but this never came off. There was always endless talk of grand schemes and ideas;

computers were mentioned a lot, though I didn't know in what context. Keith's mantra in interviews was *"We're getting into computers and graphics; we're a company, not a band."* We couldn't afford the most basic Sinclair Spectrum, let alone a high-end computer that could handle fancy graphics, even if one existed. It was a constant stream of bullshit.

Before the shows we would play a track from the newly recorded material called 'Blue Water'. It sounded dark and oppressive, and it was one of my favourite tracks from those sessions. With an odd bar of 5/4 in the rhythm, it was unsettling to listen to, but I loved it – really dark.

Showtime! We stood nervously behind the Roseland curtain as 'Blue Water' played out, and then we struck up the opening bars of another new song, 'Where Are You?'. Apparently, it was about Jeanette Lee, who left the PiL camp shortly after John returned from filming in Italy. The song started with bass and drums, and then, as the curtain drew back, Keith came launching in with his slashing Travis Bean guitar sound. It sounded immense! Bob Miller was doing a great job in front of house on the desk and producing a really great menacing wall of sound. John was leering at the packed crowd that surged forward. After John sang the first few lines, he turned round and looked at me with the biggest grin on his face I'd ever seen. He was enjoying it, and PiL was back, sounding better than ever.

This was the first PiL gig since the debacle at the Ritz in May, just four months earlier. I think a lot of people at Roseland were expecting something like that to happen again. It was just a great gig, no drama, just a little chaotic. We never wrote out a set list before the shows; we just decided beforehand what to play as our first number and then made up the rest as we went along. Someone would call out a song or just start playing an intro to one, and off we'd go. There was often a lot of time in between numbers while we decided what to do next, or we would be waiting for Keith to smoke a cigarette. John would berate the crowd.

A lot of the songs didn't even have a set structure or length to them; 'Death Disco', for instance, would start and just go on until somebody, usually Martin, decided enough was enough and ended the song, three, four or five minutes depending on what the feel or vibe was at the time. This first show was a bit special; it was a new experience for me, and it made a change to finally have a decent crowd in front of me instead of the light scattering of punters we usually saw at a Brian Brain gig. It was electrifying. As I struck up the opening bass notes to 'Public Image', there was another huge sway of fans forwards, crushing those at the front. A barrier collapsed, and suddenly, there were bodies everywhere, all struggling to stay on their feet. Complete, crazy madness. But what a buzz!

The power of music! Just two notes of a pulsing bass line was all it took to get a reaction like that. I'd never seen anything like it, and my senses were going through the stratosphere. As a performer, if you are ever lucky enough to play in such circumstances, you realise just what a high it is, drugs or no drugs. It's a massive shot of adrenaline, plus something else that you just can't fully describe.

John was in his element, and I have to admit, during this period as a frontman, apart from his early Sex Pistols days, he was at his very best. He would prowl back and forth across the stage, baiting the crowd, staring into the fans' eyes, wailing, and singing in his unique style. It didn't matter; he held the crowd in his hand and would often cadge cigarettes off people or kneel down for a chat. If anyone gave him stick or spat, he would give it right back and then some. He hated that punk parody spitting shit.

I used to love watching him work; he really is one of a kind, but he didn't like me watching and said I was *"looking at him funny"* during the shows. I didn't have to put on any sort of show like I did with Brian Brain; John was the entertainment, and all eyes were on him most of the time. So, I decided just to act the cool bass man, standing at the back in front of my bass rig, watching the show unfold in front of me. The playing was piss easy; I could play those parts with my eyes closed, so all I had for fun was to watch John swanning up and down the stage being Rotten.

We were all relieved that the first show was a resounding success. PiL were sounding immense, and it was probably one of the best times in their history. We came off stage on a high and dived straight into the booze and stimulants. There were loads of people milling about backstage. I wasn't interested in the slightest as to whom they were or if they were of any importance. I wasn't about to try and schmooze any showbiz types, no matter what their name was. I was in Public Image Limited, one of the coolest fucking bands on the planet. I just didn't care, and everyone else could go fuck themselves!

Roseland closed in 2014; Lady Gaga was the last performer to play there.

24/09/2021

○ Joan Jett, aka Joan Marie Larkin, was born in 1958 in Philadelphia, USA. Joan, as a frontwoman singer, reached the peak of her career while associated with Joan Jett & the Blackhearts. Before that Joan was a member of the all-girl band, The Runaways, who had a chart-topping single with 'Cherry Bomb'. As a soloist, she released 2 albums, the *self-titled* 1980 set (re-released as *Bad Reputation*) and *The Hit List* in 1990. Joan has also lent her hand in production and is an animal rights activist.

○ Julz Sale died on September 22, 2021, in Thailand at 63 years of age. Julz, as guitarist-vocalist, along with fellow art school members Bethan Peters and Ros Allen, formed Delta 5 in 1978; oddly, Bethan and Ros were both bass players. Drummer Kelvin Knight and guitarist Alan Riggs came into the fold a little later. It was with their debut single 'Mind Your Own Business' that Delta 5 earned notoriety. In 2021 Apple used it as the background sound to a commercial for privacy on an iPhone. Lesley Woods of the Au Pairs said of Julz, *"Such sad news of her passing. Julz was a terrific girl; she was heaps of fun to hang out with, as we had such a gas time together"*.

○ The Suburban Lawns released the one and only *self-titled* album in 1981. Suburban Lawns is an infectious, fun, and catchy POST-PUNK recording tinged with a surf-punk edge with early Talking Heads overtones. That said, even the male vocals can sound like David Byrne. The LP comes in at only about 28 minutes long, but the songs have a desirable quirky quality about them. As danceable as Devo, as witty as They Must Be Giants, and as aural as Romeo Void. Love it!

Chuck Wild by Glen Wexler

○ Chuck Wild was born September 22, 1946, in Kansas City, Missouri, USA. Chuck is a highly regarded and award-winning multi-instrumentalist known for his work with the likes of Missing Persons, Frank Zappa, The Pointer Sisters, and Michael Jackson. From 1980 to 1984, Chuck was part of the Missing Persons line-up, playing on the albums *Spring Session M* (an anagram of Missing Persons) and the Terry Bozzio/Bruce Swedien-produced *Rhyme & Reason*. Spring Session M held the very successful charting single 'Words' that was produced by the legendary Ken Scott; the single went top 10 in Australia. Aside from his session work, Chuck has since ventured deep into the world of ambient and therapeutic healing music. As of 2023, he has eighteen award-winning and charting album releases under the name Liquid Mind. Chuck's music in this area earned him the coveted President's Award from the American Music Therapy Association.

"YOU'LL BUY ME DINNER?"
CHUCK WILD
(Missing Persons, Michael Jackson, Frank Zappa et.al.)

To this day I remember my first phone call to Missing Persons' singer Dale Bozzio on September 22nd, 1980. It was my 34th birthday, and I'd just moved to Hollywood to play with a "signed group" and had gone to the Musician's Contact Service a few weeks earlier to gather phone numbers of groups playing "original" music who were looking for keyboard players. I'd called nearly 100 groups and showed up for about 35 auditions, but I wasn't wild about the original songs most bands were playing, so I kept looking.

When I called her, Dale told me about Missing Persons and said, *"Come audition tonight!"* I said, *"I can't; it's my birthday."*. Dale responded, in true "Dale" form -- *"You must come audition, and then we'll buy you birthday dinner at a great Italian restaurant a couple of blocks away. It will be a lot of fun!"* I relented, especially at the thought of a free meal at the time, and showed up at their rehearsal studio at Robertson in West LA with my Chevy van, filled with about 20 keyboards.

Actually, I failed the first audition that night because I'd never played left-handed bass before, especially with Terry Bozzio, one of the finest drummers on the planet. Still, I loved hanging out with the Zappa alums and hearing about their experiences, and I learnt that Frank had named them the "Missing Persons" because they had left his group and were now "missing".

I was so determined to re-audition that I got up at 5 am every morning and practised the songs on a cassette player until I could play them flawlessly. I asked for a re-audition and was hired two weeks later... thus began my four-year adventure with the group. This was the heyday of NEW WAVE music, and though I always thought of us as a rock band, radio and press sometimes referred to us as synth pop, alternative rock, and pop-rock (in addition to NEW WAVE). There were many, many "subsets" of NEW WAVE.

One of my funniest memories was of Missing Persons playing the second US Festival on May 30th, 1983. We were scheduled to play just after Berlin and just before U2, The Pretenders, Joe Walsh, Fleetwood Mac and David Bowie. That day we'd gotten up quite early and come to the US Festival venue at Glen Helen Regional Park, San Bernardino, California, from our hotel in Riverside, about half an hour away. To say the least, the prospect of playing for 300,000 people and also meeting several of my musical idols was exciting, but in those days, I did a lot of Hatha Yoga relaxation exercises to stay relaxed to be able to give a good performance; so, when the band went backstage, I stayed in one of our tents about 1/2 mile away to do my daily yoga.

However, I fell asleep after yoga, and the rest of the band didn't realise I was asleep in the tent, and our road manager was racing around looking for me, finally finding me asleep and said, *"Quick, wake up, it's time to play!"* I ran to the stage in a panic, though he was joking, and it wasn't actually our time yet. The joke was on me, but I was in time to sit backstage and to hear some of the greatest rock bands of the day that afternoon & evening, not to mention the fun of playing at such a large venue.

23

● This day in 1978 saw the release of the phenomenal *Parallel Lines*, this is one classy AND classic record. For this album bassist Nigel Harrison was added to the line-up and this was their first album produced by Mike Chapman who would go on to produce the band's subsequent records, *Eat to The Beat*, *Autoamerican*, and *The Hunter*. Chapman demanded tighter arrangements and every note had to be in the correct place and as close to perfection as they could achieve, he had them to practice, practice, and practice, so he could record them as "live" as possible! Chris and Debbie publicly gave Chapman plaudits for making the band what Blondie became and creating a flawless and iconic pop album. *Parallel Lines* is an incredible, NEW WAVE-POST-PUNK-pop quintessential work of art. The glittery, disco juggernaut, 'Heart of Glass' changed everything for them, it took the band finally into the mainstream. The rest of the album proved Blondie wasn't a fluke or a one-trick pony. Every track on this album is simply brilliantly performed, written, and sung. The opener, a cover of The Nerves' 'Hanging on The Telephone' is powerful and a pacesetter for what is to come, 'Will Anything Happen?' has gorgeous, blistering guitar licks and effortless tempo changes, 'Picture This' is beautifully haunting and the epic, 'Fade Away and Radiate' is filled with picturesque lyrics arguably Chris Stein's crowning achievement. All these songs are gelled by Debbie Harry's singing, and she really shines on 'Pretty Baby' and 'Sunday Girl' making them nothing short of being pop gems. All the band members get a chance to shine on 'I Know but I Don't Know', then drummer Clem Burke and keyboardist Jimmy Destri continue to deliver the goods on the anxiety-ridden, '11:59'. 'One Way or Another' and, 'Just Go Away' highlight Debbie's fiery and sarcastic sense of humour. And there's a fabulous cover of Buddy Holly's, 'I'm Gonna Love You Too' which adds a cool, unexpected fusion of doo-wop to Blondies NEW WAVE pop-punk. Some albums don't age well but *Parallel Lines* isn't one of them, it still sounds fresh, innovative, and gutsy all these decades later, and it arguably sits as Blondie's best album, it's polished, fresh and highly accomplished.

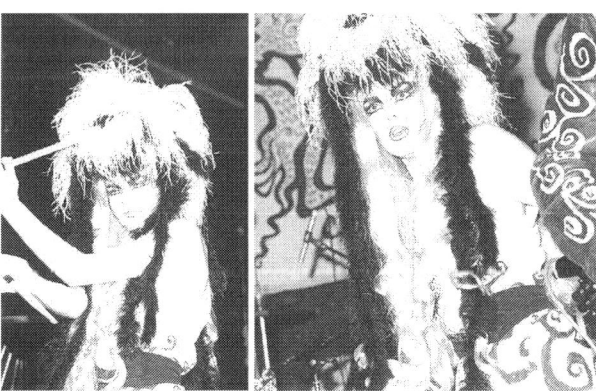

Danielle Dax by Petra Gall

● Danielle Dax, aka Danielle Gardner, was born in 1958 in Southend-on-Sea, Essex, England. Danielle is a highly underrated experimental musician and producer, most active from the late 1970s to the mid-1990s. Danielle, as a keyboardist, flautist and saxophonist, made her live debut in 1979 with the avant-garde NEW WAVE unit The Lemon Kittens, who on that occasion were billed as Amii Toytal and the Croixroads. In 1981 she appeared on Robert Fripp's League of Gentlemen's 1981 *self-titled* album, performing vocals (essentially as spoken word, it was credited as Hamsprachtmusic) on the song 'Minor Man'. From 1983 to 1990 she released four never-to-be-pigeonholed albums, each recording showing a diverse amount of experimentation. Never apologetic or compromising, she had BRILLIANT hair.

◉ Hilly Kristal was born in 1931 in Manhattan, New York, USA. Hilly was the founder of CBGB & OMFUG, the premier bar and live music venue in NYC's Bowery area. CBGB, along with Max's Kansas City, was the birthplace of much of New York's punk, POST-PUNK, new wave, and the art-rock that came to the fore in the '70s. The venue set a worldwide template for musician-friendly rock music outlets. Among the 1000s of bands that performed there were Patti Smith, Blondie, Television and Talking Heads, each cutting their teeth on the CBGB's stage. Hilly died in the place he loved, NYC's Manhattan, on August 28, 2007, aged 75.

◉ In 1984, Latin Quarter unveiled their first-ever single, titled 'Radio Africa' b/w 'Eddie'. By blending reggae, dub, and rock, Latin Quarter incorporated politically charged lyrics into their music. Unfortunately, these thought-provoking lyrics were often overlooked by mainstream UK radio hosts. However, thanks to significant airplay on alternative stations, the single managed to achieve modest sales. With its impeccable production and arrangement, this song holds a powerful message and a captivating melody that deserves to be embraced by all.

◉ At the Hollywood Palladium on September 23, 1977, a gig advertised as Punk Rock & Fashion Show had Blondie as special guest stars. Devo and The Weirdos were also on the bill, with "A SURPRISE BAND" who turned out to be The Avengers, closing out the evening performance.

◉ 'Screamin' Dave Slade came into this world screaming in 1960. As a teen in the '70s, Dave was drawn to playing guitar and bass in several bands in Lismore on the far north coast of New South Wales, Australia, most notably the legendary Gutter Cats! 1980 saw Dave relocate to Sydney, where there was a vibrant new sound in the burgeoning pub circuit. Through 1984-9, seeking his "Holy Grail" as a frontman/vocalist from Hell, he formed Frankenstein, which morphed into The Mercy Killers, then No-Man's Land, a band with an ever-evolving line-up that released 2 top five indie charting singles, with 'I Need More' going No.3 in Italy! At this time Dave and James Baker (ex-Hoodoo Gurus) established the side project The Eternal Teenagers; this band played at the unique Rock-Wrestling shows. Dave later established Savage Brides, Lovegrinder, and then the highly regarded Medicine Show, releasing a *self-titled* album. That band hit the headlines when Slash from Guns 'n' Roses joined them on stage at a Kings Cross all-nighter and proclaimed them as "*fucking awesome*". Dave took a hiatus for a few years to raise his daughters, Sarah and Paige, and released a couple of limited-edition books of prose/poetry. In the late noughties, Dave formed SLUG with Leon Beveridge, Brad Hoskins, Geoff Lynne, and Steve Reynolds. Through thick and thin, they battled on and survived Lismore's 'Great Flood' of 2022, releasing the critically acclaimed kick-ass psychedelic swamp album *Caveat Emptor* and continue to this day.

ALL IN A NIGHT'S REHEARSAL
DAVE SLADE
(Medicine Show, No Man's Land, Lovegrinder)

It's a Lovegrinder rehearsal at our rehearsal room opposite the 'Town and Country' pub St. Peters. (Yes! That's the one, as Slim Dusty says "*Where the atmosphere is great!*"). So, beer was no problem. Dave Lornie and Ramrod (Greg Leidreiter) were 'living' there on and off and Paul (Paul E Hayward) lived just up the road. On the way, I picked up Nick (Nick Potts) and Tony (Tony Robertson) "*But, can I get a lift home?*", no biggie, he lived in Lavender Bay, it's the first left turn after getting off the Harbour Bridge (*SHB). There are never any booze buses on there because they would have to close a lane to set them up, so, no worries!!!

It was a 'normal' rehearsal. (quite) a few beers, a few joints, a few lines, plenty of fun, and we are playin' great, great night! "No worries, Tony, back to yours" Lornie and Ramrod in the back. It's all very merry, beers in the car, we're yahooing! Tony in the front with his bass case and me driving, off we go!

All good, we are on the city side approach to the *SHB and on the other side of the bridge we see flashing lights, must be an accident we think, getting closer, oh no! big *RBT set up, especially for those days.

"OH NO, I'm fucked!" I'm thinking! "*maybe we will get past*", I mutter.

We are waved over, dead quiet in the car now.

A young police officer comes over and you can just tell by the way he's acting; he thinks he's got us. It must smell of alcohol and stale pot in the car.

He gives me the bag to blow in, I kind of blow out on the outer side of my mouth that he can't see, it's kind of dark too, that helps, and he takes it away.

Yep, were fucked!

He comes back a few moments later, he's obviously pissed off.

"*Your reading is negative mate*" Us: what the fuck! That's impossible! But he's not gonna let us off easy!

"*What's in the guitar case*" He's getting more aggressive, slight tittering in the car.

Yep, pushing my luck I say "*You won't believe it…a guitar*" more tittering.

Yep, he's getting even more pissed off by the second.

"*OK, so what's in the glove box*" he demands! He thinks he's got us now!

Yep, me, I couldn't help it, honest! "*gloves*" much hilarity!

By this time, he's had enough!

He comes round to the passenger side and rips the door open and starts to grab stuff!

Just then I see another policeman coming towards us, obviously a Sergeant or such, lots of stars and shit on his uniform and he's got the Sergeant hat on, he looks mean and like he means business!

OK, this time we are really fucked!

He comes over to me and says, "*Good evening, sir*", he takes one look at what the young policemen is doing and roars "*What the fuck do you think you are doing!!! Come with me son!!!*"

He turns to me and says, "*Sorry about that gentleman, on your way, have a good evening*".

As he walks off, he's tearing into the young copper and we drive off! We can't believe it!

As I write this, I still can't!!!

*SHB = Sydney Harbour Bridge
*RBT = Random Breath Testing

⊙ Armistead Wellford was born in 1959 in Richmond, Virginia, USA. In 1978 he moved to Athens to attend art school at the University of Georgia; it was there where in 1979 he struck up a friendship with Mark Cline and Mike Richmond, soon forming Love Tractor. This band, along with the B52s, Pylon and REM, defined the early Athens music scene. Between 1980 and 1990 Wellford was part of writing and producing five Love Tractor albums with the help of such notables as Alfredo Villar, Pat Irwin, Brendon O'Brien, and

Mitch Easter. Love Tractor hit the road extensively through this period, sharing bills with New Order, the B52s, Psychedelic Furs, REM, 10,000 Maniacs, Violent Femmes and The Bangles. While Love Tractor was on hiatus in the early 1990s, Wellford joined the 'supergroup' Gutterball, a band made up of members from The Dream Syndicate, The Long Ryders, House of Freaks, Silos and Cracker. Armistead would engage in broad USA and European tours with Gutterball as well as Steve Wynn on his solo tours. He also recorded with Sparklehorse for their first album release during this period. All of Love Tractor's album releases have been very well received and achieved great critical acclaim. 2023 sees Wellford back with his Love Tractor bandmates recording a new record.

Armistead Welford & Love Tractor by John Upsis

CLARINET WITH THE VIOLENT FEMMES & INTRODUCING NATALIE TO KATE
ARMISTEAD WELLFORD
(Love Tractor)

In the spring of 1983, Love Tractor was just finishing up their second album *Around the Bend* for DB Records. At the time we were doing shows in between recording and were scheduled to play with a band called The Violent Femmes at the 930 Club in Washington DC. We didn't know anything about The Violent Femmes as yet, except that we shared the same booking agent. After meeting them in the dressing room in the basement of the club, we learned they had just released their debut album on Slash records. At the 930 club, bands played two sets with a break between each. Love Tractor played first then the Femmes.

I played the clarinet on a couple of the songs from our first album as well as *Around the Bend*, even though my playing is quite imperfect, squeaks were welcomed and encouraged by my band mates rather than precise playing. It was after we each played our first sets that Brian Richie, bass player for the Femmes, came into our dressing room and says to me, "*We really want you to play clarinet with us in our second set*". I was beyond flattered, having found them to be a very different and interesting band. Unfortunately, we had planned to leave immediately after our 2nd set to get a head start back to Athens, Georgia so we missed that Femmes set. I regret that my clarinet and I didn't take the stage with the Violent Femmes. I was so complimented that they asked.

In 2023 Love Tractor had the honour of opening for The B52s for their last touring gigs in Athens, Georgia. When Kate Pierson and I were chatting after the show she said that she often sees Natalie Merchant at events and performances, and it reminded me that I had introduced them 39 years earlier! In May 1984 we were attending The New Music Seminar at Irving Plaza in New York City, it was the predecessor to SXSW, the annual conference of parallel film, interactive media, music festivals. Here Love Tractor and 10,000 Maniacs were the showcased bands for the event, it was such an amazing night, with both bands putting on fabulous performances. We were already good friends with the Maniacs, as they often played

Athens, their shows were always fantastic and not to be missed. The morning after the gig at Irving Plaza we all attended the seminar and it was there that I ran into Natalie and out of the blue I said, "*Do you want to go visit Kate Pierson?*". I knew she was about, as Kate, Ricky Wilson and Keith Strickland had come to Irving Plaza the night before for our shows. So, Natalie said "*Sure do*". So, we played hooky from the seminar and walked 15 blocks to go say hey to Kate. We had a nice visit and before we left to walk back to the seminar Natalie gave Kate the 10,000 Maniacs first record. It was so great to be present and responsible for the meeting of these 2 legendary vocalists.

24

◉ This day in 1982 announced Big Country's single 'Harvest Home', their debut single. When originally released, it met with a warm reception but was eagerly sought after later as it was a different version to that on the debut album *The Crossing*. Unmistakably Scottish with its swaying, bagpipe-like and bold Stuart Adamson. An able debut, strong and quite representative of the bigger and better things to follow.

◉ Blancmange released their first album, *Happy Families*, in 1982. The duo of Neil Arthur and Stephen Luscombe slotted into synthpop perfectly; their synth textures, bass rhythms, drum machine programming and minimalism gave a melting pot of delectable tunes. Somewhat darker than their contemporaries, the Pet Shop Boys and OMD, the total sound at times seems generic, yet interesting enough through the synthesizer fills of pops, squeaks and squeals. Rich tracks like 'I Can't Explain', 'Feel Me' and the hit 'Living on the Ceiling' bind together some great dance rhythms with world music overtones.

◉ On Wednesday, September 24, 1980, the band that was Composition of Sound took the stage for the first time as Depeche Mode at The Bridge House, Canning Town, London. The line-up was Vince Clarke, Andrew Fletcher, Dave Gahan, and Martin Gore. From here they would go on to have over 50 songs and 17 top 10 albums on the UK charts. Phenomenally, Depeche Mode have sold over 100 million records worldwide! Vince Clarke departed the band soon after the first album, *Speak and Spell*, in 1981. Alan Wilder would join just after the release of their second album, 1982's *A Broken Frame*, but left in 1995.

◉ On Friday, September 24, 1976, Eric's Club opened; this was an 'unofficial' free night. The venue site at 9 Matthew Street, Liverpool, was owned by Roger Eagle, Pete Fulwell and Ken Testi. Ken was the manager of the opening night band Deaf School. Eric's played host to the who's who of UK and international acts, with the likes of Joy Division, Talking Heads, The Stranglers, OMD, Wire, XTC, The Teardrop Explodes, The Slits and a host of other well-known bands. The 'official' opening was a week away on October 1, with The Stranglers taking to the stage. The venue closed after the night of March 14, 1980, when it was raided by the police citing rampant drug use. The Psychedelic Furs and Wah! Heat performed that night.

ED: See Ken Testi – October 30.

◉ In 1981 Surface Music from San Francisco released their one and only single, 'I Am a Janitor' b/w 'Slim Boy'. Nervous, quirky, and giving a nod to Devo, Talking Heads or The Books, the A-side has earworm quality. "*I am a ja ja ja ja ja ja ja ja janitor.*"

25

◉ Students coming from the Leeds University Art School made up Delta 5, and their debut single 'Mind Your Own Business' b/w 'Now That You're Gone' was released by Rough Trade Records and available September 25, 1979. With its funky POST-PUNK sound reminiscent of fellow Leeds bands, The Mekons and Gang of Four, the single showcased Delta 5's energetic minimalism. Propelled by a rhythm of jagged guitar and a captivating bassline, 'Mind Your Own Business' features the catchy refrain, *"Can I have a taste of your ice cream? Can I lick the crumbs from your table? Can I interfere in your crisis?"* This cheeky, infectious track exemplified Delta 5's abrupt yet entertaining musical style. Fast forward to 2021, and Apple cleverly employed it as the background music for an iPhone commercial emphasising privacy. *"Why don't you mind your own business?"*

◉ Clive Farrington (aka Clive Renteria-Farrington) was born September 25, 1957, in Manchester. Coming out of the outfit Beau Leisure, Clive was in the original line-up of When in Rome with Andrew Mann and Michael Floreale that formed in late 1986. The band came to the fore internationally with the smash debut No.11 USA single 'The Promise'. The single also topped the Billboard Clubplay Chart and was part of the *self-titled* debut album that went top 100 in the USA. Tensions caused a split, and in 1990 the band folded.

FROM DRUMS TO BASS TO VOCALS
CLIVE FARRINGTON
(When In Rome)

Growing up on the Wellgreen Estate in South Manchester. I got my first drum kit when I was 6 or 7 and had lessons all the way through school. This first, exciting experience was not as exciting as I'd wished for! I'd chosen a Red Metal Flake, Premier King copy. A parcel came for Burlington's catalogue on Christmas Eve and of course, I knew, in my head, what it was! My excitement knew no bounds!

It was Christmas Day, and I was hopping like a mad thing up and down while my dad unboxed my first ever musical instrument. The excitement turned to distress, and I was in tears as soon as I saw it appear from the box. The catalogue had been screwed up and sent me a baby kit with cardboard skins and a picture of Bugs Bunny on the drumhead! To rub salt into the wounds, the tiny kit came with plastic, illuminating sticks!!!!! A couple of weeks later, the catalogue rectified the situation and sent the proper kit. I was off!!!! I went to play drums in the school orchestra, but alas, never in a live band!

There was this guy I used to hear practicing drums about 100 yards from my house at a doctor's surgery, but never got a face to the playing. It turns out that it was none other than Simon Wolstoncroft. Simon once auditioned for The Smiths but didn't take the job because he thought the singer was arrogant. Simon went to school with Ian Brown and John Squire from The Stone Roses and formed a band with them called Patrol. In time Simon would go on to be the long-standing drummer for The Fall. In 2014 he published a really good autobiography called, *You Can Drum but You Can't Hide.*

Around 1975, I was working at an engineering factory, owned by my girlfriend's father. One day, the foreman, Dave Pine came around the workshop asking if anybody could play bass because the bass player in his cover band had taken ill and they had an important gig that coming weekend. Of course, I had to say no because all I knew anything about was drums! I also knew that they had one of the best drummers in the area, a guy called Graham Mather. Dave didn't give up and continued around the workshop asking the other workers if they could play or knew anyone who could stand in for their fallen bass player. He came back round to me and here am I, itching to just be on a stage playing live music! Well, I said yes and on my lunch break, I went to Woolworth's in Altrincham to look for and purchase a bass!

I came back to the workshop and in my hand was a fiery red Hofner Semi Acoustic copy that cost me only 30 quid! To make things simplified for me I got the band to transpose all the songs to either E, A, D or G, so that I only had to concentrate on being on the beat, leaving my left hand free to give time to the right! Basically, I was damping the strings with my left-hand fingers and playing on the beat with my right in the transposed keys.

Living in Manchester in late 1986 not as a bassist but a vocalist with the demise of Beau Leisure I formed When In Rome. We got signed to Virgin and in mid-1988 released our *self-titled* album, that album held the single 'The Promise' which went to No.84 on the US Billboard charts! Not bad for a guy who started with a drum kit featuring a cartoon character!

● On September 25, 1979, Gang of Four released their groundbreaking debut album, *Entertainment!*. The record reached No.45 on the UK charts and performed well in Australia, peaking at No.39. The first single, 'At Home He's a Tourist', climbed to No.58 in the UK, marking the highest chart position ever achieved by a Gang of Four song. The follow-up single 'Damaged Goods' cracked the top 40 in the United States. *Entertainment!* is a complete sonic experience, featuring some unforgettably edgy tracks bursting with intensity and intellect. The album captures the provocative energy of their famed live performances, with slashing angular guitars and in-your-face vocals from Jon King vividly demonstrating their signature sound. It's an explosive fusion of punk and funk, matched with literate, often inflammatory lyrics that would influence countless bands to come. Standout classic cuts include 'I Found That Essence Rare', 'Ether', 'Anthrax', and the aforementioned singles. Overall, *Entertainment!* represents a pioneering POST-PUNK statement that still sounds as vital today as it did upon its original 1979 release.

● Bassist Steve Severin, aka Steven John Bailey, was born in London, England, in 1955. Steve was a founding member and played bass with Siouxsie and the Banshees until 1996. Steve adopted the title 'Severin' from the Leopold von Sacher-Masoch character. The birth of The Banshees is one of legend. At the 100 Club punk festival in September 1976, Siouxsie Sioux and Steve, on a borrowed bass with Marco Pirroni on guitar and with Sid Vicious on drums, took the stage for a twenty-minute jam of 'The Lord's Prayer'. The event over two nights was headlined by the Sex Pistols on one night and Buzzcocks on the second night. The Banshees took the stage as an attempt to create a scene around the Sex Pistols; McLaren was grinning. Steve had first picked up a bass less than 24 hours previous. From this audacious, spontaneous beginning emerged a band who would go on to both creatively and chronologically outlast almost all their initial contemporaries, continuously evolving and revolving around Steve and Siouxsie's creative partnership for an initial 20 years and a rebirth in 2002.

26

● The EP, *Into Battle with the Art of Noise*, was the debut release by the Art of Noise and was available on this day in 1983. The studio team of Anne Dudley, Gary Langan, Paul Morley, JJ Jeczalik and Trevor Horn pushed the limits of innovation using a computer, namely the Fairlight CMI, an Australian invention. There had been splashes of the Fairlight on recordings by the likes of Naked Eyes, Kate Bush, Jean Michel Jarre & IQ from Australia but never something so comprehensive. The eight pieces here are a work of art, moody and surreal in expression, earthly in atmospherics but also mechanical in texture. Now, many years later, Art of Noise is music from the past, that remains the music of the future. It was essentially a blueprint for electro, techno, and sampling, showing where 'musique concrète' could take you.

● After a collaboration with Brian Eno and a couple of soundtracks, *Rei Momo* was the first solo outing for David Byrne. Released in 1989, we have somewhat of a departure from Talking Heads; aside from, say, *Naked,* flavoured with textures of world music, David attempts to bridge a gap between genres. Talking much from Latin American music and African feels, the album sparkles; the rhythms are bright and delicious. 'Independence Day', 'Dirty Old Town' and 'Don't Want to Be a Part of Your World' are terrific compositions, and it's difficult not to rate them among David Byrne's best. Intriguing and altogether engaging.

⊙ John Foxx, aka Dennis Leigh, was born in 1947 in Chorley, Lancashire, England. John sits as one of the most influential musicians of the late '70s and early '80s. He was the original lead singer of the band Ultravox!, who, after several name changes, including Fire of London, The Zips and The Damned, the band Tiger Lily became Ultravox! in July 1976. The group's style fused punk, glam, electronic, reggae and new wave music. It was at this time that Dennis Leigh adopted his stage name of John Foxx. After recording three seminal albums, John departed to embark on a solo career, and it was then that Midge Ure, formerly of The Rich Kids, took his place in the newly named Ultravox (exclamation mark removed). John has always primarily been associated with electronic synthesizer-based music, though he has also pursued a parallel career in graphic design and education. Gary Numan cites John as a major influence on his early career, even more so than the usually nominated David Bowie. John's debut solo album, *Metamatic*, is essential listening for those with any interest in electronic/synthpop/post-glam/art music. John went on to record three more albums in the '80s, with The Garden being best received by the public. Then after a mostly silent span of roughly 12 years in which there were a pair of early-'90s singles with Tim Simenon as Nation12, he returned more prolific than ever, operating his own label, Metamatic. He has divided his recording schedule between ambient work, including collaborations with Harold Budd, Robin Guthrie, and the Steves D'Agostino & Steve Jansen. The recordings with John Foxx and The Maths and song-based material from over 10 albums recorded with Louis Gordon that often recall that *Metamatic* sound. Keeping his hand in as a graphic artist, John has designed book covers for Salman Rushdie and Anthony Burgess, and he also co-directed LFO's video for 1991's LFO. Look into John Foxx; you won't be disappointed.

⊙ Tracey Thorn was born in 1962 in Brookman's Park, Hatfield, Hertfordshire, England. Inspired by the minimalist music of The Raincoats and The Young Marble Giants, Tracey, along with her then schoolmates Gina Hartman and Jane Fox, formed Marine Girls in 1980. Marine Girls would go on to release two albums, with 1983's *Lazy Ways* rating in NME's top 50 albums of the year. Prior to the splitting of the band, Tracey with Ben Watt formed Everything but The Girl (ETBG) in 1982, with Ben Watt with Night and Day becoming their debut single. ETBG would be highly successful, having released eleven studio albums up to 1983. Tracey has become a highly regarded solo artist with five album releases and several best-selling books.

⊙ Since August 6, 1945, more than 200,000 civilians have died from the explosion and/or resulting radiation from when an American B-29 bomber, the Enola Gay, dropped an atomic bomb over the centre of Hiroshima, Japan. It was the first time an atomic bomb had been dropped over a populated place and the first time a nuclear weapon had been used in warfare. The aftereffects of this WWII atrocity are still felt today. In memory of this event on September 26, 1980, Orchestral Manoeuvres in the Dark released their glorious 'protest' song Enola Gay.

⊙ This day in 1980 saw U2 release their first vinyl outing with the EP *Three*. The EP went top 20 in Ireland, with two of the three songs, 'Out of Control' and 'Stories for Boys', ending up being rerecorded for the Steve Lillywhite-produced debut album *Boy*. 'Out Of Control' shows even in the early days that this young band had a stadium feel. The rerecorded version shows how much a good producer is essential to a good recording. Original, forgettable, second version, unforgettable.

27

○ *Forever Young*, the debut album by the German band Alphaville, was released in 1984. Alphaville was one of the forerunners of the continent's '80s synthpop, and the album was typically that. Some great melodies and hooks to create some excellent singles, namely 'Big in Japan', 'Sounds Like a Melody' and the title track, where each has all the decadent allure of a now bygone era. Some real gorgeous synths and harmonies, and the overall production is superb.

○ Cassandra Complex released their debut album *Grenade* in 1986, a unique blend of electronica and post-punk industrial that showcased high levels of originality. Despite drawing comparisons to Cabaret Voltaire and Throbbing Gristle, the album took six years of tinkering and lineup changes by Rodney Orpheus to create. While it received critical acclaim, local sales were disappointing, with over 20,000 units sold in Europe. The band's name was inspired by a psychological state where individuals anticipate something terrible happening but feel powerless to stop it. In 2019, the album was remastered and rereleased for download and streaming.

○ The debut album *Purity* by The Essence from the Netherlands was available in 1985. Full of simple melodies and fresh jangly guitars, there's a striking resemblance to '80s The Cure, though a little thicker with keyboards. Vocalist Hans Diener's delivery is so Robert Smith, albeit with an ability of its own.

28

○ The debut single 'All the Boys in Town' that was released by the Australian rock band Divinyls on this day in 1981 was an absolute hit! This racy NEW WAVE pop song is about a young woman who has had romantic encounters with many of the young men around town and has now found her one true love. "*I must have been desperate,*" lead singer Chrissy Amphlett laments, "*Get me out of here!*" ... "*Too* much too soon". This is truly one of the greatest rock and roll songs to come out of Australia.

○ On September 28, 1979, Joy Division played at the Russel Club in Manchester. They had Foreign Press booked as a support and a surprise opener by The Teardrop Explodes. Prior to JD going onstage, singer Ian Curtis experienced an epileptic seizure, and there was doubt whether their performance would go ahead. Ian assured all that he was OK, and they took to the stage, and he gave one of his best performances ever. During the encore song 'Transmission', a fight ensued in front of the stage, and this saw bassist Peter Hook swing his guitar, taking out one of the fighters; it was Andy Outatunes, who was actually trying to settle the melee down. As Hooky took to the dance floor to enter the brawl, Andy's mates retaliated by hooking into Hooky, boots and all! JD continued with 'Atrocity Exhibition'; Hooky found his way back to the stage battered and bruised, then he abused his bandmates and left for the dressing room.

○ The debut album by Kommunity FK out of Los Angeles, USA, *The Vision and The Voice* was out in 1983. Here's a hybrid of death-rock a la Killing Joke and dark droning claustrophobia á la Joy Division. That said, they have their own gothic dark sound, but it's a shame that the production is somewhat muddled. Coming through the stifled mix is a sound representation that is atmospheric and industrial, rare from the USA.

⊙ In 1987, The Pixies made their debut in the music industry by releasing the EP *Come on Pilgrim* on the 4AD label. This EP was created using their initial demo tape recordings, which were made in the iconic Fort Apache, famously known as the home of TV's *Rin Tin Tin*. With a collection of eight tracks that amounted to just over 20 minutes, the EP perfectly captured the essence of what the Pixies were all about – screeching and wailing guitars, the intense vocals of Black Francis, and an unrelenting beat. Their sound stood out distinctively from their fellow artists on 4AD, and one can't help but feel that they set the tone for the independent music scene of the '90s in the United States.

⊙ It's good to see that not every band of wannabes took themselves seriously, as was the case with Splodgenessabounds. They immortalised themselves in the genre of 'Punk Pathetique' with the debut single available in 1981. The three songs, 'Simon Templer', 'Michael Booth's Talking Bum', and 'Two Pints of Lager & a Packet of Crisps Please', are classics in their own right! Funny!

⊙ The debut *self-titled* LP by This Heat was in the racks on this day in 1979. Abstract, ambient, ambitious, atonal, austere, bizarre, captivating, challenging, claustrophobic, disjointed, disturbing, ephemeral, exhilarating, experimental, fascinating, industrial, influential, pioneering, revolutionary, tormenting, unclassifiable! As you go through each track, you grasp at adjectives for this masterpiece of musique concrète techniques. If you haven't heard it… you must!

29

⊙ The Boomtown Rats' *self-titled* first album was released on September 29, 1977, straddling the line between NEW WAVE and punk genres. Rather than aligning closely with their punk peers in the UK, this album had a touch of The Rolling Stones' sound and an R&B influence that made it difficult to categorise. However, this unique blend of instruments, including piano, saxophone, harmonica, and even guitar solos, went against the punk conventions of the time. While it may have been less raw and more experimental, it still carried the youthful energy of the era. In fact, this debut album stands out as their most noteworthy release, as subsequent ones lacked the same level of intrigue.

Boomtown Rats by Roch Parisien

⊙ The Creatures, a side project of Siouxsie and The Banshees, released their debut recording on September 29, 1981. The five-tracker *Wild Things* was the culmination of Siouxsie and Budgie studio jamming, the result being a single A-side with 'Mad-Eyed Screamer' and four other tracks making up the EP flip side. There's a heavy accent on a percussive tribal theme, very post-punk, containing very little instrumentation, thus enabling the drumming and Siouxsie's velvety vocals to dominate. Their interpretation of the classic 'Wild Thing' is indeed fascinating.

○ *Vocabulary*, the debut album by UK group Europeans, was released in 1983. The standout here would be the voice of Steve Hogarth, the man that took over the vocals from Fish with prog-rockers Marillion. When you forget the senseless yodel in the opener of 'The Animal Song', the album moves through some atmospheric and, at times, very punchy tunes, while all the time that Hogarth vocal is absorbing and unique.

○ The year 1979 marked the first time that The Police reached the summit of the UK music charts with the release of their single 'Message in a Bottle'. Prior to this, they had only managed to secure two other Top 20 hits. The tune was featured on their album *Reggatta de Blanc* and achieved chart-topping success in Spain and Ireland. Additionally, it peaked at the No.2 spot in Canada and landed in the No.5 position in Australia.

30

○ It was September 1978 when Rusty Egan's 'Bowie Night' at Billy's, a discotheque in London's Soho, morphed into The Blitz Club. Tuesday nights at Blitz were something else, with Rusty Egan as DJ and Steve Strange as greeter/doorman; here was the birth of something new. London's art-school youth and those disillusioned with punk expressed themselves by the clothes and make-up they wore. Strange and Egan handed out flyers saying, 'Fame, Fame, Fame. What's Your Name? A Club for Heroes', these helped amass regular punters, aka Blitz Kids like George O'Dowd (Boy George), Peter Robinson (Marilyn), Jeremy Healy (Haysi Fantayzee) and Siobhan Fahey (Bananarama), to pack the venue to the sounds of Bowie, Kraftwerk, Roxy, The Normal, Lou Reed and Sparks from the turntable decks of DJ Rusty. The people, the music, the place…arguably the birth of the New Romantic movement.

○ At some point in September 1981, J.G. Thirwell, who also went by the name You've Got Foetus on Your Breath, put out his first commercially available album called *Deaf*. If you consider yourself a collector of industrial, no wave, musique concrète or noise music, you need to have some Foetus in your collection. Prior to the album's release, some Foetus tracks had appeared on underground sampler cassette tapes, but *Deaf* was the first Foetus full-length record that was available for purchase in import record and specialty music stores, exposing his music to a broader audience. J.G. was fearless in exploring any kind of noisy, experimental sound, eagerly recording and assembling sound collages from anything he could use to make noise.

○ Kate Pierson, vocalist and keyboardist for the B-52's, got arrested on September 30, 1993, along with seven other individuals from People for the Ethical Treatment of Animals (PETA), an animal rights group. They were taken into custody at the offices of Vogue magazine, where they were peacefully protesting by using bullhorns and sticking anti-fur slogans on the walls. The authorities charged them with criminal mischief and criminal trespass, and they were subsequently taken to the Midtown South police precinct in New York City.

○ Drummer and keyboardist/multi-instrumentalist Bill Rieflin was born in 1960, in Seattle, Washington, USA. Bill's work as a drummer, guitarist, programmer, and keyboardist can be found on over fifty albums with bands such as Ministry, R.E.M., NiN, Pigface, The Revolving Cocks, and King Crimson. Through the connection with King Crimson's maestro Robert Fripp, he went further to a collaboration with Fripp, Fripp's wife Toyah Wilcox and Chris Wong in The Humans, releasing three albums, until Bill's untimely passing on March 24, 2020, after succumbing to cancer.

◉ The Throwing Muses' *self-titled* debut album from 1986 was the first record put out by an American band on the 4AD label. Ivo Watts-Russell certainly struck gold with this discovery. Kristen Hersh's songwriting on the album is powerful and expressive, but it's her guitar work and vocals that instantly grab your attention. However, Throwing Muses is about more than just Hersh; the musicianship from the whole band is daring and imaginative. The rhythm section of bassist Leslie Langston and drummer David Narcizo is rock-solid and flawless. Songs like 'Call Me' and 'Rabbits Dying' demonstrate the band's careful attention to details like shifting tempos and moods, and those tracks, along with 'Green' and 'Vicky's Box', are highlights. Overall, the album showcases a band with a distinct, captivating sound and top-notch technical skills.

◉ Ash Wednesday from Adelaide, Australia, was born September 30. Ash was a formation member of JAB – 1976, Models – 1979, The Metronomes – 1979, Thealonian Music – 1981, Modern Jazz – 1983, Crashland – 1988, and The Ash Wednesday Effect – 2014, and during the years 1997-2013, he was a live performance member of Einstürzende Neubauten (E.N.). Ash is best known for his adept ability in the programming and use of synthesizers and drum machines. His solo work too is highly regarded as some of the finest of minimalist electronica; his collaborations with Karen Marks produced the astounding solo release 'Love by Numbers' and 'Cold Café' under Karen's name in 1980. The variation of design in Ash's work is bewildering; the simplicity and perfection of the product are a testimony to his prowess with equipment both live and in the studio. Through his groundbreaking approach to digital sampling, he was able to reanimate an immense sound palette into E.N.'s live performance. Dynamic sounds ranging from that of a delicate drop of water onto a plate of glass to that of explosive industrial cacophony. Returning to Melbourne in the late '90s, Ash formed The Tingler with Crashland vocalist Lyn Gordon and explored the world of recording online with the resurrected Metronomes. 2024, and there is speculation that there may be another Karen Marks collaboration in the offing.

Ash Wednesday by Richard Lewis

THIS WAS US, THIS IS IT. LIKE IT OR NOT!
ASH WEDNESDAY
(JAB, Models, The Metronomes Modern Jazz, Crashland)

JAB commanded attention! That's just the way it was. We were more of a gang than a band. When we played, we didn't care if people liked it or not. That was their problem. Fortunately…we were bloody brilliant!

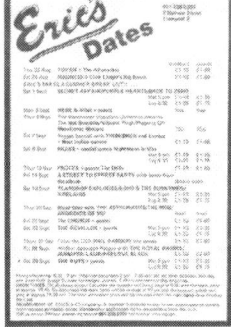
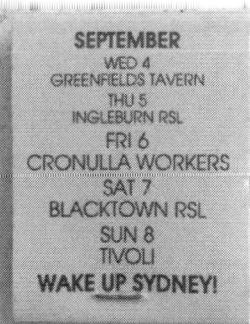

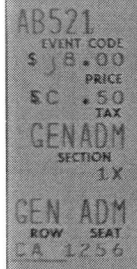
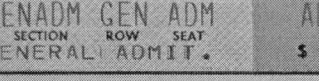
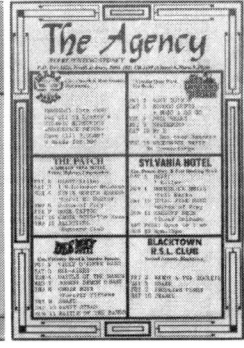

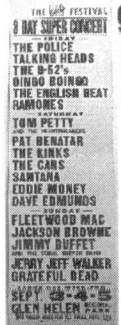
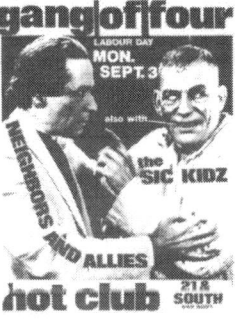

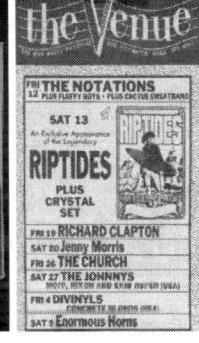

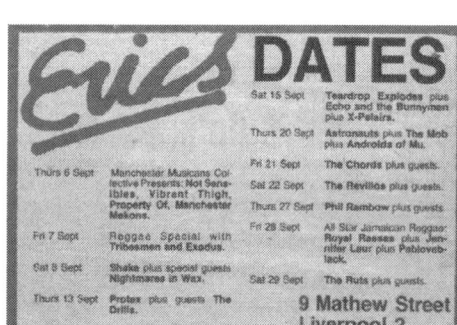

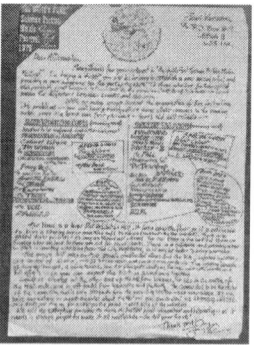

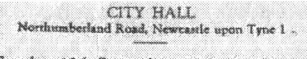

CITY HALL
Northumberland Road, Newcastle upon Tyne 1

Tuesday, 12th September, 1978, at 7.30 p.m.

STRAIGHT MUSIC

presents

BLONDIE

in concert

AREA £3.00   SEAT   N 17

Booking Agents: City Hall Box Office
Northumberland Road, Newcastle upon Tyne (Tel. 20007)
This Portion to be retained.

MCP presents

THE JESUS AND MARY CHAIN

BIRMINGHAM POWERHOUSE
SUNDAY 13TH SEPT. 7.30 p.m.
Tickets: £5.00 Advance - £5.50 on Door

000003

FESTIVAL HALL
EVANS GUDINSKI presents

Graham Parker
and the Romour

Wednesday 13th September, 1978, at 8.15 p.m.

SECTION 2
M 61

RENWICK PRIDE PRINT

marquee
90 Wardour St. W.1.   01-437 6603

OPEN EVERY NIGHT 7.00 PM - 11PM
REDUCED ADMISSION FOR STUDENTS AND MEMBERS

COWBOY INTERNATIONAL | THE BRAKES
CHRIS FARLOWE'S BLUES POWER | AXIS POINT
THE VAPORS | MERTON PARKAS
YOUNG ONES | THE MEMBERS

SUPER FLYING FUN SHOW

DE MONTFORT HALL
SIOUXSIE . . . . # 7.50
AND THE BANSHEES .
Thu 15 Sep 88 at 19.30
STANDING   05 32

Tickets cannot be exchanged nor money refunded.

the stranglers

BATTERSEA PARK
ALBERT BRIDGE ROAD SW11
SATURDAY 16TH SEPTEMBER
GATES OPEN NOON - ENDS 6pm

Harvey Goldsmith Entertainments in association with Albion Management presents

the stranglers

with Special Guest Star
Peter Gabriel
and Others
plus D.J. Andy Dunkley

BATTERSEA PARK
Albert Bridge Road, SW11
on Saturday 16th September 1978
Gates open 12.00 noon
Tickets: £4.00   N° 13476

peter gabriel
tour without frontiers

IN CONCERT

16.30

THE JESUS AND MARY CHAIN

SIDEWALKING 1988
THE GO-BETWEENS
THE BHAGWAN GUITARS
SELINAS SATURDAY SEPTEMBER 17

www.liveandloudshows.com
Presents

XTC
Live At The Rainbow, London
17 September 1979

www.liveandloudshows.com

FRI. SEPT. 18 A CERTAIN RATIO and PHYSICAL PUSH
SAT. SEPT. 19 "LAWN CHAIRS" OUR DAUGHTER'S WEDDING ROUSTABOUTS
SUN. SEPT. 20 JITTERZ
MON. SEPT. 21 SHAKIN PYRAMIDS NO MILK the UNKNOWNS
TUE. SEPT. 22
WED. SEPT. 23 DURAN DURAN
THUR. SEPT. 24 PIGBAG & the STICKMEN

Emerald City
PRESENTS

BOWWOWWOW

THIS SAT. SEPT. 19th
A provocative band from England...ex-members of Adam & the Ants...15yr. old lead-singer...mgr. Malcolm McLaren (formerly mged. The Sex Pistols.)...
Their AMERICAN DEBUT!
Route 70, Cherry Hill, NJ   (609) 488-0222

201

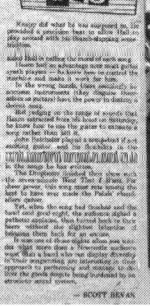

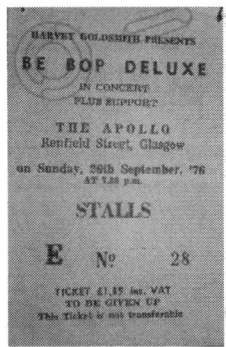
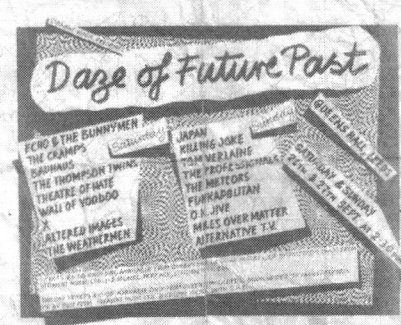

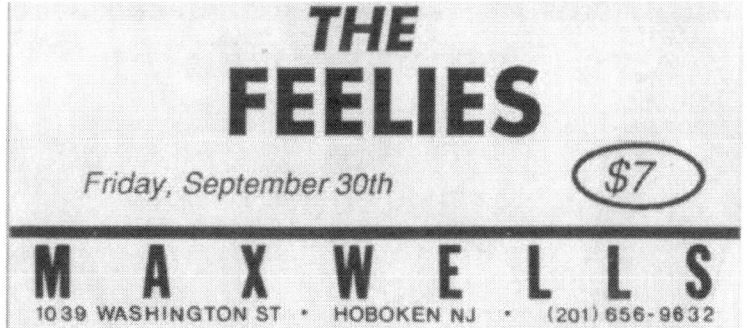

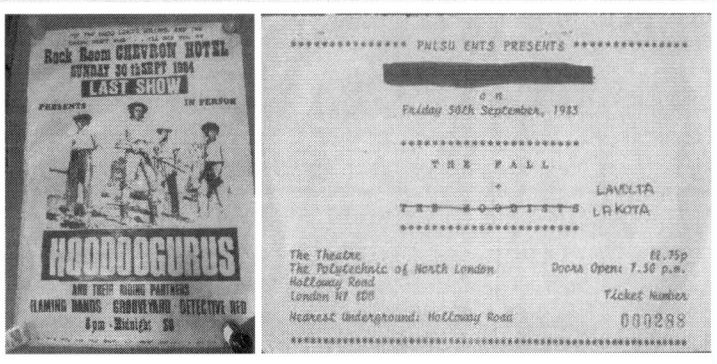

1

◉ Richard Barone was born in Tampa, Florida, USA. Acclaimed as a recording artist, performer, producer, and author, Richard was the frontman of The Bongos out of Hoboken, New Jersey. The Bongos' brand of power-pop earned them critical praise and a faithful following. Their 1982 LP *Drums Along the Hudson* is regarded as essential for the genre. It's brash yet sophisticated. Contradictory? Yes, though, when listening today, this set holds some catchy, snappy, timeless gems. With the 1987 split of The Bongos, Richard was a driver of the 'chamber pop' movement, using strings, horns, piano, and vocal harmonies. Incorporating these elements, '*Cool Blue Halo*', his first solo album - one of over a dozen - was recorded live at the Bottom Line, NYC, in 1987 and deserves special mention. Richard, as a producer, has been involved in numerous studio recordings and has collaborated with a wide array of artists, including Al Jardine, Donovan, Pete Seeger, and Lou Reed. He has scored shows and staged all-star concert events at venues such as Carnegie Hall, the Hollywood Bowl, and New York's Central Park. As an author, his published memoir, *Frontman: Surviving The Rock Star Myth* (2007), and *Music + Revolution* (2023), a history of Greenwich Village NYC in the 1960s, give insight into his life, thoughts, and influences. Currently working on a new album, Richard teaches the course Music + Revolution at The New School of Jazz & Contemporary Music, has served on the Board of Governors of The Recording Academy (GRAMMYs), serves on the Advisory Board of Anthology Film Archives, and hosts Folk Radio on WBAI New York.

Richard Barone on left with The Bongos by Phil Marino

IT DIDN'T HAPPEN OVERNIGHT
RICHARD BARONE
(The Bongos, Producer)

Sure, Patti Smith's *Horses* (1975) and the first Ramones album (1976) marked a change in the game, but in the few years prior, as well as simultaneously, Sparks, Brian Eno, Roxy Music, T. Rex, Kraftwerk, the Stooges, David Bowie, Lou Reed, and a few others had all sent up smoke signals. The seeds of punk and NEW WAVE had been sprouting like deliciously poisonous weeds throughout the more adventurous rock establishment. For the most part, it was still all happening on major or semi-major labels — from behemoths like EMI to Clive Davis's smaller but well-funded Arista, home of Barry Manilow; Chris Blackwell's heavenly Island; Richard Branson's Virgin; and Seymour Stein's regal Sire, distributed by Warner Bros. But it didn't matter where the music came from or who was distributing it. There was restlessness in the air. Fantastic as the bands were, Pink Floyd's and Led Zeppelin's outrageously overblown stadium tours and private jets — reeking of Brit Rock privilege, egomania, and supremacy in the eyes of some — simply screamed for a backlash. It came, most loudly and famously, with the Sex Pistols and the Clash in 1977. By that time, those who knew that Richard Hell and the Voidoids, the Ramones, and Television had already been there/done that in the bowels of the Bowery. But we loved it all.

The next major change occurred a year later, in 1978, Year One of POST-PUNK. In the USA, The B-52s in Athens, Georgia, and Devo in Akron, Ohio, independently put out exquisitely produced and artfully packaged debut singles that threatened, competed with, and surpassed major label releases. This changed everything. In the UK, Siouxsie and the Banshees, Joy Division, and Gang of Four had landmark releases. And, everywhere, post-punk bands released their own 7" singles, often on their own labels. This time, it *was* kind of sudden: overnight, the major record labels and A&R gatekeeper's jobs were, at best, optional. Why wait to get signed? Why not do it yourself? And from this DIY ethos, soon-to-be-important labels were created, competing with the big boys, and winning the coolness competition hands down.

That's how it was for us, anyway. Later the next year, inspired by the electricity and excitement generated by the B-52s and Ramones and the idiosyncratic worlds created by DEVO, The Feelies, and others, The Bongos formed. There were three of us, for a time living together in a sprawling railroad-style apartment in Hoboken, New Jersey. With a library of four thousand vinyl albums representing all genres, bassist Rob Norris's darkroom and camera equipment, and a view of the red neon RCA Records logo atop its building safely across the Hudson River in midtown Manhattan, we lived in a bubble of our own creation, sweetly glorifying the quaint, slightly industrial town of Hoboken in a way that echoed DEVO's dubious devotion to O-hi-o. We played in our neighbourhood bar Maxwell's and in the clubs of downtown Manhattan. Then, friend and sometimes bandmate Dennis Kelley, synth whiz kid from the band WKGB, introduced us to 21-year-old Rod Pearce, who was rumoured to have used the winnings from a horse race to start a label, Fetish Records, in London. He took a liking to us. We, in turn, were intrigued and delighted by Pearce's association with Genesis P. Orridge and Throbbing Gristle and signed with the label.

Travelling to London and touring through Europe, we recorded a string of singles for Fetish that were eventually compiled into our American debut LP, *Drums Along the Hudson*, in 1982. It was exhilarating. We were already unabashed fans of the other bands on the scene, and now we felt included, like we were a part of something bigger than all of us. It may be hard for some to comprehend, but, for us, coming up at the time we did, simply making records and touring on our own terms represented a kind of completion, a satisfaction. We felt we had done what we had set out to do. The story could have happily ended there.

Barely a year later, The Bongos signed with RCA Records. By that time, an entire alternative rock market and network of college radio stations had germinated in America, and, yes, it was seemingly overnight. But, in reality, it was the result of those first few fruitful, post-punk, DIY years in which artists were left to their own devices. For those bands who came after — some of whom would go on to embark on the same kind of outrageously overblown stadium tours with private jets we once repudiated — the path had already been paved.

◉ Martin Cooper was born in 1958 in Liverpool, England. He was a member of Orchestral Manoeuvres in the Dark (OMD) from 1979 to 89. He co-wrote songs like 'Souvenir', which reached No.3 on the UK Singles Chart. After OMD, he formed The Listening Pool with ex-bandmates and started a record label, Telegraph Records. They released one album, *Still Life*. Cooper's prize-winning artwork has been exhibited worldwide. He rejoined OMD in 2007 for a reunion tour and continues to play with them.

◉ In October 1983, Dolly Mixture unveiled their debut album, *Demonstration Tapes*. This double album showcased their unique blend of NEW WAVE and twee minimalism, presented in a straightforward and ambitious manner. The talented female trio of Rachel Bor (guitar/vox), Hester Smith (drums), and Debsey Wykes (bass/vox) personally signed and numbered each of the 1000 copies pressed. The songs on this album are not only delightful but also exhibit a minimalist and stripped-down sound. Throughout the 27 tracks, listeners can discover intriguing hooks and a nostalgic nod to '60s girl groups and perhaps even The Raincoats.

⦿ Jane Carroll Dornacker was born in 1947 in Albuquerque, USA. Jane was a touring member of The Tubes who co-wrote 'Don't Touch Me There'. Jane was Liela, the vocalist, keyboardist, and songwriter of the 1970s/1980s San Francisco "tack" rock group Leila and the Snakes. On October 22, 1986, while working as a live traffic reporter for WNBC radio in New York, she was killed in a helicopter crash. Listeners heard the terrified voice of Dornacker screaming *"Hit the water, hit the water!"*, as the helicopter from which she and pilot Bill Pate were reporting fell from the sky and crashed into the Hudson River.

⦿ Eric's, the Liverpool venue that sat as arguably the UK's most vital of the punk and POST-PUNK scene of the late 1970s, opened on October 1, 1976. And on that opening night for paying punters, it was The Stranglers performing! A week prior, on Friday, September 24, Eric's had opened its doors for an 'unofficial' free night, featuring Deaf School, who were managed by Eric's co-owner Ken Testi. The venue would go on to host the pinnacle of artists from the period, such as Talking Heads, Elvis Costello, The Buzzcocks, The Clash, Joy Division, Ramones, Sex Pistols and Siouxsie and the Banshees. This was the venue where many local bands like Dead or Alive, Echo & the Bunnymen and The Teardrop Explodes cut their teeth. The venue at 9 Mathew Street, Liverpool, owned by Roger Eagle, Pete Fulwell and Ken Testi, was shut down by the local council and police on March 14, 1980, after numerous reports of proliferating drug use; performing that night were The Psychedelic Furs and Wah!.

⦿ Moving Pictures out of Sydney, Australia, had their debut album, *Days of Innocence*, released in the first week of October 1981. Going to the top of the Australian charts in March 1982, it held the smash single 'What About Me', which became Australia's second bestselling single of 1982 behind Survivor's 'Eye of The Tiger'. The USA regarded them as NEW WAVE, but in their homeland, they were seen as more straight rock-pop; they had success in the USA as well, going top 30.

⦿ On October 1, 1975, Kraftwerk released the revolutionary album *Radio-Activity*, taking electronic music to bold new heights. Their previous album, *Autobahn*, in 1974 had already showcased the band's astonishing creativity and talent. But *Radio-Activity* was a giant leap into the future of electronic music, defined by Kraftwerk's signature cerebral aesthetic. The album was a frigid, clinical journey through a musical laboratory. Prepare yourself for layered, trance-inducing rhythms reminiscent of Bolero, paired with Ralf Hütter's detached vocals and metallic textures conveying the message that radioactivity *"is in the air for you and me"*. Kraftwerk masterfully blended melody and minimalist synthesizers, both gentle and foreboding. Tracks like 'Airwaves' have an intergalactic nursery rhyme feel. The album takes you through vocal collages in 'Intermission', the vocoder-altered 'Energy Voice', the beat-driven 'Antenna', and sci-fi lo-fi of 'Radio Stars'. The sequencing and arpeggios of 'Transistor' lead into the euphoric finale 'Ohm Sweet Ohm'. *Radio-Activity* was a landmark release, vastly influential on bands like OMD, Human League and Cabaret Voltaire. After experiencing this album, you will be energised but not overwhelmed by radioactivity, remaining charged for its full half-life, and bridging the gap between experimental electronic tinkering and the future of avant-garde electro-pop. Essential.

⦿ After years of intense effort, The La's finally released their first and only *self-titled* studio album on October 1, 1990. Founded by Mike Badger in 1983, the band underwent numerous lineup changes over the span of twelve years, with more than twenty members coming and going. However, it was Lee Mayers who emerged as the lead, showcasing his ability to infuse the melodic essence of The Merseybeat. This album presents a unique blend of psychedelia, skiffle, and blues, drawing inspiration from the best elements of The Beatles and The Rolling Stones. Notable tracks include 'Son Of A Gun', 'I Can't Sleep', and 'Doledrum', but the true standout is undeniably 'There She Goes'. This album is a stellar representation of British pop music at its finest.

● Thomas Leer, aka Thomas Wishart, was born in 1953 in Port Glasgow, Scotland. Via Thomas' early release as a soloist, the single 'Private Plane', and the 1979 *The Bridge* album collaboration with Robert Rental, he soon earned the mantle of being one of synthpop's pioneering innovators. Spanning four decades, his works have always held a level of intrigue, delving into industrial, electro-ambience, and synthpop, the latter where he was part of the 1988 duo Act with Propaganda's Claudia Brücken, recording the album *Laughter, Tears, and Rage*. Disappointingly, the Act was largely ignored, but when it was given recognition, Brücken was the name mentioned, even though without Leer's excellent work, it would have been missed altogether. This is a must for your collection.

● The *self-titled* album from the Neue Deutsche Welle movement band Liaisons Dangereuses was released in October 1981. The lineup consisted of former members of pioneering industrial/electronic groups Einstürzende Neubauten and D.A.F. - Beate Bartel on effects, Chrislo Haas on synthesizer, and Krishna Goineau on vocals. They brought with them the avant-garde, experimental sensibilities of those influential bands to create a unique fusion of dark ambient textures, pulsing electronic rhythms, drone-like synths, and samples. The result was an unsettling, yet compelling, atmosphere that paved the way for later electronic body music acts like Front 242. Please file this influential proto-techno/synth-punk record alongside classic EBM in your collection.

● Some critics have hailed Pop Will Eat Itself's album *Box Frenzy* as the most influential British album of 1987. Released on October 1, this album was known for its infusion of humour and catchy elements. If you're looking for a blend of hooks, guitars, beats, samples, and tunes, *Box Frenzy* is the perfect choice. Not taking themselves too seriously, tracks like 'Beaver Patrol', 'Grebo Guru', 'Let's Get Ugly', and their cover of Sigue Sigue Sputnik's 'Love Missile F1-11' showcase PWEI's refreshing and timeless approach.

● The 'Tanelorn Music Festival' was held over four days on the October 1-5 long weekend in 1981. The event was originally ticketed to be held January 24-26, 1981, in Picton, on the outskirts of Sydney. The event ended up being held on a huge farming property near Stroud, New South Wales, and drew upwards of 30,000 punters. With a single-lane dirt road, the only access (unless you came in by helicopter, as many of the artists did) took up to four hours to enter the festival site once you left the bitumen. The line-up featured Midnight Oil, Split Enz, Sunnyboys, Matt Finish, Men at Work, Mi-Sex, The Church and even Rodriguez! The festival had the feel of a 'mini-Woodstock', with hippies, soul food stalls, a nearby creek for bathing, and an area fenced off especially for Hell's Angels bikers.

2

● David Balfe, born in 1958, has been a musician, manager, producer, music publisher, video director, and record label head. He's best known for playing keyboards in POST-PUNK Liverpool band The Teardrop Explodes, founding and running the Zoo and Food independent record labels, signing Blur, and later being the subject of their UK No.1. Balfe grew up in Merseyside, where in the late 1970s he played bass & keyboards with bands that emerged from Liverpool's legendary Eric's club scene, including Radio Blank, Dalek I Love You, Big in Japan, the Teardrop Explodes and Lori & The Chameleons. Balfe and Drummond, having met while playing together in Big in Japan, founded the Zoo record label in 1978. The label went on to sign and release the early work of the Teardrop Explodes and Echo & The Bunnymen. They also released their own music under the name Lori & the Chameleons; singles 'Touch' and 'The Lonely Spy' were later licensed to Sire/Korova. Balfe played keyboards on and co-produced the first Bunnymen and Teardrop albums, as well as managing both bands with Bill Drummond for the years from their inception to early success. But due to lack of finance, they signed both bands to major London record companies and continued to manage them while letting the label fade into inactivity. David spent four years playing keyboards with The Teardrop Explodes, having a famously tempestuous relationship with their singer, Julian Cope. He played on their Top 10 single, 'Reward', and their two gold albums, *Kilimanjaro* (1980) and *Wilder* (1981). When the band disbanded in 1983, Balfe moved to London, where, after managing Strawberry Switchblade to a UK top 5 hit, 'Since Yesterday', and Brilliant (the post-Killing Joke band of subsequently famous producer Youth*)*, he then founded the Food record label in 1984. Food, initially funded by Balfe alone, signed Voice of the Beehive, Zodiac Mindwarp (both of whom moved on to major labels, while Balfe continued to manage them), Crazyhead, and Diesel Park West, before signing a deal with EMI to fund and distribute the Food label worldwide, while retaining creative independence. Food then signed Jesus Jones, who went on to have a No.1 album in the UK and multi-million sales internationally with their second album, *Doubt*, and a No.1 single in the USA with 'Right Here Right Now'. A year later they signed Blur. Balfe also directed Blur's first two music videos, 'She's So High' and 'There's No Other Way'. Disenchanted with the alternative scene in the years of grunge, Balfe sold the Food label to EMI in 1994 and semi-retired with his young family to the country – inspiring Damon Albarn to pen Blur's first No.1 hit, 'Country House'. David returned to the music business to take up a position at Sony Music from 1996 to 1999 as General Manager and Head of A&R of the Columbia *l*abel. His most notable success of that period was the million-selling Kula Shaker. Since then David has received a BA in Creative Writing from the University of Bedfordshire in 2003 and, in 2006, an MA in screenwriting from the University of Westminster. In June 2010, he received the Mojo Magazine 'Inspiration Award' on behalf of The Teardrop Explodes, presented by Alex James from Blur. In May 2018, Balfe was elected as a Labour councilor but did not stand for re-election in 2022. We take great pride in David's significant contribution to this book through his provision of the Prologue.

◉ Dave Faulkner was born in Perth, Australia in 1957. In 1977, as a vocalist/guitarist, he formed punk band The Victims and then, in 1979, joined The Manikins. There was a move to Sydney in 1981 where he was a founding member of Le Hoodoo Gurus, an odd line-up of 3 guitarists and a drummer, sans a bass player. Soon dropping the 'Le' and becoming The Hoodoo Gurus with the line-up of James Baker (drums), Clyde Bramley (bass), Brad Shepherd (guitar), and Faulkner, they released the impressive LP *Stoneage Romeos* in 1984, which earned the award for 'Best Debut Album' of the year. After many hard years of gigging and successful albums, 'The Gurus' split in 1998 but have since reformed several times. Over the next 20 years they appeared sporadically, with them headlining the 'A Day on The Green' concert series in March 2016. On May 6, 2009, Dave was inducted into the Western Australia Music Industry Hall of Fame, and The Gurus' iconic status on the Australian rock scene was acknowledged when they were inducted into the 2007 ARIA Hall of Fame. 2025, and The Gurus still take to the stage to enthusiastic new and old fans.

◉ Phil Oakey, born in Hinkley, England, on October 2, 1955, is known as the lead vocalist, songwriter, and frontman of The Human League. He co-founded the band with Martyn Ware and Ian Craig Marsh. Oakey collaborated with producer Giorgio Moroder on the 'Electric Dreams' theme song and recorded a *self-titled* LP in 1985. He still tours with The Human League, produces music, and DJs occasionally. The band's dark, techno-pop style, influenced by Kraftwerk, has inspired artists like The Pet Shop Boys, NIN, and Moby. John Lydon once called them *"trendy hippies"*.

Sting by Acroterion

● The son of the local milkman, Gordon Sumner, was born in 1951 and grew up in Wallsend, England. His working life started as an elementary school teacher, instructing English at St. Paul's First School in Cramlington, near Newcastle. His stage name "Sting" came from the black and yellow striped rugby shirts he wore, which gave him the appearance of a wasp. After playing in jazz and rock bands such as Last Exit and other groups, including a Dixieland jazz band, he teamed up with Stewart Copeland and Andy Summers for a decade as part of the wildly popular rock trio The Police. Sting has achieved enormous international fame, and following The Police's breakup in 1984, he went on to release several very successful solo albums and smash hit singles, including 'An Englishman in New York', 'Fragile', 'Fields of Gold', and 'If I Ever Lose My Faith in You'. He has also acted, starring in the films *Quadrophenia* (1979), *Radio On* (1979), and David Lynch's *Dune* (1984), as well as in supporting roles in many other movies.

● Drury Wellford was born October 2, 1956, in Charlottesville, Virginia, USA. Holding a master's degree in Library & Information Science from Pratt Institute in Brooklyn, Drury has a background in magazine publications such as Time-Life Books and Time Magazine. She worked at Time Magazine's news desk in New York City and was entrenched in the 'live' music scene of the '80s, particularly because her brother Armistead was a member of the famed band Love Tractor. Along with Armistead and her other brothers, Landon and Jamie, she attended a multitude of top-tier rock band concerts, ranging from Black Sabbath to Rod Stewart and Faces to the Allman Brothers, the James Gang, Jethro Tull, Grateful Dead, Traffic, Ramones, Pere Ubu and others. Drury is currently a freelance photo researcher and writer, her proudest work being the researching and licensing of images for publications by author S.C. Gwynne.

MY NIGHT WITH RUPAUL
DRURY WELFORD
(Photo Researcher and Archivist)

I had only lived in New York for a few months. It was a summer night, and Love Tractor was playing at the Peppermint Lounge. I couldn't wait for the party.

I got to the club with my friend group at around 11:30 pm. It was when the club had moved to 100 5th Avenue. It was a deserted night in downtown Manhattan, and I remember how eerie and empty the area felt and the dread that filled me when I thought about having to get to work the next morning at 8 am.

We went in, on the guest list, of course, and ordered drinks, which had to last a long time since nobody had any money. The band was supposed to go on maybe at 12:30am. Good, I thought. I'll be home by 3.00. I should be okay the next day on about 4 hours of sleep.

We sipped our drinks and smoked our cigarettes while being jostled by the crowd going back and forth to the dance floor. I'm assuming the opening band didn't come on until 12:30 because we started to hear that Love Tractor would be going on at 2:30. 2:30 in the morning, that is! That was a stretch even by my very open standards of partying 'til dawn. It was a work night, after all.

Still, we stayed on course and ordered the cheapest strong drink available at 2:00. Despair started to creep in that we would never see the band until suddenly Armistead, Mark, Mike, and Andrew walked on stage and took their positions. Then they started blasting 'Buy Me A Million Dollars', and the fans went nuts. We all surged on to the dance floor, bumping into each other as we did our wildest post-pogo moves, feet jumping and pointing out to the beat like the craziest of mediaeval dancers, curled and moussed hair swaying to the rhythm. Wild!

I was maybe 20 feet from the stage on the right side of the dance floor, boogieing like crazy. I noticed to my left a very tall, very slender man making his way up the left side of the dance floor, doing an exaggerated, athletic American Indian warrior-style dance. I was mesmerised. He wore navy blue and white striped leggings tucked into fringed knee-high brown moccasins. He had no shirt on but instead was showcasing a smooth, hairless, café au lait back and chest, long muscular arms pumping up and down to the music and his legs raised one by one in sync. He had no facial hair, and his head was clean shaven and shiny. Attached to the top of his head and trailing down his back was a large, bright red feather boa. He was moving his head up and down to the pace of his arms and legs so that the boa was swinging wildly up and down like a crazy NEW WAVE war dance. It was magnificent, and we danced all the harder, inspired by this guy's magical vibe.

After the show, the club had cleared out, and I was leaving to get a taxi home. I went to say goodnight to Armistead, who was packing up onstage. To my amazement, he was having an animated, laughter-filled conversation with the boa god, who towered over him like a tree. I walked up, and Armistead said, *"Drury! This is RuPaul. He's from Atlanta. He's in a band called Wee Wee Pole. They're great"*. RuPaul and I said our nice-to-meet-you's and talked about how great Love Tractor sounded, and I said I loved his outfit. He said thank you. Then I made my way into the night, treading some of RuPaul's twinkling stardust behind me on my way.

◉ In 1982, the Peppermint Lounge moved downtown to 100 5th Avenue. It closed in 1985. The building at 128 West 45th Street was torn down in the mid-1980s

3

◉ Georgina, aka 'Gina' Mary Birch, was born on 3rd October 1955 in Nottingham, England. Gina, as the bass-playing vocalist, was a founding member of The Raincoats. Gina is also well known as a filmmaker and producer of music videos for the likes of New Order, The Libertines, and her band The Raincoats. The Raincoats were initially mixed sex, and they played their debut gig in late 1977. By the end of 1978 they had moulded into an all-female lineup consisting of Gina, Ana da Siva (guitar/vocals), Vicky Aspinall (violin) and ex-Slits drummer Palmolive, aka Paloma McLardy. Go no further than the *self-titled* debut album, where the music is somewhat intelligently experimental, fractured, and harsh but all the while addictive. Raincoats would release four albums, all on Rough Trade. It took a long time, but in February 2023, Gina finally released her solo debut, the solo album, *I Play My Bass Loud.*

◉ *Battle Hymns for Children Singing,* the only LP by Haysi Fantayzee, was released in 1983. This was disposable pop personified. Even though they went top 20 with the two singles, 'John Wayne Is Big Leggy', a UK No.11, and 'Shiny Shiny' a No.16, there isn't more to offer here for "serious" audiophiles. All lightweight, and tongue in cheek, but granted, they stood out as very different at the time.

◉ On October 3, 1984, Killer Pussy released their sole album, *Bikini Wax*. Upon initial listening, they may come across as a budget version of The B-52's, and with subsequent plays, this resemblance becomes even more apparent. The track 'Teenage Enema Nurses in Bondage' garnered them airplay and stands out as the highlight of the album. While the band clearly did not take themselves seriously, as evidenced by song titles like 'Herpes' and 'Dildo Desire', they did delve into a risqué territory. There is certainly an element of humour present in their lyrics, such as *"I'm not a whore, I don't need men, my dildo's in the draw, it's my best friend"*. However, overall, even though comical, their music is rather forgettable.

◉ Ralph Morgenstern, aka Ralph Morgenstern-Nolting, was born in 1956 in Mülheim an der Ruhr, Germany. Ralph was a backing vocalist with Gina X Performance (GXP). GXP from Cologne were electro pioneers who formed in 1978 as a collaboration between Zeus B. Held and charismatic songwriter Gina Kikoine. GXP had a cool Euro-disco synthpop sound with an arthouse performance sensibility, as well as sexually provocative imagery. Largely unheralded, the GXP singles 'No G.D.M.' and 'Nice Mover' are pure gems which delivered sounds and beats that would go on to influence many artists for decades afterwards. Ralph has also made a name for himself as an actor, TV host and is well known in theatre and film.

◉ The album *Pauline Murray and The Invisible Girls* was put out in 1980. Pauline Murray had support musicians called The Invisible Girls, who were constantly changing. They collaborated with many artists, such as playing on John Cooper Clarke's albums from 1978 to 1982. The band featured main members Martin Hannett on guitar and bass, Steve Hopkins on keyboards and drummer Paul Burgess, as well as other musicians like guitarists Bill Nelson, Bernard Sumner, Vini Reilly, Dave Rowbotham, Pete Shelley, Wayne Hussey, bassist Steve Williams and Buzzcocks drummer John Maher. With so many talented musicians from Factory Records and production by Hannett, the album was destined to be remarkable. It departed from the usual dark Factory Records sound, with a brighter, summery feel due to Murray's sweet vocals and the skilled playing. Standout tracks include 'Sympathy', 'Shoot You Down' and 'Dream Sequence', which is simply a NEW WAVE masterpiece.

◉ The debut album *First (The Sound of Music)* by Then Jerico first charted on this day in 1987; it entered in position 35. The brainchild of vocalist Mark Shaw Then Jericho has had a long history and exists still today in 2025. Coming together in 1983, the initial incarnation of Shaw, guitarist Scott Taylor, bass player Jasper Stainthorp and drummer Steve Wren lasted until 1990. Shaw pursued a solo career until a rebirth in the late 90s. *First* was the band's best success, yielding several charting singles; of those, 'The Motive' embraced the spirit of the band, intense and emotive NEW WAVE, the single, reached the top 20 in the UK.

4

◉ On this day, The Bolshoi released their debut EP, *Giants,* in 1985, consisting of six tracks. The band blends a Goth background like Bauhaus with The Cure-styled melodies and pop sensibilities of Love and Rockets or The Church. In 1990, a re-release named *Bigger Giants* included six additional tracks, such as a long version of 'Happy Boy'. Unfortunately, The Bolshoi is one of those bands that didn't receive widespread recognition. Be sure to check out this release.

⦿ Culture Club's debut album, *Kissing to Be Clever*, made its way into the music scene on October 4, 1982, in the UK. With the inclusion of the immensely popular single, 'Do You Really Want to Hurt Me', the album achieved remarkable success, reaching the top 20 charts worldwide. Led by the unique vocals of Boy George and featuring a seamless blend of various genres such as calypso, synthpop, new romantic, and dance floor NEW WAVE, Culture Club created a timeless masterpiece of classic pop. This album not only captured the essence of the era but also stood in stark contrast to the new dominating sound of the Joy Divisionesque POST-PUNK, making it a significant contribution to the musical zeitgeist.

⦿ Chris Lowe was born in 1959 in Blackpool, Lancashire, England. In 1981, he partnered with Neil Tennant to establish Pet Shop Boys. They quickly gained recognition as one of the most successful musical duos of the 1980s. They were cheeky, smart, and pumped out extremely danceable, upbeat, catchy music that filled club dance floors all the time. The duo's ability to adapt to changing trends and their unique style of synthpop set them apart from their peers. The Pet Shop Boys seamlessly transitioned between different genres like NEW WAVE, disco, house, and techno while maintaining their distinct identity. Known for their irreverent and satirical approach, they never took themselves too seriously.

⦿ Recorded while still with Ultravox, Midge Ure released his first solo album *The Gift*, in 1985. Self-produced and not too far divorced from Ultravox, *The Gift* is full of glorious melodies, washes of icy synthesizer and of course, Midge's immaculate, precise guitar playing. Reflecting on his career, it's safe to say that this album is filled with some of Midge's finest moments. His treatment of Jethro Tull's 'Living in The Past' makes it sound like an Ultravox standard, stunning. The instrumentals 'Edo' and 'The Chieftain' are both cinematic and engaging. Midge just proves he was one of the '80s finest artists.

Midge Ure by Michael Skinner

⦿ Sad Lovers & Giants, an English POST-PUNK band, put out their record *Epic Garden Music* in 1982. The album conveyed a gloomy, dense, and cerebral tone with a heavy bassline and atmospheric synthesizer flourishes paired with melodic saxophone accents. Their style was clearly influenced by groups like The Chameleons and early The Cure, especially in the lead singer's monotonic vocals reminiscent of Robert Smith. Although obscure at the time, Sad Lovers & Giants cultivated a dedicated following, especially in Europe, and they continue to tour today. The original lineup, including vocalist Garce Allard, guitarist Tristan Garel-Funk, bassist Cliff Silver, drummer Nigel Pollard, and keyboardist/saxophonist David Wood, stayed together through 1987. On October 31, 2018, after a 16-year hiatus, the band released their seventh studio album, *Mission Creep*.

⦿ On October 4, 1982, The Smiths made their live debut at a student fashion and music event called 'An Evening of Pure Pleasure'. They were the opening act for Blue Rondo à la

Turk at The Ritz nightclub in Manchester. The Smiths blended NEW WAVE, POST-PUNK, and indie rock. They were at the forefront of the emergence of guitar-driven rock music. With a keen sense of pop music and the ability to write catchy three-minute pop songs, they etched their place in the history of mid-1980s British music. Lead singer Morrissey and guitarist Johnny Marr were very different people, but both were avid rock music fans. They embraced the do-it-yourself spirit of punk and believed that nothing was too difficult for them. Those two personalities formed one of the strangest yet most creative partnerships in rock history: a difficult songwriter and an inventive guitarist.

5

◉ The electro-pop group Depeche Mode released their first album, *Speak & Spell,* in 1981. Most of the songs were written by founding member Vince Clarke, who soon departed the band to form Yazoo with Alison Moyet and then later Erasure. The album's title was inspired by the popular children's electronic learning toy. Produced by the band and Daniel Miller of The Normal, the upbeat, hook-laden songs exemplified the emerging synthpop sound of the era. *Speak & Spell* is very much a quintessential Depeche Mode album; propelled by the hit singles 'New Life' and 'Just Can't Get Enough', it reached the UK top 10 and went gold. Though the band's initial song structures were relatively straightforward, these early works served as a foundation for the more complex, synth-driven pop sound they would later develop and refine. This evolution ultimately propelled the group to multi-million album sales and enabled them to continue performing for sold-out crowds as of 2025.

◉ On this day in 1979 record label Fast Product released *Earcom 2: Contradiction*, an EP of six tracks by three different bands: Thursdays, Basczax, and Joy Division. At the time, it was, the only way you could get hold of the Joy Division tracks 'From Safety to Where....?' and 'Auto-Suggestion'. The songs would later be part of the *Substance* singles compilation CD.

E N and FM Einheit of E N by Petra Gall

◉ The first studio album by Einstürzende Neubauten (E N), titled *Kollaps*, was released in Germany in 1981. The band's name, which means 'Collapsing New Buildings', truly reflected the unique sound of their music. Founded by German-born vocalist/guitarist Blixa Bargeld and percussionist N.U. Unruh, who was born in the United States, E N were true pioneers of industrial and noise rock. The recording of *Kollaps* also featured percussionist F.M. Eiheit. The album itself is a thrilling adventure, with tracks that combine raw industrial noises produced by their signature homemade music machines, electronic elements, and found objects. The music is filled with thumping, banging, screaming, clanging, and guitar riffs that were unlike anything else at the time, except perhaps for your little brother. This album truly set the standard for EN's unique style.

◉ Bob Geldof, aka Robert Geldof K.B.E., aka Robert Frederick Zenon Geldof, was born in 1951, in Dublin, Ireland. In 1986 he was awarded 'Knight Commander of the Order of the British Empire', a knighthood by Elizabeth II, but as he is an Irish citizen and the fact the award from the queen was honorary, he cannot be referred to as "*Sir*". Bob and the rest of the Boomtown Rats came together in 1975; they were originally called The Nightlife. The name Boomtown Rats was taken from a gang of children that Geldof had read about in Woody Guthrie's autobiography, *Bound for Glory*. The Rats started as an energetic band, oozing spirit exhibited on the UK hit 'Looking After No.1', becoming quite cultured yet remaining socially minded. The title of the smash hit 'I Don't Like Mondays' eventuated from the answer given by Brenda Ann Spencer, a San Diego schoolgirl, when asked why she'd killed her classmates. Indeed, it gave the band some international notoriety; while having moderate success in the UK, they never really broke through in the USA. The Boomtown Rats broke up in 1986 but reformed in 2013, without Johnnie Fingers or Gerry Cott.

◉ In 1979, Joe Jackson unveiled his second album, titled *I'm the Man*. This remarkable release was recorded at TW Studios, located in Fulham, London, England. Comparable to his exceptional debut album *Look Sharp*, some may argue that Joe Jackson demonstrated his prowess as a distinct artist, akin to the renowned Elvis Costello. However, it is worth noting that Joe's style leaned slightly towards mainstream appeal, making his music more accessible and less acerbic or ambiguous in its delivery. Notably, the album achieved significant success in the UK, with the single 'It's Different for Girls' reaching the impressive position of No.5 on the charts.

◉ On this day in 1980, Killing Joke released their *self-titled* debut album. This explosive record and band have been praised by many as groundbreaking and influential. The album was at the forefront of the POST-PUNK movement. Compared to their later albums, it's clear the band evolved musically in terms of arrangement and melody. However, this first album was raw, relentless, industrial, bleak, and sparse. The drumming is insistent, the guitars distorted and gritty. Jaz Coleman's vocals were confrontational and abrasive. It was an intriguing yet one-dimensional album that refused to compromise.

◉ Russell Craig Mael was born October 5, 1948, in Los Angeles, California. He and his older brother Ron formed the power pop band Halfnelson in 1971, which they soon renamed Sparks. Through their bewildering creativity and experimentalism, Sparks carved out a genre essentially their own. This prolific band has recorded over 25 albums, exerting great influence and fitting into the synthpop genre. Their 1979 single 'The Number One Song in Heaven' found them a new audience, their first major hit since 1974's 'This Town Ain't Big Enough for Both of Us'. Sparks continues to tour and record to this day, collaborating with Franz Ferdinand in 2015 on the album *FFS*.

◉ Robbie McIntosh left The Pretenders in 1987, prompting Johnny Marr from The Smiths to join the band for rehearsals. Marr performed live with the group for one tour and contributed to the single 'Windows of the World'. However, Marr's tenure with The Pretenders was brief. He departed within six months, citing personal ongoing disagreements with band members. Marr then went on to join The The and simultaneously co-founded Electronic with Bernard Sumner from New Order.

◉ Lee 'Kix' Thompson, also known as Lee Jay Thompson, was born in London, England, in 1957. He played the saxophone and contributed vocals to Madness. After the band disbanded in 1986, he co-founded a new group, The Madness, with Chris Foreman, Suggs, and Chas Smash. The band dissolved after releasing a *self-titled* album in 1988. Following this, Thompson and Foreman established The Nutty Boys and put out an album called

Crunch in 1990. Currently, Thompson tours with The Lee Thompson Ska Orchestra, a group he founded in 2011.

6

◉ Richard Jobson was born in 1960, in Fife, Scotland. Richard was a founding member and is the frontman-vocalist with Scottish band Skids. Initially, Skids attained moderate success and had a four-year career lasting from 1977 to 81. Their highest triumph was in 1979 when they went UK Top Ten with 'Into the Valley' from the debut LP *Scared to Dance*, an album loaded with loud anthemic guitar riffs and chanted choruses. "*Jobson's hearty singing sounds like an 18th century general leading his merry troops down from the hills into glorious battle*" (Trouser Press). On leaving Skids, Jobson was part of The Armoury Show, with John McGeoch on guitar and John Doyle on drums, both fresh from Magazine. Even though they held the marks of accessible anthemic rock commercially, The Amoury Show failed to impress the public from their releases of six singles and one studio album. During the 1980s Richard became a presenter on Sky Television. In June 2013, he was awarded an honorary degree (Doctor of Arts) from Edinburgh Napier University. Since then, has gone on to be a highly regarded filmmaker, director, writer, and producer.

Richard Jobson by Petra Gall

THE BAND AT CBGB'S
RICHARD JOBSON
(The Skids, The Armoury Show)

CBGB's was half full and nobody seemed particularly impressed with their set. Between the songs when he tried to talk to the audience it felt like no-one was listening as they took the opportunity with the break in the music to continue a conversation that the band had suffocated. This was their entry point to New York. The USA. A week's residence in this grimy but still legendary club. It was clear after the first two nights that New York didn't care much for the Scottish punk band trying to break into a scene that was too cool and self-referential to acknowledge their political hymns and lamentations. The band didn't fit - it was clear for all to see.

Out there in the sprawling boroughs of Queens and Brooklyn and closer in lower Manhattan on the lower east side and the ABC district bands lurked out of the shadows with a reinvented nihilism that took the shape of something deeper, more cinematic, smart and choppy - all in all a little less pale than the Scots with a message. This was the band's first major defeat. A 4,000-mile failure that had fractured the bond between each inter-dependent member. It was meant to be the beginning of something, but it felt closer to an end.

Being in a band was beginning to feel ridiculous. Embarrassing. He was moving to the sound of their music, but he was the only one in CBGB's who was dancing. They watched him like he was a dog in the sea, yelping and bouncing over the imaginary white horses. It was fun for a few seconds and then the sight and sound became repetitive and dull. He was monkey in a cage and his squawk for freedom wasn't working with the cultural evolutionary revisionists who had come out of a curiosity that was now long forgotten. Two years earlier this might have worked. But not now. The ferocity of people's ambivalence made him laugh. Not at them but at himself. Wrong place. Wrong time. Wrong music. Wrong! Wrong! Wrong! Everything was wrong yet they were only halfway through their set.

Back in the UK they had mistaken familiarity for popularity. Wrapped in that delusion they had crossed the Atlantic with a sense of entitlement. Why not. It was time. But it wasn't. You can't force people to care about something they weren't particularly interested in, in the first place. This was an era where people made their minds up almost immediately. Journalism and critics held immense power over micro and macro cultural shifts. It was them who decided who was in the cabal and who was out. And here in New York they had decided that the Scots POST-PUNKs and their blood red anthems of hope and glory were not sufficient for the NEW WAVE of musical contortionists. There was no mystery on show. No illusions. The poetry was too simplistic and ordinary - it was for "the people" not the special ones. Their music wasn't clear enough. Their soup - their cacophony had ancient beginnings and longings, but it lacked the spirit of modernism. They craved the familiar, but the audience was looking for a twist. The quirk.

The assertiveness of catching the sun come up rather than watch it go down. It was all about the new, the new, the new. And he felt yesterday and old. 24 hours is a long time in the broken allegiances of what is in and what is out. They were out. Failure was only painful to the people who understood its implications. Failure meant that what was supposed to happen next was highly unlikely. It wasn't a bad hand of cards - it felt more like a fall, a car crash. And he, the singer, felt like the driver.

JOY DIVISON IN BERLIN
RICHARD JOBSON

They arrived at the gig separately. Caroline was coming straight from work. Lang took her friend Anik for coffee. She told him about her plans for her new label Crepescule. It was a project with grand designs: spoken word, avant-garde music, European pop, torch-song nostalgia, and the input of Manchester based Factory records. It was clear to Lang that she had a deeper relationship with the band Joy Division and their singer Ian Curtis, who they were going to see tonight.

She had a soft kind face and spoke beautiful English with a gentle French accent. Her hands were long and always seemed to be intertwined which she would unclasp and bring to her face when she laughed, which she did a lot. Lang had met her in London at an event at the Belgian Embassy from where she had invited him to take part in a mixed media performance at the Plank K in Brussels. He had immediately agreed but had no idea what he would do, but it had been many months into the future, so he put it to the back of his mind. When the day arrived to fly from London to Brussels, he still had no idea what his contribution to the event would be. He had dressed foolishly in a white linen suit, knowing everyone else would be wearing black. The suit obviously drew the public's gaze in a way that now terrified Lang. In his pocket was a book of poems by the German poet Rilke. By the time he was to read he had got on the stage, accompanied by the Manchester guitarist Vinni Reilly but still had no idea what was about to happen other than Reilly would play his hypnotic ambient sounds and at some point, he would have to read something.

Plan K was an enormous warehouse in the centre of the city and had been full of people of different ages, all curious, as the night delivered new sounds and sensations. Before Reilly walked onto the stage a Parisian perfumer sprayed the area around the microphones with a smell which he thought would be appropriate to what was about to happen. Did he know something more than Lang? The smell was of citrus and pine; it reminded Lang of Spring and almost automatically he pulled out the book by Rilke and read *Vohrfruhling* as Reilly's long fingers and nails plucked his electric guitar into an echo chamber of beauty. Lang performed the poem in the original German. The gentle cadence of the words connected perfectly with the sounds coming from the guitar and Lang's soft Scottish accent was at ease with the harsher syllables and longer words. Out of nothing came something: a surprise.

Afterwards as he wandered around the event people smiled and clapped as he passed. He reached a bar area where Anik was surrounded by friends. All of them were excited by the evening's events. Lang was alive in the moment. It felt like anything was possible in this environment. It was Lang's first taste of this kind of creative camaraderie. It was liberating. In the middle of Anik's group looking back at him was the most beautiful woman he had ever seen. She crushed him with her smile and mimed "*Hello*". For Lang, the rest of the room disappeared, the fragrances, the voices, readings, music, theatre, conversations, laughter; all gone leaving the two of them in silence.

Anik broke the silence by congratulating him and telling him how much her friend, Caroline, from Berlin had loved it: the reading and the music. Caroline. That was her name. The woman now standing in front of him, still smiling, still attached to the group of people at the bar but ever so slightly moving away from them. She put out her hand for him to shake. He looked at it but instead he moved closer and kissed her on the cheek. Something he had never done before.

She laughed and kissed him back on his cheek. He was drowning, swimming under the water, trying desperately to find the surface and breathe. She spoke to him in German, telling him how much she enjoyed the reading. Rilke was one of her favourites and the music was perfect. He could see her lips move, an occasional glint of white teeth, her large black eyes and black hair held above her in a ball kept together he could see by a small pencil. Without them realizing the group had gone to watch the next performance, leaving them alone together.

"What's it like in Berlin?" He asked in German.

"Well, you know. It's my home". She answered in English.

"I would love to go there. See the city for myself. Visit the East".

"The East?"

"Why not?"

"I think that's great. Everyone who visits is too frightened to go over to the other side".

"Do you go?"

"No. I'm not allowed to. I'm originally from there. My Father got me out when I was very young. My Mother wouldn't come. She's still there".

"You're not allowed to see her?"

"No".

"I'm sorry to hear that".

"What's Scotland like?"

"Cold".

"Thats it?" She laughed and he wanted to hold her, kiss her, tell what was happening to his heart right now. At this very moment. "Nothing else?"

"Far away". He replied.

"So, you're never going back?"

"I want to live away from the UK for a while. Move around Europe. They've found me somewhere here in Brussels".

"Why not come to Berlin?"

"When?"

"With me. Tomorrow".

It had been that simple. Rilke. Reilly's music. The Plan K. Anik. And now Berlin. Did life need to be complicated. Could a decision not just be as simple as the one he had made immediately. They had spent the rest of the evening together. And he had walked her back to Anik's apartment where they kissed for hours in the doorway.

"I leave at 1pm tomorrow. Meet me at the station. I'll get you a ticket. One way. Right?"

"One way". He had said, holding her tightly not wanting this to end, refusing to slacken his grip terrified he might never see her again.

The white linen suit was left in a Brussels hotel as Lang grabbed some clothes in the morning and rushed to the station. It was busy but there she was waiting for him. Her smile lit up the dreary station as they kissed again.

"I knew you would come". She whispered in his ear. "I knew it".

And here they were In Berlin, together. Lovers. He touched the end of her fingers as they stood watching Joy Division perform. There were only a few hundred people in the old cinema, and it looked empty. The sound was terrible, and the guitars were out of tune. The new sound of Berlin was industrial and nasty. This music was fierce but romantic. The singer was like a sad Sinatra mixed with Iggy Pop. Lang loved it. He turned to Caroline and almost shouted.

"This is amazing!"

The singer seems to be in trance. The way he danced was mesmerizing. There was no communication between songs. Nothing. Just the music and him singing anthems of doomed love. Caroline and Anik were enchanted. They held hands as they sang along to the unfolding intensity and the chaotic sound. It was technically dreadful, but who cared. They were all in love with the music, the atmosphere, the words, the way he danced. It was an emotionally overwhelming experience. Lang could feel how the old cinema had been transformed into something spiritual. The beat of the drums. Urban and tribal. The guitars jangling a prettiness that seethed and deceived and then a bass line that plundered and looted through your bones before the arrival of the voice. The words.

"Dance Dance Dance to the Radio".

The excitement of just being there, being present, witnessing something important was physical. Everything was clear. It made sense. The sound of Manchester transferred to Berlin. It didn't matter that the audience were more curious than convinced. They had got it wrong. Not for the first time. This was the capital of doom and here were the archangels singing their anthems but somehow it didn't communicate directly in the same way to the audience what was obviously irrepressible to the three of them. The Berlin sneer was in the room, but it didn't matter. This was winter music for a city enclosed by a wall and death strips and floodlights, savage dogs and surrounded by the murdered. And then there were the ghosts. There were so many ghosts in this city that it was impossible not to bump into them. They were everywhere and they were here tonight in the old cinema building.

Maybe it was the name, Lang thought, Joy Division was too close for comfort, too soon. Third Reich fetish was incendiary here. Illegal. It wasn't used as a symbol of irreverence like it was in the UK. People in Berlin on both sides of the wall knew more about these symbols and what they actually meant. Nihilism was a badge of honour here on the western side but over the wall there was a belief in betterment through co-operation. The decadence seen in movies such as *Salon Kitty* and *Night Porter* would not endure here, on the contrary, people turned their backs on them, not because of shame but more importantly because these movies were imbued with a thrill, a visceral excitement. Nazi fetishism was totally unacceptable.

The name of the band was a fetish too far for the anarchists and Marxists, even the heroin addicts turned away from this perverse not so comical attachment to a bad history. Therefore, the name was a problem in this city, but the music was a spiritual experience and the words heart bracingly romantic. Some people danced along, and others stood nonchalantly looking on. By Berlin standards this was not a success but then again what were Berlin standards. What did that actually mean. Was it political determinism? Altruistic nihilism? Tribal accord? Sneering defeatism? Hopeless hopefulness? Indelible transparency? Youth's idiocy as triumph? Heroic failure?

What was the gold standard of this subterranean supernova. Lang felt it would always be superficial for the new, the incomers who could never really understand what the German word Heimat really meant for those like Caroline who were born here.

Joy Division played to indifference but not for the three people standing near the front who sang along with the anthems from haunted streets. Lang, who had seen them before knew that this was a special moment. A moment where and when different elements click together with an emerging beauty. And it was that, it was a beautiful thing to witness. Joy Division had the wrong name in the right city, but the music transcended historical fetishizing of an insane period. The music and the words were all that mattered. He kissed Caroline on the cheek as she hugged a swaying and weeping Anik. They weren't there for music that was ironic or fun, they wanted romance and the seriousness of life and death. And here it was.

There was no encore. Apart from the few who had been swept up in the music there was a general sense of apathy. But they had missed something special born from punk but coloured with a deep romanticism that spread from Goethe to Lou Reed. The happy few understood what they had witnessed. It would stay with them all forever. Lang watched as Caroline and Anik made their way backstage. He didn't follow them; he wasn't sure how to interpret the evening into words beyond sycophancy. They deserved better than that. He wanted to leave without meeting the band and walk home through Kreuzberg's side streets and try to empty his head and think clearly.

The Cinema was empty apart from the German technicians breaking down the equipment. Lang was alone. His girlfriend, the most beautiful woman in Berlin, maybe even the world, was backstage with an English band. He trusted her. He knew they would all want to know her, intimately. Knew what they would be thinking but he trusted her. She would never betray the bond they shared. Never cheapen their love for one another. It was then he saw Ian Curtis wander out with Anik and Caroline. Lang smiled as they approached lifting his hand as a gentle salute. Ian smiled back and put out his hand which Lang shook.

"Thanks for tonight. I loved it".

"The sound was terrible". Curtis replied softly.

"It didn't matter. Is this your first time in this city?"

Curtis nodded as Caroline suggested that they go somewhere else. A bar. Somewhere they could all talk. They decided to go locally rather than take a taxi back to Kreuzberg. He looked exhausted and withdrawn as Anik and Caroline continued to catch up on what they had been doing. In contrast Lang and Curtis walked quietly together.

"What's it like living here?" He asked Lang as he looked up at the dilapidated buildings and along the dark, badly lit streets. Lang could tell by his face that he considered it an impossible idea. Living in a frontier city was only for the imagination. Not reality. But this was real for Lang.

"I had no choice. It was her and here. Or nothing".

Curtis smiled understanding what that actually meant more than most.

"It's not easy". Lang continued. "The weather is extreme. I struggle a bit with the language but….but it's worth it.

"Is it dangerous?"

"It is for the kind of people who get caught up in stuff. You know, like drugs, heroin is big here. Young people think it's cool. They get hooked pretty quickly. And then that's it. They're fucked. The Wall, Music and Heroin have replaced the bear as the cities logo".

"Have you taken it?"

"No. Not for me. Besides I have the same condition as you have".

"What?" He laughed. "You're a coward too?"

Curtis was quiet again as they entered the bar and sat at a corner table and ordered beer. Lang watched him fiddle with a beer mat as if he were bored and wanted to get the hell out of this awful bar. It was as if Lang had expected somebody else, somebody more mysterious. Curtis could have been anyone from anywhere, a normal visitor to the city who was disappointed with what he found. Completely unimpressed with the Berlin of today in contrast to the Wiemar era. Seen through the eyes of a visitor it was easy to see how dull and disappointing Berlin was. A dull city surrounded by a wall. A crumbling mess where the apocalypse would begin. Berlin held none of Manhattan's glamour or the beauty of Paris or even London's boundless energy. It was not a replica of anywhere. It was a city that had to wake up to itself every day and pretend to be normal. Even the creative communities were anchored by that necessity. It was from this "normality" that came the steady flow of ideas and artistic conflict. The city was a larger version of Curtis. Normal, but anything but normal when you got to know how it all worked. It was an extraordinary city that had a bustling heart beneath its ready-made veneer. Underneath is where the truth lay.

Curtis looked up at Lang as if he had just remembered he was with him at the bar. Anik put her arm around him, and it was clear they were lovers. His eyes were hollow, dark rings appeared in the low light of the room. But he continued to stare at Lang knowing that they had shared something that few people would ever understand. Epilepsy was the strangest confidant. Both men knew the world wasn't stable, seismic ground swells, magnetic pulls and pushes, electrical shocks and the guarantee of despair as you crawled your way back out of a seizure. Sharing a few words about music was one thing but understanding the chaos, physical and mental, the dark vault with no light and the sense of a near end, were all shared as they looked at one another. No words were required.

"Hey, I'm sorry everyone but I'm so tired". He said not looking at anyone in particular.

"Of course, let's go back to the hotel". Anik replied, suddenly aware that she had spent no time with him.

"Yes. Of course. Let's go".

"Sorry". He said to Caroline and Lang through a tight smile.

They all left the bar together and Lang shook his hand again before hugging Anik as he and Caroline watched them get into a taxi. Curtis gave Lang a small wave and now under the streetlights the dark rings looked even more pronounced. And they were gone.

"He seemed so sad". Caroline said relieved to return to German. "Maybe he was just exhausted".

"The show was intense. Especially him".

"Anik loves him".

"I got that". She put her arm through his and nestled her head against his shoulder.

"Did you tell her?"

"No. We agreed we tell no-one until we're ready".

"I know".

"What did you talk about?'

"He was quite shy. He asked me why I live there".

"And what did you say?"

"Oh, you know, that I came here because of all the great gay bars".

"I see".

"And the transvestite clubs".

"Of course".

"And the fabulous Heroin".

"No doubt".

"And that I met a girl…".

"You did?"

"I did".

"And what does this girl mean to you?"

"Oh, she knows everyone so could get me into all the bars and clubs for free".

"Sounds like she's connected".

"The Queen of Berlin".

"No. You sound like you are the Queen of Berlin". She laughed.

"Nice".

"So, you use this girl like you use all the rent boys and all the heroin you take".

"Exactly. That's exactly the kind of guy I am".

"You're not very nice".

"I know".

"You're bad".

"I am".

"Very bad".

"Maybe even worse than that".

"OK Badman. Take me home and use me".

"I promise".

They clamped themselves together braced against a wind that kicked hard and cold against them. Taxis passed but they made no attempt to stop them. Lang was lost in thought about meeting Curtis. The soft-spoken man from Manchester who was the poet of isolation. He had brought a sadness to the evening that they should have expected considering his words and music. But the sadness in the bar was different from what they had seen on stage. Anik looked so happy to be with him. Lang made a silent vow to look happy to be in Berlin when he was in the company of Caroline. Not just because he was with her but because he was here. Here in this city. A city that did not inspire happiness in anything. Not even the dogs wagged their tails. Happiness was drawn from alcohol, drugs, extreme relationships, a quick death. Lang squeezed her shoulder tight. He didn't want a quick death. He wanted to live. Live here.

Lang had told Curtis that this was a city hanging by a thread at the edge of the world. Over there. Over the bridge. Over the wall. But one day it will change. Young people over there will say no more. This is where the change will come from. Or had he told him that. No, but he had wanted to. He had wanted to tell him something of value to take away with him from this German city where living ghosts are found on every street corner.

From THE KREUZBERG SONATA by permission from Richard Jobson.

⊙ Annalisse Morrow was born in 1960, in Sydney, Australia. Annalisse is best known as the vocalist, bass guitarist and songwriter for The Numbers (1978-84), MPM and the short-lived Maybe Dolls formed in 1991. The Numbers were a hard-working unit becoming hugely popular; their first 2 singles made it in the top 50, and the *self-titled* debut album peaked at No.29 nationally. Annalisse was once nominated for 'Queen of Pop' but lost out to the spandex-wearing Christie Allen. In 1985 she played the part of Laurel Lea in the Australian telemovie *Shout! The Johnny O'Keefe Story*. Today Annalise teaches interior design and does jewellery design at MisSMasH.

⊙ Salvatore 'Sal' Principato was a premature birth in 1957, in Perth Amboy Hospital, New Jersey, USA. Ironically, it was 5 days before his Liquid Liquid bandmate, bassist Richard McGuire, who was born there also! To quote Sal: "*I can just imagine the two of us wailing together in neonatal intensive care, shocked and amazed at being born. Due to my early arrival, it's been a game of catch-up ever since.*" After completing high school, Sal moved to San Francisco and immersed himself in the music and art film scene before he moved back to NYC in '79 and reunited with his friends Richard McGuire and Scott Hartley to form

Liquid Idiot. They would soon add Denis Young, and here were the makings of the famed Liquid Liquid, who had successes with songs 'Cavern', 'Bellhead' and 'Optimo' before folding in 1984. Sal then joined up with Ken "Man" Caldeira and formed Fist of Facts, putting out their unique form of industrial dub. Over the years Sal has ventured into being a DJ and drumming for the likes of Liki Outhaus and Avant Garbage. Today he runs a cultural performance space in NYC and gets back together with Liquid Liquid, who occasionally reform, playing dates in NYC and Europe.

THE SKELETAL VERSIONS OF THE LIQUID LIQUID & FIST OF FACTS STORIES
SALVATORE PRINCIPATO
(Liquid Liquid, Fist of Facts)

Part 1

In 1977 I took the long route from New Jersey to New York, passing through San Francisco; I ended up living there for two years. I returned to the east coast in the summer of 1979 with a plan to stay for only two weeks. I crashed with my hometown buddy, Richard McGuire, and a couple of other travellers, Scott Hartley and Ken Caldiera; they had recently both moved to Manhattan and were graduates from Rutgers University in New Brunswick, New Jersey. I, along with Richard's brother William and the others, was all writing music as well as staging musical happenings at Rutgers.

It was late 1979, and once in New York City, we practised all the material we had all been working on and came up with a few songs that we recorded on the cassette tape. Just so our efforts were not in vain, we took the cassette to Hilly Kristal at CBGBs, hoping and asking for a gig. He made us the fifth band on the bill. It was so much fun; I never went back to get my things in San Francisco! Soon we added Dennis Young on marimba and percussion; this marked the start of Liquid Liquid.

We evolved quickly and passionately; eventually we hooked up with Ed Bahlman of 99 Records, and after presenting him with a cassette, he took us under his wing as producer, manager, and advisor for the next four years, and in that time, we recorded three EPs, a 7" and a 12" single. 1983's 4-track release held the track 'Cavern', which became the subject of a dispute after being sampled and used by Grandmaster Melle Mel for the mega-selling 'White Lines (Don't Do It)'.

Liquid Liquid played all the clubs in New York and travelled the USA and internationally; unfortunately, we never really got to do a proper tour; they were just hit-and-run shows, yet they did establish that they were authentic. After a rollercoaster ride of events and happenings, including the drama surrounding the appropriation of our track 'Cavern', the band and the label folded in 1984.

Liquid Liquid had reunions in 2003 and 2008. We played venues and events that exposed us to new audiences and solidified our influence, evoking the milieu and illustrating the approach from which we evolved. We played at Madison Square Garden with LCD Soundsystem in 2011, marking the last time that we would perform. Over the years we re-issued our back catalogue with the labels Mo'Wax, Grand Royal, Domino, and Superior Viaduct.

Part 2

In 1983, I started creating music with Ken "Man" Caldeira; he was part of the Liquid family, so we already had rapport, and in 1985, Man came into the studio with an IBM AT computer, half a megabyte of RAM and Voyetra sequencing software. Via the new MIDI interface, this was the establishment of Fist of Facts (FoF).

FoF came together by combining me on vox and percussion, Man on bass and programming, adding horns and guitars, and Mark Cunningham (Mars), Genevieve Beaute De Monvel (Inflatable Boy Clams), Carlos Vivanco (Bardo Thodol) & Scott Hartley. We initially released one EP through Helvete Underground Record from Geneva, Switzerland, and performed mostly in N.Y.C. and in Switzerland. We were quite prolific in our songwriting and lasted until 1991, when Man went to Stanford University to gain his PhD in teaching.

In 2009, the indie label Claremont 56 out of the UK released an EP of FoF demos, along with some unreleased recordings. Then in 2019, Telephone Explosion Records (Toronto) faithfully reproduced the original EP, and we performed shows in support of the release. While booking FoF gigs. I started asking venues. Can I book a band beforehand? Can I book the band after? Can I book the whole evening? Eventually, the promoting of events at galleries, bars, small clubs, and yet undeveloped piers on the Hudson River became more important to me than performing at them. The events exhibited dance, spoken word, all sorts of music, and international and local comedy and tragedy in performance. This led me to be invited to organise a weekly event of music and culture in Greenwich Village, where we presented African and roots Caribbean performances early in the evening, with reggae well into the night. It was an inspiring blend, exciting, connecting the dots between the various cultures of Africa and the diaspora.

For 27 years now, I have organised a rehearsal space, a cultural space, and a party space in the basement of 178 Ludlow Street under the fabled Max Fish bar on the Lower East Side of NYC. Many creative types have passed through, and participated. We'd have improv sessions with a plethora of different musicians, and when it started to sound good, I thought we should go public, hence the birth of my latest project, One Seven Eight Product. In between all that I became an avid vegetarian/vegan cook, eventually doing pop-up restaurant nights, giving scratch cooking lessons, and hosting dinner parties in my tiny studio apartment and other people's homes, also developing a vegan cooking podcast.

⊙ The marvelous Tom Tom Club released their *self-titled* debut album on October 6, 1981. It's a majestic collection of funky, energetic hook laden songs, that were recorded at Compass Point Studios, Nassau, Bahamas. The cast included. bassist Tina Weymouth, her "L" sisters…..Lani, Laura and Loric, Tina's husband and fellow Talking Heads drummer Chris Frantz, along with guitarist Adrian Belew and a few of the *Remain In Light* Tour band. It's such an out and out infectious uplifting recording, that over 40 years later it remains fresh. The polyrhythms, the harmonies, the irreverence is á la Talking Heads. 'Wordy Rappinghood', rap presented in a whole new light, totally funky and rhythmic, 'Lorelei' a cruise fest of harmony and exotica, 'Genius of Love' salutes James Brown, a melodic, elegant funk wonder, 'L' Elephant' is a Belew stunt guitar showcase, the vocals bounce along like the chorus in Baptist church, simply delightful. Perfectly produced by Weymouth, Franz & Steven Stanley the album became enormously influential after its release, even Mariah Carey ripped them off with her hit 'Daydream'.

⊙ In 1978, XTC released their second album, called *GO 2* as a follow-up to their debut album, *White Music*. Although the UK version of the album did not include any singles, the North American copies featured the single 'Are You Receiving Me?'. The reason behind the album's title, *GO 2*, was a nod to the board game *Go*, with the addition of the number '2' suggested by keyboardist Barry Andrews. The album cover, which was created by Hipgnosis, served as an exposition on the utilisation of album covers to attract potential buyers. It maintained the black-and-white colour scheme from their previous album and achieved success by reaching the top 40 charts in the United Kingdom, Australia, and New Zealand.

7

⊙ On this day in 1979 The Beat from Los Angeles, USA (not to be confused with the British band of the same name) released their *self-titled* album. This was first-class 'power-pop', hook-laden, infectious melodies with clever arrangements all over. Yes, the songwriting here is superb and the playing just so. It's equal parts power pop and garage rock revival with a little touch of Ramones rawness and the band that Paul Collins toured with when he was part of The Nerves. The album is driven by some great guitar riffs that don't dominate, mainly because of the excellent pop sensibilities lyrically. The peak tracks are 'I Don't Fit In', 'Working Too Hard' and, from the movie *Caddy Shack*, 'There She Goes'. *The Beat* must rate as one of the best albums of its kind; it's way ahead of *The Knack* album-wise. The band name was soon changed to Paul Collins' Beat, then to Paul Collins & The Beat, then to The Paul Collins Band; one can only guess he could see the British Beat would not fade away and were becoming a major force worldwide. Just to make things even more confusing, in 2012 The Paul Collins Beat and The English Beat co-headlined a tour in 2012 called "The Two Beats Hearting as One Tour!"

Gene Loves Jezabel by Randee St. Nicholas

◉ Gene Loves Jezebel (GLJ) released their debut LP, *Promise,* in 1983. GLJ were glam meets goth meets POST PUNK and were one of the better 'goth' outfits of the early '80s. This album combines excellent musicianship with lush harmonising vocals by Jay & Michael Aston; this would become GLJ's trademark on later studio releases. GLJ achieved near perfection on their second album, *Immigrant,* but *Promise* has strong tunes throughout and is a classic of its time that still sounds great today, an essential and fascinating part of their story.

◉ Kevin Godley was born in 1945 in Prestwich, England. He is best known as a percussionist, drummer, singer, songwriter and a founding member of 10CC. Lol Crème and Kevin left 10CC in 1976 after the release of the hugely successful *How Dare You?* album to become the duo known as Godley & Crème. Godley & Crème were not only overly successful with recordings but were also highly regarded for their video production work, creating clips for a number of NEW WAVE bands, like The Police, Duran Duran, Herbie Hancock & Frankie Goes to Hollywood and many other major acts.

◉ It was in 1979 that the debut single by Joy Division, 'Transmission', was released on the Factory Records label. The song is totally enthralling and fascinating; the insanely good bass progression and the scorching guitar present something that is all and only Joy Division. Peter Hook is quoted as commenting about the importance of this song, *"We were doing a soundcheck at the Mayflower, in May, and we played Transmission, and people had been moving around, and then they all stopped to listen. I realised that was our first great song."* In May 2007, *NME* magazine had 'Transmission' at No.20 in a list of the '50 Greatest Indie Anthems Ever', sitting just below the classic 'Love Will Tear Us Apart'. In 2016, Pitchfork, the US online magazine, placed 'Transmission' at No.10 on its list of 'The 200 Best Songs of the 1970s'.

● Brian Mannix was born in 1961, in Melbourne, Australia. Brian has made his fame as the frontman/vocalist for Uncanny X-Men. Taking their name from a US comic book series, the band was known for a solid new-wave brand of pop. The X-Men's 1985 debut album, *Cos Life Hurts,* was highly successful nationally, reaching No.3 in the charts; the debut single '50 Years' also went top 5! The band's first incarnation folded in 1987 with a few subsequent reformations; in 2018 they teamed up with Kids in The Kitchen for one appearance and have also been part of the *Absolutely '80s* tours. Brian, being far from camera shy and with an energetic personality, featured in several TV series and, on several occasions, co-hosted Australian ABC-TV's music show *Countdown* and has appeared numerous times on the music quiz program *Spicks and Specks*. Even as a 10-year-old, Brian had panache, winning a beachside town beauty contest.

● '2-4-6-8 Motorway' b/w 'I Shall Be Released', the debut single from Tom Robinson Band, was released in 1977. The USA saw this single as 'punk' (well, it was 1977, and the USA even viewed Blondie as 'punk'), but even though TRB were from the UK, they were spitting out their version of NEW WAVE. The A-side is a rollicking belter and an epic of the period, but would any self-respecting punk band do a cover of Dylan's 'I Shall Be Released'? Highly unlikely. TRB was a candle that shone bright for one shining moment; that candle faded into obscurity, BUT this is an enduring classic.

● XTC released their debut single 'Science Friction' as an EP titled *3D EP* on October 7, 1977. Jerky, quirky pop brilliance - here comes Andy Partridge and crew. Squealing guitar and carnival-style keyboards, vocal-style changes and an unyielding rhythm section take us through a young band's entry ticket. It's bold, it's brash; they were to mature and become one of the premier artists of the end of the last millennium.

8

● Johnny Ramone was born John Cummings in 1948, in New York City. Johnny was the guitarist who, along with Joey, was the other member to be part of the band from 'Hey Ho Let's Go' (1974) to 'Whoa' (1996). The Ramones were/are arguably the most influential band of the punk rock genre. If one said that MC5 or The Stooges (or even bits of The Who) weren't punk, then The Ramones deserve the accolade as being the first. The Ramones music is raw, basically made up of 4 chords & inane lyrics. Listen to the first few albums; this is where punk is drawn from. The style has been copied by so many and will surely continue to be so. Johnny died of prostate cancer on 15th September 2004. SO! Get your prostate checked, fellas!! On the table, get lubed & get your organ fiddled with, PUNK!

● Gavin Friday, aka Fionán Martin Hanvey, was born on 8th October 1959 in Dublin, Ireland. Gavin was a founding member as the vocalist/frontman for Virgin Prunes and, in his own right, quite an accomplished songwriter, composer, actor and painter. Over the course of 1978 Virgin Prunes came from a group of teenagers growing up with the prospect of a life in the dole queue; this led to the creation of their own sanctuary from outsiders, a secretive world that they called the Lypton Village. Virgin Prunes was fronted by Gavin and joined by fellow villagers Guggi, aka Derek Rowan: vocals; Dave-id Busaras Scott, aka David Watson: vocals; Strongman, aka Trevor Rowen: bass; Dik Evans (brother of U2's The Edge): guitar; and Pod, aka Anthony Murphy: drums. Early Virgin Prunes gigs were very much performance art events, with audiences often pushed to the edges of their tolerance to the point that their appearances were regularly banned. In November 1982, on Rough Trade, the Virgin Prunes released their Colin Newman-produced debut and arguably best album, *If I Die, I Die*. They disbanded in 1986 after the departure of Guggi, Dik and Gavin with him deciding to concentrate on painting, and those that remained continued under the name The Prunes until they split up in 1990. The late 80s saw Gavin return to music, pursuing a solo career and entering into composing for film and stage, often collaborating with Maurice Seezer. To date he has released 6 well-received albums and continues to apply himself to his love of painting, culminating in several exhibitions.

...AND THEN THERE WERE THE VIRGIN PRUNES
GAVIN FRIDAY
(Virgin Prunes, Solo)

The name Virgin Prunes came from Guggi; originally it was a slang name he gave to 'freaks', 'weirdos', and 'outsiders', basically people who were different and didn't fit into the 'norm'. That was way back in 1974, before the thought of even forming a band entered our world.

But that was all soon to change with the arrival of punk rock in 1976.

Some of our Lypton Village friends were quick off the mark and formed a band called Feedback in late 1976, which morphed momentarily into The Hype in late 1977. By then punk rock had basically taken over our lives, and I and Guggi both decided to form our own band and call it Virgin Prunes.

The main conundrum would be our fellow band members, especially as neither of us could play an instrument. Although truthfully that wasn't really a worry, as the punk philosophy was 'do it yourself' and 'make it up as you go along'. It was all about the attitude, the embrace of individuality and expression, and we had loads of that. We were innocently fierce, fearless and ambitious. The angst, hunger and drive of youth are truly beautiful and forceful things.

It was in March of 1978 when Bono invited me and Guggi as the Virgin Prunes to open for The Hype, who had planned at that same live show to encore under their new name of U2. The gig was at Sutton Presbyterian Hall on March 4th, 1978. The lineup was The Hype / Virgin Prunes / Modern Heirs, and as an encore, a reformed Hype calling themselves U2. The Hype, offering to be our backing musicians, were Adam Clayton, Larry Mullen Jnr, The Edge and his brother Dick Evans.

My first task was, how do I make the musicians look original and aligned to myself and Guggi? There was no way I was going to let us just be guest performers with the Hype. Virgin Prunes had to look, sound and perform in their own unique way.

I was at that time briefly working at Dublin Meat Packers, a slaughterhouse in Cloghran, Swords, Co. Dublin. I decided to 'borrow' a load of carcass mesh, used for exporting the dead animal carcasses, along with five also 'borrowed' white slaughterhouse overalls, the idea being to dress/disguise the aforementioned musicians in the white overalls with the mesh on their heads. They looked amazing, like a gang of abattoir zombies.

Guggi dressed in ripped and torn drainpipes and stilettos with a loan of my Mam's fox fur short jacket. Myself in a plastic jumpsuit made from see-through plastic raincoats sewn together by my mother. Both of us naturally were slapped up with white theatre face paint and heavy eyeliner à la rule No.1: "You have to look the fucking part".

Regarding what we would perform... We were inspired by a band called The Worst who had just supported The Clash at Trinity College Dublin. They had played beyond the slowest, most horrendous din of an improvisation I'd ever heard. It drove the audience insane to my glee.

So, using the Worst's stance and Lou Reed's *Metal Machine Music* as musical touchstones, we would perform a cover version of The Rolling Stones' 'Satisfaction', simply because at that time I so detested that song.

All the musicians were instructed to play a slower-than-one-could-imagine-slow improvised version of the song with the main hook/guitar riff being perverted into Velvet's white noise dirge-like cacophony. Provocative?... Yes, absolutely, this was something to deliberately fuck up and aggravate the then rent-a-pogo-punter that was commonplace at all gigs in those days. We had only one rehearsal, and that was at the actual soundcheck on the afternoon of the gig, and later that evening was the first glimpse of what was the Virgin Prunes. It was a relentless mess. The improvised version of the song lasted 15 minutes, over which I and Guggi whispered and screamed like slow-motion-speed lunatics manically parading the stage. What a beautiful shambles, and we loved every minute of it even though we went down like a ton of bricks. We were bottled off stage and covered in gob – but we didn't give a fuck; in our minds, all went as planned.

Soon after the gig, Dick Evans, who was 'not' to be in the new U2 lineup, came up to me and Guggi and said he wanted to be a Virgin Prune, and we immediately christened him Dik Prune. Now we had a guitarist; all we needed was a bass player and drummer. A week later in Strongman's flat in Phibsboro, the rest of the band was formed. After seeing the Sutton Presbyterian Hall performance Strongman, Guggi's younger brother, on his own merits, went out and bought a bass guitar, which, to me, made total sense, as he, in my mind, always had the look, attitude and stance of a punk bass player; the only thing was he couldn't afford an amp as of yet. Pod, another Lypton Villager, demanded to be our drummer; he had required an old second-hand drum kit courtesy of Larry Mullen Jr..

So, we had what we felt was the perfect lineup: Dik on guitar and Strongman on bass, both plugged into Dik's amp. I and Guggi on vocals, also plugged into Dik's amp.
Then our very good friend Dave asked us, "*What about fucking me? I want to be in the band too. I'm a Virgin Prune*". So there and then, Dave was given the name of Dave id Busarus and the extraordinary task of being the band's narrator.

Over the next six weeks we worked non-stop writing and rehearsing towards our first 'official' gig. We approached Jim Sheridan of the Project Art Centre and convinced him to let us play a 30-minute set... 25th May 1978 at the Project Arts Centre, Dublin City, behold... and there were the Virgin Prunes.

VIRGIN PRUNES HISTORY
1978 - 1979 - Gavin Friday, Guggi, Dik, Strongman, Dave Id Busarus, Pod
1980 - 1981 - Gavin Friday, Guggi, Dik, Strongman, Dave Id Busarus, Haa Lacka Binttii
1981 - 1986 - Gavin Friday, Guggi, Dik, Strongman, Dave id Busarus, Mary D'Nellon***
*** *during 1985-1986 Guggi, then Dik, departed, followed by Gavin Friday, ending the band in late 1986.*

◉ Factory Records released *Still* in 1981. *Still* is a compilation album of previously unreleased and live recordings by Joy Division. The album captures the Manchester band's dark, haunting sound that was highly unique and exceptionally original for its time. Though often imitated by bands from the Factory stable, Joy Division's style has rarely been equaled. This isn't easy listening music. Rather, it reveals the band's avant-garde techniques and dynamic, an unpredictable musicality that was ostensibly incomprehensible, yet irresistibly infectious. Joy Division pioneered unconventional and groundbreaking arrangements that sparked a revolution in music. Produced by Martin Hannett, *Still* represents the band's late '70s POST-PUNK sound transitioning to sophisticated NEW WAVE. This evolution is audible from the experimental 'Exercise One' to the aggressive, danceable 'Ice Age' to their influential classics like 'Transmission' and 'Isolation'. Many songs evoke the inner turmoil and emotional despair of lead singer Ian Curtis, who ultimately lost his battle with depression. His tragic early passing only amplifies the possibilities of where his immense talents may have led, had he lived. While most appreciated by established fans, *Still* isn't the ideal introduction to Joy Division. Better entry points are their studio album *Closer* or their signature hit 'Love Will Tear Us Apart'. Although less polished than radio-friendly contemporaries, *Still* overflows with raw emotion and textured sounds central to Joy Division's identity. It's an unforgettable experience for those keen to discover the band's uncompromising artistry.

⊙ The debut album *Spring Session M* by the American NEW WAVE band Missing Persons was released October 8, 1982. The group was made up of former members of Frank Zappa's band, including lead singer Dale Bozzio, her husband and drummer Terry Bozzio, and guitarist Warren Cuccurullo, along with keyboardists Patrick O'Hearn and Chuck Wild. Their infectious, hook-filled NEW WAVE synth pop was very much a product of the early '80s. While the vibrant production was a defining aspect, the strong melodies and musicianship of Missing Persons ensured they were excellent representatives of American pop from that era. It was a standout release. Interestingly, *Spring Session M* is an anagram of Missing Persons!

⊙ In the stores on this day in 1979 was the album titled *Laughing Academy* by Punishment of Luxury, also known as Punilux. The band derived their name from an Italian painting called 'The Punishment of Lust' by artist Giovanni Segantini. This album showcased the group's unique and quirky approach to artsy POST-PUNK music, comparable to bands like Wire, XTC, and Gang of Four. At one point, Mojo magazine incorrectly listed this album as one of the worst 100 albums ever made. This was certainly an undeserved designation, perhaps because the songs were quite diverse and difficult to categorise. There were many likeable tracks, including 'Puppet Life', 'The Message', 'British Baboon', and 'Funk Me', which were on par with much of the music from that era.

⊙ *Remain in Light,* the fourth studio album by Talking Heads, was released in 1980. Talking Heads' album trilogy 1978-80 with Brian Eno culminated in what sits as one of the greatest albums of all time, *Remain in Light*. A funky, polyrhythmic art exploration born from African & Latin American influences to create textures, rhythms, and moods unlike anything about in rock music at the time. The offbeat lyrical sense of David Byrne, coupled with Eno's sense of minimalism and uncanny arrangement with percussive tangles, was now redefining the NEW WAVE dance craze. Eno brought in that Afro-jazz beat typical of Fela Kuti, and Byrne was digging into Latino emotions, which became evident much later on his solo LP *Rei Momo*. The rhythm section of Chris Franz & Tina Weymouth has never been so integral to a Talking Heads recording, though according to reports, due to studio differences with Eno & Byrne, Tina would like you to think otherwise. Even with Adrian Belew there live & in the studio, she took exception to Eno being classified as a fifth member. The album is a mass of technically flawless layering and multi-multi tracking. No better exemplified than on 'The Great Curve'. The earlier songs of Side 1, 'Burn Under Punches' & 'Cross-eyed & Painless', are the strongest danceable specials, totally infectious through the majestic combination of Tina and Chris. Side 2 becomes somewhat trancey after starting with the glorious 'Once in a Lifetime'; there's the mystery of 'Houses in Motion' with Jon Hassell's treated horns and Byrne talking his way through cryptic lyrics. 'Seen and Not Seen' is spooky and percussively minimalist. Then to 'Listening Wind', sounding like an outtake from the stunning Eno-Byrne *My Life in The Bush of Ghosts* album, except unlike *Bush,* it has Byrne's vocals, and here they sound the best they have at any time; in the background, Belew wails and squeals on his guitar. The album closes with 'The Overload', an Eno-composed dirge drone, swirling and temperate, letting the listener down easy from the euphoric preceding seven songs. You are unlucky if you have bought this already, as the remastered expanded CD has four additional unfinished out-takes. 'Fela's Riff'…where Eno pays homage to a musical idol, Fela Kuti, it's reminiscent of Philip Glass with layers of repetitive guitar and percussion. 'Unison' is real Talking Heads and like something from the *Naked* LP, with excellent layering of Byrne's voice with that ever-present percussion, a true foot-tapper. 'Double Groove' has everyone vocalising in rounds a la 'row row row ya boat' in a wonderful repetitive groove; the rhythm section works overtime here through to an unproduced abrupt ending. With the final track, 'Right Start', you get an instrumental version of what was probably 'Once in a Lifetime', guitar-y and spacious. Just perfect. Jerry

Harrison must get a mention now. His keyboard washes and textures are integral to this LP and as important as any contribution, and by the way, get his solo LP *The Red & The Black*, sensational.

9

◉ On October 9, 1984, *Limping for a Generation,* the first album by The Blow Monkeys, was available for purchase. This album blended sophisti-pop with NEW WAVE elements. The band consisted of Dr. Robert, Neville Henry, Mick Anker, and Tony Kiley and showcased smooth, classy, and stylish club tunes reminiscent of The Style Council and ABC. Standout tracks include 'Wildflower' and 'Atomic Lullaby'. The term 'blow monkeys', is an offensive title that referred to indigenous players of a didgeridoo.

Bow Wow Wow By Paul Edmond

◉ *See Jungle! See Jungle! Go Join Your Gang Yeah, City All Over! Go Ape Crazy!,* the first LP album by Bow Wow Wow was released in 1981. This creation by Malcolm McLaren sure went ape crazy! Combining members of Adam and the Ants and a 14-year-old Annabella Lwin on vocals, there was hullabaloo from the start. Having her pose nude for the album cover maintained the controversy. The music…well, there's drumming - oh yeah, ever-present busy drumming - fun with a very original sound, groovy melodic hooks and some really great guitar and bass playing…and drumming.

◉ 1986 saw *Urban Beaches,* the debut album by Cactus World News, released by MCA, being available in the UK. Cactus World News from Dublin, Ireland, came to the attention of many following the support on a 1985 UK tour with The Cult. One would be forgiven for drawing comparisons to U2, especially on the single drawn from the LP *The Bridge,* which was produced by U2's Bono. The album excites from the opening track 'Worlds Apart'. Just like U2, they sound very anthemic; the sound is big, with wailing guitar, thunderous drumming and all the telling loud vocal output. In the end, lovers of U2, Big Country or The Alarm will find something here, and if the early albums are not to your liking, this is a must to avoid.

◉ Go out on October 9, 1980, seek, and you might find the debut single release from The Fallout Club. At the time of 'Falling Years' b/w 'The Beat Boys', it was just Trevor Herion and Paul Simon, but they were soon to be joined by Matthew Seligman and wonder boy Thomas Dolby for the release of three more classic singles: 'Wonderlust', 'Dream Soldiers' and 'Pedestrian Walkway'. The A-side is synthpop excellence, it's sparse and rhythmic with Herion's vocal coming to the fore, the B-side is like a 'part 2' minimalist and intriguing.

◉ Al Jourgensen, aka Allen David Jourgensen, was born in La Habana, Cuba, in 1958 under the name Alejandro Ramírez Casas. Al has gained great recognition in the music industry as both a musician and producer, primarily for his contributions to Ministry and related projects such as Acid Horse, The Revolting Cocks, Buck Satan and the 666 Shooters. He often conceals his work under various aliases, including Alain Jourgensen, Alien Jourgensen, Alien Dog Star, Buck Satan, and Hypo Luxa.

10

○ *Icehouse*, the debut album by Australian band Flowers, was released locally on October 10, 1980, on the independent label Regular Records. Flowers had a huge following on the Sydney pub circuit with their excellent covers of glam artists like Bowie, T-Rex, Roxy Music, and Eno; they continually played to packed houses. In 1981, Flowers, so as not to be confused with a Scottish band of the same name, renamed themselves Icehouse. In 1981 the album was released internationally under the name *Icehouse* by Icehouse with different cover art.

○ Martin John Kemp was born in 1961 in London, England. While best known as the bassist for the band Spandau Ballet, Martin has also found success as an actor and occasional TV presenter, becoming famous for playing Steve Owen in the BBC soap opera EastEnders. He is the younger brother of Gary Kemp, another Spandau Ballet member and actor. Martin reflects that Spandau Ballet were defined by excesses; they had big hair, flamboyant clothes, numerous belts, and shoulder pads. He believes this over-the-top '80s aesthetic is why bands from that era didn't transition well into the more understated '90s. In Martin's opinion, 'Through The Barricades' was Spandau Ballet's most outstanding recording.

○ Kirsty MacColl was born in 1959, in Croydon, England. Signed to Stiff Records, she released a few singles which made her a known name but did not bring her immediate success. Her chart success began in 1981 with the single 'There's A Guy Works Down the Chips Shop Swears He's Elvis'. Kirsty earned a definite place in music history when she sang a duet with The Pogues on the Xmas single 'Fairytale of New York'. During her recording career from 1981, she released five albums. On December 18, 2000, while on a holiday with her family in Mexico, she was hit by a speedboat, causing fatal injuries.

○ Robert David Miles was born on October 10, 1958, in Melbourne, Australia. A son of teachers, he grew up in country Victoria, went on to study architecture at Melbourne University and became interested in the local rock scene. Being turned on by The Beatles, Rod Stewart, The Stones, and prog-rock, Robert became one of those that, as he puts it, "gets paid to drive monstrous PAs in front of tens of thousands of people". He lived in a shared house with John Archer and started mixing The Schnorts, a band with John Archer, Doug Falconer, Mark Seymour and others. That band morphed into the Jetsonnes and then into Hunters & Collectors (H&C). Robert, though always "a backroom guy", was an integral part and member of H&C since the start. As a qualified architect, Robert has designed dozens of buildings, and as a designer, artist, and photographer in the music sphere, he turned his artistic hand to creating something like fifty record covers, a hundred t-shirts, decades of tour posters and laminates, and as the coordinator for many stage designs. Look no further than the H&C record sleeves for examples of his work, his favourite… 1986's Human Frailty. Attaining production credits on many records, Robert has also been at the controls of the front of house mixer for over 2,800 live gigs in twenty-two countries. He remains active in all fields, a coordinator for many stage designs. Look no further than the H&C record sleeves for examples of his work, his favourite… 1986's *Human Frailty*. Attaining production credits on many records, Robert has also been at the controls of the front of house mixer for over 2,800 live gigs in twenty-two countries. He remains active in all fields.

A STORY ABOUT NOISE
ROBERT MILES
(The Jetsonnes, Hunters and Collectors, Graphic Artist)

I'm a sound guy. AKA, a Front of House (FOH) guy, Noise Boy, Sound Engineer, Music Engineer, Producer. I specialise in live music production. I'm also an architect, and one of the tasks an architect has, is to master is specification writing. A 'Specification' is a tome of precise instructions, where every word is placed exactly, using carefully defined technical terms. An architect has to know a fair bit about everything and make sense of a whole lot of disparate and often contradictory inputs. If anything goes wrong, it's the architect's fault. When things go right, the architect is God. Mixing music from FOH is pretty much the same gig.

"*Music is liquid architecture; Architecture is frozen music*". (Johann Wolfgang Von Goethe)
"*Rock and roll ain't noise pollution*" (AC/DC)

So where does noise fit into music? What exactly is it? Noise can be defined in various ways, not just as any genre of music you don't like. Let's begin with the colour of noise. White Noise is commonly used in a pejorative sense, as in "*that's not music, it's just white noise*" or "*all I'm hearing from you is white noise*", but what actually constitutes White Noise?

White Noise is a random signal having equal intensity at different frequencies, which sounds a bit like the wind blowing through a tunnel. The name is derived from white light, which (loosely) is a result of combining all the frequencies across the visible spectrum.

Pink Noise is a more controlled random noise which has an equal amount of energy per octave, and so contains more low-frequency components than white noise. This is what you hear when the system techs are testing the amplifiers and speaker components of the system by turning elements on one by one, and for tuning and time-aligning systems. It's not at all musical. (However, the final tune should always be done with voice or music, at the level you intend to operate at, but that's another story.) There is also Brown Noise, but you really don't want to know about that.

What other definitions do we need when we're discussing noise? I'll go over a few, starting with the unpleasant reality of the noise complaint. Noise complaints are only ever lodged by residents who have bought property next to a venue that has enjoyed a harmonious relationship with the local community for over twenty-five years. The best example of this in Australia is evidenced by the ridiculous noise restrictions placed on performances on the steps of the Sydney Opera House, right after they built that really ordinary apartment block right next to the greatest building in the country.

Noise rejection is another thing you may have heard mentioned around the traps.

Not an act of discrimination against a particular genre, but rather the proper science of eliminating noise from signal paths in audio engineering. Cables and connectors play an important part in noise rejection, especially with regard to 'balanced' or 'unbalanced' lines. Unbalanced is a technical term used to describe a type of electronic connection. (Not to be confused with the connection a stalker punter has with the Lead Singer.)

An unbalanced cable consists of two connectors with two conductors each, connected by two coaxial carriers inside the cable—a signal wire and a ground shield. The most common form is a guitar lead, with jack connectors wired to a tip and a sleeve. Unbalanced leads are used over short distances, when noise is not a significant problem. There are also balanced connections, but these are usually made between people outside the music business.

Noise Restrictions. Now we're getting to the nasty part, the uncomfortable interstitial interface that lies between the creative and the civic. For most of the history of amplified music, noise restrictions have been an unrealistic and extremely inconsistent set of petty local government regulations completely lacking engineering credibility, usually a set of numbers conjured up by Town Councilors in response to a serial noise complainant who lives three hundred and fifty-seven metres from the venue and whose life is ruined because he or she or they (a serial complainant always lives alone) can't leave their windows open in summer without the very faint perception of bass intruding on the ritual silence of their self-flagellating monastic existence.

Noise Restrictions are enforced by the Noise Police, usually represented at outdoor gigs by a small balding man in a raincoat wearing earplugs and carrying a dB meter on a tripod. At a recent zoo gig (always fraught), I was shocked to hear a Systems Engineer actually address the Noise Police representative by name and say, "*Good to see you*". Not nearly as shocked as the man being addressed, who replied that in twenty years of noise policing nobody had ever talked to him before. The rookie FOH Guy tries to argue with the Noise Police over which scale of measurement is being used or whether there has been any correlation between the FOH SPL reading and the reading at the boundary location closest to the offending complainant. Any Crusty (a title only bestowed on the most revered crew) operator simply turns down the master faders after stashing some gain elsewhere and reassures the Noise Police that the overwhelming peak he just measured was the loudest part of the loudest song and that the encore is comprised totally of ballads. To be fair, in modern times the acceptable limits are usually weighted over time. An average maximum (say, over five or preferably fifteen minutes) is much more logical than being constrained by one explosive crescendo and also much easier to comply with. This is one of the few times you want the lead singer to wax lyrical between songs at a huge outdoor festival gig, where otherwise you'd like them to start the next song as soon as you've advanced the snapshot on the console. "*Keep talking; I need to pull my average down!*" is now a common form of encouragement from the Fortress of Solitude (AKA, FOH tent).

Long before the advent of weighted averages and snapshots on consoles, there were just good old-fashioned pub gigs, the spiritual home of Australian Rock'n'Roll. One such hallowed place was the Fitzgerald Hotel in Northbridge, Perth, Western Australia. The Fitzgerald was a legendary pub gig late last century, famous for 'Sunday Sessions' in the beer garden up the north end of the block. It was one of my favourite gigs to do with H&C, even though it was an arvo gig that followed a very hectic Saturday night gig, which of course had in turn been preceded by the excess of the Friday night gig and probably the Thursday night before that.

Our exhaustion was tempered by the fact we didn't really need lights (daylight pub gigs were rare), so we made do by stringing up festoon lines with standard domestic incandescent randomly-coloured bulbs. You know, the old-fashioned backyard barbie (BBQ) twenty-first vibe. The PA was the normal ground stacks, six boxes per side plus biradial horns. (Standards must always be maintained.)

Access to the beer garden was through two eight-foot-high double cyclone wire gates, the same construction material as the rest of the boundary fence facing St Brigid's Roman Catholic Church, directly opposite. Cyclone wire fencing is rather visually and acoustically transparent and possibly not the ideal material for separating Church and State.

Because Sunday is also a popular day for church services (apparently it is long standing tradition), over time there arose some tension between these two competing community groups. Logic would suggest that the interests of twelve hundred thirsty punters should outweigh the interests of fifty guilt-stricken parishioners, but as we are talking about noise restrictions and religion, logic has no part in this story.

The Church (the weird institution, not the band) usually finished their second service by around 11.45am, and the gig-time for the Sunday Session at the Fitzgerald was 14.00, so the window for load-in and set-up was pretty tight. A compromise was reached, and it came to pass that no noise could be made until 12 noon. Being on the case, the H&C crew had the PA set up by 11.45, and one memorable day were primed for the twelve o'clock launch on the very same day a service had overrun (possible due to a longer sermon on the Children of Satan, AKA Rock Musicians).

The Church doors opened, and the parishioners were tolled down the steps with a perfectly cued twenty thousand watts of AccaDacca's Hell's Bells, turned up as far as it would go. To eleven. Those familiar with the song will know it starts with enormous bells bonging on (the other meaning) before the menacing guitar riff kicks in. To his credit, the priest moved pretty fast, but by the time he was face to face with me, hands clawing at the wire fence, I could see exactly how red in the face he had turned, and I confess I was a little worried for his health and his potential proximity to his maker. He appeared to be yelling; *"TURN IT OFF!!TURN IT OFF!!"* but my lip reading has never been strong. Not wanting to be impolite I mouthed back *"I CAN'T HEAR YOU. IT'S TOO LOUD!"*

Years later I learned that the Roman Catholic Archbishop of Perth had bought the site, once the pub had stopped operating. In a brave bid to expunge Satan's old victory, they applied for a demolition order, but were knocked back following heritage concerns. The site was on-sold to developers.

Here endeth the Story of Noise.

⦿ The synthpop band Naked Eyes put out a cover of the classic Burt Bacharach and Hal David song 'There's Always Something There to Remind Me' in 1983. The song was a big hit in Canada, New Zealand, the United States, and Australia, reaching the top 10 in each country. However, with so many exciting new acts coming out of the UK at the time, the song failed to really connect with British audiences, only managing to peak at No.59 on the charts there. Though well-executed synthpop, Naked Eyes were arguably jumping on the cover song bandwagon a bit too late, capitalising on early adopters of the Fairlight CMI sampler keyboard in a musical era where few were clamouring for yet another '60s revival.

⦿ *The Commercial Album*, released in 1980, marked a significant departure for The Residents, the peculiar San Francisco collective. Comprising 40 one-minute tracks, this album stands out as their most accessible work to date. It is a must-listen for those with a curious and adventurous taste in music. The sonic landscape created by The Residents is both unconventional and surreal, with a distinct textural quality. The album's catchy melodies explore a wide range of subject matter, including drama, love and romance, humour, human nature, and even the most abstract concepts. In the creation of *The Commercial Album*, The Residents enlisted the talents of a remarkable group of "assistants". Among them were Snakefinger, a regular collaborator; Don Preston from The Mothers of Invention; Fred Frith and Chris Cutler from Henry Cow; and the renowned Brian Eno, who contributed his synthesizer skills to the track 'The Coming of the Crow'. Additionally, the album features guest vocalists such as Andy Partridge on 'Margaret Freeman', Lene Lovich on 'Picnic Boy', and David Byrne on 'Suburban Bathers'. This diverse ensemble of artists adds depth and variety to the album, making it an essential addition to any music collection.

⦿ Werner Emil Schult was born in 1948 in Dessau, Germany. Known as Emil, he gained recognition as a painter, performance artist, musician, poet, and lyricist and is particularly renowned for his collaborations with Kraftwerk. His work, characterised by its sparse, enigmatic, and economical nature, bore a striking resemblance to a German version of Warhol. Ralf Hutter once described him as *"our medium"* who excelled in writing lyrics and managing the lights, while Florian Schneider noted that Emil's comics resonated with the group's music. Emil co-wrote the lyrics for some of Kraftwerk's best-known and iconic songs, such as 'Autobahn', 'Radio-Activity', 'The Hall of Mirrors', 'Trans-Europe Express', 'The Model', 'Computer Love', 'Pocket Calculator', and 'Techno Pop'. Although he briefly played guitar and violin with the band in the early '70s, Emil acknowledged that his musical skills were not at a professional level. Consequently, as Kraftwerk transitioned towards a more synthesiser-based sound, the need for a guitarist or violinist diminished, leading to Emil's departure from that role.

○ The Teardrop Explodes' debut LP, *Kilimanjaro,* was released in 1980. Produced by 'The Chameleons', aka Bill Drummond (KLF) and David Balfe (Big in Japan, Dalek I Love You), it is pure POST-PUNK pop-rock perfection. Listen to *Kilimanjaro,* and you will be rewarded with an album that was at the forefront of production and song structure. After all this time the music still holds up wonderfully well, frenetic and melodic and spooky. Nearly every cut is a gem. 'Sleeping Gas' with its striking drone infusions, and 'Treason', which is characterised by tempo changes and vocal variation. Released as a single in 1981, 'Reward' is one of the best tunes of that period. The trumpets and swirling orchestral arrangement make 'Went Crazy' stand out, while the toe-tapping appeal of 'Brave Boys Keep Their Promises' lies in the bouncy rhythm. Another highlight, the up-tempo and urgent 'Thief of Baghdad' has a fuller sound than the rest and a mood of intensity, whilst the spacious feel of 'When I Dream' concludes the album on an atmospheric note. Perfect.

Midge Ure by Roch Parisien

○ James Ure, OBE, was born in 1953 in Cambuslang, Scotland. Best known as Midge, he proved his talent as a multi-instrumentalist, singer, and accomplished songwriter. He has a deep love for the guitar, which is evident in his melodic and rhythmic playing style. Midge first gained recognition as a member of the Scottish band Slik, previously known as Salvation. In 1976, Slik achieved chart success with their UK No.1 hit 'Forever and Ever'. To avoid confusion with another band member named James, Midge's name was reversed to Mij and later became Midge. After leaving Slik, Midge briefly joined the band PVC2 before joining Glen Matlock's Rich Kids. In 1978, he formed the collaborative group Visage with Rusty Egan and later had a short tenure with Thin Lizzy. Midge's talent caught the attention of Billy Currie, who convinced him to join Ultravox! as their new lead vocalist after John Foxx's departure. The band dropped the exclamation mark from their name and became Ultravox, with Midge at the forefront. Ultravox's sound evolved into a more electronic and pop-orientated style, which led to their biggest hit, 'Vienna', in 1981. Despite its success, the song was kept from the top spot by Joe Dolce's novelty song 'Shaddap You Face'. Midge also co-wrote Band Aid's 1985 No.1 hit 'Do They Know It's Christmas?' and achieved his own solo success with the UK No.1 single 'If I Was' in the same year. Midge played a significant role in organising Band Aid, Live Aid, and Live 8 alongside Bob Geldof. He continues to tour as a solo artist and recently released an album featuring reimagined versions of Ultravox hits and his solo classics.

11

○ There was a swathe of jangle pop artists about in the mid '80s, like Aztec Camera and Orange Juice; Bluebelles was another of those "cute" outfits. Their debut album *Sisters*, in the racks on this day in 1984, was a perfect example of the sophisto-pop genre. From the album, the infectious 'Young at Heart' was used by Volkswagen for a saturation advertisement. Yeah, it's cheesy but has those elements that a record-buying public loves. If you see it in a second-hand bin, consider taking it home.

⦿ On Monday, 11 October 1982, Robert Fripp, a famed member of prog-rockers King Crimson, was onstage with The Damned at the Hammersmith Odeon. With Fripp they performed MC5's 'Looking at You', the Swinging Blue Jeans' song 'Hippy Hippy Shake', the Rolling Stones' song 'Citadel' and the last song of the night, their own classic 'New Rose'. Earlier in the year, Fripp joined the band in the studio for their *Strawberries* album for Bronze Records, and they recorded one track, 'Fun Factory', although it did not appear on the album.

⦿ Daryl Hall was born in 1946, in Pottstown, USA. The singer/songwriter was part of the duo Hall and Oates, who have had huge worldwide success and garnered six No.1 singles in the USA. Hall is not somebody you expect to find featured in this book, as he is essentially a mainstream artist, but in 1980 he joined Robert Fripp for the solo album *Sacred Songs*! Yes, an odd pairing indeed, but this album is a "*must-have*" for both Hall & Oates and King Crimson fans and POST-PUNK enthusiasts! In some ways, this is a missing link album between King Crimson's *Red* and *Discipline*. The vocal approach applied by Greg Lake to John Wetton, one could say, was similar, but the difference between Wetton and Belew is very broad indeed. On *Sacred Songs*, Hall's vocal approach sits beautifully between the two. Fripp has been quoted as feeling that this album was part of a trilogy along with Fripp's *Exposure* and *Peter Gabriel II*. Listen to those two, then this, and it is easy to see how.

⦿ Patrick Gibson was born in 1961, in Sydney, Australia. Patrick is known to us as a sound experimenter, musical nut, and one of the driving forces behind the Australian independent label M Squared. His musical ventures and recordings were transmitted to us via his solo work and outfits such as Scattered Order, No Night Sweats, Ya Ya Choral, Splendid Mess, Pleasant Peasants and the enigmatic (The) Systematics. Those that were there will never forget seeing The Systematics doing support for The Cure at Capitol Theatre in Sydney. Patrick shuffling through reams of paper to find the synthesizer settings between songs! Most of Patrick's output can be found on the boxed set release *A Terrace Industry M SQUARED BOX 1980-1983*. Today, this set sits as essential listening. Patrick lost his battle with cancer and passed away on May 3, 2019.

⦿ On October 11, 1979, The Human League released their innovative and pioneering album, *Reproduction*. Widely viewed as The Human League's strongest work, this album is quite unlike the pop-orientated and saccharine Human League that most are familiar with, featuring female vocalists and radio-friendly songs. Tracks such as 'Being Boiled' and 'Almost Medieval' were cutting edge and rare for that era, though comparable to Throbbing Gristle's 1977 song 'United'. It's clear that *Reproduction* had an enormous impact on Cabaret Voltaire and their contemporaries. At times dark, rhythmic, and groundbreaking, even the album cover was shocking. *Reproduction* includes some really catchy techno pop with cohesive harmonies and melodies. The Human League were well ahead of their time.

⦿ Chris Joyce was born in Manchester, England, in 1957. As the drummer, he was a formation member of The Durutti Column and played on the Factory Records EP *A Factory Sample*; Chris quit and formed The Mothmen, who released two albums. In 1982-3 Chris was working with The Mighty Wah!, Crucial & Pink Military before becoming a formation member of Simply Red. Chris' first band, Flashback, was followed by Fast Breeder, managed by Factory Records founder Tony Wilson. It was Wilson who steered Chris toward the Durutti Column, but it was with Mick Hucknall and Simply Red that he had his greatest successes, attaining huge sales worldwide. He split from Simply Red in 1991 to set up his own studio and record label, both called Planet 4. Today he works at the 'Chris Joyce School of Drums', a teaching space giving drum lessons to up-and-coming aspiring musicians.

MEETING BOBBY COLOMBY
CHRIS JOYCE
(The Durutti Column, The Mothmen, Simply Red)

One of my first visits to Los Angeles was touring with Simply Red, and I was undertaking the usual publicity rounds. Mick Hucknall and I were doing press and TV interviews, here and there. One TV show we did was 'Entertainment Tonight'; it's an American classic, and the person interviewing us was a guy called Bobby Colomby. He was very genial, and the interview went well. When the interview was over, I got to talk to Bobby, and it turned out that he was a drummer also, with quite a distinguished resume. In fact, he had been the drummer with Blood, Sweat and Tears through the Al Cooper years, 1967-77. We got on really well, and he invited me back to his house in L.A., where he played me lots of jazz records and introduced me to loads of songs and artists I didn't know. Bobby's musical pedigree was astonishing; he had worked with many artists, including the Jacksons and a favourite artist of mine, Eddie Palmieri. Eddie is legendary in Latin Jazz with over 50 albums to his name. As time passed, we became good friends, and every time I was in L.A., Bobby would come and pick me up, and we'd hang out at restaurants, parties, and various Hollywood events. Unfortunately, over the years, I lost contact with Bobby, who went on to become the senior vice president for creative development at Sony Music. Bobby had fantastic knowledge and energy, and it was a pleasure for me to spend time with the man.

Jon Langford by Petra Gall

◉ Jon Langford was born in 1957, in Newport, Wales. He is best known to us as a formation member (drummer-cum-guitarist) of The Mekons, the band that brought us the 1979 POST-PUNK classic album *The Quality of Mercy Is Not Strnen*. A much-neglected but epic album by The Mekons was the stunning 1985 *Fear and Whisky* album, cited as a precursor to cowpunk and the alt-country genre. This was a flavour he would take in the '90s when he formed The Waco Brothers based out of Chicago, USA. During his tenure with The Mekons, Jon formed The Three Johns with John Hyatt, Phillip "John" Brennan, and Hugo, their drum machine (a nod to the great Hugo Burnham perhaps), releasing five highly energetic, relentless albums from 1984 to 1990. Jon was hard to sit still; aside from a vast solo discography, he ventured over the years into numerous projects like The Killer Shrews and Pine Valley Cosmonauts. Jon is also known for his artwork on record covers and t-shirts and for having works exhibited and being the artist in residence at the Country Music Hall of Fame in 2015-16. Jon Langford and the Bright Shiners released their debut album, *Where It Really Starts,* in March 2024!

ROCK AGAINST RACISM, WHITE YOUTH-BLACK YOUTH
JON LANGFORD
(The Mekons, The Three Johns)

A recent Facebook posting by someone of an image of a gig poster from April 15, 1978, has a bunch of memories come flooding back. It said, *"Love Music/Hate Racism"*; top billed was Misty In Roots, with lower equal billing going to The Mekons and The Ruts.

A lot of the early punk gigs in Leeds were held in West Indian-owned/operated venues. This gig for the Anti-Nazi League on April 15th, opening for Misty In Roots and The Ruts at the Chapeltown Community Centre behind the Hayfields Pub, was entirely different; it embodied that spirit of consciousness and rebel stance that smarter punks like Joe Strummer, etc., dragged into the stagnant pond of white British rock'n'roll from urban Reggae culture at that time.

I recall The Mekons had opened for 999 at Roots a Reggae club in Chapeltown, and we were met with a hail of gob and Nazi salutes from politically confused members of the crowd. We were terrified, Ros Allen, our bass player, bravely told them to *"fuck off"* and it was clear it would be taken outside after the show! Fortunately, a bunch of my Rugby player mates from University were there and saw the dunderheads off. I remember some old Jamaican guys just shaking their heads at the antics.

John Peel had just made us semi-famous by playing our debut single 'Never Been in a Riot' on his late-night 'BBC Radio 1' show, and The Mekons were starting to get gigs all over the country. This was the dawn of the Rock Against Racism movement. At the very early punk gigs there weren't any actual punk records to play between the bands, so Reggae became the soundtrack to those times. Not frat-boy tropical-fruity drinks-with-umbrellas stuff but hard edged, politically conscious rebel music from Jamaica and increasingly mixed with inner-city UK sounds from homegrown acts like Steel Pulse, Aswad and Misty in Roots, a weird apocalyptic roots collective from Southall in London.

It was an amazing night. Black and white culture and youth on the same page and in the same room for once, a precursor to the 2 Tone Ska explosion that was just around the corner. The Ruts went on to have rock-Reggae hit singles with 'In A Rut' and 'Babylon's Burning' before falling foul of a heroin plague. Misty made probably my favorite Reggae album of all time, *Live at the Counter Eurovision,* and we The Mekons slid into our own, sorry, endless non-career.

One moment sticks in my mind. After the show we found our bass amp had gone missing. Chaotic scenes until our soundman located Booza, an enormous black guy from Chapeltown who worked with the Maverick Sound System and local reggae band Bodicean, he became a great friend to me later. There was some earnest discussion; I saw Booza rolling his eyes in frustration before wandering off to the payphone in the entryway.

We had our bass amp back in twenty minutes!

◉ In 1985, *Seventh Dream of Teenage Heaven,* the first studio album by Love and Rockets, was released through record label Beggars Banquet. David J, Daniel Ash and Kevin Haskins seem to blend The Beatles, The Moody Blues, The The, early-day Goth, and stray pop sensibilities for a superb first outing. Leaving off from the earlier single 'Ball of Confusion', there's a great combination of harmonies and angular guitar. Simply, a brilliant blend of vocal jigsaw production and synths, all the while driven by Daniel Ash's elegant and cleverly played guitar. David J's fretless bass slides in, out and about with lusciously structured melody lines. Haskins's drumming builds a solid base for every track; indeed, it's the rhythm section that certainly provides adhesion and is most evident on 'If There's a Heaven Above'. It is clear Ash decided to take some Tones on Tail and Bauhaus with him over to Love and Rockets. A delicate '80s release.

⊙ Simply Red is often dismissed as middle of the road; that comes from being beautifully produced, stylish and loaded with panache. With the debut album *Picture Book* released in 1985, they proved that synthpop can be soulful and funky. As with all Simply Red releases, it's Mick Hucknall's uber-impressive vocals that are the highlight, of course, and the band supporting him, the compositions, arrangements, and productions are too indeed vital components. The trio of 'Jericho', 'Money's Too Tight to Mention' and 'Holding Back the Years', served in that order, are irresistible and timeless. The surprise element was the cover of Talking Heads' 'Heaven', delivered in gospel tones; it must rate as one of the best cover versions of the '80s.

12

⊙ In 1984, Lloyd Cole and The Commotions released their first album, *Rattlesnakes,* which captures the essence of bands like The Smiths, Aztec Camera, and Orange Juice. The *title track* possesses an irresistible charm that resonates deeply even decades later. It's a timeless piece that effortlessly blends soothing vocals from Lloyd Cole with music that is tastefully understated. Songs like 'Perfect Skin', 'Forest Fire', and 'Are You Ready to Be Heartbroken?' shine brightly on this album, making it a strong contender for the best album of 1984. It's a shame that this talented group didn't achieve greater recognition, as their music remains fresh and engaging, standing the test of time like a comfortable, well-worn pair of shoes.

⊙ Pat DiNizio, the lead singer, guitarist, and songwriter of The Smithereens, was born in New Jersey, USA, in 1955. In 1980, he formed The Smithereens with high school friends in his hometown. Blending British Invasion rock with punk, pop, and baroque influences, the band became known for infectious three-minute pop-rock songs like 'Only a Memory', 'A Girl Like You', and 'Too Much of a Good Thing'. After honing their energetic live show playing small venues in New Brunswick and New York City, the band broke through commercially in 1986 with their hit 'Blood and Roses'. DiNizio continued leading The Smithereens until his death at age 62 in his home state of New Jersey on December 12, 2017.

⊙ After being together a couple of years, Friends Again out of Glasgow, Scotland, released their debut and only LP, *Trapped and Unwrapped,* on October 12, 1984. The set held the UK top 100 single "State of the Art" and "Sunkissed", which failed to chart. The album was a follow-up to the *self-titled* EP from earlier in the year. Sophisticated, infectious jangle with a taste of Aztec Camera or Haircut 100's *Trapped and Unwrapped* does not disappoint.

David Vanian by Kristan James Melik

⊙ David Vanian, aka David Lett, the frontman of The Damned, was born in Newcastle upon Tyne, England, in 1956. Vanian gained recognition for his gothic fashion sense, opting for a vampire-inspired appearance with pale makeup, slicked-back jet-black hair, and predominantly black attire, in contrast to the typical punk rock style of safety pins, spiky hair, ripped jeans, and leather jackets. Over time, Vanian's unique style became synonymous with goth rockers worldwide. He is currently married to Patricia Morrison, who has played bass for The Gun Club, The Sisters of Mercy, and Bags.

⊙ October 12, 1981, the record stores displayed the debut album titled *Painless Nights* by The Sleepers, a band hailing from San Francisco. One of the most striking aspects of this group was the unique and improvised baritone vocal style of Ricky Williams, which seamlessly merged with a brooding instrumental blend of atmospheric pre-goth rock and POST-PUNK. The band's musical talent is undeniably remarkable, with a standout track being the instrumental piece called 'Zenith'.

⊙ On October 12, 1978, John Simon Ritchie, aka Sid Vicious, aka John Beverley, contacted the authorities, claiming that someone had fatally stabbed his girlfriend, Nancy Spungen. Nancy was discovered lifeless in the bathroom of their room at the Hotel Chelsea in New York City with a single abdominal wound that appeared to have resulted in her bleeding to death. Sid was accused of committing the murder, but he passed away from a heroin overdose in February 1979 before his trial commenced. Numerous writers and filmmakers have conjectured about whether Sid really killed Nancy or if she may have actually been murdered by a drug dealer who frequently visited their hotel room. Shortly after Sid was cremated, his mother purportedly discovered a suicide note in his jacket pocket that read, *"Nancy and I had a suicide pact, and I need to uphold my end. Please bury me next to my baby and dress me in my leather jacket, jeans, and boots. Goodbye"*.

David Gedge of The Wedding Present by Petra Gall

⊙ The Wedding Present released their debut album, *George Best*, in 1987. The album features jangly guitars, feedback, and unique vocal arrangements. Dave Gedge's lyrics capture the awkwardness of relationships. The music is a nod to POST-PUNK and indie sounds. The songs have catchy hooks that stick in your head. Brand them jangly POST-PUNK; this is an excellent album, when appreciated, go listen to S*eamonsters*.

13

⊙ The debut single 'Damaged Goods' by Gang of Four was unleashed on October 13, 1978. Backed by the tracks 'Love Like Anthrax' and 'Armalite Rifle', this release was a fiery onslaught of exemplary POST-PUNK. Packed with driving rhythms, politically charged lyrics, and sexual ambiguity. Moreover, the charismatic vocals of Jon King made it one of the standout records of '78. That year was soon to bring forth a plethora of legendary POST-PUNK anthems that simply excelled, despite a couple of weak moments here and there. However, that was not the case for this single. The infectious basslines of Dave Allen, the powerful drumming of Hugo Burnham and Andy Gill's unrelenting guitar don't let up until the middle section, where the change of pace is a welcome respite, *"your kiss so sweet!"* It may not have the polished production of their subsequent *Entertainment* LP, but it was nearly flawless in all other aspects that defined the era.

Gang Of Four by Kristan James Melik

● The *self-titled* debut album by the Australian band INXS, who would go on to achieve global fame, was released in 1980 on the DeLuxe label. This marked the beginning of the band's journey as they ventured into the realm of NEW WAVE. Although this debut lacks the maturity of their later renowned songwriting, there are still some notable moments of excellence. One standout track from the album is 'Just Keep Walking', which received considerable airplay on local radio stations. While songs like 'In Vain', 'Doctor', and 'Wishy Washy' showcase the band's synthpop style, they do not reach the same level of quality as their later works. It's clear that this album marks the initial steps in their musical evolution.

INXS courtesy ATCO Records

● Rob Marche was born October 13, 1962. Out of Bristol, England, Rob played guitar with JoBoxers and was a former member of The Subway Sect. In 1983, JoBoxers went near to the top of the UK charts with the No.3 single 'Boxer Beat'.

● Henry Padovani was born in Bastia, France, in 1952. In 1977, Henry was a founding member of The Police as the original guitarist along with Stewart Copeland and Sting and was part of the recording of The Police's first single, 'Fall Out'. After being sacked by Stewart Copeland, he went to be part of Wayne County & The Electric Chairs and then in 1980 formed The Flying Padovanis, an outfit playing instrumental rock. Henry was the manager of the blues-rock soloist Zucchero Fornaciari from Italy, who was hugely successful, selling well over 15 million albums and collaborating with dozens of artists. Henry also appeared on television as a judge on France's X Factor.

● On this day in 1979, *Reggatta De Blanc* by The Police commenced its impressive four-week reign at the top of the album charts in the UK. Undoubtedly, this release stands out as the pinnacle of The Police's discography. While not as raw as their debut, it encompasses all the strengths of their initial release and much more. The band's first two singles, 'Message in a Bottle' and 'Walking on the Moon', are undeniably flawless in their execution. Furthermore, the track 'Bed's Too Big', with its underlying reggae elements, exudes an atmospheric and sublime structure. The pervasive influence of reggae throughout the album adds a distinct flavour to this exceptional representation of the NEW WAVE genre.

Public Image by Petra Gall

⊙ *HELLO! HELLO! HELLO!* 'Public Image', the debut single by Public Image Limited (PiL), was released in 1978 on Virgin Records. The single backed with '*The Cowboy Song*' went to No.9 in the UK. Who would argue that aside from one or two tracks off Metal Box, this is easily Lydon's best effort post-Pistols? John's delivery borders on the theatrical; that's not unusual for him. He tries convincing us with each angry yell and grieving howl; who are we to argue? This is a jibe at the industry, critics, his fanbase, and anybody else listening! Keith Levene really shines; the guitar lines are fantastic, and coupled with Jah Wobble's magnificently booming bass, there isn't a lot of room left for Jim Walker's drumming. The three fill every corner of the mix and ensure that PiL obtains a very distinctive, forward-looking sound; yes, there's plenty more to come.

14

⊙ October 14, 1984, saw the release of the meticulously crafted debut album by Marc Almond, *Vermin in Ermine*. This introspective masterpiece exudes an air of refinement and elegance, somewhat reminiscent of the works by Soft Cell. However, it must be noted that while *Vermin in Ermine* possesses an undeniable sense of class, it falls short in capturing those captivating hooks and enchanting melodies that came from his collaborations with his Soft Cell colleague, Dave Ball.

⊙ The iconic album *Heroes* by David Bowie was released on October 14, 1977. From a musical standpoint, this was Bowie's most innovative period, coming during his collaboration with Brian Eno. *Heroes* was Bowie's twelfth studio album and the second in his 'Berlin Trilogy'. Recorded with the help of Eno and Tony Visconti, *Heroes* built upon the ambient music experiments of *Low*, featuring contributions from guitarists Robert Fripp and Carlos Alomar, bassist George Murray, and drummer Dennis Davis. This album found the changeling Bowie venturing into largely uncharted musical territory, creating evocative, poignant rock music that was both modern and futuristic. Like *Low, Heroes* was half vocal and half instrumental, but it expanded and strengthened the sonic innovations that Bowie and Eno had developed together. The vocal songs were more fully realised, with stronger rhythms and more layers of sound in the production. Robert Fripp's guitar work gave the music a harder edge, while the instrumentals displayed Eno's influence. From the anxious, snarling opening guitar notes of 'Beauty and the Beast' to the roar of 'Joe the Lion', the title track's proclamation that "*we could be heroes*", and the despair of 'Blackout', the first half of the album rages. The instrumental 'V2-Schnieder' paid tribute to Kraftwerk's Florian Schneider, whom Bowie acknowledged as an influence. It introduced the atmospheric, awe-inspiring textures, cold synthesizers, and stark piano of the album's second half. 'Sense of Doubt' is dark and ominous, with a descending four-note piano arpeggio created by Bowie and Eno, each following instructions from Eno's Oblique Strategies cards to "*make everything as similar as possible*" and "*emphasise differences*". 'Sense of Doubt' segued into the oriental-inspired 'Moss Garden', creating a pastoral Asian feel. 'Neukoln' began industrial before shifting to Bowie's plaintive, lost-in-the-fog saxophone calls. The closer, 'The Secret Life of Arabia', moved with the rhythm of a snake charmer; Bowie's vocals are intoxicating. *Heroes* found Bowie's vocals at their peak, pure and expressive. Challenging and rewarding, *Heroes* was rare, groundbreaking art.

⊙ Thomas Dolby, aka Thomas Morgan Dolby Robertson, was born in London, England, in 1958. He played a significant role in the synthpop movement of the early '80s NEW WAVE era, alongside bands like The Human League and OMD. His hit songs 'She Blinded Me with Science' in 1982 and 'Hyperactive!' in 1984 brought him international recognition. Dolby was involved in various musical projects, from forming the band Camera Club to writing hits for artists like Lene Lovich. His collaborations extended to producing albums for Joni Mitchell and Prefab Sprout, as well as performing live with iconic musicians such as David Bowie, Peter Gabriel, Andy Partridge and Roger Waters' live show of Pink Floyd's *The Wall*. His albums, like *The Flat Earth* 'and *The Golden Age of Wireless,* are considered classics in the NEW WAVE and synthpop genres. Currently, Thomas Dolby serves as a Professor of the Arts at Johns Hopkins University in Baltimore, Maryland.

⊙ Nick 'Nero' Swan was born in Sydney, Australia, in 1959. Nero is best known to us as the bass player with Machinations, a band that, through the hard slog of the pub circuit, earned a reputation as one of Australia's premier synthpop electro bands. Nero learnt his chops as many do in a cover band; that band was Blackwater, a band that included future INXS members Jon Farris and Kirk Pengilly. He formed GreenLite in 1979, a reggae band that, as he puts it, "*were going nowhere*". After a couple of declined offers to join Machinations, all old school friends, he finally joined in 1980. The Machinations line-up was now consolidated with vocalist Fred Loneragan, Tim Doyle on guitar, and Tony Starr on keyboards. The rhythm section was Nero and a drum machine! Indeed, they were not to get a real drummer till 1983. Machinations released their first single, 'Average Inadequacy' b/w 'Arabia', in August 1981 on Phantom Records to rave reviews. 1983 saw the release of their debut album*, Esteem;* it featured the high-rotation single 'Pressure Sway'. Two more albums followed before they split in 1988. Nero joined and helped to form James Freud's touring band for James' solo album *Step into the Heat* in 1990. He enlisted Warren McLean and Toni Mott, both former members of Machinations. Alas, a second stab at a solo career was not to be for James, and they disbanded in 1991. Swan settled into a career of writing and producing music for film and television, mainly ABC-TV. Machinations have reunited several times, most recently in 2019, just before Covid hit, and you never know when they may be on stage again, alas without Tony Starr, who passed away in 2022. 2025, and Nero "*resigned*" *from* the Machs and announced on Facebook, "*I am, however, remaining active musically, so I suppose I should say, 'Watch this space!'*"

CHANCES ARE...
NICK 'NERO' SWAN
(Machinations)

I'm an old guy now, but I wasn't always old, and I certainly don't feel old ... But I was definitely young then; I was in my 20s, it was the '80s, and I'd just like to take a moment to give you a snapshot of part of my journey that had me in Machinations by 1980. That journey, as was the case with all of the new '80s bands, has its roots deep in the '70s.
NEWBOY

"You're the new boy, aren't you? What's your name again?" he asked. *"Oh yeah"*, I said, *"You're Dave, aren't you?"* He nodded, and I sat down as the train started moving out from the station. I had just started at Leo's. "I'm Nick Swan", I said, *"but you probably know me as Nero; everyone's already calling me Nero because of that cunt Taylor."* There were about 5 Nicks in my form at my new school. Paul Taylor was in my class for Ancient History and had anointed me as Nero. There was a colour plate page in the textbook with images of gold Roman coins with emperors in profile. One of the profiles looked like the New Boy, and that was the Nero coin…

Dave laughed because I called Taylor a cunt, and I relaxed. The situation had become immediately troublesome for me. As soon as I got on the train, these guys, all about my age in the carriage, had become menacing. I'd got onto the train with my bass straight from rehearsals with my new and first-ever band, Blackwater; these guys in the carriage immediately thought, muso wanker, and the vibe was ominous. It was the 70s, and kids in Sydney were really punchy at the weekend.

But they looked a little familiar. They were all from my new school, and Dave, who was the leader of this little pack and definitely one of the cool kids at school, had signalled that I wasn't to be touched. The rest of the trip home was uneventful; that is, I didn't get punched. (Dave is still a Facebook friend).

BLACKWATER

Blackwater was a great little band; we only played one gig, but we rehearsed a lot. We rehearsed up at the Farriss' place at Belrose, in the garage, along with a lot of other bands full of 15- and 16-year-olds.

Frenchs Forest wasn't my turf, but I had been hanging out there every second weekend for at least a year, at a mate's place from school. I had gotten to know a lot of his friends, been to a few parties, etc. One weekend he told me that some mates were looking for a bass player and gave me a number. I auditioned and got the gig. Johnny Farriss was our drummer and immediately grabbed my attention.

He was only 14 but already had the precision timing and the tight, economical fills of a much older player. You can build a band from the ground up with a decent drummer. In fact, it would turn out that he would be the best I'd played with until Machinations employed Warren Maclean as our first ever proper drummer. But it was 1976, and those heady days of the 80s were still way in the future. We had a kid with glasses called Kirk on rhythm guitar, who also played a bit of sax, but our main man was Martin Toole, who played lead, sang, and had the coolest guitar I'd ever seen. That guitar was an Ovation Breadwinner, and I have one in my collection right now. These Ovations were championed by Steve Marriott, who was an English 70s guitar god and leader of Humble Pie, but their coolness was almost immediately ruined by Björn from ABBA playing one, and from that point on any self-respecting guitarist refused to be seen with one. But Martin gamely continued playing his, and we respected him for it.

Blackwater played covers; we played Hendrix, Bad Company, a little Iggy Pop, ZZ Top, and Free. We were a typical mid-70s covers band, and we nailed those songs. The other bands that populated the Farriss' garage on those weekends were mostly attempting prog rock; they had names like Merlin's Circle and Isengard. One band was called Fish; they played Christian Fellowship Clubs, which were a thing in the 70s. They even had the Christian 'fish' logo.

15- and 16-year-olds trying to play King Crimson, Gentle Giant, and even Return to Forever!! This is about as rigorous as music gets, just a little too ambitious, but that's what we were faced with. (Jethro Tull songs were a little easier to play). By 1976 we had all moved on from Zeppelin, Purple and Sabbath, and prog was the thing. Only a year later, the Sex Pistols would put an end to this foolishness, with everyone relaxed and rocking out again. But that was yet to come. Andrew Farriss, I remember, played in at least two of these prog bands and was working with this new guy Michael, a singer, who had just turned up at Davidson High (where they all went to school) from Hong Kong. I remember chatting with Michael while we waited our turn at the amps. We had a bit in common, having both grown up with a colonial system in Southeast Asia in the 60s. I had been back in Australia since I was 10 but had grown up in Sumatra with servants, etc., and so had he, albeit in Hong Kong. He had just arrived back, like me, against his will and assured me that things were still awesome in Asia.

We would sit there and complain about the lack of servants and decent help. We would agree loudly so that everybody could hear that Australia kind of sucked but would be much improved with a little bit of servant action. I liked him a lot and got to know him better many years later.

But I digress, Blackwater played the simpler songs that people knew and could dance to, and I had brought a gig to the table. A gig! An actual proper gig, unpaid, of course, but with a ready-made full house. It was my new school, St Leo's, year 11 formal, and there would be at least 300 drunk kids there. Perfect! I had just started there midway through term two, having been kicked out of North Sydney Boys High after my years of misdemeanours had worn their patience thin. (That's a whole other story and too long to tell here).

But the fact that I played guitar and bass had immediately got me in with the cool kids who knew I was in a band. This had immediate dividends because the band they had booked for the formal had broken up, and they turned to me. I assured the organisers that we could play for at least an hour or an hour and a half if we repeated a few.

We were in! We were supported by a duo, Fred Loneragan and Brett Harris from our year, whom I didn't know very well. They played a few acoustic songs badly for about half an hour before we took the stage. Very exciting, the first-ever gig for me.

It went well with hardly any mistakes, and the organisers were extremely relieved. It was a long shot to take a punt on this new boy; I had rescued them from a looming disaster, and my status as 'saviour of the formal' was assured. These kids had known each other for a long time, many of them since fifth class, so they were a difficult clique to break into; being a musician breaks down a lot of walls.

Anyway, Blackwater continued to rehearse, but there were no more magical gigs that presented, and then, of course, it all fell over with a crash due to one phone call.

PERTH??

It was Martin. "*Mate*", he said, "*the Farriss's are going to Perth*". "*What are you talking about?*" I said. "*Yeah*", he replied, "*Mr Farriss has got a job there or something, and they're going to be a band over there, I think. They're going to take Kirk and Michael, and it's either going to be you or Gary. "Call Johnny,*" he said, "*that's all I know.*" "*What are you talking about?*" I replied, "*I can't go to Perth. I'm 16, and I've just started a new school; I can't go to Perth*". I repeated more to myself than anything. Needless to say, Blackwater was pretty well stuffed with the loss of our drummer and rhythm guitarist. In fact, all those bands were a bit stuffed because the Farriss's were members of at least 4 of them. Not to mention the loss of our free weekend rehearsal garage. We talked back and forth about what this meant and discussed backup plans for the continuance of Blackwater and promised to meet up the next weekend to audition new members at Martin's place, but we never did, and in fact, I never saw Martin Toole ever again.

I felt a great sense of loss. This had been part of my life for over a year now, and suddenly it was all gone. I called Johnny. It was all confirmed, and I was kind of cranky. Told him there was no way I could go to Perth even though I was pretty sure they had decided on Gary Beers. In fact, in hindsight, I never worked out how the Farriss's had convinced Michael, Kirk and Gary's parents to let them take their kids with them. Still haven't got to the bottom of that.

I threw myself into my new life at St Leos, and Blackwater gradually became a memory. Many years later, I discovered Martin Toole had been a member of the Sydney band Avion, a band I never came across but had heard of. He was a talented guy.

GREENLITE

From here on in life took over. I quickly got to know all the players at Leos, and there were a lot of them. Flotsam Jetsam, who had a moment in the 80s, also emerged from this bunch. Anyway, over the next year or 2 we put a couple of little bands together and played a few parties and a few spag dances. I think we named one of them Lemac for the night, which was camel spelt backwards. No idea why, lost in the mists of time. After school finished, a lot of us moved en masse to Darlinghurst and rehearsed there a bit, but nothing came of it. No thought of university; it was all about being in a band for me and my mates, but bands were increasingly becoming a hobby. I had a job and a girlfriend; I surfed every weekend. I did a lot of surfing in those days, pre-leash! But after a year or two of rolling along, I was becoming increasingly discontented and decided to brush the dust off my SVT, a 6-foot tall Ampeg bass rig, an incredibly heavy and loud thing made for stadium stages, not bedrooms, but I had one and was determined to use it. Eight 10-inch speakers. Had fallen into disuse over the previous year. It was 1979, and I decided to give it one last crack. I was 19, and I remember thinking in a panic that Robert Plant was 19 when they released Led Zeppelin 1, and I wasn't even in a band!!

Inspired by The Police, I had decided on a reggae band, a three-piece. I rang some mates and booked some rehearsals. The rehearsal studio was called Greenlite, and with my usual laziness, I decided to call ourselves GreenLite. With my friends Chris Rowell and Jack Whiddon on drums, we were going to be Australia's answer to The Police. I was going to try and sing as well as play bass; I had dyed my hair white and was wearing trench coats à la Quadrophenia. Had no idea how derivative it was; ridiculous! At the time I thought it was cool – kind of glad it never came to fruition, but we were a tight little unit, of course, just lots of rehearsing and no gigs. Story of my life to that point, but I was having a go and was determined to give it my best shot. We moved rehearsals down to Day Street Studios down near Chinatown. Mates of mine from Leos had recently returned from about a year overseas in the UK, had formed a band and were rehearsing down there. It was a brand-new studio with better gear, and Greenlite was a shithole. We could save some money on sharing storage space, so it made sense to rehearse down there as well. Plus, Day Street was very cool, with many of Sydney's better bands rehearsing there. Midnight Oil were rehearsing down there at the start, and they were my very favourite Sydney live band; I saw them a lot.

The best thing about Day Street, though, was that we didn't get covered in blood every rehearsal. Our drummer Jack was a bleeder and had a habit of cutting his knuckles on his snare drum. At Greenlite the rooms were so small that we would have blood spatter on each of us after every rehearsal. Even my freshly minted, white hair would have a reddish tinge to it. At Day Street we could safely keep our distance.

As we were packing up one Sunday afternoon, Freddie came up to me. The boys were fresh from OS and were rehearsing straight after us, as was their habit, so that we could catch up at the changeover. Fred was singing for this as-yet-unnamed band of buddies, but they were pretty interesting. They were supercharged after having been amongst the NEW WAVE London scene of 1979 and were following the lead of the London underground of the time, which was all synthesizers and drum machines. Gary Numan, early Human League, Depeche Mode, PiL, The Pop Group, The Cure, Gang Of Four, etc., all taking their lead from the masters, Kraftwerk.

MIDNIGHT OIL

"Hey Nero", said Fred, *"you should come down here next Friday, Midnight Oil are auditioning bass players. Dunno, maybe you should have a crack?".* *"Wow!"*

As stated, I was kind of in awe of those guys, but what the hell. As was my habit I sat in with the boys after GreenLite's rehearsal, played a little bass for them, grilled Freddie a little more about what he thought of my chances. Afterwards at home I had many second thoughts about showing up for a crack at the Oils gig. *"Who am I kidding"*, I thought. By this stage Midnight Oil already had their debut album and *Head Injuries* out and were already a pretty massive band. I loved both of those albums and still do. But after work the next day my trepidation had settled, and I set about learning as many Midnight Oil songs as I could during the rest of the week.

Friday arrived, and I showed up at Day Street with my bass promptly at 4 pm. I could hear the unmistakable sound of Midnight Oil rehearsing in one of the rooms. Strangely, I was the only bass player there waiting, I'd had visions of about 20 of them all hanging out for a chance to fill the gig. I could hear that a bass player was in there rehearsing with them though, so I settled down to wait. The people at the counter had assured me that yes, they were auditioning. Long audition though, I thought that this guy probably had the gig, as indeed he had.

After about 40 minutes, Rob Hirst came out and noticed me patiently sitting there with my bass. I stood up, *"Hi Rob"*, I said, *"Freddie told me you were auditioning so here I am"*. In those days, every musician on the North Shore vaguely knew of each other, if only through friends, it was a fairly small scene. Rob looked momentarily taken aback. *"Oh, sorry mate, I thought I'd told Fred that it was a closed audition, we're only auditioning a couple of friends"*, he said. *"Oh well, no worries"* I said. A little embarrassed I got up to go. But I must've looked a little downcast and made sad puppy dog eyes because he stopped and asked me, *"How long I'd been waiting"*. *"Oh, only about an hour or so"*, I replied, exaggerating a little of course. It worked, and Mr. Hirst took pity on me, said *"Look mate no worries, let's give you a go. I'll just go and have a chat to the lads, sort it out and I'll be back out in a sec"*. After a minute or two, he popped his head out and beckoned me in. I remember that audition very clearly, partly because I was still very green, I was still only 19 and they were a good five or six years older than me. And of course, being a little in awe of my favourite local band that I was trying to play bass for didn't help. There they all were. Peter Garrett was sitting on a couple of milk crates, smoking Kent cigarettes, and staring at me for the entire session, not unkindly, more like as if he was studying a strange object that had appeared in his lounge room. He didn't sing a note for the entire audition, just sat there, checking me out. Rob Hirst sang everything. We ran through 'Dust', 'Run by Night', 'Surfing with a Spoon', 'Bus to Bondi' and a couple of others and I did alright but the clincher and the letdown was that what they really needed was a singing bass player. *"So, can you sing?"* Rob asked after we'd run through four or so songs. *"We need a bass player that can sing backup"* he said. Confused, I said *"No"*. Even though I was the singer in my band I had not even contemplated singing in Midnight Oil. Later on, I became the go to back up vocals for Machinations, but at that point in time I really had not had much singing practice. I was only the vocalist for GreenLite by default. Vocals were an afterthought and there was no one else. I had paid no attention to any backing vocals as I had only rehearsed the bass parts during the week. I went home in a strangely calm state. I wasn't that disappointed that I hadn't got the gig but was indeed proud that I had even attempted it, and besides, my focus was still on GreenLite.

It was very gracious of them to allow me an audition. As I thought Peter Gifford already pretty much had the gig. His was the bass I had heard as I was waiting. They were just being kind, good lads those guys.

As they do in your 20s, things change in the blink of an eye. There you are moseying along, not even aware that you may be in a rut and then it all turns around. Over the course of my life, I have almost become used to things, good things, sometimes bad things turning up out of the blue to change it up.

MACHINATIONS

Freddie and the boys, Tim Doyle and Tony Starr, had a name now. They had called themselves 'machinations', no 'The', and no capital 'M'. For a little while, it was not cool to have 'the' as a preface to your name. For example, models were not 'the models'; they were models. And so it was for most bands, although whenever you appeared in print, journalists almost always ignored that instruction to drop the 'the'. We all gave up on it after a while. Tony Starr had named the band. He explained it by saying it was a word he used a lot in essays at school. I liked it. It sounded strong and modern. They had also asked me to join the band. They had gotten used to me sitting in on their rehearsal sessions and had been hypnotised by the bottom-end power of the SVT. That's my explanation anyway. I remember sitting them down and trying to convince them that they didn't need me, that what they were doing was really cool, and to stick to their guns, and of course my focus was GreenLite. That was my excuse, and I was sticking to it.

The reality, of course, was that GreenLite was actually going nowhere, I was the prime mover, I had the only vehicle, and at times I was the only one showing any enthusiasm for it. It was becoming exhausting. And of course, my focus was still on the bass. Vocals were an afterthought; we certainly weren't ready for any gigs and possibly never would be. But I persevered for a few more months. Meanwhile, machinations had already played a couple of shows. In fact, I did lights for them at the Heritage in King's Cross one night, and I had been in the audience for their first ever show at Garibaldi's.

The aforementioned turning point came after their third show, which was again at the Heritage. I had tickets that night with my girlfriend to see The B-52's at the Hordern Pavilion. The Machs were playing the Heritage that night. We were literally on the way to the Hordern with our expensive tickets when somehow, we both decided that we would prefer to go and see machinations. We promptly turned the car around and headed for The Cross. *"Fuck the B-52's"*, we thought, *"let's go and see our mates"*. I might add that machinations had a rent-a-crowd of about 100 Leos boys that showed up for almost every show, especially in the first couple of years. We needed them as extra security as well. Those days were still pretty punk, and any band with a drum machine and synthesizers were targets if you weren't careful. *"Where's your fucking drummer!!"* was the chant at many of those early shows until we shut them up with good songs and persistent abuse that we hurled back at them. Apart from drum machines being a brand-new cool thing, not to mention sequencers and synthesizers, we simply didn't know any drummers, particularly good ones. They seemed to be all used up. Indeed, it would be three years before we engaged a percussionist by the name of Henry Downes, stand up, no kick drum. We stuck to our guns as long as we could.

Anyway, the boys were good and getting better. I had enough objectivity to stand back and realise that my old mates really had a chance, a good chance of making a mark. Apart from good songs, a good name, and a good vibe, it was all about Fred. He had an extraordinarily different-sounding voice, an original voice, and in those days, it was all about having a singer with a distinctive voice, and Fred certainly had that. I was starting to regret my decision to refuse their offer.

The following week, a couple of things happened. My girlfriend had dumped me by phone; I had caused some trouble at the machinations show again, which she was not happy about. We were on the way out anyway in hindsight. It also turned out she had met someone at that very gig. Maybe we should've continued onto The B-52's. Oh well, shit happens. I was sitting there on my own despondently, beginning to make my way through a case of beer, and there was a knock at the door. Probably Cassandra coming to pick up the rest of her stuff; how was I going to deal with this? I put on my game face and answered the door. It was the boys, Fred, Tim and Tone. Confused, I immediately started with the apologies, *"Sorry boys, I got a bit pissed"*, I began, when they cut me off. *"The gig? Don't worry about that you fuckwit*", Tone said. Turned out they again had come this time to formally ask me to join the band, and this time, I said yes. With some relief, to I might add, I could go back to just being a bass player and not worry about anything else. After they left, I rang the other couple of GreenLiters to tell them it was over. I don't remember any protestations, so it was probably destiny. More likely just dumb luck though. I might add that after I had agreed to join the band, they added that I was now $20,000 in debt because the band had already racked up $80,000 and I was now a quarter of that. There's always a catch isn't there ? But I was okay with that because I really felt that I was now on the road to being a part of something special. And it was…

POSTSCRIPT

I was in a record shop in Bondi. It was about 18 months since I joined Machinations. We had recorded a single and EP at Trafalgar Studios. Five songs, 'Average Inadequacy', 'Arabia', 'Jets', 'Jon Wane' and 'EDGE'. 'Average' had become a hot single on Double Jay radio (2JJ); we were 2JJ darlings at that point. Because of this we opened the show at Parramatta Park, billed as the last Double Jay Concert. They had gone FM and changed their name to Triple J. 30,000 people, our biggest show to date. Ourselves, Mi-Sex, Moving Pictures, Matt Finish, the Radiators and of course Midnight Oil. Fantastic show, and I took great pleasure in reminding Midnight Oil that I was still around.

But back to the record shop in Bondi. I'd heard a song, 'Just Keep Walking', getting a lot of play on mainstream radio by this new band INXS. I quite liked it and had spotted the debut album. I pulled it from the rack and had a look. It had a gatefold, so I opened it up and got the surprise of my life. There they were, the Belrose boys, the Farriss Brothers or whatever. What the hell? I'd heard nothing about what had become of them. In the intervening years. Indeed, they were receding fast into my past. But there they were, and not just one or two of them; every one of those boys that went to Perth was on that gatefold! They had come good! I was proud of them. That was the first thought that came to mind. There was no envy; I had a good gig, a great gig. I was featuring as a bass player in a way that no other bass players of that time did. I was playing a kind of lead bass, and I was the envy of quite a few bass players around. I knew this because they would front me and tell me how lucky I was to have that sort of a role.

Things go around and they come around and shit happens, and I think we have very little control in our lives, certainly much less than we think.

Is there a God? No, of course, not, what a ridiculous, infantile suggestion…unless of course his name is Chance!

15

◐ The synthpop band Bronski Beat put out their debut album, *Age of Consent,* in 1984. This album includes the timeless track 'Smalltown Boy', which stands among the best synthpop songs ever made. The lyrics tell the story of homophobia and being shut out by society, mirroring the struggles faced by young gay individuals in the '80s. The music is very synthesizer-heavy, dance-ready, and easy to listen to. On the whole, the album is expertly crafted, though Jimmy Sommerville's sky-high falsetto makes the songs tricky to sing along with unless you can match his vocal range.

◐ It was a sad day indeed when, on October 15, 2006, CBGB's closed its doors. In 2005 the landlord, the Bowery Residents' Committee, which had earlier entered into a lawsuit with the venue over allegedly unpaid rent amounts, refused to renew the venue's lease. Much to the chagrin of punters and artists alike, a final concert was played with Patti Smith appearing. On December 10, 1973, the CBGB Club opened in New York City. Simply known as CBGB, it was founded by Hilly Kristal, who once explained that it was originally opened to just feature country, bluegrass, and blues music. Under the logo was the acronym 'OMFUG', said to stand for "*Other Music For Uplifting Gourmandisers!*" CBGB's was THE place in NYC; it was where bands such as Suicide, The Dead Boys, Blondie, Television, The Cramps, The Misfits, Patti Smith, and the Ramones got to show their wares. When CBGB closed its doors in 2006, Patti Smith remarked, "*There are new kids with new ideas all over the world. They'll make their own places—it doesn't matter whether it's here or wherever it is*". Today CBGB is a John Varvatos boutique.

⦿ Andrew McLennan, aka Andrew Snoid, was born October 15, 1966, in New Zealand. Andrew was a member of the bands Pop Mechanix (1980-88) and Coconut Rough (1983-85); he also joined The Swingers, led by Phil Judd, in 1982. With those bands Andrew attained chart successes in Pop Mechanix with 'Jumping Out a Window' and with Coconut Rough's 'Sierra Leone'. History was made when Pop Mechanix were involved in a lawsuit where the Australian band Popular Mechanics took Pop Mechanix's record label WEA to court over the use of their name. The plaintiff band won the case, and Andrew's band subsequently changed their name to NZ Pop for operations in Australia, but in New Zealand they continued to work as Pop Mechanix.

⦿ Yello first caught our attention on October 15th, 1980, with their debut album, *Solid Pleasure*. At that time, Yello consisted of three members: Dieter Meier on vocals and lyrics, Boris Blank on keyboards, sampling, and percussion, and Carlos Perón on tapes. Perón left the group after they recorded *You Gotta Say Yes to Another Excess* in 1983, but his absence went unnoticed. *Solid Pleasure* introduced us to an exciting musical journey, filled with constant engagement, absolute entertainment, creativity, and occasional eccentricity. Yello's distinctiveness lies in their ability to infuse their techno sound with rich moods and atmospheric elements. As they ventured forward, their electronic manipulations knew no boundaries. Very few can match the captivating storytelling skills of Dieter Meier. It is a must-listen experience.

16

⦿ ABC straddled a fine line between new romantic and NEW WAVE with their debut single 'Tears Are Not Enough' in 1981. The funky, horn-laden dancefloor track featured lead singer Martin Fry's smooth vocals over a driving beat, appealing to both camps. 'Tears Are Not Enough' appeared on their Trevor Horn-produced debut album, *Lexicon of Love*, a lush, synth-heavy set with contributions from Art of Noise members.

⦿ On October 16, 1981, the publicity hound Malcolm McLaren caused a furore in 1981 with the release of Bow Wow Wow's debut album, *See Jungle! See Jungle! Go Join Your Gang Yeah, City All Over! Go Ape Crazy!*. McLaren sure knew how to get people's attention, and he did it here with the artwork. The cover of the album was a mock-up of Édouard Manet's 1863 painting, *Dejeuner Sur L'Herbe (Lunch on the Grass)*, where he had the then 14-year-old Annabella Lwin pose nude; it became so controversial that it was banned in the USA, yet it did enter the top 200. It was very successful in the UK, reaching No.26, with the accompanying single 'Go Wild in the Country' peaking at No.7. Bow Wow Wow were an acquired taste, and this debut album is not for everybody. Wade through the bass-laden muffled mix, and you will find that the music revolves around some very irresistible melodies layered within monstrous jungle rhythms. Annabella's energetic vocals are always engaging even though they are not bright in the mix. The standout songs include 'King Kong', 'I'm a T.V. Savage' and 'Go Wild in the Country'.

⦿ The Eurythmics duo of Annie Lennox and David A. Stewart released their debut album, *In the Garden,* in 1981. Was this the birth of 'dream pop'? Formed from the ashes of The Tourists, this duo knew exactly what the others wanted, and with Conny Plank producing, they provide a provocative, at times psychedelic mixture of delicate vocals, blissful melodies, and tantalising synth wizardry. The addition of Blondie's drummer Clem Burke sets a backbeat rhythm throughout with an edge that never falters. Disappointingly, *In the Garden* is often overlooked in the Eurythmics' catalogue, probably due to the fact it doesn't hold those killer mega-selling singles. Repeated listening will show just how different it is from the band's other albums, but perhaps even better?

Eurythmics by Petra Gall

❍ The *Dare* album by The Human League debuted in October of 1981. The style of the album was the consequence of a drastic transformation from an avant-garde electronic group into a commercial pop group and marked a pinnacle of the synthpop genre. This change in direction was led by Philip Oakey following the departure of co-founders Martyn Ware and Ian Craig Marsh. Originally, Oakey, Ware, and Marsh made up The Human League and released two ground-breaking albums before disbanding in 1980, with Marsh and Ware leaving to form Heaven 17. Needing new members for his group, Oakey discovered two teenage girls, Joanne Catherall and Susan Ann Sulley, dancing at a nightclub in Sheffield. Along with Ian Burden, Jo Callis, and Philip Adrian Wright, a new lineup of The Human League was created. The music of this new iteration of The Human League represented a radical shift from experimental electronica to mainstream synthpop success. Deservedly, producer Martin Rushent won the 'Best Producer' award at the 1982 Brit Awards for his work on *Dare*, and surprisingly, the band won for 'Best British Newcomer'. *Dare* reached No.1 in the UK and produced four worldwide hits. This album remains a masterpiece due to the quality of the songs. The album was perfectly suited for the era. Kraftwerk, David Bowie, Donna Summer, Giorgio Moroder, and Gary Numan had paved the way for synthesizers in popular music, so the melodic NEW WAVE synthpop of The Human League's third album was warmly received. The fashion magazine-styled cover art perfectly embodies the atmosphere of rock music's early 1980s "new romantic" movement. Decades later, the synth and drum machine sounds are still novel, Philip Oakey's voice is ideally complemented by the female vocals, and the arrangements are superb. This classic record is undoubtedly the best album from the second incarnation of The Human League and the recommended starting point for those looking to explore the band.

● Gary Kemp was born in London, England, in 1959. Gary was the guitarist and songwriter for Spandau Ballet and has been very successful as an actor, appearing in a few successful movies, such as *The Krays, The Bodyguard & The Assassin.* Gary is the older brother of Martin Kemp, who is also a member of Spandau Ballet and an actor. In 1999, Gary was involved in a court battle over £1,000,000 in royalties against John Keeble, Steve Norman, and Tony Hadley, his three other bandmates. Gary won the case. However, in March 2009, all five members of Spandau Ballet called a truce, and they announced at a "secret gig" on the HMS Belfast in London that they would be reuniting for a world tour later in the year, alas without Tony Hadley.

Robert King (Allan) with Johnny Thunders on right

● Robert Allan was born Robert King on October 16, 1960. Robert was the vocalist for Scars from May 1977 to September 1981. Since leaving Scars, Robert recorded as a solo artist and worked as a 'producer' in demo recording studios. He has also been a member of Opium Kitchen and Groucho Handjob, as well as recording solo material. Robert also completed a degree and PhD in Ancient Near Eastern Languages. He currently lives in both Lyon, France, and Edinburgh.

TO SCARS I WAS NO WIMP!
ROBERT KING
(Scars)

May 1977 was a landmark month for me. I was standing in Hotlicks Record Shop in Cockburn Street Edinburgh, having just bought The Stooges E.P. '*Sick of You*', which cost a massive £1.50.   They had a Message Board and there I saw a smallish ad that would change my life. There was a request that would-be vocalists get in touch with a band called The Scars. They were Punk! In Edinburgh… I took down the phone number and gave them a call. We decided to meet in Edinburgh at the bus station because they lived in Currie on the outskirts of Edinburgh, so we could weigh each other up. We wandered along Princes Street, the main street of Edinburgh, and wandered into a Wimpy burger bar opposite Bruce's Records, another shop that championed Punk music. As we were chatting, a bit of bravado took over the conversation. It was debated whether or not I had the balls to leave without paying (we were all approximately 16 years old). I felt I had to, so I walked out of the café (?) without paying and walked along the road to the corner whereupon I was apprehended by a Wimpy employee who told me I was apprehended and had to stay where I was while they called the police. The wimpy person then darted off to call the police, leaving me alone on the street. Odd. I merely crossed the road and went into Bruce's Record Shop until the Scars came to rescue me. After that I auditioned and joined the band.

3/3/2024

⊙ October 16, 1938, marks the birth of Nico, born Christa Paffgen. Nico was a multi-talented individual, excelling as a vocalist, songwriter, actress, and fashion model. In 1965, she released her first single, 'I'm Not Sayin' b/w 'The Last Mile', after meeting The Rolling Stones' guitarist Brian Jones, with production by Jimmy Page. Her collaboration with The Velvet Underground on their debut album, The Velvet Underground & Nico, in 1967 further solidified her place in music history. As an actress, Nico appeared in notable films such as Federico Fellini's *La Dolce Vita* (1960) and Andy Warhol's *Chelsea Girls* (1966). In 1985, she released her final album, *Camera Obscura*, produced by John Cale, exploring new wave electronica with an experimental and dark tone. Nico's unique style and sound set her apart in the music industry. For those seeking a taste of art rock, progressive, or avant-garde music, the album June 1, 1974, captures a rare and accessible moment in music history. Featuring performances by Nico, John Cale, Kevin Ayers, Eno, Ollie Halsall, Archie Leggett, Mike Oldfield, Robert Wyatt, and others, the album showcases a blend of talent and creativity. The original release contains 9 tracks, but seeking out the out-takes copy will provide the full evening's set. Tragically, Nico passed away on July 18, 1988, after a bike riding accident in Ibiza, succumbing to a brain haemorrhage later that night.

Nico by Lampeter University

17

⊙ The debut single 'I Wanna Get Married' b/w 'Looking for Work by De Cylinders out of Noord Holland, The Netherlands, was in the racks October 17, 1980. This is power-pop perfection; it has the makings of what is a great introduction to the record market; it should have been a blistering seller. Terrific vocals by Jolanda Markus, superb instrumentation, and astounding production. Incredible that De Cylinders were pretty much missed worldwide!

⊙ Rebecca McLaine, Paul Limoli, and George Stefani, collectively known as I.M.S., had the potential for immense success with their remarkable debut album *International Music System*. Unveiled on October 17, 1983, the album's tracks have aged gracefully and remain suitable for today's club and bar scenes. The alluring, exotic, and emotional melodies are complemented by impeccable synth arrangements and programming. The sparse vocals on tracks such as 'Run Away' and 'Bubble Rap' bring a sense of playfulness that adds to the overall charm. A stellar representation of enduring electronica.

⊙ On October 17, 1978, Phantom Records opened its doors to the public for the first time at Pitt Street, Sydney. Founded by Dare Jennings, the store quickly became a hub for new releases in the punk, POST-PUNK, psyche, and NEW WAVE music genres. Over time, Phantom evolved into a record label, established by Jules Normington, and played a significant role in promoting classic Australian releases. Notable artists who debuted their music on Phantom Records included The Passengers, Sunnyboys, Flaming Hands, Le Hoodoo Gurus (later known as The Hoodoo Gurus), and Machinations, among others.

◉ Rico Rodriguez was born in Havana, Cuba, in 1934. Rico was raised in Jamaica and was the trombone player for The Specials. Rico moved to the UK in 1961 and began to play and do session work with numerous artists such as Sly Dunbar, Georgie Fame and later, Jools Holland. Jerry Dammers said of Rico, "*For me, getting to play with him was one of the greatest things about the Specials. His album Man from Wareika had been one of my all-time favourites and a great inspiration. I could not believe that he had agreed to play with us, and his contribution to the Specials was immeasurable. He provided an all-important link to authentic Jamaican ska and reggae, which we had tried to copy, and his trombone added the essential element which took us to the next level and helped offer the band a possibility of progression beyond the confines of punk*". Rico passed away on Friday, Sept. 4, 2015.

18

◉ Vanessa Briscoe Hay was born October 18, 1955, in Atlanta, Georgia, USA, and is best known as the vocalist for Pylon. The line-up of Vanessa, Randy Bewley (guitar), Vanessa Briscoe Hay, Michael Lachowski (bass) and Curtis Crowe (drums) came together in early 1979, creating a danceable texture of bright, hook-laden, *jangly guitar & want-to-foot-tap minimalist rhythms. Pylon's comparisons* with bands like Television and Gang of Four through their angular sound are unavoidable, but they had a sense of fun to complement their end product. Out front were Vanessa's vocals, vocals that cover so many adjectives: snarling, shrieking, fierce, abrasive, robotic, exclaiming and, all the time, energetic. 2024, and Vanessa is still active with the project Pylon Reenactment Society, which just released a new album, *Magnet Factory.*

1978 SPRINGTIME IN ATHENS, GEORGIA AND THE 24-HOUR PARTY
VANESSA BRISCOE HAY
(Pylon)

We were like the buds on the trees and unaware; maybe less than buds on a tree would be. April and May in Athens is a time of magic. The chill wears off very quickly, and for maybe two weeks, it is spring before it turns to summer. I was sad because it was the end of the school year, and I was graduating soon. There was an insane amount of work for me to do academically, as I was taking on an overload in an attempt to finish my degree.

In the meantime, around town, my favourite band, The B-52's had released their highly anticipated debut single, 'Rock Lobster' b/w '52 Girls', everyone was all abuzz. The first hologram most of us had seen with our own eyes was on display at Chapter Three Records, our favourite record store located directly across from the old campus and an easy couple of blocks walk from the art department. The B-52's looked good from any angle. I think Kate was blowing a kiss. It's been a long time, so it could have been Cindy? The B-52's were the hottest band in the entire country, and they were from Athens, GA!

The art department at the University of Georgia had been cobbled together from various classes taught in the College of Education and in the Home Economics Department under the College of Agriculture back in the 1930s. A young Georgia artist who had studied both the Ashcan school and American scene styles of painting in New York City, Lamar Dodd, was brought in as an associate professor in 1933 and made head of the program a year later. Dodd continued to build the department and its reputation until the 1970s, when he retired. By this time, he had made the department one of the best art schools in the Southeast. It was not uncommon after his retirement to see him loping through the halls in his trademark seersucker suits and hi-top Converse shoes.

For my final two quarters, I had taken independent art studies classes with Robert Croker; he was one of a group of professors from whom I had taken studio courses over the last four years that also included James Herbert, Richard Olsen, Judith McWillie, Harry Howe, and Mike Nicholson. Elaine de Kooning had recently taken the chair named for Lamar Dodd, and Alice Neel had taught some classes in the past, but I wasn't lucky enough to be in one of those. I did catch a discussion by Phillip Guston and gave him a gingerbread cookie from the A and A Bakery. Croker, as he was affectionately known and hated to be called, sensed the winds of destiny, and knew in the fall of 1977 that he was not going to have his contract renewed at the end of the school year. He decided to go all in and immerse himself in the study of art with the group of students who naturally surrounded him due to his willingness to discuss anything and everything and to take students back to the basics of craft and technique if they had missed it. He showed us how to construct a stretcher, stretch a canvas, gesso it. An exercise which culminated in his painting a portrait of a fellow student volunteer using traditional techniques and the oil absorption table which is used to create permanence in painting. He said that we had to know what the rules were to break them. On critique days, usually Wednesday afternoons, we would gather and share our current works with our fellow classmates and then head out to wherever the beer was cheapest and continue our discussions well into the night. Some graduate students like Michael Paxton and Watt King would also join critique and this night-time beer-fueled discussions. Later, we all might go dancing as a group at the local discotheque, which had "new music" for the last ½ hour of the night.

On October 24, 1977, I attended the wildest party I had seen so far at Croker's house in the country outside of town. He was an ex-Marine and had at some point in time become enamoured of St. Crispin's Day Eve, possibly because of the speech in Shakespeare's Henry V—a rousing speech given on the eve of the Battle of Agincourt by Henry V. A battle which the English surprisingly won and turned the tide in their favour during the 100 Years War. Vinyl record after vinyl record was spun and pretty soon the whole room was heaving and dancing as kegs gave up their magic amber fizzy drink until at some point people were being passed hand over hand overhead. In the yard, surrounded by onlookers, Croker was intoning the very speech from Henry V by the bard himself: *"From this day to the ending of the world, but we in it shall be remembered, we few, we happy few, we band of brothers"*[1].

Indeed, we all bonded like a "band of brothers" during that year. I became good friends with future Pylon bass-player Michael Lachowski and through him, his roommate, Pylon guitarist Randall 'Randy' Bewley. Close to graduation, in the spring of 1978 Croker decided to throw a party which would last 24 hours. This soirée started in the afternoon. The yard was decorated with kiddie pools and sprinklers. If you were standing in the wading pool, it was a little cooler and the bugs didn't bite as hard. Almost no one we knew at that point in time had air conditioning. All our friends and more were there. Toy airplanes. Sprinklers. Keg beer. Heat. Vinyl records being spun. More dancing. More drinking. The sun went down. I think a great many were drunk by this point. I know that I was. Someone was in a tree. Someone was on the roof. Robert Croker proceeded to read 'The Disgusting English Candy Drill', from *Gravity's Rainbow*. A fine sample of the genre that came to be called "hysterical realism" by James Wood in 2000,[2]

"Show a little backbone," advises Mrs. Quoad. *"Yes,"* Darlene said through tongue-softened sheets of caramel, *"don't you know there's a war on? Here, Now love, open your mouth"*. Through the tears he can't see it too well, but he can hear Mrs. Quoad across the table going *"Yum, yum, yum"*, and Darlene giggling. It is enormous and soft, like a marshmallow, but somehow---unless something is now going seriously wrong with his brain---it tastes like: gin. *"Wha's 'is"*, he inquires thickly. *"A gin marshmallow"*, sez Mrs. Quoad. *"Awww."*[3]

At some point, my charismatic art school pal Michael Lachowski convinced a number of us that we should form a gang to scrape the windows of recently vacated businesses downtown. We would call ourselves "The Scrapes". An initiation took place. It involved having your arm scraped by a pinecone. Mercurochrome was haphazardly applied to the wound, and a band-aid was loosely tacked across it. This went on through at least 5-6 victims until Michael himself was initiated, and he proclaimed that it hurt and put a stop to the ritual himself. The party continued. I went to put the first aid supplies back into the bathroom cabinet and noted that the tile and sink were covered in a Halloween-like explosion of red fluids, some of which was blood. I promised Croker I would come back the next day and help clean up. Well, the next afternoon I did return, and the party was still going on. Truly one for the books. At some point those who were there through the wee hours eventually slept in unusual places; under kitchen cabinets, behind the couch, in the yard, and I suppose regained their strength. A serious discussion was taking place in the living room about painting and painters while I cleaned the bathroom and cracked open a beer.

Works Cited:
1. Shakespeare, William. "The St. Crispin's Day Speech". Folger Shakespeare Library. Archived and retrieved from the original on 22 November 2020. Web
2. Wood, James (24 July 2000). "Human, All Too Inhuman: On the Formation of a New Genre: hysterical realism". The New Republic.
3. Thomas Pynchon, Gravity's Rainbow, 1973. Viking Press.

◉ The Italian NEW WAVE, synthpop duo of Franco Rago and Gigi Farina calling themselves Atelier Folie released their debut single 'When A Man Is A Man' b/w 'Madness Is Madness' in 1982. Masterfully produced and arranged the A-side must rate as one the missed masterpieces of Euro-synthpop.

◉ Catherine Ringer, the multi-instrumentalist who led the French NEW WAVE band Les Rita Mitsouko alongside Fred Chichin, was born on October 18, 1957, in Suresnes, France. Prior to her music career, Catherine had a background in stage performance as a dancer and choreographer, which also led her to venture into the world of acting in various films. Although Les Rita Mitsouko gained significant recognition in Europe, their success did not extend to a wider international audience. Following Chichin's death in 2007, Catherine embarked on a solo career under the name 'Chante les Rita Mitsouko' and released an album titled *More à la Cigale* in 2008, featuring reworked versions of Les Rita Mitsouko's songs.

Mona Soyoc by permission / KAS Product by permission

◉ Mona Soyoc was born on October 18, 1959, in Stamford, Connecticut, USA. In 1980, while living in Nancy, France, she partnered with Daniel Favre (known as Spatsz) to form the band KaS Product. Soyoc's powerful vocals and guitar combined with Spatsz's synth and drum machine mastery propelled KaS Product to the forefront of the French coldwave and electro-punk scene in the 1980s. Through three influential albums that decade, the duo cemented their genre leadership before going on hiatus. After Spatsz's passing in 2019, she reformed the band in 2023. KaS Product is releasing a new album and is back on stage with the classics and a new repertoire in 2024.

A DIRTY TWAT THAT KICKED ASS
MONA SOYOC
(KaS Product)

How does a young girl, American-born from Argentinian immigrants, raised partly in England, end up in Nancy, an eastern provincial French town that suffered 3 war invasions (and still had bullet marks on some of the walls from the last one), end up there, doing electro-punk-new-wave music? Who cares anyway?

That's where KaS Product started, in Nancy, also the cradle of Art Nouveau.

Lucky me, I had found an ad in the paper, and I had just started a job singing with a cover band in the area. We'd play every weekend for celebrations, discos, and ballrooms in neighbouring villages. But I wanted to do my music; I wanted to create the coolest music to impact.

A friend invited me to jam at Spatsz's place. He had bought a Korg dual-phonic that sounded massive! You'd press one key, and a huge, deep sound poured out of the speakers and hit you like no other sound! I started trying the mike, singing, and Spatsz said to me, *"What are you doing? You sound schizophrenic."* (He had a job at a psychiatric hospital thanks to his mom, who went there often to be treated for depression.) I thought to myself, I'll show this guy who I am!

Of course, I'd fall for Spatsz, all dressed in black leather, with jet-black hair to his shoulders and plucked eyebrows.

We'd soon play with other musicians, but after heroin hit the town, the other existing members of the band didn't show up anymore for rehearsals, so Spatsz and I decided we'd do without them. We added a little drum machine to our equipment!

At that time, we were living with other friends and would rehearse in their bedroom, as we were sleeping in the corridor. We decided we should release our first EP and went to our local record shop, Punk Records (it still exists to this day), and asked the guy if he'd like to do a record with us.

We handed him a K7 with a few songs; he said, *"I'll give you an answer Monday."* When we came back, he told us he had a friend who could record us with his REVOX tape machine.

To cut it short, that's how we started auto-producing our first record, in the living room. The first EP came out in April with the song called 'Mind'. I was obsessed with Mind Control & the dystopian world of Orwell's 1984. Then a second EP, with 'Take Me Tonight' and 'In Need (of drugs)', came out that same year in 1980.

We did our first gig playing behind a wire fence. We were concerned about the public's reaction, as they didn't like drum machines or synths. They said it wasn't music; they wanted guitar, bass, and drums! That's when we decided I would start the show behind a plastic screen that I'd stab and slit with a knife to set the tone for the evening!

Then in 1980, we borrowed some cash from my dad, and with Gérard N'Guyen, we produced our first album in the studio. In one week, we managed to pack in and mix 11 songs. *Try Out* was born!

We decided we should find a major record label in Paris. After being thrown out and told, *"This is not music!"* by most publishing and record labels we visited, somebody said there was this guy from RCA who was looking for us.

In spring 1982 we licensed our first album to RCA. And what a surprise; it was the era of the independent free radios, the Left had just won the elections (Mitterrand), and everybody was allowed to broadcast freely from their rooftop. Our songs were being played 24/7. We had sent our music to the English press, and a young journalist from London came to interview us. Unlike the French, who didn't care about what I was talking about, he analysed each song. I never felt so exposed, so naked! I didn't realise what I was writing about! I wrote 'Pussy X' in a very naive and innocent way and never gave it a second thought!

Anyway, he managed to organise 3 gigs in London at The Venue, The Embassy & The Rock Garden with Delta 5 and another French band, Orchestre Rouge.

I must say the English press loved our show and were unanimous. We kicked ass. But the coolest thing for me was that day in London; when I entered the hotel room, I turned on Radio 1 on the BBC, and John Peel was playing our song 'Pussy X'! I thought, "*What magic synchro is this?*" It was so exhilarating. A wink for me, a warm welcome! Later I asked and found out why our song 'Never Come Back' never aired in the UK like it did in France. It had been censored because I used slang: "*Never come back. You're just a dirty twat!*" Well, today I'm back, and I don't care if anyone thinks I'm a dirty twat; that song wasn't about me anyway.

After Spatsz's departure in 2019, I'm lucky to have found great new band members. I'm having the time of my life, releasing a new album in 2024 and playing in festivals and great venues! Still kicking ass and having an impact! See you soon at your local venue!

○ On this day in 1976 Throbbing Gristle were unleashed unto the world by their official live debut at the Institute of Contemporary Arts in London. The performance was part of an exhibition named *Prostitution* by COUM Transmission, a newly created collective founded by T.G. member Genesis P-Orridge. The show was explicitly confrontational; it comprised collections of rusty knives, syringes, bloodied hair, used sanitary towels and overt photographs of lesbians. Music would never be the same!

○ Did you know that 'Video Killed the Radio Star' was first recorded by Bruce Woolley and The Camera Club, with Thomas Dolby on keyboards for their album *English Garden*? The tune was written by Trevor Horn, Geoff Downes and Bruce Woolley in 1977 and later recorded and rearranged as the debut single for The Buggles. The single went to No.1 on this day in 1979 on the British singles charts, and it is renowned as the first ever music video shown on MTV in North America.

19

○ a-ha released their debut single 'Take on Me' b/w 'Love Is Reason' in 1984. There was an original release produced by Tony Mansfield, but it seemed to miss the mark, and that version didn't immediately have the trio from Norway's name up in lights. The single was remixed by Alan Tarney, and that was the rendering that was used to accompany a brilliantly conceptual film clip. It was designed around pencil sketch animation, blended with real footage, and it was soon high on MTV's playlist. The beat is infectious with a killer hook. Pure NEW WAVE perfection.

○ Murray Cook was born October 19, 1957, in Sydney, Australia. Today, Murray is a Sydney-based marine biologist/musician who is presently the coordinator of the Community Restorative Centre's Songbirds project, a prison songwriting/art and theatre program. Murray is a highly regarded multi-instrumentalist and, over the years, has formerly performed, recorded, and toured internationally with Midnight Oil, Warumpi Band, Mixed Relations, Mental as Anything, Leah Purcell, and Marlene Cummins. He worked as a music teacher at Long Bay Gaol for 21 years before all NSW prison teachers were made redundant by Premier Mike Baird. He has since written and implemented the Songbirds songwriting workshop programmes in prisons across New South Wales, from Silverwater to Broken Hill, releasing 3 CDs of prison songs. Murray was a speaker at the International Conference for Arts and Mental Health in 2019 and the Addi Road Writer's Festival in 2021 and 2023. He was a keynote speaker at the EPEA conference on prison education in Oslo, the Australian

Recreational Therapy Association, and the BAD Crime Writer's Festival in 2023. In 2004, Murray released a solo album, *Looking for Gold.*

GO BUSH TOURS 86-87
MURRAY COOK
(Warumpi Band, Mental As Anything)

It was May 1986, and the Warumpi Band were driving around lost in the back blocks of Kuranda, Far North Queensland, in Cookie's muffler-impaired Ford Fairlane 500, looking for a party. We had just played a riotous show at Kuranda's "top pub" with the local reggae giants Mantaka and were looking for the guitarist Willie Brim's house for a post-show shindig. The cops pull us over and take one look at the Black faces, reef us out, rough us up a bit, and say, *"Where are you going at this hour?" "Willie Brim's place"* blurts out Neil. Willie was no stranger to the law. The cops came back with, *"Keep on driving the fuck out of town; if we see you cunts again, we'll lock you up, no questions, okay?".* So, we wait for them to go and decide the party is worth the risk and keep looking. The party sure was.

The next day it was a struggle to drag everyone out from various women's bedrooms, couches, and verandahs and take off before sunrise. We kept driving, all of the four and a half hours to Georgetown, where we decided to swag out on the Normanton side of town. Here we light a fire, and George goes off into the bush armed with a tyre iron; he comes back with a large goanna, which, along with baked beans, XXXX beer and toast, is dinner. Sitting round the fire later, suddenly George grabs my arm, bolts off into the trees and comes back with a lovely baby Amethystine Python wrapped round his arm; he christens it 'Scrubby' after an old flame. I love snakes, so I adopted it; it wrapped itself round my head, and I drifted off replete, stoned and lost in an infinity of languid smoke and stars. For a week that snake stayed on my head and caught lizards and mice to feed her. I met an old Murri in the street in Karumba who nearly had a seizure when he patted me on the head and Scrubby reared up from under my hat. We played a show in Normanton's Purple Pub where Missy distinguished herself by sticking her head up and swaying to the beat on stage. Off to Mornington Island by charter flight the next morning, where locals were highly amused by our new bejeweled member. We played on the back of a truck after the painted traditional Lardil dancers did their thing for the entire island populace! There was one light behind us which attracted a cornucopia of giant insects, which landed on and clawed the fuck out of us. From there, then down to the beach, where the elders had cooked a dugong in the sand for 3 days prior in honour of our visit. To this day, it's the best thing I have ever tasted; I fed succulent scraps to the serpent. We stayed up to see a glorious sunrise, drinking beer, pulling on reefers, singing Hank Williams, Creedence, et al., and sang 'My Island Home' about 30 times with the local crew. We went on to play Burketown and Cloncurry, where we had the luxury of a hotel room. I woke up the next morning, and sadly Scrubby was missing. We had to get going early en route to Mt Isa via Cammooweal, and I was missing her already. We laughed about the poor bastard who had that room next to us.

Later, on that tour, I was walking down the main street of Northern Territory's Katherine with George to get a pub lunch when two big ZZ Top-type rednecks, complete with blue singlets and tough stickers, came walking up the other side with 3 bull terriers on leashes. The dogs spotted George and started straining at their leashes and snarling, *"Nigger Lover,"* spat one of them, giving me the death stare as he raised his shotgun and pointed it straight at my head, miming pulling the trigger! They continue walking, pissing themselves laughing. So, it's an early beer for me to calm my shaking hands.

Back in Queensland, and this time with Mixed Relations, we are in a broken-down tour bus en route from Laura Festival in deepest, darkest FNQ, thinking I should still be sitting by the river strumming the guitar and trying to imagine life without TV. You think they'd have replacement parts on these things, but life's like that, and to chill is too divine. It's really hot. Me? I have nothing to do except sit back and watch the world go by or at least remain stationary for a tantalizing moment.

The mighty land stretches on forever, and bus breakdowns are but a tiny sting in the scheme of things. The eucalypts bow their heads like graceful lions, and the clouds just laze through the sky with the grass paper dry, crying for that sweet singing rain. Some of these rocks are older than history and were once on the bottom of the shallow sea; maybe whales and Brachiosaurus pondered through the sleeping waters. The azure heavens, like lapis lazuli, are in infinite 3D, and yet all the lads can think of is a cold four-ex and a six-paper spliff in the artificially induced tropicana of the Lakewood Downs Jardin de Biere, as Blackfellas trudge the road and melt like sticks into the tremoloed mirage ahead, and all the time, heat, heat, heat, dry as the Palestine wilderness, enough to tax the patience of even the most saintly among us.

I guess this is the flat, brown, dull, lethargic, even lugubrious country. The land undistinguished by anything even remotely approaching pzazz or picture-postcard pristine perfection. There are no grand gaping gorges or adamantine rushing spring-fed streams. No dense palm jungles, no fabulous, rare butterflies, even more exotic Birds of Paradise, glint-eyed, oily-muscled panthers, ruby mines, mosques, magic carpet markets and microtonal modality. No! This is Australia, mate, an international destination of appallingly healthy brown Scandinavian backpackers, where it pays to belong and *'wheredyageddit'* reigns supreme. This is the bush cobber; it's fucking hard and stony. It's dry and harsh and stretches on forever. It scratches and never forgives. Even the birds just croak and give up their song to the wavy lines of heat, making the trees sing vibrato in the unbearable inferno. Yet the mountains lie massive and ancient; they wait for the day of judgement, casting their deep, dark ululations across the land.

⦿ The debut LP by Madness, *One Step Beyond,* was released in 1979. It's pretty much timeless, totally enjoyable, and today it still sounds very fresh, probably because even when it was released it was kind of, even then, revivalist. The band had quite a few hits after this debut, and there are several *Greatest Hits* collections available from Madness, but this is the real deal. There is not a dull moment, from the very first note of the *title track* to the final (goofy) track, 'Chipmunks Are Go'. Their first single, 'One Step Beyond', hit the music scene like a rocket back in 1979, and if you see them live, they'll play this for you first! 'My Girl' shows the true musical skills of the band and is followed by 'Night Boat to Cairo', which is a fantastic, fun little SKA piece. The album moves on great with 'Believe Me' and 'Land of Hope and Glory' and then builds up to one of the best ska tunes ever, 'The Prince'. The vitality and bluebeat feel stay high all the way to the end of the album, yep, until 'Chipmunks Are Go'! This is a must-have album; SKA fan or not, you'll find clever music from this clever band.

⦿ On this day in 1979, The Specials released their sensational *self-titled* album. Superlatives fail; is it one of the greatest ska albums ever? That can be debated; it's always a matter of taste. One thing's for sure: if you're into ska, you already have this album. It was through this and the Madness album, *One Step Beyond,* that most people were turned onto ska; the movement struck a chord with the UK youth, Black and white. It was old, but it was new; 'ska-mania' was becoming massive, it was sympathetic to the unemployed, and they were embraced, garnering a huge following with the Skinheads & Mods. On this album you find a band with two voices, one black, one decidedly white, but both undoubtedly British and unhappy. Where Madness was fun driven, The Specials were more about more pressing matters. The narrative was typically political and social comment highlighted by 'Too Much Too Young', a song about teen pregnancy and contraception. All the while extolling an anti-racist sentiment, the music was vibrant and upbeat. Produced by Elvis Costello, it went viral worldwide, going top 5 in the UK and New Zealand. This album catches the best version of the band in their prime. If you don't have this album, then get it!

Karl Wallinger by Roch Parisien

○ Karl Edmond De Vere Wallinger from Prestatyn, Wales, was born in 1957. Karl formed World Party in the mid-'80s after his departure from The Waterboys, with whom he played keyboards (1983–85). World Party had a minor hit in 1987 with 'Ship of Fools'; it peaked at No.4 in Australia and in the 20s in the US, UK, and New Zealand. It was a grand effort by Karl; he wrote, produced, and played all instruments on the release. 30 years later, the lyrics hold up in a particularly prescient style. Karl died on March 10, 2024, aged 66.

○ Daniel Mark Woodgate, aka Woody Woodgate, was born in 1960, in Kensington, England. Woody has always been the mainstay drummer with Madness since joining them in 1978. With the split of Madness in 1986, he became a founding member of Voice of the Beehive, who released three albums to mediocre response. Woody began his solo career in 2015, while still a member of Madness, releasing the album *In Your Mind*.

20

○ 'Stand or Fall', the first single by The Fixx to chart, was in the record store racks on October 20, 1982. The single was one of four singles released taken from the debut album *Shuttered Room*. The previous two singles released, 'Lost Planes' & 'Some People', met with very little commercial reaction. Seen as somewhat derivative NEW WAVE by critics, the album was very well received by the record-buying public and is often rated high in the best albums of 1982.

○ Girls At Our Best released their debut and only album, *Pleasure,* on October 20 in 1981. You would be forgiven to think this was a girl group, but the only female present was the lead singer Judy Evans. Born from The Butterflies that had their origin in Leeds, England, the band's only album was pure twee-pop with a side-bar Post-Punk sound. Simple music with even simpler lyrical content, mixing jangly guitar, Post-Punk basslines and some expressive synth knob twiddling, is indeed just that – a refreshing pleasure to listen to.

○ Mark King was born on the Isle of Wight, England, in 1958. Mark is most famous for being the lead singer and bassist of the band Level 42, who incorporated a hybrid of jazz-funk into a blend of NEW WAVE. Mark's style of playing was seen as influential as he popularised the 1970s slap method for playing the bass guitar and mesmerised fans with his talent for turning the bass into a drum. Mark kicked off his career with Level 42, which he founded in 1979 together with keyboardist Mike Lindup and brothers Phil (drums) and Rowland (guitar) Gould. Lindup left Level 42 in 1994, but he and King reunited in 2004 under the Level 42 banner. Level 42 has had a revolving door of members that, over the years, have included legendary players such as Billy Cobham, Gary Barnacle, and Allan Holdsworth. With moderate sales of most releases, the 1987 album *Running in the Family* went top 10 worldwide, thanks to the hit single 'Lessons in Love'.

⊙ Rocon Communications principal Roch Parisien believes that all the world's problems have a musical solution. Born on Oct. 20, 1958, in London, England, to Canadian parents, he began devouring music at a precocious age and has invested, over the years, what would amount to the gross national product of several small countries into his music collection. Roch thrives on assessing the work of others, having now served on juries for the Juno Awards, the Governor General's Performing Arts Awards, the Polaris Music Prize, the Canadian Folk Music Awards, and the West Coast Music Awards, as well as pulling duty on countless music conference panels. Where does he get off on this? Well, Roch began his career in music while still in his teens at Ottawa's CKCU-FM college radio station, where he created and hosted many specialty music programmes, including the legendary *No Future Now* – Canada's first punk rock/new wave music feature slot. It was also as a teenager in the '70s that he began taking way-cool photos of every interesting band coming through the Ottawa market, a habit he has yet to break. He launched Rocon Communications in 1991 to serve as an umbrella organisation for his music business activities. This included freelancing for a major daily newspaper, producing a syndicated record review column & becoming a pioneer of online music journalism in the '90s. He co-hosted music programmes on local TV in Ottawa and produced a national radio special for the CBC. He has worked with the Canadian Museum of Civilisation and the National Archives to evaluate and develop their collections of popular music artefacts and programmed a national folk/roots channel. Roch's writing and production work have earned him three international music journalism awards. As a music historian and archivist, he has been developing an ever-expanding database on the history of popular music. You can presently find him exploring music news, reviews, interviews, history, and photography via his daily *Roch Parisien's Rocon Communications* music blog on Facebook – also home of *The Facebook Music Interviews* series – from which several of the interviews that appear in this book are drawn. An anthology of his concert photography is currently in the works, several examples of which can also be found in this tome. Give Roch a world problem to solve, and he will assemble the perfect set list for the occasion.

⊙ On this day in 1978, The Police played their USA debut gig at New York City's CBGB. They were yet to release their debut album, *Outlandos d'Amour,* and travelled economy to the USA with their instruments as carry-on hand luggage (don't know how that happened with the drum kit). It was still early days for the fledgling band; Sting, Andy Summers, and Stewart Copeland were nowhere near the rich, world-famous rock stars they would eventually become. They hired a Ford Econoline van and travelled from NYC to Toronto, Canada, and back to NYC, playing 22 dates in between and closing the tour again at CBGB's on November 15. In his book *One Train Later*, guitarist Andy Summers happily recounts, *"No one there knew who we were or had ever heard of us. We have to prove our worth, and knowing this makes us all the more determined to blow the audience away."*

⊙ *Boy,* the debut album by U2, was released in the UK in 1980. Steve Lillywhite's production portrayed U2 as big; it's no wonder they became the label of '80s stadium rock. Nothing on *Boy* missed treatment; Bono's vox, the thundering drums, the booming, thumping bass, and the chiming, echoed guitar are all huge. Even if you turn the volume right down, the album is massive, one could argue, overdone? Such a marked difference to the Brian Eno and Daniel Lanois-produced albums of the mid to late '80s. It's definitely a landmark album of POST-PUNK but not in the discography of U2.

21

○ Paul Abrahams was born in 1958 in Sydney, Australia. Paul is best known for his production work and as the bassist and founding member of The Reels. The Reels came about in 1978 when a group of aspiring "garage wannabees" in a shared house put their inspirations together to form one of Australia's seminal synthpop outfits. The Reels would become a major drawcard themselves, but along the way they paid their dues, and the quality of their performance saw them be a support act to many local and international acts such as Midnight Oil, INXS, Icehouse, Roxy Music, and The Cure, among a host of others. 1983 saw Paul grow tired of the music industry norms, and he took to drumming with several inner-city Sydney bands. He soon returned to bass and touring with the well-known artists Peter Blakeley, James Blundell & Wendy Matthews. 2023 sees Paul writing and recording with Ricky Pannowitz as Atmospherica.

REELS BY RAIL?
PAUL ABRAHAMS
(The Reels)

I couldn't get a few facts verified, but here's the true story anyway.......

It was sometime in 1980 when The Reels supported The Boys Next Door at the Crystal Ballroom in Melbourne. We needed something special for the event, something to be remembered by. No names mentioned, but we asked a FAN, nicknamed 'Mouse', to come on stage during a song and dance. So, she came onstage in a St. Trinian's School uniform and began to take the uniform off. There were gasps and whistles from the audience as she continued until she was wearing very little, and there on the front of her bare chest was written either "*The Reels*" or "*Reels by Rail*"; no one can clarify the details. It caused quite a stir amongst the audience. We did share the stage again at the Nick Cave-curated *All Tomorrow's Parties* in 2009. For the Sydney leg of the tour, Nick asked the reformed Reels to headline.

○ Musician, producer/engineer, and film score composer Tom Ashton was born in 1963, in Staffordshire, England. Over their initial 6-year existence, Tom was a founding member and guitarist of The March Violets out of Leeds, England. As a guitarist he recorded with Clan of Xymox, had stints as a guest player with The Sisters of Mercy and The Danse Society, and also co-wrote and recorded The Batfish Boys' first album, *The Gods Hate Kansas*. Over four decades, Tom has been involved in numerous film score compositions, with his music being featured in the John Hughes-directed coming-of-age drama *Some Kind of Wonderful*. In the 1990s, while based in London, Tom played in various bands, including Amania, with ex-Violets singer Cleo Murray and Craig Adams from Sisters Of Mercy/The Mission, and also Bully, with Australian singer/songwriter/actress Abi Tucker. The March Violets reformed in 2007 and released their first proper studio album, *Made Glorious,* in 2013 and began touring extensively in the USA and Europe. His music production studio, SubVon, today operates out of Athens, Georgia, where he has recorded, mixed, and mastered many Georgia-based darkwave bands, including Vision Video, Tears for The Dying, Hip to Death and Entertainment.

ARCADE GAME AND A LEGEND HOVERS
TOM ASHTON
(The March Violets)

The March Violets were mixing new material at Right Track Studios in NYC in early 1987. We had just finished a 2-month tour and had been at Electric Lady Studio working solidly on laying down the music, so I was tired and had taken a bit of time in the recreation room to have a beer and sit at my favourite arcade game, *Outrun*.

After 10 or 15 minutes, I was aware that someone was watching me from close behind; I was totally unaware of any company, as I hadn't heard them come into the room, as I was pretty engrossed in playing.

So, I looked around, and there hovering on my right shoulder was the face of Mick Jagger, dressed in a dapper pinstripe suit and with a gently mocking expression on his face! *"You're gonna be putting a lot of money in that thing to get anything out of it"* was his comment. He nodded, then walked out.

I was speechless!

Anyway, of course I ran back to our room and told everyone. Cleo Murray made an immediate beeline for the studio he was working in to say hi!

Apparently, as it turned out, Mick was approachable and quite pleasant to her!

◉ In 1985, the first album *This Is Big Audio Dynamite* from Big Audio Dynamite (BAD) was available for purchase today! BAD were like an inexpensive version of The Clash's later era. The influences of The Clash are unavoidable among the high-tech electronic components of sampling and modern pop music. Even in the late '80s, BAD were able to be innovative, and one can only be grateful that Mick Jones's reinvention is responsible. There are some catchy songs here, they are quite clever in their use of found vocals and inventive both lyrically and musically, 'Medicine Show' displays all of that.

◉ Charlotte Caffey was born in 1953 in Santa Monica, California. Charlotte was the guitarist and songwriter in the NEW WAVE chanteuses The Go-Go's who were certainly in the running for the top female band in the 1980s. They had hits with 'Our Lips Are Sealed' and the Charlotte penned 'We Got the Beat'. She began her musical career as a bass guitar player in the early Los Angeles punk band The Eyes before joining The Go-Go's in 1978 and switching to guitar. Charlotte co-wrote the No.1 US country hit 'But for the Grace of God' with Keith Urban and collaborated in recordings with the likes of Belinda Carlisle, Red Kross and The Police's Andy Summers.

◉ Julian Cope was born in 1957 in Deri, Wales. He first found fame as the lead singer and songwriter for The Teardrop Explodes, out of Liverpool, England. After The Teardrop Explodes, he went on to have a very successful solo career, releasing nearly 40 albums to date. His 1991 album *Peggy Suicide* is often considered his best work. Over the years, Cope has been involved in various musical projects like Queen Elizabeth, Brain Donor, and Black Sheep. Before The Teardrop Explodes, he was part of a trio called The Crucial Three with two other Liverpudlians, Ian McCulloch (later of Echo & the Bunnymen) and Pete Wylie (who formed Wah!). Though The Crucial Three never officially released any music, the combination of the three musicians was historic. But it is with The Teardrop Explodes that Cope's fame is most associated, as the principal songwriter and frontman. Cope has been described as a *"rock musician, author, antiquary, musicologist, poet and cultural commentator"*. He is a recognized authority on Neolithic culture and has published several books on archaeology. He has also released three volumes of musicology: *Krautrocksampler, Japrocksampler* and *Copendium: A Guide to the Musical Underground in 2016*.

Julian Cope by Petra Gall

⦿ Lux Interior, also known as Erick Lee Purkhiser, was born in 1946 in Akron, Ohio. He took his name from an old car commercial. Lux was the frontman and original vocalist for The Cramps, a band known for their unique psychobilly-garage rock style. He was married to guitarist Poison Ivy, also known as Kristy Wallace, who was the other founding member of the band. Together, they wrote edgy songs that left an impact on their audience. Lux passed away on February 4, 2009.

Lux Interior by Petra Gall

● The The released their first album, *Soul Mining*, in 1983. This album was a significant contribution to the music scene of the early 1980s, as it combined elements of NEW WAVE, synth pop, and POST-PUNK. It stands out from other releases of that time due to its unique sound. Matt Johnson, the lead singer, expresses his emotions openly through his lyrics, and the listeners can truly feel it. While embracing the music technology of the '80s, the album also incorporates traditional instruments through clever production. It successfully avoids being weighed down by synthpop, offering a diverse musical journey. Notable tracks include 'This Is the Day' with its bluesy harmonica, 'The Sinking Feeling' with its minimalistic bass, 'Uncertain Smile' featuring a sublime piano performance, and the perfect trumpet in 'Perfect'. It is truly an extraordinary album, especially considering that it was created by a talented 21-year-old.

● 'Teenage Kicks' the debut single from The Undertones out of Northern Ireland was released in October 21, 1978. Dominant guitars don't detract from the vocal hook of this classic tune. Famed DJ John Peel was quoted as saying that "*Teenage Kicks is the standard against which all songs are now measured*". He saw the song as near to the most perfect three minutes that song could be. Melody, immediacy and defining the zeitgeist both lyrically and aurally, isn't that what you wanted?

22

● On October 22, 1976, with the release of 'New Rose' on the new independent label Stiff, The Damned became what is generally accepted as the first of the London punk bands to release a single.

● Maggie K De Monde was born October 22, Rotherham, South Yorkshire, England, and grew up in Birmingham. Maggie's first band, Playthings, supported Duran Duran on their first tour; this was before she became part of the trio that was Swans Way. Their 1984 album *The Fugitive Kind* is a pure gem; it's sleek, suave, and stylish, best represented by the tracks 'Soul Train' and 'The Blade'. The variation of tunes on the album as a whole evoke images – pastoral, film noir and urban – Robert Shaw's vocals, reminiscent at times of Martin Fry, ride to the fore. With the demise of Swans Way, Maggie and Swans bassist Rick P. Jones formed Scarlet Fantastic; their single of 1987, 'No Memory', went top 25 on the UK singles chart. It came from the debut album *24 Hrs*. In the '90s it became a huge Balearic house track; it was discovered by Andy Weatherall and played by many luminaries of the time. It seems that Maggie likes working with a limited cast, as her next couple of projects were duos Kahal & Kahal with her husband, Leif Kahal, Club Silencio with Crabbi from Pop Will Eat Itself, and Maggie and Martin with Martin Watkins, creating their *Union* album. Maggie has collaborated with many different artists internationally in recent years, and in 2016 she released an album, *Reverie,* under her Scarlet Fantastic name. Since then, she has released several singles: 'To Hell', 'Make Way for Love' and 'Better Day'. Maggie was on an album, *Metropol Nights,* alongside Boy George and Andy Bell, which was released in 2022 by German producer Roland Faber; she wrote her song 'Crazy Love' with Roland. Maggie is currently narrating and presenting a six-part documentary series called *Birmingham: A City Rooted in Talent*, a Contrary Trees production featuring many of Birmingham's most loved talents, ranging from musicians and footballers to poets and artists. Maggie is also currently recording a new album which will be released under the name Scarlet Fantastic.

Maggie K De Monde by Simon Fowler

A SPOOKY TALE
MAGGIE K DE MONDE
(Swansway, Scarlet Fantastic)

Way back in the mid '80s, I'm guessing 1984, I was recording with my band Swans Way at the iconic Trident studio in Soho, London. Our producer at the time was John Walters, who had been in the band Landscape, which had the hit single 'Einstein a Go-Go'. We were recording our song 'Illuminations', which was to go on our *Fugitive Kind* album; it's still one of my favourites on that album. The chorus lyrics are *"feeling total pleasure"*, and my job was to multi-layer my vocals with a breathy, sensuous delivery.

The vocal booth was in a sunken area in the basement of the building, while the control room where the producer sat at the recording/mixing desk was up on a much higher level. I began singing; it was quite a task I had ahead of me, as there were going to be many layers of vocals. The session started off being fine, but gradually I began to sense a feeling of unease. This feeling of unease developed until the air felt so icy and heavy that you could almost cut through it with a knife. My feeling turned to terror, and I screamed out and became uncontrollably emotional, crying and shouting for help. I fled the vocal booth, and my band members Rick P Jones and Robert Shaw came to my rescue. They comforted me and consoled me, but I think they too were pretty freaked out. After I had finally calmed down, we reset up a microphone elsewhere in the studio, and I completed my singing session for the day. I'll never forget that moment; the experience was traumatising.

We were a band from Birmingham, UK, so when recording in London, our record company would put us up in a London hotel. When I woke up the following morning, I had a circular red ring mark on my left upper arm, and I threw up a small amount of clear liquid that had a thin black streak in it. I wasn't ill in any way, but I thought that this occurrence was strange.

Several months later we were recording another song for the same album at Wessex Studios London. There was a guy there from the '80s band New Model Army, and he lent me his coat as I was chilly, and we got into a really good conversation, discussing our current recordings, gigs, etc., and then we started talking about studios, and he mentioned Trident studio in Soho. My response was *"OH MY GOD!"*, and then I started to relay my horror story to him. To my surprise he just sat quietly listening, nodding his head as if he absolutely fully got what I was saying. After I had told him about my experience there, he said to me, *"You do know what that place was, don't you?"* I could feel the hairs on the back of my neck stand up, and I got goosebumps all over. *"It was a burial ground for plague victims."* He then went on to tell me how I wasn't the only one who had experienced weird, spooky events there. Apparently, Marc Almond also witnessed strange things there, and many other engineers who worked at the studio said doors would mysteriously slam all by themselves and radios would switch themselves on in the middle of the night. This all made sense to me, and I realised how inappropriate it must have seemed for me to be singing *"feeling total pleasure"* in such a dark place full of the energy of suffering.

It was also very strange to note the red ring mark on my arm and the clear liquid that I threw up. Made me think of the old nursery rhyme that referred to the plague. *"Ring-a-ring-a-rosies. A pocket full of posies. A tissue, a tissue. We all fall down."*

This nursery rhyme originated as a song about the bubonic plague, with the *"ring around the rosie"* representing the rash that appeared on the skin of those infected. Posies of herbs were carried as protection and to ward off the smell of the disease. *"A tissue, a tissue, we all fall down"* referred to the sneezing and inevitable collapsing of those who contracted the deadly disease.

This is a memory I will never forget, and I'm amazed that our song 'Illuminations' survived as a testament to light and love. Maybe Light does overcome darkness.

There is always hope.

● Jim Sclavunos' birthday is October 22. Jim was born and grew up in New York City and has earned fame as a multi-instrumentalist, but predominantly as a drummer/percussionist. Jim was an early member of Sonic Youth appearing on their debut album *Confusion Is Sex*. Prior to Sonic Youth he was an integral part of the NYC 'No Wave' scene being a member of 8 Eyed Spy and with Teenage Jesus & The Jerks as the bass-player. Since 1994 he has been a constant member of Nick Cave & The Bad Seeds, and was a founding member of Grinderman. His credits as a producer and writer are vast collaborating and working with the likes of The Horrors, Beth Orton, Boss Hog and The Jim Jones Revue among a host of others. Look for his alias Silver Alert and you will find remixes of Depeche Mode, Alan Vega and Philip Glass.

AN INTERVIEW WITH JIM SCLAVUNOS
(Nick Cave & The Bad Seeds, Grinderman, ,
Teenage Jesus & The Jerks, 8-Eyed Spy et. al)
Interviewed by Roch Parisien (Roch Parisien's Rocon Communications)

Jim, you first came to public light as part of the POST-PUNK 'No Wave' music scene in NYC in the late '70s, working with Lydia Lunch in Teenage Jesus & The Jerks and 8-Eyed Spy, for example. What attracted you to this challenging "noise" spectrum of music and how did you first get involved?

It wasn't a challenge to my ears. It was the kind of music I had already been drawn to for years as a teenager, by way of The Mothers of Invention. Frank Zappa always made a point in those days of citing avant-garde modernist composers and free jazz pioneers alongside his rock influences (which were comparatively conservative). Much psychedelic music had a noise element. Even the Beatles had their noisy experiments such as 'Revolution No.9' off the so-called *White Album*. I just continued down that path and got interested in people like

Ornette Coleman, Captain Beefheart and his Magic Band, etc., etc. When I met Lydia, she was doing a kind of aggressive music I could relate to and so it was a natural alliance. I loved all the so-called No Wave bands, but especially Mars, who are probably the least known.

How would you describe the legacy of the NYC "No Wave" movement?

Like most legacies I think a misunderstood one. It was borne of a certain specific cultural context and was never designed to be a movement. It was a group of like-minded individuals who happened to bond together mainly because their music was unacceptable to so many people outside our small social circle. Now that it has belatedly found acceptance in a broader social circle and is seen in a broader cultural context, it has a significance it didn't have at the time. Having said that, I am glad people have discovered it or remember it, however their understanding of it may differ from mine.

Jim, Nick Cave & The Bad Seeds came 'a calling in 1994. How did that come about, what were you doing at the time, and what was your initial reaction?

I was at a very low ebb. I had been playing in several different bands, was homeless and basically living from gig to gig, Finally the gigs ran out and I simply had nowhere to go and no money and no prospects. I retreated, tail firmly between my legs, back to mom's house. About a week later, Mick Harvey called, said he heard I was at loose ends; did I fancy playing percussion and organ with The Bad Seeds on their European tour to support *Let Love In*. I replied that I would do my utmost to fit it in to my very busy and demanding schedule and off I went for 3 months of touring. Our infamous Lollapalooza tour came up immediately after that, and things just have continued on from there...

So why did the Bad Seeds feel they needed a second pair of hands-on percussion at the time? They already had Thomas Wydler well ensconced.

The *Let Love In* album had a lot of percussion and keyboard overdubs on it that the band felt were essential for adequately recreating those songs onstage. For example, the bells in 'Loverman' and 'Red Right Hand' were key parts of the drama of the song and there were no free hands to ring them chimes. My role in the band has grown from those early tours though. I started playing drums, sometimes on my own, sometimes alongside Tommy.

In terms of recording, your first full Bad Seeds album as a member was 1996's "Murder Ballads". Not for the faint of heart! Give us a glimpse of that experience.

The recording of that album was a real free-for-all, quite relaxed and convivial. Lots of guest musicians and singers passing through, throughout the whole session. Not too dissimilar to the way we record to this day. Very much a live band recording situation, everyone in there at once, the main challenge being for the producer/engineer to capture it all, because we work very, very fast. 'Stagger Lee' was done in two takes for example. No rehearsing at all. We had pretty much just come up with the idea for the song, because I handed Nick a book that contained the poem that was the basis for his lyrics. Once Marty came up with a bass line, off we went.

When I asked you ahead of this interview what Bad Seeds songs to which you believed you had contributed most and/or felt the closest affinity with, you listed 'Stagger Lee', 'Nature Boy', 'Get Ready For Love', and 'Dig Lazarus Dig'. Why those four specifically?

Well, it's maybe a bit of a misrepresentation on my part. They all just happened to have videos, and I like the songs and I did have a role in co-writing all of them, so I guess those the reasons I suggested them off the top of my head. But I like most of our repertoire, it's really difficult to name favorites.

Jim, here's the inevitable fun question for any member of The Bad Seeds...describe your experience working with Nick Cave. What he is like to work with as a person?

I'll do you better than describing working with him in a sentence; I can do it in one word: 'galvanizing'. Nick keeps the energy level very high in a recording situation. He doesn't like to linger or overwork the music, likes to keep it raw, fresh, unpredictable. He can be impatient I have to say. But he can also be very encouraging and daring.

In many ways, the Bad Seeds have been a remarkably stable and steadfast ensemble over the years, although you've undergone important shifts at the guitar position over the 2000s. First, Blixa leaving, then Mick Harvey after a 32-year association with Nick (which included musical arrangement and management contributions). Mick's departure in particular must have been somewhat of a seismic shift?

Not really a seismic shift stylistically as I think the band always strives to evolve and change from album to album. In terms of personal impact, yes, Mick's departure was strongly felt. But then, that isn't to say that Blixa's departure wasn't strongly felt as well. They were both key members, there from the beginning, so of course there was an impact. But I think musically considerable shifting was already underway.

Mick Harvey was very diplomatic about his departure, initially, but a year later came out in an interview with some pretty disparaging comments about how The Bad Seeds had been operating, especially with regard to how the band was treating "legacy..." songs (to paraphrase, in a "cavalier" manner) during live performance in his last couple of years.

As I stated above, Nick Cave and the Bad Seeds always strive to evolve and change. Sometimes this means challenging preconceptions our fans have of who we are and what we should be doing musically. I think it can and has happened internally as well, where band members see changes that have taken place in the band as something not to their liking and not conforming to their concept of what the band is/was about. I understand that Mick is unhappy with how The Bad Seeds perform some of the older material. I think that ultimately it is a matter of taste. We all take pride in what we do, and I don't think we are in any way presenting a lesser version of the band or the material, just a different one.

(Copyright Roch Parisien/Rocon Communications)

● Stiv Bators, aka Steven John Bator, was born in 1949, in Youngstown, Ohio, USA. Stiv was a frontman/vocalist for Dead Boys, Wanderers and The Lords of The New Church. Dead Boys were pioneers of the NYC punk scene and regulars at CBGB's nightclub, making appearances in several documentary films. The Lords came together in 1981 and were a 'supergroup' of sorts; their output was more refined than that of Dead Boys, and their music was melodic, better structured and played like a supergroup should. On June 3, 1990, Stiv was hit by a taxi while crossing the street in Paris, France. He was taken to hospital after the incident but left before receiving any treatment, claiming that he was fine, but then passed away in his sleep later that evening. Stiv's girlfriend later claimed that she spread some of his ashes across Jim Morrison's Paris grave but also saved some ashes to snort in an attempt to be closer to her late lover!

23

● Pauline Black OBE, the musician, actress, author, filmmaker & broadcaster, was born on October 23, 1953, in Romford, England. She has dedicated four decades to the music scene. Supporting and campaigning for racial equality throughout her work, she describes herself as first and foremost, a singer. A lifelong love of music inspired by punk and reggae artists from the 1970s led Pauline to join The Selecter and a career that has seen her travel across the world. The Selecter went on to become a platinum-selling band and one of the most influential within the 2 Tone music scene, alongside others including The Beat, The Specials and Madness. Pauline Black is one of very few women in the 2-Tone scene – she is often referred to as the Queen of Ska. After releasing their first album, Too Much Pressure, in 1980, the band went on to release five top 40 singles in the UK. Their first single, 'On My Radio', peaked at No.6 in the UK official pop charts. 2025 marks the 45th anniversary of the release of the seminal album *Too Much Pressure*. Their 17th album release in 2023, *Human Algebra*, received rave reviews. Pauline's work on stage and screen has included radio & TV presenting for BBC 6 Music and BBC 4. She has also collaborated with other artists, including Damon Albarn's Gorillaz. Based on her memoir, Pauline co-wrote and was executive producer of the Sky Arts TV-commissioned documentary *Pauline Black: A 2-Tone Story,* which premiered at the BFI London Film Festival that year and has had many UK and international screenings since.

Pauline Black at Bluesfest by Michael Krilich

ISN'T IT IRONIC?
PAULINE BLACK
(The Selecter)

In early autumn 1992, Neol Davies, founder of The Selecter, and I found ourselves reunited in a new incarnation of The Selecter and on tour in the USA. The shows had been brilliant, and it was interesting to see how a new generation of Ska/punk kids celebrated our music and were forming their own homegrown ska bands, known at the time as the 3rd wave of ska, 2-tone having been consigned to the 2nd wave.

Backstage, after a show at The Anaconda Theatre in Isla Vista, California, on September 30th, an over-enthusiastic ska fan, decked out in black and white check & a pork pie hat, with braces on their gummy teeth, showed me a paperback by an author named Fred Seaman, entitled *"The Last Days of John Lennon: A Personal Memoir"*. It appeared that Fred Seaman had been John Lennon's assistant in the last few years of his life. The dog-eared book had a bookmark in it, which he proudly opened to a page that clearly reported in the last few months before his death, John Lennon had been listening to The Selecter's debut album, 'Too Much Pressure'. I was gobsmacked by this information, instantly transported back to December 9th, 1980, when we first heard the news about John Lennon's assassination. John Lennon had died on Dec 8th at 10.50pm outside The Dakota Building in New York, but we didn't hear about it in the UK until the horrifying news hit the media the following morning.

The Selecter had been busy rehearsing at Horizon Studios in Coventry for the past three weeks, and as each of us turned up for work that morning, nobody could speak. To us, John Lennon was the ultimate maverick, a law unto himself; the mere thought that his life had been snuffed out by a gunshot seemed almost unbelievable. But it was true. A pall descended on us, and nobody spoke for a long time. Not everybody had heard, so on each new arrival of a band member through the door, the whole emotional scene & response had to be played out on some grotesque repeat.

As I stood backstage at the Anaconda Theatre with the book, some 12 years later, it was like reliving the scene all over again, but this time with the profound knowledge that The Selecter's music had been appreciated by one of our all-time heroes.

There has been much irony in The Selecter's lengthy career. We had paid our first visit to the USA in May 1980. Many things had given us pause for thought; the most obvious bone of contention was the fact that American people had guns & were not slow in using them to solve an argument or problem. We couldn't believe how many people died due to gun violence when we read some statistics. So, on our return, we wrote a song about it, which we thought was so good that it should be the title of our sophomore album. We'd finished the album by the time of John Lennon's death, and we were in rehearsal for the impending tour. That's where we were on Dec 9th, 1980, when it suddenly dawned on us that the title of the album that we had chosen was 'Celebrate the Bullet'.

How wrong can you be!

⊙ *Mix-Up*, the debut album by Cabaret Voltaire, was released in 1979 on the Rough Trade label. One could argue that this first release by the Cabs was nowhere near the epic albums like *Red Mecca, The Crackdown* or *Voice of America*, but what we get here is an adventure in sound manipulation. Mix-up is right… Indeed, it is; it's a potpourri of ideas and a sonic journey. No, not pop or rock, basically abstract art through a lo-fi recording combination of odd noises, tape loops, distorted guitar, thick bass lines, vocal yelps, a lot of delay and reverb effects. You won't be lying back relaxing to this, though innovative; it'll never be accessible to the general audience. At times it's harsh and abrasive but all the while fascinating.

⊙ In 1981, Haircut 100 dropped their first single, 'Favourite Shirt (Boy Meets Girl)', blending UK funk with a touch of rap and NEW WAVE. The track boasts catchy guitar riffs and groovy horns, reminiscent of Chic's style. Nick Heyward's talent for crafting irresistible hooks shines through, while his band adds a funky vibe to the mix. It's a fantastic introduction to their music.

⊙ Michael Mertens was born in 1953 in Stendal, Germany. Michael is best known as a member of the Dusseldorf-based band Propaganda, and for his ongoing music production work. Classically trained, Michael was integral in the composition of the music on Propaganda's album *A Secret Wish*, a set often heralded as one of the finest examples of synthpop / NEW WAVE electronica. Propaganda has folded and reformed several times; in 2025 Propaganda now only includes just Michael and original formation member Ralf Dörper. They released a *self-titled* album in 2024 to rave reviews.

Michael Mertens (on right) by Petra Gall

A CASE OF MISTAKEN IDENTITY!
MICHAEL MERTENS
(Propaganda)

My entry into the world of pop music was sideways and happened when I met Ralf Dörper. At the time I was employed by the Düsseldorf Symphonic Orchestra as a percussionist. My music room was filled with instruments: a marimba, a vibraphone and an OB-XA Synthesizer. Ralf got really interested in what I was doing, and he told me he was looking for a musical arranger of sorts for an entirely electronic band he and a friend from Cologne, Andreas Thein, just formed. That was in 1981.

To cut a long story short, I became a member of the group and was providing the compositional backbone for what turned out to become the Propaganda album *A Secret Wish*. To avoid misunderstandings, I had never seen a recording studio from the inside before. My sometimes-fragmentary ideas were refined and taken to a very high production level. Trevor Horn and Stephen Lipson did a masterful job at that. Musicians like Andy Richards and many other prolific guests, including Jonathan Sorrell, should be mentioned for helping tremendously to make that album what it finally became. In 1985/86, Propaganda was present in the charts all over Europe. We managed a small tour of around 45-50 concerts, mainly in Europe, 4 gigs in Japan, 2 in Canada, and 4 or 5 on the East Coast of the USA.

When we travelled to Portugal to play in Cascais, near Lisbon, in October 1985, a funny thing happened. We arrived at the airport and were queuing up at the passport counter. Suddenly, behind the gate, there was a commotion. Many people, lights went on, and a camera team started filming. As it turned out, the previous president of Portugal was on the same plane with us. He went over to the camera team and started to talk to them, saying how much he appreciated them coming, expressing his gratitude, but also pointing out that it wasn't necessary for them to make this effort. It took a moment to explain to him that the camera team was actually not there for him but to film the arrival of propaganda in Portugal. We were escorted out of the queue into a special seating area, and our passports were processed while we had the comfort of sitting in a private lounge to relax. That was quite hilarious. A true Beatles moment. I couldn't believe it.

I had fun doing Propaganda; it was a blast. But I also had a lot of fun afterwards. I never much liked the gatekeepers in the music industry, so I was happy to turn elsewhere. Amongst other things, I am busy with my latest work in a project with Herr Dörper.

⦿ Nigel Rennard was born October 23, 1956, in Scarborough, England, and moved with his family to Australia in 1957. From his school years he attended both Melbourne University and Swinburne Tech, which he now regards as "dead ends". Nigel's entry into music & entertainment began with a friend who was the drummer from an emerging NEW WAVE band, The Fiction. As Nigel was learning the industry ropes being involved in band management, he branched into becoming a band booking agent at a major agency. The next string in his bow was being the promoter of the iconic Melbourne venue The Seaview Ballroom. Nigel now owned one of Melbourne's best alternative music shops, Missing Link Records, and started the Man Made Record label. He handled the tours of numerous major local and international acts, including the Dead Kennedys, Screamin' Jay Hawkins, the Cramps, Nick Cave and the Bad Seeds, DRI and Morbid Angel. While all this was going on, he started Bizarre Records, a major importer and distributor of music from around the world. Then came Siren Entertainment, a music & video distributor that introduced Japanese animation to Australia in 1994 and which became the largest and most successful independent video distributor by 1999/2000. In 2022 he re-entered the live music arena with a Leonard Cohen tribute concert, the 50th anniversary of Pink Floyd's Dark Side of the Moon, in March 2023, and the 2024 concert tour of Mike Oldfield's Tubular Bells.

THE CRYSTAL AND SEAVIEW BALLROOMS 1981-1983
NIGEL RENNARD
(Band Manager, Promoter)

My story goes back to visiting the UK for the first time as a 20-year-old at the end of 1976.

The Ramones had recently toured the UK, and from there the "punk rock" explosion really took off. I arrived in November and was an avid reader of NME and Sounds in which the Sex Pistols, The Damned, The Clash, etc., were appearing. I was into the first 4 albums by Roxy Music at that time, but the energy of the punk movement and the explosion of band after band onto the scene was a burst of electricity to the brain.

Coming back to Australia in February 1977, the music scene in all "alternate" forms was also exploding. The Tiger Lounge (Laurie Richards' first venue) was going to be home to performances by The Boys Next Door, Radio Birdman, The Saints and many of the emerging punk and NEW WAVE bands. I was there to see all the above.By mid-1978, after 1 ½ years of a psychology course, one of my fellow students was talking about his band and how they needed a manager. Deal done, with no experience at all. Then the only "true" punk band in Melbourne, La Femme (all members from housing commissions in the northern suburbs), were recommended to me, and another deal was done.

After month after month of badgering the booking agencies to get bookings for my bands, the owner of the Nucleus Entertainment agency grabbed me, took me into his office and offered me a job as a booking agent. I think he just got sick of me sitting in reception!

So, there I was, working as a booking agent for Nucleus Entertainment representing the Dirty Pool agency, where the likes of The Angels, Cold Chisel, Flowers, Mental as Anything & Midnight Oil were part of the roster, along with numerous Melbourne-based bands. This meant I was dealing with the aforementioned Laurie and getting bands into the Tiger Lounge & The Crystal Ballroom along with getting La Femme bookings.

I recall that not long after the assassination of John Lennon, on December 8, 1980, I received a call from Graeme Richmond, the publican who ran The George Hotel, in Fitzroy Street, St Kilda. Why he called me was a mystery to me. I had sold a few bands to Laurie Richards during his time running the Crystal Ballroom, so perhaps he'd heard about me from that connection. In any case, he told me that Laurie would be finishing his time as promoter of the venue in early January 1981 and asked whether I would be interested in meeting with him about becoming a promoter of the venue.

Delores San Miguel had been running "little band" nights during the week when Laurie was running the bigger events in the main room on weekends. Graeme invited both of us to meet with him with the intention of a co-promoter arrangement being reached. What I deduced from that meeting was that Graeme needed the access I could provide, through my contact with the larger local and international tour agents and promoters, to draw them to the venue and maximise the numbers attending, which was obviously good for beer sales. Delores appeared to be reluctant to deal with the agencies and the big dollars they would want for the larger acts. I knew how they operated and the numbers game involved.

At the same time this was going on, I had commenced negotiations with the owner of Missing Link Records, an iconic music store in Melbourne, to purchase the business. So, at the age of 24, two of the greatest opportunities to become immersed in the world of music, a lifelong passion, fell into my lap.

1981 was "the beginning", as Delores and I agreed to run what had to be re-named "The Seaview Ballroom", as Laurie Richards had the "Crystal Ballroom" name registered and was continuing on as a promoter elsewhere, and the Missing Link deal was sealed. By September it was clear that Delores and I could no longer stay co-promoters, and the choice of who was to remain as venue operator was in the hands of the publican. I'm sure he retained me to maintain access to the big acts he wanted, and Delores departed.

Melbourne was alive with artists, musos, fashion designers, film directors and most of the punk and NEW WAVE bands in Australia. The Seaview Ballroom was a magnet for all of them. It was the place where those from Sydney, like The Laughing Clowns, or from Brisbane, like The Go-Betweens, were automatic bookings. It's the place THEY wanted to play.

Quite a number of those artists, musos, fashion designers, film directors, etc. were quite often caught trying to sneak into the venue via the fire escape or simply trying to walk past the entrance without paying. Often those that went on to play in very well-known and influential bands.

It was also the place where more new and emerging bands were offered their first gig. Running Friday and Saturday nights meant at least 4-6 bands were required, and when you are a venue that now has a target audience, it was a necessity to book the unseen and unheard. It's not every week where you can get a major headliner to fill up your room. It could be full-on hardcore punk, it could be electronica, or it could be experimental each and every week, but there was one thing for sure: the bands just kept on emerging, and you could put a night together with ease.

Behind the scenes it was a case of doing what a promoter does: organising the advertising, posters, if required, flyers, the occasional press ads and finding out about who's coming to town and when. Being there from way before the start and being there way after the finish of a night. Inhaling copious amounts of tobacco smoke and dealing with the drug- or alcohol-intoxicated.

For international acts, providing their riders with some bizarre inclusions or partying after the show in some of the upstairs rooms and being the contact or complete non-contact with them. Iggy Pop and John Lydon from PIL, straight through the door with minders, straight to the band room and straight out of the door after the show. The Teardrop Explodes, Echo and the Bunnymen and The Cure were happy to hang around after the shows.

Yes, the sex, yes, the drugs. Toilet cubicles with blood trails on the walls as they hit a rather full vein or the random observation of two people, seemingly meeting for the first time, going hard at it on the cold concrete floor, in the depths of winter, in amongst the empty beer barrels, oblivious to being discovered and going separate ways as they walked out the entrance doors.

There was also a collection of people who rented rooms, so were residents of the hotel. Anything from female and transsexual strippers, who worked up the road at the strip joint, to those with clear mental problems to those with clear drug & alcohol problems. None interested in those that frequented the place on weekends.

Having one of Melbourne's major "alternative" music stores as my "normal" weekday job was a complete tie-in with both the music and the people that frequented the venue. The bands would put out a record; we would put it in the shop. Sometimes we signed them up and released their records, with The Corpse Grinders and The Sacred Cowboys being two of them... regulars at the Ballroom.

If I were going to list the major achievements during my time there, they would be the major overseas tours by Simple Minds, The Cure, Echo & the Bunnymen, PiL, The Gun Club, Iggy Pop, The Fall and Dead Kennedys.

Launching the first Melbourne Fashion show, 'Fashion 82'

Julie Purvis was a 3RRR radio presenter, manager at Inflation and postgraduate student at the Victorian College of The Arts (VCA), and Jillian Burt was a budding music journalist. In 1982 they hatched the idea of an art/fashion parade to be held at the Seaview Ballroom. As fashion illustrator and graphic designer Robert Pearce said, *"It's looking at fashion as the most confrontational of the art forms: you wear it, you have to confront it."*

'Fashion 82' billed a mere seven designers, *"playing with fashion as art and art as fashion"*. From the haute couture of Desbina Collins to the leather uniforms of Peter Bainbridge and the work of four artists, Ian Russell, Tobsha Learner, Maria Kozic and Rosslynd Piggott.

Essendon Airport and comedians Mandy and Melanie Salamon performed.

To top it all, there was a demonstration of how to tease your hair to Pink Flamingo heights compered by Robert Pearce. Tobsha Learner, a VCA graduate, evoked a tribal feel in sync with the 'hideous to the eye' vision of The Birthday Party's Nick the Stripper music video of 1981, shot as a promo by The Rich Kids (Paul Goldman and Evan English).

'Fashion 83'

'Fashion 83' was an altogether more ambitious affair with twenty-one designers, many of them with a growing professional reputation in the fashion world, such as Inars Larcis and Clarence Chai. Louise Neri, barely wearing Jenny Bannister, was held aloft by well-oiled musclemen, and Alannah Hill buffalo-girled her way down the catwalk in Galaxy.

Giving the opportunity to perform to so many new and emerging bands, some that went on to bigger and better things like Lisa Gerrard, from Dead Can Dance, who did their first ever gig there. Having Nick Cave, under his various incarnations, perform every New Year's Eve show from 1981 to 1983.

Running a venue where the cream of the alternative music, fashion, and film communities intermingled and started their journey to bigger things.

Doing my first overseas tour promotion, in 1983, with The Dead Kennedys and having the largest crowd ever at the Seaview Ballroom. It was so packed; one of my favourite memories was hearing a shout from the very back of the room, *"Make another layer!"*

After 40 years it's hard to remember finite details, but this covers the time, the place, the people and specific events. Hopefully this portrays an image of what it was like. If there is anything specific you want to know about and would like a recollection of, I'd be happy to try and remember.

❍ Graeme Revell, an award-winning composer and pioneer of the industrial music genre, was born on this day in Auckland, New Zealand. Revell is renowned for his innovative contributions to the experimental band SPK, whose performances incorporated a unique blend of synthesizers, steel drums, corrugated iron sheets, anvils, and even power tools, creating a distinctive auditory and visual experience. SPK operated under various aliases, including SoliPsiK, SepPuKu, Surgical Penis Klinik, System Planning Korporation, and Sozialistisches Patienten Kollektiv, with Revell adopting the moniker Operator. Since the late 1980s, Revell's compositions have been featured in numerous film scores and television soundtracks, with his first significant achievement being the score for the film *Dead Calm*.

❍ Rock music lost one of its greats in 2017 when George Young passed away! A founding member of the sixties pop group The Easybeats and then Flash & The Pan in the late '70s, George was co-writer of the MEGA hits 'Friday on My Mind' and 'Love Is in the Air' with Harry Vanda; the pair were also AC/DC's early producers. The band featured his younger brothers Malcolm and Angus. With Harry Vanda, the studio project Flash and The Pan slotted right into the zeitgeist of '80s NEW WAVE. 'Hey St. Peter', 'Down Among the Deadmen' and 'Walking in the Rain' are certified classics. Their songs were always melodic, infectiously catchy, and very arty. There's no forgetting though that the 1965 Vanda & Young composition 'Friday on My Mind' has been voted as Australia's "greatest" pop song.

24

❍ The Blue Aeroplanes' debut album *Bop Art,* was available on this day in 1984, with an album launch party held at The Red House; it was Bristol's first warehouse gig. Here's an interesting fusion of post-punk, jazz, and art rock; though a little raw in production, the back music is funky and engaging. The lyric content by Gerard Langley can be at times a little over the top, but knowing the history of the band, that was his intent for the music to be a vehicle for his poetry. Well worth a listen.

◉ Helen Carter was born in 1959, in Marrickville, Sydney, Australia. Helen, "the Queen of funk", plays bass and was a formation member with Do-Re-Mi. When Do-Re-Mi formed in Sydney in 1981, the line-up consisted of vocalist Deborah Conway, Dorland Bray on drums, percussion & backing vocals, guitarist Stephen Philip with Helen on bass guitar and backing vocals. Do-Re-Mi garnered a huge following and, from their inception were regarded as one of Australia's premier and successful POST-PUNK groups. The band was born from the amalgamation of members of The Benders (Conway & Bray), Friction (Carter) and Philip from the legendary Thought Criminals. When Do-Re-Mi disbanded in 1988 Helen moved on to work with the bands Lupi with Stephen Philip and Underfelt. In 2019 Do-Re-Mi reunited with an all-female line-up of Helen, Deborah Conway, Julia Day (drums), Bridie O'Brien (guitar) and Clio Renner (keyboards) for some Australian concert dates, being on the bill with Icehouse, Sunnyboys & Mental as Anything.

FRACTURED PASSION: FRICTION 1978
HELEN CARTER
(Friction, Do-Re-Mi)

I was born in Marrickville, suburban Sydney, in 1959 but grew up in country NSW, where my parents worked on sheep stations. Being remote from the "big smoke", I learnt to read and write via correspondence school. Farm life was great for the young Helen; I loved the freedom to play in the dirt while not being tutored by my loving and rather lenient mother. A move back to the city when I was 6 years old meant no more correspondence schooling, as I was now attending Bondi Beach Public School, where I excelled at being the lunch monitor. Obviously, I loved being bossy! Everyone would have wanted to live beachside in Sydney in the '60s – surf and sun, what could be better? This was in the days when Bondi was a blue-collar suburb, not the swanky multi-million-dollar place it is today. My stepfather was a beach inspector at Bondi, Bronte and Tamarama beaches, so that surf and sun was always nearby. I took a short-lived turn at being a 'surfie chick', and as a long-haired and tanned, bikini-clad girl, I made it as the Daily Telegraph newspaper 'Page 3 Girl'. Those testosterone-loaded teens were now swooning! I soon realised the error of my ways; aged 16, she left high school, left home, left Bondi, and moved into the inner-city Darlinghurst squats to become a feminist and play the bass guitar. I never shaved my armpits again! My boyfriend at the time was the bass player in the Thought Criminals, and he fancied himself as a guitarist. One rehearsal day he shoved his bass towards me and said, "*Here, play this.*" A few notes later, I was smashing out the Pistols' 'Pretty Vacant', and I now had found my creative love. Not long after, I co-founded Friction with Ruby Davies and the late Fiona Warner, sister of Thoughties vocalist Bruce Warner. We wrote a number of songs together and, with Danny Rumour on guitar, recorded lo-fi demos on a dusty radio-cassette player. Remarkably, these recordings survived decades and were released in 2018 by Blank Records. Following Friction's demise, I met Dorland Bray at Brownies Paddington Inn after overhearing Dorland talking to someone about wanting a bass player. Releasing the pushy hairy feminist inside, I immediately butted in and introduced myself as Dorland's new bass player. Soon after, Dorland and Deborah Conway moved from Melbourne to Sydney, Stephen Philip joined the band, and the rest is history.

1978 was a year of noise in Sydney, Australia. Punk bands popped up in every dingy flat along Oxford Street Darlinghurst, and the city's pubs opened their cellars and back rooms where unholy screams were barely heard over three chords and unmic'd drums. In Taylor

Square other noises marked the start of another cultural revolution, the coming out of our gay and lesbian brothers and sisters. Darlinghurst was considered a poor and dirty part of the inner city and very affordable for musicians, artists, budding filmmakers, drag queens and fringe dwellers. It was a strange and exciting mix.

I was 18 and living in the Darlinghurst squats known as The Compound. I was invited to move in by Ruby, an artist, photographer, and drummer who was a mentor and inspiration. Our house was a two-storey terrace with a shared backyard that connected the other houses. Some handy residents had hooked up the block to electricity. Ruby had made the house quite nice, and there was an adequate kitchen. I can't remember if there was a bathroom, but I do remember showering in an open bathroom where other compound residents went about their day, barely noticing the naked person in full view. I slept on a mattress at the front of the terrace. I stuffed blankets under the French doors to keep out the noise, dirt, and smell of the traffic on Stanley Street, just feet away. I got scabies. I lost a lot of weight and survived on the dole. Ah, those were the days!

Ruby and I started playing in the upstairs bedroom of the terrace, decorating the room with egg cartons as was the practice at the time, in a vain attempt to contain the noise. The floorboards were beyond wonky, and we wanted to turn up our amps. Bob Nimmo lived in the squat with us; he ran the Day Street rehearsal studio space, which doubled as a screen-printing business. I'd only recently started playing bass, and Bob helped me buy my 1976 Fender Precision after my beloved Gibson EB3 was stolen from the squat by a woman called Johanna, who blamed me for the theft of her camera. My parents had bought me the EB3 and then very generously found the money for the Precision. It was a lot of money even then.

We started rehearsing at Day Street and auditioning guitarists. We invited Fiona Warner, Thought Criminals singer Bruce Warner's sister, to sing with us. Danny Rumour, who would go on to form Sekret Sekret and The Cruel Sea, played guitar with us for a while, and we recorded some original and cover songs at rehearsals. Originals included 'Death Cult 911', 'Fractured Passion' and 'Help Me Make It Thru the Nite'. Later, we found a guitarist called Carol who co-wrote some of our original songs.

Friction played a handful of shows at places like The Royal Hotel Bondi, the Sussex Hotel (whose publican at the time, Stella, earned a legendary status), Garibaldi's and a few others. We often got ourselves into trouble simply by being women in a band, especially in places like the front bar at The Sussex, which we shared with fat, drunk and narky union members who thought women should fuck off back to the cleaning and cooking. Stella often had to calm these blokes down in our defence. It was the time of our lives, and we felt strong, creative and in control, making noise and changing our world.

I went on to play bass with Do Re Mi. Ruby is a respected teacher and photographer.

● The debut single 'King' b/w 'The American Way' by British '80s synthpop band Hohokam was in the racks in 1984. Produced by Gary Numan and released on his label Numa Records, the band members were Dave Earl (guitar), Steve Devier (vocals), Tony Alum (drums), and George Kamm (synths & bass). The single received little airplay and minor sales and is regarded today as somewhat of a lost gem. When Kamm left the group, Gary Numan's engineer Andy Reilly joined the band as drummer, and Tony Alum took over keyboard duties, then Devier left with Skip Collins coming in as vocalist. It was this line-up that the hard-to-find *Seven Deadly Sins* album.

● Rowland Stuart Howard, born in Melbourne, Australia, in 1959, was an influential musician in the Australian post-punk scene. In the mid-1970s, "Rowie" played guitar for the bands The Young Charlatans and The Boys Next Door, which later became The Birthday Party, where he remained until they broke up in 1983. He then joined Crime & The City Solution for a year before forming These Immortal Souls in 1987. Howard collaborated with many other artists, including Lydia Lunch, Henry Rollins, KaS Product, Barry Adamson,

Frank Tovey (of Fad Gadget), and Nick Cave and the Bad Seeds. His impact on Australian post-punk was immense and led to a laneway in St Kilda being named Rowland S. Howard Lane in his honour. Tragically, Howard passed away in 2009 at the age of 50 while awaiting a liver transplant to treat hepatocellular carcinoma and cirrhosis.

Rowland S Howard by Petra Gall

o Ignatius Jones was born Juan Ignacio Trápaga Esteban in Manila, The Philippines, on October 24, 1957. Ignatius was the frontman of the NEW WAVE – shock rockers Jimmy and the Boys, who came into being in the mid-1970sand existed until 1982. With Jones and Joylene Hairmouth (William O'Riordan) as the mainstay central figures, the band was formed from members of the exclusive private schools Riverview and Cranbrook. They exhibited performances that included choreographed simulated sex, sadomasochism, self-mutilation, and audience abuse; they were out to shock, and shock they did! Jones was double-jointed, and the positions he achieved on stage had the audience aghast, earning blood-curdling screams. The bold lyricism of the Jimmy and the Boys setlist too held shock value; 'Product of Your Mind', the cover of The Kinks' 'I'm Not Like Everybody Else' and 'They Won't Let My Girlfriend Talk to Me' garnered high rotation on radio and club dancefloors. In 1982 Ignatius moved out of pub gigs to the theatre stage, initially performing as Eddie and Dr Scott in the Australian review of *The Rocky Horror Show.* He then signed a record deal with Warner Bros. for limited releases; the Steve Kilbey-penned 'Like A Ghost' fared well, peaking at No.83 nationally. Ignatius would move into performance and event design, most notably with David Atkins, as the opening and closing ceremonies creative directors for the *2000 Sydney Olympics* and *The Man from Snowy River: Arena Spectacular,* and he was the creative director of the annual multimedia festival Vivid Sydney from 2011 to 2019. After a short illness Ignatius died on May 7, 2024, at home in the Philippines.

o The debut LP *Jumpcut* by the synthpop band Man Jumping was released in 1985 on Bill Nelson's Cocteau Records label. The five-piece band, comprised of keyboardists and a drummer, ambitiously crafted a clever album of synthpop and electronic music. The track 'Belle Dux on the Beach' seems to pay homage to Yellow Magic Orchestra with its diverse ethnic rhythms. 'In the Jungle' is another standout, driven by an addictive bassline and danceable groove that evokes a minor comparison to the rhythmic interplay of David Byrne and Brian Eno on their collaboration *My Life in the Bush of Ghosts.* Overall, *Jumpcut* showcases Man Jumping's creative range across synth-driven pop.

25

o In 1959, Christine Joy Amphlett, also known as 'Chrissy', was born and raised in Geelong, Victoria. After a chance encounter at the Sydney Opera House, Chrissy and future manager/bassist Jeremy Paul met guitarist Mark McEntee and discussed forming a group. They were later joined by drummer Richard Harvey and keyboardist Bjarne Ohlin. Together, they worked hard performing in various city pubs. Chrissy's unique style, including wearing a school uniform and fishnet stockings, made her hugely popular and earned her the reputation of being someone to watch. The Divinyls gained success with their debut biographical single 'Boys in Town', which received plenty of airplay and reached the top 10 nationally. They continued their success with follow-up singles 'Science Fiction' (13) and 'Pleasure and Pain' (11). In 1991, The Divinyls reached their peak with 'I Touch Myself', which became No.1 in Australia, No.4 in the USA, and No.10 in the UK. Sadly, Chrissy passed away at the age of 53 on April 21, 2013, after battling breast cancer and multiple sclerosis. It is worth noting that Chrissy was a cousin of the famous Australian pop singer from the 1960s, Little Pattie.

O Victor DeLorenzo was born in 1954 in Milwaukie, USA, and was a founding member of the Violent Femmes. The Violent Femmes, oddly enough, often labelled as folk-punk, captured the essence of teen angst with extraordinary precision; they were raw and quirky. With that, the trio's music initially found little commercial success but was still grasped by a throng of followers, creating a somewhat cult status. The group formed in Milwaukee, Wisconsin, in the early '80s and comprised singer/guitarist Gordon Gano, bassist Brian Ritchie, and, of course, percussionist Victor, who was famed for his use of a beer keg.

O Richard Lloyd was born in Pittsburgh, USA, in 1951. Richard is an American guitarist, singer and songwriter, best known as a founding member of the band Television. Television was born out of the mid-'70s New York rock scene that produced the Ramones, Talking Heads, Blondie, et al. Their critically acclaimed debut album *Marquee Moon,* released in February 1977, had Richard and Tom Verlaine laying down contemporary punk power chords in a progressive jazz-inspired interplay that marked it as one of the seminal albums of post-punk. It's a multi-layered masterpiece recording, with melodic lines and counter-melodies that was unlike anything before. There are no three-minute throwaway songs on *Marquee Moon*; it's unique for the time, with the title cut and 'Torn Curtain' lengthy numbers, both close to 10 minutes each; here they show off the band's sharp musicianship. *Marquee Moon* is one of those albums that not many people have heard of but everybody with a credible music collection should own. In 1978 Television folded, and Richard entered a successful solo career. 1979 saw the album *Alchemy,* but there was a halt through the early '80s due to his well-documented drug addiction. He returned with *Field of Fire* in 1985, which was recorded in Sweden with the local band Lolita Pop. Television reformed in 1992, and Richard remained until 2007. Lloyd published his memory book in 2017. The book is titled '*Everything Is Combustible: Television, CBGB's and Five Decades of Rock and Roll'*.

AN INTERVIEW RICHARD LLOYD
(Television)
Interviewed by Roch Parisien (Roch Parisien's Rocon Communications)

From the '70s to the present, a lot of good young players who have been influenced by "classic" blues-based rock end up in bands that are little more than the current decade's "tributes" to those bands from the '60s and '70s. How were you guys in Television able to take those influences and somewhat subvert them, contort them differently, and do something original with it?

Frankly, in Television, I don't think we thought we had any influences, and we certainly didn't give a shit if someone compared us to anyone else. I only heard the Velvet Underground record once when someone took me after school to a place where they were shooting up to it – and it didn't look very appealing. I had listened to all sorts of music, but basically loved electric Chicago blues, psychedelic guitar, The Rolling Stones, and so many other things I could hardly list them, but I never learned anything of that. When I helped to form Television, I could not play a single cover song. Really. I refused whenever anyone tried to show me the newest hot guitar lick or song, because I didn't want it to influence me unduly. We were just two guitars, bass and drums like kids that ran away to the circus and were dead serious both about being dead serious about having fun…if that makes any sense.

The classic dual-guitar approach to rock, bands like the Allman Brothers and Derek & the Dominos say, were again blues-based in structure and feel. How did what you and Tom Verlaine develop differ from that, from a lay-person's technique approach?

This seems to me as an unanswerable question. It's not up to me and shouldn't be up to me to analyse and dissect something that is and was an organic whole. Unless you want me to examine an organic hole. That would be different.

My music journalist colleague Stephen Thomas Erlewine wrote at allmusic.com that you created "an influential new guitar vocabulary. While guitarists Tom Verlaine and Richard Lloyd liked to jam, they didn't follow the accepted rock structures for improvisation – they removed the blues while retaining the raw energy of garage rock, adding complex, lyrical solo lines that recalled both jazz and rock, with its angular rhythms and fluid leads…" Can you live with that?

I like what the president of Atlantic records said as I was passing close by on my way to the bathroom – a fellow named Jerry Wexler really wanted to sign us but his boss had to okay it – Ahmet Ertegun. I heard him say, "*Jerry! I can't sign this band. This is not Earth music!*" Maybe Tom and I are from a different planet, or rather different planets. I'm not kidding. That's as good of an answer as the one your journalist friend wrote. Television was extraterrestrial. I mean, we are beaming 'I Love Lucy' out into the Universe. From my perspective, that's just as wacky…

How did you and Tom work out who was going to play lead from song to song?

Tom and I always had a certain rivalry as to who was going to play the solos. I always played the leads while Tom was singing and then we "fought" over the solos, sometimes Tom doing one night and me doing the next and then deciding. The rivalry, if you can call it that, could be riveting, because it was like watching two sports cars, like Maseratis, sitting next to each other going the speed limit. Even when they are parked, people look at them because they know that they can go 225 miles an hour easily. So, it was like being two sports cars on stage and you had to pay attention to find out what was going on. On the first record, we put down who did what solo, but not who played what leads, which were mostly myself.

How did you and Tom first meet? Do I correctly understand that [eventual Television manager] Terry Ork brought you to see him at an audition night at a NYC club called Reno Sweeney's?

That is true. I saw Tom play three songs at an audition night at a club in the village that catered to gay Broadway singers – and I turned to Terry during the second song and told him that if he could put the two of us together, he would create something memorable, although 'memorable' is not the word I used. So, I asked Terry to ask Richard to ask Tom to come see me, which he did, along with Richard, and we discussed putting a band together. I played them some stuff, and Tom played some stuff. I was a very quick study when I saw something played in front of me, so when Tom played something and handed me the guitar, I could replicate it, or bend it or warp it or whatever. So, Tom and Richard went off in a corner and whispered blah blah blah, came back and said "*Okay*", let's go for it. I relinquished the role of leadership only because I preferred a more rock'n'roll lifestyle, whereas Tom was straight as a plank and only had something like three drinks a year, and he had a good idea about being serious about the music, as was I. But I had much more to do with the actual building of the CBGBs scene, because Tom never went there unless we were actually going to play.

I knew we needed both, not just a place to play but some kind of historical burgeoning movement around us. That was absolutely crucial and since Tom wasn't going to participate in that part, I took it.

How did you guys manage to convince Hilley Kristal to give you a shot at converting his "country, bluegrass & blues" club (CBGBs) to present new alternative rock music?

We knew we needed a place to play regularly, and we knew it had to be some kind of dive where no one else would really want to play. Tom spotted it while walking to rehearsal and he and I went up and visited Hilly who was straightening out the awning. He showed us around and we asked him if he was going to have music and he said yes, country blues and bluegrass and other music for undernourished gormandizers. We asked him if we could play there but when we told him we played a strange kind of rock'n'roll he said no. He grilled us about some other questions, like where to move the stage, etc..

The next day Terry Ork and I went up without Tom and convinced Hilly to let us play on his worst night, Sunday. Terry guaranteed that he would make money at the bar promising to bring only alcoholics. So we got a show there and at the end of it we each got a dollar, which made us professional musicians…sort of.

I read somewhere that you guys actually built the first stage at CBGBs...true?

I don't think we built the first stage there, because there had been other people who discussed playing there before us, mostly acoustic music. But before we did play, we most definitely moved the stage, halfway down the club on the right-hand side in three tiers, so that the drums could be on the top tier, and you had a built-in drum riser. Then you could put the amps on the second tier and stand on the first tier, singing and playing and falling down (and getting back up maybe). That was the reason the stage was three layers or levels. Then we decided that there should never be more than two bands on any given evening but that each band would play twice – one, because we wanted to play more than we were able to otherwise, and second, it came from the idea of the movie double feature. This meant that the two bands would cross-pollinate audiences and make it more likely for people to stay in the club rather than go someplace else. It worked, but it took something like a year and a half before we started to pack the place. A lot of people wouldn't come down – too scared of urine. It used to drip down through the ceiling sometimes.

Yeewww!! So, the influential scene that built up around that club with you, The Ramones, Blondie, Patti Smith, Talking Heads, etc.; what was the perception being inside the eye of that particular hurricane? Were you aware from early on that something important was happening, or did the full magnitude only develop later in hindsight?

I don't know about anyone else, but I knew exactly what I was doing, what my intentions were for the club, the band and the scene and it happened exactly as I wanted it to. Arrogant smaragant, I had a certain quality of what best might be called magnetic or magical force, and although I never laid claim or wanted credit for it, it is far enough now in the past and I am old enough that I might as well reveal something of what was going on inside of my own conscious intentions. So I absolutely knew that something extraordinarily important was happening, or I would've stormed the gates of fucking hell and pulled down heaven to make it happen.

Amongst the bands themselves, was it more a sense of community and support, or was it highly competitive? Or were there cliques/sides chosen perhaps..?

The answer to your question is: extremely both!

Do you think the scene created in NY in the 1970s could ever happen again?

Even though the notion that lightning never strikes twice in the same place has been scientifically proven to be incorrect, because of the factors involved what happened in the late 70s in New York will never happen again, in my opinion. There have been scenes in Minneapolis, Athens Georgia, Seattle, Los Angeles, etc., but historically none of them match the historical integrity and force of pivot that the scene we created in New York had on the entire history of musical enterprise.

(Copyright Roch Parisien/Rocon Communications)

● Peter Coyle was born in Liverpool, England, in 1962. In 1982, Coyle and Jeremy Kelly formed the band The Lotus Eaters. Their debut single, 'The First Picture of You', became a hit in the UK, peaking at No.15, as well as in other European countries like France, Italy, and Spain. The song's success landed Coyle and Kelly, the vocalist and guitarist, respectively, on some magazine covers. However, when the group released their first album, *No Sense of Sin*, a year later, much of their initial fanbase had lost interest. With their airy, rich, and ornate sound, The Lotus Eaters had a similar style to the band China Crisis. They were a group of British young men dressed in bright long-sleeved shirts, thin dark neckties, and hair slicked with gel. This was at a time when goth culture, known for its spikes, skulls, and black velvet outfits, was also prevalent. The Lotus Eaters' cheerful sound alienated the gloomy goth scene. Captivating and sometimes haunting, their ability to enthrall listeners seemed to stem from their focus on emotional themes rather than intellectual ones.

● On the 25th of October 1980, New Order performed their inaugural concert as a four-member band at The Squat in Manchester. This significant event took place nearly three months after Peter Hook, Stephen Morris, and Bernard Sumner showcased their untitled debut performance at Manchester's Bach Club. The inclusion of Gillian Gilbert as a keyboardist-guitarist marked the completion of the New Order line-up. They would soon propel themselves to the top echelon of POST-PUNK bands.

26

● The Beat's *self-titled* debut album was released in the United States on October 26, 1979. This American band should not be confused with the British band of the same name, as their musical styles are completely different. The US band's album showcases power pop at its finest, in contrast to the UK band's Ska sound. The songs are brief and punchy, brimming with infectious melodies, hooks, and boundless energy. Tracks like 'Different Kind of Girl', 'You Won't Be Happy', and 'Let Me into Your Life', written by Eddie Money, are prime examples of the record's catchy songcraft.

● On October 26, 1979, Killing Joke's debut single 'Turn to Red'/'Nervous System'/'Are You Receiving' was released. The three-tracker missed out on charting, but in time it became much sought after by completists. To make it tricky for collectors, it came out as a promotional (not for sale) and non-promo. It was also on a 12" four-track E.P. Then, just in time for Xmas, it was in the record stores as a 12-inch on December 14

● The debut album *Steps in Time* by King was available October 26, 1984. Born out of the remnants of The Reluctant Stereotypes, vocalist Paul King formed an outfit named after himself, adding to the royalists of the period, Queen and Prince. Holding a very diverse number of textures, the album's singles are the strongest, sparkling, infectious and very cool dancefloor synthpop. 'Won't You Hold My Hand Now' went top 25 in the UK, but what missed by most was 'Fish".

● The groundbreaking electronic music group Liaisons Dangereuses released their *self-titled* debut album on this date in 1981. Adopting their name from an 18th-century French epistolary novel, the band came together in Düsseldorf, Germany, and consisted of Beate

Bartel, who handled effects and synthesizers (and was also a member of Einstürzende Neubauten and Mania D), Christo Haas, who played synthesizers (and was also in the group D.A.F.); and vocalist Krishna Goineau from Barcelona. Together they created a dark, hypnotic, rhythmic blend of electronic music. Their album intrigues and rightly earns them a place among the best artists in the genre. An undeniable classic.

O Loop's debut album *Heaven's End* hit record stores on this day in 1987. The psychedelic POST-PUNK band from Surry, England, created a hypnotic, dark sonic atmosphere on the album, channeling influences like Hawkwind and Can into droning, melody-free soundscapes. Rather than relying on catchy hooks, *Heaven's End* pulls listeners into its foreboding world through textures and rhythms designed to permeate open minds.

O Natalie Anne Merchant was born in 1963 in Jamestown, USA. As a 17-year-old Natalie joined 10,000 Maniacs and became the main vocalist after the departure of Teri Newhouse. Natalie not only brought a stunning vocal delivery but also the ability to write poignant topical lyrics. Natalie remained with the band until 1993, being part of 6 studio albums and 1 live album. Natalie has gone on to record 7 solo albums, with her debut, *Tigerlily* going 5 times platinum in the USA; it held 3 top 20 singles! Natalie has been very charitable to causes involving women and children and has volunteered in Harlem's homeless shelters and is a member of Artists Against Racism.

O Keith Julian Strickland was born in 1953 in Athens, Georgia. Keith is known to us as one of the founding members of The B-52's. Keith was originally the band's drummer but switched to guitar after the death of guitarist Ricky Wilson in 1985. He also plays keyboards and bass guitar and has occasionally provided backing vocals.

27

O *Steeltown*, Big Country's second album release, reached No.1 on the UK charts in 1984. This remains the band's sole chart-topping LP. Many argue it surpasses the band's debut album both lyrically and musically. Loaded with impassioned, wailing guitars, the production quality exceeds that of the first album. Lyrically, *Steeltown* explores darker political themes, offering keen social commentary on the struggles of the British working class. Yet the music remains triumphant - bombastic and rampant, with ingeniously controlled tempos. For Big Country, *Steeltown* marked a career peak, both musically and lyrically.

Crime & The City Solution by Petra Gall

O *Room of Lights*, the debut studio album by Crime & the City Solution, was released in 1986 on Mute Records. Crime & The City Solution formed as an offshoot of Nick Cave & The Bad Seeds, with Bad Seed members Mick Harvey and Rowland S. Howard contributing to the writing and performance. Their dark, chiming guitars and Bronwyn Adams' haunting violin create a tense, film noir atmosphere reminiscent of Joy Division. While evoking the blues, *Room of Lights* crafts a tighter and more coherent POST-PUNK sound than The Bad Seeds' early work. Largely, it's an impressive debut.

⊙ Peter Dodd was born on October 27, 1955. Pete as a guitarist-vocalist was part of the original Thompson Twins lineup formed in 1977 that consisted of Dodd, Tom Bailey on bass and vocals, John Roog on guitar, and Jon Podgorski (known as "Pod") on drums. Dodd and Roog left The Thompson Twins in 1982 and stayed with a side-project, Big View, a band that also had included Tom Bailey. Big View recorded one single, 'August Grass', then folded. Today Pete lives in Chesterfield, England, and works as a freelance journalist.

⊙ Simon Le Bon was born in Bushey, England, on October 27, 1958. Well known as the vocalist for Duran Duran, he was also a founding member of Arcadia. Duran Duran went to the top of the UK charts in 1983 with the single 'Is There Something I Should Know' and had over 20 other UK Top 40 singles. In the USA in 1984 they had a No.1 single with 'The Reflex', and the same year 'The Wild Boys' went top 5 around the globe.

⊙ The debut single 'Slave Girl' by The Lime Spiders from Sydney, Australia, was in the record racks of your favourite store on October 27, 1984. The single was the second release following the well-received *25th Hour* EP the previous year. The band was and has been continually fronted by the hyperactive Mick Blood. They earned a reputation for flat-out, energetic, live performances, and that vibrance of their power pop POST-PUNK is well captured on this single. The line-up over the years has somewhat seen a revolving door; they earned the honour of having the first video clip played on the long-lasting ABC-TV program RAGE with 'Weirdo Libido'.

⊙ Pulsallama had a brief existence; the multi-membered, all-girl group out of Manhattan, USA, only had two single releases, and the first, 'The Devil Lives in My Husband's Body' b/w 'Umgawa Pt.II', was in the racks in 1982. Described as "*13 girls fighting over a cowbell*", the sound is percussive and chaotic. The Slits manager Dick O'Dell gave them an avenue via his Y Records label, also the label for Pigbag, Shriekback and The Pop Group. They achieved great exposure as an opener for The Clash on their 1982 '*Combat Rock*' tour. But bitchiness and infighting led to the band dissolving in early 1983.

28

⊙ On October 28, 1986, music retailers were filling their shelves with the Close Lobsters' debut single 'Going to Heaven to See If It Rains' from Paisley, Renfrewshire, Scotland. Following the success of 'Firestation Towers', featured on the *C86 New Musical Express* compilation, the band secured a contract with Fire Records, resulting in the release of three albums and multiple singles. Despite disbanding and reuniting multiple times, they returned to the studio in 2019 and unveiled the album *Post Neo Anti: Arte Povera in the Forest of Symbols* in 2020.

⊙ The *Days of Wine and Roses* debut album by The Dream Syndicate was released in 1982. Take a touch of Velvet Underground, a gallop of Crazy Horse, a thrash of The Clash, soup it with some POST-PUNK and '60s garage, and there you have it. Jagged guitar, bits of feedback and immediate vocals make *The Days of Wine and Roses* a highly desirable album. At times it's abrasive and very psychedelic, but every time you find it an absorbing listen.

⊙ The debut album *Monarchie und Alltag* (Monarchy and Daily Life) by the German POST-PUNK band Fehlfarben from Düsseldorf was released on October 28, 1980. Firmly rooted in the Neue Deutsche Welle movement, this classic POST-PUNK record contains hints of Gang of Four, Joy Division, and Killing Joke, making for an intriguing listen. However, the album is hampered somewhat by Paul Hein's monotonous vocal delivery, which rarely rises above a shouted chant. The atmospheric 'Paul Ist Tot' stands out as the most nuanced and subtly crafted track.

○ A press release was issued on October 28, 1982, that The Jam would be splitting after their current tour. A comment from Paul Weller was, *"We need to explore new musical possibilities"*. Their last appearance was at The Brighton Centre on December 11, 1982. In the new year Weller teamed up with keyboardist Mick Talbot to form The Style Council, Bruce Foxton went solo and soon had a minor hit with 'Freak', and Rick Buckler formed Time UK.

○ Spencer P. Jones was born in Te Awamutu, New Zealand, in 1956. Spencer, as a vocalist, a guitarist, and a songwriter, earned celebrity status via his band, The Johnnys, who pioneered 'cow-punk' in the southern antipodes. After moving to Australia in the mid-seventies, he went on to work with some excellent, if largely unknown, Australian outfits, "paying his dues" on the Aussie pub circuit. It was with The Johnnys, though, that Spencer really stamped himself as a force; the release of their debut album *Highlights of a Dangerous Life,* ensured the band would be known internationally. 1989 saw The Johnnys split, and Spencer moved onto Beasts of Bourbon, a band with its own form of blues rock that was fronted by the enigmatic Tex Perkins. Spencer was a real journeyman musician, always turning up with different bands in different places. Some of the bands he worked with include Olympic Sideburns, Paul Kelly and The Coloured Girls, Hell to Pay and The Sacred Cowboys. Spencer released several solo albums, mostly flying under the commercial radar, but *The Last Gasp,* produced by Tony Cohen, is definitely worth seeking out. It was quoted as being a record where *"you can feel the smoky bar rooms this music was born in; the atmosphere here is thick with music and attitude."* In 2018 Spencer announced he had been diagnosed with inoperable liver cancer in March and entered palliative care. He died on 21 August 2018.

○ Drummer Stephen Morris, born on October 28, 1957, has made significant contributions to the music industry. He is renowned for his drumming skills in bands like Joy Division, New Order, and The Other Two (alongside his wife Gillian Gilbert). Morris's precise and mechanical drumming style played a crucial role in creating the atmospheric sound of Joy Division. Despite being primarily a percussionist, he also showcases his talent on keyboards and is the mastermind behind the programmed sequencing that defines New Order's iconic recordings, including the timeless track 'Blue Monday'. Interestingly, during the mid-eighties, Morris even lent his drumming skills to Echo and the Bunnymen while New Order was recording in the same studios. Hence, it is Morris's drumming you hear on Echo's 'Soul Kitchen'.

○ William Reid was born in Glasgow, Scotland, in 1958. In 1983 William and younger brother Jim formed The Jesus and Mary Chain, producing a "wall of sound" and acquiring the label from many as the premier 'POST-PUNK outfit'. Their debut album, *Psychocandy,* was released to critical acclaim in 1985, and they went on to release five more studio albums before disbanding in 1999. They reunited in 2007 and have been constantly gigging ever since.

29

○ Frankie Goes to Hollywood released the first of their two albums, *Welcome to the Pleasuredome,* on 29th October 1984. This is such an interesting album, full of oomph, classy production, hooks, and style. We all remember the hit, 'Relax', but this album has much more to offer than that little bit of '80s nostalgia. "Overhyped", "controversial", "ambitious", "progressive", "weird" and "mediocre" are some of the adjectives used to describe FGTH. Nonetheless, WTTP is an aural journey, a potpourri of feels, textures, samples and even impersonations. The music presentation is experimental and diverse; we get a great mix of pop music and a plethora of styles and techniques. The remakes of older songs in 'Ferry', 'War', and 'Born to Run' are worthy of the effort and are arguably better than the originals. The original compositions, ranging from the '80s pop style 'Relax' and 'Two Tribes' to the melodic epic 'Welcome to the Pleasure Dome', are massive. The recording quality is excellent, as is the production. And speaking of the production, that is where this album truly excels. There is a spacious depth to the melodies and instrumentation that was not common to the minimalist production of most '80s pop music. This recording is one of the best examples of the use of the Fairlight CMI, but the credit here lies with the album's producer, Trevor Horn. Horn was responsible for the recording's depth and structure, giving it his signature expansive mood. Overall, this is an excellent album, one that can be listened to over and again, offering the listener something new every time. It was and will remain a classic, arguably the epitome of synthpop. It still has an undated feel about it and is worth a listen again today, if you have it!

⦿ Stephen Luscombe was born in Middlesex, England, in 1954. Steven was a foundation member and keyboardist for Blancmange. Essentially a duo with Neil Arthur, Blancmange initially found some minor success in 1982 with the release of the single 'God's Kitchen' b/w 'I've Seen the Word'; it went to No.65 in the UK. It was the release of their next single, 'Living on The Ceiling', which reached No.7 on the UK singles chart, that earned them international success.

⦿ Men At Work hit the top of the US singles chart with 'Who Can It Be Now?'. It was the first of their two number ones, with 'Down Under' topping the list later that year.

⦿ Roger O'Donnell was born on this day in 1955, in London, England. Roger is a highly regarded keyboardist who made his first major stage appearance as a 21-year-old with the legendary Arthur Brown. In 1983 Roger played keyboards on tour with Thompson Twins, moving to part of the line-up with The Psychedelic Furs and then Berlin. Roger joined The Cure in 1987 with the departure of Lol Tolhurst and co-wrote much of the acclaimed album *Disintegration*. As a solo artist, he has released over a dozen albums.

Einar & Bjork - Kukl by Petra Gall

⦿ Einar Orn, aka Einar Örn Benediktsson, is from Iceland but was born in Copenhagen, Denmark, in 1962. Einar was a vocalist and played trumpet with The Sugarcubes. In the days after The Sugarcubes, he also worked in concert promotion on gigs for Björk, The Prodigy, Fugees and Massive Attack. In Iceland, he was one of the founders of Reykjavík's first cybercafe, The Siberia Cafe: *"We were too early. Those who knew what it was all about preferred to do their internet hacking at home"*. Since 2001 he has been active with Curver Thoroddsen in Ghostigital, releasing several albums. Currently he has been active as a visual artist working in cross-disciplinary media.

FROM BAD TASTE TO TASTY
EINAR ÖRN
(Kukl, The Sugarcubes)

So, what an idea to ask me to write something from the past. Currently, I am more concerned with the present and what I should do next in my art since visual art is now my major mainstay. Am I a 'has-been'? No, I would not say that. I have been active in music and visual arts since 1981, so there's no point in stopping now. When it comes down to writing, I needed prompting; thankfully, Michael has been patiently applying to me.

It all began in March 1981, when I, Bragi, Fridrik and Asgeir set up a rehearsal for a band due to play the day after at a college concert evening. I was going to do noises with a flanger or some other gadgets. I remember that the only instrument which intrigued me at one of the local music instrument shops was a Roland Space Echo. I thought that it had endless possibilities and a Höfner bass, just like Paul played. Three years ago, I finally bought a Space Echo. Anyway, that first rehearsal day, Asgeir handed me a microphone and said, "*Sing*", and sing I did. We made 9 songs that day; they were from 9 seconds long to 90 seconds long. It fitted. Wire and Swell Maps had short songs, so why not us? This band was called Purrkur Pillnikk. It was August 1986 when I returned from London from my studies. I was lucky enough to have friends in London who were members of punk bands: Flux of Pink Indians, with whom I played trumpet on a tour, and CRASS. My trumpet playing was wicked; at least some thought that, as I was the only one getting bottled on stage at ULU. Bragi is returning from Spain, Friðrik is in Reykjavík, and we start hanging around at Nesvegur. We are in a cultural limbo, but our discussions lead us to the conclusion that good taste was killing everything. It was probably Thor who pointed out what Picasso said, "*Good taste is the killer of creativity*." We formed a company, a publishing house which would publish our garbage; who else would? We called the company Smekkleysa SM (Bad Taste SM). We realised that to achieve that we needed to be a pop band, so we put together a band. With the addition of Björk Guðmundsdóttir, the band would later be The Sugarcubes, and we got a break with our first single, 'Ammæli' b/w 'Birthday'. That B-side became the single of the week with both Melody Maker and NME, and what followed was a whirlwind journey around the world. We met loads of people. Different people. Some of them are my best friends today. We had our peculiarities; we did not really take no for an answer, so we managed to do a lot of things over a relatively short time.

AND we are still remembered... at least in some quarters!

◉ Richard Ploog was born in 1962 in Adelaide, Australia, where he established his formative years as a drummer with bands such as Loose Kicks, Exhibit A and The Dagoes. In 1981 Richard joined The Church as the drummer and backing vocalist; he was present for half of the recording of their debut album *Of Skins and Heart*. He stayed until 1990, touring and recording six albums. He sat behind the kit for Damien Lovelock's debut solo album, *Wig Wig Wig Wig World*, in 1988 and with fellow The Church member Peter Koppes in 1991, in the band The Well to tour and record the albums *From the Well* and *Iridescence*. Since 2014 Richard has been part of Groom Epoch, who have to date released three highly regarded albums.

30

◉ Guadalcanal Diary from Georgia, in the USA, had their debut album *Walking in the Shadow of the Big Man,* on the record store shelves on October 30, 1984. Jangle pop with a country rock, R.E.M. flavour, this full album set followed their 1983 4-track, independent EP *Watusi Rodeo,* and it proves that they were tragically overlooked internationally. The album opener 'Trail of Tears' and the anthemic 'Fire from Heaven' are far from forgettable. The variation within this album is wide and varied; there's the country rock styled 'Ghosts on the Road', the twangy surf-rock of 'Watusi Rodeo', and the '60s Byrds-coloured 'Why Do the Heathen Rage'. The instrumental title track is an absolute gem, moody and atmospheric. Worth seeking out.

● The debut 3-track 12" single by the Canadian synthpop outfit Rational Youth was on the shelves October 30, 1981. The A-side held 'I Want to See the Light' and included an instrumental version, 'Light Instrumental', on the B-side. Minimalist and somewhat giving a nod to OMD, Rational Youth was driven was by Tracy Howe and had releases as late as 2014, the last being a collaboration with Psyche, doing an electronic version of AC/DC's 'Thunderstruck'

● Ken Testi was born on October 30, 1950, in Taunton, England. Ken is best known as an impresario who was a co-creator of the iconic Liverpool music venue Eric's. Ken delved into event promotion and band management while still at school with the band Ibex, being the first of the notable acts he was involved with. Ibex is famed as being the band that had Farrokh 'Fred' Bulsara as frontman-vocalist in 1969. Ibex had a name change to Wreckage, as did Fred Bulsara, to Freddie Mercury! The early '70s saw Ken manage the "*only Liverpool band that mattered other than The Beatles*", Deaf School, who he still manages to this day. Eric's opened on September 24, 1976, and closed in 1980. Throughout those four years, Eric's was arguably the premier venue in the UK, showcasing the leading NEW WAVE and POST-PUNK band of the day.

AN INTERVIEW WITH KEN TESTI
(Erics, band manager)

Hi Ken, how and where are you and what are you up to?

Hi Michael, I'm well, and presently I'm in Chester, kind of my hometown these days, where I am the foster carer for my grandson, but usually, for the past 13 or so years, I've lived in St Agnes, Cornwall, with my lovely partner Lesley; she has a business down there. I'm presently getting ready for 3 shows next week, 2 Deaf School shows in London and Liverpool, and also one in Liverpool, a breakout show with Deaf School's keyboardist Max Ripple, better known as John Wood.

Do you have a musical background to speak of, and how did Erics come about?

As a teen in the sixties, I went to grammar school and associated with those kinds of pupils that were engaging in music. I played around with some instruments but really never gave them the time to be proficient as a player. But I did take to gigs, loved going to them, and started arranging them at church and school halls, youth clubs and the like. In 1969, on leaving school, I became the driver, the fixer, and the booker for what was essentially then the school band, Ibex. I had a girlfriend staying in London that summer, so I took the band down there; we were going to hit the big time! But that didn't happen, yet we did meet some interesting chaps in a pub; their names were Roger Taylor, Brian May and Freddie Bulsara. At the time Ibex was a 3-piece without a dedicated singer, so Freddie joined the band; he did fit the bill, so to speak. Ibex split in 1970, and it was then that Fred teamed up with Brian and Roger. My parents ran pubs in the UK, so I had a fair idea of that side of hospitality. We went from pub to pub – Chester, St Helens, Widnes, that sort of thing – in Southwest Lancashire; it's called Merseyside these days.

You managed Deaf School, and still do. When people speak of music out of Liverpool the bands mentioned are of course The Beatles and then Deaf School.

I loved The Beatles; it was a breath of fresh air, and I just loved it. But when they left Liverpool, the creative lights of Liverpool went out too. Blues was taking off, and progressive rock was being born; Cream, Led Zeppelin and the like were embracing both, and there were loads of cover bands. It was uninspiring stuff, but in saying that, some of the best musicians I have ever met played in those bands. There was not a real lot happening creativity-wise; some great players, but they were lacking the creativity of the Beatles. As I said, that creative light had gone out and didn't come on again until Deaf School turned up. There was this band, we'll call it that, that wanted to do a Xmas gig; those guys, Clive Langer, Steve Allen, etc., and over a dozen others were looking for a suitable venue at the art college, or the polytechnic as it was known then, and the only space available was at the old deaf school. Hence the name.

What was one of the unusual scenarios around the Eric's nightclub.

A lot of the kids that wanted to go to Eric's were under 18; that was the age where you were allowed to enter licensed premises, so we started to do matinees on a Saturday to cater to the underaged ones. That way the younger record-buying public could get to see the bands, and the first one we did was with The Stranglers. So, if you talk to any of those punters, you are sure to get varied answers to the same question. As many of them remember being at the Blondie show, even though it was cancelled and it was going to a bigger venue, they will swear they were there! (laughs).

It was 1976. You and Roger Eagle opened Eric's. How and why Eric's.

Roger has some experience in getting gigs done and overseeing a venue. He was a big guy, barrel-chested, and could shout out orders, and people listened. He said that he was keen to open a club, and I said, *"I'd be in for some of that."* Through tour-managing Deaf School, I got to know all the bookers in the country, or at least most of them, as well as the venues. Roger eyed what was a pretty derelict building opposite The Cavern in Liverpool, the place made famous by The Beatles. The brief was we'd get the place and split it into two levels, the basement named The Revolution Club (channelling Che Guevara) and the upper floor Gatsby's (after the successful film). This was even though we had the original intention for Eric's to be 'transportable'; wherever we were that night, it would be Eric's. It was important for us to become a cardinal point on the tour circuit. There was a mindset with club owners to give their clubs "inspirational" female names, such as Tiffany's, Rebecca's, and Cinderella's, and the like; it was a prevalent theme for names from the '60s into the '70s. The club owners thought, Get the girls in, and naturally the guys will follow. So, I was of the mind to reject the previous generation's thought process. I'm looking around for an Anglo-Saxon male title as a counterbalance to all those others, so Eric's came to mind. No real relevance to anything for anybody.

Opening night, October 1, 1976. You had The Stranglers on, Deaf School warmed up the week before, then The Runaways, week two. Eric's became 'members only'. How did this work?

The Stranglers were hugely successful, BUT Liverpool had never seen anything like The Runaways. They were to play at Gatsby's venue, but we didn't want to bring our Eric's crowd through the glitzy, neon-lit entrance; that just wasn't us. So, the entrance was through a narrow fire exit. Our queue is going to the left around the corner, and as I look up the street, I see another queue. I asked, *"Who are those people queuing for?"* They say, *"That's the end of this queue…"* The line went right around the block! Not even The Beatles managed something like that! From that point on, every agent in the country wanted to get their bands into Eric's, and it was that gig that made us that cardinal point for band tours. We never had to look for another act; the bands came to us! As part of the licensing laws at the time, you closed at 11.00PM on the weekend and 10.30PM during the week. But if you had a supper licence, where you sold hot food, you got an extra hour. Then, to go to 2.00AM, you need a 'special hours' certificate, but that only applied to members clubs, with a membership book that had to be signed on entry. So, we played that game; people signed themselves and their guests in. That scenario too worked to our advantage; we had the members' addresses, and we'd mail them out our flyers, those bands, those nights, that kept them coming back. Those flyers are highly prized pieces of memorabilia now.

Who or what was the most memorable night for you?

Joey Ramone's 21st birthday, with Talking Heads as the support band. A story goes with that. There was a rumour that Ramones believed you played faster at the end of your set than the beginning, so they would go through their entire set before they went on so that they were ready for breakneck maximum speed from the get-go. I can confirm that rumour! Stanley Clarke, August 6, 1977, was highly memorable; it was suggested to Stanley by the Ramones, *"You just have to do Eric's; it's the best vibe."* Who were we to say no to one of the greatest bass players alive? He was to be recording a 'live' album through his tour of Europe, and was using the Virgin mobile studio, subsequently I had to apply for a street closure order as I'm told this is for a 40-foot trailer plus prime mover, and as it turns out there were 2 of these units! Using that system, a 48-channel recording studio in the street, with a return feed to our PA, gave us the best sound Eric's ever had.

A great vibe as you say. Was there ever any trouble to speak of?

We had little or no trouble from the punters. The only trouble was when the police turned up. One night, and it was my mistake; a group turned up who were part of a buck's party. I signed them up at the door. They were loud and rude and wanted to get on stage with The Damned, and unluckily there was a photo of one of our bouncers bringing a microphone stand down onto one of their heads; that didn't go over well. Pete Wylie, I think, has that photo.

1980, Eric's was closed by the police reportedly because of rampant drug use. How was different to anywhere else?

Let me be clear, we were no strangers to drugs ourselves. That said, we didn't condone drug use near or at our licensed premises; it was toxic. We had a zero-tolerance policy. We even threw out people that we knew, friends; we took them outside for lighting up a spliff. The lack of 'brown paper bags' (wink) didn't help us at all. The cops didn't understand Eric's; it was full of punks. They looked different but were great kids.

What are you doing presently and what are you listening to?

I was going to go to the supermarket, but this was more fun. As mentioned, we are getting ready for the upcoming Deaf School gigs. I don't play music anymore. So, send me the link to your radio station; I'll try to listen. I do have some vinyl records and a few CDs. I do treasure an album by Brian May, Roger Taylor, and Tim Staffell when they were called Smile; it was pre-Queen; it was never released in the UK; it's a Japanese pressing. Oh! Please go listen to the guitar on Baker St. Filter out the sax solo – that's Hugh Burns; it's fantastic. If I get back to Sydney to see my brother, I'll check you out! Good talking to you; look after yourself. Cheers.

The *Sound of the Sand and Other Songs of the Pedestrian*, the debut solo LP by David Thomas was released in 1981, on the Rough Trade Records label. Bizarre? Of course, it is when David Thomas is involved. There are all sorts of things going on here, vastly different to Pere Ubu, yet strangely the same. 'The Crickets in The Flats', an instrumental, has a tribal jungle theme that centers on drummer Anton Fier, bongos and squealing brass abound.

'Sound of the Sand' is as mellow as David has ever sounded, with Richard Thompson's jangly guitar a treat! David is supported by four different bands on this, so from track to track there are vast distances travelled, nothing is the same as it ever was! Try this out!

⊙ The Van Vliet brothers Simon and Peter from Hijmegan, The Netherlands, created the outfit Mekanik Kommando in 1980 and by October 30 their debut album *It Would Be Quiet in the Woods If Only a Few Birds Sing* was released. Little known, but they were forerunners in minimal synthpop, with echoes of Peter Bauman, The Normal and Leer & Rental. It's not surprising it was released on the Tone Float label named after the album by Kraftwerk's earliest incarnation Organization. 'Replay' sounds very reminiscent of The Residents, and the intrigue goes further with 'Birds'. On the whole inventive & creative electronica.

31

⊙ Feargal Sharkey was invited by Vince Clarke and Eric Radcliffe to provide vocals for a one-off single released on this day in 1983. Under the moniker of The Assembly, 'Never Never' b/w 'Stop-Start' presented a perfect combination of Clarke's glorious synth sound selection and subtle arrangement coupled with Sharkey's pleasant and easily identifiable voice. The quality of Radcliffe's production here leaves one wondering what might have been with a little more time together.

⊙ October 31, 1978, saw the release of Joe Jackson's smash debut single 'Is She Really Going Out with Him?'. *"Is she really going out with him? Is she really gonna take him home tonight? Is she really going out with him? My eyes don't deceive me; there's something going wrong around here"*. A sad statement by the envious guy who misses out. A statement with an infectious hook that just won't go away. A statement that led him to be the one the girls wanted to go home with.

⊙ Annabella Lwin was born in 1966. Annabella is of Anglo-Burmese background, born to a Burmese father and an English mother in Rangoon, Burma. As a fourteen-year-old she was plucked by Malcolm McLaren from a dry cleaner's shop where she worked to join Bow Wow Wow in 1980. She was quickly "rechristened" by McLaren from her real name, Myant Myant Aye, and made an immediate celebrity. In 1983 Annabella was sacked from the band and she pursued a solo career. In the '90s Annabella put together her second band, The Naked Experience, having moderate success with 'Car Sex' & 'Do What You Do'. Annabella has featured on many collaborations with the likes of Utah Saints and Guy Chambers, and today she works as a record producer and tours as Annabella's Bow Wow Wow.

⊙ 1981 saw MDK's (Mekanïk Destrüktïw Komandöh) debut album, *The Path to Peace,* released on cassette tape. Taking their name from the 1973 album title by French prog-rock outfit Magama, MDK formed in 1979 in Berlin and became a dominant force in the early '80s Neue Deutsche Welle (New German Wave). The tape explored various styles of post-punk and industrial themes; it's incredibly intense, theatrical, and dark with occasional jazz overtones with loads of atmosphere.

⊙ Johnny Marr, aka John Martin Maher, was born in Manchester, England, in 1963. Johnny was the guitarist and co-songwriter of The Smiths along with Steven Morrissey. He has also been a member of the bands Electronic, 7 Worlds Collide, The Cribs, The The & Modest Mouse. Few British groups have had the far-reaching impact of The Smiths, and few guitarists are as celebrated as Marr. He was recently named NME's ultimate guitarist, ahead of Jimmy Page and Jimi Hendrix (ahead of Jimi?). THAT is saying something!). Johnny was given an honorary doctorate by Salford University for "changing the face of British music". Always very vocal, he is quoted as saying: *"We (The Smiths) invented indie as we still know it…With The Smiths 100 percent of my focus was on providing interesting guitar hooks and putting some kind of space-age twist on the guitarist's role. The pop guitarist crossed with the mad professor. That's how I thought of myself...I seem to attract and be attracted to very willful, fascinating people...I've almost never played any of The Smiths' records once they've gone out. I was always like that, and probably always will be. There isn't enough of me to be heard on them".*

⊙ Larry Mullen Jr, aka Lawrence Joseph Mullen, was born in 1961 and raised in Artane, Dublin, Ireland. We all know Larry as the drummer in U2. He had to add the "Junior" to the end of his name to distinguish himself from his father, Larry Mullen, Sr, because as Larry's career blossomed, so did his tax bills, and his father was the unlucky recipient of them in the early 1980s. Before U2, Larry's previous gigs included playing drums for the Post Office Workers Union Band. Larry is the youngest member of U2 and was only 14 when he had the idea to start the band by putting up ads at his school. He then held auditions in his living room; Bono, The Edge, and Adam Clayton showed up. Before U2 took the name, they were known as the Larry Mullen Band (as Larry said, "*for about 10 minutes*"), then Feedback and The Hype! Luck came their way when, in early 1978, they won 500 pounds in a talent quest; this cash enabled them to get studio time to make demos. Larry is noted for his dislike of the Passengers venture with Brian Eno and even more so of the album: "*There's a thin line between interesting music and self-indulgence. We crossed it on the* passenger's *record*". and later Mullen in a doco stated, "*It still hasn't grown on me. Though 'Miss Sarajevo' is a classic.* And in the same doco, Bono said, "*Larry just didn't like [Passengers] because we didn't let him play the drums*". And then there is a great quote from Larry: "*If Bono left U2, we could carry on. If I left, we'd be screwed.*"

⊙ The first of two collaborations by Andy Summers (The Police) and Robert Fripp (King Crimson), *I Advance Masked* was on the store shelves October 31, 1982. This duo are guitarists's guitarists, and this album is a must-have for any guitarist or guitar-playing enthusiast! Purely instrumental, largely showcasing Summer's guitar synth and Fripp's Frippertronics, the playing is far from self-indulgent hot-licks playing, but more a trip into the tones that guitar can achieve. To the average listener, the aural landscapes achieved here are fascinating; they're intricate and very complex, a lesson in design, structure, subtleness, and prowess to the guitar player. QUIET! Geniuses at work.

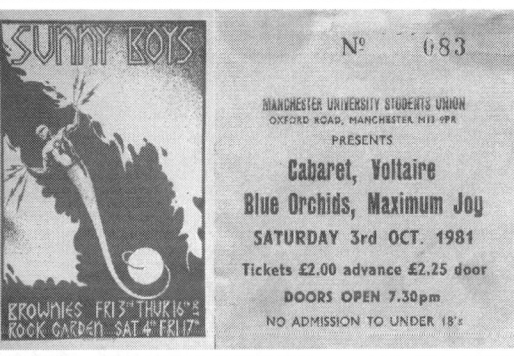

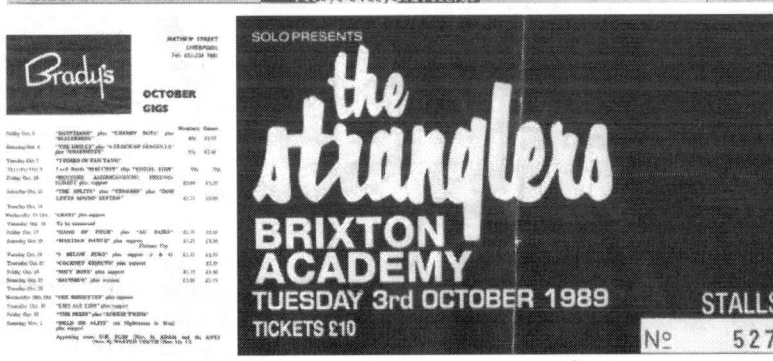

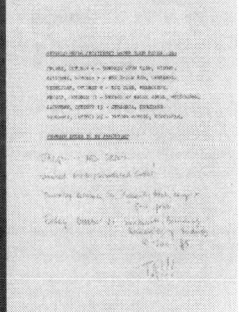

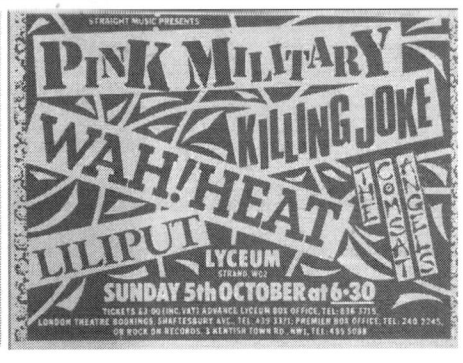

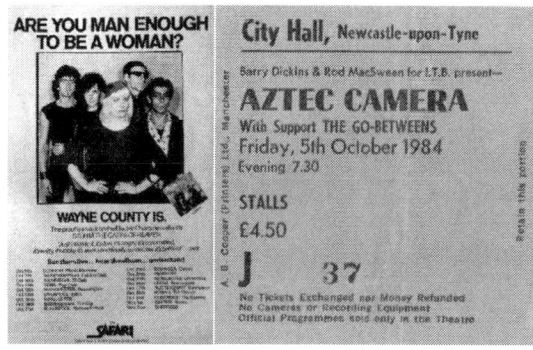

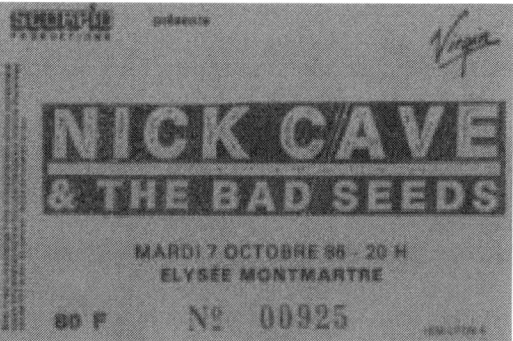

PUNK MUSIC BY

SUICIDE

nasty cut
cool p. liebegott
reverend reverby

Sat. Oct 10, 10 PM   at Museum

FREE   729 B'way, 2nd fl.

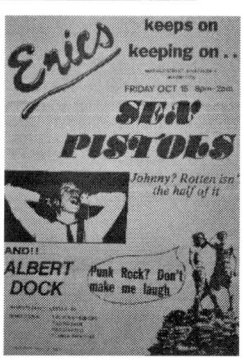

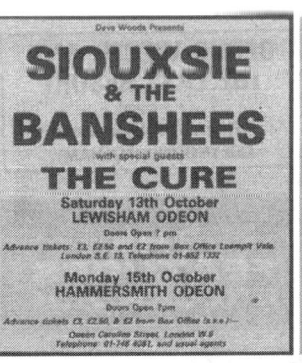

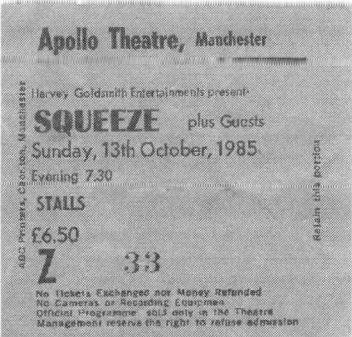

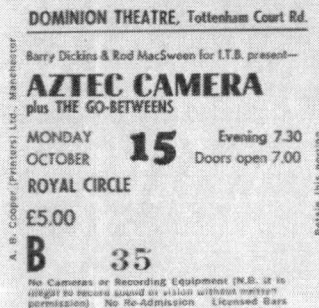

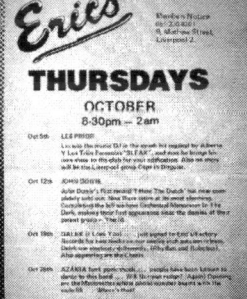

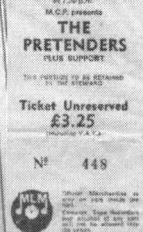

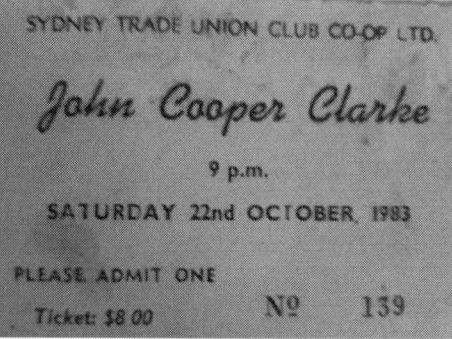

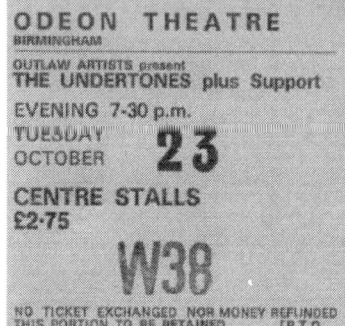

YACHTS
FRI. 27. OCT.
Erics

M.C.P. presents
UB40
PLUS SPECIAL GUESTS
BIRMINGHAM INTERNATIONAL ARENA NEC
The big heart of England
00PM MON 28 OCT 85
BLOCK 5 F 102
doors open
6.30PM
AGNT
GOULD
2-OCT-85

FRI. 28th and SAT. 29th
TIM FINN
in concert
WITH 11-PIECE BAND
IN THE BALLROOM

WIRE FACES PERFORMING AS
TELEVISION
WITH GUESTS BLONDIE • TALKING HEADS
RICHARD HELL & THE VOIDOIDS
RAMONES
HI-DIVE~DENVER OCT 29 8PM

BANDSTAND presents
COCTEAU TWINS
plus Support
FRAZIER CHORUS
THE HUMMINGBIRD,
DALE END,
BIRMINGHAM
MON 29TH OCT/90
7.30PM
£7.50 Advance
000633

CABARET VOLTAIRE
YOUNG MARBLE GIANTS
MONITOR & VICTORY ACRES

SCHLITZ ROCKS AMERICA
THE WHO
THE CLASH
FRI. OCT. 29
COLISEUM
Schlitz - The Taste That Rocks America

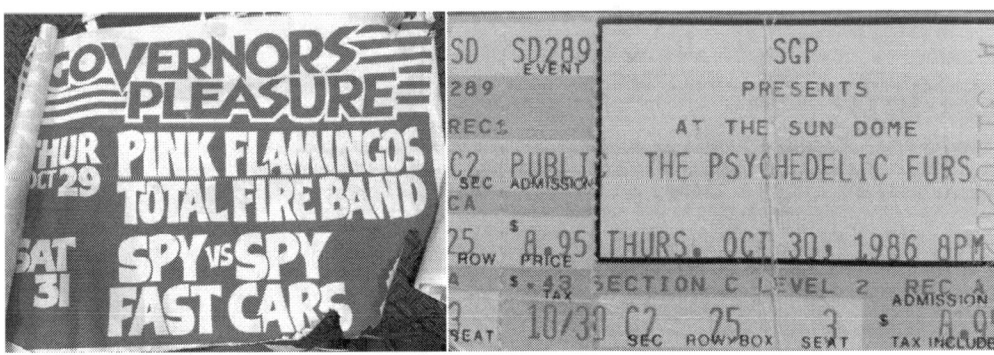

GOVERNORS PLEASURE
THUR OCT 29 PINK FLAMINGOS
TOTAL FIRE BAND
SAT 31 SPY vs SPY
FAST CARS

SGP
PRESENTS
AT THE SUN DOME
THE PSYCHEDELIC FURS
THURS. OCT 30, 1986 8PM

SCAPA FLOW
DEAD TRAVEL FAST
SYSTEMATICS
LOVE MUM
AND THE
URGENT RING MES
TRADE UNION CLUB
FRIDAY, 30th OCTOBER

PARIS LIVE
NEW WAVE
SUNDAY 30th
FEATURING
JOHNNY DOLE AND THE SCABS
PSYCHO SURGEONS
SUBVERSION

with love party (ex leboyer boys)
southern cross saturday 30th october 8.30-12

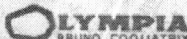

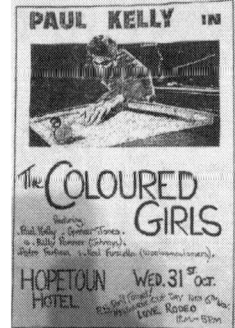
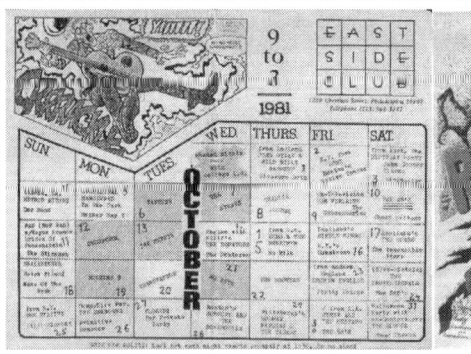

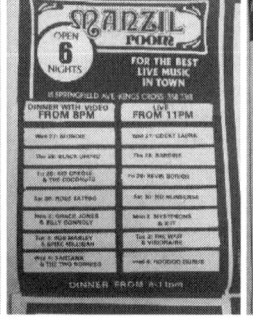
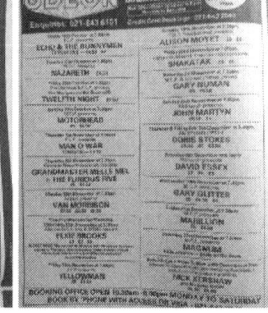

1

◉ On November 1st, 1980, The Birthday Party released their *self-titled* album. It was a confusing release for several reasons. Originally, the album was credited under the name The Boys Next Door on The Missing Link label. Then CBS re-released it, jointly crediting both The Birthday Party and The Boys Next Door. In 1982, 4AD reissued the album again with new artwork, only crediting The Birthday Party, with no mention of The Boys Next Door. This convoluted release history suggests Nick Cave intentionally made things complicated, staying true to his contrary nature.

Birthday Party from Nigel Rennard

◉ On November 1, 1979, capitalising on the recent success of their single 'No G.D.M.' in Austria, Gina X-Performance (GXP) made their live debut in Vienna. The Euro-disco synthpop group, featuring Zeus B. Held and vocalist Gina Kikoine, performed before a sell-out crowd of 14,000. On stage, vocalist Gina and music controller/keyboardist Zeus B. Held were joined by drummer Lazlo Czigany, along with backing singers and dancers. That night, they shared the bill with Boney M, Clout, and Ludwig Hirsch. GXP's performance was critically acclaimed for successfully presenting their recently released album *Nice Mover* live.

◉ Eddie Macdonald was born on this day in 1959. In 1981, he was the bassist for the band Seventeen, later renamed The Alarm. Along with Mike Peters, they were the main songwriters for the band. Their single 'Sixty Eight Guns' reached the top 20 in the UK in 1983 and appeared on the top ten album *Declaration* in 1984.

◉ Mental As Anything released their debut album, *Get Wet*, in November 1979. Bringing together their diverse influences, the five art-schoolers created a classic Australian album that remains remarkably fresh today. Starting with the opening track, 'The Nips Are Getting Bigger', the album immediately showcases the band's brilliant lyrical wordplay and excellent group dynamics, revealing them as a significant new force. While producer Cameron Allen's approach doesn't fully capture the band's effervescent live energy, it successfully shapes them into a cohesive and clever studio act, delivering a set of undeniably catchy tunes. The Mental as Anything discography is filled with great songs, and *Get Wet* contributes several key tracks, including 'Business and Pleasure', 'Talk to Baby Jesus', 'Insurance Man', 'Egypt' and, naturally, 'The Nips Are Getting Bigger'.

◉ Midnight Oil released their *self-titled* debut album on November 1, 1978. Already renowned as one of Australia's premier live acts, the band successfully captured that powerful energy on this record. Midnight Oil possessed a truly unique sound, distinct from any other artist before or since. Their music combined power with a fine musicality that was always evident. The album features Peter Garrett's supreme vocals, Rob Hirst's unbelievable drumming, and superb guitar work from Jim Moginie and Martin Rotsey. Highlights include 'Run by Night', 'Head Over Heels' & 'Surfing with a Spoon'. This is widely considered an Australian classic!

● The Australian band The Reels put out their *self-titled* debut record in 1979. The album was bursting with infectious, eccentric NEW WAVE pop tunes, including their first nationally charting single, 'Love Will Find a Way', which cracked the top 40. In the late 1970s, The Reels stood out as completely unique and rejuvenating, compared to the typical "pub rock" or avant-garde inner-city music happening in Australia at the time. Live, they flawlessly recreated their studio sound through an enviable sound system, crystal clear digital audio pumped through cutting-edge BOSE speakers that was the envy of most live performers in the country then. The Reels were always fascinating and enjoyable.

● In 1980, the album *Easy Listening for the Hard of Hearing* was launched, it was collaborative effort by Boyd Rice and Frank Tovey. Despite its title, the album presents a very challenging listening experience. The compositions are primarily built upon repetitive, pulse-like samples and loops, often layered with synthesiser textures. The album exhibits a notable lack of conventional musical complexity. It is typically classified within the 'Industrial' genre, sharing characteristics with artists like Throbbing Gristle or even early Kraftwerk.

● The Sound's debut album, *Jeopardy*, was released in 1980. Hailing from the southern part of London, this band had a unique sound that drew comparisons to Magazine and came close to Echo and The Bunnymen. Led by Adrian Borland, The Sound is often overlooked when discussing the early '80s music scene. They skilfully blended the dark tones of POST-PUNK guitar and rhythm with subtle synthesizers, resulting in a captivating and introspective texture. The standout tracks 'Heartland' and 'Missiles' perfectly showcase this combination. Unfortunately, despite their talent, The Sound's five subsequent albums went largely unnoticed, leading to their split in 1988. Tragically, Adrian Borland, who had been battling a schizoaffective disorder, took his own life in 1999.

● Stephen Vineburg was born in Sydney, Australia, in 1956. He has developed a portfolio of interests in business, art, film, and music. Stephen was a fixture of the inner-city rock scene in Sydney for many years. He organised several music venues and was a director of the Sydney Trade Union Club. He also contributed to the first EP, *But Jacques, the Fish?* by The Celibate Rifles. After a short career as a rock writer, he became the lead singer for The Professors and The Fifth Estate. The Professors took their name from Vineburg's friendship with Chris Bailey of The Saints. They were influential on a range of other young bands and feature in Clinton Walker's seminal compendium of the era, Inner City Sound. In 2018, The Professors released an EP, *Go Out Tonight*, on Buttercup Records, and in 2019, they appeared as part of the Sedition Festival alongside Ed Kuepper, The Flaming Hands and Shy Imposters.

THE DAY THE EARTH STOOD STILL
STEPHEN VINEBURG
(The Professors, The Fifth Estate)

I guess my mother is to blame. It all goes back to a wet June morning in 1964 when I was seven years old. For the only time I can remember, my mother allowed me to stay home and be late to school. I sat on the floor with my school bag, glued to a grainy black-and-white TV image as The Beatles landed at Sydney Airport. It was the most exciting thing I had seen. I was hooked.

At the schoolyard that morning we discussed how we could form our own pop group and who would get the prized role of drummer. Everyone wanted to be Ringo. Given that we were also equally enthralled with the idea of being astronauts, being in a pop group seemed a slightly more achievable ambition.

As a child of the Sixties, I received a transistor radio as a Christmas present, which became a constant companion, and I regularly fell asleep with the earpiece still in. I picked up the weekly Top 40 list from the local record store and pored over it with the enthusiasm of a gambler studying the form guide.

Next, of course, came the stage of devouring all pop music-related newspapers and magazines. The big breakthrough came when Lillian Roxon began filing reports from the New York underground scene for, of all places, a conservative Sunday newspaper – The Sun Herald. Suddenly, my suburban home was filled with the goings-on of Warhol and Reed and The Plastic Exploding Inevitable. She wrote with such an enthusiasm and vigour that you felt you had to be there, or if not there, create your own facsimile.

So, a high school boy began organising 'dances' with light shows and other forms of 'happenings', sadly all done without the benefit of a driver's licence or many of the other life skills which would have been handy for a 16-year-old. It was a DIY mentality, maybe born of more innocent times, that said, "Why not?"

University was the next step and the opportunity to write rock music and film reviews for Honi Soit, the student newspaper of the

One day in early 1977, I was given the assignment of interviewing The Saints, who had recently arrived from Brisbane and were staying in a semi-derelict block of flats on Berry St, North Sydney. The Saints had arrived in Sydney after EMI Australia had been instructed by Head Office in London to sign and record them on the strength of their self-released single, 'I'm Stranded'.

Next door to the flats was the office of their recently acquired managers, Together Management, who had been brought in as part of the upsurge in interest from EMI. Together consisted of Chris Gilbey and Tommy Moeller. Gilbey was also the manager of Jon English, and Moeller, who had written 'Concrete and Clay' while in the band, Unit 4 Plus 2, was now writing TV jingles.

I have to declare that I had acquired at that stage what might be called a 'Glebe' sensibility and regarded The Saints as a pale Antipodean response to the emerging news of 'punk rock' from London. Anyway, on the train across the Harbour Bridge, I read through the press pack and was intrigued to read the famous NME assessment of 'I'm Stranded' as "the single of the week and every other week". How could this be?

Anyway, I arrived at Berry St to meet Chris Bailey, a dishevelled version of Brendan Behan crossed with Oscar Wilde (if Wilde had smoked Winfield Reds). Also, an obviously highly intelligent, if somewhat remote, Ed Kuepper; a very likeable and down-to-earth Ivor Hay; and Kim Bradshaw, who was perhaps finding the adjustment from Brisbane to Sydney the most difficult. Jeffrey Wegener and Bob Farrell, later to feature in the Laughing Clowns and other influential groups, were also living there.

I opened the interview in a somewhat combative tone; weren't they just cashing in on the latest trend? This provocative line of questioning was met with indifference from Ed Kuepper, no doubt borne out of the fatigue of dealing with ignorant know-alls. Chris Bailey, however, was a real verbal pugilist, and there was a heavy tussle about originality, the state of the music industry and The Saints' reason for being.

None of this, I thought, however, was going to contribute to a useful press interview, although with the benefit of hindsight, in fact, it could have made a very interesting interview. It is often hard to jump out of the confidence of your preconceptions.

Having reached a stalemate, I suggested we adjourn to the pub, just up on the corner of Walker St. The disorderly and disarrayed nature of our table sitting slightly ajar with the ranks of North Sydney advertising types.

One thing led to another, or more correctly, one beer led to another. As the afternoon wore on, we uncovered common ground. Suddenly, the press article seemed much less important than me joining the ranks of those committed to taking on the status quo and being literally outside the realm of normal society.

As the long afternoon blurred into evening, it was decided we should go to The Funhouse, a band venue above the Oxford Tavern at Taylor Square. The Funhouse had been established by Radio Birdman as a place for them and their friends to play following rejection by all the other music venues in Sydney.

Now here it gets a bit hazy. My recollection is that we saw the Hellcats that night, featuring Ron Peno on vocals. Ron, of course, went on to have a successful career with Died Pretty. Later, when the pub closed at 10pm, we all climbed into a Mini Moke and headed to a house party in Five Dock. At the party, the music was a curious selection of '60s nuggets and the latest from New York and London. Definitely no Supertramp or Frampton Comes Alive!

There I met Clyde Bramley, later of the Hoodoo Gurus; Jim Dickson, then of The Survivors but later of the Barracudas and Radio Birdman; and Janine Hall, later of The Saints and Weddings Parties, Anything. Quite an introduction to the burgeoning underground rock scene. In many ways it reminded me of the Sydney Push, the infamous school of writers, poets, and actors, including Clive James and Germaine Greer, who in previous decades had stood outside the Sydney establishment.

So, a wild night and a life-changing day. Chris Bailey and Ed Kuepper remain two of the most remarkable people I have met. It certainly gave me, and as it turned out, an awful lot of other people, the inspiration to think, "Well, you know what – why not?"

The episode brought an abrupt end to my career as a rock critic. Who wants to write about mainstream bands anyway? There were only a few bands who really mattered. More to the point, who wants to write about bands when you can form your own one? The next steps were to do just that.

2

● 'Nowhere Girl', the most successful single for the English band B-Movie, was originally released on 2nd November 1980 to lacklustre response. After being remixed and reworked in 1982, it was re-released and reached No.67 in the UK. Again, the song was reworked for B-Movie's first studio album, *Forever Running*, in 1985.

● 'The Message' by Grandmaster Flash and the Furious Five (GFFF) was released on the Sugar Hill label on this day in 1982. It made a significant impact, establishing GFFF as one of the pioneering rap groups with meaningful lyrics that resonated with society. The song was later recognised as the "Greatest Hip-Hop song of all time" in a 2012 list by Rolling Stone magazine. Achieving commercial success, 'The Message' reached No.4 on the Billboard R & B singles chart. However, the overwhelming success led to internal conflicts within GFFF, resulting in the group splitting into different factions, with Flash, Melle Mel, and The Kidd Creole going their separate ways.

● Rick Grossman was born in Sydney, Australia, in 1959. Rick is a bassist/vocalist and has been a member of The Divinyls, The Hoodoo Gurus, Matt Finish, The Ghostwriters, The Persian Rugs, The Kelly Gang, The Hellcats, Parachute, Bleeding Hearts, The Traitors and Men at Work....wow! He's been around! From 1980 he played with Matt Finish and was part of the recording of the top 20 LP *Short Note*. Rick moved onto The Divinyls from 1982 to 1987 until he entered rehab for heroin addiction. In 1988 Rick replaced Clyde Bramley in The Hoodoo Gurus, and still he plays with them today; that is, whenever they decide to play.

YOU DON'T DO THIS
RICK GROSSMAN
(Matt Finish, The Divinyls, Hoodoo Gurus et al.)
Melbourne 1978

Once upon a time, I lived in a house on Hoddle Street in East Melbourne. The music scene was very lively, and everyone knew everyone. The house was big, with six bedrooms and one tiny room at the bottom of the stairs in which one had to do their time before graduating to a proper bedroom. The guys were all from Adelaide and had been together in a band called Spare Change. I had been in The Bleeding Hearts the previous year... a story in itself... John Dowler, the singer of Spare Change, left; the Hearts broke up, and we formed a band called Parachute with Chris Langman, Graeme Perry, Bob Kretchmer and me. The house echoed with the music of Patti Smith, Television, Dylan, Velvet Underground, Bowie, Ramones, Roxy Music, etc. I got a real bedroom, and Paul Kelly moved in under the stairs fresh from Adelaide. He would later write 'Leaps and Bounds' about that house.

No TV, so we'd spend hours in a huge front room playing and finally got a set together, a publicist, and started gigging furiously around Melbourne. Parachute had a kind of lo-fi sound... not really punk, but more like The Band/Dylan. We attracted the interest of Ross Wilson, who would come and listen in our front room. It was soon arranged for him to produce our recordings. After one long session with Ross, we had heard about a party on that night, so I, Ross and Chris headed out. Chris borrowed Paul K's treasured leather jacket. We went to the party and were followed out by two guys who had the "punk" look, spiky hair, boots, safety pins, etc. As we got to the car, one of them said, *"We want to kill Wilson because he's a boring old fart!"*. This dickhead actually said that!!! They laid into us and tried to break Ross's arm. They seemed to know kickboxing or some martial art. I got kicked, Ross badly punched and Chris got a black eye. They also tore the leather jacket off Chris. We were hurt and humiliated, but losing the jacket was the worst.

We circulated a rumour that all the Melbourne roadies were very angry that a legend like Ross had been beaten up. Back then, roadies were hard men, quite often guys who'd done time in jail and were used to violence... quite often at the end of gigs in the pubs. But of course, no roadies even knew about this incident... we made it up. As I said, everyone knew everyone. After a week we got a note saying, "You can have the jacket back; just call the roadies off". It arrived a few days later.

Paul had his jacket back and was clothed again, and Parachute recorded a song called 'Big Beat' and then were destined for a couple of obscure collections of Melbourne music. Good band. We supported a band called Mother Goose who had a hit called 'Baked Beans'. Their singer was in a sailor suit, and their keys player had a big red beard and wore a ballerina outfit, bizarre! We played our songs about existentialism and broken dreams in our Dylan style and got bottles thrown at us. I then realised we were fighting a losing battle. It was disheartening and all kinds of introspective. Other than inner-city venues, we would die terribly supporting bigger acts in the suburbs. I learnt that you have to grab hold of an audience instead of almost apologising.

Martin Armiger was starting a new band. He was in Bleeding Hearts, and I was a huge admirer of his. The band was pretty "punk': loud, fast, and great songs, some of which later turned up on albums when Martin joined Sports. Chris later played and wrote songs with Paul Kelly and became a TV director, and the drummer Graeme Perry and guitarist Bob Kretchmer played with me the following year in Eric Gradman's Man and Machine – Bob later ended up in Icehouse.

I loved that time, the people, and the songs. We were all just starting out, and I guess part of the journey was learning WHAT NOT TO DO!

● Mick Karn released his first solo album *Titles* in 1982. After the split of Japan, he ventured away from the Asian influence predominantly used by Japan to that of Africa and the Middle East, a perfect example being the exotic 'Saviour, Are You with Me'. Always innovative and individualistic as a bass player, he took to various woodwind and brass instruments like clarinet and bassoon to augment a truly expressive album. But it's with the bass that Mick Karn excels like no other, the track 'Tribal Dawn' is a true exhibition of his prowess. *Titles* was well received publicly and peaked at No.74 on the UK Album Chart. There's a wide variation of textures on Titles, each tune exhibits his virtuosity at playing bass, giving each song an iconic, almost trademarked sound.

⦿ Lindy Morrison (OAM) aka Belinda Morrison was born in 1951. Lindy is best known to most as the drummer in The Go-Betweens who appeared on all the band's releases from their first LP, *Send Me a Lullaby* in 1981, until the band's first break up on 26 December 1989. Lindy gets around, she also played with Cleopatra Wong, Shrew, Zero, The Four Gods, Deep Blue Sea, Tuff Monks, The Rainy Season, Cassy Judy and Alex the astronaut. She now performs with Rob Snarski in SnaraskiCircusLindyBand and in the UK with Newcastle on Tyne band The Girl with The Replaceable Head. Using her knowledge of the industry and connections Lindy authored an important student handbook *Australian Women in Rock & Pop Music*. In 2013 her work as a performer, an advocate and for her contributions to community was recognized by being awarded a prestigious Order of Australia Medal. In Covid 19 time, 2021, Lindy found her way onto television in an advert as a roadie for herself!

Lindy Morrison by Petra Gall

10 QUESTIONS: AN INTERVIEW WITH LINDY MORRISON

Hi Lindy, You were born and grew up in Brisbane and became a drummer, unlike the wannabe up-front singers; how come?

Well, when I left school, I went to university and achieved a Bachelor of Social Work in 1972, but that field ended up wearing me out. I loved drumming, and when I first sat behind a kit, there were little or no women instrumentalists on stage. Being in a dress was a love of mine, and sitting there open-legged on a drum stool was a shock for most people. I am aware that I have a legacy as one of the first female drummers in Australia, which makes me very proud. That said, I don't think my chosen profession is what my parents would have wanted; I think they would have preferred me to be married with kids.

How did your joining The Go-Betweens come about?

I lived in a house in inner-city Brisbane, and Robert Forster used to come around to visit me. At the time I was in a band called Zero, and it wasn't long until we started jamming together, and then he started playing in the band, but he left soon with Grant McLennan to go to the UK. It was on their return they asked me to join up with them. These guys really interested me with their mindset, and musically we synced well too. It worked for us all, as we wanted to get out of Brisbane, and being in a band was a great way to do that.

What are your thoughts on the music you were involved in?

Well, Robert and Grant were exceptional songwriters with two very different styles of writing, and the dynamic of male-female band members relationships gave an extraordinary level of excitement. Though it wasn't surprising that we weren't embraced by Australia, the local culture of the mainstream didn't fit with our quirkiness and intelligent lyricism. But with the departure of Robert Vickers around the time of the album *16 Lovers Lane*, we lost a great chemistry of a very gelled rhythm section. I had been playing with Robert for about five years, so learning to play with a new bassist was a bit of a downer for me.

What can you say about you and Amanda being in the band?

There's a great story about that. We were sitting relaxed in 301 Studios in Sydney, and in walked Robert Gudinski; it was our first meeting with him. Hovering about, moving here and there, he settled his gaze on us and said, *"Girls in the band, you'll break up in a year!"* …... we proved him wrong… we went 19 months! (laughs)

The band toured pretty intensely; it can be hard on relationships and cameradery. What are your thoughts on that?

We toured relentlessly; it was how we survived. We never stopped touring. We always looked forward to it, and touring as support to Alex Chilton was something else. Yeah, touring was our bread and butter; without it, we couldn't survive. The World Tour took its toll; it became the death of us. We were doing it so tough overseas, while in the UK it seemed that in Australia everyone was doing so well and we were just losers, and on December 27, 1989, Grant and Robert decided to disband The Go-Betweens. Even though I didn't see it at the time, it was good for me personally.

What recording/s have given you the most pleasure?

A difficult question, easier to say, "What was the most unhappy experience?" Recording Spring Hill Fair in France, even though it was a beautiful setting with vineyards and waterfalls, the producer, John Brand, wanted me to record in a way I wasn't familiar with, using a click track and rhythm machines, which didn't sit well. And 16 Lovers Lane, I was just unhappy; I guess it was because I felt a bit lost back in Australia, and a new bassist didn't help.

Looking back, is there anything you'd like to have done differently, any regrets?

(Laughing) Yeah! I would have behaved differently (laughs).

At the split of the band, did you know what direction you wanted to go in? What about Cleopatra Wong?

No, not really. I had just had a child, Lucinda, and all I owned was my '64 Ludwig drumkit. I settled in Sydney and moved into teaching there. Both Amanda Brown and I wanted to write songs; this was something denied us with the Go-Betweens, so Cleopatra Wong was a great vehicle for Amanda, really, as she is an excellent songwriter. We were able to tour Asia and record and release two, in my opinion, glorious EPs, *Egg* and *Cleopatra's Lament*. Yet, touring with kids, mine and Amanda's, was a nightmare, so something had to give. Amanda went into music and film, and she's been very successful with that.

Away from bands, what did you move into?

For a long time, I've been involved in what is called community music, where I would meet all varieties of drummers and rhythmists in country towns doing drumming workshops. This would include school kids preparing them for performing; it was just fantastic. I'm also very proud of my work as musical director with The Junction House Band and what it's done for awareness of the skills and abilities of people with intellectual disabilities.

So where is Lindy Morrison now that we've moved out of COVID-19?

I'm pretty much in love with drumming. I can do it while on my own and be engrossed with being in the moment. Music is and will be my life; I won't retire from it. I get to play with so many different people. 2023 saw me begin a collaboration with Rob Snarski of Chad's

Tree and Backeyed Susans fame as SnarskiCircusLindyBand, lots of dates and lots of fun. Now, I have about 5 years left in me, that's if I'm lucky, and I like to be fit. I go kayaking and swimming and practice drumming every day, which helps with that. Even today, after so many years of drumming, I'm finding new ideas, and that excites me. I never stop learning.

◉ Pylon, an innovative rock band from Athens, Georgia, put out their album *Gyrate* on November 2nd, 1980. This outstanding debut album unjustly flew under most people's radar. Pylon had a distinctive sound characterised by jagged, choppy guitars and commanding lead vocals from Vanessa Briscoe. There were detectable similarities to contemporaries like Television and Gang of Four in Pylon's abrupt, angular musical approach. Songs like 'Cool', 'Dub', 'Feast on My Heart', 'Gravity', and 'Danger' featured catchy, jangly guitars and Briscoe's in-your-face singing. Although overlooked at the time, *Gyrate* was a gem stacked with listenable, replayable tracks that deserve rediscovery.

◉ Dave Rowbotham, a Manchester native born in 1958, was tragically discovered murdered in his flat by his girlfriend on November 2, 1991. Throughout his life, Dave played a significant role in the music scene, being an early member of The Durutti Column, The Mothmen, and The Invisible Girls. He was also a regular session player for Factory Records. Despite the heinous nature of his death, justice has never been served, and to honour his memory, The Happy Mondays released the heartfelt song 'Cowboy Dave' as a tribute.

◉ 'Suffer The Children' the debut single by Tears for Fears was released in 1981. The single version, the album, and the remixed versions all have their own levels of complexity, each engaging. The single's production was less polished with backing vocals much more prevalent, but this didn't affect the power and beauty of the song. Hearing this meant that owning the debut album, *The Hurting*, would be a must.

◉ On November 2, 1979, Visage released their first single "Tar"; it failed to chart. Visage was formed in late 1979 when Steve Strange and Rusty Egan got together in the studio to record some demos. Steve had briefly been in the punk and NEW WAVE bands The Moors Murderers and The Photons, while Rusty was working with Midge Ure in the band The Rich Kids. Soon Midge was invited in, and the trio recorded a demo session which included a cover of the Zager and Evans hit 'In the Year 2525'. The Visage line-up was completed with the addition of Ultravox keyboardist Billy Currie and three-fifths of the band Magazine – guitarist John McGeoch, keyboardist Dave Formula and bassist Barry Adamson, who left after the poor response to the single "Tar". Success did not elude those that remained, though, as within a few months they had released their breakthrough single, 'Fade to Grey', which peaked at No.8 in the UK and reached No.1 in Germany.

3

◉ In 1980 Bauhaus released *In the Flat Field*. The debut LP was the complete antithesis of mainstream rock; it invented what still today is regarded as the stereotype of 'Goth Music'. Steeped in a gloomy mood, and with Pete Murphy's grim, despairing vocal delivery, we get songs of desolation, tragedy, and irony. "*I get bored*," he wails! The astonishingly precise rhythm section of David J and Haskins pulls off a variety of jaw-dropping performances, including the high-paced tension of the title track and the brooding crawl from 'Spy in the Cab'. Daniel Ash's screaming guitar slots in perfectly, but the best thing about these songs is not what they sound like but what they don't sound like. Murphy channels as much Iggy Pop as he does Bowie, proving not to be a simple copyist of either, able to both maniacally sing-shout and take a somewhat lighter touch throughout. The songs are meteoric, as in the Alice Cooperish opener 'Double Dare' or the intense dirge demonstrative overtone of 'Stigmata Martyr'. Some of the lyrical content is simply sublime, as in 'Small Talk Stinks' with the line "*there's no idle gossip in braille*"; it's a killer. The set concludes with the seven-minute 'Nerves', an aptly titled piece that alternates between understated energy and unleashed power toward a dramatic ending. Bauhaus and Peter Murphy were unique; this album was an apex moment in POST-PUNK.

⦿ Adam Ant, aka Stuart Goddard, was born in 1954 in Marylebone, England. In 1981, as part of Adam and the Ants, he scored a No.1 hit single with 'Stand and Deliver', and a No.1 album with *Kings of the Wild Frontier*. The Ants also had over a dozen Top 40 hit singles. 'Antmusic' and 'Goody Two Shoes' both went to No.1 in Australia. At 21 years of age, he was diagnosed as having bipolar disorder, and this led to some radical actions. He was charged with throwing a car alternator through a pub window and then threatening staff and patrons with an imitation gun. He was arrested after attempting to smash in his neighbour's patio door with a shovel. During a gig in early 2018, he was heckled by fans who left in droves as Mr. Ant rambled and raved on about his distrust of women, his divorces, and the way the media & industry have treated him over the years. A newspaper report stated, "*Fans left behind debated his mental state, whether he was intoxicated and whether their memories of their 80s idol had been ruined forever. He stood, but certainly did not deliver!*" After 18 years away from the studio in 2013 he released the album *Adam Ant Is the BlueBlack Hussar in Marrying the Gunner's Daughter* to mixed reviews. Today Mr. Ant's shows are sellout smashes; he toured the UK in 2016 and North America in early 2017, performing his *Kings of the Wild Frontier* album in its entirety, then taking the tour to New Zealand and Australia.

⦿ In 1979 Robin Scott went by the moniker M, and he went to No.1 on the US Billboard singles chart with 'Pop Muzik'. The song was the opening track of Scott's debut album, *New York, London, Paris, Munich*. It was nothing less than a monster. The single peaked at No.2 in the UK and topped the charts in Europe and North America.

⦿ Ian McNabb was born Robert McNabb on November 3, 1960. Hailing from Liverpool, England, he served as the singer-songwriter/guitarist and frontman of The Icicle Works, achieving success in the UK with the top 20 single 'Love Is a Wonderful Colour' in 1983. Additionally, he played a significant role in The Wild Swans until their dissolution in late 1990. Following this, Ian released a couple of singles that did not receive much attention. However, he made a comeback in 1993 with a collection of demos that laid the foundation for his debut solo album, *Truth and Beauty*. Throughout his solo career, Ian has collaborated with notable artists such as Ringo Starr, Neil Young/Crazy Horse, Mike Scott of The Waterboys, and Danny Thompson of the folk band Pentangle.

⦿ When The Nightingales released their debut album, *Pigs on Purpose*, on Cherry Red Records in November 1982, it marked a strong and distinctive first effort. The songs feature driving double guitar riffs and the deadpan vocals of Robert Lloyd. Tracks like 'The Crunch', 'Hedonists Sigh', 'It Lives Again', and 'Don't Blink' shine with energetic POST-PUNK guitar bursts set against a propulsive beat. While Lloyd's monotonic delivery risks tedium, the lack of any guitar solos keeps the focus on the band's unique musical ideas and energetic execution, capturing the essence of the POST-PUNK era.

⦿ On this day in 1978, Pere Ubu, hailing from Cleveland, Ohio, unveiled their second studio album, *Dub Housing*. Like their previous works, Pere Ubu's latest offering may not immediately captivate everyone, and some might not connect with it at all. However, nestled within the album is 'Ubu Dance Party', arguably the closest the band's original lineup ventured towards a pop-infused track. Leading the charge is Dave Thomas, a vocalist with a style that defies comparison, yet somehow perfectly complements the unconventional sound of this truly unique collective. At times, their music ventures into the avant-garde, while at others, it delves into the realm of sheer peculiarity. Thomas unleashes his vocal prowess, intertwining with the instrumentation's twangy, jangly, abrasive, and chaotic nature, resulting in an overall challenging listening experience. Undoubtedly moody, unsettling, and far from easy listening, Pere Ubu's *Dub Housing* remains an indispensable auditory encounter.

⦿ The Police's debut studio album, *Outlandos d'Amour*, was released in November 1982 and featured their distinctive fusion of punk rock, NEW WAVE, POST-PUNK, and reggae. While hit songs like 'So Lonely', 'Roxanne', and 'Can't Stand Losing You' propelled the band into the spotlight, the album also contains excellent lesser-known tracks like 'Truth Hits Everybody', 'Peanuts', and 'Hole in My Life'. With Sting's clever bass playing and singing, Andy Summers' eccentric guitar work, and Stewart Copeland's splashy drumming, *Outlandos d'Amour* showcases The Police's one-of-a-kind sound and powerful musicianship that made them stand out. Though best remembered for the iconic singles, this strong debut album demonstrates the breadth and diversity of the band's musical talents.

⦿ On November 3, 1979, The Raincoats released their *self-titled* debut album. Filled with catchy rhythms and unique instrumentation, the band, fronted by Gina Birch and Ana de Silva, boldly explored uncharted territory. Their raw sound, reminiscent of The Slits, featured edgy harmonies, powerful drums and bass, jagged guitar riffs, and even a violin. The Raincoats aimed to prove that innovative songwriting will never go out of style.

⦿ The debut single by Spandau Ballet, 'To Cut a Long Story Short', was released in 1980 and reached No.5 on the UK Singles Chart. It appeared on the album *Journeys to Glory* and was produced by Richard James Burgess. Spandau Ballet took the lead of the 'new romantic movement' with their unique style. The band's musicianship was top-notch, and Tony Hadley's vocals were outstanding.

4

⦿ Christopher Henry Difford, aka Chris Difford, was born in 1954 in London, England. Chris was a founding member of Squeeze and is renowned most notably for his song-writing partnership with Glenn Tilbrook; the pair have often been quoted as the "Lennon and McCartney of the '80s". Their compositions, among so many others, 'Cool for Cats', 'Pulling Mussels (From the Shell)', 'Tempted', 'Black Coffee in Bed', and 'Take Me, I'm Yours', are timeless classics! Throughout his career Chris has released 6 solo albums with his lyrics chosen by the likes of Elvis Costello, Paul Young, Jools Holland, Elton John & Wet Wet Wet to cover. A little-known fact about Chris is that in 1972 he was a member of David Bowie's road crew on the UK tour of David Bowie's Ziggy Stardust UK tour!

⦿ On November 4, 1956, in Hereford, England, James Honeyman-Scott was born. He was renowned as a founding member and guitar player for The Pretenders, establishing himself as one of the most innovative and adaptable guitarists during the NEW WAVE movement of the early 1980s. Unfortunately, James became another tragic victim of the music industry's drug culture, passing away on June 16, 1982, due to heart failure triggered by an adverse reaction to cocaine. His untimely demise occurred just days after The Pretenders dismissed their bassist, Pete Farndon. Prior to his death, James had expressed to Chrissie Hynde his inability to deal with Pete's heroin addiction, stating that Pete had to leave, or he would depart from the band.

⦿ The debut album *Try Out* by French NEW WAVE duo KaS Product cemented their status as pioneers of the 'cold wave' scene. Released in 1982, the record showcases Spatsz's brooding electronics and Mona Soyoc's impassioned vocals and guitar over dark, yet delicate synths. While not pure synthpop, *Try Out* reveals influences of Nina Hagen's theatricality and The B-52's off-kilter style, with Soyoc's enthusiastic, dramatic delivery evoking Toyah Wilcox. Creative and idiosyncratic, *Try Out* heralded the arrival of a highly inventive new act.

⦿ Cosey Fanni Tutti, aka Christine Carol Newby, was born on this day in 1951, in Hull, England. Cosey, a performance artist/vocalist/multi-instrumentalist, was part of Throbbing Gristle (TG) & Chris & Cosey. She took the name Cosey Fanni Tutti, which comes from Mozart's opera Così fan tutte, meaning literally "They [women] all do the same", before which she performed under the name Cosmosis. With the demise of Throbbing Gristle (TG) in 1981, Cosey, TG member and life partner Chris Carter continued recording and performing under the guises of Chris & Cosey, Carter Tutti and CTI (Creative Technology Institute). The duo's output trod the path of being both rhythmic and ambient, producing some glorious synthesised symphonic arrangements reminiscent of the works by Brian Eno and Autechre. The duo's 1981 debut album release, *Heartbeat*, was groundbreaking; a decade before rave and trance came to the fore, they melded those genres with industrial for an indeed awesome listening experience. Cosey and partner Chris have gone on to record well over 30 albums together and collaborated with many musicians. Cosey has released two solo albums and composed the original soundtrack for the 2020 film Delia, about the electronic music pioneer Delia Derbyshire.

⦿ Sinead O'Connor, as she was known then, released her debut album, *The Lion and the Cobra*, in 1987. Considered a landmark for female artists of the 1980s and 1990s, the album features a diverse mix of musical textures reflecting O'Connor's eclectic personality. Drawing inspiration from artists like Siouxsie Sioux, Peter Gabriel, Kate Bush, and Prince, O'Connor showcases impressive vocal skills on songs like 'Jerusalem' and 'Just Like You Said It Would Be'. Authentic, original, and expressive, *The Lion and the Cobra* deserves acclaim for its artistry. Though some dismissed O'Connor due to her publicity, the album rewards close listening.

⦿ The *self-titled* first album by They Might Be Giants in 1986 brought forth a distinctive sound. Filled with captivating and peculiar tunes centered on enigmatic lyrics and unusual musical arrangements, it is impossible not to be captivated by its one-of-a-kind charm. The addition of whistling, accordion, and tuba enhances the delightful themes. Tracks such as 'Number Three', 'Hide Away Folk Family', and 'Boat of Car' truly stand out. Nothing quite like it had been heard before or since, with maybe the exception of Olivia Tremor Control's *Black Foliage*. It remains intriguing and unforgettable.

⦿ On November 4, 1982, Virgin Prunes released their debut album ...*If I Die, I Die* on the Rough Trade label. Produced by Wire's Colin Newman, the record epitomizes POST-PUNK adventurism and creativity. Layers of tribal drums and angular, mysterious guitar intertwine with unusual bouzoukis. Fronted by Gavin Friday (Fionán Martin Hanvey) and featuring Guggi (Derek Rowan), Dave-id Busaras Scott (David Watson), Strongman (Trevor Rowan, Guggi's brother), Dik Evans (Richard Evans, brother of U2's The Edge), and Pod (Anthony Murphy), the Virgin Prunes were known for live shows akin to confrontational performance art, frequently resulting in banned appearances. Each eclectic song differs vastly from the last, intriguingly pushing listeners to their limits like early PiL and Throbbing Gristle. As dark and apocalyptic as any band, the Virgin Prunes crafted a lush, foreboding, beautifully unsettling nightmare with this masterful debut.

5

⦿ Helen O'Hara, also known as Helen Bevington, was born in 1956 in Bristol, England. She was the violinist for the band Dexys Midnight Runners from 1982 to 1987, playing on their albums *Too-Rye-Ay and Don't Stand Me Down*. O'Hara eventually became the musical director and producer for the band. She even co-wrote the song 'This Is What She's Like', which was reportedly about her.

◉ The excellent 4-track debut EP *Watusi Rodeo* from Guadalcanal Diary was released in 1983. Taking their name from the book/movie of the same title, this 4-piece jangle pop band from Georgia is often compared to R.E.M., but they have their own distinct sound. Two standout tracks that highlight the talented rhythm section are 'Michael Rockefeller', with its clever arrangement, and 'John Wayne'.

◉ On this day in 1976, the Scottish punk rock band The Rezillos played their first gig at Teviot Row House, a student union building at the University of Edinburgh. The original line-up that day featured Fay Fife and Eugene Reynolds on vocals, Gail Warning on backing vocals, Jo Callis and Hi-Fi Harris on guitars, D.K. Smythe on bass, Angel Patterson on drums, and William Mysterious on saxophone. Over the years, the band has undergone multiple line-up changes through several reformations, including when Fife and Reynolds created the spinoff band The Revillos after a split in 1979. The Rezillos later reformed in 2001 with a new lineup.

◉ Mike Score, born in 1952 in Beverely, England, has been the keyboardist, guitarist, and lead singer for A Flock of Seagulls since the band's inception. Initially gaining attention for their eccentric haircuts, A Flock of Seagulls found success with their catchy synthpop songs and striking stage presence, becoming one of the iconic NEW WAVE bands of the early 1980s. After a successful run of albums and tours, during which they opened for major acts like The Police, the band disbanded in 1988. Mike soon reformed the band with new members and continues to tour as A Flock of Seagulls, focusing on their timeless music rather than outlandish hairstyles. Their smash hit 'I Ran', with its memorable video in heavy rotation on MTV, epitomized British NEW WAVE and cemented A Flock of Seagulls' reputation as a top band of the era.

◉ The Tube was a groundbreaking TV music program that ran from 1982 to 1987, it kicked off its first episode on this day in 1982. Paula Yates and Jools Holland served as hosts, and the show commenced with a lively performance of 'She Goes to Finos' by Toy Dolls. The episode also showcased The Jam, who rocked the stage with their popular hits 'Town Called Malice', 'Move on Up', and 'Beat Surrender'. The show derived its name from the plexiglass tunnel that served as an entrance to Studio Five at Tyne Tees TV, the filming location.

6

◉ Rozz Williams, aka Roger Alan Painter was born in Pamona, USA in 1963, Rozz was a prolific and influential musician, vocalist, writer, painter, and performer. As the founding frontman of the gothic rock band Christian Death, formed in October 1979, Williams helped pioneer the American goth scene with the band's slow, doom-laden guitar riffs, ambient synth textures, and theatrical live performances inspired by David Bowie, Roxy Music, Alice Cooper, and Throbbing Gristle. After departing Christian Death, Williams continued his prolific output across various musical projects like Shadow Project, Premature Ejaculation, and Daucus Karota, cementing his status as a groundbreaking figure in alternative and gothic rock music. Rozz committed suicide on April 1, 1998, at 34 years of age.

◉ Released in 1983, the debut album *The Politics of Dancing* by Re-Flex featured the minor hit single and title track. Despite Re-Flex's strong musical pedigree – including vocalist Baxter's Bowie-esque phrasing, lush synthesizers, and dynamic percussion – the album missed out on the acclaim it deserved. With influences of Heaven 17 and production quality to match, Re-Flex had all the elements for success.

◉ The Australian POST-PUNK band The Triffids released their first non-independent album, *Treeless Plain*, on Hot Records in November 1983. Prior to this major label debut, they had self-released six cassette tapes between 1978 and 1981, simply titled *1st* through *6th*. After honing their sound through years of live performances and indie releases, they were very much a vehicle for the poetry of David McComb and built a reputation in Australia that began to spread internationally. With influences of The Smiths, Echo and the Bunnymen, and Teardrop Explodes, the band brought a unique blend of melancholy and confidence to Treeless Plain. Though underrated at the time, *Treeless Plain* stands alongside other seminal Australian POST-PUNK records from The Saints, The Church, The Stems, and Laughing Clowns.

◉ Seek and you may find the debut single 'Shoot the Truth' by the Greek band Yell-O-Yell on Creep Records. With a dark, angst-ridden sound reminiscent of The Birthday Party, the Athens trio of Phil Scars Vascalis (vocals, guitar), Vangelis Casillieris (drums), and Haris Kirkilis (bass) released two albums in their short but successful career. Their 2012 retrospective album *(Still) Warm Like Worms* is worth seeking out for fans of macabre music.

◉ George Young, born in Glasgow, Scotland on November 6, 1947, was a founding member of the 1960s pop group The Easybeats and later Flash and the Pan. Along with Harry Vanda, he co-wrote the mega hits 'Friday on My Mind' and 'Love Is in the Air' and was also the producer for AC/DC, which featured his younger brothers Malcolm and Angus. As the lead vocalist and synthesiser player in Flash and the Pan, Young was joined by guitarist and vocalist Harry Vanda, bassist Les Karski, drummer Ray Arnott, and pianist Warren "Thumping Pig" Morgan. The band achieved major success with the singles 'Hey St. Peter' and 'Down Among the Dead Men' and their 6 highly regarded albums. The rock music world lost one of its greats when Young passed away on October 23, 2017.

7

◉ Colourbox released their debut *self-titled* mini-album in 1983 through 4AD Records. This release should not be confused with their later 1985 *self-titled* full-length album, itself a brilliant piece of work. When listening to modern genres like trance, trip hop, techno, and electro rave, it becomes clear that Colourbox were ahead of their time. As pioneering samplers, they were part of the vanguard of electronic music. Their music remains timeless and hip, even today. Unlike the cheesy synthpop of the era, their songs are soulful and funky, with intricate sampled overlays. 'Shotgun', the opening track, demonstrates their genius cut-and-paste sampling skills. Overall, this important 1983 EP represents a milestone in the early days of electronica.

◉ Karen Marks was born in Melbourne, Australia, on November 7th. Her first forays into rock music were as a journalist for several music magazines. In the late 1970s, there was a burgeoning music scene in Melbourne, and Karen secured a position as manager for The Boys Next Door, gaining experience that soon led her to manage JAB, a band that would morph into Models, one of Australia's most successful groups. With her tough, uncompromising attitude, Karen pushed Models to great heights. In 1980, she ventured into recording, releasing 'Cold Café', a sought-after single that was later included on Julien Dechery and DJ Sundae's compilation *Sky Girl*. More recently, following the overwhelming international success of the rerelease of Cold Café, Karen and long-time collaborator Ash Wednesday performed a sellout concert at the Melbourne Town Hall in April 2023. 2024 and more performances in Australia and overseas are being looked into along with new material for an album. A documentary is in the offing.

10 QUESTIONS: AN INTERVIEW WITH KAREN MARKS

G'day, Karen. In your teenage years you attended an all-girls school in Melbourne. Were you learning music there at that time?

Yes, I studied violin, and being interested in singing, I was a soprano in the choir and part of the Madrigal group. Madrigal singing was a style developed in Europe during the Renaissance based around polyphony with parts for four to six voices.

After school you moved into rock journalism; what magazines or newspapers carried your articles?

There were numerous like Observer Pop, Sweet, Scream and various band 'fanzines', such as one for John Paul Young & The Allstars. These were mostly about 24 pages in size.

As everywhere, Melbourne in the late '70s was very exciting musically. Who and how did you come in contact with during that period?

Everybody! My sister Jandy had the 'Dear Jandy' column in arguably Australia's most famous magazine at the time, Go-Set. Jandy also worked at Teasers nightclub, and I often tagged along with her, meeting up with members of The La De Das, The Dingoes, Ayres Rock & AC/DC. It was like one big family hanging out together, with us ending up at parties at Michael Gudinski's or Molly Meldrum's. At the height of his fame, I was sharing a house with Greg Macainsh, the bass player with Skyhooks, and to this day he is still one of my best friends. I guess hanging out with the likes of Ross Wilson, Joe Camilleri and Keith Glass drew the attention of the up-and-coming new 'punks'; hence, Phill Calvert approached me and asked me to manage Boys Next Door.

So, this led to you being the first manager of The Boys Next Door and then JAB. What was that like, and where did the individuals from those bands end up?

It was so interesting; so many of them attained high levels of distinction in the music world. Phill Calvert went to play with the Psychedelic Furs, and Mick Harvey went on to the Bad Seeds and, as a soloist, became very successful as both a musician and producer. Ash Wednesday made some great music with The Metronomes and later went to Berlin, Germany, and was part of Einstürzende Neubauten. Of course, Nick Cave has become a leading artist worldwide, and then there's me. I'm so thankful to have gained international success and critical acclaim after only my first release.

Was there one event that happened as a manager that still strikes a chord with you?

I'm proud of the fact that I stood up to Dirty Pool Management, who tried to muscle a The Stranglers tour support away from Models for one of their bands, Flowers. Models got the gig!

1981, and you start recording a great debut, "Cold Café". What led you to doing that? Can you tell me a little about the process and who helped that come to fruition?

At the time Ash Wednesday had left Models, and I too had ceased managing them, and Ash had a loft space full of equipment on Brunswick Street, Melbourne, so we played around with ideas and brought in different people. The end result is "Cold Café".

Cold Café is now available on the digital platform Bandcamp; what has the response to that been like? It must be rewarding to know that the tune was also included on the "Sky Girl' compilation created by Julien Dechery and DJ Sundae?

All I know is that "Cold Café" has done incredibly well; as for actual numbers, I really have no idea. Thanks must go to Michael Kucyk of Efficient Space, who has been distributing it on Bandcamp.

Are you presently working on any musical projects?

I'm always jotting down melodies, words and ideas. I really want to take these into a rehearsal space and studio with Ash Wednesday as soon as possible. An aim would be to do some music festivals in Europe.

In the world of music, what has been the most rewarding for you?

Wow, my love goes to the people I have met for the pleasure I gained from their music. The great loves in my life have been musicians; to me, that is everything. Heart & Soul.

One last question. Is there one thing that you would like to go back to the '70s & '80s and tell the impressionable young Karen Marks?

Karen, you can do it too! Just go for it!

Thanks very much, Karen.

● *Alphabravocharliedeltaechofoxtrotgolf,* the debut album by the Australian band Models, was released in 1980. Although the album cover stated it was "produced by no-one", Tony Cohen and the band members themselves handled production while Models were still unsigned. While *Alphabravocharliedeltaechofoxtrotgolf* sounds dated today due to advances in technology, it was well regarded in Australia at the time of its release. Over the course of their career, which saw several line-up changes, Models explored a diverse musical output, from glam and raw POST-PUNK to quirky NEW WAVE and synthpop.

● Frank Tovey was one of the more intriguing NEW WAVE artists; using the moniker of Fad Gadget, he released his debut album *Fireside Favourites* in 1980. Tovey's music bridged the gap between synthpop and industrial bands like Throbbing Gristle and Cabaret Voltaire, blending bleak, icy synthesizers with catchy electronica. Though often disturbing and not radio-friendly, his work was sadly overlooked by the larger NEW WAVE audience. Tracks like the title song, 'Newsreel', 'Pedestrian', 'The Box', and 'Arch of The Aorta' showcase Tovey's dark electronic style.

● Released in 1983, Real Life's debut album, *Heartland*, showcased the Melbourne-based band's synth-driven sound. Produced by Steve Hillage, this album was a key moment for the group; it featured atmospheric, melodic synthesizers and rhythmic electronic drums from a Simmons kit. Coming right after their hit single 'Send Me an Angel', *Heartland* intrigues with its diversity and complexity beyond that massive synthpop song. Other highlights are the varied tracks 'Under the Hammer', 'Always', 'Exploding Bullets' and the catchy 'Catch Mc I'm Falling'.

● The Canadian band Strange Advance released their debut album, *Worlds Away*, in 1982. Featuring the minor hit single 'Worlds Away', a melodic synth ballad, the album fits into the synthpop style of Ultravox. With great melodies built around electronic percussion and synthesizers, the record contains plenty of synth-driven songs.

8

● Blue Peter released *Radio Silence*, their first full-length album, in 1980. The album held the smash single 'Radio Silence', a song that packed club dance floors, and the lead track 'Video Verite' must rate as one of the band's strongest tracks and a definite lost power pop classic. Packed with power-pop tunes, it was produced by Jasper, Kevin Doyle, and Chris Wardman.

● The Dancing Did released their fifth and most popular single, 'Badger Boys', in 1982. The Dancing Did (a "did" is a gypsy) had their origin in Evesham, Worcestershire, UK. This band was rather unique and was once described as "a brand of rustic rock 'n' roll, coming from a mix of The Clash and Steeleye Span sprinkled with Fairport Convention!" The band comprised Tim Harrison (vocals), Martyn Dormer (lead guitar, synthesiser, vocals), Roger Smith (bass) and Chris Houghton (drums) coming together in 1980. They released two independent singles on their own Fruit and Veg label before moving to Stiff Records. Their only album of 1982, *And Did Those Feet*, was ranked by NME magazine in The 100 Greatest Albums You've Never Heard.

◉ The Dream Academy released their *self-titled* debut album in 1985, when NEW WAVE and POST-PUNK were on the decline. With its sophisticated production, *The Dream Academy* is an album that reveals more of itself with each listen. It contains fantastic songs like 'Life in A Northern Town' (a classic), 'The Love Parade', and 'The Edge of Forever'. Delicate and refined, this very good album only seems to get better with time.

◉ The only album recorded by the Mo-Dettes, *The Story So Far*, was released on November 8, 1980. The band emerged from an earlier project called The Bomberettes, and their music showed the influence of bands like LiLiPUT, The Slits, and The Raincoats-unsurprising given that founding Mo-Dettes member Kate Korus had also played with those groups. *The Story So Far* is considered one of the seminal "all-girl" POST-PUNK records, though its rough, bass-heavy production gives it a distinct DIY aesthetic with a mod/pop-influenced garage rock sound with echoes of The Raincoats, LiLiPuT, and The Slits, though in a more pop-orientated, reggae-less direction. The album compiles most of the Mo-Dettes' recordings up to that point, including the semi-hit single 'White Mouse Disco', along with other highlights like 'Dark Park Creeping', 'The Kray Twins', and their Edith Piaf tribute, 'Sparrow'. The Story So Far represents an enjoyable example of the DIY ethos applied to POST-PUNK pop.

◉ Paul Stephen Thompson was born November 8, 1957. During his tenure with The Cure, he was known as Porl, and it's for his work with The Cure that he is best known. He was actually an original member when they were known as Easy Cure but dropped away prior to the name change and recording. Porl re-joined the band for the recording of the album *The Top* as a saxophonist, keyboardist, and guitarist, but he was never going to be too far away, as he is Robert Smith's brother-in-law, being married to Robert's sister. Porl performed on the next four studio albums, *The Head on the Door, Kiss Me, Kiss Me, Kiss Me, Disintegration* and *Wish*, before leaving to join Jimmy Page and Robert Plant for a tour in 1995. These days he is not currently a member of The Cure; he is a painter and is collaborating on various artistic projects, and he now goes by the name Pearl Thompson.

9

◉ In 1984, Julian Cope released his second solo album, *Fried*. This psychedelic cult classic will always be regarded as one of Cope's most adventurous and mystifying works. The *Fried* album cover, portraying a naked Cope with a tortoise shell on his back looking at a toy truck, just adds to the mystique. Coming off the success of his first solo album *World Shut Your Mouth*, and his frontman role in The Teardrop Explodes, Cope's creativity continued to shine on *Fried*. Sparkling with undeniably brilliant pop tunes and quintessentially quirky, cryptic Cope tracks, the album remains neo-psychedelic while showcasing the artist's inventiveness. Highlights include the rocking 'Reynard the Fox', the spaced-out 'Holy Love', and the sensational 'Sunspots'. Both Julian Cope's solo work and his time with The Teardrop Explodes deserve a revered place in any '80s music collection.

◉ Sean Kelly, the singer, guitarist, and songwriter, was born November 9, 1958. Sean, after the split of The Teenage Radio Stars, joined the second incarnation of Models, the band originally founded by Ash Wednesday & Janis Freidenfeldson, aka Johnny Crash. After Models split in 1987, Sean became a founding member of the 'supergroup' Absent Friends and then The Harbour City Dukes (aka The Dukes) in 1990. That year saw him awarded an ARIA as producer of the 'Australian Single of the Year' for his work with the aforementioned slick R'n'B outfit Absent Friends, a band featuring Wendy Matthews, GANGgajang's Mark Calaghan, and the INXS bassist Garry Beers. Nobody could argue that it is with Models that he has etched a place in Australian music history. Models since its early days had a revolving door membership of POST-PUNK/pop royalty, with the likes of Wednesday, Andrew Duffield, and Roger Mason on keyboards; Mark Ferrie and James Freud on bass guitar, and Crash, Duster Stiggs, and Darton Price on drums and percussion. They were rounded out with James Valentine on saxophone and Wendy Matthews as backing vocalist. Models highly acclaimed album, *The Pleasure of Your Company*, was ranked in the Top 100 Australian Albums, and Models were inducted into the ARIA Hall of Fame in 2010. Through their time, Models were able to earn support with the likes of David Bowie, Bryan Ferry, The Ramones, Midnight Oil, and The Birthday Party, and today a Models lineup of Kelly, Duffield, Ferrie, and Ashley Davies still perform sporadically. In 2020, amidst lockdowns, Kelly also began solo performances and gigs with Trio, which featured singer-guitarist Billy Miller and bassist Rosie Westbrook.

● The debut album *Business as Usual* by Men at Work was released in Australia on November 9, 1981, and in the United States in April 1982, going to the top of the charts for 4 months. While viewed as NEW WAVE in the USA, Men at Work were considered more mainstream rock in Australia. The album was a worldwide success, selling over 15 million copies and earning the band several music awards in both Australia and the USA. It featured three hugely popular singles – 'Who Can It Be Now?', 'Be Good Johnny' and the anthemic 'Down Under'. After the TV quiz program Spicks and Specks asked the question, "What children's song is contained in the song Down Under?" The answer was "Kookaburra". It then resulted in phone calls and emails to Larrikin Music the next day, this culminated in a lawsuit for copyright infringement of the original song 'Kookaburra'. The band lost the case, and frontman Colin Hay has since suggested the deaths of his father in 2010 and bandmate Greg Ham in 2012 were linked to the stress of the lawsuit.

● Alison Moyet's soulful voice transcends the synthpop genre on her 1984 debut solo album *Alf*. As one half of Yazoo, Moyet had already impressed critics and fans alike. On the album *Alf*, her warm, perfectly toned vocals elevate standout tracks like 'Love Resurrection' and 'All Cried Out' above typical '80s synthpop. While some songs sound formulaic, Moyet's majestic voice remains captivating throughout.

● The Raincoats played their debut gig on November 9, 1977, at The Tabernacle in Notting Hill, London. The line-up then consisted of Gina Birch (bass & vox), Ana da Silva (guitar & vox), Ross Crighton (guitar), and Nick Turner (drums). By 1978 they became an all-female lineup consisting of Birch, da Silva, Vicky Aspinall (violin) and ex-Slits drummer Palmolive, aka Paloma McLardy.

● *La Folie*, the sixth studio album by The Stranglers, was released in 1981. With this album, The Stranglers made a conscious effort to deliver more commercially acceptable songs. The French album title translates to "madness", foreshadowing the band's bold new musical direction. *La Folie* contains the international hit 'Golden Brown' and other melodic, pop-orientated songs like 'Non-Stop', 'Tramp' and 'Pin Up'. The album closes with the haunting 6-minute semi-acoustic ballad 'La Folie', sung partially in French, about the notorious cannibal murderer Issei Sagawa. This atmospheric, romantic track was a dramatic departure from The Stranglers' earlier work and unsurprisingly failed to chart when released as a single. Overall, *La Folie* showed The Stranglers exploring a more accessible, radio-friendly sound.

10

● Peter Bramall, better known as Bram Tchaikovsky, was the singer and guitarist for the British rock band The Motors. Born in 1950 in Lincolnshire, England, Tchaikovsky helped The Motors achieve their greatest chart success - the 1978 UK top 5 single 'Airport'. After splitting from The Motors, Tchaikovsky formed his own band, Bram Tchaikovsky, releasing the power pop classic 'Girl of My Dreams'. The Motors' debut album *1* is considered a seminal power pop record, despite emerging concurrently with the punk scene. Songs like 'Dancing the Night Away' led to The Motors being included on punk compilations, yet their melodic sound was far removed from punk. The Motors pioneered the NEW WAVE/power pop sound, inspiring countless garage and pub rock bands. Though The Motors lacked vocal finesse, their energetic debut still stands as a prime example of pub rock style.

● In early 1982, Kraftwerk were working on a new album in their Kling Klang studio with the tentative title *Technicolor*. Due to trademark issues, it was soon re-titled *Techno Pop*, and upon its release by EMI on November 10, 1986, it became known as *Electric Café*. This landmark album had a profound influence on electronic music, with its six innovative tracks - the rhythmic overture of 'Boing Boom Tschak', the infectious 'Techno Pop' with its blistering groove and arpeggios, the female vocal of 'Musique Non-Stop' in tribute to artist Rebecca Allen, who created the computer images of their faces that they use in concert and on the *Electric Café* album cover. To quote Ralf Hutter, "*You made computer images of four men, so we made a computer image of a woman's voice*". There are sublime beats and telephone sounds of 'The Telephone Call', the unusual emotion of 'Sex Object', and the epic closing track 'Electric Café' with melodies reminiscent of *Trans Europe Express*. In 2009, it was renamed and re-released as *Techno Pop*. Kraftwerk fans have mixed opinions, some finding it more pop-structured and accessible, bringing new listeners, while others missed the previous sound of their sprawling trademark compositions. Yet with its catchy electronic beats, it brilliantly showcases Kraftwerk's talent for melodic pop sensibilities fused with their pioneering electronic aesthetic. For any fan of electronic music, it serves as an engaging introduction to Kraftwerk's influential genius.

● Frank Maudsley, who was born Francis Lee Maudsley in 1959 in Liverpool, England, was the bass player for the NEW WAVE band Flock of Seagulls. The band had several international hit songs in the '80s, including 'I Ran (So Far Away)', 'Space Age Love Song' and 'Wishing (If I Had a Photograph of You)', each released in 1982, and 'The More You Live, the More You Love', from 1984. After the band split in 1986, Mike Score reformed the band without Maudsley in 1988. However, Maudsley reunited with the original Flock of Seagulls lineup of Mike Score, Ali Score, Paul Reynolds, and himself for a one-time performance on the VH1 show Bands Reunited in November 2003. Although no longer part of Score's touring band, in June 2011 Maudsley performed with former bandmate Paul Reynolds at the Croxteth Park Music Festival in Liverpool under the name "A Flock of Seagulls". Maudsley's current activities and whereabouts are uncertain.

● On November 10, 1984, the band Frankie Goes to Hollywood rocketed to No.1 on the UK album chart with their debut record, *Welcome to the Pleasure Dome*. The album set a record with over one million advance orders. On the same day, the band made their television debut, performing 'Two Tribes' and 'Born to Run' on Saturday Night Live, further propelling their meteoric rise to fame.

● Throbbing Gristle's debut album, *Second Annual Report of Throbbing Gristle*, released in 1977, presents a challenging and avant-garde soundscape. The album's chilling yet hypnotic atmosphere blends industrial noise, drones, and bleak sound collages with Genesis P-Orridge's wailing vocals, evoking the experimental psychedelia of Pink Floyd's *Ummagumma*. Though raw in technique, the inventive and uncompromising nature the *Second Annual Report* marks it as a landmark recording in the birth of industrial music. However, its dissonant and disturbing aesthetic certainly makes it an acquired taste, not the most accessible entry point into Throbbing Gristle's catalogue. For new listeners, *20 Jazz Funk Greats* offers a more approachable introduction to the band's radical sonic assault.

◉ Visage released their hit single 'Fade to Grey' and their *self-titled* first album on November 10th, 1980, through Polydor Records. 'Fade to Grey', which featured spoken French interludes by Brigitte Arens, became a smash hit internationally, cracking the Top 10 in the UK and the Top 5 in several other countries. It also reached No.1 in Germany and Switzerland and was certified silver in the UK. However, the songwriting credits sparked controversy when Visage's frontman Steve Strange argued in his 2002 memoir that it was unfair to only credit Billy Currie, Chris Payne, and Midge Ure, as he felt his leadership of the group was the integral role in their success and should have earned him a writer's credit. In 2005, Kelly Osbourne's single 'One Word', written by Linda Perry, was accused of copying 'Fade to Grey', resulting in an out-of-court settlement where Osbourne's team agreed to give Visage a cut of the royalties.

11

◉ Chris Connelly was born on November 11, 1964, in Edinburgh, Scotland. In 1980, he formed the band Finitribe but shifted his focus after collaborating with Al Jourgensen in London's Southern Studios in November 1986. Shortly thereafter, Connelly moved to Chicago and became an integral part of the burgeoning industrial music scene, earning recognition for his contributions to albums by Pigface, Murder Inc., KMFDM, and especially Ministry and The Revolting Cocks. His solo work marked a departure from industrial into more pop-influenced styles reminiscent of the 1970s. In 2007, Connelly penned the memoir *"Concrete, Bulletproof, Invisible + Fried: My Life as A Revolting Cock,"* chronicling his studio and touring experiences between 1986 and 1992.

FINI TRIBE LIVE IN GLASGOW, 31ST OCTOBER 1986
CHRIS CONNELLY
(Fini Tribe, Ministry, Revolting Cocks)

Oh dear, oh dear, oh dear. I do accept a huge portion of the responsibility for this particular caper. You see, Fini Tribe really didn't give a fuck; we ploughed our own furrow, always had, and, at that point, about six years into our existence, it sort of felt like nobody wanted us. We could not compete with the blue-eyed pigswill of upcoming Scottish combos like Hipsway and Wet Wet Wet, nor the mildly annoying feel-good paisley kindermusik of the BMX Bandits, etc.

After a slam dunk performance art fiasco at the assembly rooms in Edinburgh a while before, where we apparently ruined the floor by spraying paint on the audience by way of a suspended and punctured rubbish bag, we were cautiously invited to play at the prestigious 'Third Eye Centre' in Glasgow as part of the "Glasgow Style" fortnight. We were playing with a band called The Boy Hairdresser; we hoped to scare seven kinds of shite out of them, but we presented our most benign and tepid faces and promised there would be NO "stunts" like at the assembly rooms, HONEST, MISTER!!! *"We'll keep our heads down and just play a few wee songs; it'll be braw!"*

Meanwhile, amid hushed demonic laughter, we plotted, and through some tenuous contact with the great improvisationalist and artist Paul Burwell, we picked up a few tips to use in our performance.

What did the staff of the 'Third Eye Centre' think as we loaded in a recently "procured" shovel from an excavator truck? It had to have been six feet wide, and lo and behold!? Why was the inside covered in cotton balls!? And why are they stuck on with cow gum!? A (now obsolete) adhesive made from rubber dissolved in highly volatile and flammable petroleum spirits!? *"Oh, it's a percussion instrument; the cotton just dulls the sound a wee bit...".*

At the climax of what was probably a very loud, unnerving, and visceral show, a flame was taken to the volatile and huge shovel, and it just went up like a bonfire, spectacular, very hot, and pretty scary!

The fire was extinguished fairly quickly, and the Fini Tribe were told in no uncertain terms how banned they were from the Third Eye Centre, from Glasgow, from Scotland, and from the fuckin' WORLD!

I was delighted! We were delighted! Another layer of acrimony between us and the music bigwigs of Caledonia: no airplay on late-night Radio Forth or Clyde for you, you boundary-pushing experimental bastards!!!

It would not be long before I parted ways with the Fini Tribe, amicably, and went to push more stupid boundaries in the USA. The Finis went on to have well-deserved success with dance music.

And we all lived happily ever after!

● *Doot-Doot*, the debut album by the UK band Freur, was released in 1983. Freur was formed in Wales by Karl Hyde and Rick Smith, who later went on to form the successful electronic act Underworld. Freur was their second band, following their earlier art school collaboration, Screen Gemz. Drawing influence from Kraftwerk, Freur experimented with synthesizers, techno beats, tapes, and electronic rhythms, supplemented by guitar and live drums. The title track became a dancefloor staple of the New Romantic era, selling well in New Zealand and Germany. With its similarities to The The, the album featured some solid tunes beyond 'Doot Doot', like 'Runaway', 'Riders in the Night', and 'Theme from the Film of the Same Name'.

● The Australian band GANGgajang released their *self-titled* debut album on November 11, 1985. Considered one of the best Aussie albums of the '80s, *GANGgajang* sold over 120,000 copies, earning it Platinum status. The album is consistently strong from start to finish, with no weak tracks. Frontman Mark Callaghan, formerly of the band The Riptides, brought his songwriting talents to GANGgajang, penning eclectic, high-quality songs that defy easy classification. 'Sounds of Then' is regarded as an Australian classic, with 'Gimme Some Lovin'', close behind, as another standout track.

● Ian Craig Marsh was born in Sheffield, England, on November 11, 1956. A founding member of the pioneering synthpop band The Human League, he left in 1980 to form the British Electric Foundation (B.E.F.) and later the synthpop band Heaven 17 with Martyn Ware. Heaven 17 took their name from the fictional band mentioned in the movie A Clockwork Orange. Marsh and Ware first collaborated in 1977 on the avant-garde project Dead Daughters, where they integrated synthesizer patterns with tape loops and samples. After Dead Daughters, they formed The Future and then The Human League with Philip Oakey and Adi Newton. Newton soon departed, after which the band became known as The Human League. In 2008, Marsh ended his involvement with Heaven 17 to pursue a career as a music teacher.

● Andy Partridge, aka Mr. Partridge, aka Sir John Johns, aka Sandy Sandwich, born Andrew John Partridge in 1953 in Malta, is a renowned British singer-songwriter and multi-instrumentalist. Best known as the founding member and principal songwriter of XTC, Andy established himself as a leading figure of '80s music thanks to his melodic pop sensibilities and playful, experimental vocal and musical arrangements. Beyond his seminal work with XTC, Partridge has also collaborated as a performer, writer, or producer with diverse artists like The Residents, Thomas Dolby, Robyn Hitchcock, and the ambient musician Harold Budd. For a treasure trove of Partridge's work beyond the XTC catalogue, seek out the 8-CD box set *The Fuzzy Warbles Collector's Album*, featuring over 100 rarities and outtakes spanning his prolific career. Today, Partridge continues to live and work in his hometown of Swindon, Wiltshire, where his unique creative spirit first took root.

Andy Partridge by Roch Parisien/Units – Brad, Scott &Rachel by Chester Simpson

⦿ The San Francisco-based band The Units released their *self-titled* debut 7" EP in 1979, pioneering a synth-punk fusion of pulsing synthesizers and robotic vocals reminiscent of Cabaret Voltaire and Devo. Labelled "synth-punk", their futuristic sound eschewed guitars in favour of synthesizers led by Scott Ryser's hypnotic rhythms. The EP featured the singles 'High Pressure Days' and 'Warm Moving Bodies', a stunning encapsulation of late '70s techno. Their creative use of synthesizers was groundbreaking for punk bands of the era. Seek out The Units' influential first album, *Digital Stimulation* from 1980 on the 415 label, which expanded on their unique POST-PUNK electronic sound.

⦿ Bruce Woolley, a multi-instrumentalist, record producer, and songwriter, was born in 1953 in Shepshed, England. He is best known for co-writing the smash hit 'Video Killed the Radio Star' with Geoff Downes and Trevor Horn while a member of the band The Camera Club, which also featured Thomas Dolby. Originally released on The Camera Club's album *English Garden* in 1979, 'Video Killed the Radio Star' later became a huge hit for The Buggles in 1979. Bruce is a prolific songwriter; his compositions have been covered by a diverse array of artists, including Tom Jones, Grace Jones, Stereo MCs, Cher, Cliff Richard, John Farnham and Nikki Minaj.

THE WORLD'S FIRST MODERN POP RECORD
BRUCE WOOLLEY
(Camera Club, The Buggles)

London in the 1970s was a pretty run-down place, with its Dickensian alleys, seedy accommodation, shabby pubs enforcing draconian drinking hours, and crumbling, neglected architecture adjacent to WW2 bomb sites. The IRA dominated the headlines, while trade union-mandated strikes left tonnes of uncollected refuse rotting in the streets. Beacons of light included American Trash Cinema, Capital Radio (the UK's first independent radio station), and an incredible, new, underground music scene: punk rock.

In 1976, as the iconoclastic Sex Pistols were causing outrage, I escaped to London from the 'Grim' North of England's cover-band circuit to join fellow musicians Rod Thompson and Trevor Horn. We were naive and broke, but miraculously we found a patron in Alex Everett – son of a wealthy music publisher – who gave us all a job. Trevor became the house producer. We joined forces with keyboard player Geoff Downes (Tina Charles) and singer Kip Trevor (Black Widow) and proceeded to make a string of spectacularly unsuccessful pop records. Alex quickly ran out of money, mainly due to Trevor's extortionate and unsustainable studio bills, and the party was over before it had started.

Emerging from this chaos, Trevor and I wrote our first song together – 'Clean Clean'. We regrouped with Geoff Downes and began jamming as a group, but progress was slow, so when A&R legend Muff Winwood offered me a singles deal with CBS Records, I seized the opportunity. Although the first record, 'Bobby Bad', disappeared without a trace, I was feeling the support of a major label – and the explosive energy of the London NEW WAVE scene. I was ready to go on the road.

My management reluctantly agreed to fund a band. "*Why give yourself a lobotomy?*" they cautioned. So, I enlisted my schoolfriend guitarist David Birch (The Vibrators) and drummer Richard Wernham (The Motors), whose girlfriend Marion Fudger played bass. I'd discovered a young keyboard player, Tom Robertson, from the small ads section in the Melody Maker. The Camera Club was born. We put on a showcase at Streatham's Orchestra Pit (another bomb site) for CBS – and they loved it. The 'suits' demanded the album.

A few days later, Tom Robertson came to rehearsal with some news. He explained that he and his friend Tom '2-4-6-8 Motorway' Robinson had made a pact one night in Nashville, the famous Kensington pub rock venue. This was the deal: whoever became famous first, then the other "Tom" would have to change their name to avoid any future confusion. When our keyboard player announced his alias, we fell about – he must be joking – but he was deadly serious. Overnight, he'd become Thomas Dolby!

I kept in constant touch with Trevor, and in 1978 he and I wrote 'Video Killed the Radio Star (VKTRS), and some months later, with a demo budget from Tina Charles, we recorded the song together with Geoff Downes at Sound Suite Studios in Camden. While the Camera Club gigged and recorded, Geoff and Trev landed a deal with Island Records. In a bizarre, parallel universe, two different versions of 'VKTRS' began to emerge. One night, Trevor saw us play at the subterranean Rock Garden, where I sang a new line: "Put the blame on VTR". He admitted later to thinking, "Right – I'll have that." It's a continuous source of frustration for me that Trevor misheard it as "VCR!"

During a CC rehearsal I was on a payphone to Geoff about another song we were writing, 'Baby Blue', which was to become our first UK hit for Dusty Springfield. In the background, Geoff couldn't help overhearing Mr Dolby interpreting the keyboard solo from 'Clean Clean'. Now, while Geoff hadn't had any part in writing that song, nor 'VKTRS', it was apparent that Tom was using versions of Geoff's solos and motifs – including instrumental passages from 'VKTRS' on which Geoff and I had collaborated. I could feel Geoff bristling down the wire.

Trevor and Geoff called a meeting, and they stated their case: if I was going to be using duplicate riffs with the Camera Club, then Geoff should get a co-write on 'VKTRS' and 'Clean Clean'. You have to realise that the newly christened Buggles were now negotiating a publishing deal with Island – so it would be highly advantageous for them if Geoff was perceived as a co-writer; but the fact remained that Trevor and I wrote those songs – musically and lyrically, on piano and guitars. Geoff had effectively come in later as the 'arranger'. However, I could see their point, and so I agreed to share the writing credits but suggested that only one of the songs be split three ways and that the other be split 50% to them and 50% to me. They agreed, and Trevor said, "*How do we decide which song is 50/50?*" We ended up tossing a coin. I called Heads. The coin landed on heads. Trevor said, "*Congratulations, Bruce – you've got 50% of Video Killed the Radio Star,*" which, everything considered, still seems like a fair deal.

With the support of CBS, I went off to tour America, living the Spinal Tap Rock Dream, and gained a certain cult following – in fact, to this day I get fan letters praising the original Camera Club's version of 'VKTRS' (broadcast some weeks before the Buggles' record release) as the "best" version; but I know that in reality, our version fell short. The evidence is that the Buggles went on to sell millions of singles internationally, and, as Pete Waterman observed, in 1979 they created the world's first "modern pop record".

Some years later, when Trevor was a tax exile in Dublin, I went to stay with him for a working holiday. On the first night, he played me the Presidents of the United States of America's version of our famous song. We both agreed it might have sounded like that had we stayed together as a band all those years ago. We then went to the pub and sank several pints for old time's sake.

BW Surrey, England, 2020

12

○ The debut album *Difficult Shapes & Passive Rhythms Some People Think It's Fun to Entertain* was released by the British band China Crisis in 1982. Formed in 1979 in Kirkby near Liverpool, China Crisis initially consisted of vocalist/keyboardist Gary Daly and guitarist Eddie Lundon experimenting with synthesizers and drum machines in a living room. Difficult Shapes spent 17 weeks on the UK Albums Chart, peaking at No.21 in February 1983. The album featured the singles 'African and White', 'No More Blue Horizons' and 'Christian'. China Crisis was part of the explosion of new bands from Liverpool in the late '70s and early '80s, alongside contemporaries like OMD, Echo and the Bunnymen, The Teardrop Explodes and Frankie Goes to Hollywood. With clever instrumentation and infectious melodic hooks, China Crisis were one of the few that stood out from the pack.

○ 'Tally Ho', the debut single by The Clean from Dunedin in New Zealand, was in the racks November 12, 1981. 'Tally Ho' became much sought after upon its release, as it was the first release to highlight the new Flying Nun label; it peaked at No.19 in the New Zealand charts. Formed by brothers Hamish and David Kilgour in 1978, The Clean pioneered what was regarded as the new emerging POST-PUNK 'Dunedin Sound'.

○ On this day in 1984, the duo Pete Murphy and Mick Karn released *The Waking Hour* under the name Dali's Car. Murphy had recently departed from Bauhaus, and Karn was fresh from working with Japan and Gary Numan. Though possessing distinct talents, the two clashed creatively in the studio. "*It was a particularly difficult project,*" Karn recalled in a late '90s interview. "*We were two very different people*". Despite their differences, they produced a mystically spooky album, with each of its brief songs being compellingly distinct. Karn's freakishly melodic bass and Murphy's deep, rich voice were engrossing. In late 2010, cancer-stricken Karn and Murphy briefly reunited in the studio to record a second Dali's Car album, managing five tracks before Karn's passing on January 4, 2011. Those final recordings were released in 2012 as the EP *InGladAloneness*.

○ Jean-Luc De Meyer was born in 1957, in Brussels, Belgium. Jean-Luc is the vocalist and lyricist with Belgian group Front 242. Front 242 are highly successful in Europe with their industrial/EBM sound. Formed in 1981 by programmers Patrick Codenys and Dirk Bergen, they were soon joined by another programmer, Daniel Bressanutti and Jean-Luc. Jean-Luc was also a mainstay of the outfits C-TEC, Cobalt 60 and, most recently, 32Crash.

○ On November 12, 1980, Depeche Mode played as a support act to Fad Gadget at the Bridge House in Canning Town, London's East End. Daniel Miller, who was there to support his good friend Frank Tovey (Fad Gadget), was so impressed with Depeche Mode that he signed them to his label Mute Records that same night! Eager to sign with any label after being rejected by several record companies despite hand-delivering demo tapes, the band was thrilled to join Mute Records.

○ Dave Jackson, born in 1957, in Liverpool, England, is a frontman and vocalist best known for forming the bands 051, The Room, Benny Profane, Dust, and Dead Cowboys. In 1979, Jackson formed The Room, which released several critically acclaimed yet commercially unsuccessful singles and albums, including *In Evil Hour*, which was partly produced by Tom Verlaine and featured guitar-driven NEW WAVE reminiscent of bands like Echo & The Bunnymen and Teardrop Explodes. From 1985 to 1990, Jackson was part of Benny Profane, which followed a similar trajectory of critical success but limited commercial appeal. Throughout these projects, Jackson frequently collaborated with bassist Becky Stringer, who was a member of all his bands except The Room. After years with these bands, Jackson went solo in 2010, releasing a *self-titled* album. In 2023, he revived The Room for the album *Restless Fate*, and 2024 saw the release of the album *The Telling*.

IN THE SUMMER 1981
DAVE JACKSON
(051, The Room, Benny Profane, Dust and Dead Cowboys)

The Room had released 2 singles and a cassette album on our own label Box, receiving the pressings at our Prince's Park Gates East HQ, which was a flat that Becky Stringer and I rented because it had a basement where we could practice. Our neighbour, John, a massive fan of The Fall, helped us put singles into sleeves that arrived in separate boxes. Becky's sister had emigrated to live in San Francisco, and with some friends who worked at Damage Magazine, she had arranged a semi-official tour of the West Coast for us. The plan was to go over on holiday visas and hire equipment from a music shop in San Jose. There were gigs arranged in Los Angeles, Berkeley, San Francisco, Sacramento, Seattle, and even Vancouver. But, in those days, you had to go down to the US embassy in person to get visas, show some proof you had a reason to come back, state that you were not a communist, had no drug convictions, and had some form of gainful employment.

I was the only member of the band at that point who was officially unemployed, and I had heard horror stories of people being sent back from the States by US immigration. Rob and Clive had a gardening business and renovated old furniture, so I lied that I worked for them on my application and was overjoyed that it worked. Clive was the only one of us who said that he already had a visa. So, we arrived in LA, to be met by Helen. Rob, Becky, and I breezed through immigration. But Clive was nowhere to be seen. Helen made enquiries and came back panicked. Clive's visa wasn't valid! It was a merchant seaman's visa, so he was going to be taken to a hotel and then sent back to the UK! Helen got in touch with her dad, Professor John Stringer, who worked at Stanford and for a government contractor called EPRI, and he performed a miracle. He must've pulled some major strings as he got Clive released into his custody pending a San Francisco hearing. I was fuming on our flight from LA to SF, but Clive seemed blissfully unaffected by his ordeal.

The court hearing went okay, and, to my delight, I discovered that our first gig was going to be a matinee show at a place called The American Indian Centre (AIC), where we were to be supporting The Fall, and also that we'd be playing at a party that evening at the Mabuhay Gardens, a venue associated with the Dead Kennedys. We rehearsed in the Stringer's garage with our rented gear. It was weird being in California just as the Toxteth riots of 1981 were making even the myopic US news. We'd left about a week after the riots started and the first night we returned to Prince's Gate after playing The Royal Court with Dead or Alive and The Ponderosa Glee Boys, we found riot police lined up opposite our flat. The day we left, we passed the smouldering rubble of The Rialto, a former dance hall (turned carpet warehouse) where my mum and dad had met.

I went to see The Fall at the I-Beam the night before we were due to play with them, and they were great. I was a massive fan back then. The following afternoon we took the stage at the AIC and played a blinder. Finally getting to sing out some of the tension that had built up was great. That evening we played the Mabuhay, and I got chatting with Mark Riley, the Falls bass player.

Over the following weeks we played in Sacramento and Berkeley and drove down to LA, where we played four gigs at two venues, one of which was on Sunset Boulevard. We used to encore with a manic version of The Move's 'Flowers in the Rain'. I only knew one verse and repeated it; the 2nd and 3rd verses were the same as the first, Ramones style. One night a bunch of drunken cockneys joined us, jumping round on stage to it. They had all just burnt their passports and were planning on staying in the US, having met some rich American girls. I was incensed with the sound guy; in the UK there had been a tendency to be brusque with uncooperative sound guys. On the second night at the Sunset Strip venue, the sound engineer was clearly off his head (on mushrooms, it turned out), and I was getting a bit annoyed with him, but my attitude toward him changed when Rob pointed out that he had a pistol in the waistband of his jeans.

Back in San Francisco, we had a return gig, headlining this time, at the AIC. We were all big Captain Beefheart fans, especially Rob, and had been to see the band recently when they played Liverpool. And who should we see in the audience at our gig but Eric Drew Feldman, the bass player, who had been first onstage wearing a fireman's helmet, unmistakable with his square goatee? To our surprise, he was first backstage to congratulate us on our set. It also turned out that he had a girlfriend in Vancouver and could find us a place to stay there in return for a ride.

We drove up via Seattle, where I nearly got done for jaywalking, an offence that doesn't even exist in the UK, and we played a great club (the name escapes me) where the promoters gave us one of their apartments for the night. In Vancouver, we stayed with Eric's friends. We were booked to play three nights at a place called Gary Taylor's Rock Room and discovered that the basement room was a strip club. Eric joined us onstage and played a souped-up Casio keyboard on a couple of songs. Gary Taylor was quite an odd character, wearing a cowboy hat and timing our set to make sure we played at least a full hour. To fulfil this, we improvised a new song called 'Prisoners of Gary Taylor's Rock Room', where I ad-libbed a sort of shaggy dog story vocal about the place. On the last night, Gary brought in a mobile recording unit to get us down on tape.

We returned to play one last gig in Seattle, and Becky and I flew back from there. It was quite a bizarre experience, thinking back. We didn't have work permits for the USA but managed to get them to cross over into Canada. Clive's escape from immigration was so unusual. If he'd been sent home, the whole enterprise of the West Coast Tour would have been messed up. I remember trying to tell John Peel about it when he called us when our second session aired, but my voice went up an octave when I realised I was live on air, and it all came out in something of a jumble!

Started by Roger Huddle and Red Saunders, on 12 November 1976 at the Princess Alice pub in Forest Gate, London, Carol Grimes and the Boogie Band performed at the first Rock Against Racism gig. The event was the birth of the movement that would awaken the UK to bigotry; it brought together rock, punk, and reggae in a powerful stand against discrimination. Annually, future events would include performances by the likes of The Clash, Graham Parker, The Mekons, Gang of Four, The Fall and Buzzcocks, among a host of others.

13

○ The landmark album *Tin Drum* by Japan was released in 1981. This album is often quoted as the creative pinnacle of the band's career. Having achieved considerable success in Japan and developed close ties with local artists, the group created their most unique, stimulating, and striking recording. With *Tin Drum*, Japan completely shed the trash glam-rock of their early work and the subtlety of Gentlemen Take Polaroids, forging a new sound fusing exquisite funk rhythms, exotic Asian influences, and minimalist textures. Songs like 'Ghosts', 'The Art of Parties', and 'Visions of China' highlighted the talents of each member and evoked a moody, Chinese cultural aesthetic. Sylvian's rich vocals soared over Barbieri's atmospheric keyboards, Jansen's polyrhythmic percussion, and Karn's fretless bass. Sparse, esoteric arrangements complemented the Asian-inspired subject matter. *Tin Drum* was arguably the peak of Japan's career, a culmination of the band's artistic vision.

○ New Order released their debut album, *Movement*, on November 13, 1981. After Joy Division disbanded following the tragic death of lead singer Ian Curtis, the remaining members – guitarist Bernard Sumner, drummer Stephen Morris, and bassist Peter Hook –

forged ahead to form New Order. With the addition of Gillian Gilbert on synths and programming, they took a forward, yet sideways, step from Joy Division's stark POST-PUNK sound. Producer Martin Hannett helped the band experiment more in the studio to develop a shimmering, atmospheric sound that almost defined a new genre. The blend of Morris' live drums with drum machines and the interplay of different vocalists gave Movement an intriguing energy. While seeking their sound, the album showed New Order's transition from Joy Division's resolutive POST-PUNK to the dancefloor classics like 'Blue Monday' that would soon define them. With infectious bass and guitar riffs, 'Chosen Time' is an underrated gem and arguably the closest they ever sounded to Joy Division. Later releases like 'Everything's Gone Green' and 'Mesh' built on Movement's foundations into a masterpiece debut that would be a career highlight for any POST-PUNK band. Though succeeded by even greater work, *Movement* established New Order's signature sound.

⦿ On the 13th of November in 1976, an announcement was made in Melody Maker magazine regarding an upcoming significant punk tour. The tour was set to feature the Sex Pistols and the Ramones as co-headliners, with support from Talking Heads, the Vibrators, and Chris Spedding. However, in line with the rebellious nature of the punk movement, the tour ultimately did not materialize.

⦿ When the debut album *The Scream* by Siouxsie and the Banshees was released on November 13, 1978, many hailed it as the "birth of POST-PUNK". Recorded in just one week and mixed in three during August 1978, the album came on the heels of the band's hit 'Hong Kong Garden', which had reached No.7 on the UK charts. Though sympathetic to punk in ethos, *The Scream* marked a clear musical and sonic progression from basic punk. Tracks like the atmospheric 'Pure' and the slowly building 'Overground' showed the band's willingness to experiment. Their cover of 'Helter Skelter' paid homage to the past while also establishing the song as distinctly their own. The album featured tribal rhythms, metallic guitar dissonance, and unique chord progressions from John McKay, all anchored by Siouxsie's commanding vocals. Many years later, *The Scream* remains an impressive landmark recording in the evolution of POST-PUNK.

⦿ Roger Steen, guitarist and vocalist for The Tubes, was born in Pipestone, Minnesota, USA, on this day in 1949. As a founding and mainstay member of the San Francisco-based band, Steen helped pioneer their satirical, often controversial style. The Tubes built their shows and songs around themes of pornography, media satire, consumerism, and politics. They released their *self-titled* debut album in 1975, featuring the hit single 'White Punks on Dope'. The single reached No.28 in the UK charts in 1977.

14

⦿ Brian Eno's influence on rock, electronic, ambient, and synthpop musicians is well documented. Revered as the 'Godfather of Ambient', his acclaimed solo work pioneered the genre, and his vocal releases are quoted by many as being highly influential. His innovative ambient sound first emerged on 1975's Discreet Music and continued to his brilliant third solo album *Another Green World* (*AGW*). Released on November 14, 1975, AGW featured an all-star lineup including Phil Collins, Robert Fripp, Percy Jones, and John Cale. Eno was exploring instrumental landscapes and textures, simply unheard of in rock music at the time. On *AGW* Eno used synthesizers, found sounds, and studio techniques to create a groundbreaking work. The album's opener, 'Sky Saw', moves like the helicopter scenes in *Apocalypse Now*, contrasting the gentle lushness defining much of the record. Tracks like the tranquil 'Becalmed' and rich 'Sombre Reptiles' showcase Eno's textural mastery. Though several tracks are under two minutes, the slightly longer 'Everything Merges with the Night' exhibits Eno's subtle, soothing vocals. With standouts like 'Spirits Drifting', 'Zawinul/Lava', and 'Little Fishes', *AGW* features mellow, sublime tracks with intricate textures. While Eno's "rock" albums broke ground, *AGW* showcases his inventiveness and artistry at their peak. For those new to Eno, this 1975 classic is the ideal starting point and an essential listen. AND… It is no surprise that on this day in 2012, Brian Peter George Jean-Baptiste de la Salle Eno received the prestigious Royal Designer for Industry award from the British Royal Society for Arts, recognising his pioneering use of sound in technology and media to promote long-term sustainable thinking. Eno remains the only recipient of this honour specifically for sound design.

⦿ The synthpop trio Fiat Lux, originally featuring Bill Nelson's younger brother Ian Nelson on keyboards and saxophone, released their debut single 'Feels Like Winter Again' in 1982 through Bill Nelson's Cocteau label. After putting out a half dozen singles, the band dissolved in 1985, but vocalist Steve Wright and multi-instrumentalist David Crickmore reunited as a duo in 2017 to resume recording. In 2021, without the late Ian Nelson, Wright and Crickmore released their fifth Fiat Lux album, *Twisted Culture*.

⦿ The debut album *Standing on Ceremony* by Figures on a Beach from Detroit, Michigan, USA, hit store shelves on this day in 1987. Though the UK NEW WAVE sound was rare in the US at the time, Figures exemplified that genre. Tight production and intriguing arrangements on the album draw some comparisons to The Fixx and INXS.

⦿ The Mission (known as 'The Mission UK' in the USA) released their debut album *God's Own Medicine*, on November 14, 1986. This seminal goth record, produced by Tim Palmer, reached No.11 on the Top 40 and went gold. Palmer captured the vibrant energy of the up-and-coming band. Frontman Wayne Hussey brought experience from his previous groups like The Invisible Girls, Dead or Alive, and The Sisters of Mercy. With hits like the goth anthems 'Wasteland' and 'Severina', God's Own Medicine is quintessential goth: dark, brooding, and essential for any fan of the genre's shadowy aesthetic.

⦿ Released in 1980, Polyrock's *self-titled* album could be found on this day in record stores. Formed in 1978 in New York City, the band was led by singer and guitarist Billy Robertson and featured Catherine Oblasney on vocals, Tommy Robertson on guitar, Joseph Yannece on percussion, keyboardist Lenny Aaron, and bassist Curt Cosentino. With the positive influence of producer Philip Glass, Polyrock created infectious melodies and intriguing arrangements that resulted in timeless music. They blended quirky NEW WAVE reminiscent of Talking Heads and The Books, as in 'This Song' and 'Go West', and ethereal textures akin to Cocteau Twin on 'Romantic Me' and 'No Love Lost'. The clever compositions on this overlooked gem remain fresh decades later.

15

⦿ The debut album *Two by Two* from the British band Blue Zoo was released in 1983. Produced by Talk Talk's Tim Friese-Green, the album's heavy David Bowie influence is undeniable, especially in frontman Andy O's vocals. However, the band's skilled musicianship and arrangements keep the album cohesive, with few weak spots. Riding this success, Blue Zoo managed to achieve four top 50 UK singles from the album, including 'Cry Boy Cry', which reached No.13.

⦿ David Cairns was born in 1958 in London, England. David was a founding member of Secret Affair (SA), a band without knowing it or aiming at it, who were part of the Mod Revival and were clearly identifiable by their sharp dress and mohair suits. SA's 1979 debut single Time for Action, penned by David, was a hit and peaked at No.13 with sales of over 200,000. After 3 albums and half a dozen singles, SA split in 1982, and David formed The Flag and subsequently Walk on Fire, releasing the MCA album *Blind Faith* in 1989 to critical review. After which David was appointed Special Projects Manager for Gibson Guitars USA throughout the '90s. Since then, David rebirthed SA who still plays, albeit sporadically, and he has been actively involved in music for TV commercials. SA reformed in 2002 and went on to produce their 4th studio album *Soho Dreams*, in 2012, which received 5-star reviews in Classic Rock and other magazines.

THE RAINBOW THEATRE
DAVID CAIRNS
(Secret Affair)

As a fourteen-year-old schoolboy in 1972, my friend Kevin Hill and I were becoming big prog-rock music fans and buying vinyl albums when we could afford it and decided to go and see some bands live in concert, starting with Genesis in June of 1972, at the Shoreditch Town Hall in East London, where no more than fifty-odd fans were sat on old chairs in the hall. I think they were still promoting their *Nursery Cryme* album or maybe previewing the next album, *Foxtrot*, that came out later that year, and Peter Gabriel was in full performance artist mode, I seem to recall.

Not two months later, on August 19th, Kevin and I had bought tickets to see David Bowie presenting *Ziggy Stardust and the Spiders from Mars* at the legendary Rainbow Theatre, Finsbury Park, North London (Roxy Music as support).

We could only afford the cheapest seats "up in the gods", and with no video screens in those days, Bowie was this tiny man in his wonderful outfits strutting the stage and singing and playing that amazing album with Mick Ronson on guitar, of course. It was only one of two London shows, as Ziggy, after he played several shows in the US, disbanded the whole concept and moved on, so we were lucky to have been there.

Imagine then how I felt when several years later, here I was on the very same stage headlining the Rainbow on Dec 8th, 1979, and with an audience of 3000 people, a sell-out show. Secret Affair had climbed up from the East End pubs to the Marquee Club in Soho to the ultimate venue.

I remember at the sound check that our sound engineer Lawrence surprised me with one of the early cordless guitar systems connecting the guitar through VHF radio receivers and a unit in my back pocket, so I was free to go anywhere I wanted in the theatre, so during a drum break, I ran with our security man off the stage, up the back stairways and burst out into the upper circle and started my guitar solo not far from the seats I'd sat in watching Ziggy Stardust, a big show-off moment, but I felt I'd come full circle in my dreams of making it in a band!

Six months later we went on to sell out the Hammersmith Odeon, which had a 3,600 capacity, another great achievement for us, but it didn't have that same special feeling for me as that night at the Rainbow.

August 2023.

◉ Indochine, a Parisian band, released their debut album *L'Aventurier*, in 1982. Over a 30-year career, they have released over a dozen albums, achieving great popularity in France but only minor sales outside Europe. 'L'Aventurier', the award-winning title track, was a moderate European hit in the 1980s, embodying the French NEW WAVE sound. With twangy Shadows-esque guitars over simple drum machines and meandering synths, the album has a confusing, chaotic soundscape. The French vocals evoke comparisons to Plastic Bertrand's eccentric style.

◉ The Lemon Kittens' experimental debut EP *Spoonfed & Writhing*, released November 15, 1979, ventured into bizarre and original territory reminiscent of Captain Beefheart and The Pop Group. Band members Karl Blake, Gary Thatcher, Mylmus, and Danielle Dax presented insanely inventive tunes, including a delightfully raw cover of 'Shakin' All Over'. Unafraid to explore the avant-garde, their boldness ironically contributed to their obscurity.

◉ *Dantzig Twist*, the debut album by French POST-PUNK band Marquis de Sade, was released on November 15, 1979. Vocalist Philippe Pascal's inflections at times echo David Byrne and Eyeless in Gaza's Martin Bates, but the album's shallow, muddy production obscures his vocals. Within the talented band, Frank Darcel's ringing guitar echoes Television's interplay. While not an everyday listen, this inventive French album certainly holds curiosity value.

◉ Jeremy Saxon Oxley, born on November 15, 1961, who grew up in Kingscliff, New South Wales, Australia, was the frontman, lead vocalist, primary songwriter, and guitarist for the Australian rock band Sunnyboys. Formed in Sydney in 1980, Sunnyboys originally consisted of Jeremy, his brother Peter Oxley on bass, drummer Bil Bilson, and guitarist Richard Burgman. Very few bands garnered the excitement of the public like Sunnyboys; their energy knew no bounds, and the band quickly rose to fame for their energetic live performances. However, Jeremy's public struggle with schizophrenia was captured in the documentary film The Sunnyboy. Through it all, his prodigious musical gifts have persevered.

Jeremy Oxley by Jenny Tubbs / Chrome by Petra Gall

16

◉ On the shelves on November 16, 1977, was the innovative and futuristic album *Alien Soundtracks* by Chrome out of San Francisco. Experimental dystopian music that lent a beginning to a new burgeoning industrial genre. With this blend of Hawkwind meets Tuxedomoon meets The Residents, it's so surprising that it missed general acclaim. The UK had everyone's attention, and San Francisco, USA, just wasn't where people were expecting a revelation to come from. Damon Edge (Thomas Wisse) and Helios Creed (Barry Johnson) presented a mixture of sly and often abrasive guitar, electronic noodling and sound effects; it was a melting pot of psychedelia. This recording is unique, or at least it was then; one might guess it was because of Creed's belief that he had contact with aliens!

◉ In the early 1990s, Ian McCulloch and Will Sergeant of Echo & the Bunnymen formed the band Electrafixion with bassist Leon de Sylva and drummer Tony McGuigan. Electrafixion's angular, gritty, guitar-driven sound marked a departure from Echo & the Bunnymen's sparser, more melodic style. The band released their debut single 'Zephyr' on this day in 1994.

◉ Gilbert Gabriel was born November 16, 1956. Gabriel first became known worldwide as part of The Dream Academy when they released the hit tune 'Life in a Northern Town' in 1985. As a multi-instrumentalist, Gilbert's part in The Dreamy Academy's output was exemplary; he co-wrote most of the band's *self-titled* debut album which peaked at No.20 in the USA. Gilbert parted ways with Nick Laird-Clowes and Kate St. John in 1991 venturing into solo, collaborative works and the formation of Colour of Love, releasing a couple of singles in 1992. Today Gilbert is involved in a project called Dreamadelica, a concept comprising the sounds of world, jazz, and dreampop electronica.

○ On November 16, 1987, former Clash drummer Nicholas "Topper" Headon was sentenced to 15 months in prison at Maidstone Crown Court in England after supplying heroin to a man who later died. Success with The Clash didn't really agree with Topper or rather, it agreed too much! Headon, who joined The Clash in 1977, originally planned to stay with the band for only a year to gain name recognition before moving on. However, he found The Clash explored a diverse range of musical styles beyond punk, their roots. Headon remained with the band for five years of intense performing, partying, and drug use. By 1982, his heroin addiction was unmanageable, forcing Clash frontman Joe Strummer to fire him.

17

○ Amanda Gabrielle Brown was born in Sydney, Australia, in 1965. During her time with the band The Go-Betweens from 1986 to 1989, Amanda toured extensively with the group and contributed violin, oboe, keyboards, guitar, and backing vocals on their highly acclaimed albums *Tallulah* and *16 Lovers Lane*. Outside of The Go-Betweens, Amanda co-founded the band Cleopatra Wong with Go-Betweens drummer Lindy Morrison in 1991. Her skills as a versatile musician have also led to in-demand session work with artists like Silverchair, The Vines, The Church, and R.E.M.. Her musical talents have earned her credits and awards for the TV series *On the Ropes, Grace Beside Me*, and the documentaries *Suburb for Sale, The Family* and *Red Obsession*. She has also contributed music to the feature films *Monkey Puzzle, Kings of Mykonos*, and *Son of a Lion*.

○ Catherine "Kate" Ceberano AM (Australia Medal) was born in 1966 in Melbourne, Australia. Along with her AM, Kate has received the highest awards in the Australian music industry, including the ARIA for Best Female Artist, and achieved massive success as a songwriter, especially with the hit 'Pash' receiving a gold sales certification in 1998. Emerging from the remnants of the experimental group Essendon Airport, Kate became the lead singer with I'm Talking, a NEW WAVE/pop/funk band formed in 1983. During a 4-year life, the band was successful with 3 top ten singles and an album *Bear Witness*, that peaked at No.14 nationally. I'm Talking briefly reunited in 2019 for a series of acclaimed reunion shows, proving the enduring popularity of their catchy pop songs and Kate's vocal talents.

○ Pat Place was born on November 17, 1953, in Chicago, USA. Pat studied art at Northern Illinois University, where she attained a Bachelor of Fine Arts degree. To be where art was at its strongest, Pat moved to New York City in 1975 and, within a couple of years, was exhibiting her own work in NYC's galleries. Pat's influence in NYC was strong, being involved in the burgeoning 'No Wave' movement through being the 1977 founding member-guitarist of The Contortions. In 1979 Pat moved from The Contortions to form Bush Tetras with vocalist Cynthia Sley. The music of Bush Tetras' was a marked departure from that of The Contortions, being less frenetic with a perception of space and less aggression. The single 'Too Many Creeps' is a POST-PUNK collector's essential, filed right next to Au Pairs and Delta 5. In more recent times Pat's photography work was integral to the exhibition No Wave, Post Punk, Underground New York 1976-80 curated by Thurston Moore in NYC.

10 QUESTIONS: AN INTERVIEW WITH PAT PLACE

Hi Pat, What's going on in your life today? How is COVID-19 impacting?

Well, obviously there are tons of negatives as a result of Covid. The upside for me was we all had to jump off the fast-paced treadmill of life and slow down! Time to reflect and realise what is essential. I made art, and wrote songs remotely with Bush Tetras; also, the BT's are putting out a box set of 33 songs covering 40 years on Wharfcat records, which will be released in Nov. 2021. So, we were all busy with the details of getting that together, and BT did one live stream show in the winter and, of course, like everyone else, a lot of TV bingeing!

Today is so far removed from the late '00s when you were part of part of the New York City 'no wave' movement; it must have been a thrill for a young 20-something. Being in Contortions, you were part of those recordings on the Eno-produced 'No New York' album. He was just attaining 'celebrity' status; do you remember what your thoughts on him were?

Yes, these times are far different from the late '70s when I was in the Contortions, etc..!! And yes, it so was exciting, and it all happened very quickly. Much to everyone's surprise! My thoughts on Brian Eno? I was a fan of his solo work and knew it well, so I felt very fortunate to be part of the No New York recordings. We had one afternoon; it was quick, and we were busy, so it was very cool, but just part of the bullet train we were on!

You've earned a name for your photography through exhibitions; what's your favoured subject matter? What part of that art form are you most proud of?

My photography? I went to art school and have a BFA in painting and sculpture. I moved to NYC at 21 right out of art school. I could not afford a studio, so I started taking photos of everything, but the stuff I showed were staged scenes with coloured lights and toys that I found in Chinatown or anywhere, really – – the weirder, the better!

That was the work I had several shows with in the early '80s, and the BTs have subsequently used several of those photos for album covers, etc. I continue to photograph various subjects, and I am making sculptures also.

Jumping to Bush Tetras. I understand you opened for The Clash; that must have been something else. What would be your most memorable gig?

Opening for the Clash was definitely a high point; we did a few nights with them at Bonds, which led to Topper Headon producing the 3-song *Rituals* EP for us, which we recorded at Electric Ladyland. We also opened for Gang of Four several times in NYC and London; those were memorable because I loved the band, and we were a good match.

Where does the name 'Bush Tetras' come from? Did you consider yourself "punks?" You were more musical than that, in my opinion.

The name Bush Tetras comes from an amalgam of Dee's idea of Bush Babies and Laura K, and I came up with Neon Teras – hence Bush Tetras! We really did not consider our music punk; we were taking influences from all sorts of music, including funk (which I learned lot about playing in the Contortions), reggae, and some African music. We used a lot of different percussion, and I always purposely avoided using the 3-bar chord cliche!! We definitely had the punk DIY attitude and I suppose had that look.

How did you guys feel when "Too Many Creeps" started getting airplay? It's one song that you are well known for. Is there something else you made that that you wish got more exposure?

Yes, 'Too Many Creeps' put us on the map as a kind of NYC anthem. 'Can't Be Funky' was actually on the Billboard charts. We never made an album in the '80s, just singles and EPs – 'Things That Go Boom in the Night' came out much later and was a compilation of our '80s songs.

Who did you see play in the late '70s or early '80s that blew you away, if anyone?

The late '70s and early '80s were a constant flow of great music and shows, too many to list,, but some that stand out were PiL, Iggy Pop, Patti Smith, Television, X-Ray Spex, Gang of Four and The Voidoids. I saw a then-unknown band called U2 play to 50 people at the Mudd Club on a cold January night! Ramones, and I loved seeing the no wave bands like DNA, Teenage Jesus and the Jerks, and Mars in that short no wave period.

What was the music that you grew up on? I guess you could say influenced you to become a musician?

I grew up listening to all the amazing great 60s music, but I was intent on visual art at that time, and still am; music was a constant for me and got me through my teenage years. I was very young when the Beatles first performed on Ed Sullivan, and seeing that made me want a guitar, which I couldn't really play, but that and the usual piano lessons and an oboe were my first instruments. I fell into music after art school because I was attracted to the no wave scene, where you didn't need much experience or know how to play in a traditional way; it seemed a musical version of Dada, which I was a huge fan of as an art student.

Pat's sitting at home, it's raining outside and you're at a loose end. What will be your go-to albums for the rest of the afternoon?

HA! My musical tastes are extremely diverse. If I had to choose one, it would probably be the Stones… from the *Beggars Banquet – Let It Bleed – Sticky Fingers – Exile* period.

Is there something you can tell us about Pat Place that people don't already know?

I'm sure!! Let's go with -I love Joni Mitchell- – sorry to any hardcore fans!!!

You don't need to make apologies for the wonderous Joni Pat…Thanks very much.

Great to be here Michael.

◉ On November 17, 2006, The Sugarcubes reform and take the stage in Reykjavik for the first time in 14 years! Björk reassembled the band to celebrate the 20th anniversary of its debut single, 'Birthday', with all profits going to the non-profit entity Smekkleysa SM established by the band to promote Icelandic music.

18

◉ The *self-titled* 5-track EP by the short-lived Los Angeles trio Bone Symphony was released on November 18, 1983. Centered around vocalist Scott Wilk's stunning vocals, the group had minimal output beyond this EP. However, their song 'One Foot in Front of The Other' appeared in the movie *The Nerds* and can be found on the film's original soundtrack album, though it was not included on the EP.

◉ Chris and Cosey released their groundbreaking debut album *Heartbeat* on Rough Trade on November 18, 1981. Fresh from the first dissolution of Throbbing Gristle, Chris Carter and Cosey Fanni Tutti (Christine Newby) provided a majestic futuristic venture into dark rhythmic electronics, defining themselves as serious innovators. Bridging synthpop and industrial, it's fair to say this may be the birth of 'Trance'. It was early days for analogue drum machines and sequencers, and there's no doubt that *Heartbeat* would be grasped as influential to new artists in post-industrial, synthpop and electronica.

◉ On November 18, 1985, *Psychocandy*, the debut album by The Jesus and Mary Chain, was released. This is arguably where "shoegaze" was born, or it was majorly influenced by it; you can argue that with your friends. It's guitars, guitars, and more beautiful abrasive guitars. A load of feedback and low-tech production, reminiscent of Velvet Underground, and of course you can hear Joy Division here on 'Something's Wrong' and 'In a Hole'. Many quote this as 'the album of '85' competing with *Meat Is Murder* or *Songs from The Big*

Chair… You'll hear some of the most heavily distorted guitar riffs ever recorded, like chainsaws in a cyclone, with vocals recorded in a tunnel, but somehow, they were able to lay down some very infectious songs. The song, a short but power-laden 'Something's Wrong', runs four minutes, but the other thirteen tracks hardly push three minutes. A must have in your '80s music collection.

Graham Parker by Roch Parisien

○ Graham Parker was born in 1950, in London, England. He is best known as the lead singer of Graham Parker & The Rumour, the band he fronted in the 1970s and early 1980s. In his early days with The Rumour, Parker coupled punk rock's raw energy with his deeply rooted love of American R&B, country, and soul music. The band built a reputation as an incendiary live act as well. With his raspy, snarling vocals and swaggering stage presence, Parker had the attitude of a punk rocker but the musicality of a soul singer adept at crafting catchy pop songs. His album *Howlin' Wind* was released in 1976; it well preceded the arrival of punk and the latter NEW WAVE, yet it had all the flavour of POST-PUNK, ensuring that he would now be embraced by the followers of those movements. Parker's persona and music are believed to have been major influences on many British musicians who followed him, most notably Elvis Costello, Paul Weller, and Joe Jackson.

"ahhhh…PIG HEAVEN"
GRAHAM PARKER
(& The Rumour)

I've never quite seen any concrete connection between me and NEW WAVE, which was always stripped down and quite minimal compared to my dense recordings. Plus, in 1976, when I released my first two albums, the term NEW WAVE seemed to be being floated by a few critics about a few bands – mostly yet to make much of a splash – but until 1977, when I was making my third album, it seemed more hypothetical than real.

Then they all appeared along with punk, and it hit the High Street, as it were. My only rather facile link to this alleged genre, I suppose, was when I released *Squeezing Out Sparks* in 1979, and in the United States, it made a bigger impact by far than the three preceding albums, and because it didn't feature the horn section along with the other dense instrumentation of the preceding albums, it got a bit of a NEW WAVE tag. People thought it was my first album and erroneously pegged me as a latecomer to NEW WAVE, I guess.

It has to be said, though, that the hangover from the by then pompous and flatulent denim suit and hair bands needed to be kicked down a peg or two, and the irreverent style of NEW WAVE acts, and especially punk, presented the logical and necessary step to break the chokehold of something that was already past its prime by 1972, let alone '77.

Frankly, I preferred disco anyway. Give me a KC and the Sunshine Band collection and a car ride, and I'm in pig heaven.

06/09/2021

◉ On this day you might have been able to find the self-released debut single 'Skank Bloc Bologna' by Scritti Politti on their own St. Pancras label. One might regard the title a little off-putting, but this song with angular guitar, a reggae-styled rhythm section and oblique lyrics is astounding for the period. Emblazoned with hand-stamped serial numbers on the sleeve, it has become a real collector's item.

◉ That charismatic pop singer Kim Wilde was born in 1960, in Chiswick, Middlesex, England. She is the daughter of singer Marty Wilde and the sister of Ricky Wilde. Kim shot to fame in the 1980s with several hit singles, most notably her debut, 'Kids in America', which showcased her synth-driven pop sound aligned with the NEW WAVE movement. After early hits like 'Chequered Love', her momentum slowed as subsequent releases lacked the strength of her initial singles. However, in late 1986, she made a comeback with a dance cover of The Supremes' 'You Keep Me Hangin' On', which reached the Top Ten internationally. Though Wilde continued releasing music in the '90s and scoring occasional hits in dance or adult contemporary genres, she faded from the limelight. In recent years, Wilde has embarked on revival tours, including a recent co-headlining tour in Australia with Howard Jones, though it garnered a lukewarm response.

19

Swimming Pool Q's and The Police

◉ Jeff Calder was born November 19, 1951, in Charleston, South Carolina, USA. Through the '70s Jeff drew on his background as a creative writing student of Harry Crews at the University of Florida to pursue a career as a music journalist before moving to Atlanta in 1978 to form The Swimming Pool Q's, today, the only extant band from the city's original NEW WAVE & Punk era. His long essay, *Living by Night in the Land of Opportunity: Reflections on Life in a Rock & Roll Band* (1992), was published in Duke University's South Atlantic Quarterly. He's written liner notes for the Q's' *The Deep End* and *To Understand: The Early Recordings of Matthew Sweet*. Since 2013, he's been a book reviewer for the Atlanta Journal-Constitution. In the 1990s, Calder served as an A&R rep for Brendan O'Brien's Sony imprint, 57/Shotput Records, where he coordinated the reissue of *Music to Eat*, the classic avant-garde 1971 album by the Hampton Grease Band. He assisted Pylon's reissue projects for the albums *Gyrate* and *Chomp*, and in 2003 he co-produced the Q's 2003 magnum opus, *Royal Academy of Reality*, released on the Bar/None label. At Atlanta's legendary Southern Tracks Studio, Jeff was the associate manager during recordings by artists such as Pearl Jam and Bruce Springsteen. 2023 saw him playing with the Glenn Phillips Band and their side project, The Supreme Court, as well as the guitarist for the Atlanta group The Hot Place, fronted by Lisa King. Their debut album *Language of Birds* featured Television's Richard Lloyd and David J of Bauhaus & Love and Rockets appears on their *self-titled* new album. That album features several tracks mixed by Ed Stasium (Ramones, Talking Heads, Smithereens), who, incidentally, co-produced and engineered the Q's' 1984 first A&M Records release, The Swimming Pool Q's.

LOU REED AND THE POLICE
JEFF CALDER
(The Swimming Pool Q's)

LOU REED

When we got our deal with A&M Records in 1984, we began looking for a professional manager to act as a go-between—record companies were quite complicated at that time. We talked to people all over the country, but there was a manager in Atlanta, Charlie Brusco, who had managed The Outlaws and worked with some other classic Southern Rock bands. Charlie wasn't someone that you would necessarily think would be right for an egghead band like The Swimming Pool Q's, but he had extensive contacts in the industry and really wanted to handle the group. And he knew Lou Reed's manager.

Our *self-titled* album had just come out, so we were on the West Coast visiting A&M and playing some dates, including one with R.E.M. at the Greek Amphitheatre. The next day, Charlie, who was yet to be our manager, said, *"Do you want to go on a national tour with Lou Reed?"* We said, *"Yes,"* and he became our manager.

Lou's album, *New Sensations*, had just been released. It was his first album in quite a while, his comeback really, and it was doing well. 'I Love You, Suzanne' was in heavy rotation at MTV. He was recovering from drug and alcohol problems—there was no big secret about that, even then, and he was successfully dealing with them.

Lou was really kind—he'd give us little pep talks in passing—but he was generally quiet and didn't socialise much. It was important for him to stay sequestered from the backstage reality of the rock grind. We toured for several months, from coast to coast, and the last show of the American tour was at the Fox Theatre in Atlanta, where we jammed with him on the encore, 'Sweet Jane'. Lou wanted us for the European leg of his tour, but, inexplicably, A&M, a hyper-intelligent label, didn't see enough benefit in that to help us with tour support.

Among the notable musicians Lou had in his band were Fernando Saunders and Robert Quine. Fernando was a wonderful bassist who played a fretless in drop D tuning and was thus able to get a big, full sound.

Lead guitarist Robert Quine was well known in the NEW WAVE and punk world. He had been an original member of Richard Hell and the Voidoids, playing on their first album, *Blank Generation*, the seminal punk statement for sure. It's kind of surprising that more people don't talk about it, because it wasn't conventional punk; it was way more abstract, what at the time would have been called "angular". That's what Robert was, the master of angular, and Lou loved him for it, though his playing was in contradistinction to what was going on with New Sensations, which was fairly straightforward rock and roll. Robert Quine didn't really sound like the intention of that record, which, of course, made things all the more interesting.

We talked to Robert a lot during the tour. We were on the same wavelength since we were from a "Pure Wave" background, so we related to him on a number of levels. He was a very good musician, often unintentionally funny, and really smart. I believe he had been a law student—he wore a herringbone sport coat, charcoal the shade. Robert was related to an important American philosopher named William Van Orman Quine. He was from the Midwest somewhere, I think Kansas. He had been a lawyer before moving to New York and getting involved in the punk underground. He was eccentric and unpredictable, audacious, and personable, just the way you would think and want him to be. He was quite a character.

At some point, midway through the tour, Lou had to shoot a video, but he didn't ask Robert to be in it, so Robert got his feelings hurt. Briefly, the whole thing was a really fraught scene. We were playing a theatre in Albany, New York, and just before showtime, as he was about to go on, Quine was trying to take a Valium, but it fell out of his hand—it was a big Valium too; it was like this giant disc—and, in slow motion, it fell on the floor and rolled under a locked closet door. And it was a complete panic on Robert's part. They had to hold the curtain and find a janitor to open the door and retrieve Robert's Valium. Which they did!

But it put him on edge. On top of not being asked to be in the video, which had happened in the past few days, there was the thing with the Valium. So they were playing the gig, and Anne, Bob, and I were standing by the mixing console on the side of the stage, and Quine was performing his solo – I've forgotten what the song was, maybe 'Satellite of Love' – and he walked over to the console, still fuming, and I don't know whether the Valium had kicked in or not, but he walked over to the three of us and, without missing a note, said, "I've hated everything he's done since the Velvet Underground." Playing the whole time, he ambled back to the centre of the stage and finished the solo. Just phenomenal.

THE POLICE

We toured the South with The Police in the spring of 1979, just when they were breaking nationally with 'Roxanne'. While they had been to the States maybe six months before, it was very early on for them, and it hadn't been much of a tour. What happened was Stewart Copeland's brother, Ian, really put together the whole Police concept of low-budget touring for the band. They had a station wagon, and they may have also had a van or a small truck. It was a bare-bones operation. They were playing 1000-1500 seat venues at that point because the record was really hitting. Ian launched all of this out of a booking agency in Macon called Paragon. He later started FBI/Frontier Booking International based in New York. But at that time, he was operating out of Paragon, which was somewhat of a strange pairing, given that all the bands that Ian was working with were NEW WAVE and punk bands, mostly from England.

Paragon had been the agency for the Allman Brothers, and they were closely intertwined with Capricorn Records, so they booked almost all of the era's Southern Rock bands. Ian was working there along with a couple of other chaps who would later become booking agents with him at the FBI. He wanted to make sure that we were "wavish" enough to be playing with The Police. So, at some point, he came to see us play at the Agora in Atlanta, and I guess we passed, because when the Police came to the South to tour, and there were a lot of dates, we became an opening act along with another group from Athens, called the Tone Tones.

The Police were terrific, and their soundchecks were mesmerising because they would jam on new material like 'Message in a Bottle' for an hour. I don't know if they even had ten songs then, but they would stretch them out for long periods of time to fill out a 90-minute set. They could just play forever. They were a really good band and great fun. They were not guys that fought all the time, or anything like that. They really liked The Swimming Pool Q's, so we got to be friendly with them—I think they related to us because we had musical skills, to some extent.

We played half a dozen dates with them in the South—Birmingham, Atlanta, Tampa, Orlando, maybe one other date in there—and ended up in Gainesville, at the University of Florida, where I had gone to school, so it was interesting. It was certainly the biggest show that we had played, but it was also the biggest show that The Police had played. It was an outdoor event, with maybe seven thousand people. It was a totally successful concert. They ended up bringing us out to play on a song that I didn't really know at the time, called 'I Can't Stand Losing You'. I thought that the song was titled 'I Can't Stand Music'. Anne was on one side of the stage singing with Andy Summers, and I was next to Sting, who, you know, was not a small guy. Sting was a powerful presence. He was muscular, and I'm not saying he towered over me, but I did have to look up at him, and he was a real singer. He was belting it out. I don't know what I'd been doing before, but it wasn't singing. When you're standing next to Sting singing on stage, that's actually singing. So, I was just doing the best I could, but when the chorus came around, I started singing, "I can't stand music," because I thought that was the name of the song. I mean, it wouldn't have been odd in 1979 to have a song called 'I Can't Stand Music', given where we came from. So, Sting is looking at me, a little bit cross-eyed; I guess he thought I was being sarcastic, and then he realised that, no, I actually thought those were the words. So, he started singing, "I can't stand music!", and then we all started singing, "I can't, I can't, I can't stand music!" I think the crowd liked it!

● The 4-track EP *Roman Candle*, released in 1983, was the debut release by Flesh for Lulu. Driven by Nick Marsh on vocals and guitar and drummer James Mitchell, FFL was undeservedly lumped in the Goth category, even though they seem to be chasing a glam identity. There is not a load of diversity amidst the POST-PUNK strains and clear, crisp production. There's some excellent drumming and basslines, but largely through lacklustre songwriting and variety, the songs just kind of blend together. They got dumped by Polydor after a poor commercial response, and one can only say that probably inspired the later impressive releases.

● Hipsway's *self-titled* debut album was released in 1986. The album was rather uneven but had a couple of standout tracks on side one, 'The Honeythief' and 'Long White Car', but weaker material on side two. Overall, Hipsway's sound on the album was comparable to other NEW WAVE pop bands like Curiosity Killed the Cat and Go West. The band released one more album, 1989's *Scratch the Surface*, before disbanding. In 2019, a reformed version of Hipsway led by original member Graham Skinner released the album *Smoke & Dreams*, but it received little attention.

● Alan Murphy was born in London, England, in 1953. Alan was a highly proficient guitarist and was a member of Go West from 1985 to'88, Level 42 from 1988 to'89 and was with Scritti Politti during 1989. He also worked on tour with Kate Bush and in the studio with Mike & the Mechanics. On October 19, 1989, he died from pneumonia, a complication related to Aids.

● Eddie Rayner was born Anthony Edward Charles Rayner in 1952, in Lower Hutt, New Zealand. Known as "Kiwi Eddie", he spent twelve years as the keyboardist for the iconic New Zealand band Split Enz. Rayner has also played with influential groups like The Orb, Crowded House, and Phil Manzanera's 801. He has released two solo albums—the all-instrumental debut *Horse* and *Play It Straight*. Rayner is an acclaimed session musician and producer, having worked with artists such as Paul McCartney, Models, and Dame Kiri Te Kanawa. Some consider his best contributions to be on Split Enz's 1980 album *True Colours*, especially the instrumentals 'Double Happy' and 'The Choral Sea', though it also features classics like 'I Got You' and 'I Hope I Never'. While not as experimental as Split Enz's uber-creative debut, *Mental Notes, True Colours* showcases infectious melodies, superb musicianship, and Rayner's creative flair. It remains a NEW WAVE classic that has stood the test of time.

● When the British music magazine Sounds named 'Anarchy in the UK' it's single of the week on November 19, 1976, it marked the debut of The Sex Pistols, who had just released the inflammatory punk anthem. After the song's release, the band appeared on a British talk show hosted by Bill Grundy. They repeatedly swore at and berated Grundy on air, sparking controversy. As a result, the band's record label EMI dropped them and withdrew the single. But you were already familiar with this infamous TV incident, weren't you?

● Mark Taylor was born in 1960 in Folkestone, Kent, England. In 1980, Taylor came to Australia for a one-year working holiday, staying with an aunt who had emigrated in the

1960s. Before he knew it, this self-taught keyboardist was playing organ in Australia's first dedicated ska band, The Allniters. The band went from cramped gigs at the Sussex Hotel in downtown Sydney to headlining major venues nationwide. When he came from the UK, Taylor brought a collection of over two hundred songs co-written with his childhood friend Peter Young; one of these was 'Hold On', which became the Allniters' first top 40 hit several years later. Between 1981 and 1985, the Allniters toured extensively, becoming one of Australia's most popular live acts. With three top 40 and two top 20 singles, plus a top 20 album called *D,D,D,Dance*, the band was arguably the most popular ska group in the Southern Hemisphere. The Allniters disbanded in 1985 due to the usual musical differences and exhaustion, but the front line of the band reformed later that year and continues to perform to this day. Mark has written a three-book series featuring Club Ska on tour.

Allniters by permission

THE ALLNITERS FIRST GIG
MARK TAYLOR
(The Allniters)

The Sussex Hotel once stood on the block bounded by Kent, Liverpool, South and Harbour streets in Haymarket. Built in 1923, the hotel had been run by a grey-haired publican named Stella since 1973. Home to trade unionists, lesbians, women's groups and journalists, the fledgling mod scene had co-opted the Sussex as their base, having abandoned the Heritage to the punk scene. Stella was a great supporter of live music, and if fresh young pimple-faced musicians could put two or three chords together, she'd give them a go. The pub was on two levels, a large upstairs bar with a small cozy 'snug' hosting an old jukebox in one corner and a smaller downstairs bar with a cellar once used for black liquor marketing during the war. The cellar could comfortably hold thirty people and had a small stage at one end lit by a single naked fluorescent light strip. We named the cellar 'The Pit' and had sixties garage-influenced bands like The Clones, Proteens, The Introverts, Jump Vision, The Sets and Fast Cars playing to a rapidly growing audience. Then on Monday, 22nd September 1980, came the Allniters.

The previous evening I'd called round to Graham's house in Forbes Street with Martin to see Janet, to buy her Yamaha CY-10 organ for $150. We then headed into the city to Kent Street Studios for our first rehearsal. Martin (Fabok), the guitarist and founder; Graham (Hood) on bass; and vocalists Peter (Travis) and Umberto (Rullo) had played one show the previous week with Greg Noise, the Introverts' singer, on drums. After last week's gig, Martin realised a regular drummer was required and asked me, Brett (Pattinson), and Phil (Ayres) if we'd like to join his band. We would be playing support to the introverts and beatboys.

"Ah, it's a bit small," said Peter, standing on the stage, scratching his head.

He was right; it could at best host a modest four-piece lineup. There were seven of us. Now our Phil didn't get to be a ladies' shoe salesman without having some ingenuity.

He had an idea which consisted of Brett, Phil and me driving down the road to Chinatown and the site of the future Entertainment Centre to find a stage. Half an hour later we were back in the Pit, setting up old boards and planks on blue plastic milk crates as a stage extension. We began setting up our equipment on the main stage. Travis and Bert, as we called Peter and Umberto, were expected to risk broken ankles on the rickety extension we'd constructed.

"Brett, where are your drums?" asked our observant bassist.

Yes, Brett Pattinson was our drummer. He'd used the rehearsal room's kit last night and had been waiting for the right moment to tell us that he didn't actually own a drum kit. I decided now was a good time to inform my bandmates that I didn't have an amplifier for the organ. It seemed that Phil was the only one of the three new recruits who had the 'gear' to do the gig. He'd blown the last of this pay packet on various percussion instruments. He'd told us that he'd play saxophone, but…well, you've guessed it.

The bands that played the Sussex were very easygoing, and many were good mates with members of the mod scene. It didn't take much persuasion to get The Introverts to lend us a drum kit and guitar amp for our set. The resident sound system (P.A.) consisted of two large white speakers, two foldback speakers and a couple of microphones supplied and operated by Jeff Fatt, a future Cockroach and Wiggle. His P.A. was affectionately dubbed the 'washing machine' by all who used it. With our borrowed gear, and with Pete and Bert avoiding the stage extension as much as possible and with sweat streaming down the walls and Sta-Prest Levis, we played our way through numbers by Toots and the Maytals, Merton Parkers, Sam the Sham and the Pharaohs, Nancy Sinatra, Desmond Dekker, Symarip, The Beat, Smokey Robinson, Eric Morris, The Specials and Junior Murvin. Were we an instant overnight success? Fuck no, but the fifty or so mods crammed knee-deep in the Pit seemed to like us, and we had fun, so all in all, it was an ok debut. We even had a mention on 2JJ the following day, and I quote from my diary of the time: "a piano player who leans against a wall looking cool and a madman next to him who hits everything in sight". But what's more, we were paid for the gig. Yes, we each received the princely sum of $3!

"Three bucks a gig, eh?" mused Martin, leading the way to the bar, *"How long will it take you to buy a drum kit, Brett?"*

20

❍ Jimmy Brown, born in 1957 in Birmingham, England, serves as the drummer for the reggae group UB40, a position he has held since 1978. Raised in the culturally diverse inner city of Birmingham, where Caribbean, Indian, and Pakistani communities thrived, Jimmy, along with UB40 guitarist Ali Campbell and bassist Earl Falconer, were heavily influenced by the eclectic local music scene. They began practising and crafting their unique style of reggae music, composing original songs. Their talent caught the attention of fellow musicians, such as percussionists Yomi Babayemi and Norman Hassan, saxophonist Brian Travers, keyboardist Jimmy Lynn, and Ali's brother Robin Campbell. With all eight members on board, UB40 officially formed. Following a performance at a local pub, where they caught the eye of Chrissie Hynde, the band was invited to open for The Pretenders. It was during this gig that representatives from Graduate Records discovered them, leading to the release of their debut single 'King' b/w 'Food for Thought', which peaked at No.4 on the UK singles chart.

❍ In 1978, Richard Davis made his first-ever recording called 'Methane Sea', comprised of two distinct parts on alternate sides titled 'Prelude' and 'Aftermath'. This initial foray into the world of experimental electronica showcased Davis's talent and set the stage for his future endeavours. Eventually, he became a pivotal member of the Detroit-based group Cybotron with Juan Atkins. When discussing the inspiration behind Methane Sea, Davis revealed that his time serving in the Vietnam War and witnessing the tragic events of the Jonestown Massacre had a profound and lasting impact on his mindset.

⦿ Gail Ann Dorsey is a renowned session bassist and vocalist who has collaborated with many high-profile artists. Since the 1990s, she has been most closely associated with David Bowie, touring with him and contributing bass and vocals to his albums *Earthling, Heathen, Reality*, and *The Next Day*. Her three solo albums and work with bands like Gang of Four, The The, Tears for Fears, and The Indigo Girls have also earned her acclaim. Born on this day in Philadelphia in 1962, Dorsey's versatility, musicality, and skill have made her an in-demand session player.

⦿ *From Brussels with Love* was originally released on November 20, 1980, on the Belgian label Les Disques du Crépuscule. It was a cassette compilation that featured 22 exclusive tracks from the premier artists dabbling in the new avant-garde, ambient and NEW WAVE, as well as several artists from the distinguished Factory Records stable in Manchester. Included in the sampler were the likes of John Foxx, Thomas Dolby, Bill Nelson, Durutti Column and even an interview with Brian Eno. *"This tape, a long mysterious piece of collective modern overdrive, points to a future somewhere. And it looks more crimson than rosy, it's that good"* (sic) (Sounds Dec. 1980). Today, with some searching, it can be found on CD.

Nina Hagen Band by Petra Gall

⦿ Nina Hagen Band's *self-titled* debut album entered the German charts on this day in 1978. Though sung in German, it found an appreciative audience in the English-speaking punk scene when released elsewhere. This unique album introduced Nina's captivating vocals and became an instant cult classic in the NEW WAVE movement. Songs like the gems 'Unbeschreiblich Weiblich (Indescribably Feminine)' and 'TV-Glotzer (White Punks on Dope)', the great cover of The Tubes' song showcased Hagen's impressive vocal range. On operatic rock excursions like 'Natuertraene' and 'Heiss', her classically trained voice shines. Hagen was perhaps too quirky for the mainstream, but this album shows her creative spirit burning brightly. Seamlessly fusing punk, rock, and opera, it pushes boundaries with rhythmic innovations and superb musicianship. Atmospheric yet experimental, these captivating arrangements make the album highly original and timeless.

⦿ Paul King was born in Galway, Ireland, in 1960, relocating to Coventry, England, when he was still a young boy. Paul was the lead vocalist and frontman for the band King, releasing two commercially successful studio albums in 1984 and 1985. By 1989, as the popularity of King started to decline, Paul transitioned into broadcasting, becoming well known as a television presenter and MTV video jockey. This exposure led to him hosting a series of commercials promoting various music compilation albums. As a solo musician in 1987, he released the album *Joy*, which included two tracks, 'Follow My Heart' and 'I Know', that were collaborations with Dan Hartman and charted moderately.

◉ Marc Scully was born in Sydney, Australia, in 1963. Marc today is known as 'Omegaman'. As Omegaman, Marc is a producer and audio engineer for Studio 57, which has become very well known for its recording, mixing, and mastering. Marc, as a bass player, moved into the music circuit when his first 'major' band, MX Warheads, came to fruition in 1980. His next band was the cowpunk outfit Love Rodeo, with Greg Perano and Roddy Radalj releasing one single, the much sought after 'Love Yodel No. 9'. After some on-the-road slog, Scully & Perano formed The Deadly Hume, attaining a solid and faithful following while active from 1985 to 89. During that period, they went international, playing in New Zealand and the USA. The Deadly Hume found themselves as support to the likes of New Order and The Damned, among others. Marc's next four-year stint as a bassist saw him relocate to Melbourne, joining Nick Barker and The Reptiles, who were a major touring act. Success again came Marc's way with Ratcat; the band played nationally at large festivals and small pubs, and they also toured Asia. In the mid-'90s, tired of that touring life, Marc established Omegaman DJ'ing in numerous clubs, pubs, bars and festivals. Today, Marc is involved in production and runs the Studio 57 recording studio.

MEMORIES OF A ROCK AND ROLLA
MARC SCULLY
(MX Warheads, Love Rodeo, Deadly Hume, The Reptiles, RATCAT)

Like many aspiring teens, I started garage jamming with a few local Sans Souci fellas. Our set included a couple of covers: the Stooges' 'Wanna Be Your Dog' & 'No Fun' and 'Louie Louie', etc. Our first & only gig was at the James Cook High School Dance.

I was about 17 when I ended up forming MX Warheads with Donnie Bourke, guitarist and singer from The Eyes. At the time I was a sometimes resident at the infamous Darlinghurst Squats, known as The Compound. MX played the local haunts: French's, Mosman Hotel, Hopetoun, Vulcan Hotel, etc. We did a stint in Melbourne, where we stayed at Macy's in Toorak. Many touring or interstate bands stayed there. Highway (Sherbet) were our neighbours, and we spent many a late night post-gigs jamming in one of the rooms.

After a long, hard drug- & alcohol-fuelled haze, we finally returned to Sydney & continued on for a year or so.

After MX Warheads, I was part of The Love Rodeo; we were a wild cow-punk trio that was Roddy Radalj – guitar (Hoodoo Gurus, Scientists, Johnnys), Greg Perano – drums (Hunters & Collectors), and me on bass. We played around Sydney, did a few trips to Melbourne, and thrived on audience participation; that was a big part of the Love Rodeo's appeal. We were short-lived, but we had a lot of fun; we released one single, 'Love Yodel No.9', on Timberyard Records.

In 1985, Greg & I then formed The Deadly Hume. Greg moved from drums to vocals, I was Stephen "Bones" Martin on guitar, Stuart Brown was the drummer, and there was yours truly on bass. John "the sound hound" Bassett was an integral part of our sound; he was our audio engineer both live & in the studio. We played a heap of shows up & down the Eastern seaboard from Brisbane to Melbourne and even did a couple of trips to New Zealand.

Midway through the Hume years, Bones was replaced by Ron Hadley as our new guitarist, and we travelled to New York & Los Angeles. After the US trip we had a few different drummers, with Richard Ploog (The Church) and Johnny MacKay (Machinations) among them. During our 5-year life, we gained quite a few supporters for international bands like Screaming Jay Hawkins, New Order, The Damned and The Pogues.

Ahh, the Pogues – I can't ever forget that night when the Hume supported them in 1988 at the Enmore over 2 nights. After watching The Pogues' somewhat chaotic and incredibly exciting soundcheck, we were hanging around in our dressing room when Shane McGowan and Spider popped their heads in the door to ask, *"Do you lads have anything to drink?"* We said, *"No, sorry"* – we weren't getting a drink rider. They said, *"Well, that won't do; you lads need a drink!"* They soon came back with a bottle of whisky and a case of beer for us! Yes…no rider, but fortunately, we received a lot of support from 2JJJ radio & released some great records on the Phantom label.

My next stop was playing bass for Nick Barker & The Reptiles; this meant relocating to Melbourne. We had a gruelling schedule, playing 3-5 nights a week, and often we'd be driving hours to & from the shows in Wagga Wagga, a 5-hour trip away. Unfortunately, we didn't always stay overnight; we'd pack and head back home! Quite a few shows were as support acts for the likes of Jimmy Barnes (post-Cold Chisel years), Noiseworks and Boom Crash Opera, etc. We played in all kinds of venues, big & small: sweaty pubs & a couple of wild biker festivals. We made it on to TV's *Hey Hey It's Saturday* a handful of times & did a lunchtime show for the prisoners at Pentridge Gaol. We started a tour in far north Queensland in Cairns, heading south through Townsville, Rockhampton, the Sunshine & Gold Coast, and into New South Wales, with gigs on the North Coast, Mid-North Coast, Newcastle, on to Sydney, then Wollongong, the South Coast & beyond. We played and we played, circling the outskirts of Melbourne, Geelong, Ballarat to Adelaide & back around countless times, flew to Tasmania & played Perth a number of times. We were super tight; match fit & ran like a well-oiled although somewhat dysfunctional cock rock & roll machine!

Toward the end, in 1992, I was asked to audition for Boom Crash Opera; alas, it wasn't to be, as it was torpedoed due to the situation between my former housemates Nick & Dale! That's another story for another time! Around the same time legendary Ian Rilen had asked me to play with Hell to Pay, I turned it down, something I regret. The Reptiles disbanded not long after, Nick took off overseas & I was called in to play with old Sydney mates Ratcat.

The Ratcat years were awesome, & we toured a lot! We travelled as far away as Darwin, including a trip to Kakadu & Broome. Then down to Perth for a few shows, then back home to Sydney for a few weeks, & then we'd head off again for more adventures on the road.

The luxury of having your own room at the Hilton was nice, real nice. It was in stark contrast to those arduous days with *the Reptile,* that's for sure.

Spring & summer was usually starting a tour up north; the Cairns run down the coast over a couple of weeks. Crazy 'O-week' gigs at universities, with summer gigs in all of the usual coastal towns. We would have a week or two off, then back on the road, to Melbourne, to Adelaide, back to Perth, rinse and repeat! We went to New Zealand, where apparently no-one had heard of us! We travelled to Asia a couple of times and played an outdoor MTV music festival in Wan Chai, Hong Kong, with Apache Indian & Techno-tronic, plus a festival in Manila & some shows in Singapore, etc..

After 4 years or so, I decided to leave. It was an incredibly hard decision to make. My last show was a side show set at the Big Day Out Festival with Simon.

I gave up playing live, as it had become a chore & my anxiety was getting out of control.

It was 21 years until I played a benefit show in 2017 with Ratcat in honour of Simon Holmes from the Hummingbirds, who had tragically taken his own life earlier that year. I also played bass for the Hummingbirds that night; it was an all-star lineup with Smudge, Custard, Ups & Downs, Disneyfist, Arial Maps, Dusty Ravens, and The Tall Grass among the acts appearing. Currently I play bass with Alannah Russack (ex-Hummingbirds), and I have a solo project called Omegaman; it's mostly reggae, Latin, funk & beats. For 25 years I have been kept busy DJing clubs, bars, and festivals.

Omegaman tunes are released on US label Fort Knox Recordings, Washington.

21

⦿ Released in 1978 by Rough Trade Records, the debut EP *Extended Play* introduced listeners to Cabaret Voltaire, one of the most creative bands of the latter part of the 20th century. Adventurous yet minimalist, the EP displayed the band's expert use of prehistoric drum machines, monophonic synthesizers, Casios, and effects devices like echo, flanging, and vocal reverb. This groundbreaking EP established Cabaret Voltaire's innovative avant-garde sound. For any music lover, *Extended Play* is an essential and highly influential release worth seeking out.

◉ Simon Fisher Turner was born in 1954 in Dover, England. He is well-known in the music world as a composer and sound designer and earned a name early for involvement with the band The The, when he and Colin Lloyd Tucker were part of the group for about a year before going off as the duo Deux Filles in 1982 to record two albums. Turner also recorded two solo albums and toured under the name King of Luxembourg in the late 1980s. In the late 1990s, he played in the Hangovers, a band led by Gina Birch of the Raincoats. Throughout his career, Turner has collaborated on and recorded numerous soundtracks. He continues to release albums on Mute Records under his own name, Simon Fisher Turner.

Jakob Magnusson and Bjork / Bjork – Kukl by Petra Gall

◉ Björk Guðmundsdóttir, the acclaimed Icelandic musician known mononymously by her first name, was born on November 21, 1965, in Reykjavik. Her unique artistry has earned her the label of musical genius. Raised on a hippie commune by her activist mother, Hildur Rúna Hauksdóttir, Björk began studying flute and piano at age six. Impressed by her talent, teachers sent a recording of Björk singing 'I Love to Love' by Tina Charles to Iceland's sole radio station, RUV. The recording was broadcast nationwide, catching the attention of Fálkinn Records executives who promptly signed the precocious 12-year-old. In 1977, Björk released her *self-titled* debut album and became an instant celebrity in her homeland. The early '80s saw Björk out front of the bands Jam-80, Tappi Tikarrass and Kukl, where her vocal acrobatics became the main talking point. In 1986 she formed Sykurmolarnir, aka The Sugarcubes; they would have minor success with the single Birthday and the debut album *Life's Too Good*. After two more moderately received album releases, they split in 1992. Since then, the often-controversial singer-songwriter and multi-instrumentalist has consistently pushed musical boundaries with her avant-garde, genre-blending releases. While intensely complex and challenging for some listeners, her 2011 album *Biophilia* displays Björk's signature eccentric artistry. Her music is modern, music of the new millennia, a great album and arguably Björk's best. So, if you don't want to be challenged, just buy some music that is a rehash of the '60s, '70s or '80s, and maybe this is not for you. This is today...and tomorrow, next week and many days into the future. Listen...Learn...Create.

◉ Peter Koppes was born in Canberra, Australia, in 1955. Peter is a highly talented multi-instrumentalist, but best known as the guitarist, keyboardist, and vocalist who was a founding member of The Church. The Church came together in 1980 and became a regular, paying their dues on the Sydney pub and club circuit. Their first album *Of Skins and Heart*, was released in April 1981 and is often cited as one of the great Australian debut recordings.

Disillusioned with the band's progress, he left the line-up after the release of their 7th album, the stunning *Priest=Aura*. He returned after four years in 1992 and continued as a solid member until 2019. During his hiatus and departure, Peter has recorded several solo albums, ventured into multiple collaborations with the likes of Margot Smith and the late Damien Lovelock on the *It's a Wig Wig Wig Wig World* album, and created the project Peter Koppes and The Well, releasing 2 critically received albums. In 2022 Peter released *Music Evolution Therapy*, an album of 56 short instrumental pieces of new scale theory; it features what is known as the Seven Note Scale or Mode for the Dominant E7#9 'Hendrix' Chord.

THE NS 10s
PETER KOPPES
(The Church)

In 1981 the most famous mixing engineer in the world was Bob Clearmountain, and he had arrived in Australia to record and produce the second album by The Church called *The Blurred Crusade*.

He had just come from the USA, mixing *Tattoo You* with The Rolling Stones, following his reputation for creating the new big, lush sound of Roxy Music, Bruce Springsteen, The Pretenders and Bryan Adams.

Every engineer and producer in the world wanted to know how he achieved his sound, as he rarely worked around other people.

He installed his equipment to record The Church at EMI 301 Studios in Sydney, and suddenly many local producers wanted to inspect those studios for their prospective jobs, but they were also likely spying on his setup.

Bob may be the humblest man in the music business and would not have minded, so I will let you know the gear he was using due to his significant influence on modern music.

He would only ever listen on small bookshelf speakers called 'Yamaha NS10' that were identifiable for their black boxes with white speaker cones and even now are seen perched on top of almost every professional mixing desk that anyone has seen in a photo or documentary.

The Yamaha NS10s became the standard industry reference speakers, but Bob would also stick a piece of square tissue paper (possibly from the head cleaner or toilet variety) over the tweeter to soften its harshness.

But many engineers complained about the 'bland' sound of these speakers, and so I asked Bob why he used them.

His answer was, "If the music sounds good on them, it will sound good on everything else."

● Brian Ritchie was a founding member and bassist of Milwaukee's Violent Femmes, which has been touring the globe since 1981. The band's *self-titled* debut album is a killer; 'Blister in the Sun', 'Kiss Off', 'Add It Up', and 'Gone Daddy Gone' are just plainly excellent. 'Please Do Not Go' and 'Good Feeling' are just a tiny bit behind. Brian has also performed and recorded with innumerable artists, including Rodriguez, the Australian Chamber Orchestra, Pierre Henry, ad infinitum. He currently resides in Tasmania, where he is the Artistic Director of Music at Mona (Museum of Old and New Art).

LOU, BONNIE, AND CIGARS
BRIAN RITCHIE
(Violent Femmes)

Violent Femmes were touring The Fatherland with an unusual bill of Bonnie Raitt, Lou Reed, Lyle Lovett, and The Femmes. I was hanging around backstage when I spotted Lou puffing on a little cigarillo. I asked him if he liked cigars, to which he replied in the affirmative but admitted that he only smoked those minis. So, I pulled out a very large Romeo and Julieta Churchill Havana and offered it to him. While we were fiddling around with the cigar cutter and matches, getting ready for Lou to join the world of big boy cigars, we were approached by Bonnie Raitt.

Bonnie was a great person to be on tour with because she's engaging, funny and bawdy. She looked at me, looked at Lou, looked at the cigar, then looked at me again and asked, *"Brian, do you have anything about that size I can put in MY mouth?"* This was the only time I saw Lou embarrassed and at a loss for words.

So goes the story of how I introduced my musical hero to cigar smoking. He influenced my entire musical outlook, and I returned the favour by turning him on to proper cigars. That may not have been an equal trade, but there you have it. The End.

Brian Ritchie by Roch Parisien

⦿ Chris Watson, born Christopher Richard Watson in 1953 in Sheffield, England, was a founding member of the pioneering industrial POST-PUNK band Cabaret Voltaire. Watson is renowned for his skill in manipulating sound using tape loops, electronics, and effects. His work entailed crafting structured compositions by supplementing recordings with an array of unconventional instruments and processed voices. These experimental techniques, developed alongside Cabaret Voltaire partners Richard H. Kirk and Stephen Mallinder, ensured the band was regarded as "ahead of its time". He has also earned high praise for his award-winning solo work and collaborations with Andrew McKenzie as The Hafler Trio with their sound art and design. Chris is acclaimed as a field recordist, with recognition coming for his wildlife recordings featured in documentaries by David Attenborough. His work with Icelandic composer-musician Hildur Guðnadóttir on the 2019 Chernobyl miniseries soundtrack earned a Grammy nomination.

22

⦿ Dave Ball, the technical half of Soft Cell, released his debut and sole solo album, *In Strict Tempo*, on November 22, 1983, on Stevo's Some Bizzare label. The album is a departure from Soft Cell's melodic, hook-laden songs, the industrial synthpop LP *Non-Stop Erotic Cabaret*. Much of the music has an uneasy, challenging, yet intriguing quality, particularly the 12-minute-plus funk-disco-techno-jazz epic 'American Stories'. Featuring Gavin Friday and Genesis P-Orridge, it's not always an easy listen; *In Strict Tempo* offers rewards for the adventurous listener.

⦿ The Portraits released their debut single, titled 'Released and Available', in 1979. Soon after, the NEW WAVE band renamed themselves first The Fix and then The Fixx, following little response to their first two singles. Over the next 30 years, keyboardist-vocalist Cy

Curnin, drummer Adam Woods, keyboardist Rupert Greenall and guitarist Jamie West-Oram remained the core members of The Fixx, contributing to a dozen album releases.

⊙ Martina Michèle "Tina" Weymouth, born in Coronado, California, in 1950, is best known as the bass player for the highly influential and innovative band Talking Heads. In 1980, alongside her husband and Talking Heads drummer Chris Frantz and guitarist Adrian Belew, Weymouth was a founding member of the side projects, The Tom Tom Club, and the Heads. With Talking Heads, Weymouth recorded nine acclaimed studio albums and also recorded six albums with Tom Tom Club and the Heads, an album called *No Talking, Just Head*. The Heads line-up included fellow Talking Heads members Frantz and Jerry Harrison and featured guest vocalists like Andy Partridge, Michael Hutchence, Debbie Harry, and Shaun Ryder. When Weymouth and Frantz formed Tom Tom Club, they built on the funk and polyrhythmic style of the Talking Heads album *Remain in Light*. The 1981 *self-titled* debut album generated two huge dance hits, 'Wordy Rappinghood' and 'Genius of Love'. The album also marks a point in music history when the New York alternative scene and the burgeoning hip-hop scene were influencing each other, when both parties were on to something new. With its lush funk grooves, inventive rap vocalizing, and Weymouth's propulsive bass, the album still holds up as an innovative snapshot of the early 1980s music scene.

23

⊙ Chris Bostock, hailing from Bristol, England, was born in 1962. In 1983, Chris showcased his bass skills as a member of Jo Boxers, a band that achieved almost top ranking on the UK charts with their No.3 hit single 'Boxer Beat'. Additionally, Chris collaborated with Rob Marche, who was also part of Jo Boxers, in the band Subway Sect. Furthermore, Chris's musical journey included stints with The X-Certs, The Stingrays, and Dave Stewart's ensemble.

⊙ *Back In the D.H.S.S.*, the debut vinyl album by Half Man Half Biscuit, hit UK record store shelves on November 23, 1985. The DHSS was referring to Dept. of Health & Social Security. Released on the Probe Plus label, this rollicking, irreverent POST-PUNK record exhibits jangly guitar and bass lines as the band skewers English culture with razor-sharp wit and wordplay that even Morrissey would have envied. With its uniquely British ironic references, the lyrics may prove challenging for those outside the UK. Song titles like 'Fuckin' Ell, It's Fred Titmus', '99% Of Gargoyles Look Like Bob Todd', and 'I Hate Nerys Hughes (From the Heart)' exemplify the band's witty approach.

⊙ Craig Hooper was born in 1959 in Sydney, Australia. Growing up in Dubbo, a central New South Wales town, Hooper's first musical experience was playing in a primary school recorder group. One member of that group was Glennis "Glad" Reed, who later joined Midnight Oil. As a teenager, Hooper taught himself guitar and piano and joined the local band The New Gold Stars. There he met John Bliss, who introduced him to Dave Mason. The three formed the core of The Reels, whose 1981 song 'Quasimodo's Dream' was voted one of the top 10 Australian songs of all time. The Reels took a hiatus in 1984, during which Hooper played on The Church's 1984 EP *Persia* and helped form The Mullanes with Neil Finn, Paul Hester, and Nick Seymour. Hooper left The Mullanes in 1985 prior to a US tour, allowing him to rejoin most of The Reels' original members when the band reformed. The remaining trio of The Mullanes went on to become Crowded House. Throughout his career, Hooper worked as a consummate professional musician - producing and doing session work with bands like The Rockmelons and Ross Wilson, as well as for advertising jingles, to pay the rent in leaner times. One highlight was his work on The Reels' *Beautiful* album, which included the band's first No.1 single 'This Guy's in Love with You'. For that album he did all the arrangements and programming and played almost all the instruments, using, among other things, an early version of the Fairlight CMI sampler.

STRANDED IN AOTEAROA
CRAIG HOOPER
(The Reels, The Mullanes)

After recording your first album, there is an expectation that you will play that album live until your next one and that the style/genre captured in that album is what the band is all about. Growing up in the country, we (The Reels) were exposed to a broad range of music, and we used to change the arrangements of our songs, often quite radically, all the time. For us, an album is more of a snapshot of what you happened to be playing around that time. Being locked into reproducing our first album every night for the next year was soul-destroying. So, when we finally took a break and onboarded a new member, Karen Ansell, we disappeared into an underground (literally) rehearsal room for several weeks, put down the guitars and picked up (figuratively) synthesizers and made almost random noises for hours on end. Out of that period emerged a new sensibility that led eventually to the *Quasimodo's Dream* album, via an EP of covers, *Five Great Gift Ideas*.

This was years before most equipment had microprocessors and memory and presets. We each had a ring binder file and a torch because between each song we would have to manually recall the settings on our synths, the only exception being the Roland Jupiter 4, which had a massive 8 individual memories. This meant that on stage the first note of every song was an anxious moment, as one missed switch or wrongly adjusted knob could be cacophonous or nothing. This new configuration didn't lend itself to a "standard" stage setup of "back line" guitar, bass, and keyboard amplifiers and foldback wedges; it required a lot more subtlety and control. We ditched the instrument amplifiers, and each person got an analogue parametric equaliser and an analogue delay to give a bit more control over the sound of what were fairly primitive synthesizers (Korg 700S and MS-20s), as well as for guitar and bass, which were now effectively DI'd (direct input) like the synths. We each had a custom-designed speaker cabinet which was general purpose, which looked like a large bass cabinet, fed from the foldback mixer so each person had their own monitor mix. We also ditched the traditional Shure SM-58 vocal microphones and replaced them with headsets so that we weren't constantly adjusting stands as we switched between instruments.

The new stage configuration also didn't fit well with the traditional PA systems with 4560 bins, etc.; we needed something that was more suited to the "everything is DI'd" approach, something that would at least in theory allow a bit more of the nuances to come through. There weren't many options that were both high-quality sound and tough enough to actually tour with, and we eventually settled on 32 Bose 802 speakers. We were not very much cashed up, nor did we have a respectable credit rating, so we actually had to get our parents to go guarantors on a large hire-purchase deal, which included the PA, the headsets, a couple of keyboards, and some drums and bits and pieces.

The wisdom of this financial obligation came to be questioned over the next few years. We toured New Zealand in early 1981 and took our PA with us. Meanwhile, 'According to My Heart' had moved up the charts and was in the top 5 in most states, our first commercial success. As we were at the airport in Auckland, in the departure lounge waiting for our boarding call, excited about coming home and doing our biggest tour ever, suddenly every flight on the board switched to "Cancelled". It turned out to be a pilot's strike.

Our equipment had already gone through customs, and our luggage had been checked in. We had no choice but to go back into town and try to find accommodation for the band and crew for what we thought was one night. The news reports said that they expected to resolve the strike that day, every day, so we spent roughly a week traipsing out to the airport, sitting around bored and then going back into the city to look for more accommodation. Meanwhile, we had to cancel the first week, then two weeks, of what would have been our biggest tour ever.

We obviously couldn't continue sitting around the airport indefinitely, so we ended up having to hire a light plane to fly out from Australia to pick us up. By this stage we had our luggage back, and somebody had managed to have some, ahem, "quiet words" with some customs official or maybe airport staff and managed to get us back a few of our instruments. But the PA was stuck at Auckland airport for the unforeseeable future.

So we had cancelled the first few weeks of our triumphant national tour and spent a fortune hiring a private plane to fly from Australia to pick us up (and that's another whole story in itself, flying across the Tasman Sea in a dangerously overloaded light plane, barely making it to Lord Howe Island before running out of fuel); we had to hire new equipment, including a PA, for the rest of the tour while still making payments on the equipment stuck in NZ. We went heavily into debt, a factor that played into other tensions in the band once it became obvious that we would be working for at least the next year to pay off the debt resulting from that cursed NZ tour. As people gradually left the band, their parents were removed from the hire-purchase agreement, and eventually, when Dave got sick and The Reels stopped for a couple of years, Dave's and my parents had to take over paying the hire-purchase payments until we eventually managed to sell the equipment we still had and finally paid it out.

But we did get to play at Sweetwaters Festival in front of 30,000 people, so there's that.

O The Kelpies' debut single 'Take Me Away' b/w 'Second by Second' was released on November 23, 1982. This inner-city Sydney POST-PUNK band's single was released on Phantom Records # PH-17. The Kelpies were born out of the bands The Bedhogs and Suicide Squad, with guitarists Brian Connolly, Mark Easton, bassist Con Murphy, drummer Ashley Thompson and James Gelding handling the vocals.

O The second album release by Public Image Ltd, *Metal Box*, made its debut on November 23, 1979, presented in a unique metal can packaging by Virgin Records. After astounding initial sales, it was later reissued in the more traditional cardboard sleeve format as *Second Edition* in February 1980. *Metal Box* marked a significant departure for PiL, pushing the boundaries of POST-PUNK music into uncharted experimental realms, introducing a challenging new 'jazz-like' style that drew comparisons to the innovative Captain Beefheart. Jah Wobble's commanding basslines displayed a newfound precision and wider dynamic range compared to their earlier work. The stark, icy, and relentless drumming contributed by Martin Atkins, David Humphrey, and Richard Dudanski delivered intense rhythms. Keith Levene's sharp, wailing guitar added percussive elements to the chaotic musical landscape. John Lydon's unmistakable vocalisations and exclamations, combined with subtle synth textures from Levene, rounded out the distinctive sound of *Metal Box*. Despite being recognised as a groundbreaking and uncompromising album, the recording's sound quality and musicianship were acknowledged as raw and unpolished for its time.

O 'Starry Eyes' the debut single by The Records, was available November 23, 1978. It was a power-pop classic from a much-underrated band. The single should have been a big seller, and even though it sounded great on the radio, it was missed by the greater record-buying public. The subject matter? It was one of the ultimate kiss-off songs, to their duplicitous manager of all people. You can file this next to Cheap Trick.

24

O Clem Burke was born November 24, 1955 in Bayonne, New Jersey. Clem brought unexpected rhythm to punk and NEW WAVE; Burke's combo of crisp backbeat and kinetic, Keith Moon-influenced bluster helped set Blondie apart from the pack. With Clem behind the kit, Blondie put everything from disco grooves and reggae to hip-hop beats into the group's smash hits, and he had a presence and charisma beyond your typical sticksman. Debbie Harry is quoted as saying, *"He was into jumping over his drum kit fairly regularly; he was a real star. He could play, and you could tell that it was his life."* After a battle with cancer, Clem died on April 7, 2025; he was 70 years of age.

⊙ Care's second single, 'Flaming Sword', peaked at No.48 on the UK charts on this day in 1983; it followed their debut single, 'My Boyish Days'. This passionate, bright classic featured rich, melancholy vocals by Paul Simpson over Ian Broudie's classy production. As a founding member of Big in Japan and Original Mirrors, Liverpool native Broudie imbued the timeless track with his signature sound.

⊙ Michael William Head, the driving force behind the jangle-pop masters The Pale Fountains, was born in 1961 in Liverpool, England. With The Pale Fountains, Head wrapped sophisticated, intelligent lyrics around the band's silky music, though they were sadly missed by the wider audience and folded in 1987. Their two album releases remain timeless modern-day listening. After The Pale Fountains dissolved, Head and his brother John formed Shack, releasing 5 studio albums. In 2022 Michael formed The Red Elastic Band and released the well-received album *Dear Scott*.

⊙ Gary Numan's first album with Tubeway Army was released on November 24, 1978, and it peaked at No.14 on the UK Album Chart. The *self-titled* album held a lot of similarities to the pop-punk release 'That's Too Bad' from earlier in February. It predominantly showcased guitar with subtle yet impactful synth embellishments in the beginnings and endings. Numan's distinct, detached, robotic, staccato vocals perfectly complemented the album's infectious, concise songs filled with memorable hooks. The driving rhythms were provided by Numan's uncle Jess Lydiard on drums, while Paul Gardiner's flawless bass provided a solid foundation for the powerful guitar work. This groundbreaking album by one of the most influential and innovative musicians of the 20th century hinted at the creative advancements yet to come.

⊙ The Undertones, formed in Derry, Northern Ireland, in 1975, ceased to exist on November 24, 1983, after a decade of success. Originally consisting of Feargal Sharkey, John O'Neill, Damian O'Neill, Michael Bradley and Billy Doherty, the band released their debut EP, *Teenage Kicks*, in 1978. The title track captivated BBC's DJ John Peel; he named it as his favourite song of all time and gave it high rotation. The exposure led to a major record deal and the release of their *self-titled* debut album the following year. After issuing two more albums, their fourth, *The Sin of Pride* in 1983, proved to be their swan song. The band reunited in 1999 without Sharkey, who went on to have a solo career and later became head of UK Music. The Undertones have since toured extensively, performing several tours across the UK, Ireland, Continental Europe, Japan, and Turkey. In 2017 they played the Isle of Wight Festival and toured the USA & Australia.

25

⊙ Recorded on November 25, 1984, and released just a week later, the song 'Do They Know It's Christmas' by Band Aid quickly rose to the top of the charts worldwide. This single set a record as the fastest-selling single in the UK, with over one million copies sold in the first week and three million by the end of the year. The song raised more than £10 million for charity. Written by Midge Ure and Bob Geldof, the recording featured a star-studded lineup of over 40 music industry vocalists. The music was composed by Midge Ure of Ultravox, Phil Collins of Genesis, and John Taylor of Duran Duran.

⊙ The Brisbane band The Go-Betweens released their debut album *Send Me a Lullaby* on November 25, 1981, as an eight-track mini-album recorded earlier that July. In February 1982, four more tracks were added for the expanded UK release. The three-piece lineup consisted of Robert Forster (vocals, rhythm guitar), Grant McLennan (vocals, bass guitar, lead guitar), and Lindy Morrison (drums, vocals), with guest appearances by James Freud, Nick Cave, Roland Howard, Mick Harvey, and Dan Wallace-Crabbe. Somewhat embryonic and adolescent, this was a disjointed debut; the band had already attracted a loyal following with their classic single 'Lee Remick' and were sure to improve, which they did. The Go-Betweens were always able to weave together beautiful, delicate melodies, harmonising bass and guitar. Morrison provided rock-steady percussion with first-class fills and punctuation. 'Arrow in a Bow' evoked an artsy Talking Heads feel with exceptional bass, while 'Hold Your Horses' and 'One Thing Can Hold Us' exemplified their talent for catchy melodies.

⦿ The first day of the Jamaica World Music Festival was held in Montego Bay, Jamaica, on November 25, 1982. The lineup featured NEW WAVE artists including The B-52's, Squeeze, Joe Jackson, The English Beat, and The Clash, as well as classic reggae artists like Peter Tosh, Rita Marley and The Melody Makers, Bobby and The Midnites, Jimmy Cliff, and Toots and The Maytals. Over the three-day event, other classic artists performing included The Beach Boys, Aretha Franklin, and Skeeter Davis.

⦿ The Nuns, hailing from San Francisco, USA, emerged from the punk scene, but their catchy, bombastic pop-punk hooks bridged the gap between POST-PUNK and NEW WAVE. After five years of live performances, they released their *self-titled* debut album in 1980. The excellent musicianship and Jennifer Miro's passionate vocals evoked the gritty sound of Penetration and Blondie's punk roots, rather than the band's later releases. The album's catchiest tracks, 'Walkin' the Beat', 'Wild', and 'Suicide Child', showcase Miro's melodic keyboard work providing texture throughout. This is a recording that remains worth revisiting.

⦿ Robert Vickers was born in Brisbane, Australia, on November 25, 1958. Best known as the bassist for the influential Australian band The Go-Betweens from 1983 to 1987, Vickers first gained musical experience playing with local Brisbane bands like The Numbers in the late 1970s. After a brief stint in the New York band Colors, who were managed by CBGB owner Hilly Kristal, Vickers joined The Go-Betweens when they were recording in London in 1983. He played on their classic albums *Spring Hill Fair, Before Hollywood*, and *Tallulah*, leaving the band in late 1987. Since then, Vickers has toured and recorded with artists like Amy Rigby and Lloyd Cole, worked as a publicist for Jetset Records in New York, and currently runs his own marketing and PR agency, Proxy Media PR, out of New York City.

BERLIN
ROBERT VICKERS
(Riptides, The Go-Betweens)

I was always fascinated by Berlin. I loved the movie *Cabaret* and the Christopher Isherwood book it was based on. Anything about Berlin between the wars, during the Weimar Republic era, interested me. When I was a teenager, backpacking through Europe in 1977, I visited the city and spent the day in East Berlin, marvelling at the still extant bullet holes in walls. Berlin was a time capsule, an unusual city; divided by the Berlin Wall, East Berlin on one side, with all of Soviet-occupied East Germany backing it up, and on the other, West Berlin, an island inside communist East Germany populated by old people who refused to move and young people who the West Germans encouraged to live there by making them exempt from military service.

Years later, on May 24th, 1987, I made another visit. I was in an Australian band called The Go-Betweens who regularly toured Germany, so I had been back a number of times. Usually playing at a midsized club called The Loft Metropole, which was always a great show. A large percentage of young people in the city made it into a kind of fantasy playground for rock bands at the time. Like an underground Disneyland.

Prior to going on this tour, my partner, Janie Heath, had given me the phone number of a friend of hers, Kid Congo Powers, whom she had met years ago when a group of the early LA punks had visited New York. By this time, after stints in The Gun Club and The Cramps, Kid had joined Nick Cave and the Bad Seeds, who were now living in Berlin. I had met him in London, where he had his own band, Fur Bible, for a while. I intended to call him when I got there.

We had played an odd gig in a small German city the night before but, due to some freak accident of scheduling, had been given two nights off in Berlin. This was highly unusual, and we were anxious to enjoy this mini holiday in one of our favourite cities. So much so that we drove there nonstop in a 12-hour, 800 km marathon, including the always tense transit through the DDR (East Germany) via a corridor to West Berlin.

We arrived at the hotel around midnight, but I was determined to take full advantage of my nights off. The rest of the band went to bed, but I managed to convince our driver to go out with me to see if we could find a bar for a quick drink. We did immediately. It was a shoebox, ominously dark, with a few tables and chairs and a small bar with a portable television set on it playing the Tod Browning film Freaks. In other words, perfect. On earlier tours I had had wild nights out in Berlin, and although this was a subdued one, it was also very special in that I got to know two fascinating people.

I found a public phone and called Kid hoping just to make contact for the upcoming show, but to my surprise, he wanted to come right out. In the meantime, other people were coming in. It was the kind of town where the really important things only happened in the wee small hours of the morning. I chatted to a girl who was the singer in a band called The Idiot Cards named Billie Ray Martin, who later had hits in the UK under her own name.

Presently a three-headed vision came sweeping into the bar, laughing and surveying the scene: Kid, extravagant in a dark suit with his jet-black hair slicked back and a pencil moustache, and flanking him, to my surprise, two darkly glamorous women also in black with raven hair and bright red lipstick, Anita Lane and Katie Beale. I knew of both from Melbourne and London, where they had lived and were known as part of the Birthday Party camp. The Birthday Party was Nick Cave's band prior to The Bad Seeds.

Katie Beale was a painter and the girlfriend of Birthday Party guitarist Mick Harvey, who had made the move to The Bad Seeds with Nick Cave, and Anita was Nick's girlfriend and had written some of the Birthday Party's songs with him. She was also embarking on her own singing career at this time. These were fabulous and talented women who made the Melbourne rock scene the most interesting of the Australian scenes and the most like the New York one I had recently left.

Despite seeing these women at gigs and parties for a few years, this was my first chance to find out who they really were and enjoy some reflected glamour. They were in fine form. They seemed very at home in the Berlin band ecosystem, and after the travails of following around the dysfunctional Birthday Party, The Bad Seeds' relative stability had to be a relief.

In the years since that night our paths continued to cross, and although I saw much more of Katie than of Anita, it was always eventful to run into her. Anita Lane recently passed away in Melbourne. Katie Beale is still painting.

December 2023.

◉ When Yellow Magic Orchestra released their *self-titled* debut album in 1978, they put the bleeps, bloops, and electronic sounds of video games into a pioneering and cohesive album, years ahead of most musicians. The Japanese trio of Ryuichi Sakamoto, Yukihiro Takahashi, and Harouomi Hosono, assisted by Hideki Matsutake, created catchy songs with an unmistakable Eastern techno flair. Tunes like 'Simoon' and 'Mad Pierrot' have an almost Western lounge music style, while 'La Femme Chinoise' at times evokes the feeling of playing Space Invaders in an amusement arcade. This innovative album was created before the era of digital sampling and preset synthesizers. YMO had to manually patch together banks of analogue waveform generators and homemade sequencers; it was quite similar to how Kraftwerk worked, indeed a difficult and laborious process. While the sound is dated by today's standards, Yellow Magic Orchestra's influence and inspiration remain significant, and their debut album was groundbreaking.

◉ Dave Hewson was born in London, England, on November 25, 1953. During the 1980s, Dave was a pivotal figure in various synthpop groups, most notably the trio Poeme Electronique, alongside Sharon Abbott and Julie Ruler. The 1980 single 'The Echoes Fade' by Poeme Electronique, which exceeds 6 minutes in length, is considered the quintessential example of dark, minimal electronic music and is currently highly coveted by dedicated collectors of the genre. At that time, Dave was also known for his role as a producer and composer for the works of Twins Natalia and Techno Twins. Over the years, up to the present day, Dave has earned a reputation as a distinguished composer of scores for both television and film. Among his most notable contributions is the theme music for ITV's coverage of the funerals of Queen Elizabeth and Prince Philip, as well as for the Coronation of King Charles and Queen Camilla.

A WARDROBE MALFUNCTION LEADS TO SUCCESS
DAVE HEWSON
(Poeme Electronique, Twins Natalia, Techno Twins)

Over the years we had performed a number of gigs in South London. I remember on one occasion we had entered a competition for best live band. Sharon had forgotten her stage clothes so she went on stage in a black rubbish bin bag.

She was renowned for her amazing presence on stage and her performance, but on this occasion, she flung her arms out to the audience, and in doing so, rocketed her bra into the front row causing consternation as unfortunately the black sack fell down at the same time. Needless to say, we won the competition/

26

◉ The Liverpool-based band Big in Japan had a short career, releasing just one shared single with The Chuddy Nuddies and four-track EP in November 1978. Despite their brief time together, the band had a significant influence. Members went on to find success with bands like KLF, Frankie Goes to Hollywood, Echo & the Bunnymen, and The Teardrop Explodes. The 1978 EP, titled *From Y to Z and Never Again*, was released as a final effort to pay off debts before the band broke up, but it led to the founding of Zoo Records. The track 'Suicide A Go Go' is catchy and playful, reminiscent of The B-52's. 'Nothing Special' has an interesting start-stop rhythm. 'Taxi' showcases excellent POST-PUNK sounds, while 'Cindy & the Barbi Dolls' is an odd track that defies categorisation. Despite its short duration, Big in Japan left a lasting mark on the POST-PUNK genre.

◉ On November 26, 2016, in London, Joe Corre, son of Sex Pistols manager Malcolm McLaren and fashion designer Dame Vivienne Westwood, allegedly burnt punk memorabilia said to be worth millions of dollars. He torched the items alongside effigies of politicians rigged with fireworks as part of a protest near Albert Bridge in Chelsea. Wearing a top hat and bandana, Corre told the gathered crowd before igniting the blaze, *"Punk was never meant to be nostalgic. You can't learn it in a museum workshop. Punk has become just another marketing tool to sell you something unnecessary: the illusion of an alternative choice, conformity in a different uniform"*.

⊙ The band The Godfathers released their first album, *Hit by Hit,* on November 26, 1986. The record combined tracks from their initial three releases, along with a cover version of John Lennon's 'Cold Turkey' and some instrumental interludes. Formed after the breakup of The Sid Presley Experience, The Godfathers consisted of singer Peter Coyne, his brother and bassist Chris Coyne, guitarists Kris Dollimore and Mike Gibson, and drummer George Mazur. With their blend of abrasive POST-PUNK, pop, and R&B, the album marked an excellent debut for the band, who went on to release nearly a dozen critically acclaimed albums over the course of their career. Lacking pretension, *Hit by Hit* showcases guitar-centered '80s rock music with catchy melodies and hooks.

⊙ The Sound released their second album, *From the Lion's Mouth,* in 1981, but despite their U2-like sound predating U2's own, the band did not achieve the same level of recognition as their peers. The album is a front-to-back masterpiece that should be recognised alongside other early '80s classics for its excellence and cohesiveness. Adrian Borland's exploration of humanity's darker aspects is subtly uplifting, making the album a standout in the POST-PUNK genre and a tragically overlooked gem of its time.

27

⊙ The Australian NEW WAVE band Beargarden released their debut album, *All That Fall,* in 1986. Originally known as The Ears, Beargarden secured a record deal with Virgin after years of honing their sound through extensive gigging. However, tensions arose, and the band was dropped by Virgin, though they eventually found a new home with Chase Records. Propelled by Sam Sejavka's powerful vocals and backed by driving synths and percussion, *All That Fall* showcases Beargarden's prodigious talents and '80s flair. Despite their label troubles, the album proved a triumph, rewarding fans with catchy songs delivered with panache.

⊙ Charlie Burchill, hailing from Glasgow, Scotland, was born November 27, 1959. Renowned as the co-founder and guitarist of the band Simple Minds, Charlie has remained a steadfast member of the group since its inception in 1977, working in tandem with vocalist Jim Kerr. In their early experimental albums, Charlie showcased his versatility by playing a wide array of instruments, such as the violin, keyboards, saxophone, and his elegant white Gibson 335 guitar. As time went on, he advanced to his iconic 1962 Gretsch White Falcon guitar, which he continues to strum to this very day.

⊙ The Human League's synthpop smash hit 'Don't You Want Me' was released in 1981 as the band's first No.1 single anywhere. Preceded by three other singles from their massively successful album *Dare,* it remains the band's best known and most commercially successful recording to date. 'Don't You Want Me' was the 1981 Christmas chart topper in the UK, where it has sold over 1.56 million copies, making it the 23rd most successful single in the history of the UK Singles Chart!

⊙ Quando Quango released only one album, *Pigs + Battleships* on November 27, 1985, on the Factory label (Fact 110). This sophisticated techno-synthpop album features beautiful synth sounds and intriguing samples wrapped inside smooth dancefloor grooves. The band originally came together in Holland but relocated to Manchester. Their sound evokes influences like Rip Rig and Panic and Yello without getting bogged down into any one style. Tracks like the reggae-funk 'Happy Boy', reminiscent of The Slits, and the jazz-funk toe-tapper 'Rebel' stand out. The true highlight, though, remains the intro track 'Genius', which lives up to its name.

⊙ Soft Cell's debut LP, *Non-Stop Erotic Cabaret,* made its way into the UK music scene in 1981. Widely regarded as the pinnacle of synthpop albums from that year, it captivates listeners with its enthralling melodies and thought-provoking lyrics. From the rhythmic allure of 'Tainted Love' to the introspective musings of 'Bedsitter' and the audaciously bizarre 'Sex Dwarf', the album exudes a theatrical quality infused with film noir undertones. It effortlessly emanates an air of sleaze, romance, and humour, captivating audiences with its meticulously crafted production and track sequence. *Non-Stop Erotic Cabaret* stands as a testament to the brilliance of synthpop, through David Ball's ability to seamlessly blend keyboards, percussion, and the mesmerising vocal interplay between Marc Almond and Vicious Pink Phenomena. Undoubtedly, it is an indispensable addition to any synthpop collection, showcasing the genre's finest offerings.

28

⊙ The Jam released *Sound Affects* on November 28, 1980. It has been said that *Sound Affects* is the only Jam album that feels complete, with both variety and cohesion. With the melody of 'Man in the Corner Shop', to the immediacy and tightness of 'Start', a brilliant homage in both the production and the riff of The Beatles' 'Taxman', and to the stark, early '80s NEW WAVE feel of 'Set the House Ablaze'. The album opens with the simple but memorable bass line of 'Pretty Green', moves into the anticipatory love song 'Monday', and then we're fully immersed. Every track is remarkable and benefits from a harsh, metallic production style where the vocals are almost secondary to the driving music. Was this Paul Weller's attempt to recreate the Beatles' Revolver in a modern style? It captures The Jam at their peak of songwriting, even without their hit 'Going Underground'. Don't bother with compilations and greatest hits; engage yourself in this brilliant album.

⊙ Jerry Harrison's inaugural solo album, *The Red and the Black*, was available on this day in 1981. Like a companion piece to Talking Heads' *Remain in Light*, Harrison's album brims with funk, mystery, and atmosphere. Many of the same musicians from *Remain in Light* lend their talents here, including the brilliant guitar work of Adrian Belew. The backing vocalists, led by Nona Hendryx, provide depth and contrast to Harrison's mostly monotonic lead vocals. What Harrison lacks in vocal range he makes up for with inventive songwriting and keyboard playing. The songs remain fresh decades later, a testament to Harrison's artistry. Astounding in its synergy.

⊙ David Rowley was born in Sydney, Australia, on November 28, 1958. Best known as a drummer, he had his first impromptu gig at age 14 in a church hall with renowned bassist/guitarist Murray Cook, who later played in The Warumpi Band and Mental as Anything. After finishing high school, Rowley spent a gap year in London, arriving in late 1976 just after the Sex Pistols' infamous interview with Bill Grundy. The punk explosion made a mark on society and on Rowley. Returning to Sydney, he played in several bands, including The Critics, followed by Jump Vision in 1980, who recorded the well-regarded single 'I Can't Get Used to You' b/w 'The Jump', which got heavy airplay on Radio 2JJ. Rowley then joined the MKII version of Brisbane band The End with Brett Myers, later of The Died Pretty, during what he calls his "British progressive POST-PUNK cyclical drums phase". After leaving The End and releasing the dance-sound single 'Sound of God' with Watusi Now, Rowley decided to get serious about his music career and moved back to London in mid-1984. Already a trained journalist, he almost accidentally scored the role of London Editor for *Countdown* Magazine. Just months after arriving in London, he quickly found a band, Salvation Sunday, fronted by vocalist Joanne Winterbottom. With access to every record label in the UK, the band soon got a deal with Polydor and management by Outlaw (Tears for Fears, Julian Cope, Level 42). They released three singles, including 'Cold Grey Eyes'. In late 1987 Rowley left the band and took a job with EMI in London, later heading A&R for Air Chrysalis in Stockholm. After 24 years abroad, he returned to Sydney and rejoined The Prison Wives, featuring vocalist Rebecca Hancock and guitarist Ged Corben. In 2012, Rowley's obsession with Lee Hazlewood led him to form The Nancy

Sinatra/Lee Hazlewood Experience with friends, playing faithful renditions of their pop and country classics. He continues drumming with bands like The Amazing Woolloomooloosers, The Band of Gold, and at Sydney's El Rocco jazz club.

○ Wire's debut studio album, *Pink Flag*, was released in the United Kingdom in 1977. Although it initially went unnoticed, the album quickly gained widespread recognition and solidified its status as a groundbreaking POST-PUNK masterpiece. *Pink Flag* marked the beginning of Wire's influential trilogy, which also includes *Chairs Missing* and *154*. Produced by Mike Thorne with a minimalist approach, the album's raw and unembellished sound allowed Wire's innovative interpretation of rock music to shine. Led by Colin Newman, *Pink Flag* exemplifies Wire's forward-thinking vision by blending abstract and minimalist lyrics, catchy hooks, and layers of distortion to create an electrifying and imaginative whole. These three albums established Wire's exceptional reputation and laid the foundation for the POST-PUNK sound that would define the early 1980s, affirming their position as pioneers of the movement.

29

○ "Brain" was the pseudonym used by Elvis Costello for the writing of most of the songs on *Mad About the Wrong Boy*. Disappointingly, the absence of his vocals as the lead singer prevents what could have been an outstanding album by The Attractions, which was released in 1980. The instrumental work on the album is characterised by tight, precise arrangements and incredibly infectious melodies, showcasing the talent of the musicians. However, the mediocre quality of the vocals falls short in comparison to Costello's exceptional songwriting. Nevertheless, the album still manages to provide an intriguing glimpse into the potential of the songs if Costello had performed them himself.

Chris Bailey by Petra Gall

○ Chris Bailey was born Christopher James Mannix Bailey in 1957, in Nanyuki, Kenya, where his father, Robert, was stationed with the British Army. Bailey grew up first in Belfast, then in Brisbane after moving to Australia at age 7. In 1973, Bailey co-founded The Saints in Brisbane along with Ed Kuepper and Ivor Hay; originally called Kid Galahad and the Eternals, the band soon changed their name to The Saints. They released their debut single '(I'm) Stranded' in September 1976, preceding the Sex Pistols' 'Anarchy in the UK' and the Damned's 'New Rose'. Over the years, The Saints had a revolving cast of over 30 members, but Bailey remained a constant driving force. As a solo artist and with future Saints lineups, he moved toward R&B-influenced roots rock, folk, and more austere instrumentation. Bailey released seven solo albums, with his debut, *Casablanca*, receiving the most critical acclaim and commercial success. He passed away on April 9, 2022, in Haarlem, Netherlands.

○ Michael Dempsey, born in Salisbury, Southern Rhodesia (now Zimbabwe), on 29 November 1958, has enjoyed a highly influential music career spanning more than four decades. He played a pivotal role in the formation of The Cure, contributing as a bassist and lead vocalist on their early singles and albums in the late 1970s. Following his departure from The Cure in 1979, Dempsey embarked on a journey as a bassist for various seminal bands, engaging in session work. It is worth noting that one of his most notable contributions was as a bassist for Roxy Music's hit single 'Avalon'. In 1983, Michael assumed the role of bassist for Liverpool's The Lotus Eaters and soon became a collaborator with the duo Act, consisting of Claudia Brücken and Thomas Leer. Since the 1990s, he has dedicated his time to audio production and remastering. A career highlight was his production of a performance of Pink Floyd's *Atom Heart Mother* in 2008, featuring composer Ron Geesin and a special guest appearance by David Gilmour. Throughout his extensive career, Michael Dempsey has left an indelible mark on the British music scene, collaborating with numerous influential bands and artists.

○ Bob Geldof's debut solo album, *Deep in the Heart of Nowhere*, was released on November 29, 1986. The album featured an array of talented musicians, including Eric Clapton, Midge Ure, Jools Holland, Clem Burke, and Dave Stewart. On the album, Geldof delivered a collection of catchy, rock-infused, emotive songs. Unfortunately, Geldof's musical work did not receive nearly as much praise as his concert organising efforts. However, he penned some fantastic songs for this record. With backing vocals provided by Maria McKee, Annie Lennox, and Alison Moyet, the performances on the album were superb. Notable tracks on the album include 'The World Is Calling', 'In the Pouring Rain', and the poignant 'I Cry Too', which featured Eric Clapton's signature sound.

○ Arguably, nobody in the last century capitalised on new trends as adeptly as Malcolm McLaren. Having moved on from his commercial interests with The Sex Pistols, Bow Wow Wow, and Adam Ant, McLaren released his debut solo single 'Buffalo Gals' in 1982. This catchy, genre-bending track exemplified his knack for harnessing the zeitgeist. 'Buffalo Gals' was an eccentric fusion of hip hop, techno, and country square dancing that scratched a peculiar itch. The story behind McLaren pitching this avant-garde idea to producer and co-writer Trevor Horn would be fascinating to hear. In any case, the infectious single climbed the charts in seven countries, captivating the hungry record-buying public.

○ The debut album *A Thin Red Line* by TV21 was on the record store shelves on this day in 1981. This Scottish band lasted only one album, but at the time, this one album marked them as a group with enormous potential. TV21 had all those great elements that made The Teardrop Explodes, Echo & the Bunnymen and The Chameleons so well known. There are touches of a moody, atmospheric sound not unlike Joy Division, yet with all these comparisons TV21 were still able to have their own sound. The opener 'Waiting for the Drop' and single, 'Snakes and Ladders' are highlights. Impressive debut and end.

30

Murray Attaway (in the hat) - Guadalcanal Diary by permission

◉ Murray Attaway was born in Atlanta, Georgia, USA, on November 30, 1957. He is best known as the lead singer and rhythm guitarist of Guadalcanal Diary (GD) out of Marietta, Georgia. Taking their name from a 1943 war movie, over an 8-year period, they recorded four studio albums, which were a mix of Byrds style jangle and cow punk flavoured rock/pop. After GD's breakup, Murray recorded two solo albums, *In Thrall*, released in 1993, and *Delirium*, recorded 1994-5, which to today remains unreleased. Murray reunited with GD briefly in 1996, recording a self-released live album, *At Your Birthday Party*. Murray has written music for several independent films as well as having had songs placed in numerous films and television shows. He happily exited his career in the music industry in 1997, becoming a web developer and full-time parent. In 2019, he created the satirical *Dazzle Dudes* podcast, which tells the fictional story of a group of inept young males who attempt to start a glam rock band in central Georgia in the 1970s. The show was written, performed, and produced by Murray, with his wife Layla as co-writer. 2023, and Murray began work on a new album titled "(tense music plays…)". We Wait!

ATHENS AND ATLANTA IN THE "GOLDEN AGE"
MURRAY ATTAWAY
(Guadalcanal Diary)

So much has been written about the music that came out of the towns of Athens and Atlanta, Georgia, in the 1980s that both have attained a mythical status, not unlike Liverpool, London, San Francisco, and LA of the 1960s.

The state of Georgia in the USA has always produced a lot of great music: Ray Charles, Otis Redding, Johnny Mercer, James Brown, and Little Richard were all native Georgians. The Georgia Sea Islands contain communities wherein the "ring shout" and Gullah/Geechee music are still alive, having originated with enslaved people from the area which is now Angola. And for years, Atlanta has been rightly recognised as a centre of hip-hop, birthing the "Dirty South" style.

Athens and Atlanta are roughly sixty miles apart. Athens, which is home to the University of Georgia, was a fairly typical college town in the late '70s and early '80s. When I finished high school, it was where you went for a weekend of partying if you lived in the Atlanta area. A lot of my friends had already moved there for college, cheap beer, and insanely cheap rent.

One of those friends was Curtis Crowe, who later became Pylon's drummer, but at that time, he and I were in a band called Strictly American. (That name was intended as irony then, in a way that would be hard to explain now.) Curtis and our friend Bill were renting two upper floors in a semi-neglected building downtown near the campus, and they decided to throw a party on the vast third floor on Halloween of 1978. They christened the place The 40-Watt Club, and, though the legendary venue moved to at least four locations before landing at the address where it still operates, this was the first iteration. Strictly American was the band that night. Somewhere there's a tape of that performance, which is regrettable.

Around that same time, the B-52s formed. I first saw them play on two picnic tables pushed together in a friend's house in Athens. Soon after, Danny Beard, who was/is the owner of Wax'n'Facts record store in Atlanta, put out their first single, 'Rock Lobster', on what became one of the most engaging record labels of the time, DB Recs. DB Recs would go on to release albums by Pylon, Love Tractor, The Coolies, and a whole bunch of other great music. Guadalcanal Diary's first album was on DB (it was later re-released when we moved to Elektra).

So, in Athens, there was a pretty big eruption of bands, a lot of whose members went to art school at the university: Pylon, Love Tractor, REM, Oh OK and the Method Actors, just to name a few. The town also had its share of more straightforward rock bands like The Michael Guthrie Band and Strawberry Flats.

In Atlanta, there were The Fans (a great and seriously overlooked early punk/alternative group), the Swimming Pool Qs, Bruce Hampton's various ensembles, The Brains, Arms Akimbo, The Nightporters, Vietnam, The Coolies and Guadalcanal Diary. Again, just a few of the names.

Atlanta had a slew of good clubs, the most influential of which was 688, run by Steve May. Guadalcanal's big goal in life at our inception was to headline a Friday night at 688 (we did).

If I were pressed to describe differences between the two music scenes, I'd say that Athens was the arty one and Atlanta was the gritty one. Maybe think '60s San Francisco vs New York City. Pretty broad assessment, but accurate enough.

In both places, there was a lot of camaraderie between everyone as well as familial connections; for instance, Rhett Crowe, Guadalcanal's bass player, is the sister of Curtis Crowe, the aforementioned drummer of Pylon. Danny Beard of DB Recs is actually my cousin by marriage, although we didn't know this until well after we'd made a record together.

Atlanta's scene was a little more to my taste, and I felt comfortable in it. However, the lure of cheap housing and so many friends in Athens inspired a lot of people to relocate there, including my bandmates, first John Poe, then Rhett Crowe and Jeff Walls. I was reluctant and was the last Guad to move (although technically Warren Chilton, who was the band's first manager, videographer and ersatz "fifth Guad", moved there after me).

My problem was that "Athens' music" had by then become synonymous with a sort of POST-PUNK "don't think, just dance" trend, and Guadalcanal wasn't part of that. We were an Atlanta band. But you could dance to us, and people did, so why not?

By this time, the B-52s had been signed to a major and were becoming globally known. REM signed with IRS (and later Warners) and started to take off. We had made our first record, started touring and then signed with Elektra for four more. A newer band, and a terrific one, Dreams So Real, had gotten a deal with Arista. Still, at that point, Athens was pretty chill, and you'd go to brunch on a Saturday at the Bluebird Cafe and run into all your friends from the other bands.

Back in Atlanta, The Coolies had made two great albums, and a cool new duo called the Indigo Girls were starting to get some traction, while a sort of loose group of eccentrics calling themselves Now Explosion pushed boundaries everywhere they were allowed to play. This group also spawned RuPaul, who did unforgettable shows with his band WeeWeePole.

It's worth mentioning WRAS, the college station at Georgia State University in Atlanta. This station was so good and so influential that major record labels would court and service them like a commercial station. This was before labels had a "college radio" department and way before commercial alternative radio showed up. WRAS stood alone.

Both cities had cool independent newspapers that covered all the goings-on. In Atlanta, it was Creative Loafing and, later, Stomp and Stammer. In Athens, it was Tasty World and then Flagpole.

I suppose that this mythical time ran from around 1978 to somewhere in the early '90s. This is not to suggest that there were not great artists and music coming from both cities afterwards. There were plenty and still are. This is just a specific time sort of frozen in amber.

When I sat down to write this, I thought I'd downplay the mythical status and just describe it as a collision of art schools, affordable housing, and interesting record collections. As I began to recall people and places and the feel of the time, I realised it really was pretty cool.

Frozen in amber. Or better, frozen in Lucite.

⊙ Richard Barbieri, born in London, England, on November 30, 1957, is a renowned synthesizer player, keyboardist, and composer. Emerging in the late 1970s and early 1980s as a member of the glam/NEW WAVE band Japan and their later reincarnation Rain Tree

Crow, Barbieri went on to record with Steve Jansen as The Dolphin Brothers and with Jansen and Mick Karn as JBK. In the mid-1990s, Barbieri and his wife Suzanne formed the band Indigo Falls, releasing their acclaimed *self-titled* album in 1996. Since 1993, he has been the keyboardist for the progressive rock band Porcupine Tree. Highly regarded for his instrumental virtuosity and production skills, Barbieri is credited with helping develop the modern electronic synth sound, citing Karlheinz Stockhausen as a key influence. His subtle yet integral approach has drawn comparisons to ambient musicians like Brian Eno. Barbieri's influence as a producer shines through on albums like Japan's *Tin Drum*. He continues to release evocative soundscapes that excite the senses.

◉ Born William Michael Albert Broad in London, England, in November 1955, Billy Idol initially gained recognition as the lead guitarist for the punk rock group Generation X starting in 1976. Following the band's breakup in 1981, Idol moved to New York City with guitarist Steve Stevens. Though Idol's first solo *self-titled* album in 1982 included popular songs like 'Hot in the City' and 'White Wedding', it was his follow-up record 'Rebel Yell' that propelled him to widespread fame around the world.

◉ The album *English Garden* was the only album release from The Camera Club, released on November 30, 1979. It served as an early showcase for Bruce Woolley before his later success with The Buggles and Thomas Dolby. With its blend of NEW WAVE and power pop styles, the album contains the original versions of 'Video Killed the Radio Star' and its B-side 'Clean Clean'. The infectious melodies and back-to-back hooks make for an energetic listen, with stellar performances from vocalist Woolley, bassist Matthew Seligman, drummer Rod Johnson, guitarist Dave Birch, and keyboardist Dolby. Though short-lived, The Camera Club established a template of catchy, synth-driven pop that Dolby and Woolley would continue exploring.

Jonas Almquist - The Leather Nun by Petra Gall

◉ The debut EP *Slow Death* by Swedish four-piece The Leather Nun (known locally as Lädernunnan). Following the premier of the title track on Swedish national radio on December 22, 1978, the EP was on the shelves on this day in 1979. The 4-track release on Throbbing Gristle's Industrial Records label made the top of the German Musik Express chart and caused some controversy at the time, as the original cover art designed by Throbbing Gristle's Peter "Sleazy" Christopherson displayed an image of Roberto Crescenzio, who died from burns during a protest in Turin, Italy. The reprint/re-release cover art was changed to an array of skulls looking like the shape of the African continent.

◉ Martha Davis released *Policy*, her first of three solo studio albums, on this day in 1987. This solo project followed the breakup of her band, The Motels, earlier that year. With meticulous production and a collection of well-crafted songs, *Policy* stands as a much stronger album than any of The Motels' records. While not breaking new ground, the album showcases a mature Davis demonstrating all she had learnt from her years with The Motels.

Policy deserved more notoriety than it attained as a polished effort from an experienced artist.

● Released just in time for the 1981 Christmas holiday rush, Les Disques du Crepuscule, a Belgian label, unveiled the festive LP *Ghosts of Christmas Past* on November 30th. This album displayed a diverse lineup of POST-PUNK artists who contributed their talents to an unconventional collection of holiday songs. Among the notable artists featured were Tuxedomoon, The Durutti Column, Paul Haig, Michael Nyman, Aztec Camera, Thick Pigeon, The Names, and many more. This unique Yuletide compilation appealed to the discerning taste of POST-PUNK enthusiasts, who would have taken pride in playing it. As time went on, fans had the opportunity to enjoy an expanded edition of the album, which included additional tracks from artists such as Antenna, Mikado, The French Impressionists, and the Pale Fountains.

● On November 30, 1979, The Mekons released the album *The Quality of Mercy Is Not Strnen*, whose title refers to the 'Infinite Monkey Theorem', a concept that concludes that an infinite number of monkeys hitting keys at random on a typewriter will eventually almost type the Shakespeare quote "the quality of mercy is not strained", which is a line in his play The Merchant of Venice. This album marked the beginning of the band's career, which followed a couple of singles released in 1978. Over the past 40 years, The Mekons have been constantly creative and uncompromising, producing around 20 albums and featuring as many as 20 members. While The Mekons may not be considered as influential as bands like Wire or Gang of Four by some, their witty, cynical lyrics and ever-evolving yet faithful POST-PUNK sound have earned them a dedicated following.

The Mekons by Petra Gall/The Mekons - Jon Langford by Carmen Knoebel

● Walk into your local record store on November 30, 1979, and you could buy the debut single 'Disgracing the Family Name' b/w 'Work Song' by Skafish on Illegal Records. With quirky power pop nodding to Sparks and/or Zappa, the A-side and B-side are as eccentric as Skafish's Chicago-based frontman, Jim Skafish. After gaining exposure through an appearance in the movie *Urgh! A Music War*, Skafish went on to release a couple of albums in the '80s on Miles Copeland's I.R.S. Records.

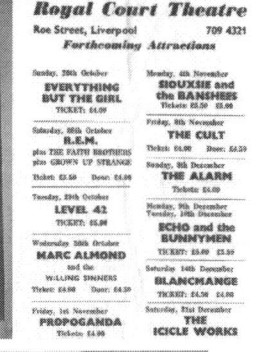

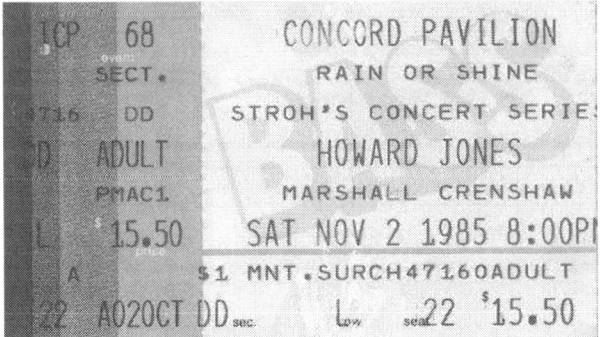

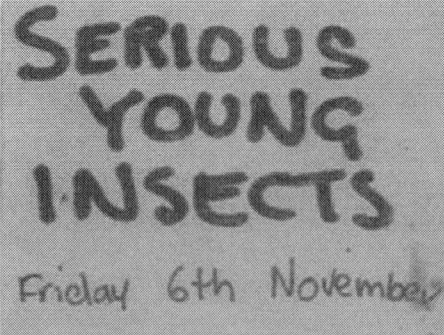

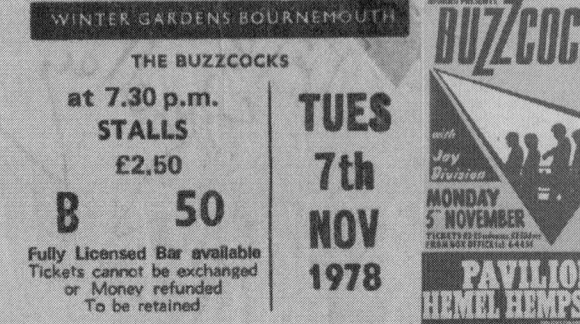

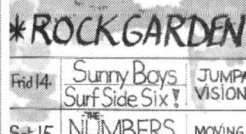

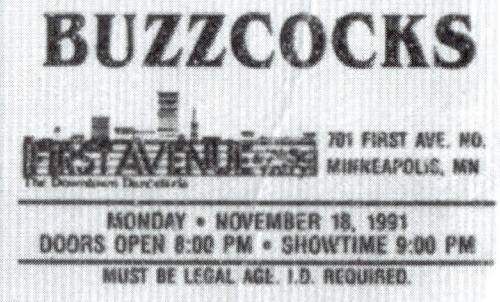

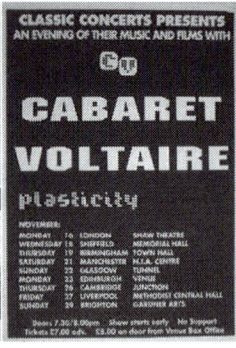

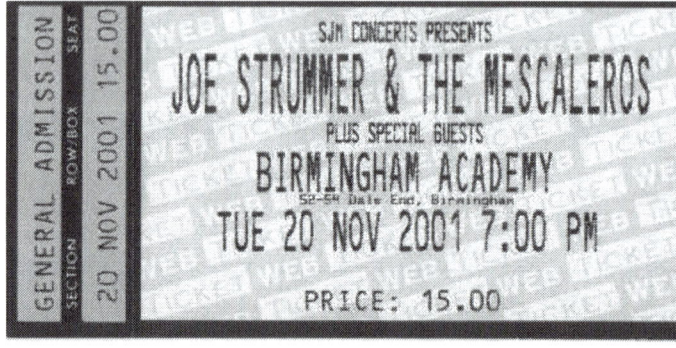

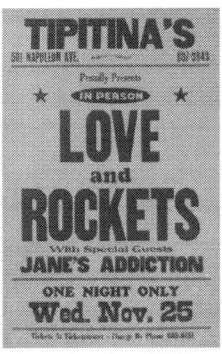

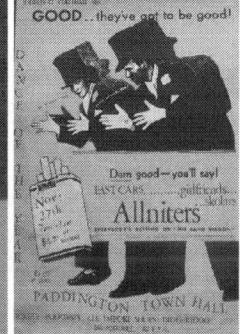

1

◉ Viv Albertine was born in Sydney, Australia in 1954. She grew up in North London and became an icon of punk/POST-PUNK music as the guitarist for the pioneering all-female punk band The Slits. Prior to joining The Slits, Viv formed a band called The Flowers of Romance with Sid Vicious, Sarah Hall, and Palmolive (Paloma McLardy); the band was named by John Lydon. At age 17, Viv bought her first guitar, a Les Paul Junior with money left to her by her grandmother. She was fortunate to receive guitar lessons from childhood friend Keith Levene and punk legends Joe Strummer and Johnny Thunders. After her music career, Viv became a highly regarded film director and published two memoirs: *Clothes, Clothes, Clothes. Music, Music, Music. Boys, Boys, Boys* and *To Throw Away Unopened*, each recounting her days in the punk/POST-PUNK scene.

◉ On December 1, 1982, the band Alien Sex Fiend, which one could say was broadly a vehicle for Nicholas Wade aka Nik Fiend made their debut performance at The Batcave Club in London's Soho district. This club is widely considered the birthplace of the goth subculture. It was where patrons entered through a coffin and were greeted by cobwebs covering the black walls and ceilings. The venue hosted avant-garde films and live shows by bands with gothic aesthetics like Siouxsie and the Banshees and Bauhaus. Specimen became the resident house band, while Alien Sex Fiend frequently performed as guests. After their debut, Alien Sex Fiend went on to record over a dozen albums that blended dark electronica with acid dance guitar music.

◉ Blondie's *self-titled* debut album was released in December 1976. The album bridged punk and NEW WAVE with infectious '60s feels and surf flavour. While their first two albums had found significant success in Australia, New Zealand, and the UK, it wasn't until the critical acclaim of their Mike Chapman produced third album, *Parallel Lines*, in 1978 that the band, who were initially regarded as an underground punk band, attained greater public appeal in the USA. The world was their oyster, and Blondie has since gone on to sell over 40 million records worldwide and continues to actively perform. The cover of Blondie shows a band with resolve and strength and what inside today remains an enjoyable listen. In all it showcases a small-time band breaking into one of the most exciting musical movements since the halcyon time of flower power.

◉ On December 1, 1981, Vince Clarke left Depeche Mode to form the duo Yazoo with Alison Moyet, an old schoolmate. Although Alison had placed an advert seeking a "rootsy blues musician", Vince saw the ad and contacted Alison despite not fitting that description, and the unlikely pairing led to the formation of Yazoo. With the single 'Only You', a song Vince had originally offered to Depeche Mode, Yazoo reached the top of the charts. Soon after, Vince and Alison recorded their debut album together, *Upstairs at Eric's*. Yazoo released a few more successful singles and a second album, *You and Me Both* in 1983, proving themselves one of the most original bands in music history.

◉ Julee Cruise, born in 1956 in Creston, Iowa, USA, first gained recognition through her collaboration with director David Lynch and composer Angelo Badalamenti. She was featured in Lynch's film Blue Velvet before recording 'Falling', an ethereal dream pop song from her debut album *Floating into the Night*, which became the instrumental theme song for Lynch's TV series *Twin Peaks*. Cruise made cameo appearances in *Twin Peaks* as a singer performing at the town's Roadhouse bar. In the 1990s, she toured with the B-52's, filling in for Cindy Wilson while she was on hiatus to raise her children. Cruise released four albums over the course of her career until her death by suicide in June 2022.

◉ Flash and the Pan released their *self-titled* album to rave reviews in 1978. Featuring synthpop, NEW WAVE, and even progressive rock influences, the album defies easy categorization. The creative duo behind the project, ex-Easybeats members Harry Vanda and George Young, boldly explored new sonic territory. With quirky, fun, and complex songs like 'Hey, St. Peter', 'Down Among the Dead Men', 'Walking in the Rain', 'Lady Killer', and 'First and Last', the album showcased Vanda and Young's innovative musical talents. Though released decades ago, Flash and the Pan's imaginative debut remains timeless. If you missed this gem back in the day, it's not too late to discover it now, indeed they were no flash in the pan.

◉ Stephen Batt, known by the stage name Steve Jansen, was born on December 1, 1959, is the younger brother of David Sylvian. He was a drummer for the bands Japan, Rain Tree Crow, The Dolphin Brothers, JBK (with Richard Barbieri and Mick Karn), and Nine Horses. Jansen has also collaborated with Barbieri as a duo and with Barbieri and Nobukazu Takemura on the album *Changing Hands*. In addition to drumming, Jansen was the lead vocalist for The Dolphin Brothers. He has worked extensively as an engineer, producer, and live performer, contributing widely to the music industry and entered collaborations with a multitude of artists, that includes the likes of Anja Garbarek, Maiya Hershey, Annie Lennox, Ryuichi Sakamoto, and Yukihiro Takahashi. Along with Swedes Charles Storm, Thomas Feiner and Ulf Jansson he formed EXIT NORTH, that partnership has released 2 much admired albums. Beyond music, Jansen has had photographic exhibitions documenting his time touring with the band Japan.

HOTEL TO VENUE TO HOTEL...VERY BEATLESQUE
STEVE JANSEN
(Japan, Rain Tree Crow, Dolphin Brothers)

In 1979 we struggled to sell out a small venue in the UK; however, we had an almost Beatlemania-like fanbase in Japan. As a consequence, on our first visit we suddenly found ourselves thrust into the limelight, surrounded by a team of bodyguards and subjected to various escape plans from concerts by the local promoters.

For the largest venue (Budokan), we were ushered straight off stage into the back of a waiting truck so that fans sitting patiently in taxis wouldn't initiate tracking us back to the hotel we were staying at (it all seemed a little over the top). The truck was a windowless box, the type not connected to the driver cab, so once we were inside (with a makeshift builder's lamp swinging from the ceiling), we were cut off from anyone else on the exterior. It would be a short 10-minute hop to a waiting limo somewhere clear of the venue.

On the second night, as the truck pulled away with us in the back, the rear double doors weren't secured properly, and one side swung open. Our Scottish hard-man tour manager grabbed the edge of the door and pulled it closed as best he could with his fingers curled around the opening. Meanwhile we resorted to hammering on the cab partition to alert the driver, who eventually pulled over and rushed around. He immediately realised the door was ajar but didn't notice the hand holding it, slammed the door shut and bolted it. He pulled off at speed and failed to hear the screams of agony from the tour manager. Again, we hammered on the cab while he almost passed out from the pain of having his hand literally bolted between the doors, unable to free it. If there was any upside from this, fortunately, as the pinch-point was across the palm of his hand, no fingers were lost; however, he was permanently scarred, as I think we all were.

The local promoters must have had their reasons for these escape plans – perhaps to avoid dangerous collisions. The taxi drivers seemed to enjoy the 'follow-that-car' moment, giving little amused glances as they dared to overtake on behalf of the far too many passengers in the back hanging out of windows wielding flashing cameras. A convoy of taxi drivers all in the same game and others daring to scoot alongside on mopeds. Regardless of being subjected to various covert manoeuvres, whether it was at venues, hotels or railway stations, fans seemed to track down bands by more basic methods of deduction, as there were always a few hundred in and around the lobby, with the more affluent booked into the same hotel or even on various internal train and flight journeys between performances. After these first experiences of 'stardom', arriving back in London, where we couldn't even have confidence in finding transport home, things felt a bit surreal, but at 19 you tend to take a lot in your stride.

◉ Cyndi Lauper's iconic debut solo album, *She's So Unusual,* was released on this day in 1983. Brimming with Lauper's flamboyant musical flair, the album epitomised the NEW WAVE and pop sounds of the 1980s. While it featured several covers, the record also included Lauper's timeless ballad 'Time After Time', which gained credibility when Miles Davis recorded a jazz version. Fuelled by smash hits like 'Girls Just Want to Have Fun', 'She Bop', 'Money Changes Everything', 'When You Were Mine', and 'All Through the Night', *She's So Unusual* became an essential album for any NEW WAVE and pop music collector.

◉ Thomas Leer's debut single, 'Private Plane' b/w 'International', was released in 1978 on his own private label Oblique. Recorded in his flat over 3 days, the single reflected inspiration from Kraftwerk with its complex, ethereally minimalist raw electronica. At a time when electronic music was rare, Leer's single stands as essential listening for its pioneering sound and high quality.

◉ Marlene Marti, better known as Marlene Marder, was born in 1954 in Zurich, Switzerland. She gained fame as the guitarist of the Swiss POST-PUNK band LiLiPUT, originally called Kleenex. Formed in 1976, Kleenex released several singles and a 1978 *self-titled* EP before being forced to change their name due to trademark issues with the Kleenex company. As one of the first bands on the Rough Trade label, LiLiPUT helped define the POST-PUNK sound. In 1986, Marlene published an autobiography titled Kleenex/LiLiPUT chronicling her time in the band while running a record store and concert agency. She passed away from cancer on May 15, 2016, at the age of 61, leaving behind definite rock music legacy.

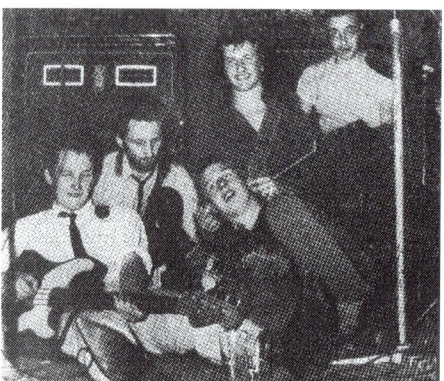

Mental as Anything

◉ The debut vinyl release from Mental as Anything, *Plays at Your Party*, was released in December 1978. The EP contained three tracks: 'Golfshoes', 'C.Y.O. Dance', and 'The Nips Are Getting Bigger'. 'The Nips Are Getting Bigger' was rereleased as a 7-inch in mid-1979 with 'Instrumental as Anything' on the B-side. The initial pressing of 1,100 copies sold out in three weeks, and the second pressing sold out in just one day, still today making the EP a highly sought-after record among collectors.

2

◉ Released in 1977 by London's Radio Stars, *Songs for Swinging Lovers* is an enjoyable debut album defined by crafty, hook-laden power pop and NEW WAVE. Driven by ex-

John's Children vocalist Andy Ellison's playfully irreverent attitude, the album's clever songwriting deserves appreciation. Fans of Cheap Trick will enjoy Radio Stars' melodic sensibilities.

◉ The single 'Where's Captain Kirk' was released by Spizzenergi in 1979. Spizz was known for constantly changing band names, reportedly in an effort to break the record for most releases under different monikers. These included Spizz 77, Spizzoil, Athletico Spizz 80, The Spizzles, Spizzenergi2, Spizz's Big Business, Spizzsexual, Spizz Orbit, Spizzivision, and Spizzenergi2000, among countless others. 'Where's Captain Kirk' was an infectious, quirky, and tongue-in-cheek song reminiscent of the styles of DEVO, The Dickies or The Rezillos. Its vibrant and catchy sound made it a forerunner to Spizzenergi's next single, 'Spock's Missing'.

◉ In 1983, the Icelandic band Tappi Tíkarrass (roughly translating to "cork the bitch's arse") released their debut album *Miranda*. The album featured the energetic vocals of a 17-year-old Björk, her soaring voice floats over and weaves between the twangy and at times abrasive guitars. While the intriguing song structures are catchy, the Icelandic lyrics remain indecipherable for non-speakers, though this matters little as the songs do not aim for profound meanings. A superbly tight rhythm section of bass and drums anchors the brash, in-your-face guitars. Interspersed are nice melodic parts that blend with bold harmonies. Though not groundbreaking, *Miranda* fills in crucial gaps in Björk's early career, showcasing her sensational talent even in these formative years.

◉ Chris Wilson, a highly regarded harmonica player and blues-roots guitarist, was born in 1956 in Aphington, Australia. Although known mostly for his blues influences, Wilson also contributed to POST-PUNK artists such as Hunters & Collectors, Paul Kelly and The Coloured Girls. In 1999, he was chosen by Elvis Costello as his opening act. In 1987, Wilson formed the band Crown of Thorns with guitarist Barry Palmer and bassist Chris Rodgers. A journalist described the group as "a diverse amalgam, recalling everything from Tim Buckley to Captain Beefheart and American blues". Wilson passed away from pancreatic cancer on January 16, 2019, at the age of 63.

3

◉ On December 3, 1978, a performance by Elvis Costello & The Attractions at Sydney's Regent Theatre sparked a riot when Costello played just a break-neck set of 12 songs, for what was reportedly less than one hour. The audience became agitated when they were made aware that there would be no encore, it was announced that "Elvis has left the building". Incensed by the band's refusal to return the crowd destroyed a significant portion of the theatre's seating. The opening act, Jo Jo Zep and The Falcons, and its frontman Joe Camilleri were backstage during the incident. Camilleri later admitted he was "absolutely freaked out" by the violence, stating, *"Elvis left straight after the set. I could hear the crowd getting restless as I sat backstage. It got pretty violent at one stage".*

◉ The NEW WAVE power pop album *The Right to Be Italian* by Holly and The Italians was released on December 3, 1981. Led by singer and guitarist Holly Beth Vincent who cultivated a tough girl image, the band delivered crisp, guitar-driven pop songs. While not groundbreaking, the album contains several highlights, including the catchy singles 'Tell That Girl to Shut Up', 'Rock Against Romance', and 'Youth Coup'. Though uneven at times, Vincent's energetic performance and knack for pop hooks make The Right to Be Italian an enjoyable slice of early '80s NEW WAVE. After briefly joining The Waitresses following Patty Donahue's departure in 1984, Vincent was unable to sustain momentum. By the end of that year, The Waitresses had dissolved entirely.

Fred Maher, born in Manhattan in 1962, first gained recognition as the drummer for Material, the innovative funk and electronica band led by renowned bassist and producer Bill Laswell. In the early 1980s, Maher contributed to Material's first two albums before leaving to study architecture. However, after just one semester, the chance to join Scritti Politti's rising synthpop act in 1984 pulled Maher back to music. Scritti Politti's hit singles like 'Wood Beez (Pray Like Aretha Franklin)' and 'The Word Girl' earned acclaim and brought their album *Cupid & Psyche 85* into the top 5 in the UK, with Maher's skilled drumming and programming attracting notice. During this period, Maher also teamed up with former Voidoids guitarist Robert Quine for the instrumental album *Basic*. Quine introduced Maher to Lou Reed, beginning a collaboration that led to Maher producing Reed's album *New York* in 1989. Beyond drumming, Maher is an acclaimed producer who has worked with artists like I'm Talking, Information Society, Lloyd Cole, Matthew Sweet, and The Breeders.

I MADE HIM SOUND LIKE LOU REED
FRED MAHER
(Massacre, Material, Scritti Politti, producer)

I'm struggling to come up with a story from my days with Massacre or Material that is of any interest, but there is one interesting factoid, though, of how Massacre (the original trio of Fred Frith, Bill Laswell and myself) got its name. Peter Blegvad, who back in 1974 had been a member of Henry Cow with Fred, had a show coming up at The Kitchen in NYC, and he asked Fred if he wanted to open the show. I'm not exactly sure when we started rehearsing as a band, but it was decided that Blegvad's show was going to be our debut. The show date was on Valentine's Day, and so that's where the name comes from.

Another story is how I got the job as producer of Lou Reed's *New York* album.

I played drums with Lou for a few years and was brought in by the late, great Robert Quine. My first gig with Lou was actually "miming" drums for the video that accompanied the song 'I Love Women', from the *Blue Mask* album. To be clear, I did not play drums on The Blue Mask, but for whatever reason, Lou decided that he didn't like the drummer and wanted somebody else to "play drums" in the video. Quine suggested me, and that was the first time I met Lou. I guess he liked me, and that led to me actually playing drums with him. The next project was Lou's album *Legendary Hearts*. After that were three nights, with two shows a night at NYC's The Bottom Line. It was filmed and eventually became a DVD many years later (interestingly, you can find it on YouTube). Then came the album *New Sensations*. By then, Lou and Quine had one of many fallouts.

At the time I was a full-time architecture student at Cooper Union College, so Lou scheduled the basic track recordings entirely around my winter break from school; it still amazes me that he would do that.

Fast forwarding, I eventually dropped out of Cooper to join Scritti Politti, disappeared for a while, and Lou moved on. After the Scritti album *Cupid & Psyche '85* was completed and I was back home in New York, I got a call from Lou asking if I would play drums on his next record, to which I said, *"Of course!"* He had a new deal with Sire Records and was shopping for a producer. He asked me about producers, and I suggested a few who were "hot" at the time, but it seemed that nobody was interested. It was at this point that I, being young, arrogant, and ambitious, suggested that I could be the producer. He laughed and asked what the hell I knew about recording guitars and real drums because all I had done was "Synth Pop". So, I talked him into getting one day in a studio as an audition of sorts. Lou agreed, and in one day we recorded and mixed Romeo Had Juliette at Media Sound with just Lou, guitarist Mike Rathke and me. I also engineered, again with the confidence and arrogance of being a 20-something. At the end of the day, rough mixes were put on cassette, and that was that. The next morning, Lou called me up, and he said, *"I sound like Lou Reed again,"* and that I had the job!

◉ In 1981, Klaus Nomi released his *self-titled* debut album after completing a tour with David Bowie. His album featured eclectic covers of songs and one original composition, it showcased his operatic vocals and NEW WAVE style. Nomi's unique approach and singular voice made the songs his own, bearing little resemblance to the originals. The album established Nomi as a captivating and innovative artist.

◉ Sadly, the innovative synthpop band Testcard F released only two treasured singles before disbanding. Skilled in crafting their own synthesizers, drum machines, and other gear from found objects and tapes, Testcard F showed great promise when they won a 'battle of the bands' competition in Norwich in 1982. However, the pressures of success ultimately broke the band apart shortly after putting out their debut single that same year, 'Bandwagon Tango b/w 'Unfamiliar Room', a single that stood out among the synthpop releases of the day.

4

◉ Steve Barton was born on December 4, 1954, in Los Angeles. He was the vocalist, guitarist, and songwriter for the band Translator, which formed in L.A. in 1979. Originally a trio with bassist Larry Dekker and drummer Dave Scheff, they soon added guitarist and songwriter Robert Darlington before relocating to San Francisco in 1980. Barton grew up influenced by classic pop/rock acts like The Beatles and David Bowie, as well as Frank Sinatra and Bizet's Carmen. He began as a drummer before switching to guitar, after being inspired by Mick Ronson and seeing Bob Marley live. Barton played a Gibson Les Paul guitar on every Translator album. The band's jangly NEW WAVE sound had hints of contemporaries like R.E.M. and Gang of Four. Translator released four albums before disbanding in 1986. Since then, Barton has been a prolific solo artist, releasing 7 solo albums and several singles. He has collaborated with artists including Peter Buck of R.E.M., Debbi Peterson of The Bangles, Scott McCaughey of R.E.M. and The Minus 5, Steve Berlin of Los Lobos, and Translator's Dave Scheff. Barton plans to release a new solo album in 2024.

GOT ALL EXCITED AT LOAD-IN!
STEVE BARTON
(Translator)

The years-long relationship that I was in had come crashing apart. I was now living alone in a small bungalow in Los Angeles. I loved it. There was a small kitchen, a tiny bathroom and a place for my bed and stereo – even a little deck outside. I lived there for exactly one year. Most of the very early Translator songs were written in that place. On October 28, 1980, we moved en masse as a band up to San Francisco. Once there, I traded in my delightful bungalow for a sleeping bag on the floor of a friend's flat in the Castro section of San Francisco. The band started to gig around town, getting a really good following, and within a year or so, we got signed to 415 Records. We had a hit single, 'Everywhere That I'm Not', released 4 albums, and toured a lot. We played everywhere, from dives all the way up to opening for Bowie at Oakland Stadium! Our tours with some of our favourite bands were so great – Gang of Four, Psychedelic Furs, and B-52's – and our own shows to our strong core group of fans.

One memorable story…before we were signed, we were playing at a legendary club in SF called the Mabuhay Gardens (known as "the fab Mab", or simply as "the Mab"). It was run by an edgy, cool impresario named Dirk Dirkson. We played there tons of times. To load in, there was an alley that ran between the back door of the Mab and the building next door. Bands would bring their equipment in, then move their car to start the search for parking – which could be an adventure itself. We were on stage. I was in the middle of singing some song, and I suddenly thought, *"Did I move my car after we loaded in?"* When our set ended, I opened the side door to see my Datsun station-wagon still in the alley! People from the other band had simply picked it up by the fenders and moved it out of the way. The fenders got a little bit banged up, but I couldn't have cared less. I thought that was such a cool solution. I'm not so sure I'd feel the same way if that happened today.

These days I put my own albums out, almost always with Dave Scheff on drums. From time to time, Translator gets together to put out a single or an album, maybe play a few shows. The four of us are all still very close. The future is always up ahead – I continue to run or stagger or stumble or fly into it. Onwards.

◉ On December 4, 1989, the first single 'Getting Away with It' by Electronic, was released. The supergroup Electronic was comprised of New Order's Bernard Sumner, former Smiths guitarist Johnny Marr, and Pet Shop Boys vocalist Neil Tennant. The single featured prime songwriting that provided a simple chord progression amidst lush orchestration arranged by Anne Dudley of The Art of Noise. It peaked at No.12 on the UK charts.

◉ On December 4, 1982, The Jam's single 'Beat Surrender' reached No.1 on the UK singles chart, marking the band's fourth chart-topping hit in the UK and their final single release. Later that month, frontman Paul Weller broke up the group and went on to form The Style Council.

Sonic Youth by Petra Gall

◉ In 1984, Sonic Youth released their debut single 'Death Valley 69', featuring no-wave icon Lydia Lunch on supporting vocals. The single showcased Sonic Youth's ability to fuse experimentation and dissonance with melody and structure. While noisy and unsettling, the classic track marked the beginning of Sonic Youth's blend of avant-garde and accessible that would define their signature sound.

5

◉ *Kill Me in the Morning*, the sole album by Float Up CP, was released in 1985 by Rough Trade Records. Comprised of former members of The Pop Group and Rip Rig and Panic, the record is an energetic fusion of POST-PUNK, dance, and jazz. Neneh Cherry's soulful vocals echo her work with Rip Rig more than The Pop Group, complemented by Ollie Moore's saxophone and Bruce Smith's propulsive drumming. Despite its distinctive sound and talented personnel, the album was overlooked upon release. However, its adventurous blending of genres makes *Kill Me in the Morning* a one-of-a-kind album worth revisiting.

◉ Peter Godwin's debut solo release was an EP titled *Dance Emotions*, which was available for the Christmas market in early December 1982. With similarities to the synthpop sound of The Human League, the British musician delivered a collection of club-ready synthpop tracks. Standout songs included the well-received single 'Images of Heaven', 'Emotional Disguise', and 'Cruel Heart'. Unfortunately, Godwin did not expand his stylistic range much on his 1983 LP *Correspondence*, which closely resembled *Dance Emotions*. Earlier in the 1970s, Godwin was part of a band called Metro that later changed their name to Public Zone and released a single, 'Naïve' featuring Stewart Copeland on drums. Copeland declined an offer to join Public Zone full-time, opting instead to remain with The Police.

⊙ The Human League's 'Don't You Want Me?' soared to the top of the UK charts on December 5th, 1981, cementing the band's place at the peak of the NEW WAVE and synthpop movement. With its flawless pop sensibilities, the infectious single planted the Human League's flag at the summit, much like Hillary's on Everest. 'Don't You Want Me' would continue its triumphant ascent, hitting No.1 in the US on July 3rd, 1982.

6

⊙ Adrian Borland was a guitarist and frontman for the British POST-PUNK band The Sound, which formed in South London in 1979 after the dissolution of Borland's previous band, The Outsiders. Born on December 6, 1957, in London, England, Borland initially started The Sound with bassist Graham Bailey ("Green"), drummer Mike Dudley, multi-instrumentalist Belinda "Bi" Marshall, and guitarist Adrian Janes, who contributed ideas and lyrics while studying away at university in Wales. After releasing their debut album, *Jeopardy*, in 1980, Marshall left the band and was replaced by Colvin "Max" Mayers. Over the next several years, The Sound went on to release four more albums before disbanding in 1988. Borland later pursued a solo career and played in other bands as well. However, he struggled with schizoaffective disorder and tragically died by suicide in April 1999 at age 41 after jumping in front of a train.

⊙ Rick Buckler, born Paul Richard Buckler on December 6, 1955, in Woking, England, was the drummer for the band The Jam. The Jam reached the top of the UK charts in 1980 with the songs 'Going Underground' and 'Start' from their album *Sound Affects*. The band played their final concert in Brighton on December 11, 1982. After The Jam disbanded, Rick formed the band Time U.K. with former members of Masterswitch, The Tom Robinson Band, and Sparks. Their debut single, 'The Cabaret', sold nearly 70,000 copies. When Time U.K. ended, Rick worked in music production and ran a recording studio. In 2005, he started a new band called The Gift, which played covers of The Jam's most popular songs. He later spent 4 years playing with The Jam's original bassist Bruce Foxton in the band From the Jam. In Rick's last years he lived in Woking, creating unique handcrafted wooden furniture. Rick passed away after a short illness on February 17, 2025.

Pink Military (L-R Nicky Hillon, Martin Dempsey, Jayne Casey, Neil Innes) by Francesco Mellina/

⊙ Jayne Casey was born in 1956 in Wallasey, England. She first gained recognition as the vocalist and early member of Liverpool's Big in Japan (BiJ), a band whose shifting lineup over two years also included Ian Broudie, Holly Johnson, David Balfe, and Budgie. Though BiJ released just one single and one EP, they garnered an enormous following and proved influential to the pioneers of POST-PUNK in the UK, often mentioned alongside Deaf School. After BiJ's split, Casey went on to form Pink Military, who produced the hypnotic album *Do Animals Believe in God?* on Eric's label, a recording outlet for bands playing at the Liverpool venue of the same name. In late 1981, Casey formed the electronic duo Pink Industry with former BiJ member Ambrose Reynolds and a revolving cast of guest musicians, releasing 3 albums before disbanding in 1987. She later moved into television production and organizing artistic and cultural events in Liverpool, while also co-founding the successful nightclub Cream in the '90s.

Jayne Casey at Erics by permission

A GIRLS TALE
JAYNE CASEY
(Big In Japan, Pink Military, Pink Industry)

It was the summer of 81. I was 24 years old and had taken time out of music to give birth to my son. I didn't have family support, so it was hard work, and I was unsure if I'd have the time to make music again.

One sunny day I was walking my baby when I bumped into one of the 'crucial 3'. A group of lads from Eric's scene who had always taken the piss. I was conscious of looking a bit of a mess; I was tired and was still carrying weight from having just given birth. He looked me up and down, laughed in a snide way and said, *"Ha! That's you finished".*

His words stung; I held back my tears, and fury rose inside of me.

I went back to my flat burning inside; I hated those boys!!

The sink was full of dirty dishes, and I had 100 things to do – maybe he was right – maybe I'd never make music again.

I went into my bedroom and dug out my metronome, set it to a 4/4 signature and placed it next to the sink, and as I washed the dishes, I wrote a song called 'Don't Let Go'.

Later that evening Ambrose Reynolds rang me. My best friend Holly Johnston had been bugging me for ages, telling me I should work with him. I explained to Ambrose that I was housebound and didn't think I had the time to go into a recording studio. Ambrose said, "Let me come up to your flat with my bass guitar and 4-track, and we'll just start writing together."

The next day he turned up, and I sang him 'Don't Let Go'. He put an amazing bass line to it, and we knew instantly that we had a sound.

For the next 18 months he would call up to my flat, and in-between housework and breastfeeding, we'd write and record Pink Industry's first album, *Low Technology*. It had a dark electronic sound which we knew didn't fit into the mainstream, so we released it on our own independent record label.

We continued releasing material independently, but the sound we had created didn't really come into its own until long after our demise, when dance music happened a decade later, and DJs started using the raw material for remixes.

40 years after its release, much to our delight, 'Don't Let Go' was used in the USA as an advert for Converse. The ad featured a champion skateboarder who had used the song as inspiration to stay on his skateboard since he was a kid. The impact was huge; suddenly a

song that had received a few thousand hits in its lifetime on YouTube was up there in the millions. A few years later, the same song was picked up by the House of Dior for a fashion advert.

Nearly 43 years on, I am so thrilled that Pink Industry still has life, and every time I receive a cheque for that song, I thank that boy who laughed at me from the very bottom of my heart.

● Ed Tudor Pole (ETP), aka TenPole Tudor, was born December 6, 1954. When Lydon left the Sex Pistols, TenPole Tudor joined and wrote 'Who Killed Bambi' and sang it in The *Great Rock & Roll Swindle*. ETP formed Tenpole Tudor in 1979. 'Swords of 1000' was their biggest hit, and when the band imploded, ETP wrote 'Ted Ain't Dead' for the film *Absolute Beginners*, in which he played Ed the Ted. He drifted into acting for a while, working with Clint Eastwood in *White Hunter Black Heart* and with Ed Harris in Alex Cox's *Walker*, filmed in Nicaragua with Joe Strummer. Discovering that acting was an "empty, frivolous occupation" and realizing above all he is a musician, Ed embarked on a fifteen-year solo UK tour, playing every weekend until the pandemic stopped it. Tenpole then wrote his memoirs: *The Pen is Mightier*. He plays on.

THE DEATH OF ROCK & ROLL
EDWARD TUDOR POLE
(Tenpole Tudor)

I'd think of ways to break the conventional boundaries of the rock show and to make it more interesting, more theatrical, and more original. Our most elaborate concert was The Death of Rock & Roll, performed some time in 1984 in a student hall near the Post Office Tower in London.

Frank Sidebottom, a very annoying man who wore a giant circular cartoon head and sang to a backing tape, was also on the bill. The place was packed, we were headlining, and the show began with me coming on with a guitar and singing a couple of songs.

Then I greet the crowd. *"Hang on, this would be much better if we had a proper band, wouldn't it?"* I said.

"Yes!" they agreed. *"I know, let's form a band! Can anyone play the drums?"* This question always elicits volunteers, but Sarah was in the audience, planted and primed, and was the first to make it onto the stage.

"But you're a girl!" I said, *"Girls can't play drums!"* Sarah punches me indignantly, and I fall realistically to the floor using stage-fight techniques we'd rehearsed. I get up, concede the point, and she gets the job as drummer.

"As we've got a girl drummer, let's form an ALL GIRL GROUP!' I now say to the audience, *"Is there a girl bassist and guitarist and sax player in the house?"* As I hoped for and expected, no-one volunteered, so I say, *"Well, we've got some girls in the dressing room. Let's get them on stage, and we'll ask them if they can play anything."*

Now on come Matt Fisher, Sean Poe and Mick O'Donnell, all dressed up as women, wearing wigs, make-up, false eyelashes and padded white blouses. The costumes affected them differently. Matt looked very pretty, Sean like the girl next door and Mick looked like an old charwoman. I briefly interviewed them in turn, asking about their hobbies, etc., and, finding out they could all play, we picked up our instruments and played a few Chuck Berry rockers. After which, in a pause, I spot a copy of Melody Maker on one of the amps and pick it up.

"Let's see if we've got a review," I said to the audience, bending time as I leafed through the pages. Suddenly I saw something that made me freeze, eyes growing wide in shock. I looked up at the crowd, appalled. *"Oi! It says here that rock & roll is dead! Why didn't anybody tell me?!"* I demand indignantly. Awkward silence. Becoming very angry, I pull

out a Stanley knife and approach the girls. I grab Sean from behind with my arm around his neck, waving the blade in his face, *"Oi Sharon, why didn't you tell me rock & roll was dead?"*

"I'm sorry!" sobbed Sean, whereupon I start stabbing the red paint-filled Durex strapped to his chest beneath his blouse until it bursts, blooming red, and Sean falls dying to the floor.

I then killed Matt in similar fashion, and more blood poured. By now some very spooky prepared soundtrack music was playing over the PA. As I crossed the stage to do Mick, I suddenly turned upon the audience and gave a quick thrust of the dripping blade in their direction.

I was astonished by how quickly and intently these rough-looking men down the front recoiled very sharply backwards, creating a space as if in serious danger. (Surely, they didn't believe my homicidal maniac act was real?) After I did Mick, it left only Sarah. I mowed her down with an invisible, audible machine gun, and as she fell, the drums were kicked over by her death spasms.

Then the music changed to Mozart's requiem as I faced the audience in horror at what I had done. Lit only by a single spotlight in a sea of black, I plunged the knife into my own blood pack, strapped on to a biscuit tin lid that I wore around my neck under the shirt like a bib. I have a scar which marks the night I learnt the wisdom of wearing body armour. (It can be surprisingly tricky to pierce the rubber).

I freely admit that all these theatrics were borrowed wholesale from Lindsay Kemp, but the Tenpole Tudor audience was never going to go to Sadler's Wells and see his shows, so let's bring the best bits to them.

I had bitten down on a blood capsule, and with my mouth shaped like Munch's The Scream (I don't mean Munch Universe), in a vignette of horror, the blood dripped out of my mouth in the shrinking spotlight until only my face was lit. The spooky music climaxed, and the light faded to blackout and a stunned silence.

My regret is that we only performed this piece once. It took massive preparation and rehearsal, creating the intro and outro tapes, costumes, make-up, hair, etc.

7

Claudia Brücken by Petra Gall

● Born on December 7, 1963, in Berching, Germany, Claudia Brücken was the lead vocalist for Propaganda, one of the premier synthpop groups of the 1980s. Formed in 1982, Propaganda was among the first bands signed to Trevor Horn's influential ZTT label. In 1985, ZTT released Propaganda's brilliant debut LP, *A Secret Wish*, which reached No.16

on the UK album charts. After Propaganda's short but illustrious run, Brücken went on to form the duo Act with Scottish electronic composer Thomas Leer, releasing the album *Laughter, Tears and Rage* in 1988. She later fronted the duo Onetwo with Orchestral Manoeuvres in the Dark's Paul Humphreys, putting out the EP *Item* in 2004 and an album, *Instead*, in 2007. Brücken has also released three solo albums: *Love: A Million Things, The Lost Are Found,* and *Where Else.....* In early 2018, she collaborated with Jerome Froese, son of electronic music pioneer and Tangerine Dream founder Edgar Froese, on the album *Beginn*. After several failed attempts at reforming Propaganda, she recently established xPropaganda with former bandmate Susanne Freytag.

⊙ Tim Butler, born Timothy George Butler in 1958 in Teddington, England, was a founding member and the bassist of The Psychedelic Furs, alongside his brother Richard, the lead singer. Tim compiled the band's career-spanning compilation album *Greatest Hits*, which includes seventeen of their most popular songs. Tracing the band's evolution from their early Bowie and Roxy Music influences on the POST-PUNK soundscapes of their beginnings to their pop-infused later work, this collection contains many of their most iconic hits, like 'Pretty in Pink', 'The Ghost in You', 'Sometimes' and 'Heartbeat'. While it covers many of the essentials, some favourites like 'Should God Forget' are omitted. Overall, *Greatest Hits* provides an excellent, if incomplete, overview of The Psychedelic Furs' standout moments and chart successes for both longtime fans and newcomers alike.

⊙ The influential experimental group The Legendary Pink Dots released their debut vinyl LP, *Brighter Now* in 1982, though they had put out a couple of limited-edition cassette releases beforehand. Over their long and highly creative career, the band has defied genre categorization, blending minimalist, jazz, synthpop, and other eclectic influences. This early album exhibits the group's diverse style, with highlights like the gently minimalist 'Louder After 6', reminiscent of Young Marble Giants, and the atmospheric, subdued 'Hanging Gardens'. Already adept at techniques like reverse tape and delicate vocoder vocals, The Legendary Pink Dots were showcasing their sonic originality and versatility even on this first full-length release.

⊙ On December 7, 1979, Talking Heads headlined a show at The Electric Ballroom in Camden Town, London, with Orchestral Manoeuvres in the Dark as the opening act.

8

⊙ Warren Cuccurullo was born on December 8, 1956, in New York. In 1980, he was the guitarist and a founding member of the band Missing Persons. As an avid Frank Zappa fan, Warren would travel far and wide to attend Zappa's concerts and soon befriended members of Zappa's backing band and then Zappa himself, ending up having a role in a segment of Zappa's concert film *Baby Snakes*. Impressed by his knowledge of Zappa's repertoire, Frank invited Warren to join his band and to tour with them through 1978-79; this led to him taking part in the recording of Joe's Garage. After his time with Zappa, Warren co-founded Missing Persons with drummer Terry Bozzio and vocalist Dale Bozzio. The band found early success with hit singles like 'Words' and 'Destination Unknown' from their gold-certified debut album *Spring Session M* (an anagram of Missing Persons). After Missing Persons disbanded in 1986, Warren joined Duran Duran as their new guitarist. He went on to record and write for Duran Duran's albums *Notorious, Big Thing,* and *Liberty*, remaining a long-term member until 2001.

⊙ Sydney's The Deadly Hume's second single and their first with Phantom Records was released December 8, 1986. The 7" 'Passenger Blues' b/w 'Bed as Big as a Boat' (PH-22) was a sell-out success due to an intense following. The lineup of Greg Perano (vocals & guitar), Stephen Martin (guitar), Marc Scully (bass), and Stuart Brown (drums) gave out a sound that was rhythmically strong, bluesy, swampy, and rather infectious. The band took their name from the highway that stretched between Sydney and Melbourne.

◉ Buster Stiggs, aka Mark John Hough, was born in Essex, England, in 1954. Buster was an Australasian music legend, well known as part of New Zealand's first punk band, Suburban Reptiles. He would later join his old schoolmate Phil Judd in The Swingers, who are famed for the timeless hit, and one that some say may be the greatest song in NZ rock history, 'Counting the Beat'! Buster left The Swingers in 1981 to join the Melbourne based Models and was part of the recording of the insanely good mini-album *Cut Lunch* but departed in 1982 to concentrate on graphic design. Buster died in 2018 aged 63 from health issues stemming from diagnoses of blood and bone marrow cancer.

◉ Sinead O'Connor, who converted to Islam in 2018 and took the name Shuhada Davitt, was born on December 8, 1966, in Dublin, Ireland. Though petite and waiflike in appearance, she had an outsized persona and commanding voice. O'Connor never shied away from controversy, often pushing people's buttons with her blunt commentary on social issues. She attributed this rebellious spirit to the abuse she endured in childhood, once remarking, "*I'm not a nice person, I'm trouble*". O'Connor rejected the pop star label, drawing inspiration instead from protest singers, yet her distinctive visual style with a shaved head made her one of the most iconic artists of her era. Her 1987 debut, *The Lion and the Cobra*, was a critical and commercial success, pioneering the atmospheric sound that would define her career. Propelled to stardom, O'Connor earned a Grammy nomination for her searing vocals on the album. Her cover of Prince's 'Nothing Compares 2 U' topped charts worldwide, cementing her status as a generational talent. Over a decades-long career, Sinead released 10 acclaimed albums before her untimely passing on July 26, 2023, in London. Though complex and contradictory, her towering voice and fearless artistry made her an indelible star, a star she didn't want to be.

◉ When Public Image Ltd. released their first album, *Public Image: First Issue*, on Virgin Records in the UK on December 8, 1978, many considered it the genesis of what would later be called POST-PUNK. The band, formed by ex-Sex Pistols frontman John Lydon (aka Johnny Rotten) and featuring guitarist Keith Levene, bassist Jah Wobble (aka John Wardle), and drummer Jim Walker, produced a genre-bending sound combining elements of dub, progressive rock, Krautrock, noise, and atonality. Their excellent second album *Metal Box*, rightfully gets most of the attention and praise, possibly because *First Issue* is much more confrontational and less melodic. Half of the eight-track album was hastily written and recorded after funding was depleted, resulting in uneven audio quality. Songs like 'Public Image', 'Theme' and 'Low Life' are the standouts, with 'Fodderstompf' considered by many a "throwaway" and "antagonistic" track, though here Wobble's bass here remains a highlight of the album. Tensions were also high after Wobble attacked producer Bill Price's assistant; it led Price to bar the band from their preferred Wessex Studios. Virgin Records was initially hesitant about promoting the release, given its overt critiques of organized religion in several tracks.

◉ Paul Rutherford was born in Liverpool, England, on December 8, 1959. Paul's first foray into the music world was in the late '70s as the vocalist with Liverpool locals, The Spitfire Boys. At the time, Paul went by the moniker of Maggot! Paul would go on to join Frankie Goes to Hollywood in 1982 as a keyboardist, backing vocalist, and dancer. Frankie was huge! Through 1983-4 they dominated the charts; the singles 'Relax' and 'Two Tribes' went to No.1 worldwide, as did the album *Welcome to The Pleasuredome*. Frankie fell apart in late 1986, and from here Paul went solo to release a few singles and his underappreciated debut album, Oh World. Paul was part of the first Frankie 3-year reformation in 2004, and then again in 2023. Today he lives in New Zealand with his partner, Perry.

LIFE BEFORE FRANKIE
PAUL RUTHERFORD
(Frankie Goes to Hollywood)

I became friends with Holly Johnson before punk rock took off; we used to meet and come across each other at some of the gay clubs; that was in 1976. A music venue in Liverpool called Eric's had just opened up; it was run by Roger Eagle, Ken Testi, and Pete Fulwell, and I used to go there with Jayne Casey, who was in a band called Pink Military, who were very well-known in Liverpool. Jayne was my best friend; she and Holly were part of one of Liverpool's first punk groups, Big in Japan. For me, that's how it all began. I was studying art and wanted to work in fashion and worked for Jayne at her vintage clothes shop, where she designed outfits too. Then Eric's opened; it was the first place the Sex Pistols played in Liverpool, and as I remember, all the key music industry people from Liverpool were there that night, like Peter Burns of Dead or Alive, Pete Wylie of Wah Heat, and Julian Cope of The Teardrop Explodes. It sparked a burst of beautiful creativity. I do recall that Susan Ballion (Siouxsie Sioux) and Peter Clarke (Budgie) were around too.

I got asked to jam with some guys at an old prison called The Clink where bands used to rehearse, and we became known as The Spitfire Boys, a lineup that included the Pete's... Clarke, Wylie, and Burns. That was my start in music; I sang lead, but the band over time would have a few different lineups. I always thought fashion and clothes design would be my path. While still going to art school, I was making clothes and getting picked up by the guys, driving to Leeds or Glasgow to play a show. Then I'd sleep and go back to school; all this was exciting for a 17- or 18-year-old. Bands were getting signed left and right in England, and fortunately we secured a record deal and put out the single, 'British Refugee'. Punk was increasingly aggressive and violent; Skinheads and Meatheads had got into it and were dominating, for Holly and me. It was time to move on.

We started The English Opium Eaters; a name was suggested to us by Mick Jones of The Clash, and luckily, we were able to play support for them on several occasions. Life at the time was rehearsing, playing, then watching bands until dawn and talking for hours; that went on for years. It was a period about finding yourself. You went with it because it was your life. No one was famous; just being was the antithesis of that. Big names like Iggy Pop and Bowie were totally relevant and inspirational and would show up at gigs. With them around, we thought that we were part of that bigger thing. It just felt like success was close and totally possible. The music was suddenly there. I'd be on the guest lists. Regardless of that great moniker, The English Opium Eaters never got past practice sessions.

In 1980, after a trip to New York to see my sister, Holly asked me to join his new band, Sons of Egypt, which eventually morphed into Frankie Goes to Hollywood. I was very fortunate when a Greek guy from Liverpool named Hambi asked me to tour Europe singing backup for his band Hambi and the Dance. When Hambi played Liverpool, Frankie supported them, and I got to sing with both bands. That first show was awesome. And that marked the beginning of Frankie Goes to Hollywood.

9

◉ On December 9, 1979, The Cure, under the pseudonym Cult Hero, released the single 'I'm A Cult Hero'. The song was originally recorded as a demo with Robert Smith experimenting with different band lineups in the studio. The vocals were sung by Smith's friend Frank Bell, a postman from Crawley, Sussex. In the UK, the single was released on Fiction Records with 'I Dig You' as the B-side, but internationally 'I'm A Cult Hero' was listed as the B-side instead.

⦿ The debut album *The Absence of a Canary* by the Canadian band Ceramic Hello was released in limited quantities in 1981. Fans of John Foxx's *Metamatic* or Gary Numan will appreciate the Numan-styled vocal lines and Foxx-inspired synth textures. However, the album crafts its own unique sound, with computer game-esque tones reminiscent of Yellow Magic Orchestra's *Technodelic*. This seminal minimal synth record is a must-have for any aficionado of the genre.

⦿ The British NEW WAVE band The Lucy Show released their debut album, *Undone*, in 1985. Despite their strong songwriting and infectious melodies reminiscent of The Teardrop Explodes and Echo and the Bunnymen, The Lucy Show remained overlooked through their two albums. Undone bursts with swirling synthesizers, ragged guitars, and psychedelic rock, especially on the catchy single 'Ephemeral'. While 1985 lacked many musical highlights, Undone stood out as a gem worth owning thanks to songwriters and vocalists Mark Bandola and Rob Vandeven, who drew inspiration from 1960s rock and pop. With major label backing in the USA and everything going for them except promotion, The Lucy Show had the misfortune to never find their audience.

⦿ Michael Coffey (aka Tee), who was born on December 9, 1958, in Blackburn, Lancashire, UK. Michael emigrated to Sydney, Australia, with his family in 1965. As he puts it, he came "online" after hearing a few 1960s highlights such as 'I Am the Walrus', 'See Emily Play' & 'Revolution 9'. One night in 1971, the cogs were connected when he first heard 'Hot Love' by T. Rex; then it was from T. Rex to Bowie, to Roxy Music, to Lou Reed & Velvet Underground, the Stooges and Robert Fripp, Eno and the like. Michael's next epiphany and inspiration came with the so-called 'krautrock' of early Tangerine Dream and Faust and Brian Eno's groundbreaking *Obscure Records* releases. Michael's first recording was circa 1974-75 when he delved into a reconstruction of the Beatles' 'Revolution 9', toying with cassette loops and drones (from song fade-outs). Michael has been making "art damaged music" and new hybrids ever since, thoroughly committed to generating variety and change rather than sticking to genre or being obsessed with authenticity or technique ("I will leave that to the authentic musician/tradies"). He bought a Revox A66 and started recording as A Cloakroom Assembly (ACRA) in 1978, with the Barons in 1979, then co-founded the M Squared label, studio, and Scattered Order in 1979 with Mitch Jones. Michael "tinkily bonked" through 1981-85 with various hybrid M Squared bands, including the much-misunderstood Ya Ya Choral with partner Fiona Graham as it morphed from tinkily-bonk into a hard rockin' (as Michael put it) "metal(ish)" guitar band that toured the UK in the late '80s, morphing into electro buzz pop in the early '90s. Always in the wrong place at the wrong time. ACRA was reactivated in the mid-'90s, and this marked a return for Michael to dronescapes, sound collages and sonic incense. In 2009, after lots of interest from overseas labels to reissue M Squared material, he reconnected with Mitch Jones (and later Shane Fahey) to reactivate Scattered Order. Scattered Order has been quite prolific and still active in 2025, loosely categorised as 'POST-PUNK' or 'art noise', releasing new material every 12 months or so. So they toured Europe, always experimenting, changing, growing, and evolving under the names ACRA, Space Therapy Robinson, Frosty and Tee Marshall. Sadly, Michael passed away on May 15, 2024, from the effects of multiple myeloma and amyloidosis.

WE JUST WEREN'T PART OF THE BOYS CLUB
MICHAEL COFFEY
(A Cloakroom Assembly, Scattered Order, Ya Ya Choral)

In the early days, in the early 1980s, it was still a big boys club; other musos and promoters in the Sydney and Melbourne scene didn't take us seriously because we had boys, girls and drum machines in our bands and didn't play that 'meat and potatoes' style of pub rock,

Birdman, Detroit or corporate NEW WAVE Oz-rock. Of course, this limited our options for playing live and kept us in the inner city

I remember one guy from an 'emerging' big Melbourne band getting upset (after I had organised their first Sydney debut shows) because we got The Cure supports at the Capitol Theatre; he told me, *"We should have got that spot, not you, cos you aren't doing this seriously, like we are!"*

We had enough friends in more open-minded bands who helped us out though. Ironically, later on when Ya Ya Choral morphed into a metal(ish) rock band and got rave reviews in Kerrang! and Metal Hammer and toured the UK, the knives came out again. Always in the wrong place at the wrong time, am I being contrary?

10

◎ On December 10, 1973, the iconic music venue CBGB opened its doors in New York City. Founded by Hilly Kristal, the name originally stood for "Country, BlueGrass, and Blues", though its stage would soon host artists that defined the punk and NEW WAVE scenes. With the slogan "OMFUG" (meaning "Other Music for Uplifting Gourmandizers") under its awning, CBGB became the place for seminal acts like Talking Heads, Suicide, The Dead Boys, Blondie, Television, The Cramps, The Misfits, Patti Smith, and The Ramones to develop their revolutionary sounds. After over 30 years as a hub of underground music and subcultures, CBGB closed its doors for good on October 15, 2006, following a rent dispute with landlords the Bowery Residents' Committee. Patti Smith, who had helped put the venue on the map, played a final concert that night, though she remarked, *"There's new kids with new ideas all over the world. They'll make their own places-it doesn't matter whether it's here or wherever it is"*. Today the former home of CBGB houses a John Varvatos boutique, but its legacy as the birthplace of punk lives on.

◎ The *self-titled* debut album from Fine Young Cannibals, released in 1985, was an excellent mid-1980s album that still sounds fresh today, thanks to its timeless retro Motown-soul quality. This texture showcased frontman Roland Gift's distinctive vocals and blended NEW WAVE and soulful R&B into a set of catchy songs. Highlights included the hit single 'Johnny Come Home', covers of 'Suspicious Minds' and 'Blue', and the infectious 'Move to Work'. These standout tracks anchored a strong debut album that established Fine Young Cannibals' signature sound, blending vintage soul with contemporary NEW WAVE.

◎ Paul Hardcastle was born in Kensington, England, on December 10, 1957. As a producer, mixer, composer, programmer, and keyboardist, he made his recording debut in 1981 with 'Don't Depend on Me', a minor hit on the UK dance music scene. His breakthrough came in 1985 with the worldwide major hit '19'. Using audio snippets of news reports about the Vietnam War, he created a thought-provoking tune that went to No.1 in thirteen countries, but in the USA, it only topped Billboard's dance-club chart. Paul has also recorded under the pseudonym Silent Underdog, gaining production and remix credits for works by Ian Dury, Carol Kenyon, LW5, and Phil Lynott's last-ever recording, 'Nineteen'. From his home studio, where he still releases records under aliases like the Deff Boyz, Beeps International, Kiss the Sky, and the bestselling *Jazzmasters* series, Hardcastle put out some of his most popular releases through the '90s and into the new millennium and continues to sell well in the specialty dance market.

◎ Jeremy Ryder, better known by his stage name Jack Hues, was born on December 10, 1954, in Chatham, Kent, England. In 1979, he co-founded the NEW WAVE band Huang Chung as the guitarist, keyboardist, and lead vocalist. The band later changed their name to Wang Chung in 1983 to make it easier to pronounce. Despite going through periods of hiatus, Wang Chung has released seven albums and numerous singles between 1982 and 2019. Their biggest hits were 'Dance Hall Days' (1984) and 'Everybody Have Fun Tonight'

(1986). Outside of the band, Hues has released two solo albums and several jazz albums, collaborating with various jazz musicians. He partnered with Tony Banks of Genesis on Tony's 1995 *Strictly Inc.* solo album and composed film scores - most notably for William Friedkin's *The Guardian* and two short films by Hues' son Jack Ryder, *Act of Memory* and *Dog*.

YAMAHA BASS FOR RENT?
JACK HUES
(Wang Chung, Strictly Inc., Solo)

Through the 14-year period that Wang Chung existed, there are all sorts of funny stories, like Darren walking into a plate glass door in a club in LA because he kept his sunglasses on to look cool after coming in from the blinding California sunlight outside. Nick falling backwards offstage – all the slapstick stuff.

We recorded our second album, *Points on the Curve*, at Abbey Road Studio 2 in deliberate homage to The Beatles. Chris Hughes and Ross Cullum, our producers, and I were huge Beatles fans; Nick too, of course. We wanted to soak up the residual energies and have that experience of actually working day after day in that magical space. We worked there for six or seven months and mixed the album there too, sending everything off to Geffen Records in LA for approval. Obviously, there was no internet to send things instantaneously in 1983. All the mixes went on 1/2" stereo tapes via FedEx or whatever.

Eventually we heard back from John Kalodner, our (legendary) A&R guy. He loved the album but said, *"Why don't you guys spend a bit more time on Dance Hall Days and see if you can get it better?"* Abbey Road was booked out, so we found a room at AIR Studios, which in those days was located above Top Shop right on Oxford Circus in London, the very centre of town. It was owned by George Martin, The Beatles producer. I remember redoing the guitar solo on 'Wait' there.

One afternoon Chris said we should look at Nick's bass part on Dance Hall Days, but Nick, in classic fashion, hadn't brought a bass with him. As he is left-handed, I joked, *"Why don't we borrow one of Paul's basses? He's left-handed."* Paul McCartney was recording down the corridor in another room. I thought no more of it, but after a couple of hours our studio door opened, and in walked Macca with one of his basses. He stood at the door and said in his deepest Liverpool accent, *"Maurice Plaquet bass hire here; you guys ordered a bass?"* Maurice Plaquet's was the go-to instrument rental place in London at the time. There was a rather stunned silence. He then walked over to me and handed me the bass and said, *"Is it you who wanted to borrow it? Here you go!"* I was so stunned I just took the bass and mumbled, *"Yeah, err, thanks..."* and felt utterly star-struck, speechless. He then sat on the sofa and chatted with Chris, whom he knew because Chris and Linda were friends, saying, *"Linda's heard the song; she loves it,"* and after a few minutes, got up and left. I was still speechless…

So, Nick used Paul's bass, and I think that those parts are the ones that ended up on the final mix of 'Dance Hall Days'. So, we got a bit of that Beatles energy after all, as if we hadn't absorbed enough in Abbey Road, and, of course, the subsequent success of 'Dance Hall Days' is a contribution to the ongoing legacy of which we are so fortunate to be a part.

Jack Hues, Canterbury: May 2023

On December 10, 1979, music took a U-turn on its highway when the industrial legends Throbbing Gristle (TG) released their third studio album, *20 Jazz Funk Greats (20 JFG)*. The album collided head-on with listeners, as it was neither jazz nor funk but TG's attempt at accessible mainstream music. *20 JFG* is a genre-defying masterpiece that touches on electro, ambient, industrial, pastoral and goth styles. As a cohesive work, it excites the auditory senses like nothing else. With 20 *JFG TG* made a prolific leap toward accessibility on their own terms. While much of the Class of '79 were slowing down, TG gave us a sharp, percussive, dark, and slimy potpourri. The formal elegance of Chris Carter's synthesizers is scrawled upon by Genesis P-Orridge's bass riffs and Cosey Fanni Tutti's fuzz guitar freakouts, spiced with her violin and cornet honks. *20 JFG* is TG's most accessible release and a great starting point. 'Hot on the Heels of Love' is a great synthpop song, while 'Beachy Head' and 'Exotica' are Eno-esque ambient pieces. Most tunes still maintain Genesis P-Orridge's signature subversive lyrics and vocals, as epitomised by the lyric *"I've got a little biscuit tin to keep your panties in"*.

11

◉ After a couple of demo cassettes and an EP, the first full-length LP album outing, *Europa Is Hier*, by the Dutch band deDIV, was on the shelves December 11, 1982. The band came together at the end of 1979 and exemplified the approach into POST-PUNK. The new emerging Dutch NEW WAVE scene was taking hold, and deDIV, who initially exhibited their songs in the Dutch language, were leading the way. Growing from a three-piece to five in the mid-'80s and shortening their name to DIV, they would present recordings and live performances in English and were regarded as innovators, especially with drummer Peter de Wolf's self-designed 'Unit Drumkit', a one-of-a-kind setup that was its own road case, a drum-riser incorporating a horizontal bass drum! After several striking yet poorly received releases, DIV dissolved in 1990.

◉ Leigh Gorman was born on this day in London, England, in 1961. A classically trained musician, Leigh mastered just about any instrument and style he put his hand to. At the tender age of 16 in 1977, his skill saw him venture into studio session work, and he was a member of 57 Men, a band that featured Glenn Gregory (Heaven 17) and Jack Hues (Wang Chung). In 1979 Leigh became a member of Adam and the Ants, who were managed by Malcolm McLaren; this was a stepping stone to Bow Wow Wow in the next year. With the pressures of touring taking a toll and interest in Bow Wow Wow waning, he formed Chiefs of Relief; they released the one *self-titled* album and several singles. The late '90s saw Leigh enter into some successful production work, most notably the 1989 single 'Twenty Seconds to Comply' by Silver Bullet. Through several reformations of Bow Wow Wow, Leigh continues to tour with them today.

◉ On December 11, 1982, The Jam played their final concert together at the Brighton Conference Centre. Afterwards, each member went their own way. Lead singer-guitarist Paul Weller teamed up with keyboardist Mick Talbot, formerly of the mod revival band The Merton Parkas, to launch The Style Council. Weller wanted to incorporate more soul, R&B, and jazz into his music - a direction he felt his punk orientated Jam bandmates could not follow. Drummer Rick Buckler formed Time UK with former members of Masterswitch, The Tom Robinson Band, Sparks, and bassist Bruce Foxton went solo for a short while, recording the album *Touch Sensitive* which held the UK Top 20 hit 'Freak'.

◉ On December 11, 1987, Kitchens of Distinction (aka KOD) out of Tooting, England, released their debut single, 'The Last Gasp Death Shuffle', which was named Single of the Week by NME. This acclaim attracted several record labels, leading the band to sign with One Little Indian. KOD progressed sonically and matured into one of the few dream pop bands that emphasised emotive songwriting as much as swirling guitar atmospherics. The band formed in 1986 with singer/bassist Patrick Fitzgerald, guitarist Julian Swales, and drummer Daniel Goodwin, taking their name from a magazine advertisement. Their 1989 debut album *Love Is Hell* earned critical praise and aligned them with the shoegaze scene alongside bands like My Bloody Valentine, The Chameleons and Cocteau Twins. Many bands and fans now look back at this seminal KOD album as an important influence. With its solid rhythms, bristling energy, gorgeous guitars and vocals bursting with passion and even anger, a listen to the album Love Is Hell is rewarding. Standouts like 'In a Cave', 'Shiver', 'Prize' and 'The 3rd Time We Open the Capsule' showcase the band's brilliant songcraft. *Love Is Hell* is a superb yet overlooked album.

12

◉ Cyril John "Cy" Curnin was born in 1957, in Wimbledon, England. Cy is the main songwriter and lead vocalist for The Fixx. The Fixx came about after the incarnations of first Portraits and then Fix. College friends Cy and drummer Adam Woods got together in the late '70s and advertised in the national music papers for additional members. Responses came from guitarist Jamie West-Oram, keyboardist Rupert Greenall, and bassist Charlie Barret…The Fixx was fixed! The music of The Fixx has always flirted with the mainstream with their catchy, keyboard driven almost formula-style pop. Their single, 'One Thing Leads to Another', went top 5 in the USA and Canada; it opened the door for the *Reach the Beach* album to go top 10.

◉ Belouis Some, aka Neville Keighley was born December 12, 1959, in London, England. Belouis immediately comes to mind for his 1985 hit 'Imagination', the video clip for which caused a furore at the time because of its full-frontal nudity. Although the single peaked at No.17 in the UK chart, it was a big European hit and top 5 in the US dance charts. The follow-up single 'Some People' from the album of the same name was used in the USA for a nationwide Swatch Watch TV commercial, which successfully tapped into '80s US fashion and youth culture; both singles charted on the Billboard Top 100. Belouis Some was one of the opening acts for Queen on their Magic Tour in 1986. 'Round Round', which was part of the *Pretty in Pink* movie soundtrack, found Belouis a worldwide audience, which aided in exposure and sales of his *self-titled* 1987 album. In 1989 he formed The Big Broadcast, and in 1993 the album *Living Your Life* was released to critical acclaim. Belouis Some has been part of several '80s-themed festivals.

OPENING FOR QUEEN
BELOUIS SOME

In May 1986 a massive roll call of current '80s bands performed at the Montreux Pop Festival in Switzerland, promoted by MTV out of the USA. The event lasted two days; we performed one song each night, and it was broadcast on live TV all over the world… so everyone was there! INXS, Frankie Goes to Hollywood, Eurythmics, A-Ha, Talk Talk, Simply Red – you name it!

Of course, as well as performing, the event was party central. We all went a little crazy, and it ended up culminating with a massive party cruise held by Queen on a steamship hired by EMI Records on Lake Geneva to announce their upcoming 'Magic Tour'. The party was going strong, then Queen arrived to announce what would be their groundbreaking summer stadium tour; there was a throng of press and untold numbers of photos, and of course we then carried on partying.

A short while later I got a tap on the shoulder from the worldwide managing director of EMI Records, Peter Jamieson, and in front of everyone he asked if I could come upstairs with him, as Freddie Mercury would like to meet me.

Freddie was charming and very complimentary; we talked about the TV show, the bands, and the cruise. Freddie then turns to Peter and says, *"I'd like Belouis to open for us on the Magic Tour, please."* Peter looked horrified, as I was already massively unrecouped to the record company. Of course, he agreed, and the party went from strength to strength!

By the way, the next day we flew to New York and played the Beacon Theatre, headlining the Swatch Live Show.

The newly named jangle power-poppers The Three O'Clock, from Los Angeles, released their debut full-length album, *Sixteen Tambourines*, on December 12, 1983, on the Frontier label. Well produced with a touch of '60s psychedelia, the album holds some mighty hooks and infectious choruses. 'And So We Run', 'Tomorrow' and 'Seeing is Believing' are play-it-again-and-again tunes. Overall, an admirable recording from one of the original groups to come out of Los Angeles' paisley underground movement. It has been said that their debut was actually the eponymous LP *The Salvation Army*, but they ran afoul of The Salvation Army organization, which threatened legal action, hence a name change, and The Three O'Clock was born; the album would be rereleased as *Befour Three O'Clock* in 1986.

13

GANGgajang released their debut single, 'Gimme Some Loving', on December 13, 1984. The band was formed by guitarist and lead vocalist Mark 'Cal' Callaghan, formerly of the Riptides, along with ex-members of The Angels - Chris Bailey on bass and Graham 'Buzz' Bidstrup on drums. The three had met during the recording of the ABC-TV show *Sweet and Sour*. The single reached No.33 on the Australian charts, and the song was included on their 1985 album *GANGgajang*, which went platinum.

Psyche by Alain Duplantier

The Canadian EBM/synthpop duo Psyche released their debut album *Insomnia Theatre* on December 13, 1985. Driven largely by sequencers and drum machines, Psyche explored dark, atmospheric sounds and basic dancefloor rhythms, though rarely venturing beyond the conventions of their British and German contemporaries. There are noticeable similarities to Soft Cell and Cabaret Voltaire throughout the album. While the Edmonton-based Huss brothers, Darrin and Stephen (aka Evan Panic), did not garner much publicity, they found success in Germany with strong initial sales. Steeped in synthpop with gothic flair, *Insomnia Theatre* requires a few listens to fully appreciate but rewards with some worthwhile discoveries across its 8-track double EP length. Taking inspiration from Fad Gadget, Psyche's outrageous live shows would feature one of the Huss boys covered in shaving cream. Standout tracks include 'Maggots' and 'Children Carry Knives'. Stephen died in 2015, but Darrin has continued with the name and continues to perform as well with a new electronic project named Jetlag.

Rough Trade Records was born in 1977 with the release of the French band Métal Urbain's second single, 'Paris Maquis'. Rough Trade would prove itself to be an important outlet for artists such as Cabaret Voltaire, The Go-Betweens, Monochrome Set, The Normal, Scritti Politti, Spizz and The Smiths.

Patti Smith's seminal 1975 debut album *Horses*, produced by John Cale, captured the raw energy of punk before the genre fully emerged. While too artistic to be strictly punk, *Horses* proved massively influential, often cited as one of the most impactful albums ever made. Smith's vocals range from sultry to shamanic, channeling the spirit of the Velvet Underground. *Horses* defined the musical ethos of its time, not because it sounded dated, but because it presaged the punk explosion soon to come. The album's artsy ambition shaped its prog rock-length tracks like 'Land' and 'Birdland', which stretched past nine minutes, a prog approach that her contemporary Tom Verlaine entered into with *Marquee Moon*. Though Smith wanted to be a three-chord rocker sporting wrap-around shades, her talent propelled her beyond the constraints of short, sharp rock songs. She yearned to be a punk monster, but her words and ideas destined her for something more.

◉ Tom Verlaine was born in 1949, in Denville, New Jersey, USA. Tom was highly influential through his exploratory guitar improvisations and poetic songwriting, sitting on the fringes of punk, jazz, and progressive rock. Television never really achieved huge commercial success, but their masterpiece debut album *Marquee Moon* deservedly achieved critical acclaim when released yet sold poorly in the USA, but it did hit the top 30 in the UK. Tom would go on to record 9 solo albums, each highly regarded, with his compositions being covered by the likes of David Bowie, Sonic Youth, Echo and the Bunnymen, and Siouxsie and the Banshees. Throughout his career he collaborated with numerous bands and individuals, such as Patti Smith, and Patti is quoted as saying, "*Tom plays guitar like a thousand bluebirds screaming*". Tom was also part of the "supergroup" The Million Dollar Bashers, who were the support band for the Bob Dylan biopic *I'm Not There*. Tom died on January 28, 2023, after battling prostate cancer.

14

The Clash by Roch Parisien

◉ On December 14, 1979, The Clash released their landmark album *London Calling* in the UK (January 1980 elsewhere). Rhythm guitarist and lead vocalist Joe Strummer, lead guitarist and vocalist Mick Jones, bassist and vocalist Paul Simonon, and drummer and percussionist Nicholas "Topper" Headon presented a bold statement on the political, social, and cultural zeitgeist. Unafraid to experiment, they masterfully blended rock, POST-PUNK, ska, rockabilly, R&B, pop, and reggae. *London Calling* arrived as punk rock was declining worldwide, with most bands shifting toward POST-PUNK artistry and NEW WAVE. With this album, The Clash transcended punk's limitations while retaining its raw energy and conviction. The first half of *London Calling* is flawless. The anthemic title track opens with Strummer's gritty, apocalyptic call to arms over ragged guitar and Simonon's thundering bass. 'Brand New Cadillac' injects rockabilly spirit into a cover of Vince Taylor's song. 'Jimmy Jazz' recounts an outcast always staying ahead of the cops. 'Rudie Can't Fail' rivals any reggae classic, while 'The Right Profile' is rockabilly mastery with killer horns. 'Lost in the Supermarket' redefines pop within a punk ethos. The second half falters slightly compared to the first, as expected for a double album, though the addictive pure pop of 'Train in Vain' closes it perfectly. Being sophisticated in songcraft and production, *London Calling* represented a creative peak for The Clash, one they would be unable to top, though the excellent triple set of *Sandinista!* followed. Growing divisions between Strummer and Jones soon destroyed the band. *London Calling* remains a must-have for its music and its significance in rock history. A little trivia: The title 'Train in Vain' and track position never made the cover printing on the original double-album vinyl record. The title though, was scratched into the vinyl in the needle run-off area on the fourth side of the album. If you have one of those, you indeed have a collector's item!

◉ On this day in 1979, Fingerprintz released their debut album, *The Very Dab*, an excellent and unique record that defied categorisation. The band blended NEW WAVE with a brooding POST-PUNK aesthetic, creating a dark, sparse, and unconventional sound. Vocalist and guitarist Jimme O'Neill's distinctive delivery, paired with minimalist production and eccentric compositions, gave the album a gritty, back-alley feel that stood out in 1979 and still feels fresh today. Three instrumental tracks especially shine: the ominous '2.A.T.', 'Fingerprince' with its wailing saxophone, and the foreboding 'Wet Job'.

◉ Mike Scott, born in Edinburgh, Scotland, on December 14, 1958, was a founding member of The Waterboys. Over nearly 40 years, The Waterboys have had over 60 different musicians come and go, but Scott has remained the constant throughout the band's history. As a solo artist, Scott released the albums *Bring 'Em All In* in 1995 and *Still Burning* in 1997. The Waterboys achieved great success, especially during their "Big Music" period in the late 1980s when they released the folk-influenced album *Fisherman's Blues*. With its polished production and Celtic influences, *Fisherman's Blues* featured over 20 guest musicians and spawned the band's most commercially successful single, 'Fisherman's Blues'.

◉ Paul Scott (no relation to the aforementioned Mike) was born December 14, 1958, in Waimate, New Zealand, and began his career in music, writing and playing bass in the angular NZ group Pop Mechanix. Despite court cases, a revolving cast of singers and multiple record labels, their single 'Jumping Out a Window' became a staple of New Zealand pop culture. Paul relocated to Australia, and Paul formed Montana with Ken Stewart (Mr Blonde), Michelle Margherita and Steve Melville. Their first release featured 'Koolest Band', which received national airplay and high rotation on radio JJJ. A brief tour of the USA and a performance at SXSW led to 'Koolest Band' being included in the Hollywood movie You Drive Me Crazy. The subsequent album *Bubblegum Love* was released in Australia, Spain, France and the USA. Scott has since plied bass for various Australian acts, playing everywhere from community halls and malls in Sydney, Melbourne, and Brisbane to the Sydney Opera House. During this time, he has released a series of solo records under his 'Insufferable' moniker, which have been warmly received.

I'M NOW A FILM DIRECTOR
PAUL SCOTT
(Pop Mechanix aka NZ Pop)

Ahhhh… The Manzil Room! The uncharitable might describe it as a seedy late-night bar; I preferred to think of it as a room full of possibilities, most of them ill-advised, but not all.
For our sins or more likely at the behest of our manager and patron, Michael Chugg, NZ POP had a regular Sunday night residence there. The venue was always lively, bordering on riotous, and the audience usually had a high quota of post-gig musicians and industry folk networking over their refreshments of choice.
On the night in question, Chuggy, the famed entrepreneur and promoter, was in attendance, and just as we were about to start our second set of the evening, he approached with an unusual request: *"My friend wants to sing some songs with you."* Initially we weren't terribly keen on the idea until he revealed that 'his friend' was none other than the Animal's legendary vocalist Eric Burdon. Oh boy! *"What do you want to sing?"* We asked, *"Blues in A!"* he replied, and so off we went on a 15-minute jam led by that glorious electric voice; it

was a fantastic moment and one of the highlights of my performing life. Fast forward 30-odd years, and a friend, Justin Andres, who was Eric's MD and bass player, invited me to their show at the Enmore Theatre. After the gig, we went backstage to pay our respects, and there was the man himself, sitting on a couch, politely holding court. I shuffled forward to offer my appreciation for what was a truly enjoyable gig when Justin prompted me, *"Tell Eric about the time you played with him in the '80s."* So, I sat down next to the great man and recounted the Manzil Room gig blow by blow; he listened intently and patted my knee encouragingly. When I finished my tale, he nodded and smiled. *"Thanks,"* I said, *"you were in great voice tonight."* As I got up, I heard him say to one of his crew, *"Who was that? Was that Quentin Tarantino!"*

15

◉ The debut single 'Tael of the Saeghors' by The Makers of the Dead Travel Fast was available in selected stores in Sydney, Australia, on this day in 1980. Backed with 'The Dumb Waiter', the single was destined to become a cult hit through high rotation on radio station 2JJJ and their inspiring sporadic live appearances. Released on the M Squared label, 'Tael' is a delectable mix of experimentalist electronica and sea-shanty with an exquisite sax melody. The band who took their name from a quote in Bram Stoker's Dracula was at the time a studio project; their first recording, 'The Dead Travel Fast', appeared on the M Squared compilation *Growing Pains*. Going live, they added the 'prefix' The Makers Of. The single now is a rarity, but the tune can be found on the M Squared boxed set *Terrace Industry*.

◉ On December 15, 1985, The Mighty Lemon Drops' debut independent single, 'Like an Angel', was released on Dreamworld Records. The song bursts with energy, evoking shadows of The Doors, Echo & The Bunnymen, and even The Jam. Vocalist Paul Marsh's rich, strong voice resembles a young Jim Morrison, complemented by the band's dark, ultra-solid rhythm section. With such a powerful sound, it's no surprise the single sold around 15,000 copies. Martin Gilks' sensational drumming further amplifies the track's excitement, which propelled the band's subsequent success with their debut album *Happy Head*.

◉ Paul Simonon, born in London, England, on December 15, 1955, was the backbone of the legendary punk rock band The Clash. Along with Joe Strummer and Mick Jones, Simonon formed The Clash in 1976 and remained the only constant member until the group dissolved in 1986. After The Clash broke up, Simonon continued making music and went on to establish himself as a successful painter. The Clash were inducted into the Rock and Roll Hall of Fame in 2003, cementing their status as punk rock pioneers. In the 1980s, Simonon married Pearl E. Gates of the band Pearl Harbor and The Explosions, who had opened for The Clash on tour. Simonon and Gates were married for seven years before divorcing in 1989. In 2023 Paul teamed with vocalist Galen Ayres to release the country-latin America-tinged album *Can We Do Tomorrow Another Day?*.

◉ The debut solo album *Chewing Hides the Sound* by Snakefinger was released in 1979 by Ralph Records. Snakefinger, whose real name was Philip Charles Lithman, co-produced and co-wrote the album along with the avant-garde rock band The Residents. Snakefinger was a brilliantly eccentric guitarist who took creative approaches to playing rather than relying on standard guitar techniques. This album, made in collaboration with the highly experimental Residents, allowed Snakefinger to fully explore his gift for bizarre and humorous songwriting and, of course, a unique guitar style. The album opens with a melodic, sparse cover of Kraftwerk's 'The Model', with Snakefinger cleverly replacing the synth lines with his own distinctive guitar riffs. The left-field humour of Snakefinger and the Residents comes through on songs like 'Kill the Great Raven', 'Here Come the Bums', and the sacrilegious but comical 'Jesus Was a Leprechaun'. Overall, the album has a quintessential

Residents sound, but with Snakefinger's experimental guitar work pushing into new territory, it's a true underground NEW WAVE avant-rock hybrid all of its own. Each track displays Snakefinger's one-of-a-kind approach to the electric guitar, proving he had a relationship with the instrument quite unlike any other player. This album is an eccentric classic that will continue to appeal to serious music fans across eras and genres for its bold artistic vision.

16

◎ Lizzy Mercier Descloux, born Martine-Elisabeth Mercier Descloux in Lyon, France, on December 16, 1956, was a boundary-pushing musician known for her eclectic style. In 1978, she formed the avant-garde duo Rosa Yemen with Didier Esteban, releasing a *self-titled* EP that fused no wave and mutant disco. The following year, Descloux recorded her acclaimed solo debut, *Press Color* at Bob Blank's Blank Tapes studio. Her innovative solo career produced five aurally outrageous and eclectic albums where she made her mark with unique covers of songs like 'Mission Impossible', 'Fever', and 'Fire'. A self-described "bohemian musical sponge", Descloux's genre-bending artistry intrigued critics before she passed away on April 20, 2004, from ovarian and colon cancers.

◎ The debut single-EP by Minutemen from California was out December 16, 1980. Paranoid Time is a 7-track set of arty POST-PUNK, where the songs are uncompromising, immediate and without melodies to tap along to, yet with a catchiness that most similar bands were without. What the songs lack in polish, they make up for in the song structure and design. It's easy to see the influence of Wire.

◎ On December 16, 1982, German DJ Ralf Behrendt brought together Stefanie Lange and Claudia Hossfeld to form the group Saâda Bonaire and produce the sensational dance single 'You Could Be More as You Are' b/w 'It's a Man's Man's World'. Producer Dennis Bovell, using Kraftwerk's Kling Klang studio, created an epic dance floor anthem by layering synths, drum machines, pops, and squeaks behind Lange and Hossfeld's blistering vocals. With his studio expertise, Bovell crafted a rare masterpiece from this amalgam of sounds supporting Saâda Bonaire's scorching vocals.

17

◎ In December 1980, New York POST-PUNK band the Bush Tetras released their debut single, 'Too Many Creeps', on 99 Records. With its distorted guitar, in-your-face vocals, and pulsating funk bassline, the single became a staple at holiday parties that year. Formed in 1979, Bush Tetras originally comprised vocalist Cynthia Sley, guitarist Pat Place (formerly of The Contortions), bassist Laura Kennedy, and drummer Dee Pop. Though angular and funky like The Contortions, Bush Tetras had a less frenetic, more melodic sound, particularly on their 1995 reunion album *Beauty Lies*, which was produced by funk-rock pioneer Nona Hendryx. Despite its critical acclaim, the reunion album failed to gain commercial success, leading to the band's second dissolution. Back together again in 2005, they continue to perform sporadically, albeit with lineup changes after the passing of both drummer Dee-Pop and bassist Laura Kennedy.

◎ Sara Dallin was born in 1961 in Bristol, England. Sara was a founding member of Bananarama, along with Siobhan Fahey and Keren Woodward. The trio have-been hugely successful from the day they started in 1980, with well over 25 top-charting singles. With that, they earned a place in the Guinness Book of World Records for achieving the most UK chart entries by an all-female group, and worldwide they have sold over 30 million units. Original member Siobhan Fahey departed in 1988, with Jacquie O'Sullivan being the third member for 3 years; this left Sara and Keren to continue as a duo.

● The debut album *The Guilty Have No Pride* by Death in June was released in 1983. The album featuring Douglas P., Tony Wakeford, and Patrick Leagas is considered the genesis of the neofolk-goth genre. With its haunting, texturally complex, and expressively varied sound echoing Bauhaus and Joy Division, some of the production techniques are exceptional. Douglas P.'s vocals are consistently distant, sinister, and reverberating, shielded by deep industrial bass and militaristic drumming. Death In June have released over 20 albums from 1981 to the present day, and this one especially is well worth seeking out.

● Mark Gane was born on December 17, 1953. Coming together in Toronto, Canada in 1977, Mark along with Martha Johnson and David Millar was a founding member of Martha and the Muffins, the band that initially became internationally known after the release of his composition and smash hit single 'Echo Beach'. The band should not be singularly defined by 'Echo Beach', as the quality of the later album releases such as *This Is the Ice Age* proves. With a willingness to experiment, that album displays some superb, dreamy soundscapes; 'Swimming' and 'One Day in Paris' are icy-cool. In 1982 Mark and Martha took their explorations one step further with the venture M+M engaging with session players; they filled dancefloors with the hits 'Black Stations/White Stations' and 'Song in My Head'. Forty-eight years and nine Martha and the Muffins albums later, Mark continued his sonic explorations with his solo album, *Garden Music*, an instrumental album, 11 tracks based on common plant names.

ECHO BEACH
MARK GANE
(Martha and the Muffins)

Let's go back – February 1978 – to the Ontario College of Art Experimental Arts Department located at 60 McCaul St in the former Brink's Express building in downtown Toronto. A lot of interesting bands, sound and video artists and events passed through there long before it was demolished for a condo in 2017. As part of the facilities, the Sound Lab was home to a very basic 4-track recording studio, an EMS Synthi, the synthesizer (famously used by Brian Eno and which I later bought from the college), some microphones and not much else.

The lighting is barely adequate to illuminate the burlap-covered, soundproof walls. I'm sitting on a chair looking down at the Les Paul on my lap where a circular riff has landed. In my hands. Out of the blue. No songwriter can fully explain, either to themselves or to others, where it comes from, and I'm not going to attempt to do that now.

The first draft of the lyrics was written down in my art school notebook, alongside sketches, class schedules and experimental music scores. Being heavily influenced at the time by Roxy Music, I wanted to evoke a similar feeling often found in the lyrics of Bryan Ferry, that tongue-in-cheek insouciance, channelling Noël Coward et al. Thus, "I know it's out of fashion and a trifle uncool…". The key word is "trifle". You can't help being tongue-in-cheek with a word like that.

Around the same time, I recorded a rough demo of the song in The Sound Lab, no vocals (maybe the lyrics hadn't been written yet), just two guitar tracks – the riff along with a possible song structure. It's the earliest recorded version of the song, not yet fully formed, but well on its way. Few people ever heard that song sketch, but two years later 'Echo Beach' would become a different story.

Many years later, my father told me he thought the success of the song was due in part to its feeling of nostalgia, something I never consciously thought about when I was writing it. But given the emotional hold the song has had over so many people for 40+ years, I think he must have been right.

● The band from Newcastle, Australia, Pel Mel, had their debut album, *Out of Reason*, available for the Xmas present-buying public on December 17, 1982. This is a set of beautifully crafted songs that are superbly produced by the late Tony Cohen. Pel Mel showed that one could move from that POST-PUNK rawness of their live performances to funky pop. Jude McGee's voice leads the way over the funk-driven bass and minimalist keys; melodies abound. Extremely tasty.

⊙ On December 17, 1978, Voigt/465 released their debut single 'State' b/w 'A Secret West'. The lineup of vocalist Rae Macron Cru, Lindsay O'Meara on bass, guitarist Rod Pobestek, Phil Turnbull on keyboards and drummer Bruce Stalder had a short but stellar career; they were highly regarded not only for their few recordings but also for their engaging live performances in inner-city Sydney. Today, this single is all but impossible to find, but 'State' can be found on the double CD set *Inner City Sound* which is a superb document of Australia's premier early POST-PUNK.

18

⊙ The British POST-PUNK band Joy Division performed their sole concert ever in Paris, France, on December 18, 1979, at the famed venue Les Bains Douches. A partial recording of the concert was made and later issued in 2001 by the record company NMC.

⊙ Grantley Evan Marshall, aka Grant Marshal, aka Daddy G, was born in 1959. Daddy G is a founding member of the band Massive Attack, who are arguably the premier band of the trip hop genre. They formed in 1988 in Bristol, with members consisting of Grant "Daddy G" Marshall, Robert "3D" Del Naja and Andy "Mushroom" Vowles ("Mush"). The band spun off from a collective called The Wild Bunch, which included vocalists Horace Andy and Shara Nelson, and they have produced some of the most intriguing & often beguiling music of the last 30-odd years. With their roots in the Bristol club scene of the early '80s, the members of Massive Attack originated trip-hop, one of the most influential sounds of the '90s, combining the rhythmic urgency of hip-hop, the freewheeling samples of the DJ's craft, soul-rich melodies, and dub-reggae's hefty, intoxicating bottom end.

⊙ Elliot Easton, the left-handed lead guitarist for The Cars, was born Elliot Steinberg on December 18, 1953. Elliot played on all six of the Cars' albums up to the split of the band in 1988. In 1984 he recorded his solo LP *Change No Change* and collaborated with vocalist Jules Shear on several projects, the best known being the *Eternal Return* album. Elliott returned to The Cars for their final recording, *Move Like This*, in 2011 and has always continued with session work and other projects like The Band of Angels, Nelson, The Immediate Family and also touring with Creedence Clearwater Revisited for 10 years.

Martha Johnson by Phil Kamin

⊙ Martha Johnson was born in Toronto, Canada, on December 18, 1950, and was a founding member and lead vocalist of the Canadian art pop band Martha and the Muffins. Best known for the international hit single, the famed 'Echo Beach', Martha and the Muffins have had a number of high-charting hits in Canada, and as M+M they charted at No.2 in the Billboard Dance Charts with their 1984 hit 'Black Stations/White Stations'. In addition to releasing 9 studio albums with Martha and the Muffins, Martha has released two solo albums, *Solo One*, in 2013 and her 1995 children's album, *Songs from the Tree House*, which won a Juno Award, (Canada's equivalent to The Grammys) for Best Children's Album. Despite being diagnosed with Parkinson's Disease in 2000, Martha has remained active as a recording artist, collaborator and mentor to younger songwriters, as well as advocating for greater awareness of Parkinson's Disease.

ONE DAY IN PARIS
MARTHA JOHNSON
(Martha and the Muffins)

'One Day in Paris' came during a time of contradiction in my life when the band was at its peak with a top ten hit around the world. 'Echo Beach' had thrown us into a spotlight that we were trying to quickly adapt to. Success and strife went hand in hand.

During our European tour, we had a day off in Paris. I found myself wandering alone, trying to make the most of it while feeling abandoned by the rest of the band, who had already left the hotel. It seemed ironic to be the toast of the town, yet feel so alone and unsettled about how the six members of the band would survive all the changes and challenges we were facing.

When we came to record the song during the *This Is the Ice Age* sessions, our first of three albums co-produced with Daniel Lanois, my simple piano and voice arrangement was transformed into the atmospheric piece that appears on the album.

A beautiful ending to a melancholy day.

Bill Nelson by Bill Nelson

○ The enigmatic Bill Nelson was born in 1948 in Yorkshire, England. Bill first came to the fore when in the band Be Bop Deluxe; they had a UK top 20 hit with 'Ships in The Night'. Bill is a supreme multi-instrumentalist and prolific recorder of over 100 albums! He has recorded under several guises, namely, The Revox Cadets, Orchestra Arcana, Channel Light Vessel, The Lighthouse Signal Mechanism Orchestra, and, of course, Bill Nelson. Bill's music couldn't be more fascinating and varied, venturing from guitar-driven pop to ambient music. After Be Bop Deluxe folded in 1978, he moved to a NEW WAVEy guitar project called Bill Nelson's Red Noise and released the essential and defining album *Sound on Sound*. From the '80s he concentrated mostly as a solo musician and received critical acclaim for his experimental synthpop releases, namely the single 'Do You Dream in Colour?' and the marvellous albums *Quit Dreaming and Get on the Beam* and *The Love That Whirls (Diary of a Thinking Heart)*. His skilful use of samples, loops and the studio is mesmerizing and best exhibited on the Orchestra Arcana mini-LP *Sex, Psyche Etc*. Continuous recording through the '80s saw Bill become increasingly esoteric. He delved into found sounds, samples and music based around his personal interest in occult and Gnostic beliefs.

Soundtracks and voluminous ambient albums are the norm while still releasing the arty sound he is so well known for. The desire to share Bill's genius is shown by his collaborators in the likes of David Sylvian, Harold Budd, Roger Eno, Cabaret Voltaire and Yellow Magic Orchestra, all names with unquestionable musical credentials. His production works include the likes of The Skids, Gary Numan, Flock of Seagulls & Nash the Slash. Some of his output is not immediately "accessible", but he has something for everyone in his catalogue of a staggering amount of music.

◉ If you looked on December 19, 1981, you would have found Carlos Peron's debut solo album, *Impersonator*, a worthy Christmas present. This is an essential album for any Yello fan and was created while Peron was still part of the Swiss electronic band. Impersonator is a wonderful collage of cut-ups and soundbites that, while somewhat distant from the rhythmic, melodious works of Yello, remains intriguing. Combining ever-changing vocal samples and percussion from track to track, it is an absorbing, if challenging listen, that reveals more with repeated plays. Yello aficionados will enjoy hearing familiar sounds on this solo set, even as Peron would soon part ways with core members Boris Blank and Dieter Meier. Nonetheless, his influence remains with them to this day.

◉ Kevin "Geordie" Walker, the guitarist and a founding member of the POST-PUNK band Killing Joke, was born on December 18, 1958, in County Durham, England. In 1978, Geordie responded to an advertisement placed by vocalist Jaz Coleman and joined Killing Joke despite having never played in a band before. Geordie and Jaz went on to become the only constant members in Killing Joke over the decades. Geordie also played in the supergroups Murder, Inc., Pigface and The Damage Manual. Geordie died on November 26, 2023, 2 days after suffering a stroke.

19

◉ Limahl, born Christopher Hamill on December 19, 1958, in Lancashire, England, was the lead vocalist of the 1980s NEW WAVE band Kajagoogoo. Limahl, an anagram of his last name, fronted the pop group known for splashy, melodramatic songs that were hits with young fans. Shortly after Kajagoogoo released their debut album, *White Feathers*, Limahl was fired over creative differences. He went on to pursue a solo career, releasing three albums and several singles. Limahl is possibly best remembered for singing the theme song to the 1984 film *The Neverending Story*.

◉ To circumvent contractual restraints that prohibited him from releasing experimental music under his own name, Bill Nelson founded Orchestra Arcana in 1986 as an outlet for his avant-garde inclinations. This pseudonym gave Nelson the freedom to incorporate novel techniques like digital sampling and found sounds on the project's debut album, *Iconography*, which was released on December 19th of that year. With synthesizers, guitars, and an array of sampled human voices, the record allowed Nelson to indulge his creative spirit as sampling technology emerged. Tunes like 'Clock Conscious', 'The Gods Speak', and the title track showcase Nelson's adventurous embrace of this nascent art-form to craft music that is intriguing, seductive, and ahead of its time.

◉ It's Christmas 1982, and you rush out to get the *self-titled* debut EP by Visible Targets as a gift for your NEW WAVE friends. They would be thrilled with this first release from the Seattle band. Frontwoman Laura Keane's vocals are complemented by the harmonies and guitar work of sisters Rebecca Hamilton (bass) and Pamela Golden (guitar), rounded out by Greg Morlan's tasty guitar and Ron Simmons' methodical, precise drumming. The catchy melodies and hooks stand up to anything released that year. Impressively, the band was able to get Mick Ronson to produce their follow-up EP *Autistic Savant*, on which he reworked their excellent track 'Twilite Zone'.

20

⊙ Billy Bragg, born Steven William Bragg on December 20, 1957, in Barking, Essex, England, was dubbed 'The Bard of Barking' for his passionate social commentary set to a mix of punk rock and protest music. Though not revolutionary, Bragg struck a chord with his raw, heartfelt songs - just him and his electric guitar, inspired by Dylan and Guthrie. While widely popular for his original compositions, Bragg's only No.1 single was a cover of The Beatles' 'She's Leaving Home'.

⊙ Patrick Huntrods, born December 20, 1957, in London, England, was better known by his stage name Pat Fish or Black Eg. As the frontman of The Jazz Butcher and its many iterations, Fish was the only constant member across the band's revolving door of musicians. First debuting in Oxford on February 20, 1982, The Jazz Butcher developed an eccentric, left-field sound influenced by artists like Syd Barrett and Brian Eno. Fish became known for his surreal, imaginative lyrics as the band released a dozen critically acclaimed, yet moderately selling albums. After nearly 40 years with The Jazz Butcher, Fish passed away on October 5, 2021, at age 64, leaving behind a legacy of bizarre and brilliant music.

⊙ After releasing a couple of glam-rock albums, Japan made a mature transition to NEW WAVE with their album *Quiet Life*, released December 20, 1979. The band members openly disassociated themselves from their first two albums, saying this is where they found their direction. Artfully produced and skilfully arranged, the songs on *Quiet Life* are melodic, moody, and infectious. The individual performances here excel. Steve Jansen's ever-changing and inventive drumming creates rhythms that drive each track. Mick Karn's exquisite bass playing takes the instrument to another level that few at the time could equal, and his sublime horn playing also deserves mention. Keyboardist Richard Barbieri is meticulous in his sound selection and tonal work. Rob Dean's intricate yet subtle, understated guitar work provides the perfect background. Then there are David Sylvian's vocals - he croons and sways, enriching the high-quality music. *Quiet Life* represents an important step in Japan's progression toward greater things. It is a vital album.

Ed Keupper by Jude Keupper

⊙ Edmund "Ed" Kuepper, born in Bremen, West Germany, in 1955, migrated with his family to Brisbane, Australia, in the 1960s. Kuepper was a founding member of the seminal punk band The Saints in 1973, widely credited as pioneers of the punk genre. After The Saints disbanded in 1978, Kuepper formed the experimental POST-PUNK group Laughing Clowns in Sydney. Lauded for their unique jazz-punk fusion, Laughing Clowns gained a devoted following, especially for their critically acclaimed 1979 *self-titled* debut EP. Since then, Kuepper has forged an esteemed career as one of Australia's most prolific and revered recording artists, regularly releasing solo albums and touring extensively. He has collaborated on projects with diverse artists like Judi Dransfield-Kuepper, Nick Cave and the Bad Seeds, and the Queensland Symphony Orchestra. Kuepper also composes soundtracks for films such as Last Cab to Darwin and The Christmas Cake. Concurrently, he formed The Aints in the 1990s, an offshoot of The Saints. The Saints and The Aints have since reunited for performances and new recordings. Among his accolades, Kuepper received the inaugural GW McLennan Lifetime Achievement Award in 2012 and ARIA Hall of Fame induction with The Saints in 2001. His 2015 solo album *Lost Cities* earned widespread critical acclaim. Kuepper continues to record and perform as a solo artist and with his bands.

⊙ On December 20th, 1976, the band Malice performed their first ever concert at St. Wilfrid's Secondary School located in Crawley, England. This band would later change their name to Easy Cure and then finally settle on the name The Cure, which they are known as today.

⊙ On this day in 1982, Psychic TV released their debut LP, *Force the Hand of Chance*, on Some Bizzare Records. It marked the departure from Throbbing Gristle by Genesis P-Orridge and Peter "Sleazy" Christopherson. However, this record was no departure from the avant-garde for the duo. Force the Hand of Chance is an enigmatic work, traversing diverse musical territory from the pop stylings of 'Just Drifting' and 'Stolen Kisses' to the stark 'Terminus' to the POST-PUNK dancefloor jam 'Ov Power'. While perhaps unexpected from former Throbbing Gristle members, the genre-defying experimentation of Force the Hand of Chance aligns with Psychic TV's pioneering spirit.

⊙ Public Image Limited, aka PiL, played their debut "live" gig in Brussels, Belgium, on December 20, 1978. The lineup for this show was John Lydon – vocals, Keith Levene – guitar, Jah Wobble – bass, and Jim Walker – drums. Thankfully, the night featured the only time the B-side tune, 'The Cowboy Song', off their debut single, would ever be played, and it was played twice, in succession!

⊙ 'Voyage, Voyage', the debut single by Desireless, was rocketing up the European charts on December 21, 1986. Desireless was Claudie Fritsch-Mentrop, and her single went to No.1 in 10 European countries and even topped the charts in Thailand! Sung in French, it is plainly catchy and melodic and stood out amongst a plethora of Europop flooding out at the time. The success of this single would give her a great birthday present on Xmas day!

21

⊙ Ready for the Christmas market, *Forever Running*, the debut album by B-Movie, was released on December 21, 1985. The album featured re-recorded versions of the band's two hit singles, 'Remembrance Day' and 'Nowhere Girl'. Unfortunately, the album sold poorly. As a result, the band lost interest and split up, only to reappear about twenty years later. Aside from the two singles and the title track, there was little groundbreaking material. However, the album showcased B-Movie's solid synthpop sound, which stood out among many of their '80s peers. If you come across *Forever Running* in a second-hand store or bargain bin, consider picking it up to hear B-Movie's catchy melodies and synth lines.

⊙ On December 21, 1981, LiLiPuT, aka Kleenex, released their *self-titled* debut album in their homeland of Switzerland; it subsequently had a wider release in wider Europe in early 1982. This female four-piece was a true contender for the mantle left by The Slits: punchy, raw with a great sense of melody. The debut held textures wide and varied; it's quirky, it's boisterous, it's angular and at times abstract. The track 'Birdy' is a fine example, almost like The Residents or Velvet Underground. The vocals sit mostly in the back of the mix; there's a strange blend of chants and undecipherable harmonics. *LiLiPuT*, the album, is a sonic adventure in a way; the ladies are very experimental, and there's often an unexpected twist adding to the delightful journey. In 1980, Kleenex had to make a name change due to the threat of legal action from Kimberley-Clark, the worldwide manufacturer who held the trademark of 'Kleenex'.

Liliput by Petra Gall

⊙ Tony Lewis was born December 21, 1957, in London, England. Tony was best known to us as the bass player/vocalist for The Outfield. They had moderate sales success, but the single 'Your Love' went over big when in 1986, in the United States, the song reached No.6 on the Billboard chart. The song's success was largely due to its AOR sound and Lewis's delivery sounding like a Sting clone. Tony died on October 20, 2020.

22

⊙ Minimal Compact's *self-titled* EP was available December 22, 1981. This 5-piece from Israel had a dark atmospheric sound and was totally minimalist. The 5-track debut is worth buying if you ever see it for sale in a second-hand bin.

Minimal Compact by Petra Gall

⊙ The Cure released their debut single 'Killing an Arab' b/w '10:15 Saturday Night' on this day in 1978. Even though recorded during the sessions for the debut LP *Three Imaginary Boys*, the A-side was not included on the album. Internationally, with the aim to attract a new market, the album was renamed *Boys Don't Cry* with different track listing; 'Killing An Arab' was included on that LP. Essentially this was a compilation album of sorts.

⊙ On December 22, 2002, Joe Strummer, aka John Graham Mellor, died of a heart attack aged 50. Joe was the singer/guitarist with The Clash & The Mescaleros, the 101ers, Latino Rockabilly War, and the Pogues, as well as a successful solo career. If nothing else, Joe can always be connected to one of the greatest recordings of modern music, The Clash's *London Calling*, arguably one of the best, if not the best, LPs of the era.

23

⊙ December 23, 1955, is the birthdate of bassist and producer Dave Allen. Dave was an enormously influential part of the music scene from the late '70s and certainly developed a solid fan base through his superb bass playing. Dave was the second bassist with Gang of Four, joining in 1977 with the departure of Dave Wolson. In 1981 he left to form Shriekback with Barry Andrews, formerly of XTC, and Carl Marsh from Out on Blue Six. In 1988, after being part of the recording of 5 albums, he split from Shriekback to be part of King Swamp and then onto The Elastic Purejoy, who recorded on his label, World Domination Recordings, based in Los Angeles. Dave would go on to concentrate on production in advertising. Born in Kendal, England, at the age of 69, after living with early-onset dementia, Dave Allen died on April 6, 2025.

⊙ Guitar virtuoso Adrian Belew was born on December 23, 1949, in Covington, Kentucky. With an impressive resume envied by guitarists worldwide, Belew has extensively worked as both a session and touring musician. He is most well-known for his collaborations with influential artists and bands, including Talking Heads, David Bowie, Frank Zappa, Laurie Anderson, Paul Simon, The Tom Tom Club, and King Crimson. He is primarily recognised as a guitarist and singer with a highly unconventional and unique guitar style. Rather than relying on standard guitar tones and chords, he uses the guitar to produce unusual sounds that are often indistinguishable from animal noises or machine sounds. This limitless creativity defined his work with King Crimson from 1981 to 2009, during which he was the frontman and second guitarist to Robert Fripp on a dozen of their studio and live albums. The trilogy of *Discipline*, *Beat* and *Three of a Perfect Pair* showcase Belew's talents, especially on the NEW WAVE influenced track 'Elephant Talk'. Beyond performing, Belew has contributed to guitar design innovations including the Parker Fly. With nearly 20 solo albums released, 2023 saw Belew team up with Jerry Harrison for the *Remain in Light* tour, paying homage to the seminal 1980 Talking Heads album.

Adrian Belew with Bowie by Roch Parisien

FUCK YOU CAPTAIN TOM
ADRIAN BELEW
(Frank Zappa, David Bowie, Talking Heads, King Crimson et.al)

In 1978 I did my first tour of Europe as a guitarist and singer for Frank Zappa's band. One night when we played in Cologne, Germany, unbeknownst to me, Brian Eno was in the audience. Brian knew David Bowie was looking for a new guitarist for his upcoming tour. He called David after seeing our show and told David he should come to see the guitarist for Frank's band.

The next night we performed in Berlin. There was a part of the show where Frank took an extended guitar solo, and most of the band members, including myself, left the stage for a few minutes. As I walked to the back of the stage, I looked over at the monitor mixing board and saw David Bowie and Iggy Pop standing there.

Wow! I couldn't believe it!

So, I walked over to David Bowie, shook his hand and said, "*I love what you've done; thank you for all the music.*" And he said, "*Great, how would you like to be in my band?*" I motioned back towards Frank and said, "*Well, I'm kind of playing with that guy.*" David laughed and said, "*Yes, I know, but when Frank's tour ends, my tour starts two weeks later. Shall we talk about it over dinner?*".

David said he would meet me back at our hotel, and sure enough, when I arrived back at the hotel, David Bowie and his assistant Coco Schwab were sitting on a couch in the lobby. As I walked past them, they whispered to me, "*Get into the elevator, go up to your room, come back down in a few minutes, and meet us outside. We have a car waiting*".

It was like something out of a spy film!

When I came back down and went outside, there was a black limousine waiting. The driver opened the door, and I went in the back with David and Coco and he started telling me his plans for his upcoming tour, all the songs we would play, how the stage was set, the staging, and the like and so on, and how much he loved my guitar playing! It was so exciting! He said they were taking me to one of his favourite restaurants in Berlin.

How many restaurants are there in Berlin? 25,000?

We arrived at the restaurant, went in the front door, and who should be sitting at the very first table but Frank Zappa and the rest of the band! So, the three of us sat down with Frank and the band. David, trying to be cordial, motioned to me and said, "*Quite a guitar player you have here, Frank.*"

And Frank said, "*Fuck you, Captain Tom.*" (here Frank demotes David from being Major Tom to Captain Tom)

David persisted, "*Oh come on now, Frank, surely we can be gentlemen about this?*"

Frank said, "*Fuck you, Captain Tom.*"

I was stunned. David said, "*So you really have nothing to say?*" Frank said, "*Fuck you, Captain Tom.*"

David and Coco and I got up and went back out the front door. Getting in the limo, David said in his wonderfully British way, "*I thought that went rather nicely!*"

Adapted from YouTube: Thanks, Otis Gibbs.

◉ Grace Knight, born in Manchester, England, on December 23, 1955, first rose to fame as the lead singer of the NEW WAVErs Eurogliders. Forming in Perth, Australia, in the 1980s, Eurogliders enjoyed major chart success with hits like 'Heaven (Must Be There)', which reached No.2 in Australia and No.65 on the US Billboard Hot 100. After Eurogliders disbanded in the late 1980s, Knight embarked on a successful solo career as a jazz singer, releasing eight albums. She also had a small acting role in the 1989 TV miniseries *Come in Spinner*. In 2005, Knight briefly reunited with Eurogliders guitarist Bernie Lynch, and they have been touring festivals as Eurogliders since 2013. Most recently, in 2021, Eurogliders released a new album called *Blue Kiss Project*, and in 2023 Grace has teamed up with Wendy Matthews, performing as a duo.

EUROGLIDERS BY CHANCE
GRACE KNIGHT
(Eurogliders)

I worked my way to Australia on a cruise ship; my boyfriend and I got a spot on the ship providing some of the on-board entertainment. We were a singing duo called 'Kris & Kelly'.

When I was young, I thought Grace was an old-fashioned name, so for a couple of years or so, I was 'Kelly Knight'. My sister had moved to Australia a few years earlier as a 'ten-pound pom', and I missed her terribly. The job was supposed to start and finish in the UK, but I had no intention of going back there, so we 'jumped ship' when it docked in Perth. I arrived in sunny Australia in September 1977.

My boyfriend and I parted ways, and with no other marketable skills, I took any singing job I could find. I worked at Dirty Dick's Theatre Restaurant for a while. They had a Robin Hood and His Merry Men themed show, and I was featured as Maid Marion. I also went on to some cabaret work and eventually found my way into a cover band called 'Lumiere', which had two female lead singers and covered all the hits of the day.

One day I met Bernie Lynch at a BBQ at my sister's place; he was the lead singer in a band called 'Rip Torn & The Stockings'. At some point he worked out I was a singer and asked me to come and sing some backing vocals on a record he was making. Doing a recording back then was a pretty big deal, so I jumped at the opportunity. I remember Bernie plied me with Stone's Green Ginger Wine on the pretext it would help me relax!

When Bernie parted ways with The Stockings, he formed a band with Amanda Vincent called 'Living Single'. They'd probably been going for a few months or maybe a year when he asked me to join the band. Given he's a great singer, I wondered why he wanted me in the band; I think I just assumed it was because he fancied me. We'd been doing gigs around Perth for a while when we found out there was a band in the UK called Living Single. With the notion that one day we would become world famous, we decided to change the name to avoid confusion. We put a bunch of words in a hat, and the first two pieces of paper pulled out were 'glider' and 'euro', so we became Eurogliders!

Most of the successful bands in Perth at that time were playing covers; there really wasn't much of an appetite for unknown bands playing originals. In the early days we'd do any gig we could get, and often there would be nearly as many people in the band as in the crowd. Our big break came via a TV advert for a meat pie. A much more well-known artist that had the same management as Eurogliders was offered the gig; he was a vegetarian and didn't want to be associated with a meat pie and declined the offer. Somehow our management talked the client into hiring us for the job. The advert was for the 'Rage Pie' and was to promote the pie as a convenient bar snack while you were enjoying a night out at your favourite pub. The advert featured us landing in a helicopter with 'EUROGLIDERS' emblazoned on the side. It gave the impression we were an uber-rich and famous international rock band. The week before the advert went to air, we had only a handful of punters turning up at each show. As soon as the advert started, hundreds of people were turning up at each show thinking they were going to see the latest sensation from overseas.

With our now-expanding fan base, we were starting to get noticed by music industry folk, and soon enough we ended up with a recording contract. The 'Rage Pie' didn't take the bar food market by storm and disappeared as quickly as it had arrived; it worked an absolute treat for us though!

◉ Ollie Moore was born in Birmingham, England, on December 23, 1959, and grew up in Bristol, where his father was Head of Music at the BBC. As a saxophonist in 1980 Ollie joined Pigbag, the sensational horn-driven dance-punk unit who in 1982 had a No.3 UK charting single with the instrumental 'Papa's Got a Brand New Pigbag'. Inspired by jazz greats like Coltrane, Kuti and Cherry, he practised and refined his playing, and with Pigbag, played the same stage as his heroes at the Bracknell Jazz Fest. Pigbag earned respect from the media and critics alike, so much so that the famed punk documenter Don Letts met and filmed the band at Berry St. studios in London as they recorded the track live. The story goes that the "footage" never saw the light of day, as he didn't have any film in the camera! Ollie was also part of Float Up CP, who released only one studio album, *Kill Me in The Morning*, in 1985.

THE STORY OF PAPA'S GOT A BRAND NEW PIGBAG
OLLIE MOORE
(Pigbag Float UP CP)

It's important to say that the song was written collectively, as that was always the way we worked as a band; everyone had an equal input to the music that evolved. I think it's fair to say that Pigbag, the band, and the song 'Papa's Got a Brand New Pigbag' were inseparable in many people's views.

I will endeavour to explain my part in how this tune came to be. I am the only remaining member to live in Bristol; this is how my career in music started and the journey to 'Papa'.

My father wanted me to learn the clarinet whilst at Bristol Grammar School, and my uncle, who played clarinet in the London Symphony Orchestra, sourced a reasonable student model for me to play. I still remember the pleasant aroma of the instrument in its furry case with its cork and "woody" aroma. Any pleasant associations with this intriguing instrument were soon to be dashed by an extremely abusive, bad-tempered, impatient teacher called Mr Stone. I was 12 years old. He was a lumbering figure of a man who stood at about 6 feet three and wore a suit several sizes too small for him. He would correct my mistakes with a thrust of the base of the clarinet upwards against my teeth if I made a squeak or played a wrong note, his face bulging and turning puce in colour, as if he were about to burst a blood vessel, as he spat angry words in disgust at my incompetence. Consequently, after a few lessons with this monster, I stopped going altogether. I didn't tell my father, who was Head of Music, until the end of term.

1979, and I sold my year-old motorcycle, which I had saved up to buy, as the insurance had risen drastically, and bought a car for £95. I then bought a Martin tenor saxophone in silver from the music store in Hotwells. It cost £240. I was over the moon and so excited to learn how to play it...BY MYSELF!

I had met Simon Underwood; he was the bass player with The Pop Group. I had got to know him through going to their gigs. I knew the lead singer, Mark Stewart, having been at the same school together. Simon was becoming disillusioned with the band, and the inevitable clashes, personal and musical, had come to the fore. It was time for him to move on. He was becoming more and more interested in jazz and world music and was eager to experiment in that direction. He shared a lot of this music, and I was eager to lap it up, and I ended up buying a lot of records from him and from Tony's record store at Focus in Clifton village. I was devouring artists like John Coltrane, Archie Shepp, Don Cherry, Fela Kuti, Funkadelic, James Brown, and, of course, the totally out there Sun Ra and his Arkestra, just to name a few.

My parents were divorced by the time I had reached 18. The family house was sold, and I went to live with my father, who had bought a flat in Clifton. Unfortunately, my father wasn't very keen on me playing the sax in his flat, and I had several complaints from an elderly retired Austrian doctor, who lived in the flat below. A toilet roll stuffed down the bell of the saxophone wasn't a very effective mute. I was looking to move out within a few months. Fortunately for me, I moved in with old school friend Rich Beal (artist, singer, and songwriter with Head and Pregnant) in a tiny room at the top of the house on Regent St, Clifton. I was lucky enough to have friends who lived in a basement flat, and they would let me use their cellar to go and practise my saxophone without fear of upsetting too many neighbours. This was just a temporary move until I moved into a squat in Hotwells. This was called Trinity Rooms and was a great place (and free!) to live, as there was a rehearsal room there, where we could play pretty much whenever we wanted. It also had an empty church hall out the back with a great natural reverb echo.

My first band was called Fish Food, featuring the (now sadly departed) hugely talented and eccentric singer/poet Andy Fairley, who went on to record with the mighty Adrian

Sherwood and On U Sound. Howard Purse was on guitar; Daniel Swan, former Cortinas drummer, also featured. The Cortinas were the first proper punk band I ever saw. They supported The Damned at Malvern Winter Gardens in 1976. They were riveting.

The first gig I played was at the Granary in Bristol on Welsh Back. A band called Double Vision was playing, featuring Melanie Dicks on vocals and Rob Merrill on drums. I ended up on stage with Mark Stewart, who was singing a version of Max Romeo's 'Chase the Devil'. I had been playing sax for about 3 months by now! A little while later I hitched up to Hitchin in Hertfordshire and played with The Pop Group. On this occasion they had two drummers, Bruce Smith and Brian Nevill, who later joined Pigbag after Chip had left in 1982.

In the spring of 1980, I was jamming with Simon, and we had been put in touch with some guys in Cheltenham who had heard that Simon had left The Pop Group and asked if he would be interested in playing with them. We would go up to Cheltenham and play in a place called Beech House in a room with black walls. Sadly, early recordings of these sessions were lost from an Akai reel-to-reel tape recorder. These were the sessions where 'Papa' was born, and it would go on for about 20 minutes in a frenzy of percussion, including frying pans and horns! The band was James Johnstone and Chip Carpenter, who were in a punk band called Hardware. Roger Freeman was on timbales and percussion, and Chris Hamlin on congas and clarinet, and I was with Simon Underwood. Chris Lee was on trumpet.

After a trip to France picking fruit, I returned after a six-week stay on the day The Pop Group played their last gig at a huge CND rally in Trafalgar Square on 26/10/1980. Coming back to Bristol, things had moved on; Pigbag had played their first gig supporting the Slits at Romeo and Juliet's, and fortunately, I was welcomed back to the fold.

Dick O'Dell had approached Simon with a view to managing us, and he wanted to record 'Papa'. We rehearsed at Janine Rainforth's dad's house in a village outside Keynsham, called Burnett, near Bristol. Janine was a keyboardist vocalist who was a co-founder of the band Maximum Joy. I remember that it was the day that John Lennon was shot and killed in New York by Mark Chapman. 8th December 1980.

My first gig with the band was at a Bristol Recorder event at the Anson Rooms at Bristol University. We were supposed to be top of the bill; that is, we were to play last.
The other acts, including the Electric Guitars, played over their allocated times, and we were left with 20 minutes before the curfew. The porters turned the power off, and we carried on acoustically, banging frying pans and blasting away on the horns for a good 20 minutes longer.

We continued rehearsing with a view to arranging 'Papa' to around 3 and a half minutes. This took place in Cheltenham, and we were booked into the studio in Berry St. Studios in Clerkenwell, London. This was March of 1981. Legendary filmmaker and documenter of the punk movement Don Letts was there with his video camera.

He filmed us as we recorded it. Unfortunately, despite trying to obtain the footage, the story goes that he didn't actually have any film in the camera!

As we were still raw, rough, self-taught musicians high on energy, we didn't have a grasp of bar lengths and sections, so when it came to recording the solos, it was decided that Roger would stand in front of us with a stopwatch, and after 1 minute of free blowing, he would signal us to end!

Dick O'Dell, in what turned out to be a very shrewd move, withheld the official release of 'Papa'. This was after a year or so of regularly selling 1000-odd singles weekly and attaining top position in the independent charts of the time. The strategy worked, and in the summer of 1982, the single entered the top 40 playlist, and Radio 1 had to give it airplay. The preorder sales had built up over 6 weeks or so, and at that time the chart positions were based on weekly sales. We got to No.30, then No 9, then No 3! We were denied the No.1 slot by Bucks Fizz and Paul McCartney and Stevie Wonder with 'Ebony and Ivory'!

I remember it well, on a sunny Tuesday afternoon, on the green outside my flat, listening to the radio, hearing the chart countdown. Happy times. It makes me want to thank my clarinet teacher, Mr Stone, who ensured that I was going to teach myself the saxophone and play it in my own way.

Recently at work, one of my colleagues introduced me to two other workers at Bristol docks.

"Do you know who this is? ...Do you remember Pigbag?"

"Yeah", one of the guys, who was about my age, replied, "My mate was the only one who could dance to that song."

Back in the day there had been some discussion about whether we should do TOTP. We were concerned about "selling out". Luckily, we decided to do it. Roger Freeman wasn't happy though, as he claimed we had told him that he couldn't wear his donkey jacket, which he always wore. He decided not to appear and subsequently left the band. That was a shame. He is a very talented musician and taught himself trombone in a short space of time. He played a solo on the 12-inch extended version of the song. My only regret now is that we didn't include the single on our debut album, *Dr Heckle and Mr Jive*. Our worthy reasoning was that we wanted people to hear new material, as we felt we had moved on since recording 'Papa', and people could hear it by buying the single.

A couple of my most enduring memories are from the summer of 1982. Pigbag played the Bracknell Jazz Festival, and a subsequent review in the Guardian described my saxophone tone as like being in an iron foundry! And when we supported the Specials at the Rainbow in Finsbury Park (later to become infamous as a mosque where the radical Muslim Abu Hamza made his hate speeches). The Specials had just written 'Ghost Town' and were playing it in Soundcheck with the great late Rico Rodriguez on trombone. Wafts of ganja smoke drifted out from the open door of the dressing room as the legendary trombonist warmed up on his instrument. We were very nervous to be playing in front of a huge crowd of mods and skinheads and ended up playing at nearly twice the tempo. Jerry Dammers was grinning at the side of the stage, encouraging us. We were on for about 25 minutes.

After a couple of numbers, one of the youths at the front shouted, *"Oi, what's the name of the band?"* (The single wasn't in the charts at this time.) James Johnstone, our guitarist, percussionist and keyboards player, leant forward and politely said, *"Pigbag"*.

"What? Pigshit?"

We were then met with chants of *"PIGSHIT"* after each number; regardless, I think they enjoyed it really, though.

I have enjoyed writing this piece and recalling that period of my life. So, to anybody who has chosen to give time to read about this era, I am proud to have been a part of Bristol's musical history.

◉ Martin Plaza, aka Martin Murphy, was born in Sydney, Australia, in 1956. Martin, who took his name from a Sydney pedestrian mall, is famed as a founding member, vocalist, guitarist, and songwriter with Mental as Anything and a solid member until 2015. With the Mentals, he was part of all their 14 album recordings. He also was part of Beatfish with James Freud, in The Stetsons, and leading Martin Plaza and The Lost Vegans. As a soloist, in 1986 Martin went to No.2 on the Australian charts with his cover of the 1960s Unit 4+2 song 'Concrete and Clay'.

24

◉ Ian Burden, born in 1957 in Sheffield, England, is best known as the bassist and keyboardist for the band Human League. After studying audio and visual arts at Sheffield Hallam University, Burden took inspiration from German electronic bands like Neu!, Kraftwerk, and Tangerine Dream to form the band Graph with some old friends. When Graph disbanded, Burden was invited by Phil Oakey to initially work as a session musician on Human League's album *Dare*. He later joined the band full-time from 1981 to 1987, until touring fatigue and a lack of creative experimentation diminished his enthusiasm. During his tenure with Human League, Burden co-wrote many of the band's hit songs with Oakey, leaving a strong legacy. Following his departure from Human League, he ventured into a solo career, releasing Loot in 1990 and, after a considerable hiatus, Hey Hey Ho Hum in 2018. In the early 2000s, he contributed to the first two albums by the Melbourne darkwave band The Tenth Stage, as well as the album *State of Decay* by the German band Parralox in 2009.

I'M HUMAN
IAN BURDEN
(The Human League)

Like anyone, I've had my share of embarrassing and interesting experiences.
Embarrassing:

In Stockholm, Sweden, when backstage with The Human League, I was in one of my very rare bad moods. Nobody had told me about a photo opportunity for the Swedish national press. So, I wasn't at all prepared. When asked, *"We'd like you to pose next to Frida,"* my grumpiness led me to ask, *"Who the f**k is Frida?"* I turned, and sitting within earshot of me was this attractive blonde woman. I wasn't too familiar with ABBA at the time, and I hadn't recognised her, so how was I to know?
Interesting:

We were in George Martin's Air Studios for the recording of what was to be Human League's 1984 *Hysteria* album. Needing a break, I walked into the recreation area and discovered one legendary Paul McCartney staring fixedly at a wall, completely unresponsive to my cheery *"Hello,"* as I waved a hand in front of his face. There was no blinking, facial expression, or movement whatsoever. I panicked and ran down to our control room exclaiming what I'd seen, thinking he might be dead (even though we all know Paul died many years ago!). Our producer laughed, explaining, *"Paul often sleeps with his eyes open. Paul is only sleeping... Please don't wake him; he's drifting upstream!"*

It's unfortunate that so much synthpop from France did not reach a wider audience. This is certainly true of Taxi Girl, whose music could rival bands like OMD and Human League. Their debut single in 1979, the pulsating, infectious 'Mannequin', unmistakably signalled vast promise for the band. With its melodious sound, it's a song that's hard to get tired of.

25

⦿ Robin Campbell, the guitarist for the reggae band UB40, was born in 1954, in Birmingham, England. He is the brother of UB40's vocalist Ali Campbell and the son of the Scottish folk singer Ian Campbell. Before joining UB40, Robin worked as an apprentice toolmaker. His brother Ali persuaded him to buy a guitar and join Ali's band, which already included six other friends. In addition to his music career with UB40, Robin has worked as an actor and appeared in several films.

⦿ Claudie Fritsch-Mentrop, born in Paris on December 25, 1952, first gained fame as the Euro-synthpop artist Desireless. Her debut 1986 single 'Voyage Voyage' reached No.1 in 11 countries. Still active today, Claudie has released a dozen albums and numerous singles and EPs under the Desireless moniker over her decades-long career.

⦿ Annie Lennox, born in Aberdeen, Scotland, on December 25, 1954, is arguably one of the premier female pop/rock artists of the '80s. After the split of The Tourists, she partnered with Dave Stewart to form Eurythmics. Her work with Eurythmics is often underrated, as the vocal arrangements and production on many of their recordings were largely due to

Annie's tireless hours alone with an engineer in the studio without Stewart. Following a decade of collaboration, Eurythmics dissolved in 1990, and Lennox released her first solo album, *Diva*, in 1992. *Diva* showcased a soulful, mature departure from the electronic Eurythmics sound of the 1980s. Throughout her career, Lennox continued to push boundaries with her live performances, including male backup dancers in ballet attire and bear costumes.

◉ Shane MacGowan was born on Xmas Day 1957 in Pembury, Kent, England, to Irish parents and grew up in Tipperary, Ireland. In 1976, using the pseudonym Shane O'Hooligan, he formed the punk rock band The Nipple Erectors, his first foray into music. After playing in several bands, MacGowan became the bassist and vocalist for Pogue Mahone (which translates to 'Kiss My Arse'); they later changed their name to The Pogues. Pogue Mahone played their first gig in October 1982. While The Pogues did not find great international success, they were hugely popular in the UK and Ireland, especially after their 1987 single 'Fairytale of New York' featuring Kirsty MacColl brought them some worldwide recognition. The Pogues split in 1991, after which MacGowan formed Shane MacGowan and The Popes, releasing two albums. The Pogues reunited in 2001 for a reunion tour before disbanding again in 2014. Until his passing on November 30, 2023, MacGowan made occasional live appearances, most notably with The Pretenders in 2019.

◉ On Christmas Day 1978, Public Image Ltd (PiL) played their first UK gig at The Rainbow Theatre in London. This was the first of 2 nights. The band, consisting of John Lydon, Jah Wobble, Keith Levene and Jim Walker, had started rehearsing in mid-1978 but were yet to decide on a name. Lydon chose the name 'Public Image' after the Muriel Spark novel The Public Image. A few months later, they added the suffix 'Ltd'. Their first release was the single 'Public Image' apparently written while Lydon was still a member of the Sex Pistols. The single performed well, reaching No.9 on the UK charts and charting respectably as an import in the USA. The B-side of their debut single, 'The Cowboy Song', was played live only twice, back-to-back, at PiL's debut performance in Brussels, Belgium, a week earlier.

◉ Merry Xmas. After his pioneering work with Suicide, 1980 marked the release of Alan Vega's *self-titled* debut solo album. This recording carries Vega's signature style - detached, cold, and alienated - yet with a slightly more subdued energy. Propulsive rhythms permeate the record, often with a rockabilly twang that evokes rock and roll's past. 'Fireball' especially highlights Vega's Elvis Presley-inspired vocals. Though still unmistakably Alan Vega with his chilling, hypnotic atmospherics, the album points toward new directions for this extraordinary singer and performer. There's no escaping that singular Suicide sound, with its beguiling mix of electronics and vocals, but here Vega's solo work carves out fresh territory that deserves to be heard.

26

◉ Amanda Kramer's birthday is December 26, 1961. Amanda has one of those resumes that any keyboardist would find enviable; in recent times, since 2003, she has been part of the touring band of The Psychedelic Furs and in the past worked with numerous artists and bands such as World Party, Lloyd Cole, Steve Kilbey, Tom Bailey, Julee Cruise and Siouxsie Sioux, among others. In the late '80s Amanda had a tenure of a couple of years with Information Society before departing and joining The Golden Palominos; she appears on their 1989 album *A Dead Horse* as vocalist. As a highly trained musician, aside from her foray into the music of film and television, she released a solo album in 2004 called *Fallen Light Renew*.

◉ Steven Pearse, better known as Stevo, was born in Haverhill, Suffolk County, England, on December 26, 1962. He is best known as a music producer and owner of the record label

Some Bizzare Records. In January 1981, Stevo released the seminal compilation LP *Some Bizzare Album*, which featured unsigned artists who would soon achieve worldwide fame. With genres like New Romantic and synthpop still emerging, Stevo took a gamble by exposing acts like Soft Cell, Depeche Mode, The The, and Blancmange. In the early 1980s, Stevo also hosted Stevo's Electro Tunes events in London, providing exposure to avant-garde electronic acts like Fad Gadget, Psychic TV, and DAF. His foresight and risk-taking helped launch the careers of many influential bands in the nascent synthpop and NEW WAVE scenes.

SOME BIZZARE HISTORY
STEVO PEARCE
(Producer, Label Owner)

I spent my childhood in a small Suffolk town, playing in local cornfields and woods, or at the aptly named "newt pond". These days of innocence evaporated when my family moved back to the East End of London in the summer of 1973. I was ten. It was like being propelled from innocence to ignorance overnight. Everyone in London seemed much more grown-up and worldly wise than I was. Survival meant "growing up" fast.

I was only thirteen when punk exploded. It was part of the "growing up". I got into the POST-PUNK avant-garde. I enjoyed the new synthesizer-driven music of the POST-PUNK late '70s: Cabaret Voltaire, early Ultravox (led by John Foxx before the arrival of Midge Ure), Kraftwerk, the Normal (Daniel Miller), early Human League, and early OMD. I was listening to these bands long before almost anyone else had heard of them. At that point, only Kraftwerk had made any dent in the charts.

I started a weekly "futurist" night club upstairs at the Chelsea Drug Store on the King's Road, which had been made famous in the lyrics of the Rolling Stones' You Can't Always Get What You Want. Word spread, and soon I was invited to compile a weekly "futurist chart" for Sounds, which, at that time, was an influential music paper. I began to receive tapes from new and unknown bands, including Depeche Mode and Soft Cell. The spell at the Chelsea Drug Store didn't last long. The heavy metal crowd downstairs didn't think much of their bizarrely dressed and made-up neighbours dancing to the weird and wonderful sounds upstairs. One night, they invaded our space, physically abusing those in attendance and causing damage. The owners of the drugstore did not want to see a repeat of the violence and unceremoniously shut us down. The moral of the story would seem to be that violence pays! By this time, however, I was already being offered gigs at other venues and was making connections with new artists, including Depeche Mode and Soft Cell, who were invited to record tracks for the *Some Bizarre Album*, the compilation album which launched Some Bizarre Records.

The rest, as they say, is history. After Tainted Love became an international bestseller, I was catapulted into the stratosphere of the music business, travelling the world and earning more money than I could have imagined in my wildest dreams. It was a roller-coaster ride, a blur. Henning Schmitz, born in Germany on December 26, 1953, is a member of the band Kraftwerk. He officially joined the group as a full member in 1991 after keyboardist Fernando Abrantes left. Well prior to 1991 Henning had been working as Kraftwerk's chief sound engineer in their Kling Klang studio in Dusseldorf and earned a credit on their 1986 album *Electric Café*. Henning operates production services from his X.1 studio.

27

◉ Terry Bozzio, born on December 27, 1950, is renowned for playing one of the largest drum kits in the world and for his work with Missing Persons and Frank Zappa. With Missing Persons, Bozzio appeared on 5 albums and an EP. He also played on 26 albums with Zappa and has released over a dozen solo albums. After drummer Bill Bruford left the prog-rock band UK in late 1978, Bozzio joined Eddie Jobson and John Wetton to continue UK as a trio. In 1997, Bozzio was inducted into the Modern Drummer Hall of Fame. His daughter Marina and son Raanen have both followed in his footsteps as drummers, with Marina playing in the heavy metal band Aldious.

◉ Ged Duffy was born on December 27, 1960, in Manchester, England. In 1980, he was a founding member of the band Stockholm Monsters, which released several singles and one album, *Alma Mater*, on Factory Records. The album was produced by Peter Hook of New Order. In 1981 and '82, Stockholm Monsters toured as the opening act for New Order, with Hook handling their live sound mixing. In 1982, Duffy formed the band Lavolta Lakota, releasing one single and opening for bands like Death Cult, The Fall, and New Order. Once again, Peter Hook mixed the live sound for Duffy's new band. Ged Duffy is also known for working as a DJ at the famous Manchester clubs Russell and Hacienda. He later wrote a candid memoir, Factory Fairy Tales, documenting his experiences at those legendary venues.

MANCHESTER TALES
GED DUFFY
(Stockholm Monsters, Club DJ, Roadie, Author)

THE LAST GIG BY JOY DIVISION IN MANCHESTER, APRIL 11, 1980.
Joy Division played Russell with Mini Pops, and Crawling Chaos, this was the last time I ever saw them. I DJed that night and the place was packed with 900 in, but I think that there were a few more than that as Alan was never known to turn anyone away. Due to the trouble at their last gig here, Rob had hired some Hells Angels from Wythenshawe to do the security. These guys were rough and caused a lot of tension with the crowd all evening. Crawling Chaos were absolutely shit. Minny Pops were good - a bit quirky, a bit industrial, a bit pop. They were Dutch and their singer, Wally, was a great laugh.

I was loving being the DJ and The Furs, The Bunnymen, Teardrop Explodes, The Banshees, Killing Joke, and The Doors all got a blasting on the night. Gretton told me that they would be on in 15 minutes, so I lopped on 'Sister Ray' by The Velvet Underground, all 17 minutes of it. Rob immediately turned round and said, *"You twat"* and I said, *"Give us three or four songs in its place"*. In due course they came on and played the best I ever saw them. Included in the set were 'Shadowplay', 'Love Will Tear Us Apart', and a few songs off the soon to be released Closer. They finished with 'She's Lost Control'. Slim and I watched them from the DJ Box at the rear of the stage, so I was standing directly behind Hooky and saw first-hand what an amazing drummer Stephen Morris was. I was fascinated by Barney playing the synthesiser on some of the songs and it was weird watching Ian dance from behind as opposed to being in front of him. It was such a brilliant gig and I still recall it at times when I'm listening to Closer or Unknown Pleasures.

As soon as they went off Gretton walked on stage and grabbed the mike and said *"Joy Division will not be coming back on again tonight and if any of you bastards throw a bottle at me there definitely will be hell. I'll come and kick you all in"*. At this he got bombarded with bottles and ran off the stage with a big grin on his face. They came back on to the sort of cheers that a gladiator might expect, the Ged Duffy 114 115 audience erupted. I looked at Slim and said, *"These fuckers have finally made it, they're going to be fucking massive"*. They played 'Atrocity Exhibition' and sent the crowd wild.

As they went off Rob nodded to me to put a song on as they were not coming on again so since my Velvet Underground album was still on the deck I played 'Pale Blue Eyes'. I'm actually welling up as I write this as they were so fucking good and it's such a shame what happened a few weeks later. I've recently read that 'Pale Blue Eyes' was one of Ian's favourite songs. I don't know if that is true or not but if it is then he would have been pleased walking into the dressing room listening to it ringing out in the Russell on the night that Joy Division finally conquered Manchester.

OPENING NIGHT AT THE HACIENDA, MAY 21, 1982

On 21st May 1982 The Hacienda (FAC 51) opens its doors. Terry Mason, Slim, 'Rocking' Dave Holmes and I were the first stage crew and we got there in the afternoon to set up for an all-female band from New York called ESG. First thing we noticed was that they had changed the design totally from what Rob Gretton had told us when he had been taken round a few months ago. The stage was now in the middle of the club on the right-hand side. We noticed that the stage had a low ceiling which meant that most bands would not be able to use their own lighting rig when they played here. It also stopped bigger bands from using their own backdrops as they wouldn't fit. It was a terrible design.

The DJ Booth was tucked away in the corner of the stage, and they couldn't see anything that was happening in the club, and no one could approach them to request a song. A few weeks late, it was relocated to the middle of the balcony, which was a great spot. The area in front of the stage where the crowd would stand had walls and bollards round it so it was enclosed, and it had a step to get onto it which you would not see in the dark. Health and Safety would have made them change this design and make the floor open. The way it was designed drastically cut down the number of people who could see a band.

The ceiling was the same as before, mega high with a glass roof. This would bugger up the sound and in the summer months, bring daylight into the club. You want a dark club, not a sunlit one. When you came through the doors and turned into the club it looked amazing, but as a venue to see a band it was dreadful. The dressing room was massive, clean, had working plug sockets, was well lit, and even had flowers set up in there. It was nothing like the shitholes that we had been in at all the clubs we worked or played. The Russell was nothing like this.

We set up the stage and it was Oz doing the PA and then waited for the place to open. The club had to be "Members Only" to obtain the drinks license so Terry, Slim, Dave and I were given Honorary Membership cards with our names embossed into them, but Peter Saville hadn't delivered them yet. We got them about a week later. The cost of a membership was £5.25. This membership guaranteed a free ticket to see New Order and a free ticket to see ACR. They sold 3,000 memberships and most of them never got to see New Order.

On this first night, the audience were made up of a lot of press who came up from London and important movers and shakers from Manchester, so it was a free bar. We noticed that there was a token machine next to the bar which you took a token from, and you would get served when your number came up. They used this system for the first two months and finally realized that a club audience waiting for a drink act differently than Mrs. Jones waiting for her bacon in Asda, so they scrapped it.

We went downstairs and discovered a small cocktail bar called The Gay Traitor with a list of cocktails from A to Z. Slim and I tried everyone in order and then stuck with a Zum Zum which was double vodka, double gin, and fresh orange juice. It took us a few weeks to get to this decision but then we would start each night in there with one of these. Halfway down these stairs there was a seating area and most times Rob, Wilson, and the Factory lot could be found there. Slim and I used to spend time sitting there with them when we weren't busy.

There was also a restaurant area with tables and chairs where we introduced ourselves to the chef and Suzanne the waitress. I can't remember the name of the chef and he would only be there for two months. Opposite the stage there were American Diner style seating: long, padded bench seats with a table separating them. These cubicles were all along the side of the wall and at each end there were stairs going up to the balcony. There were more tables and chairs set upstairs there.

After it opened, we went outside to see how large the queue was, and it went round the corner of the street. Paul Weller from The Jam turned up and walked past the whole queue and tried to get in. He didn't have a membership and wasn't on the guest list, so he got turned away. He used the "Do you know who I am" line but it didn't work. He turned round and walked off and took some abuse off the waiting queue. At this time, The Jam were probably the biggest band on the planet, but he wasn't welcome at the Hac.

The club was opened by Bernard Manning, a famous blue Manchester comedian and when he came out on stage he got heckled by the crowd. He took one look at the place, turned to Tony Wilson, and said, "Worse fucking club I've ever played in", walked off, didn't accept his fee and went home. ESG were three sisters from New York who played a set of bass heavy funk which frankly bored me to tears. This would become the norm for Slim and I as Mike Pickering booked some utter dross over the next few months. Once they had gone off Vinny Reilly from Durutti Column played a Grand Piano on stage while Tony Wilson joined with him to sing a bit and play a bit. We had so much fucking fun getting that stupid grand piano on and off the stage.

It was impossible to hear anything as the acoustics of the place were awful due to the amount of open space the sound could travel. To be honest I don't think the audience missed much by not hearing it. When the DJ played his records, the sound was dreadful too as everything he played just went Boom, Boom, Boom Rob Gretton said that the sound system had cost £30,000 to be installed and I told him that they must have seen him coming as it sounded wank. He agreed with me - it would be upgraded in a couple of months. The new sound system improved the sound from the DJ, but the stage sound was still awful. A few months later they installed large solid plastic strips hanging from the ceiling to the floor which acted as a barrier to the main area of the club. You would come into the club and then push open these strips to enter the stage and bar area. They were like a giant fly screen that you would find in cafés and shops. They looked awful and didn't match the décor of the club, but they improved the live sound of the bands and helped to get rid of some of the echo. I also think that they should have installed a false ceiling as this would have helped as well.

The club was open seven nights a week and at lunchtime on Saturday and Sunday. They did this for the first six months and then dropped the Saturday lunchtime and completely closed on a Sunday. There was a giant video screen at either side of the stage, and they hired a video guy called Claude to control these screens. He would mix lots of images and just play them when the DJ was playing his records. So, you could see an image of Hitler giving a speech followed by Mickey Mouse eating an ice cream. Every band that played there got filmed by Malcolm Whitehead and would be given a copy of their gig before they left free of charge.

The following night Cabaret Voltaire played to a crowd of about 70 people all bunched together on the dance floor. This would turn out to be the norm. Slim and I went along on each night of the first week and there were about ten people in each night. We got free food off the chef, free cocktails downstairs, and free beer at the bar. This would become our routine. Next up was Teardrop Explodes who played a secret word-of-mouth gig and only seven people turned up. There were more staff than customers. Fair play to the band who put on a proper show, but it was a very informal gig, and they were followed by 23 Skidoo who also played in front of a small crowd again. I enjoyed them.

(With permission: extracted excerpts from Ged Duffy's Factory Fairy Tales)

⦿ After 12 years of making music together, the Australian indie rock band The Go-Betweens broke up in December 1989, much to the surprise of drummer Lindy Morrison, violinist Amanda Brown, and bassist Michael Armiger. Though critically acclaimed for their intelligent lyrics and unique sound, which blended unusual instrumentation with literate songwriting, The Go-Betweens had struggled to find commercial success in their home country. Years of relentless touring and fraying relationships between singer-songwriters

Grant McLennan and Robert Forster ultimately led the duo to decide to disband the group. The Go-Betweens had released six albums between 1977 and 1989, developing an international cult following despite their lack of mainstream popularity in Australia. McLennan and Forster briefly reformed the band with new members in 2000, but after McLennan's sudden death from a heart attack in 2006, The Go-Betweens split up once more, ending the influential group's three-decade run.

◉ Youth, aka Martin Glover, was born on 27th December 1960 in Slough, England. Adopting the moniker Youth (originally Pig Youth, as a nod to the reggae deejay Big Youth), as an 18-year-old he was a founding member and bassist of Killing Joke, and he was also the first of the original lineup to leave, though he re-joined them on three occasions. Dissatisfied with KJ's goings-on, he first parted ways after the release of 1982's *Revelations* album and formed Brilliant with KLF's Jim Cauty. From here, intrigued with music design, he has concentrated on production work with a vast array of artists, from Wet Wet Wet to U2 to Tom Jones to Crowded House & The Orb, among many others. The effect he has had on finished products cannot be overstated; go no further than The Verve's glorious 'Bitter Sweet Symphony', for example. Not many people get the chance to work with Paul McCartney, and with him, Youth released three albums as The Firemen, the first being 1993's stunning ambient/trance set *Strawberries Oceans Ships Forest*.

AN INTERVIEW WITH YOUTH aka Martin Glover (via Zoom)

Hi mate, what do you prefer to answer to, Youth or Martin? I understand that the name Youth was borrowed from the DJ reggae artist, right?

I prefer Youth and yes, the name comes from him indirectly. Though he is an inspiration for the Dub music I'm known for.

Growing up, your formative years, what drove you to music? Was it a household thing? Pop music or prog-rock as a teen?

Dancing in front of a mirror with a tennis racquet when I was about 9 years old, miming The Sweet, David Bowie, Marc Bolan, and The Beatles. Prog really wasn't a thing for me, maybe a little bit. I was definitely into Pink Floyd and Zeppelin. In London we were known as Soul Boys when I was 14 /15, right into jazz and funk, I progressed into dub and reggae.

As a musician, were you trained, took lessons or self-taught? Why bass, you're known for that as your weapon of choice?

I was self-taught, yeah. I learnt guitar like most. I could play guitar, and I went to an audition as a bass player, I had never played bass, but I passed the audition with Rage and joined the band. My favourite bass-players were and are Paul McCartney, Robbie Shakespear, Jaco Pastorius and Carol Kaye.

What was it like in those early days, your first band?

It was a great experience, we did it cheap. We had the dole, 20 quid to live on. I lived in a squat, it wasn't just handy, it was smart, the houses weren't occupied, so we occupied them. We'd just hang out and got stoned, telling stories, so easy going.

Killing Joke has been around for 40 plus years what do you attribute that longevity to?

It has been a constant struggle and to put it simply, chaos really.

You've toured the world, played everywhere. What gig sticks in your mind?

(Long Pause) Reading, The Hexagon 1981. It was just a magical time. Just before the band imploded, those gigs at that time were just so special. I was tasking a lot of LSD back then, so it was pretty magical and psychedelic.

As for KJ recordings, do you have a favourite?

I don't look back that much; I'm usually thinking of what is to come or where I am presently. Recording has peaks and valleys, I suppose the *Pandemonium* album and doing the vocals in the King's Chamber of The Great Pyramid of Giza, that was outstanding. The recording of What's This For, the second album, with Nick Launay was pretty special. Those couple and the earlier recordings would have a great influence on what I was to do in the future as a producer and writer.

Can you extrapolate on the Giza thing?

What!? Geezer Butler? (both laughing). Love Geezer Butler, Love Sabbath. I was listening to Sabbath the other day and I thought, they are quite Beatlesy, the song structures and even the melodies. Very Beatles in a weird way. Anyway, I've diverted.

Tell me something about your travels and music history?

I remember, we had a promotion in New York City, Ruth Polsky first took us there. We were booked to tour with Joy Division, but Ian died. New York in 79-80 was incredible. We had some amazing gigs in the United States. The club scene was so different to playing pubs in London. You know, we had only played 15 gigs before we headlined The Lyceum, it came together very fast. We were introducing elements like dub and disco, and not everyone got us, they do more now than back then. We did the support for Joy Division's last tour; I learnt a lot from those gigs and the atmosphere they created. Before Killing Joke, I was in The Rage, and luckily, we scored a residency at Eric's, at the time I was living in a that squat with Budgie who went on to be in Big In Japan and later on The Banshees and that's when I learnt to play.

Eric's in Liverpool was pretty important as a venue?

Yeah, most certainly, Eric's was the showcase venue, and Liverpool was the cornerstone for POST-PUNK and psychedelia, and still is. When I left Killing Joke and started my other band Brilliant, we had David Balfe from Teardrop Explodes and Bill Drummond managing us, they were closely connected to Eric's, so we had close connections there.

What do you know of Australian bands? It's been said and sparks many an argument, that The Saints from Brisbane were the first true punk band?

The first tour, by my first band The Rage, was being third on the bill for 32 dates as support to The Adverts and The Saints. The Saints just blew my mind every night, an incredible band! That tour was the catalyst to getting that residency at Eric's, so much exposure with such a killer band. Such great things in Australia, I loved the Bad Seeds out of Melbourne, they were amazing.

What's on your turntable at the moment?

Nothing is constant, I'm flipping through jazz, free jazz. Alice Coltrane, Pharoah Sanders. I'm listening to all sorts, seventies, The Shadows, a lot of ambient like Popol Vah and the Kompakt Label, Popol Vah are probably my favourite band at the moment. Of course, Roedelius, all that ambient noise stuff. Sixties psychedelic punk, world music, Indian music. All kinds. My taste is rather eclectic.

Youth! The clock is ticking!... We are running out of time! OH NO!, we have run out of time..............Lost him! Couldn't reconnect... bummer!

⦿ Sandii, born Sandi A. Hohn in Tokyo, Japan, on December 27, 1952, is a Japanese-American singer who has performed under many names. The daughter of a US Navy officer and a Japanese mother, she first gained fame as the vocalist for the band Sandii & the Sunsetz. Led by her husband, Makoto Kubota, the band spent significant time recording and touring in the UK with artists like David Sylvian, Fun Boy Three, YMO, Japan, Eurythmics, INXS, Blondie, and David Bowie, building a loyal following and moderate album sales between 1981 and 1988. Aside from the band, Sandii has also had a successful solo career in Japan and Asia, in addition to working in Japanese animation. Today she runs two popular hula dance schools in Tokyo and Yokohama, where she is raising the popularity of hula in Japan and incorporating it into her recent recordings of Hawaiian and Pacific Island styles. Though she has performed under various names over the years, she currently goes by Kumu Hula Sandii Manumele Laniākea.

◉ Even though The Pretenders were based in London, their debut album *Pretenders*, was first released in the USA in 1979. The US label Sire released it ahead of the UK release on January 11, 1980. The Pretenders were situated at the precise point where punk and NEW WAVE met. The album reached No.1 in the UK a week after the single 'Brass in Pocket' did the same. Many found Chrissie Hynde's bold, cocky persona as an independent woman who wouldn't take no for an answer irresistible. The timing was perfect, as The Pretenders fused punk and NEW WAVE. Pop gems like 'Brass in Pocket', 'Private Life', 'Precious' and 'Kid' exemplified this sensibility. The brilliant, dynamite album was ranked the 20th best of the 1980s by Rolling Stone in 1989.

◉ John Watts was born in 1954 in Surrey, England. After studying clinical psychology, he began a career as a mental health worker. However, he soon found success in music when he formed the band Fischer-Z with Steve Skolnik while attending Brunel University in 1976. Riding the wave of punk, NEW WAVE, and art rock in the 1970s, Fischer-Z secured a record deal with United Artists in 1978, joining stablemates like The Buzzcocks, The Stranglers, and Dr. Feelgood in 1982. Fischer-Z were becoming well known; they would soon earn support spots with the likes of Bob Marley, Dire Straits, The Police and James Brown, in turn lifting their exposure. In 1982 Watts released a solo album called *One More Twist* while still performing with Fischer-Z, and over the decades, he has released 11 albums as a soloist using several monikers, such as The Cry, Watts, and J.M.Watts. John has continued to tour and record new music with various incarnations of the band, releasing over one dozen excellent albums. He currently lives and works as a musician in Brighton, England.

JUST CHRISTMAS 1980 AT THE RAINBOW THEATRE
JOHN WATTS
(Fischer -Z)

Just back from The States.
Just 3 days rest.
Got married … Just.
Just honeymooned.
Just got back home.
Just felt in love.
Just entertained.
Just unconcerned.
Just played the first.
Of two Dire Straits shows.
Just climbed The Rainbow.
Just sat astride.
Just boggled restless as a child.

JW2023

Fiat Lux by permission

● Steve Wright was born December 27, 1958, in Glasgow, Scotland. Steve, as the keyboardist/percussionist/lead vocalist, was a founding member of Fiat Lux. Fiat Lux was a trio that, along with Steve, originally included David Crickmore (guitars and keyboards) and Ian Nelson (keys and saxophone), the younger brother of the iconic Bill Nelson. During their first period of existence, from 1982 to 1985, they released a handful of singles and a 6-track mini-album, *Hired History* (1984); their debut single, 'Feels Like Winter Again', was produced by Bill Nelson and was put out on his Cocteau label. Prior to the formation of the band, Steve worked as an actor with The Yorkshire Actors Company, learning skills that took him to Yorkshire Television and into freelance production and directing. In 2017 Steve rebirthed Fiat Lux and reunited with Crickmore, and to date they have released three albums.

RECOGNITION: CAN BE GOOD OR BAD.
STEVE WRIGHT
(Fiat Lux)

Sometimes it's good to be recognised in public; sometimes it's bad. Sometimes it has surprising results! After having performed on the Euro-networked TV show 'Music Laden' in Germany, I and Fiat Lux took a short flight to Holland to perform at a festival there.

In the long passport control queue at Schipol Airport, a policeman (with a gun!) came up to me and said, *"Show me your passport, please."* I did.

Then he said, *"Come with me."*

I turned to the rest of the band and crew and said something like, *"Fuckinell, lads, help!!!"*

The police guy then asked me which people were with me. I told him.

He said, *"You must ALL come with me!"* So, we did.

Unsmiling and silent, he led us down past the whole murmuring queue to the front. He opened a gate and escorted us through. Then came the killer words...

"Have a great gig. I love your music; I'll see you tonight!"

From fear to fun in 2 minutes! True!!!

28

● Tex Perkins, aka Gregory Stephen Perkins, was born December 28, 1964, in Darwin, Australia. Tex is famed as the front man of quite a few bands, such as Tex Deadly and the Dum-Dums, The Cruel Sea, Beasts of Bourbon, James Baker Experience and Salamander Jim & quite a few others. Tex is also a prolific recordist as a solo artist. More recently as Tex Perkins and The Tennessee Four, consisting of Shannon Bourne, guitar; Shane Reilly, guitar; Steve Hadley, bass; and Dave Folley, drums. Tex has performed a series of shows in Australia and New Zealand titled 'The Man in Black – The Johnny Cash Story' to rave reviews. With Tex's latest venture, he collaborates with Matt Walker in swampy-blues under the guise of Tex Perkins & The Fat Rubber Band.

Tex Perkins by Petra Gall

◎ Suicide's debut *self-titled* album was released in 1977. The album is a masterpiece-utterly unique, unprecedented, mesmerising, and without any pretensions or sense of compromise. For a band merely consisting of a singer and a guy with a beat-up old keyboard plugged into a few distortion pedals, Suicide in 1977 truly made one of rock 'n' roll's all-time essential albums. With no other electro-punk acts to emulate, Suicide was far ahead of their time on this record. Always minimalist and intense, the album's power stems from Marty Rev's trance-like, repetitive keyboards and Alan Vega's unpredictable, howling, frenzied vocals. The primitive Farfisa organ and rudimentary drum machines create a raw, abrasive sound akin to Throbbing Gristle, Can, and The Residents. Freakish, frightening, and awe-inspiring, this genre-defining album is highly recommended and deserves a perfect 10/10 rating.

◎ Wire came together in London in 1976 when Colin Newman initially teamed up with guitarists George Gill and Bruce Gilbert, bassist Graham Lewis, and drummer Robert Gotobed, aka Robert Grey, to form one of the most celebrated POST-PUNK bands of the time. After Gill's departure, the remaining Wire lineup recorded the debut album, *Pink Flag*, released on this day in 1977. The album had punk trappings yet took a new route with its commanding yet unconfrontational style. With *Pink Flag*, Wire showed they were vastly different from their punk contemporaries. This release was just the beginning, as two more remarkable albums followed: *Chairs Missing* and *154*, which cemented Wire's reputation as a pioneering force. In 1980, the members pursued solo work and collaborations, departing from Wire for a time. Wire reassembled in 1985 with a new electronica-based strategy, embracing the sequencers, synthesizers, and drum machines of the era on *The Ideal Copy* and *A Bell Is a Cup Until It's Struck*. With *The Ideal Copy* as the first DAT format release, Wire was again at the forefront of innovation. Since 1987, Wire has released over a dozen albums, and often refer to as the "most famous band you've never heard of". Their evolution of sound and direction arguably positions them without equal, their class and style finding them constantly discussed alongside the likes of New Order and Pink Floyd as forefathers of POST-PUNK and contemporary artistic music.

29

◎ *White Souls in Black Suits*, the debut album release by Clock DVA, was available December 29, 1980. Clock DVA was formed in 1978 by Adolphus "Adi" Newton and Steven "Judd" Turner, and this release was initially only available as a cassette; it has since become available on CD and on vinyl but only in Italy. The album lays out a chilled atmosphere textured by experimentalism. Through the poor production and sound quality, comparisons to Throbbing Gristle or even Captain Beefheart are unavoidable. Amidst the angst, there is a serene feeling of calm. Seek it out.

David Smylie Byrnes by permission

◉ David Smylie Byrnes was born in Sydney, Australia, in 1964 to a musical family; his father was a member of the original Deltones band. With this musical upbringing, it was unsurprising that Byrnes pursued music himself. Influenced by Hendrix, King Crimson, and Pink Floyd, he learnt guitar and bass. Byrnes was a member of the psychedelic POST-PUNK band The Moffs from 1984 to 1989 before moving on to Lazarus. The Moffs released two albums and several singles, with 'Another Day in The Sun' regarded as a classic of that era. As a skilled session musician, Byrnes also plays violin, piano, banjo, saranji, and, as he puts it, "most things with strings". Today, Byrnes works in his Electric Church studio as an engineer and producer. Outside of music, he has a passion for sports like cricket, rugby league, fishing, and golf.

ROCK AND ROLL AND RUM & COKES
DAVID SMYLIE BYRNES
(The Moffs)

A fire which is not normally associated with POST-PUNK bands happened, and I was a firsthand witness to it not once, but two times!

It was a Thursday back in 1984, and my band at the time, The Moffs, were getting a large following at the Southern Cross Hotel in Sydney. It was as packed as The Southern could get that night, all sweaty, with shoes sticking to that ever-present sticky floor.

Our keyboardist Nick Potts had blown a fuse in his amp in the earlier soundcheck/rehearsal, so we borrowed a Vox guitar amp off Kieren Fitzpatrick, the guitarist from Division 4. Three quarters of the way through the gig, I could see from stage right, where I was positioned, Nick's (or Kieren's) amp had flames coming out of the top. Greg Smyrell, aka 'Quick', who was The Scientists road manager before they went overseas, was in the side bit where the crew would hang. In his confidence and compassion, he decided to throw his drink on the flames to douse it. His favourite drink at that time was rum and Coke. Well, the fire got worse before it got better, and on resumption, Nick had to play harmonica for the remaining songs.

We told Kieren about his amp and that we would pay for it; it was then that Kieren said that he had used the foil out of a cigarette packet as a fuse in said Vox amp!

Two months later, the Lime Spiders are playing the same venue with Greg 'Quick' Smyrell in their crew. Drummer Richard Lawson was trying out the fab new oil-filled tom drum skins.

It was 'Cracker Night', and someone threw a sparkler onstage, and it lit up one of Richard's drum skins. Ever quick to the rescue was Quick, and he again threw that favourite drink of his, a rum and coke, over the kit; this time disaster. The whole kit went up; we all had to evacuate the venue, and the gig was over.

That's Rock and Roll and Rum & Cokes at the Southern.

○ The up-and-coming punk rock band Department S released their first single, 'Is Vic There?' b/w 'Solid Gold – Easy Action', on Demon Records on December 29, 1980. Featuring guitarist Mike Herbage, bassist Tony Lorden, drummer Stuart Mizon, and vocalist Vaughn Toulouse, Department S had previously performed as Guns for Hire, releasing one single titled 'I'm Gonna Rough My Girlfriend's Boyfriend Up Tonight'. Propelled by the strength of the infectious A-side track and an excellent cover of Marc Bolan on the B-side, Department S's debut single was a huge success, earning ample radio play and peaking at No.22 on the UK charts.

○ Jim Reid, the lead singer for The Jesus and Mary Chain, was born in Scotland on December 29, 1961. Along with his older brother and guitarist William Reid, Jim formed the band where he was born in East Kilbride, on the outskirts of Glasgow, in 1983. Seeking to become the premier POST-PUNK outfit of the mid-'80s, the band released their critically acclaimed debut album, *Psychocandy*, in 1985. Over the next decade, The Jesus and Mary Chain put out five more studio albums before disbanding in 1999. However, they reunited in 2007 and have been constantly touring ever since.

30

○ Darrin Huss was born in Toronto, Canada, in 1965. Along with his brother Stephen, when living in Edmonton, they formed Psyche, venturing into a dark form of synthpop. At the time, Darrin was 17 years of age, and his brother was merely 15 years old! Psyche was pioneering and counted as one of Canada's foremost synthpop bands. The group have been creating their signature dramatic, atmospheric music blending synthesizers and drum machines for over 40 years. They have long been recognised as influential in independent electronic music, through exploring various styles from harsh industrial to warm synthpop to minimal dance music to darkwave. They are best known for hit songs like 'Unveiling the Secret', 'Eternal', 'Misery', 'Sanctuary', '15 Minutes', and their well-known cover of Q Lazzarus's 'Goodbye Horses', which first gained fame appearing in the film *The Silence of The Lambs*. They have released 11 official albums and numerous compilations and remix sets. Known for his smooth vocal delivery, Darrin has collaborated with several synthpop artists, such as Fading Colours & Icon of Coil. Darrin continued the Psyche project after his brother's passing in 2015.

UNVEILING THE SECRET – WE ARE CANADIAN NOT EUROPEAN
DARRIN HUSS
(Psyche)

We were the first electronic band in Edmonton, Alberta. Canada.

I started making music with my brother, initially playing bass, and my brother played keyboard and occasional guitar. By the time we had a drum machine and Sequential Circuits Pro One synths to make our grooves, I had ditched my bass and concentrated on lyrics and singing to my brother's soundtracks. By 1981 we were already performing and doing some covers of our favourite synth groups. We did 'New Life' by Depeche Mode, 'Back to Nature' by Fad Gadget, 'The Model' by Kraftwerk, and even 'Alle Gegen Alle' by DAF!

Songs like 'Cars' and later the *Telekon* album by Gary Numan completely changed our lives. There were punk elements too, such as Dead Kennedys, Plasmatics and The Cramps. As well as the Goth side with Bauhaus, Siouxsie, and The Cure.

The name Psyche was finally realised after we tried a few other names, such as Youthenics, which was probably a mashup of our Canadian heroes Rational Youth and Eurythmics. Psyche came out of the B-side to Killing Joke's 'Wardance' single that was spelt "Pssyche", actually. I wanted a name that could be seen as an insight into what we wanted to express lyrically and musically. I loved the earthshaking sound of early Killing Joke and all their themes, but also the lyrical intelligence and pondering of Fad Gadget, Gary Numan, and Robert Smith.

Psyche seemed to cover the sound and words that we would stand behind even as we got older. By the time we were writing our own songs, my main influence would be Soft Cell. I felt that Marc Almond had the most perfect synthpop voice. It was honest, emotional, and personal sounding. Our first song, 'Krieg', was so named because that was our NEW WAVE club in Edmonton, as well as the fact that I was learning German because of listening to Deutsch Amerikanische Freundschaft, which also heavily leaned on the sound of early Soft Cell. By the time 'Love Is a Stranger' and 'Sweet Dreams' became massive hits in Canada, I would have added the inspiration of Annie Lennox's vocal stylings to my repertoire. Eurythmics and Soft Cell definitely had an influence on our looks as well. Slowly, Psyche became its own brand of dark synthpop.

Many a cassette demo was made. Many a show had been played, but we still hadn't created an album. When the whole family moved back to Waterloo from whence, we came, there was a period of finding ourselves anew and my brother finishing school. I became a DJ and ended up spending nearly two years with that, as well as an internship at a radio station. At some point we managed to get enough new material together to finally make an album called *Insomnia Theatre* and release it independently in 1985 after failing to secure a contract with Nettwerk Records, which at the same time was considering Psyche or Skinny Puppy and went with the latter as they were already establishing themselves in the label's home of Vancouver.

My brother and I, now literally at the opposite end of the country, decided to set our sights on Europe, and after sending out demos to Mute Records in the UK, like probably every electronic act on the planet would've done, we ended up getting signed to New Rose Records in Paris, France.

I must digress to point out that we are once again a DIY project, but for a certain period we learnt what labels could do and how the music business is just that, a business. You must have both, or you may never be heard. One of the most exciting days of our lives was when we received a phone call from New Rose Records, and they said they would pay us to update our debut album for the European market. As well as the fact that they liked the songs so much, it would be a double album! 2 x 45 rpm 12" discs to showcase 2 songs on each side. I have always believed that we were doing something groundbreaking that could stand the test of time, and now we had support from a company that was going to form our image and showcase us to the best of their abilities. And boy, did they!

We were disappointed at first that Mute didn't answer, and there were a few other label rejections. However, we became the first electronic band to be signed to the label that had Damon Edge of CHROME, as well as the recently signed The Cramps. This is how Psyche was able to maintain its uniqueness and influential sound on the dark electronic scene from the beginning. The irony of this is that we became a European act that actually never set foot in the UK until decades later. We learnt quickly that although our label was well known on the French market, our sales were somewhat higher in Germany. We received some cool reviews in the UK papers; however, it was mostly Sounds magazine that championed our *Insomnia Theatre* album and the follow-up EP.

This all happened before we even played a single show across the ocean. That changed when New Rose Records decided it was time for the follow-up, and I would say this is when Psyche truly began to be discovered and branch out.

The weird thing is that our second album, *Unveiling the Secret*, was going to end up being fully ignored by the UK while gaining us even more ground in France, Germany, Scandinavia, and the USA. Before that all happened, however, we were advanced money to come to Paris and record our second album, with which we would make our stage debut as opening act for the first-ever synth duo, Suicide, at the prestigious Elysée Montmartre, in front of 2000 people!

We, like many '80s synth fans, were more aware of Soft Cell, Blancmange, Yazoo, and Eurythmics, the synth duos that followed, and would never have heard of Suicide had it not been for Soft Cell doing a cover version of 'Ghost Rider' with Jim Foetus at a live show. New Rose had just licensed the Suicide debut for a re-release, as well as a solo album from Martin Rev, and was eager to showcase us. This proved to me that if you were truly unique and ahead of your time, there would eventually be possible futures reliving your past. I wasn't aware that you could embrace this possibility at the time, so all we wanted to do was go on stage and blow them away! Disrespectful, I know, but we felt we were worthy of being heard and just as ahead of our time as well. We pulled out all the stops: a complete B-movie horror show with fake blood and a girl lying on a table and twitching like a zombie. I can't remember our entire setlist, but I'm pretty sure we played 'Unveiling the Secret' and 'Screaming Machine'. Our album and single would come out a month after this show, but we definitely made our mark, and 'Unveiling the Secret' became our calling card.

The album only contained 8 songs, but they represented the Dark EBM (which wasn't a term we adhered to) and poppier elements of our now somewhat sleeker 'electro sound'. Whereas 'The Saint Became a Lush' and 'Black Panther' leaned more towards 'Goth Industrial', 'Unveiling the Secret' and the next single, 'Prisoner to Desire', were heading in the direction of Yazoo, with a twist of Divine meets Pet Shop Boys. I am incredibly proud of having one of the few, perhaps the only, 'dark synth club hits' that doesn't even have a repeated chorus lyric.

'Unveiling The Secret' and 'The Saint Became a Lush' are poetry set to an electronic soundtrack. Both songs have been added to many compilations over the years and became our first hits in Latin countries Spain, Brazil, Argentina, and Chile. An interesting breakthrough that has continued Psyche's renown to this day.

◉ Robert Quine was born in 1942 in Akron, Ohio. Robert first rose to fame through his work with Richard Hell & The Voidoids. He was by no stretch of the imagination your typical punk rock guitarist; he was innovative and eclectic in style, a style that embraced fractured guitar runs and discordant noise, always displaying influences from jazz, rock, and blues. Robert was not very keen on touring and was always busy with a variety of studio projects and played sessions for Tom Waits, Marianne Faithfull, Brian Eno, and Lloyd Cole, among others. Robert died on May 31, 2004, from a heroin overdose.

◉ Patti Smith, who was born on December 30, 1946, in Chicago, Illinois, is an iconic American singer-songwriter, poet, and visual artist who became a driving force in the punk rock movement of the '70s in New York City. With the release of her acclaimed 1975 album *Horses* and its hit single 'Because the Night', co-written with Bruce Springsteen, Smith cemented her status as the "Godmother of Punk". 1979 saw Patti move to Detroit with MC5's Fred "Sonic" Smith; they married, and they went on to have two children. This time together in self-imposed exile enabled them to write together, and in 1988 they recorded Dream of Life. In 2007 Patti became a Rock and Roll Hall of Fame inductee and the same year was named a Commander of the Ordre des Arts et des Lettres by the French Minister of Culture. She has also been listed as No.117 on Rolling Stone's list of the 200 Greatest Singers of All Time.

◉ Trevor Tanner was born in London, England in 1962. As a child, he began exploring music by playing piano and singing in his school's choir. At age 11, hearing David Bowie's 'Watch That Man' on the radio was an epiphany for Trevor; it inspired his interest in guitar. "I grew up in the whole punk thing," Tanner said, setting the course for his music career. Tanner became well-known as the singer-guitarist for The Bolshoi, releasing four critically acclaimed studio albums: *Giants, Friends, Lindy's Party,* and *Country Life*, although 1989's *Country Life* was never completed until it was re-constructed in 2015 by Tanner's label-head, David Paul Wyatt Perko in a joint venture with Beggars Banquet, and finally released on CD-only, inside the 5 CD box-set, *The Bolshoi* on Beggar's Arkive initiative. In mid-2024 Perko again collaborated with Beggar's Banquet and Country Life was released as a double LP on grass green and sun orange vinyl with Tanner recording a bonus version of the song, Dolores Jones, as an acoustic re-imagining for the last track of the album. Beyond The Bolshoi, the early 2000s were an intense period of productivity for Tanner, who put out five solo albums on the Emperor Penguin Recordings label, including the highly popular album *Eaten by the Sea*, which was released a number of years after the highly praised, 3 CD box-set *Bullish, Bellyache,* and *Belch*. In 2015, Tanner selected 15 of his favorite Bolshoi tracks and re-imagined them as acoustic versions, which were release in 2016 on CD and vinyl as the self-homage album, *Trevor Tanner's The Bolshoi Favourites No.1*. Today, Tanner continues to play live while continuously working on new material for his next solo release.

THE BOLSHOI, MORE THAN A BALLET
TREVOR TANNER
(The Bolshoi)

Back in the early eighties, the world was a much different place. Being in a band was something a bounteous array of English folk attempted via someone's garage – or less. All it took was an acute magical ability to shake a tambourine, and the next "Ziggy Stardust wannabe" fever dream was born. What separated the priests from the altar boys, though, were the steady exercises in self-punishment that, like an ugly cat startled by a gesture of affection, had two very distinct sides: playing live and recording in a studio. This isn't to say that both weren't more fun than an Arctic beach full of horny Odobenus rosmarus in Prins Karls Forland, but sinking my own eager tusks into both made for an often-endless barrage of ill humour.

I became a pulchritudinous showman of sorts during the era of the *Giants* EP. I once found myself on a bus in California with my mates, being interviewed prior to the worldwide release of our video for 'Happy Boy'. That in itself was fortuitous, but it was an event leading up to it, earlier that morning, that is still writhing around in my brain. Headed out for a pack of smokes, I guardedly made my way across a somewhat traffic-gorged Los Angeles street. Next thing I knew, I was on the verge of being arrested for jaywalking. I couldn't believe it. Here's this authority figure that I am supposed to take seriously, and all I can see is Erik Estrada from CHiPs, outfit, sunglasses, and all. As hard as I tried, I could not stop laughing, and Officer Estrada was not amused. As the rest of the world witnessed the Bolshoi divulging our turn-ons and turn-offs via city bus – followed by the fast-paced, monochromatic world premiere of the 'Happy Boy' music video – I was slightly hungover, barely awake, and happy to have avoided jail time.

By the time the songs and videos for the *Friends* album began, dealing with rapidly moving schedules and an army of prima donnas annoyingly shoving things into my face was somewhat old hat for me. I'll note though, that, as I shook the end of my guitar into the camera and lurked around in a rather appealing London flat for the Away video, no one realised that we had broken into that space and weren't supposed to be there, which led to an aggressive eviction. Film hides so much, doesn't it? Ahhh... the tinsel-laced world of showbiz.

At some point during or just after the *Lindy's Party* album, all the record execs, enthusiastic producers, tour managers, and a general lot of narcissistic creative kings and queens probably had enough of tangling with us, and it was time to throw in the proverbial towel. Perhaps it came way too early. Maybe it was way too late.

Before we officially left, though, we worked feverishly on our fourth album, tentatively titled *Country Life*. We believed that *Country Life* was our greatest achievement, but due to ongoing friction in prior years, we were dispelled by the powers that be, and *Country Life* began gathering dust in an attic for nearly 30 years. It has since been found, polished up, and in 2024, given a well-deserved proper release on grass green and sun orange vinyl.

Headed out of the big-label circus, I ventured into the nineties knowing one thing for certain: life is way more conducive when you are working alone or with co-conspirators of similar minds. Developing an ever-unfolding, diabolical friendship with creative director David Paul Wyatt Perko, in the late nineties, by way of a random off-kilter interview in Fright X Magazine, was undeniably my golden ticket to board the solo train of self-realisation straight into the new millennium. Gone were the gruelling days of ten outsiders hammering together one song; these were now the oh-so-much-happier new days of one person in glorious control of ten songs. That one person being me, your incessant, humble yet pompous, truculent bigot. Jump aboard all my post-Bolshoi exploits at TrevorTanner.com. Lock the door; live in dread.

March 25, 2024

31

⦿ Hilary Blake released her 4-track *Kinetic* EP in late 1982, launching the career of producer Stephen Hague. Though not a commercial success, the EP found critical acclaim for its inventiveness and became a staple on dance floors and college radio across the USA. Due to its popularity, Hague expanded the original two tracks to four for the vinyl and cassette release. He played most instruments on the EP before going on to produce hits for OMD, Pet Shop Boys, New Order, Peter Gabriel, The Pretenders, PiL, Pere Ubu, and many others, becoming one of the most successful NEW WAVE and alternative producers of the 20th century.

Ken Davis

⦿ Ken Davis was born in December in the late 1940s in the United Kingdom. Originally playing the trumpet in school, he went on to become one of the world's leading composers and musicians of healing, relaxation, ambient, and environmental music. In 1960, Ken's family migrated to Australia, where he experimented with Farfisa organs in music stores until acquiring a Korg synthesiser and guitar, using tape loops and sound synthesis. During the 1980s, Davis teamed up with Mars Lasar to form the electronic duo IQ. As pioneers of musical instrument technology, IQ were one of the first groups to record with the innovative Fairlight CMI, which is prominently featured on their album tracks 'The New Tomorrow', 'Time Travelers', and 'Rhythmatic Stereo'. Given their proficiency with the instrument, IQ was selected by Fairlight to promote and exhibit this new technology in Japan. In the mid-1970s, Davis could be found every Sunday playing nine keyboards and two drum machines on the forecourt of the Sydney Opera House, attracting hundreds of onlookers drawn to his live performance. This successful marketing outlet grew into his business of over 1500 listening stations in Australian Geographic, tourism and airport stores across Australia and

New Zealand. Ken Davis cares for our environment and included nature sounds in many of his 60 albums and nature DVDs now streaming the world for all to experience.

ROCK TO SYNTHESIZED TO COMPUTERIZED
KEN DAVIS
(IQ, Solo)

The original band Khan was formed in Adelaide by me, and after supporting bands like AC/DC, Ted Mulry and many more, we moved the band to Perth, Australia, and, as bands do, we went through several lineup changes before moving to Sydney. The Dellafranca twins, Toni on bass and drummer John, were a very striking-looking pair. They loved to wear all the stage gear and make-up for stage presence; it was something that we needed when we performed at prime venues like The Bondi Lifesaver. Living together in a Bondi Junction hotel, I found it all too hard keeping the band fed and paid, so our time together only lasted about three months, and the Dellafrancas headed back to Perth.

Change had to happen, so I then added a new bassist and drummer and called the band IQ. We soon earned a reputation in the Australian music business as an original band with original ideas. We recorded some demo tracks for submitting to record companies, 'Andromeda: Is There Life On Mars' & 'Put a Smile on Your Face', and a few others. These raised some eyebrows but just didn't get us across the line.

Andrew Sacaroitz, our keyboard player, left the band, and that opened the door to the very young and talented Mars Lasar. I watched him on a television programme playing Jean-Michel Jarre's 'Oxygene' and called him, and after much persuasion, he joined the band. Our output grew ever more modern and electronic in approach, with synthesizers now as a solid foundation sound. Mars had a creative mind, and I encouraged him to write music for the band, so with that, we wrote songs both solo and together and recorded the *self-titled* mini-album *IQ*. It proved to be the one and only release by IQ on the independent label Cream Music. IQ had a small but faithful following, and through sponsorship by a friend of the band called Andy, we were able to record a single called 'Put A Smile on Your Face' at Fatboy Studios in Balmain. The album and single received little airplay; this initially didn't discourage us, as we sold a few copies to our fans at gigs and inner-city import stores. Disheartened, after numerous live gigs and a year of hard slog and so many previous years of trying to be recognised, I decided to disband that lineup and went on as an electronic duo with Mars; I kept the name IQ.

IQ was lucky to have a very enthusiastic fan named Christophe Vali, who actually became our manager, and after a chance meeting with Kim Ryrie from Fairlight Industries, he mentioned that he managed IQ. Kim was very interested in IQ's performance and music when he had seen us as the support act at a Mike Oldfield concert the week before. This opened a door for us! Kim and Peter Vogel had recently developed the Fairlight CMI, the most elaborate music computer system in the world at the time. One of the first owners was Stevie Wonder, followed by Peter Gabriel and Kate Bush, amongst others! We began talking, and IQ was invited to Fairlight in Darlinghurst, Sydney, where I was very vocal about acquiring a Fairlight CMI and performing with it live. Kim agreed, and not only did we get one… we got two! It expanded our thinking; the possibilities of this device were endless, and we spent a great deal of time creating music on them. This scenario elevated our profile, and we started to get television appearances on Sounds, hosted by Donnie Sutherland, and Simon Townsend's Wonder World. I had always wanted to go to Japan, and that dream was realised in 1982 when I went to Tokyo and Osaka to showcase and display our skills on the Fairlight CMI; it was such a great experience!

After Japan, Henk Visschedijk joined as lead vocalist, and together we recorded 'Humans'. I wrote the music and collaborated with him on the lyrics. We recorded a film clip for one of my compositions, 'The New Tomorrow', at the club-venue Jamison Street in

Sydney, and as far as airplay was concerned, it was a success; however, it did not lead to a recording contract.

Through Fairlight I had been introduced to the Linn Drum machine and modern mixers; it gave me a great opportunity to realise the potential of the new genre happening, labelled 'Dance Music'. Soon after, Mars Lasar decided to go it alone, and he moved to the USA, continuing his career with Fairlight USA. Henk had garnered solo gigs and was sought after as an actor. That line-up of IQ, Mars, Henk, and I recorded 'Humans' and 'The New Tomorrow'; these are both now featured on YouTube under the name IQBand Australia 1980-1990.

I loved synthesizers and sequencers; these allowed my mind to create music of a new era soon to be known as 'New Age Music'! I soon acquired more synthesizers such as the early Roland SH2, SH101 and TR 707 drum machine, linked together via MIDI. I was able to produce a sound that I knew would be popular. I spent day and night for many months experimenting with all my new gear but still incorporating my guitar playing in the music. I felt confident that this new music was going to give me an opportunity to go it alone. No more was I going to rely on other members of a band. With all my new gear, I could produce everything!

I had a gift for melody and was overly disillusioned with the business of the Australian music industry, and I just did not know what to do with my creative and innovative compositions of ambient and melodic music, so I looked for the alternative solution. The answer? Release my own music as Ken Davis Music, and to date I have released over 50 albums on CD, cassette, and DVD. My music has been featured in the Qantas A380s inflight entertainment programme *Floating on Air*. I am passionate about the environment and care about the future of planet Earth. Seek and you may find me performing under the pseudonyms of Ambassador of the Future and World Environmental Composer and, of course, Ken Davis.

● Were you lucky enough to get a copy of the exquisitely packaged *A Factory Sample* (FAC 2), the double 7-inch debut record release by Factory Records? Released in December 1978, the four sides held two Joy Division classics, 'Digital' and 'Glass'; there were two lost classics from The Durutti Column, 'No Communication' and 'Thin Ice (Detail)'; and a couple of gems from Cabaret Voltaire, 'Baader Meinhof' and 'Sex In Secret'. That left 3 tracks by John Dowie that are oddly out of place on this record. The two discs were beautifully presented in a silver-dyed rice paper cover in a sealed plastic bag.

● The debut *self-titled* album Pearl Harbor and The Explosions was released worldwide by Warner Bros. at the end of 1979. Vocalist Pearl E. Gates, backed by Hilary Hanes (bass), John Hanes (drums), and Peter Dunne (guitar), followed up their well-received single 'Shut Up and Dance' with an upbeat, melodic, and accessible NEW WAVE sound inspired by UK punk. Stacked with hooks, the album's catchy material made it a must-have for any music collection. Although short-lived, Pearl Harbor and The Explosions created an enduring legacy and influence with this classic release. After touring together, Pearl married Paul Simonon, bassist for The Clash, beginning a 7-year marriage.

● Andy Summers, born Andrew James Somers in 1942, in Pouten-le-Fylde, Lancashire, England, was the guitarist for the rock band The Police. The Police had only one No.1 hit in the USA with 'Every Breath You Take' but topped the charts in the UK five times, and all but their debut album *Outlandos d'Amour* reached No.1 in both the UK and Australia. Before joining The Police, Summers was already an accomplished guitarist, playing with acts like Zoot Money's Big Roll Band, The Soft Machine, and Eric Burdon & The Animals. Andy has released over one dozen albums, been part of several soundtracks and entered into many collaborations. During his tenure with The Police, he entered into a partnership with Robert

Fripp, releasing the exquisite instrumental albums *I Advance Masked* and *Bewitched* in the early 1980s to critical acclaim.

David Thomas of Pere Ubu by Petra Gall

⬤ What was the birth of POST-PUNK? Here's a candidate. The debut single '30 Seconds Over Tokyo' b/w 'Heart of Darkness' by Cleveland's Pere Ubu was in the record store racks in 1975! This is POST-PUNK, even before punk! Born out of Rocket from the Tombs, the notorious Cleveland rock band led by David Thomas, these guys were experimenting with their Krautrock influences. This was groundbreaking and very special. If you haven't got Pere Ubu, start with this!

⬤ Paul Roberts, who took over the vocalist role with The Stranglers when Hugh Cornwell left in 1990, was born 31st December 1959, in Chiswick, England. Not being a guitarist like Hugh, they commissioned John Ellis and later Baz Warne to be the guitarists. Paul stuck with The Stranglers for 16 years before moving on to do many stage and acting roles: he is noted as co-creator of the show Let's Dance, paying tribute to the great David Bowie.

⬤ The stunning *self-titled* debut EP by The Sunnyboys was released on December 31, 1980, by Sydney's Phantom Records. It was four infectious songs of NEW WAVE/garage pop tinged with a Remains influence that everybody just had to have. Even though the songs are simple and uncomplicated, they shine with a level of sophistication that allows Jeremy Oxley's compositions to come to the fore. Overall, the EP is very jangly and melodious POST-PUNK power pop; the songs 'Alone with You' and 'Love to Rule' simply rate amongst the best Australian songs of the era.

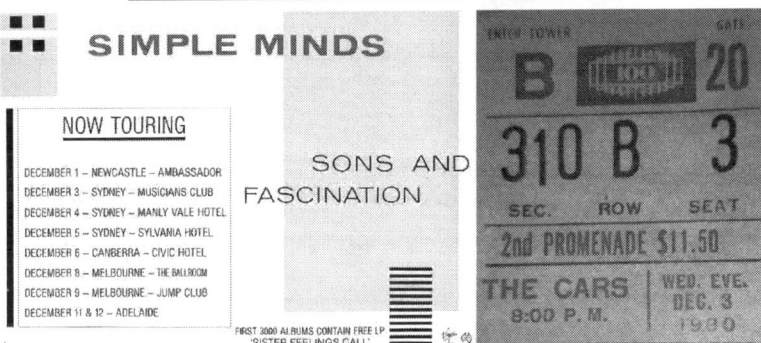

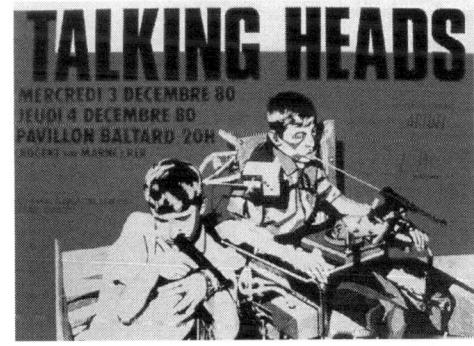

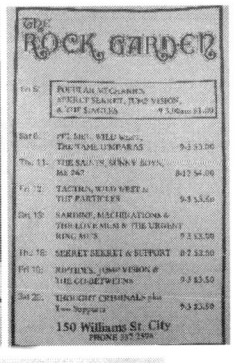

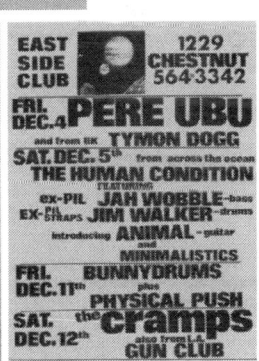

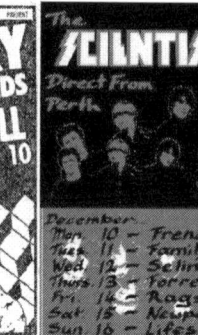

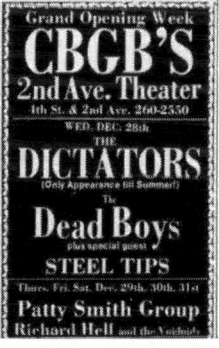

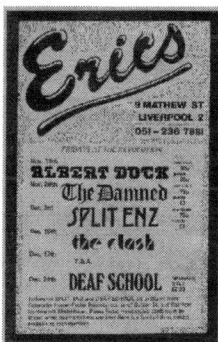

ABOUT THE AUTHOR

Michael Krilich's musical background goes back to when he started buying records at age 12. Not content to just listen, he researched all he listened to, discovering who the musicians were, who the tracks were produced by and the history of the record companies. This knowledge led to opportunities to be a published writer in several music magazines and to be asked to provide liner notes for several releases. His work sees him pegged as a musicologist, historian, and blogger.

The 1980s saw Michael as a columnist and an occasional contributor a number of street press magazines such as On the Street, T.A.G.G, Noises and Happenings, and Byron Beats. In 1979 Michael was the co-presenter of The New Music Show on 2NCR-FM.

During the late '70s and early '80s, Michael turned his interest towards electronic music. Inspired by the likes of Kraftwerk, Eno and Jean Michel Jarre, he collected various synthesizers, electronic devices and tape machines. He arguably became the first to combine samples of Australian Indigenous music and electronica on his independent cassette release *Thematic Variations*, it was featured on the national radio program 2JJJ's Demo Show and received some ongoing rotation. From that, many years after its original release, Michael's ground-breaking 'sample' piece *Arnhem Land* was picked up by Left Ear Records out of Melbourne, Australia and in January 2025 the label released it digitally and on 12" vinyl. Since its release *Arnhem Land* has been selected by the Australian National Film and Sound Archive to be saved in perpetuity.

Today Michael is the programmer and manager of a community radio station on the Mid-North Coast of New South Wales, Australia. FRESH FM is unique and ad free. He has established a concept where the songs are introduced by the artists rather than an announcer and the feedback on this has been overwhelmingly positive from listeners and artists alike. The diversity and quality of music played has contributed to the overall success of the station. FRESH FM can boast to being one of the only stations that promotes new local artists without question or favour. Michael searched the radio world and FRESH FM can now boast syndications of programs from the UK (Dick O'Dell), the USA (John Wooler) and locally (Pete Matthewman). The station via the internet is proud to have a growing worldwide listener base.

For several years now it has been Michael's vision to share his in-depth knowledge of the New Wave & Post-Punk period with the world, so he created the Facebook group '70s & '80s New Wave and Post-Punk (& Sub-Genres) History & Music.' The group is dedicated to the subject matter of this book and presently is approaching 50,000 global members. Here he posts daily trivia on musicians' birthdays, releases, and events. This group has become a meeting place not just for fans, but also noteworthy musicians worldwide.

ACKNOWLEDGEMENTS

It's fair to say that the success and outcome of a project such as this takes the input, encouragement, support and assistance of many people. With the creation of this book, I have been extremely fortunate to have got this over the past 10 years while compiling data and in the writing of the manuscript.

There are so many people that need and deserve thanks. Firstly, my life partner Libby Permezel who I had to call on many, many times for help with the intricacies of word processing. Without her help the script you are reading would appear to be by someone from another planet or a chimpanzee. Indeed, The Quality of Mercy Is Not Strnen. Thanks Lib.

Then there are the moderators and members of my Facebook group. They have been a continuing and valuable source of inspiration and information. I must say that I was driven to start this project by them in the first instance, they wanted my daily blogs in one place, in a printed form, so here it is. It was with the bass player Jimmy Jay Rothery who I initially planned and drafted the concept of the Facebook group concentrating on the period and genres herein. Jimmy no longer graces this mortal coil, rest in peace friend.

Thanks to Stuart Coupe for inspiration, guidance and his foreword. Thanks to David Balfe for an intriguing insightful prologue. And thanks John Perriott, Jo Forster and Fiona Hammond for their ideas in design, stylizing and editing. And special thank you to Michael Palmer and Andrew Sparke for their help with cover design and the internal graphics.

Where would I be without the contributors and interviewees? They are what can really be termed as 'icing on the cake.' So many celebrated and illustrious personalities sharing their experiences, memories, images and perceptions, all gathered in one place, and doing it gratis. To the 300 plus of you, my heartfelt thanks.

Then there are those that provided images. It's through the flyers, posters and artist photos that we transport ourselves back to the time. We find it respectful to give credit where credit due for the images used herein. An inordinate number of enquiries have been made into who were the artists/designers of the flyers and posters, mainly to no avail. We scoured websites, Facebook groups and even made phone calls, so if you recognize any of your work that is uncredited, please contact us so we can ensure that you are credited in the second edition.

Professionals and amateurs alike have provided and given permission to use their works and sacred possessions. Thanks to: Tony Beesley of Days Like Tomorrow Books for the copyrighted photos by Kristan James Melik, Joey Bruno, Jon Foy, Jason Gross of Perfect Sound Forever, Peter Hartinger, Graham Macindoe, Maggie K de Monde, Roch Parisien, Skull Printworks, Peter Torcher and Schwules Museum for allowing the use of Petra Gall's work. Many artists that are included in the book provided me with images of themselves and/or their band, where possible we have credited the photographer, but through the sands of time and faded memories some names are unknown, if you are amongst these, I thank you. Again, should your photo be uncredited or incorrect, please reach out to us so we can credit you appropriately in the upcoming second edition.

Now, to you, the reader. I hope you get a fraction the enjoyment out of this that I have had putting it together. Without you this book is merely a lump of paper.

Printed in Dunstable, United Kingdom